THE ROUTLEDGE HANDBOOK OF EDUCATION TECHNOLOGY

This handbook offers a comprehensive understanding of the use of technology in education. With a focus on the development of Education Technology in India, it explores innovative strategies as well as challenges in incorporating technology to support learning.

The volume examines diverse learning approaches such as assistive technology and augmentative and alternative communication for learners with disabilities and creating more social and accessible environments for learning through Collaborative Learning Techniques (CoLTS), massive open online courses (MOOCs), and the use of AI (Artificial Intelligence) in modern classrooms. Enriched with discussions on recent trends in ET (Education Technology), university curriculum and syllabi, and real-life examples of the use of ET in different classroom settings, the book captures diverse aspects of education technology and its potential. It also discusses the challenges of making technology and resources available for all and highlights the impact technology has had in classrooms across the world during the COVID-19 pandemic.

This book will be of interest to students, researchers, and teachers of education, digital education, education technology, and information technology. The book will also be useful for policymakers, educationalists, instructional designers, and educational institutions.

Santoshi Halder is a Professor at the Department of Education, University of Calcutta, India. She is a Board-Certified Behavior Analyst (BACB, USA) and Special Educator Licensure (RCI, India). Her specialization and primary focus of research range from Educational Technology (ET), Special Needs Education (SEN), and inclusion of people with diverse needs, to marginalized communities and minorities. Her recent book publications include *Inclusion, Disability, and Culture* (2017), *Inclusion, Equity, Access for Individuals with Disabilities* (2019), and *Routledge Handbook of Inclusive Education for Teachers* (2022). Her research work focuses on video modeling behavioral intervention for people with autism, marginalized and secluded communities, and finding constructive strategic pathways for the inclusion of people with diverse needs in low-, middle-, and high-income countries.

Sanju Saha is an Assistant Professor at Ghoshpukur College, Siliguri, West Bengal, India. His research interests include instructional design, technological innovation for teaching-learning, instructional visualization, and technology-based design of learning materials to utilize human cognition.

THE ROUTLEDGE HANDBOOK OF EDUCATION TECHNOLOGY

Santoshi Halder and Sanju Saha

LONDON AND NEW YORK

Cover image: © Getty Images

First published 2023
by Routledge
4 Park Square, Milton Park, Abingdon, Oxon OX14 4RN

and by Routledge
605 Third Avenue, New York, NY 10158

Routledge is an imprint of the Taylor & Francis Group, an informa business

© 2023 Santoshi Haldar and Sanju Saha

The right of Santoshi Haldar and Sanju Saha to be identified as authors of this work has been asserted in accordance with sections 77 and 78 of the Copyright, Designs and Patents Act 1988.

All rights reserved. No part of this book may be reprinted or reproduced or utilised in any form or by any electronic, mechanical, or other means, now known or hereafter invented, including photocopying and recording, or in any information storage or retrieval system, without permission in writing from the publishers.

Trademark notice: Product or corporate names may be trademarks or registered trademarks, and are used only for identification and explanation without intent to infringe.

British Library Cataloguing-in-Publication Data
A catalogue record for this book is available from the British Library

ISBN: 978-1-032-27196-5 (hbk)
ISBN: 978-1-032-27619-9 (pbk)
ISBN: 978-1-003-29354-5 (ebk)

DOI: 10.4324/9781003293545

Typeset in Bembo
by Deanta Global Publishing Services, Chennai, India

Let us unravel and extend the potential of technology for good of all

CONTENTS

List of figures   ix
List of tables   xii
Foreword   xv
Preface   xvii
Acknowledgments   xix

PART I
Fundamental Concepts and Theories   1

1. Origin of Technology and Philosophy of Educational Technology   3
2. Conceptual Orientation of Educational Technology   6
3. Historical Evolution of Educational Technology   19
4. Instructional Design in Education   31
5. Communication and Communication Strategies   56
6. Models and Patterns of Communication   74

PART II
Design, Evaluation, and Implementations   97

7. System Analysis or System Approach in Education   99
8. Micro-teaching   109
9. Programmed Instruction   129
10. Models of Teaching   142
11. Cooperative Learning   152

12	Theories and Techniques of Cooperative Learning	164
13	Co-teaching Approach in Education	177
14	Blended Learning in Education	196
15	Assistive Technology and Augmentative and Alternative Communication	207
16	Models and Universal Design Principles of Assistive Technology	220
17	Intelligent Tutoring System (ITS) in Education	233

PART III
Large-Scale Instructional/Administration Tools, Techniques, and Initiatives — **245**

18	Distance Education	247
19	E-Learning in Education	266
20	Massive Open Online Course (MOOC)	282
21	Learning Management System (LMS) and Learning Content Management System (LCMS) in Education	294
22	Social Media Applications in Education	305
23	Various Social Media Platforms and Applications in Education	314
24	Open Educational Resources (OER)	325

PART IV
Emerging Trends — **337**

25	Computer in Education and Its Application	339
26	Information Communication Technology (ICT) in Education	351
27	Games, Gamification, and Simulation in Education	363
28	Mobile or M-Learning in Education	378
29	Artificial Intelligence in Education	390
30	COVID-19 Pandemic: Educational Strategies and Resources during Crises and Emergencies	400

Index — *417*

FIGURES

2.1	Present scope of educational technology in the context of the instructional procedure, educational administration, and educational testing and feedback	10
2.2	Hardware and software approach	13
2.3	System approach of educational technology	14
2.4	System approach to teaching model (SAT)	14
3.1	Abacus math	22
3.2	Old Chinese abacus or counting frame which was used as the original calculator. It consists of a wooden frame with wooden beads and bamboo rods	22
3.3	Image of Stonehenge standing in Southern England	23
3.4	Gutenberg printing press	24
3.5	Napier's bones	24
3.6	Keuffel & Esser Slide Rule, model 4081-3 (c. 1940)	25
3.7	NMS Jacquard loom	25
3.8	Panasonic 16-mm film projector and vidicon camera, 1957	26
3.9	Sputnik 1	27
3.10	Skinner teaching machine	27
3.11	Integrated circuits	28
3.12	HP 1000 E-Series minicomputer	29
4.1	The basic structure of instructional design	36
4.2	Timeline for ADDIE model of instructional design	38
4.3	Analysis phase of ADDIE model of instructional design	39
4.4	The structural aspect of a formative and summative evaluation of the ADDIE model	43
4.5	The ASSURE model of instructional design	44
4.6	The Dick and Carey systems approach model for designing instruction	47
5.1	Diagrammatic representation of the process or cycle of communication	62
5.2	Oral communication process	64

5.3	Nonverbal communication process	65
6.1	Wheel network pattern of communication	75
6.2	Chain network pattern of communication	75
6.3	Y network pattern of communication	76
6.4	Circle network pattern of communication	76
6.5	Star or all-channel communication pattern	77
6.6	Intrapersonal communication process	78
6.7	Dyadic communication process	78
6.8	Small-group communication process	78
6.9	Public communication process	79
6.10	Mass communication process	79
6.11	A linear model of communication	80
6.12	Shannon Weaver communication model	81
6.13	Components of Lasswell's communication model	83
6.14	Aristotle's communication model	84
6.15	Berlo's SMCR communication model	86
6.16	Transactional model of communication	88
6.17	Barnlund's transactional model of communication	90
6.18	Becker's mosaic model of communication	91
6.19	An interactive model of communication	92
6.20	Fishbone diagram or cause and effect diagram	93
7.1	Parameters for instructional system	101
7.2	Schematic flow chart of the system approach	102
7.3	Stages of the instructional development system	105
7.4	Goal determination	106
8.1	The microteaching cycle	114
8.2	The phases of microteaching	115
8.3	The standard microteaching model	117
11.1	Co-operative learning environment	153
11.2	Traditional learning environments	157
13.1	The parallel model of co-teaching	180
13.2	The station model of co-teaching	181
13.3	The teaming model of co-teaching	183
13.4	The alternative model of co-teaching	184
13.5	The one teaches one observes model of co-teaching	185
13.6	The one teaches one assists model of co-teaching	186
13.7	Present stages of the co-teaching process	188
13.8	Components of the co-teaching approach	192
14.1	Process of blended learning	202
14.2	The constructive alignment model of curriculum design	203
14.3	The 4Q model of evaluation	204
15.1	Categories of assistive technology by Blackhurst and Lahm, 2008	209
17.1	Interaction in components in an intelligent tutoring system	237
17.2	Siemer and Angelides's general intelligent tutoring system architecture	238

17.3	Costa and Perskuchisk's Architecture of MATHEMA for IT learning environment	239
18.1	Guided didactic conversation: BorjeHolmburg (1995)	256
19.1	Information systems success model	273
19.2	Updated information systems success model	274
21.1	Components of Learning Management System (LMS)	295
21.2	Overview of the functional aspect of Learning Management System	301
21.3	Overview and features of Learning Management System	301
24.1	Difference between all right reserved, open license, and public domain	332
25.1	Process of computer-assisted instruction	344
26.1	Representation of ICT and its various uses	352
26.2	Scope of ICT in education	354
27.1	Elements of gamification classified by Oxford Analytica in a global analysis report (2016)	370
28.1	Basic elements of mobile learning	382
28.2	Teacher role in the present technology era	383

TABLES

2.1	Differences between technology in education and technology of education	16
3.1	Technology for teaching (1500 BC–AD 1990)	21
4.1	Difference between instructional system design and instructional design	34
5.1	Difference between vertical and horizontal communication	67
6.1	Components in the Shannon Weaver communication model	81
6.2	Components of Lasswell's model of communication	83
8.1	Comparison between microteaching and traditional teaching	112
8.2	Phases of microteaching with specific activities and components	115
8.3	Presents various teaching skills explained by Allen and Ryan (1969)	116
8.4	Present list of different stages of the lesson and the components of teaching skills	119
8.5	Present components of explaining skills for microteaching	120
8.6	Format sample	120
8.7	Gradation index	121
8.8	Component-wise grading	121
8.9	Sample format skill of illustration	122
8.10	*Gradation Index*	122
8.11	Component-wise grading	123
8.12	Sample format for the skill of reinforcement	124
8.13	Grading index	124
8.14	Component-wise grading	125
8.15	Phases and timing for microteaching	126
10.1	Concept Attainment Model of Teaching	149
11.1	Timeline on the history of cooperative learning	155
11.2	Comparison between traditional learning and cooperative learning	158
13.1	Present applicability of co-teaching and level of planning	187
16.1	Present various models of assistive technology	221

16.2	Assistive technology for people with visually impaired	224
16.3	Assistive Technology for Hearing Impaired	227
16.4	Assistive Technology for People with Physical Disabilities	228
16.5	Assistive Technology for People with a Communication Disability	228
16.6	Assistive Technology for People with Cognitive Disability and Learning Disorder	229
16.7	Agencies and organizations for assistive technology	230
16.8	Some vendors for assistive technology resources	230
17.1	Historical chronology of intelligent tutoring system	236
18.1	Details of the name of the theory and contributors with year	253
18.2	Distance teaching program based on dialog and structure	256
18.3	Types of independent study programs by learner autonomy	259
20.1	Difference between online learning and MOOC	286
20.2	Categorization of MOOC-based on their massiveness and openness	286
20.3	MOOC-based learning platforms and their web addresses	292
21.1	Historical overview of Learning Management System	297
21.2	Comparison of LMS and LCMS	299
21.3	Learning management platform commercial and open-source	300
22.1	Differences between social and industrial media	310
23.1	Comparison between traditional newsletter and eNewsletter	315
23.2	Comparison between traditional classroom communication and Facebook-based classroom communication	317
23.3	Some other social media platforms for education	320
23.4	Name of the websites, their functions, and official website link	321
24.1	Present historical overview of open educational resources	327
24.2	Present repository-based OER platform	329
24.3	OER for complete courses	330
24.4	Six types of Creative Commons licensing	333
24.5	Present various institutional repositories in India	334
25.1	Advantages and Disadvantages of Computer-Based Instructional Visualization	349
26.1	ICT tools in education	353
27.1	Difference between game, game-based learning, and gamification	364
27.2	Brief history of gamification trajectory	368
27.3	Present game-design elements and motives	370
27.4	Some of the various gamification-based learning applications/platforms	373
30.1	Tools to create infographics and charts for teachers	403
30.2	Tools to create infographics for teachers	404
30.3	Tools to create text-to-speech for teachers	405
30.4	Digital storytelling tools for teachers	405
30.5	Podcast tools for teachers	405
30.6	Screen recorder tools for teachers	405
30.7	Social bookmarking for teachers	406
30.8	Bibliography and citation tools for teachers	407

30.9	Sticky notes tools for teachers	407
30.10	Photo and image editing tools for teachers	408
30.11	Testing and quizzing tool for teachers	408
30.12	Web or video conferencing tools for teachers	409
30.13	Authoring tools for teachers	409
30.14	Video tools for teachers	409
30.15	PDF tools for teachers	410

FOREWORD

It is an immense honor and privilege to write this foreword for 'Educational Technology' authored by two passionate and informed scholars, Prof. Santoshi Halder and Dr Sanju Saha. Readers may be tempted to wonder what yet another book on educational technology can possibly add to the already available books dealing with educational technology. As well as the wealth and scope of already available literature in the field of educational technology, authors attempting to provide fresh insights or a novel angle to educational technology are also faced with the speed and scope with which technology, in general, and specifically educational technology are changing. Often educational technology is outpacing critical reflection on its value contribution, the hype surrounding the "new", the potential and risks, as well as the critical question pertaining to whose interests are ultimately served. We therefore increasingly need authors with a critical disposition who write about educational technology and who recognize that the field of educational technology is an intensely contested field with developers, venture capitalists, educators, students, and education providers negotiating the often-perilous intersections between value, profit, and educational gains. Too often it is almost impossible to distinguish, on the one hand, the potential of (new) educational technologies to address existing, new, or perceived pedagogical problems and, on the other hand, the claims and rhetoric surrounding educational technology. As such, this book provides a comprehensive overview of educational technology and will contribute to more informed and critical discussions on the potential, risks, and challenges of using educational technology in appropriate, ethical, and effective ways.

This book consists of 30 chapters divided into four different parts. Part I deals with "Fundamental Concepts and Theories", and Part II addresses "Design, Evaluation, and Implementations". Part III introduces "Large-Scale Instrumental/Administration Tools, Techniques, and Initiatives", and the concluding part (Part IV) addresses "Emerging Trends". In these four parts, each chapter is dedicated to a specific aspect of the vast and expanding educational technology landscape. The chapters are uniform in firstly foregrounding the learning objective, and then introducing several gateway questions. This is followed by, depending on the focus, definitions, core characteristics, and an informative overview of the chapter focus.

The book provides a very comprehensive overview of educational technologies ranging from foundational concepts to discussing some of the latest forms and uses of educational technology. As such, the book is an excellent introduction to educational technology and should be an invaluable introduction to those looking for an informed introduction to the field. Particularly valuable is the inclusion of a detailed discussion of different models of "Instructional Design in Education", different "Models and Patterns of Communication", "Models of Teaching", and "Cooperative Learning". The inclusion of chapters on "Assistive Technology" for those living with, or teaching those living with, a variety of disabilities is of immense value. Two chapters in the book address "Games, Gamification, and Simulation in Education" and "Mobile or M-Learning in Education".

While the book may be valuable for scholars, educators, and students from a range of international contexts, the book will add immense value to the specific context of India. For example, inter alia, the phenomenon of "Microteaching in India", "Programmed Instruction", evolution of "Distance Education", "Market and Structure of E-Learning", "Barriers of E-Learning in the Context of India", Open Educational Resources (OER) and some latest trend in educational technology, e.g., "Artificial Intelligence in Education". The book culminates with an overview chapter on the application of "Educational Strategies and Resources during Crises and Emergencies" with special reference to the COVID-19 pandemic.

I would like to congratulate Prof. Santoshi Halder and Dr Sanju Saha for this invaluable contribution to mapping the field of educational technology, and specifically for the immense value this book will add to the making of more informed and appropriate choices in the context of education in India.

Paul Prinsloo
Research Professor in Open and Distance Learning
University of South Africa, (UNISA), Pretoria, South
Africa

PREFACE

Human resource is surely the most significant natural resource. Living a quality life and enjoying every moment of human existence is perhaps the right of every individual. However, we are not all born having the same personal or social/context-driven attributes. Differences and diversity are natural phenomenon that needs to be accepted, celebrated, rejoiced, and facilitated. Individual differences can be enhanced and facilitated for maximum utilization through the application of technology in education. The application of innovations in technology can facilitate inclusion not only in education but also in every sphere of life and human existence and make life comfortable. The key to equality, equity, and access can be successfully achieved through technology and its strategic and appropriate application. Hence, it is pertinent to know and understand technology and its various aspects most comprehensively so that its crucial elements can be implemented in real-life applications most appropriately.

The idea for drafting this comprehensive book on educational technology was initiated and conceptualized back in 2011 while understanding the needs of the students and became further crystallized and shaped through cumulative efforts, thought processes, and brainstorming. It appeared that despite many books being available in the market, there is always room for betterment to bridge the persistent lacuna. The demand for a more comprehensive book on the subject covering updated areas and topics based on the most recent revised courses and syllabi provided more impetus to this ongoing endeavor.

This book is an attempt to provide the most updated resources on educational technology and its various crucial aspects to students, scholars, teachers, and educators. To successfully and most effectively achieve the objectives, the entire existing and latest courses and their syllabi were reviewed. A detailed list of chapters and subheadings was laid down after careful thought followed by stimulating discussions. The content has been prepared based on all existing resources available in India and abroad on each topic. All of the content has been prepared and drafted in easy language to make it more accessible and easily readable for a much wider audience, mostly in the developing countries, with a primary focus on the Indian context so that it can provide the most updated content in one comprehensive book most effectively. I believe the book is going to benefit numerous students, scholars, and trainee teachers, as well as educators, and facilitate their quest and goal of getting acquainted with educational technology with its crucial aspects and application.

Preface

The book is categorized into four sections:

Part I: Fundamental Concepts and Theories
Part II: Design, Evaluation, and Implementations
Part III: Large-Scale Instructional/Administration Tools, Techniques, and Initiatives
Part IV: Emerging Trends

The book is designed to be of use to a wide range of students, scholars, researchers, teacher educators, and teacher trainees covering most of the syllabi of graduate and postgraduate courses: Bachelor's in Education, Master's in Education, teacher training courses (B.Ed. and M.Ed.), research-oriented courses (MPhil. and PhD), etc.

ACKNOWLEDGMENTS

The initial idea of a well-conceptualized and comprehensive book on educational technology evolved while teaching educational technology courses in higher educational institutions. The raw ideas gathered crystallized, culminated, and got refined and shaped through multiple academic and nonacademic means, including teaching, and research exposures and opportunities, over the years in various divergent contexts. Teaching in a heterogeneous classroom and addressing the multifarious needs of learners with varied abilities and backgrounds has been one of the most interesting and adventurous challenges and one that I thoroughly cherish. Bringing out the best in every learner most creatively through an enriched stimulating environment that includes scaffolding, brainstorming, and critical thinking is one of the significant goals of any educational system and the role of the teachers is paramount.

The content of the book is an accumulation of thoughts over the years through multiple exposures and engagements in India and across various countries of the world (low, middle, and high income).

First and foremost, I am thankful to the University of Calcutta for providing me the scope, platform, opportunity, and continuous support to flourish my multifarious research and academic endeavors most strategically, effectively, and significantly.

I would like to acknowledge the various organizations who have supported me through prestigious funding opportunities, namely the United States-India Educational Foundation (USIEF), New Delhi; Institute of International Education (IIE), New Delhi; The Rockefeller Foundation, USA; Shastri Indo-Canadian Institute (SICI), New Delhi; Japan Society for the Promotion of Science (JSPS), Tokyo; Department of Education and Training, under the Australian government; Australian High Commission; Endeavour Australia India Council; Indian Council of Social Science Research (ICSSR), New Delhi; University Grants Commission (UGC), New Delhi; and National Institute for the Humanities and Social Sciences (NIHSS), South Africa. These fellowships/awards entrusted me with the role and responsibility of getting engaged with exceptional academicians in different interdisciplinary fields through significant collaborations across various countries through the interchange of thoughts that shaped my thought process further and added to my drive for contributing to the community and its people.

From the outset, I would like to thank my co-author, who is also my former PhD. and postdoctorate scholar, Dr Sanju Saha, with his ever-inquisitive mind for the quest for knowledge, who readily and most enthusiastically agreed and accepted my invitation to take this academic plunge and collaborated with me on this book project. His contribution to materializing and manifesting the ideas most concretely in the form of this book is noteworthy and appreciable. Without his efforts of working with me tirelessly and extracting his valuable time and following my guidance and assistance most enthusiastically, this book would not have attained its current form. Moreover, his sincere efforts reflected throughout the book show his enormous passion for technology. I am glad to be able to extend and continue our academic relationship further in a different role through this significant academic contribution. The book is the result of the cumulative collaborative and cooperative efforts of both of us together through continuous stimulating discussions, brainstorming, debates, and positive arguments.

I acknowledge the support and assistance of the publisher, Routledge India, for supporting us for this book project and for providing us the needed assistance at every phase.

Finally, I would like to thank my husband, Dr Arindam Talukdar, Principal Scientist, Indian Institute of Chemical Biology (IICB), Kolkata, India, my daughter Mihika, my son Kiaan, my parents, and the almighty God for instilling in me the inspiration, drive, energy, passion, and consistent effort without which the book would not have been possible.

Finally, I would like to state that this is just a part of our multiple continuous efforts to provide needful comprehensive resources for enhancing the sphere of teaching and learning in our capacity as a teacher, academician, and researcher in the field. The entire journey of bringing this amazing book to fruition has been a learning experience in itself that has been extremely refreshing, and we are sure to continue our efforts with more future endeavors.

Prof. Santoshi Halder

PART I

Fundamental Concepts and Theories

1
ORIGIN OF TECHNOLOGY AND PHILOSOPHY OF EDUCATIONAL TECHNOLOGY

Introduction

It can be assumed that mixed types of learners will read this book, such as completely novice learners who for the first time are getting introduced to the new buzz term "Educational Technology" (ET), at the same time, some may have some basic knowledge about ET, while others may have some advanced knowledge about ET. It is imperative to say that whatever level the learner is at, one has to accept the reality that we all are living in a "technological era", where every aspect of our life and society is changing unprecedentedly, mostly due to the advancement of technology. Therefore, as a learner of ET, one must know about "technology" and its origins. Taking this into consideration, the introductory chapter of the book has been designed to delve into the "origins" of technology through the lenses of the philosophy of technology. This chapter, at the outset, will focus on the origin of "education" and explain how technology works as a catalyst for education. Besides this, the core aim of education and basic knowledge about technology will also be discussed. Further, the relationship between technology, its value, and technology as determinism will also be elaborated. Eventually, the chapter will discuss the various aspects of technology in the field of education. The chapter will be concluded by laying out the journey from technology to technology education and the philosophy of technology education.

Concept of Education and Technology

"Education" is derived from the Latin word "*Educatum*", which means "the art of teaching". However, the modern approach to education is very dynamic. The aim of education is varied based on factors like cultural context, environmental context, personal traits, etc. However, the collective aspect of the various educational aims mainly focuses on three fundamental aspects:

- To transfer culture and improve the way of life
- To improve the social and physical environment
- To fulfill and improve individual life

To achieve the three fundamental objectives of education, various countries developed pathways or policies. For example, the United States has the pertinent Educational Need of Youth (1944) (cited by Gilchrist, 1951), India has a National Policy on Education (1986), Australia has the

Common Agreed National Goal for Schooling in Australia (AEC, 1986), and so on and so forth (Vries, 2012). All these policies mainly focused on the development of self-confidence, achievement of personal excellence, etc. To achieve these goals, various subjects, curriculum, school systems, and subject-based development of education have occurred.

Besides this, technology is a different concept and has a long history. In the early stages of the development of human beings, technology was developed and used as a "survival strategy" as well as for the "development of lifestyle" through improvement or environmental impact, when technology was not a subject. Therefore, the philosophical aspect of technology in that period was not explicit. In the early stages of human development lots of problems were faced and every time mankind tried to find a possible pathway to solve the problem by inventing various technological innovations. For example, weapons were invented by using stones through repeated trial-and-error learning or attempts to get good weapons. Furthermore, the knowledge and skills which were gathered from the trial-and-error learning method were transferred to the next generation and, by this process, one specific technology became more modern, updated, and usable. This is called modern technology, and its long evolutionary journey began with primary innovation.

Now, the fact is that in the ancient period there was no such separate subject related to "technology education". Technology education or technology as a subject of education is a very recent concept. The concept regarding the philosophy of technology was first introduced by Ernst Kapp in 1977. It is very surprising that although technology takes a vital role in present civilized society there is a lack of answers regarding how technology is significant for human life. Or how it impacts society, the relationship between advancement in technology and advancement in a civilization, the impact of human engagement with technology, and so on and so forth. Therefore, a basic gap can be seen in the context of acceptance of technology by teachers, parents, and students and their attitude toward technology as a subject as well as for school administration. Moreover, another interesting fact is that in the past it was thought that the use of technology in the context of education was basically for slow learners, and it is not known why this type of misconception or attitude formed regarding "educational technology". Maybe this type of misconception happened due to a lack of knowledge of the philosophy of technology.

However, this kind of rigid conception regarding technology changed after the Industrial Revolution and the knowledge of technology became a professional one, a way of thinking that brings about improvement in society and the environment.

The present chapter aims to provide a basic conception of the philosophy of educational technology. Philosophy denotes a branch of fundamental concepts of the nature of technology, beliefs about technology, the value of technology, the determining factors of technology, etc.

Philosophy of Technology Education

A comprehensive discussion about the philosophy of technology cannot take place without discussing the relationship between technology and technology education from a philosophical viewpoint. Therefore, it is imperative to create a learning environment where the learner has some opportunity to work with technology to understand the pivotal methods and principles of technology. Besides this, a student needs to adapt various cognitive and technological skills to understand the functional aspect of technology, which may only come from technology education.

It is also noted that there is a difference between technological knowledge and technological activity; technological knowledge is always scientific, whereas technological activity should be focused on the design-like process.

Somehow, technologists and technological designers function separately. The designer of technology produces original ideas and technologies to work with the design. Nevertheless, technologists also produce the original ideas in the context of functional activities of a specific design.

From the philosophical point of view, technology education functions in two ways; one is in a liberal art context and the second one is in a vocational training context. In the *liberal art context*, technology education focuses on mainly the "methodology of technology", whereas the *vocational aspect* focuses on competency and skill-based knowledge. But the link between these two aspects occurs when an acquisition of skills determines the specific methodology for technology education.

Now the use of technology is ubiquitous throughout the world. All countries have been gradually adapting technology education for economic and social development. However, there is still a lack of knowledge about the philosophical aspect. One doesn't know what school technology should belong to. How a student can learn through it? What are the effective teaching strategies for technology education? And so on and so forth. Furthermore, this kind of lack of consciousness creates fear in the teacher and, as a result, they are very suspicious of or pessimistic about accepting new technology.

Through this introductory chapter, the learner will know that in the context of technology education, there is a great degree of diversity throughout the world. For example, in Japan, there is no core technology education; in Israel, it's a compulsory subject; in Sweden, it has a humanistic approach; the United States focuses on the context of technology education, etc. Therefore, whatever the nature of technology education, the policymakers should design the curriculum of technology education by taking into consideration the country's needs and also know that teachers' beliefs about technology will broadcast the social context.

References

Gilchrist, R. S. (1951). Are schools meeting the imperative needs of youth? *Bulletin of the National Association of Secondary School Principals, 35*(180), 82–87.

Vries, M. J. de (2012). Philosophy of technology. In P. J. Williams (Ed.), *Technology education for teachers* (pp. 15–34). Sense Publishers.

Suggested Readings

Archer, B. (1986). *The three R's in technology in schools* (A. Cross & B. McCormick, Eds.). Milton Keynes: Open University Press.

Benson, C., & Lunt, J. (Eds.). (2011). *International handbook of primary technology education: Reviewing the past twenty years* (Vol. 7). Boston USA/ London, U.K: Springer Science & Business Media, D. Reidal Publishing Company.

De Vries, M. J. (2016). *Teaching about technology: An introduction to the philosophy of technology for non-philosophers*. Berlin: Springer.

Erneling, C. E. (2010). *Towards discursive education: Philosophy, technology, and modern education*. Cambridge: Cambridge University Press.

Ihde, D. (2012). *Technics and praxis: A philosophy of technology* (Vol. 24). Boston USA/ London, U.K: Springer Science & Business Media, D. Reidal Publishing Company.

Knight, G. (1982). *Issues and alternatives in educational philosophy*. Berrien Springs, MI: Andrews University Press.

Mitcham, C. (1994). *Thinking through technology: The path between engineering and philosophy*. Chicago, IL: University of Chicago Press.

Scharff, R. C., & Dusek, V. (Eds.). (2013). *Philosophy of technology: The technological condition: An anthology*. Chichester: John Wiley & Sons.

2
CONCEPTUAL ORIENTATION OF EDUCATIONAL TECHNOLOGY

Introduction

In the present times, we are living in a liberal global economy where technology is a power for change and information is the fuel. Throughout the world, if we look around every corner, the common thing to get noticed is the application of technology for living and the availability of information. Therefore, the 21st century is also called the era of the knowledge economy. The revolutionary innovations and applications of technology impact every aspect of human beings and the education sector is not exempted from it. The overall teaching-learning scenario is gradually changing due to technological excogitations. School, or any learning environment, is more than a knowledge tank through which knowledge can be distributed and is rather an environment that promotes learning and a process of acquisition that produces knowledge and skills for lifelong learning and technology is the holder and carrier. Over the last few decades, the impact of technology on education has been very large and seeks to explore the meaning of educational technology, the various approaches of Educational Technology (ET), etc. Therefore, the present chapter aims to discuss and provide a bird's-eye view of the application of technology in education.

Concept and Definition of Educational Technology

To get an overall view about educational technology it is imperative to form a separate concept of "technology" and "education", and then merge and present them as a comprehensive definition of technology from the established literature survey in the field.

What Is Meant by Technology?

In a very basic view, the term "technology" is derived from two Greek words namely "*Technic*" and "*Logia*". The term "*Technic*" denotes "art or skill" and "*Logia*" denotes "science or study". Therefore, combining the meaning of these two words is a science of the study of an art or skill.

In that point of view technology is a systematic understanding and application of "science" to achieve a specific objective effectively and efficiently. Professor Galbraith discussed two essential characteristics of technology:

- Systematic application of scientific knowledge into practice
- Deviation of any task into its components

The following are some of the explicit definitions of technology provided by Cass G. Gentry in his book chapter, "Educational Technology: A Question of Meaning".

Simon (1983) discussed "Technology as a rational discipline designed to assure the mastery of man over physical nature by using scientifically determined laws".

Jacquetta Bloomer (1973) defined "technology as the application of scientific theory to practical ends".

Mc Dermott (1981) explained that "Technology, in its concrete empirical meaning refers fundamentally to a system of rationalized control over large groups of man, event and machines by small groups of a technically skilled man operating through an organized hierarchy".

In *Random House Kernerman Webster's College Dictionary (2010)*, "Technology refers to applications, methods, theories, and practices that are used to reach desirable ends, especially industrial and commercial ends".

From the above definitions, it is very clear that technology is a pivotal component in every aspect of a human being. Now one should know what is meant by education and what are its fundamental objectives.

What Is Meant by Education?

The word "education" is derived from the Latin word "*Educatum*" that means "to bring out". In this context, education aims to bring out better qualities of the individual.

The Universal Dictionary of the English Language defines education as:

- To provide training, to educate
- Developing the brain and characteristics of a learner
- A particular state of an education system

From this point of view, "education" is a process that promotes modification of behavior, social efficiency, socialization, actualization, harmonious and all-round development, and adjustment to the environment.

John Dewey (1916) defined education as "the enterprise of supplying the conditions which ensure growth, or adequacy of life irrespective of age".

What Is Meant by Educational Technology?

From the separate view of "technology" and "education", it is quite clear that "educational technology" is an application part of the technological aspect to promote various educational objectives. By using various processes of technology and resources, educational technology generally emphasizes the teaching and learning process and communication aspects through the diverse application of multiple devices. By using devices or strategies of educational technology instructors or teachers developed various unique and organized teaching-learning processes by utilization of modern technological development. Though plenty of discussion regarding ET has evolved over the years by various researchers, there is, however, still no concrete or universal definition of ET, maybe this is because of the dynamic nature of the field of educational technology.

Definitions of Educational Technology

For a better understanding of the definitions of educational technology, following are some of the definitions provided by the eminent researchers and scholars from the various fields of study.

S. S. Kulkarni (1986) discussed that "Educational Technology may be defined as the application of the laws as well as recent discoveries of science and technology to the process of education".

Dieuzeide (1971) defined educational technology as a "body of knowledge resulting from the application of the science of teaching and learning to the real world of the classroom, together with the tools and methodologies developed to assist these applications".

Takshi Sakamato (1971) said, "Educational Technology is an applied or practical study which aims at maximizing educational effect by controlling such relevant facts as educational purposes, educational environment, the conduct of the student, behavior of instructors and interrelations between students and instructors".

Cleary et al. (1976) explained that "Educational Technology is concerned with the overall methodology and set of techniques employed in the application of instructional principles".

Collier et al. (1971) stated that educational technology involves the applications of systems, techniques, and aids to improve the process of human learning, … It is characterized by four features in particular: the definition of objectives to be achieved by the learner; the application of principles of learning to the analysis and structuring of the subject matter to be learned; the selection and use of appropriate media for presenting material; and the use of the appropriate methods of assessing student performance to evaluate the effectiveness of courses and materials.

AECT (Association for Educational Communications and Technology) Task Force (1977) explained that educational technology "is a complex, integrated process involving people, procedures, ideas, devices, and organization, for analyzing problems, and devising, implementing, evaluating and managing solutions to those problems, involved in all aspects of human learning".

Jacquetta Bloomer (1973) said, "Educational Technology is the application of scientific knowledge about practical learning situations".

Richmond (1970) stated, "Educational Technology is concerned to provide appropriately designing learning situations, holding in view the objectives of the teaching or training, bring or bear the best means of instruction".

Januszewski and Molenda (2008) defined that "Educational technology is the study and ethical practice of facilitating learning and improving performance by creating, using and managing appropriate technological processes and resources".

UNESCO (2001) explained that "Educational technology is a communication process resulting from the application of scientific methods to the behavioral science of teaching and learning. This communication may or may not require the use of media such as television broadcasts, radio, cassettes, etc.".

Kumar (2002) stated:

> Educational Technology is a systematic way of designing, implementing and evaluating the total process of learning and teaching in terms of specific objectives, based on research in human learning and communication and employing a combination of human and non-human resources to bring about more effective instruction.

NPE (National Policy on Education) (1986) says, "Educational technology offers the means to reach large numbers in remote and inaccessible areas, remove disparity in educational facilities available to the disadvantaged, and provide individualized instruction to learners conveniently suited to their needs and pace of learning".

Besides all the mentioned definitions of educational technology, it is also imperative to provide the latest and more acceptable definition provided by the Association for Educational Communications and Technology.

The *Association for Educational Communications and Technology (AECT) (1977)* defines "Educational technology as the study and ethical practice of facilitating learning and improving performance by creating, using and managing appropriate technological processes and resources" (cited by Richey et al., 2008).

From the above definition, one gets the view that educational technology is the application of scientific knowledge and technology in education. Now, if we try to separate the two views, we can see that science is a search of knowledge and technology is an application of scientific knowledge to the solution of a problem. Therefore, ET is a systematic approach to the teaching-learning process. With a simplistic view of ET, educational technology is:

- The scientific aspect and systematic approach to using technology in education to achieve the aim of education
- A scientific aspect of preservation, transmission, and development of knowledge through technology
- The application of scientific knowledge and devices to enhance the meaningful contextualization and productivity in education

Characteristics of Educational Technology

After the critical discussion on definitions, the following are some of the major characteristics of educational technology.

Application of scientific principles: One of the essential characteristics of educational technology is that it is scientific. The development of a field of science is a parallel indication of the development of a field of educational technology. The application of scientific principles in the field of educational technology ensures a maximized benefit of teaching and learning scenarios. Educational technology as a field of study always tries to adopt various technological, mechanical, and scientific knowledge to encounter various educational problems and find out a required solution.

Dynamic, flexible, and modern discipline: The field of educational technology is dynamic, flexible, and based on modern disciplines. It is dynamic because every day various new technologies are developed to find out a specific solution. It is flexible because day by day old technology is becoming obsolete and one embraces new technology. And it is a modern discipline because this field is ready to face future challenges.

Mass communication approach: By using various modern communication technologies, the field of ET has been impacted by the mass approach of teaching and learning processes. By using educational technology, mass numbers of students can learn irrespective of their socio-economic status, demographic background, location, language, etc.

Personalization teaching and learning: Another unique characteristic of educational technology is it encourages individual differences and by using various scientific methods of design it can nurture every student in respect of their specific needs.

Scientific solution to methods and techniques of instructions: Educational technology provides various scientific solutions to specific problems. It also encourages development of various instruments to accelerate the learning process and to improve the teaching and learning environment.

Systematic approach: Educational technology is a systematic approach. On the one hand, it utilizes various hardcore hardware- and software-based technological knowledge and, on the other hand, a systematic use of multidisciplinary field knowledge to achieve educational objectives.

Facilitates educational system and management process: Another essential characteristic of educational technology is that it helps to facilitate and manage the educational environment in an effective as well as an efficient way.

Research-based discipline: Educational technology is a more sophisticated field of study. It includes a multidisciplinary field of knowledge and psychosocial and behavioral knowledge to solve a specific problem related to teaching and instruction.

Scope of Educational Technology

From the previous discussion one gets some basic knowledge about the concept of educational technology and its characteristics. From this general discussion one can understand that the field of educational technology is not only limited to the use of audiovisual tools in the teaching-learning process but rather is a multidisciplinary field of knowledge. It encompasses several domains of knowledge, such as behavioral science, engineering and mechanical knowledge, psychological principles, knowledge of learning theories, use of computer-based media, etc. This huge spectrum of inclusion of different fields of knowledge expands the scope of educational technology so that it is much wider. Therefore, the scope of educational technology includes, but it is not limited to, the discussion of selection and use of media and method, management of resources, and evaluation. Following are some basic scopes of educational technology as proposed by Derek Rowntree (1973):

- Development of goals and objectives for specific teaching and learning processes
- Arrangement of suitable teaching and learning environments
- Structuring and scientific development of course materials
- Selection of effective teaching strategies, learning media, and instructional instruments
- Evaluation of the effectiveness of certain teaching and learning process
- Last, but not least, provision of appropriate feedback for future development (see Figure 2.1)

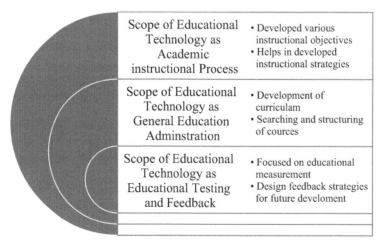

Figure 2.1 Present scope of educational technology in the context of the instructional procedure, educational administration, and educational testing and feedback.

From the above discussion of the scope of the study of educational technology, the following conclusions can be made in this regard:

- Educational technology as a "theory and practice"—focused on approaches of learning
- Educational technology as "technological tools and media"—assists in communication, development, management, and exchange of knowledge
- Educational technology as "learning management system"—helps in curriculum, information, and content management

Assumptions of Educational Technology

The following are some of the basic assumptions in the context of educational technology:

1. *The assumption of productivity:* One of the major aims of the present educational system is to increase productivity in the context of education as a system approach and, in that case, technology is one of the weapons or means to do so. For the productivity aspect, dichotomous contexts are needed such as quality and productivity. In the context of cost-effectiveness, therefore, it is assumed that the use of technology can create a balance between them.
2. *Assumption of technology as a bridge between strategies and tactical aspects:* It is assumed that technology can work as a lever to increase the quality aspect of education. Technology is not a strategic tool but rather a technical tool that bridges between strategies and applications to reach a certain goal of education.
3. *Assumptions of cost-effectiveness:* As technology can work accurately and repetitively in a specific job, it is therefore assumed that the use of technology in the field of education can make education cost-effective.
4. *Active learning assumptions:* It is a known fact that active learning is a more motivating learning strategy than passive learning. As technology can serve education in a more personalized way to the larger community, it is therefore assumed that technology can produce an effective active learning environment for the benefit of learning.

Approaches of Educational Technology

From the discussion of the previous section, one gets a basic view that the field of educational technology is the application of various modern and advanced skills to achieve various aims and objectives of education and training. Therefore, educational technology as a scientific aspect is a multifaceted concept. Lumsdaine (1964) has classified the field of educational technology into three distinct approaches:

- Educational Technology I or Hardware Approaches
- Educational Technology II or Software Approaches
- Educational Technology III or System Approaches

Educational Technology I or Hardware Approach

Educational Technology I or the Hardware Approach originated from the field of physical science and engineering. This is a concept that Silverman (1968) denotes as "technology in education". For example, suppose a teacher wants to communicate with several students in a big classroom, then amplification of the teacher's voice is imperative for effective communication.

In this specific scenario, the use of a microphone can be an effective device for teaching and learning. Therefore, as a simplified view, the use of a hardware device like a microphone is an "Educational Technology I or Hardware Approach". Like the microphone, the use of a model, chart, slide, filmstrip, projector, audiovisual aids, radio, tape recorder, teaching machines, computer, etc. are all hardware approaches in educational technology. One of the unique characteristics of ET I or hardware approaches to educational technology is that all equipment is developed in a different field like engineering or mechanics and is utilized for educational purposes.

Educational technologist Davis provides a similar conception that hardware technology of education purely uses innovations of different fields like physical science, engineering, or mechanics which helps to mechanize the entire teaching and learning process to promote and achieve the objective of education in a very specific and easy matter. In addition, these approaches also help the teacher to deal with more students in an effective as well as a personalized way. Nickson (1978) explained that the hardware approach of educational technology is an application of the science of many other fields to the field of education to meet the needs of an individual as well as society. Therefore, Silverman (1968) also called this approach "Relational technology" which means the application of technology, machines, and devices in the context of the process of teaching and learning.

Therefore, hardware approaches to educational technology mainly focus on "machine technology". They believe that the application of machines in the context of instruction helps in the advancement of the teaching and learning process as well as the cognitive aspects of instruction. Educational Technology I or the Hardware Approach of education emphasizes three basic facts: *preservation*, *transmission*, and *advancement*.

It is also noted that various mechanical devices used in the field of education are not specifically designed for teaching and instruction but rather ithey are designed only for effective communication, information, and recreation. Therefore, as a teacher or instructor, one needs to be aware or cautious about using various hardware devices to achieve the educational objectives.

Educational Technology II or Software Approach

As the hardware approach originated from physical science and applied engineering, the software approach originated from "behavioral science" and "psychology of learning", for bringing desirable change in the learner.

As approaches of Educational Technology II originated from "theories of learning", they therefore mainly focus on questions like: What is the process of learning? What are the factors for effective learning and communications? What kind of mental preparedness of students is required for effective learning? So this approach deals with various aspects like prior knowledge of the learner, expert knowledge of the teacher, method of the teaching process, the motivation of the learning process, etc. for optimizing the teaching and learning process. To do so, the ET II Approach is focused on the technique of developing and utilization of software. Therefore, this approach is also called the software approach of educational technology.

In this software approach context, the National Centre for Programmed Learning UK defined ET as: "Application of scientific knowledge about learning and conditions of learning, to improve the effectiveness and efficiency of teaching and learning. In the absence of scientifically established principles, educational technology implements techniques of empirical testing to improve learning situations" (cited by Kumar, 1996; see Figure 2.2).

The software approach of educational technology is also called "constructive educational technology" by Silverman (1968). Generally, the software approach of educational technology is focused on analysis, selection, and construction to achieve any desired educational aim and

Conceptual Orientation

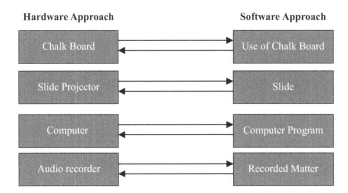

Figure 2.2 Hardware and software approach (based on Kumar, 1996).

objectives. In this aspect, education is technology enriched from the various interdisciplinary fields like psychology, management, cybernetics, philosophy, sociology, etc.

The software approach of educational technology is mainly designed for the application of various psychological theories for bringing desirable change in the learner through the principle of the instructional procedure, teaching behavior, and behavior-modification process. The software approach of educational technology is also called "instructional technology", "teaching technology", and "behavioral technology". According to Davis (1971), "The software approach of educational technology closely associates with the modern principles of programmed learning and is characterized by task analysis, writing, precise objectives, selection of correct responses and constant evaluation process" (Aggarwal, 1995). It is imperative to say that though the fields of "hardware technology" and "software technology" are independent approaches of educational technology, both the approaches are very interlinked and both are very much dependent on each other. The hardware approach deals with machines, and the software approach deals with the principles of learning and teaching.

Educational Technology III or System Approach

This is a third and comparatively more recent approach to educational technology. It originated from the concept of system engineering. This is a concept of "technology of education". The system approach of educational technology mainly focused on a systematic way to design, carry out, and evaluate the whole process of an education system to achieve the educational objective. The concept of the system approach became popular after World War II. In that specific period, there was a great demand for scientific decision-making as well as the administration and management of military problems. Therefore, this approach is also called "management technology". Generally, the system approach of educational technology deals with a complete aspect of the teaching and learning process.

The US Commission on Instructional Technology defines it as follows:

> System approach of educational technology is a systematic way of designing and implementing and evaluating the total process of learning and teaching in terms of specific objects based on research in human learning and communication and employing a combination of human and non-human resources to bring about more effective instruction.
>
> *(cited by Reiser & Ely, 1997; see Figure 2.3)*

Fundamental Concepts and Theories

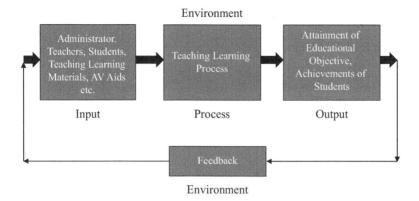

Figure 2.3 System approach of educational technology.

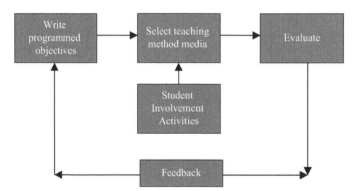

Figure 2.4 System approach to teaching model (SAT) (adapted from Smith, 1991).

From this definition, one can get a complete view about the system approach of education as follows:

- A system approach is a complete process of teaching and learning designed for the utilization of scientific procedures like research, communication, and evaluation in an instructional process.
- It encourages the utilization of various valuable resources, irrespective of human and non-human, to achieve a certain educational goal.
- A system approach is a process of a complex whole. Various parts of a system work together with a mechanism or interconnecting process to achieve a specific objective.
- It is an intelligent combinational process of hardware and software approaches to achieve the desired result.
- A system approach to education is considered as a whole educational process in the context of input–output system (see Figure 2.4)

The Technology of Education and Technology in Education: Overview

The concept of "educational technology" can be classified into two independent but mutually interlinked concepts:

- Technology of education
- Technology in education

Technology of Education

Technology of education is the core aspect in the context of education. It is a combinational aspect of an application of the various fields of knowledge of behavioral science, knowledge of psychology principle, knowledge of management and administration, etc. to solve various learning problems and find out effective teaching and learning solutions. Technology of education has a broad spectrum covered with various scientific system approach techniques of curriculum planning transaction and evaluation processes through the means of input–process–output techniques.

Following are some of the technical aspects that fall under the spectrum of the technology of education:

- System analysis
- Programmed learning
- Designing of an instructional objective
- Evaluation process and selection of instruments
- Strategies of the teaching-learning process
- Designing of instruction and analysis of instructional problems
- Designing a model of teaching

Technology in Education

Technology in education is the application of technological knowledge, devices, and machines in education. In the context of education, technology includes the use of various devices like projectors, film, television, radio, Internet, etc. As previously discussed, technology education is an application of the engineering principle. Silverman (1968) explained that approach as "relative technology" and "constructive educational technology" (see Table 2.1).

Forms of Educational Technology

As readers now have a comprehensive knowledge about the concept of educational technology and its versatile applicability in the different fields, the subsequent section aims to provide information about various forms of educational technology:

- Teaching technology
- Instructional technology
- Behavioral technology

Teaching technology: Teaching is a unique activity to promote the aim of education effectively. The most significant aspect of teaching is to bring about the all-around development of children. This is one of the essential scientific aspects of education. Teaching as a science studies various teaching strategies objectively and scientifically. Generally teaching technology is concerned with a justification of various teaching activities theoretically and in a systematic way to provide effective and motivational teaching methods to the teacher. The early exponents of teaching technology are Davis, Gagne, Robert Glaser, etc. One of the

Table 2.1 Differences between technology in education and technology of education

Context of Differentiations	Technology in Education	Technology of Education
Theoretical aspect	Technology in education is mainly based on behavioral science and psychological principle	Technology of education is theoretically based on physical, engineering, and mechanical science
Approach	It is mainly based on the software approach of ET	It is based on a hardware approach
Application	This approach is focused on learning aids	It is related to teaching aids
Dynamism and flexibility	This approach is more dynamic and flexible	It a fixed and rigid approach
Scope	This approach is more scientific and aims to understand the need of learners to achieve the educational goal	This approach is more effective in the context of mass education
Type	Silverman called this approach of educational technology "constructive educational technology"	This approach of educational technology is also called "relative technology"
Cost	This approach is less costly	This is expensive due to the use of various hardware devices

major assumptions of teaching technology are the three basic vital domains of educational objective—cognitive, affective, and psychomotor—that can be achieved by the use of technology and can be organized through three levels of teaching—memory, understanding, and reflective. Furthermore, teaching technology is the combinational knowledge of philosophy, sociology, and scientific knowledge of education.

Instructional technology: Instruction is a very important aspect of the human learning process. In a narrow concept "instruction" denotes communication of various information, except for by the teacher. For instance, web-based learning or an open education system communicates with learners through mediums such as radio, television, press, etc. One of the major aims of instructional technology is the development of the cognitive aspect of the learner. Instructional technology as a form of educational technology mainly is the application aspect of scientific and psychological principles. Programmed instruction is one of the most essential examples of instructional technology. It is also imperative to say that instructional technology is based on the assumption that every individual is unique and has different needs and capacities, and therefore the process of instruction needs to be personalized to serve the major aims of education. Instructional technology also believes that the student is a more active component and assumes that students can learn without a teacher if instruction is provided effectively and scientifically. The major proponents of instructional technology are Skinner, Glaser, Crowder, Gilbert, etc.

Behavioral technology: Behavioral technology is based purely on psychological principles. It is based on the behavioral science of learning. Behavioral technology places teachers as a secondary component. It believes that communication is one of the major components in the educational process. This form of educational technology is focused on scientific knowledge or modification of teacher behavior. This form of technology is also called "training technology". Major exponents of behavioral technology are B. F. Skinner, Anderson, Amidon, etc. Behavioral technology is based on the assumption that the behavior of a teacher should always be as social as well as psychological and that teacher behavior can be modified by training and reinforcement.

References

AECT. (1977). *The definition of educational technology.* Washington, DC: AECT.

Aggarwal, J. C. (1995). *Essentials of educational technology.* Vikas Publishing House.

Association for Educational Communications and Technology. (1977). *The definition of educational technology.* Washington, DC: Association for Educational Communications and Technology.

Bloomer, J. (1973). What have simulation and gaming got to do with programmed learning and educational technology? *Programmed Learning and Educational Technology, 10*(4), 224–234. https://doi.org/10.1080/1355800730100402.

Cleary, A. et al. (1976). *Educational technology: Implications for early and special education.* New York: John Wiley and Sons.

Collier, K. G. et al. (1971). *Colleges of education learning programmes: A proposal (working paper no. 5).* Washington, DC: National Council for Educational Technology.

Dewey, J. (1916). *The school and society.* Chicago, IL: University of Chicago Press.

Dieuzeide, H. (1971). *Educational technology: Sophisticated, adaptive and rational technology.*

Gentry, C. G. (2016). *Reflection Paper on Educational Technology, Instructional Technology, and Material development* by Merve BÖLÜKBA. https://bolukbasmervew.wordpress.com/2016/05/15/educational-technology-written-by-cass-g-gentry/

Januszewski, A. & Molenda. (2008). *Educational technology: The development of a concept.* Libraries Unlimited.

Kulkarni, S. S. (1986). *Introduction to educational technology.* Oxford: Lott Publishing Co. New Delhi.

Kumar, K. L. (1996). *Educational technology.* New Age International.

Kumar, K. L. (2002). Internet-based interactive design for students, teachers and practitioners, proceedings of the international conference. In *A millennium dawn in training and continuing education* (pp. 379–380). Bahrain.

Lumsdaine, A. A. (1964). Educational technology, programmed learning and instructional science. *Theories of learning and instruction, 63rd yearbook of NSSE.*

McDermott, J. (1981). Technology: The opiate of the intellectuals. In A. Teich (Ed.), *Technology and man's future.* New York: St. Martin's Press.

Reiser, R. A., & Ely, D. P. (1997). The field of educational technology as reflected through its definitions. *Educational Technology Research and Development, 45*(3), 63–72. https://doi.org/10.1007/bf02299730.

Richey, R. C., Silber, K. H., & Ely, D. P. (2008). Reflections on the 2008 AECT definitions of the field. *TechTrends, 52*(1), 24–25.

Richmond, W. K. (1970). *The teaching revolution.* London: Methuen.

Rowntree, D. (1973). *What is educational technology? A problem-solving approach to education.* London: Open University, Institute of Educational Technology, Harper and Row.

Sakamoto, T. (1971). United nations educational, scientific, and cultural organization, Bangkok (Thailand). Regional office for education in Asia and Oceania. In *The development of educational technology.* Washington, DC: Distributed by ERIC Clearinghouse. Retrieved from https://eric.ed.gov/?id=ED084795

Simon, Y. R. (1983). Pursuit of happiness and lust for power in a technology society. In D. C. Mitcham & R. Mackey (Eds.), *Philosophy and technology.* New York: Free Press.

Silverman, R. E. (1968). Two kinds of technology. *Educational Technology, 8*(1), 3–3.

Silverman, R. E. (1968). Using the SR reinforcement model. *Educational Technology, 8*(5), 3–12.

Smith (1991). https://journals.sagepub.com/doi/abs/10.1177/030582989102000031001

The National Policy on Education (NPE). (1986). www.ncert. Retrieved from nic.in/oth_anoun/npe86.pdf.

UNESCO (2001). Information and communication technologies in teacher education: a planning guide - UNESCO Digital Library. https://unesdoc.unesco.org/ark:/48223/pf0000129533

Suggested Readings

Educational Technology. (2010). *Word reference random house unabridged dictionary of American English.*

Frant, A. S. (1991). *Instructive instructional strategies: Ways to enhance learning by TV in designing for learner access: Challenges & practices.* Madison, WI: University of Wisconsin.

HRD Ministry, Govt. of India. (1986). *Report of national policy on education*. New Delhi: Department of Education.

IGNOU. (2000). *ES-361: Educational technology*, B.Ed. Programme (pp. 9–11). New Delhi: IGNOU.

IGNOU. (2009). *MES-031, introduction to educational technology?* (pp. 1–19). New Delhi: IGNOU. (Unit-1).

Katherine, S. C., John, D. S., & Ertmer, P. A. (2010). Technology integration for meaningful classroom use: A standard based approach. *Cennamo Ross Ertmer*, xvii, 4–11.

Kulkarni, S. S. (1986). *Introduction to educational technology* (pp. 143–144). New Delhi: Oxford & IBH Publishing Co.

Kumar, K. L. (1997). *Educational technology: A practical textbook for students, teachers, professionals and trainers*. New Delhi: New Age International.

Mahandiratta, M. (1997). *Encyclopaedia dictionary of education* (Vol. I, p. 252). New Delhi: Sarup & Sons.

Mishra, P., & Koehler, M. J. (2006). Technological pedagogical content knowledge: A framework for integrating technology in teacher knowledge. *Teachers College Record, 108*(6), 1017–1054.

NCERT (2012). *Proposed syllabus of educational technology and ICT for teacher education programme*. New Delhi: CIET.

Nickson, M. (1994). The culture of the mathematics classroom: An unknown quantity? In Lerman, S. (eds) *Cultural Perspectives on the Mathematics Classroom. Mathematics Education Library* (Vol. 14, pp. 7–35). Dordrecht: Springer.

Rao, R. R., & Rao, D. B. (2006). *Methods of teacher training* (p. 416). New Delhi: Discovery Publishing House.

Sharma, R. A. (2004). *Technological foundations of education* (3rd ed.). Meerut: R. Lal Publications.

Skinner, B. F. (1968). *The technology of teaching*. New York: Appleton-Century-Crofts.

Walia, J. S. (1997). *Educational technology* (pp. 104–120). Jalandhar: Paul Publishers.

Wikipedia. (2012). *Educational technology*. Retrieved December 14, 2012, from http://edutechwiki.unige.ch/en/Educational_technology.

3
HISTORICAL EVOLUTION OF EDUCATIONAL TECHNOLOGY

It is not an overwhelming assumption that after reading the previous two chapters of this book one may have built some reasonable and comprehensive knowledge about "Educational Technology (ET)", including its application and impact in education. From the previous discussion, it is explicit that educational technology helps in the advancement of the instruction and assessment process and provides a pathway for preparing scientific instructional procedure and framework at all levels of instructions such as formal, non-formal, and informal aspects of education. In addition, it also encourages the use of a wide range of media and upgraded technological innovations in various instructional environments such as in an audiovisual teaching-learning environment, in modern Web 3.0 technology, in textbook-based learning approaches, in online-based teaching-learning communication, etc. However, the modern development of educational technology is certainly an innovation, it has a long history, and day by day this field has been gradually enriching from various concepts from the multidisciplinary fields while communicating across different innovations and frameworks. Moreover, it is also notable that the advancement of technology (specifically media-based innovation) draws a parallel advancement of the field of ET in the context of global innovation including innovation in India. Therefore, to know more about the origin of ET a learner must gain comprehensive knowledge about the historical overview of ET from the early aspect of human society. This chapter is designed to provide an explicit knowledge of technological innovation in the context of instruction. This chapter will provide more about the global context of the development of educational technology from the root level of innovation to the application of ET in the context of India.

Global Historical Development of Educational Technology

To obtain comprehensive knowledge about ET, it is imperative to go back to the early stages of innovation. This section will discuss the innovation of technology in the context of education from the period of the Stone Age to the age of information and communication technology. Following are the evolutionary phases of educational technology and innovations.

Stone Age Period

If we take drawing and writing as an early phase of educational technology, then the man of the Stone Age will be recognized as a progenitor of ET because they used to draw various day-today activities and their thoughts on the surface of rocks on cave walls or on a flat surface. It is notable that in this stage transfer of the knowledge of the use of stones, pebbles, counting sticks, slabs, etc. was the most primary aspect of instruction.

The Age of Book and Chalkboard

This is a great revolutionary time of educational technology. This phase is revolutionary in the sense that, in 1456, Johannes Gutenberg invented the printing machine. With this innovation, the exploration of information, expansion, and access of knowledge was more open and interesting because of "one-to-one" and "self-learning" which was impossible before the innovation of printing technology. Therefore, printing technology is a more obvious and essential innovation in the context of teaching and instruction.

Furthermore, another essential innovation at the end of this period is the chalkboard which is popularly known as a blackboard. This innovation changed the way of instruction and opened the pathway of group communication in a specific place. This innovation also provides a space for teachers and instructors to write down important points, diagrams, or symbols and communicate with the group of students.

Mass Communication Age

Another milestone of the historical age of educational technology is the age of media innovation for mass communication. The innovation of radio and television is an historic point of advancement of technology in the global context. Before this innovation, communication with a mass audience was extremely limited. Therefore, the innovation of early-stage mass media like radio and television expanded the opportunity for mass instruction.

The Information Communication Age/Computer Age

The development of the microcomputer is more recent and one of the most effective innovations in the field of educational technology. This innovation surprisingly changed the way of instructional processes throughout the world. The innovation of computers expanded the scope for access to more data from anywhere at a low or no cost. Therefore, this is also called the "Information Age". Conway (1990) discussed some of the specific development that takes place through the advancement of computer technology in the context of education or instruction, as follows:

- Blackboard converted to white smart board with advanced features of the touch pen
- Multimedia-based system added with sound blaster and speakers
- CD-ROM player and DVR-ROM player
- A personal computer equipped with a videodisc player and a videotape controller
- Conference-based computer on PC-PC
- Touch screen and voice-recognizing/communication devices
- The innovation of digital cameras and editing features of digital images
- The innovation of virtual reality

The next section will discuss very specific evolutionary aspects of ET from the year 1500 BC to AD 2018.

Technological Development (1500 BC to AD 2018)

This section is intended to align an overview of technological innovation in the context of education from 1500 BC to AD 2018. In this context, Tony Bates in his blog post listed various technological innovations from 1500 BC. Table 3.1 presents the innovation of educational technology from 1500 BC to AD 2013 (for an extract from the blog post of Tony Bates see his site at www.tonybates.com).

Table 3.1 Technology for teaching (1500 BC–AD 1990)

Development	Year
Teacher	1500 BC
Printed book	1450
Postal service	1850
Blackboard	1850
Telephone	1890
Radio	1920
Film	1920
Broadcast television	1950
Cable television	1950
Audiocassettes	1965
Computer-based instruction	1970
Satellite television	1975
Laser videodiscs	1975
Audioconference	1975
Personal computer	1980
Audio-graphics	1980
Viewdata/teletext	1980
Computer conferencing	1980
Compact discs	1985
E-mail	1985
Videoconferencing	1990
Projector	1990
Smart board	1990
Internet	1990
World Wide Web	1990
Simulation and games	1990
Learning management system	1995
Browser/web portal	1995
Wireless network	1995
Mobile phones	1995
Learning objects/open education resources (OERs)	1995
Fiber-optic cable	2000
DVDs	2000
Search engine	2000
Virtual reality	2003
E-portfolios	2005
Clickers	2005
YouTube	2005
Lecture capture	2008
E-books	2009
Cloud computing	2010
Learning analytics	2011
MOOC (massive open online course)	2013

Some Cornerstone Innovations in Education and Technology

The above discussion provides a general outline of the evolution of educational technology from 1500 BC to AD 2018. The next section discusses in detail some of the technological innovations since the inception of the abacus in 3000 BC.

Abacus: This is an early-stage innovative device for calculating. The abacus is marked as the first computer, invented in 3000 BC (see Figure 3.1)

Suan pan: This is a surviving early-stage counting board which dates back to 400 BC. In China, it is called a saun pan and in Japan it is called a soroban. A soroban is a type of abacus still used for calculation (see Figure 3.2).

Figure 3.1 Abacus math. (Image Credit – Peter Griffin. Source: publicdomainpictures.net).

Figure 3.2 Old Chinese abacus or counting frame which was used as the original calculator. It consists of a wooden frame with wooden beads and bamboo rods (Image Credit: Catalogocollezioni (in it). Source: Museoscienza.org. Museo Nazionale della Scienza e della Tecnologia Leonardo da Vinci, Milano).

Stonehenge: Stonehenge is the earliest form of astronomical calculator. It was created around 2300 BC and took 2000 years to complete. Stonehenge is in Southern England (see Figure 3.3).

Leonardo da Vinci calculator: Around 1502, the first mechanical calculator was invented by Leonardo da Vinci. It is now known as "Codex Madrid". In the year 1968, IBM hired Dr Roberto Guatelli to make a replica of the da Vinci design of a calculator.

Gutenberg printing press: Between 1452 and 1456, Johannes Gutenberg developed the printing press. This is one of the greatest innovations of all time. The first book published by the Gutenberg printing press was the Bible (see Figure 3.4).

Napier's bones: John Napier is the inventor of logarithms and he developed an aid for calculation in 1617 known as "Napier's bones". Napier described a method of multiplication by using his innovative "numbering rods". The numbering rods look like bones and are made of ivory (see Figure 3.5).

Slide rule: In 1654 Robert Bissaker invented the slide rule which is an early innovation of the electronic calculator (see Figure 3.6).

Magin Cataoprica: The Magin Cataoprica is a kind of magic lantern which was invented in around 1646. It is also called a magic lantern and used to play slide shows or educational material in the classroom. The Magin Cataoprica is an early-use projection media for theaters or home events.

Jacquard loom: It is amazing to know that modern computer programming was influenced by the innovation of Joseph-Marie Jacquard namely by the "Jacquard loom". It is a mechanism of punched cards that control the machine as required. This punch-card mechanism is one of the fundamental ideas of the first computer (see Figure 3.7).

Educational film: Educational film is one of the greatest innovations in the field of teaching and instruction. The early innovation year of educational film is controversial. Some research-

Figure 3.3 Image of Stonehenge standing in Southern England. (Source: www.flickr.com/photos/garethwiscombe/1071477228/in/photostream/Authorgarethwiscombe).

Fundamental Concepts and Theories

Figure 3.4 Gutenberg printing press. (Source: https://commons.wikimedia.org/wiki/File:Gutenberg .press.jpg. Author: Ghw at English Wikipedia).

Figure 3.5 Napier's bones. (Source: https://commons.wikimedia.org/wiki/File:Napier%27s_calculating _tables.JPG. Author: Kim Traynor).

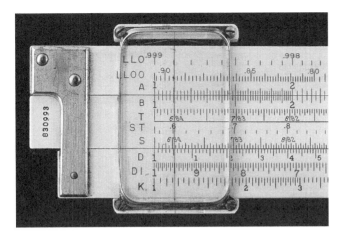

Figure 3.6 Keuffel & Esser Slide Rule, model 4081-3 (c. 1940). (Source: https://commons.wikimedia.org/wiki/File:Keuffel_%26_Esser_slide_rule,_model_4081-3_(ca._1940)_-_Detail.jpg. Author: s58y).

Figure 3.7 NMS Jacquard loom. (Source: https://commons.wikimedia.org/wiki/File:NMS_Jacquard_loom.JPG. Author: Ad Meskens).

ers think that the first educational film was invented in St Petersburg in 1897, while some researchers explain that early innovation of educational film was inspired by film, namely newsreel, in 1913. Nevertheless, from 1900 onward plenty of educational films were made which influenced the field of teaching and instruction. It is also noted that Thomas Edison is the producer of the first educational film.

16 mm film: Another revolutionary innovation in the field of education is 16 mm film. It is revolutionary because it was less expensive with 35 mm. It was first introduced by Eastman

Fundamental Concepts and Theories

Kodak in 1923. Further, one can see that 16 mm film has been used in many ways in various universities and colleges for instruction (see Figure 3.8).

Educational radio: Educational radio was one of the greatest distance learning mediums. The first educational radio was licensed to the University of Salt Lake City in 1921. After that the University of Wisconsin and the University of Minnesota also received licenses for setting up a radio station in 1921. The early development of educational radio was mainly initiated for farmers in 1914 by the US Department of Agriculture. After a few years, educational radio became famous in the context of correspondence education in various fields.

Television: Television is another of the greatest influential innovations during the period of the 1900s. In the context of education, an early public demonstration of education was conducted in 1927. Moreover, educational television or learning television was used to provide instruction by distance mode. Various educational programs were performed through television such as adult educational programs, children's television series, etc.

Differentiate analyzer: This is an early innovation of the mechanical analog computer that was invented to solve a differential equation. The general architecture of a differential analyzer is the integration of a wheel and disc for computing or performing complex analysis. In the early part of 1836, Gaspard-Gustava de Coriolis designed a mechanical device that could perform differential equations very easily. This was also an early stage of innovation of the modern computer.

Turing machine: The Turing machine generally refers to a mathematical model of computation. The Turing machine was invented nine years before the introduction of the digital computer by Alan Turing in 1936.

Electronic Numerical Integrator and Computer (ENIAC): ENIAC was the first electronic computer. In the context of functionality, ENIAC can solve a large class of numeric problems. It consisted of 17,468 electronic vacuum tubes to make the calculation. ENIAC was invented in 1945 and started working on 10 December 1945.

Figure 3.8 Panasonic 16-mm film projector and vidicon camera, 1957. (Source: https://commons.wikimedia.org/wiki/File:Pantason_16_mm_film_projector_and_vidicon_camera,_1957_(21709473451).jpg. Author: Yle Elävaarkisto - Yle Archives from Yleisradio, Finland).

Sputnik 1: This is another revolutionary approach toward the modern information age. Sputnik 1 is the first artificial earth satellite in the world. It was launched on 4 October 1957 and it orbited for three weeks before the batteries were discharged. It looked like a polished bucketball with a 58 cm (23 in) diameter with four antennas to catch the radio signal (see Figure 3.9).

Teaching machine: A teaching machine generally refers to mechanical devices to present educational material for teaching and learning. The first invention of the teaching machine was made by Sidney Pressey in the mid-1920s. The early innovation of teaching machines mainly aimed to administer multiple-choice questions. However, further innovation of the teaching machine was found in the work of Norman Crowder. B. F. Skinner, an eminent researcher, developed a teaching machine named "GLIDER" that was based on the idea of how positive reinforcement effects or directs any teaching and learning process (see Figure 3.10).

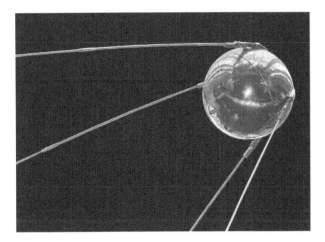

Figure 3.9 Sputnik 1. (Source: https://commons.wikimedia.org/wiki/File:Sputnik_satelitea.jpg. Author: Carlos Moreno Rekondo).

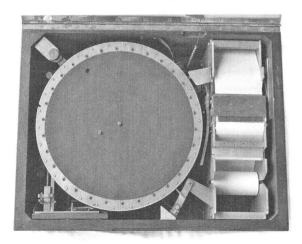

Figure 3.10 Skinner teaching machine. (Source: https://commons.wikimedia.org/wiki/File:Skinner_teaching_machine_09.jpg. Author: Silly rabbit).

Fundamental Concepts and Theories

Programmed instruction or learning: Programmed learning is another essential teaching and learning approach. This approach was generally based on the theory of Skinner's behaviorism.

Integrated Circuits (IC): Integrated circuits are also called monolithic integrated circuits and sometimes referred to as an IC, a chip, or a microchip. An IC is a pivotal innovation that accommodates a huge number of tiny transistors in a small plate systematically. ICs are used in many electronic devices like televisions, mobile phones, computers, digital home appliances, etc. (see Figure 3.11).

Minicomputer: The minicomputer is another historical innovation in the context of educational technology. From the mid-1960s onward, minicomputers were developed costing less than 25,000 USD. It was the early stage of innovation of the personal computer that further influenced the overall educational system in many ways (see Figure 3.12).

FORTRAN (formula translation): The first high-level programming language was developed by Konrad Zuse between 1942 and 1945, namely "*Plankalkül*". However, the most famous high-level commercial language was developed by John Backus and his IBM team in the year 1956. The name of this language was FORTRAN. FORTRAN has become famous for facilitating the porting of any code to a new computer.

Programmed Logic for Automatic Teaching Operations (PLATO): This was a cornerstone innovation in 1960. It was the first Computer-Assisted Instruction (CAI), which was promoted by the University of Illinois. PLATO was a multiuse computing mechanism that included online testing, e-mail, chatrooms, etc.

Computer-Assisted Instruction (CAI): As discussed earlier, after the introduction of computers in education various strategies were undertaken by researchers to use the computer in the context of education. CAI is one of the essential innovations for providing instruction through the computer.

Information and Communications Technology (ICT): The acronym ICT is familiar to all, as it is ubiquitous throughout the globe ICT. ICT in a simplistic view refers to the integration of

Figure 3.11 Integrated circuits. (Source: https://commons.wikimedia.org/wiki/File:Integrated_circuits .jpg. Author: Mataresephotos).

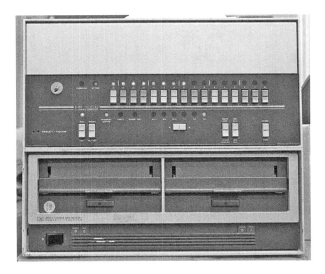

Figure 3.12 HP 1000 E-Series minicomputer. (Source: https://commons.wikimedia.org/wiki/File:HP_1000_E-Series_minicomputer.jpg. Author:Autopilot).

a telephone or wireless signal and a computer as a medium of communication. Currently, devices like smartphones, computers, the Internet, etc. are all a part of ICT.

Artificial Intelligence (AI): Artificial intelligence sometimes also refers to machine intelligence. This is a very recent and powerful innovation in the field of computer science as well as in education. In a general view, AI is machine intelligence like we have human intelligence. Through this process, a machine or device can "Learn", "Create", or "Solve" various problems based on the situation. It is just like the "cognitive function" of a machine as a mind is to a human. The first AI research started in 1956 with the help of eminent researchers like John McCarthy (MIT), Marvin Minsky (MIT), Arthur Samuel (IBM), etc.

Bibliography

Bates, T. (2011). Retrieved December, 2012, from http://www.tonybates.ca.
Conway, K. (1990). *Master Classrooms: Classroom Design with Technology in Mind.* Academic Computing Publications, Incorporated, 26 pages
Ellington, H., Percival, F., & Race, P. (2005). *Handbook of educational technology.* New Delhi: Kogan Page India Pvt. Ltd.
Ely, D. P. (1991). Trends and issues in educational technology, 1989. In G. J. Anglin (Ed.), *Instructional technology: Past, present and future.* Englewood: Libraries Unlimited Inc.
Glaser, R. (1976). Components of a psychology of instruction: Problems in defining the field. *Review of Educational Research, 46*(1), 1–24.
Knowles, M. (1975). *Self-directed learning.* New York: Association Press.
Kulkarni, S. S. (1986). *Introduction to educational technology.* New Delhi: Oxford & IBH Press.
Kumar, K. L. (1996). *Educational technology: A practical textbook for students, teachers, professionals and trainers.* New Delhi: New Age International.
Merrill, M. D. (1983). Component display theory. In C. M. Reigeluth (Ed.), *Instructional theories and models.* Hillsdale, NJ: LEA.
Moore, M. (1989). The theory of distance education: Some recent literature. In A. Tight (Ed.), *Integration and independence: Student support in distance education and open learning.*
Mukhopadhyay, M. et al. (1993). *Utilisation of media facilities in school: An evaluation study of the ET scheme of the ministry of HRD.* New Delhi: NCERT.

NCERT. (2006). *Position paper: National focus group on education technology*. New Delhi: Ational Council of Educational Research and Training.
Panda, S. (1990). Educational technology and distance education: The convergence and the futures. *Media & Technology for Human Resource Development, 3*(1), 27–40.
Panda, S. (1995). Tele-teaching in higher education. In K. B. Powar & S. Panda (Eds.), *Higher education in India – In search of quality*. New Delhi: Association of Indian Universities.
Panda, S. (2009). The world wide web and lifelong learning. In P. Jarvis (Ed.), *The Routledge international handbook of lifelong learning*. London and New York: Routledge.
Power, M. (2008). The emergence of a blended online learning environment. *Merlot Journal of Online Learning and Teaching. 4*(4). Retrieved from http://jolt.merlot.org/vol4no4/power_1208.htm.
PricewaterhouseCoopers. (2010). *Survey of ICTs for education in India and South Asia*. India: PricewaterhouseCoopers.

4
INSTRUCTIONAL DESIGN IN EDUCATION

Introduction

Every person is unique and has different needs and learning styles. But our conventional educational practice or method often does not quite encourage this individual differentiation and provides a system or process that is based on a predetermined instructional approach with a fixed amount of content and time. Therefore, slow learners are forced to move faster before they achieve mastery in specific content. This paradigm of instructional approach was developed in the industrial age when there was very little scope to provide individualistic learning due to the high cost and lack of proper scientific design. However, the modern technological revolution expands the scope toward creating a learning environment that is more personalized and need-based. Therefore, various researchers and educationists look for a scientific design of instruction. This chapter discusses a pivotal innovation in the field of teaching and learning called "instructional design" (ID).

Meaning and Definition of Instructional Design

Instructional design is not a new concept in the context of the modern education system. Therefore, before discussing what instructional design is and how it functions, it is imperative to know about the basic functions related to instructional design. In general terms, we all know that education is comprised of knowledge about the curriculum, counseling, administration, evaluation and another pivotal aspect, "instruction". But the basic difference between "curriculum and "instruction" is that the former is more concerned about "what to teach and then further 'How to teach'" (Snelbecker, 1974). Furthermore, "curriculum" is the goal of education while "instruction" mostly deals with the method of instruction.

Branch and Merrill (2012) state, "Instructional Design (ID) is a system of procedures for developing education and training curricula consistently and reliably".

Mustaro et al. (2007) define ID as "(a) systematic process, based on educational theories, on the development of instructional strategies, and specifications to promote the quality learning experience".

Reiser and Dempsey (2007) define it as a "systematic process that is employed to develop education and training programs consistently and reliably".

Miner et al. (2005) state that "The instructional design process incorporates the theoretical considerations presented above into a practice-based framework that bridges the gap between learner needs, learning objectives, delivery of instruction, and evaluation".

Crawford (2004) defines instructional design as "the distinct systematic process through which evolves a superior instructional product as delineated through an instructional design model. It guides designers to work more efficiently while producing more effective and appealing instruction suitable for a wide range of learning environments".

Gustafson and Branch (2002) state that "Instructional design is a complex process that is creative, active and iterative".

Siemens (2002) states: "Instructional Design is the art and science of creating an instructional environment and material that will bring the learner from the state of not being able to accomplish certain tasks to the state of being able to accomplish those tasks. Instructional Design is based on theoretical and practical research in the areas of cognition, educational psychology, and problem-solving".

Gredler (2001) defines it as

> The development of instruction for specified goals and objectives in which (i) the organized sequential selection of components is made based on based on information, data, and theoretical principles at every stage and (ii) the product is tested in real-world situations both during development and at the end of the development process.

Smith and Ragan (1999) put forth that "The term instructional design refers to the systematic and reflective process of translating the principles of learning and instruction into plans for instructional materials, activities, information resources, and evaluation".

McNeil (retreived from http://www.coe.uh.edu/courses/cuin6373/whatisid.html) defines instructional design as the following:

Process: Instructional Design is the systematic development of instructional specifications using learning and instructional theory to ensure the quality of instruction. It is the entire process of analysis of learning needs and goals and the development of a delivery system to meet those needs. It includes the development of instructional materials and activities and tryout and evaluation of all instruction and learner activities.

Discipline: Instructional Design is that branch of knowledge concerned with research and theory about instructional strategies and the process for developing and implementing those strategies.

Science: Instructional Design is the science of creating detailed specifications for the development, implementation, evaluation, and maintenance of situations that facilitate the learning of both large and small units of the subject matter at all levels of complexity.

Reality: Instructional Design can start at any point in the design process. Often a glimmer of an idea is developed to give the core of an instruction situation. By the time the entire process is done the designer looks back and she or he checks to see that all parts of the "science" have been taken into account. Then the entire process is written up as if it occurred systematically.

(Retrieved from Sara McNeil, www.coe.uh.edu/courses/cuin6373/whatisid.html

The Origin of Instructional Design

To make any instructional process more effective and scientific is a fundamental aim of any instructor. Therefore, various researchers developed plenty of innovative approaches making the instructional process more scientific and goal oriented. In this context, an instructional design approach is not a new concept. The roots of instructional design approach can be seen through the early Greek philosophers. However, we can see a concrete approach toward the scientific design of instruction in the work of Thorndike on instructional design and learning in 1913, Bobbitt's work on job analysis in 1924, Tyler's work on the objectivity of learning as well as criterion reference testing in 1942, etc. Furthermore, during World War II, there was a huge need for the systematic application of behavioral psychology in the process of instruction and scientific design of instruction. During that specific period, the major aim was to provide a self-paced individualistic instructional approach to the learner. For instance, eminent researchers like Skinner, Pavlov, and Thorndike proposed various theories of learning and provided scientific pathways to make instruction more scientific. During World War II, various technological devices were also developed to provide effective instruction to the soldiers and this kind of innovation expanded the scope of scientific instruction for the future design of instruction. As well as all such early approaches, another revolutionary innovation for the development of instructional design was the development of the field of "cognitive psychology". The field of cognitive psychology and the development of microcomputer innovation significantly contributed to what we call modern instructional design. Cognitive psychology focused on the psychological state of a learner and the microcomputer revolution expanded the scope of sophisticated design and simulative learning approaches. The most recent next-level innovation in the field of instructional design is the use and development of artificial intelligence in the instructional system to increase the personalization of learning (Knirk & Gustafson, 1986).

Instructional System Design (ISD)

Those who are familiar with instructional design may assume that they also know about "instructional system design". Actually, in the field of education, various interchangeable terms are used to provide an overview of various methods of instruction such as instructional design, instructional system design, instructional technology, instructional design, instructional development, etc. (Gustafson & Branch, 2002). But, in terms of scope and expansion of instructional process ISD is much broader. Various eminent researchers such as Smith and Ragan in 2005 and Kemp, Morrison, and Ross in 1998 explained that ISD is a process, a discipline, a field of study, a science, and a reality in the context of instruction. ISD is mostly responsible for providing a process of instruction that is closely related to theories of instructional design. It is intended to describe the required process or procedure to be followed by instructors or teacher for the utmost utilization of a learning environment for effective instruction to achieve the instructional goal.

Instructional system design is a broader concept when compared with ID because the ISD model is mainly focused on five phases—analysis, design, development, implementation, and evaluation—whereas the ID model only covers the first two phases, i.e., analysis and design (see Table 4.1).

Strategies for Instructional Design

It is important to know about the various strategies applicable to effective instructional design. The types of learning strategies will be discussed as proposed by the eminent researcher Reigeluth in 1983. He proposed three types: organizational, delivery, and management.

Table 4.1 Difference between instructional system design and instructional design

Subject	Instructional System Design	Instructional Design
Scope	Instructional system design is broader in scope in the context of the development of instructional materials	Instructional design is narrow in scope
Process	ISD typically divided the instructional design process into five phases: analysis, design, development, implementation, and evaluation (ADDIE)	ID only deals with two phases: analysis and design
Evaluation	The ISD model uses both formative and summative evaluation processes	ID can only consider one approach
Flexibility	The ISD model is more flexible. One instructor can use both ADDIE models or can plug any required theoretical aspect at any time	ID is not very flexible compared to ISD
Fundamental aspect	The ISD model keeps and monitors the overall training program on the correct path to reach a specific goal	The ID model is used to support the learning process being designated

Organizational Aspects

In an organizational aspect of ID, an instructional designer should be conscious about sequencing and structuring a learning module on a microlevel or macrolevel. Sequencing and structuring will help to perform any learning module properly.

Sequencing and Structuring of the Learning Module

The fundamental aspect of sequencing and structuring is to ensure whether the learning objective is met. Notably, the sequencing process of instruction helps the learner to generate a pattern of relationships to achieve a definite purpose. The overall learning process will be easier and effective by providing the learning materials in a more meaningful way. Therefore, in the sequencing process learning material is presented in an organized and meaningful way. It helps to avoid inconsistency and duplicity or repetition of content of instruction.

Some of the sequencing techniques or processes are as follows:

1. *Simple to complex:* In this context, the objective and content of instruction sequencing are based on the complexity of context material.
2. *Critical sequence:* In this aspect, learning objectives are sequenced based on the relative importance of the topic or content.
3. *Known to unknown:* This is a unique sequencing approach in ID. Here most known or familiar content is presented before the unknown.
4. *Dependent relationship:* In this sequencing style design, the learner needs expertise in one specific topic or aspect before mastery of other aspects.
5. *Supportive relationship:* This is another unique approach. Here various common elements are included in each objective and each objective should be close to the other for the maximum transformation of learning.
6. *Cause and effect:* Here all the objectives of the learning process should be sequenced based on cause and effect.

Delivery Strategies

The term delivery mainly concerns communicating or transforming something from one place to another. In any instructional design the delivery strategies denote the transfer process of learning objects to the learner. The medium of delivery may vary due to the availability of resources or the environment. For example, when the learner and instructor are at a distance, then learning materials may be presented or delivered through E-learning or distance learning. The following are some of the delivery strategies in the context of instructional design:

- Social media
- Classroom
- E-learning
- Distance and corresponding learning
- Lecturing strategies
- M-learning
- Video or multimedia-based

Management Strategies

Another essential strategy in the context of an instructional design process is "management strategies". The management aspect in a view of instructional design refers to decisions and processes which help the learner interacts with learning materials to increase the knowledge and skill in specific learning content. Some of the strategies are:

- Lockstep
- Personalized system of instruction
- Programmed learning
- Fishbowls
- Boot camp
- Action learning

Besides these strategies, some of the strategies discussed by Marzano in 1998 are described in the following section.

Linguistic learning mode: In the linguistic learning mode learning content is presented linguistically and learners are often expected to respond linguistically.
Nonlinguistic learning mode: In the nonlinguistic mode of learning the learner experiences and processes learning information through sensation (smell), kinesthetic sensation (touch), auditory sensation (sound), and taste sensation (Marzano, 1998).
Affective mode of learning: In an effective learning mode the fundamental aspect is to reinforce learning by use of the power of feelings and emotions.

Model and Theories of Instructional Design

Generally, the model of any design represents a prototype of an object in a structural way. In a similar aspect the model of an instructional design refers to the procedural framework of any representation of a design for the systematic production of instruction. Moreover, a model of the instructional design process includes an analysis of the audience, discussion of a different learning context, specific goals, and objectives of any learning goal. From the overall discussion of instructional design, one gets the concept that in the context of instructional design, no universal design exists or is applicable for any learning situation, rather the design of ID is more situational and needs to be customized based on various critical factors related to the learning environment. However, in that context, the model of instructional design provides an explicit guideline for a specific educational initiative (Morrison et al., 2004). In addition, Morrison, Ross, and Kemp also discussed that instructional design models and theories are more situation specific and the model identity of discussion is about a situation where some strategies, activities, or models should or should not be used. In this particular case, an instructional design model is the most appropriate guideline to develop course material and encounter various challenges related to the specific context of learning. Gustafson and Branch (2002) discussed that any model is a fundamental guideline to conceptualize the representation of reality. They also discussed four essential components related to instructional design, those are:

1. Analysis of the learning environment or setting and learner needs
2. Designing an effective, efficient, and relevant environment for the teacher
3. Development of all learners and strategies for management learning materials
4. Evaluation of results in summative and formative ways

Besides this, Seels and Glasgow (1998) discussed the following specific purposes for the development of instructional design models:

1. Visualizing a systematic process
2. Development of a tool for managing processes and projects
3. Development of a practical model set for required tasks (see Figure 4.1)

Before one starts to gain in-depth knowledge about various instructional designs, it is imperative to know the list of prescriptive instructional design models. As discussed, the instructional

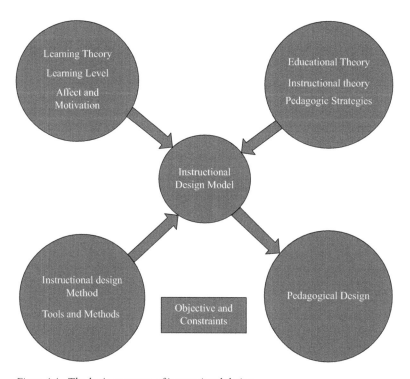

Figure 4.1 The basic structure of instructional design.

module provides guidelines and framework about the structure and process of development of instructional material or activities. The following are some of the commonly accepted instructional design models:

- 4C/ID Model (van Merriënboer)
- Algo-Heuristic Theory (Landa)
- ADDIE Model (analysis, design, development, implementation, and evaluation)
- Weaknesses of the ADDIE Model
- ARCS (Keller)
- ASSURE (Heinich, Molenda, Russell, and Smaldino)
- Backward Design (Wiggins and McTighe)
- Cognitive Apprenticeship (Edmondson)
- Conditions of Learning (Gagne)
- Component Display Theory (Merrill)
- Criterion-Referenced Instruction (Mager)
- Dick and Carey Model
- Elaboration Theory
- Gerlach-Ely Model
- Hannafin-Peck Model
- Knirk and Gustafson Model
- Instructional Systems Design (ISD)
- Integrative Learning Design Framework for Online Learning (Debbaugh)
- Iterative Design
- Spiral Model (Boehm)
- Rapid Prototyping (Tripp and Bichelmeyer)
- Kemp Design Model (Morrison, Ross, and Kemp)
- Organizational Elements Model (OEM) (Kaufman)
- Transactional Distance (Moore)
- Cognitive Apprenticeship
- Discovery Learning
- Empathic Instructional Design
- Goal-Based Scenarios

ADDIE Model of Instructional Design

The ADDIE model is one of the commonly used instructional designs. It was developed by Royce in 1970. Generally, the ADDIE model is a guideline for the content developer, teacher, and instructional designer to create an efficient and effective teaching design. The acronym ADDIE stands for the steps detailed in the following section.

- Analyze
- Design
- Develop
- Implement
- Evaluate

The ADDIE model of instructional design can be used in an online teaching-learning model or in face-to-face communication or a blended learning approach. Each phase of the ADDIE

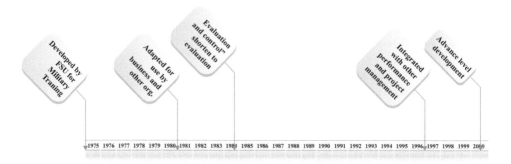

Figure 4.2 Timeline for ADDIE model of instructional design.

model is related to each of the others. The following is a detailed discussion of each phase of the ADDIE instructional design model (see Figure 4.2).

Analysis Phase

The analysis phase is the most important in the ADDIE model. In the analysis phase, instructional goals and objects are established, instructional problems are clarified, a possible solution is determined, the learning environment is considered, the delivery option is found, and the time line for the project and the existing knowledge and skills are identified. This stage of the ADDIE model requires an extensive amount of research in the context of need analysis and task analysis, as well as job analysis. Generally, in the analysis phase, the instructional designer mainly focuses on the basic aspects of analysis. These are as follows:

a. Analysis of learner
b. Analysis of the instructional goal
c. Developing instruction analysis
d. Analysis of learning objectives

Analysis of Learner

Analysis of the learner is a very essential stage in the context of the ADDIE model. This stage considers the analysis of the following:

- Analysis of the learner includes in-depth knowledge about what the learner already knows about any topic. After the detailed analysis of existing knowledge of the learner an instructional designer can build a design plan as to how much information is required for the learner.
- The need to know the specific needs of the learner and the problems they are facing.
- The need to have an in-depth analysis of the learner as the instructional designer is required to make a survey, interview, pretest, and posttest assessment of the learner for designing a strategy.

Analysis of the Instructional Goal

In the stage of analysis, an instructional designer needs to identify the obvious goal of a specific instruction. The stage of analysis of the instructional goal mainly tries to find out the answer to what the learner wants to learn. That is the entire matter of specification of the learning goal. Without an analysis of instructional goals, the instructional situations may not be very efficient and effective.

Developing Instructional Analysis

This stage is very essential and complicated, as after the specification of the instructional goal there is a need to start writing the important steps and details to achieve the instructional goal. This requires expert knowledge and skills for developing the instructional analysis.

Analysis of Learning Objectives

This is a very crucial stage. In this phase, the following aspects are needed to be taken into consideration:

- The need to specify what a learner should be able to perform after finishing the instruction
- The formalization and specification of skill, behavior, and knowledge of learner as a learning objective
- The specification of a measurable behavior that can indicate the attainment of the goal (see Figure 4.3)

Design Phase

Another important aspect of the ADDIE model of instructional design is the design phase. In the design phase, the instructional designer always thinks about how to design instructional

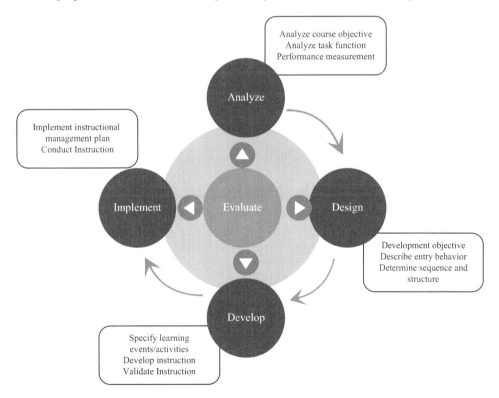

Figure 4.3 Analysis phase of ADDIE model of instructional design.

material that will be effective for achieving the instructional goal and facilitate student learning and instruction. In addition, in the design phase, the instructional designer designs assessments for a specific topic and creates strategies. In the design phase, the instructional designer needs to take into consideration the following aspects:

- Analysis and design of assessment
- Design of specification of the form of course
- Designing instructional course strategies

Analysis and Design of Assessment

The design and analysis of the assessment of learning objectives or outcomes is a vital step for the successful design of instructional material. The following are the basic points needed to be taken into consideration by the instructional designer when they have to analyze and design the assessment:

- In-depth analysis of student data is collected at the former stage, namely the analysis stage.
- A designer needs to ensure the overall design of assessment is related to content and context of learning objectives.
- Avoid miscommunication or misunderstanding by the learner which comes from confusion in the design of assessment or task questions which are written by the designer or content writer.

Design of Specification of the Form of Course

The form of course denotes the representation of any instructional material about a specific topic. This is all about the context of the delivery system of any instructional material. The following are some of the steps that the structural designer can take into consideration to design a successful specific form of course:

- A designer can use various forms of courses to deliver instructional material such as the lecture method, the online teaching-learning method, self-learning workbooks, a blended learning approach, etc.
- The form of course should match the design assessment.

Design Instructional Course Strategies

The design of instructional course strategy is a combination of the various methods which help the learner increase their understanding of a specific topic. The methods should be lecture-based, discussion-based, reading and writing activities, etc. In this stage motivation of the learner is very important to recognize the importance of specific courses. Furthermore, in this stage, student participation is a very crucial aspect that can be gained through feedback.

Developmental Phase

The development phase is another very essential aspect in the context of the ADDIE model of instructional design. This is the third stage after the analysis and design of instructional material. The development phase involves some kind of soft and hard technology in an educational setting or process. It also describes the backup plan if a technology is not working properly. Developmental phases include the following substages:

Development of an Initial Sample of Instructional Material

Before the development of the final instructional material, it is imperative to develop a sample design of the overall material and test it through varied opinions and feedback from the learner. This is very important because through this process the success rate of any developed instructional material will increase. In addition, various problems and weaknesses can be identified before the final development of any instructional material.

Development of Final Course Material

After the sampling process, another stage is to develop the final course material and try to make a list of various instructional strategies that need to be included to achieve the learning objective. However, after the final development, advice should be taken from the supervisor or an expert and comments gathered from a client, friend, or learner to get more feedback, suggestions, and criticism.

Practice for Pilot Test

After the final development of the overall instructional material, another important stage is to pilot run the overall test. This is the stage when you will actually use all the developed material in practice or on pilot-run mode. Instructional designers or teachers can implement it with their peer groups, friends, etc. Through this pilot an instructional designer can develop an assessment of feedback to find out weaknesses or problems of any design and improve the overall instructional material as is required.

Implementation Phase

The previously discussed three stages focused on analysis, design, and development of any instructional material. However, the fourth stage of the ADDIE model of instructional design is purely focused on the application of any instructional material. To increase the engagement of learners with how to successfully apply the developed instructional material, there is a strong need to follow the following stages:

- Provide the appropriate training to the instructor.
- Prepare the learner.
- Organize the learning environment.

Provide the Appropriate Training to the Instructor

At the implementation phase of the ADDIE model of instructional design, one of the critical aspects is to train the instructor appropriately so that they can successfully apply the developed instructional material. To successfully apply the instructional material the instructor or teacher needs to gain knowledge and skills about the course material, course objectives, multimedia uses, assessment, activities about the course material, etc.

Prepare the Learner

Besides the preparation of the teacher, another essential aspect is to prepare the learner simultaneously. Before participating in a specific instructional scenario, it is imperative to ensure that all the materials, tools, and experience, as well as the prerequisite knowledge of the learner, are adequate for a specific course.

Organize the Learning Environment

Another essential aspect of the implementation stage is to organize an effective learning space. The preparation of the learning phase is not just the arrangement of a teacher but also providing the chairs, tables, boards, etc., all the required material and handouts, and arranging a computer as required for the online instructional material, etc.

Evaluation Phase

The evaluation phase is the last and extremely vital stage in the ADDIE model of instructional design. This stage is important because in this stage the teacher or instructional designer can review whether the developed instructional material achieves an instructional goal or meet the learner's needs. In the evaluation phase the instructional designer mainly focuses on two types of evaluation: (a) formative evaluation and (b) summative evaluation. Formative evaluation is a continuous process of evaluation through which overall instructional material can be valued step by step on the ADDIE model. The following section describes some of the stages for formative evaluation and summative evaluation.

- One-to-one formative evaluation
- Small-group evaluation
- A trial-in-field formative evaluation
- Summative evaluation

One-to-One Formative Evaluation

This is a particularly basic-level evaluation process of instructional material where every aspect of instructional material is evaluated at once to find out problems, strengths, and weaknesses of any instructional material.

Small-Group Evaluation

This is a second-level evaluation after the one-to-one formative evaluation. After getting various comments and feedback from the one-to-one evaluation, the overall instructional material will be applied in a small group to find out the effectiveness and achievement of changes made in the one-to-one evaluation phases.

A Trial-in-Field Formative Evaluation

This is the final stage of evaluation after the previous two phases. In this stage of evaluation, the instructional design needs to create an environment that will be similar to a real environment. At this stage, it is vital to ensure the clarity, effectiveness, and practicability of instructional material which will be then ready to be delivered.

Summative Evaluation

Summative evaluation is also very important because it helps to find out the real value of an instructional material after the completion of the whole course. Through the summative evaluation, one can evaluate the outcome of the learner as well as the effectiveness of instructional material and the design of instruction. The instructional designer can use a Likert-type scale (viz.

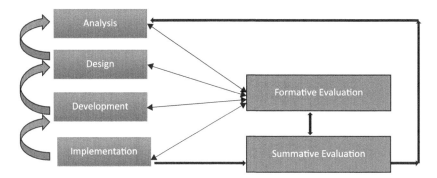

Figure 4.4 The structural aspect of a formative and summative evaluation of the ADDIE model.

agree, neutral, disagree, strongly disagree) with an opinion given by the student on a specific instructional material. In addition, instructional designers can use an open-ended questionnaire to find out more in-depth evaluation for improving instructional material (see Figure 4.4).

ASSURE Model of Instructional Design

Another important instructional design model after the ADDIE model is the ASSURE model.

The ASSURE model is a six-step guideline for planning, designing, and delivering instructional material to achieve the learners' needs. The ASSURE Model of instructional design is a constructivist approach, proposed by Robert Heinrich and Michael Molenda from Indiana University and James D. Russell from Purdue University in 1999. The major assumption of the ASSURE model is that "careful planning will increase the effectiveness of instruction" (Daniel Callison, 2002). ASSURE is the acronym for the following six steps:

- A—Analyze learners.
- S—State standards and objectives.
- S—Select strategies, technology, media and materials.
- U—Utilize technology, media, and materials.
- R—Require learner participation.
- E—Evaluate and revise (see Figure 4.5)

A—Analyze Learners

The first step of the ASSURE model is that to analyze a learner to develop effective instructional material, the teacher must be involved adequately to analyze his learner attributes and needs. This process includes the analysis of learner characteristics that are associated with learning outcomes. Through the analysis of learner teachers, the instructional designer can make specific strategies to achieve the specific learning objective. The following are some of the general as well as the specific attributes of the learner to analyze before designing:

- *General characteristics:* Age, gender, sex, socioeconomic level, ethnic group, work background, interest, health, culture, etc.
- *Entry competencies:* Prior knowledge, current skills, attitude, biases, etc.
- *Learning styles:* Visual, auditory, tactile, logical, etc.

Fundamental Concepts and Theories

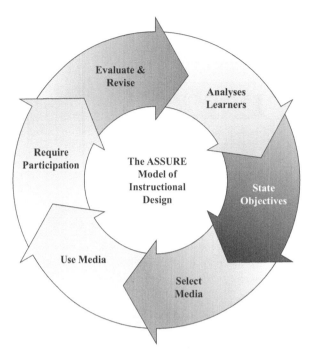

Figure 4.5 The ASSURE model of instructional design.

S—State Standards and Objectives

After the analysis of learner attributes, other essential stages state the standard and objective of learning. A statement of objectives includes specification of the result of an instruction which will be achieved by the learner. The objectives of the description of learning outcomes are written in ABCD formation. The ABCD format in the ASSURE model of instructional design is as follows:

- *A for audience:* For whom is the objective intended? Or who is the audience?
- *B for behavior:* The need to state what the learner will do. As per the behavior aspect, the instructional designer needs to specify the objective in an observable and measurable manner. Additionally, the capability of the learner needs to be demonstrated as a learner performance as per a real-world skill. The instructional designer can use action verbs if required.
- *C for condition:* This aspect denotes in what condition the learner can demonstrate his skill. It also demonstrates tools, materials, various teaching-learning aids, references, etc. the learner may or may not use and the discussion of the learning environment where the learner needs to perform.
- *D for degree:* It denotes how well a learner will demonstrate their mastery. It includes mastery of new skills and competence of performance of a learner. For example, the execution, accuracy, and time limit proportion of required correct responses, the quantity and quality standard, etc.

S—Select Strategies, Technology, Media, and Materials

After the standardization of objectives and essential aspects in the context of the ASSURE model is the selection of strategies, technology, media, and instructional material. This is very important because an appropriate selection of instructional material can bring the effective results that an instructional designer or teacher wants to achieve.

Throughout the stages of selection of appropriate strategies, media, and instructional material the first stage is to find out the appropriate delivery medium or method of instruction. At an early stage in the selection of instructional material the designer selects the proportion of teaching methods, such as whether it will be teacher-centric, student-centered, or a mixed approach to the instructional process. With the teacher-centric instructional process, an instructional designer has to design an overall instructional method, as well as a lecture-based process, as per the student-centered method it requires group discussion and a cooperative group work approach.

After the selection of the method, another essential approach is to find out the appropriate strategies of instruction. Generally, the best strategy of any instructional design is a student-centric approach where students are encouraged to discover the correct answers.

After the selection of strategies, it is essential to select appropriate media and material which will be the best support for teaching and learning. The selection of appropriate, relevant media or content material is a vital aspect for effective learning outcomes. Philip Swain (2003) explains, "As we know, Instructional Technology—the convergence of Communication Technology within the realm of teaching and learning has already had a profound effect on education at all levels".

U—Utilize Technology, Media, and Materials

This step of the ASSURE model mainly focuses on the utilization of various media, technology, and materials to achieve learning objectives effectively. In this context, instructional designers need to take into consideration the following five "Ps".

- *Preview and preparation of instructional material, media, and technology:* It means that before the application of final instructional media, it is very essential for the instructional designer to pilot run overall instructional media to ensure that the lesson will go smoothly and seamlessly at the final stage.
- *Preparation of environment:* The second most important aspect is to prepare and set up a learning environment where adequate required teaching-learning components are available. Furthermore, if possible, it is very important to create a noise-free learning environment.
- *Preparation of learner:* This is very crucial in any teaching and learning process. Before applying instructional material, it is imperative to inform the learner about overall learning objectives. This overview can provide a mental map to the learner as to what they have to focus on throughout the learning process. Moreover, the instructional designer or teacher should give a brief overview to the student on how they will be assessed, what their assignment will be, what the process of gradation will, etc.
- *Provide the learning experiences:* This is the final stage before the application of any instructional material. In this step, the instructional designer needs to ensure that every prior step is followed properly and effectively to achieve a successful instructional process.

R—Require Learner Participation

A well-established fact is that students will learn better when they are actively involved in a teaching and learning process. Whatever teaching strategy will follow, the essential consideration is the engagement of the student with the learning material. To achieve this, the instructional designer needs to incorporate various activity-based learning approaches. Furthermore, it requires questions and answers, group discussion, group work, etc. to ensure the motivation and engagement of the learner in a specific teaching-learning scenario.

E—Evaluate and Revise

This is the final and one of the most vital stages in the ASSURE model of instructional design. In this stage, the instructional designer requires evaluation of teaching strategies, technologies, media, material, etc. carefully and in-depth. The following are some of the questions that need to be asked by the instructional designer during the evaluation process of any instructional material:

- Are the designed lessons meeting the learning objectives of the learner?
- How, as a teacher, can one determine if any student is achieving the instructional objective?
- How can one judge the weakness of presentation?
- Will alternative technology, media, or material increase the performance of a learner?

The step of evaluation also focuses on feedback from the learner, whether they are gathering positive experiences from the overall teaching scenarios. The overall process of the ASSURE model is a strategy to integrate technology into the curriculum.

Dick and Carey Model of Instructional Design

The Dick and Carey model (DC model) is one of the popular models in the field of instructional design. It is based on the system approach design of instruction. The DC model was first released in 1968 and after that the model was published in a book titled *The Systematic Design of Instruction* by Walter Dick and Lou Carey in 1978. The overall DC model starts by identifying an instructional goal and ends with a summative evaluation of the instructional process. The following ten components were discussed in the DC model. These all are parallel aspects rather than linear ones.

- Assess needs to identify the instructional goal.
- Conduct instructional analysis.
- Analyze learner and context.
- Write performance objective.
- Develop assignment instruments.
- Develop instructional strategies.
- Develop and select instructional material.
- Design and conduct a formative evaluation of instruction.
- Revise instruction.
- Design and conduct a summative evaluation.

The DC model explained instruction as a complete system, where each element of the system such as context, content learning, and instruction is interrelated. It is also notable that the

Instructional Design in Education

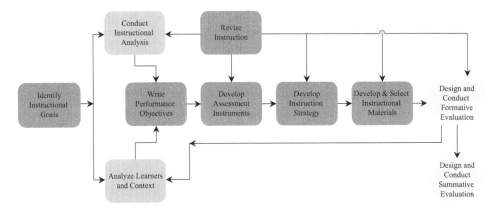

Figure 4.6 The Dick and Carey systems approach model for designing instruction (adapted from Dick et al., 2009).

DC model is based on Gagne's nine events of an instructional framework (Moallem, 2001). Following is a brief discussion of each stage of Dick and Carey's model (see Figure 4.6).

Stage 1: Access needs to identify the instructional goal
- Need to figure out all instruction goals.
- Need to identify a broader spectrum of learning objectives.
- Requires need analysis of learner.

Stage 2: Conduct instructional analysis
- The instructional designer needs to determine specific skills required to achieve an instructional goal.
- Requires task analysis to find out the specific procedure.
- Analysis of information processing.
- Analysis of intellectual skills required to achieve the specific learning objective.

Stage 3: Analyze learner and context
- Analysis of learner's intellectual skills.
- Analysis of verbal comprehension and spatial orientation.
- Analysis of personality traits of the learner.

Stage 4: Write performance objective
- Write the need and goal of any learning scenario into a specific and detailed learning objective.
- Find out whether any instruction is related to the goal.
- Develop measurement scale to measure the performance of learners.

Stage 5: Develop assessment instruments
- To diagnose individual and their requirement for learning new skills.
- Assessment of student performance during the lesson.
- Documents of the progress of learners for their parents or administrator.
- Evaluate the instructional system.

Stage 6: Develop instructional strategies
- To determine how instructional activity will accomplish instructional strategies.
- Choice of a delivery system such as teacher-led instructional design, learner-centered instructional design, etc.

Stage 7: Develop and select instructional material
- Selection of media as instructional material such as paper-based, printed, electronic, etc.
- Reuse of existing material if possible.
- Development of new material.
- Based on the selection of media, the role of the teacher also needs to be aligned.

Stage 8: Design and conduct a formative evaluation of instruction
- An evaluation of data is needed for improving instructional material.
- A revision is needed of the instructional material.

Stage 9: Revise Design
- Revision of the instructional material.

Stage 10: Design and conduct a summative evaluation
- To find out or follow up on the effectiveness of the instructional system as a whole.
- This is needed to make a summative evaluation on a small as well as large scale.

Gagne's Nine Events of Instruction

Robert Mills Gagne (1916–2002) was an American psychologist who worked on the sequencing of learning as an instructional event in the classroom situation. One of the legendary works of Gagne in the field of instructional design is "The Nine Events of Instruction" which are based on the cognitivism approach. In 1985, Gagne proposed a framework for an effective learning process. Good and Brophy (1977) described the

> Nine step model of Gagne general consideration to be taken into account when designing instruction. Although some steps might be needed (or might be unnecessary) for certain types of lesson, the general consideration provides a good checklist of key design steps.
> *(cited by Brophy, 1979)*

In a basic sense, one can say that Gagne's nine-step model is some kind of condition of learning. The following are the nine specific steps of instruction proposed by Gagne:

1. Gain the attention of the learner.
2. Inform learner of learning objective.
3. Stimulate and recall prior learning.
4. Present the content material.
5. Provide learning guidance.
6. Elicit performance.
7. Provide feedback.
8. Assess performance.
9. Enhance retention and transfer.

The following is a detailed discussion on the nine steps of Gagne's learning event adapted from Gagne, Briggs, and Wager (1992).

1. *Gain the attention of the learner*
   The first event is all about the readiness of the learner and the preparation of stimulation to gain the attention of the learner. The following are some of the methods to gain the attention of students:

- Use the storytelling approach.
- Stimulate students through uniqueness, uncertainty, or surprise.
- Ask interactive and interesting questions.
- Present a problem.
- Provide a detailed overview or realistic context about why a specific learning topic is important for them.

2. *Inform learner of learning objective*

Another essential aspect is to provide a view to the learner about why a specific topic will be learned. To do so it is very essential to inform the student about the overall learning objective and outcome of the teaching and learning scenario. It is a very helpful strategy to organize the thoughts of learners. The following are some of the methods to inform the learner about any learning objectives:
- Describe the required performance.
- Provide knowledge to the learner about specific preset criteria for standard performance.

3. *Stimulate and recall prior learning*

At this stage, the major aim is to help the student assimilate all the new information they gained with their prior knowledge or their existing knowledge. That can be done through the following methods:
- Providing some questions through which a teacher can gain knowledge about the level of prior knowledge of the learner.
- A teacher can have a formal discussion with the student to understand their previous concept of the specific topic.

4. *Present the content material*

This is to some extent similar concept to Skinner's sequenced learning event. This stage or event mainly focuses on the effective approach to provide instructional material so that the cognitive overload of the learner can be overcome or ignored. Additionally, it focuses on meaningful organization and a chunk of instructional material so that learning objectives can be achieved effectively and efficiently. The following are some of the methods for effectively providing content material:
- Provide an adequate and relevant example.
- Organization of instruction in a simple to complex manner.
- Provide content material in a segmented way.
- Use of audio as well as video as a medium of presentation of instructional material.
- Presentation of material through demonstration, podcast, group work, lecture, etc.

5. *Provide learning guidance*

Provide an overview to the learner as to how they can learn a specific skill. It means learners need instructional support through cues, hints, prompts, or other methods. This is very important to increase learner participation and metacognitive skills of the learner. The following are some of the methods to provide learning guidance:
- Provide a model of various learning strategies such as brainstorming, concept mapping, mnemonics, mind mapping, visualizing, etc.
- Providing an example and non-example is another essential method of learning guidance. Through the non-example method, a student can understand the opposite of some examples.
- Provide metaphors, visual images, case studies, etc.
- Provide cues, prompts, hints, etc.

6. *Elicit performance*
   This is an outcome part, by letting the learner do something by internalizing new skills and knowledge, through which a teacher can confirm the correct understanding of a learner-specific concept. The following are some of the ways to activate learner performance:
   - Provide an opportunity for the student to collaborate with their peers.
   - Ask deep-learning questions.
   - Follow up, recite, and revisiting the procedure.
   - Provide real-world examples.
7. *Provide feedback*
   Providing feedback is a very vital aspect as explained by Gagne in his nine-event model. For effective learning immediate feedback of learner performance is a very essential aspect. In addition, there needs to be some consideration that just providing common feedback like "good job", "well done", "fantastic" is not enough. The following are some of feedback strategies:
   - *Confirmation feedback:* This feedback explains to the learner whether they did right/wrong in the context of what they are supposed to do.
   - *Connective and remedial feedback:* Provide information to the learner regarding the accuracy of performance.
   - *Remedial feedback:* Engage and direct the learner in the right direction without providing the correct answer.
   - *Informative feedback:* Provide additional information or suggestions to the learner to confirm that students are actively learning.
   - *Analytical feedback:* Provide students suggestions and recommendations regarding the performance of the learner.
8. *Access performance*
   This is the confirmation stage of whether the learning outcome has been achieved by the learner. The following methods are used to access the performance of learners:
   - Use a pretest and posttest approach.
   - Apply various questioning strategies.
   - Apply criterion-referenced performance.
   - Identify normative reference performance.
9. *Enhance retention and transfer*
   At this stage, the major intention is to develop the expertise of learners and internalize new knowledge effectively. The following methods are used to enhance retention and transfer it effectively to the learner:
   - Give knowledge to the learner about similar problem situations.
   - Provide additional practices.
   - Prepare various types of content.
   - Gather various examples.
   - Concept mapping, references, template, etc.

ARCS Model of Motivation by John Keller

We all know that motivation is one of the essential key elements for the teaching and learning process. The ARCS model which was proposed by John Keller in 1983 is a problem-solving approach to make a learning activity more engaging in an E-learning environment. Keller

(2016) mainly focused on a "motivational design" concept: "Motivational design is the process of emerging resources and procedures to bring about changes in motivation". As per Keller's (1983) explanation, "motivational design" can enhance the motivation of learners through the process of attention, relevance, confidence, and satisfaction (ARCS).

John Keller proposed that the fundamental context of attention could be obtained in two ways:

1. *Perceptual arousal:* As per Keller's opinion the perceptual arousal is one of the fundamental aspects that could be gained by surprises, doubt, and disbelief.
2. *Inquiry arousal:* Inquiry arousal mainly focused on the stimulation of the learner's curiosity that could be gained through a challenging situation to the learner and how they solve it.

Guideline 1—Attention

Keller has proposed several methods to grab the learner's attention:

1. *Active participation:* In the ARCS model John Keller has emphasized the active participation process of the learner. He explained that active participation generally comes from role-play, games, simulation, and various hand-on activities.
2. *Variability:* Variability generally denotes the application of various methods or modalities such as group discussions, infographics, videos, short lectures, etc.
3. *Humor:* Application of various cartoons and humorous activities to gain the interest of the learner. One also needs to be aware that too much humor can distract the learner's attention.
4. *Incongruity and conflict:* John Keller discussed that "A devil's advocate approach in which statements are posed that go against a learner's previous experience.
5. *Specific examples:* Content need to be developed in a way that must represent specific examples properly through images, stories, or motivational biography.
6. *Inquiry:* To increase more engagement the content should be encouraged by posing questions, brainstorming, activities, presenting problems, etc.

Guideline 2—Relevance

To increase the motivation of the learner, it is very important to connect the content that could help relate to the learner's real world. To do so, the instructional designer may apply concrete language and examples which are familiar to the learner. In addition, content should connect to the goal, motivate, and relate to past experiences of the learner. In the ARCS model, Keller has proposed the following methods of active relevance to the learner:

1. *Experience:* Experience generally refers to accumulation of previous knowledge with present knowledge. Keller proposed that the design of instructional content must be developed in a way that could show the learner how to present learning that will be enhanced by using existing skills and experience.
2. *Present worth:* Explore to the learner how the content will be useful for them.
3. *Future usefulness:* Learner needs to explore how the present content helps the learner in future aspects, how the present subject matter is helpful for me tomorrow.

4. *Needs matching:* Learner needs to explore how the present content connects to the learner's needs.
5. *Modeling:* In this aspect, an instructional designer should make clear to the learner what students have to do to achieve a specific goal. This can be achieved through the process of a video that functions as a tutor.
6. *Choice:* The learner needs to be allowed to choose various strategies and methods in order to decide how to pursue and organize their work.

Guideline 3—Confidence

As Keller states, before a student is going to learn something they must feel confident that they can fully succeed in a specific learning activity. If students feel that the learning content is difficult, then they may not try to learn the content effectively.

- In a teaching and learning process, it is important to help the student to understand that they can fully succeed in a specific course of study in the context of achieving the objective. If they fail then student motivation will be decreased.
- There is a need to provide explicit objectives and prerequisites to the student so that they can understand the learning path.
- There is a need to provide appropriate and instant feedback to the learner.
- It is important for the students to feel some degree of control over the content.

Guideline 4—Satisfactions

- The learner must receive proper rewards based on their performance.
- There is a need to make the learner feel that the application of new knowledge will be helpful for a real setting.
- Satisfaction is based on motivation, so it is important to increase student motivation intrinsically or extrinsically.

Advantages of Instructional Design

Following this discussion of instructional design, one gets a view that instructional design is a systematic application of the instructional method or material to increase the effectiveness of any instructional learning environment. This section is intended to provide some of the essential advantages of systematic instructional design in a teaching and learning scenario:

- *Encourage the advocacy of learners:* In an overall systematic instructional process, instructional designers spend a great amount of time designing and developing instructional material by following a systematic as well as a scientific procedure, and therefore it helps to increase the participation of learners and encourage the advocacy of learners.
- *Support effective, efficient, and appealing instruction:* A teaching and learning process can only be effective when the overall teaching and learning scenario is effective, efficient, and appealing as per instructional strategies. Simply, these three factors are considered as success factors of any instructional process. Systematic design of instructional analysis provides a systematic guideline to the instructor so that they can increase the following factors appropriately.

- *Provide support to the designer, developer, and instructor:* A systematic process of instructional design is an organized procedure of providing instruction so that it encourages increased communication and cooperation between the designer, developer, and instructor in the context of producing and developing instruction. As a result, it helps to achieve a learning objective efficiently and effectively.
- *Facilitate diffusion/dissemination/adaption:* After the development of any instructional material through a systematic instructional procedure one of the essential benefits is it can be distributed, duplicated, or can be reused in a different field if required.
- *Achievement of learning objective accurately and appropriately:* The systematic design of the instructional objective helps to ensure that through a proper systematic guideline a learner can determine learning objectives accurately and appropriately.
- *Provide a systematic framework when encountering problems related to learning:* One knows that learning is a complex procedure. Throughout the learning process a learner can encounter various problems. In this context, a systematic approach of instructional design provides a scientific framework and guideline about how a learner can deal with a specific problem or solution for the problem, etc.

Disadvantages of Instructional Design

Though instructional design is a very effective approach for learning and teaching, it also has some limitations:

- Sometimes it is very hard to identify learning objectives in advance.
- Instructional system design can be criticized in the context of the heuristic design approach. This means it indicates what to do but ignores the specific context of "how to do it". However, this criticism is not true in recent contexts as various researchers have conducted considerable research and provided a guideline on how various processes in the instructional system design model can be applied.
- Another criticism in the context of instructional design is that it is very time-consuming when there is limited knowledge about the application and maintenance of the instructional model.

Bibliography

Branch, R. M., & Merrill, M. D. (2012). Characteristics of instructional design models. *Trends and Issues in Instructional Design and Technology*, 8–16.

Brophy, J. E. (1979). Teacher behavior and its effects. *Journal of Educational Psychology*, 71(6), 733–750. http://doi.org/10.1037/0022-0663.71.6.733.

Callison, D. (2002). Instructional models (part III). *School Library Media Activities Monthly*, 19(3), 36–37.

Crawford, C. (2004). Non-linear instructional design model: Eternal, synergistic design and development. *British Journal of Educational Technology*, 35(4), 413–420.

Dick, W., Carey, L., & Carey, J. O. (2009). *The systematic design of instruction*. Upper Saddle River, NJ: Merrill.

Gagne, R. M., Briggs, L. J., & Wager, W. W. (1992). *Principles of instructional design* (4th ed.). Fort Worth, TX: Holt.

Gredler, M. E. (2001). *Learning and instruction: Theory into practice* (4th ed.). Columbus, OH: Merrill Prentice-Hall.

Gustafson, K. L., & Branch, R. M. (2007). What is instructional design? In R. A. Reiser & J. V. Dempsey (Eds.), Trends and Issues in instructional design and technology (2nd ed., pp. 16–25). Upper Saddle River, NJ: Merrill-Prentice Hall.

Keller, J. M. (1983). Motivational design of instruction. In C. M. Reigeluth (Ed.), *Instructional design theories and models: An overview of their current status*. Hillsdale, NJ: Erlbaum.

Kemp, J. E., Morrison, G. R., & Ross, S. M. (1998). *Designing effective instruction* (2nd ed.). Upper Saddle River, NJ: Prentice-Hall.

Keller, J. M. (2016). Motivation, learning, and technology: Applying the ARCS-V motivation model. *Participatory Educational Research*, *3*(2), 1–15.

Knirk, F. G., & Gustafson, K. L. (1986). *Instructional technology: A systematic approach to education*. Holt Rinehart & Winston. 432 pages. (November 1985)

Marzano, R. J. (1998). *A theory-based meta-analysis of research on instruction*. Washington, DC: Office of Educational Research and Improvement (ED).

McNeil, Sara, http://www.coe.uh.edu/courses/cuin6373/whatisid.html in What is Instructional Design? - eLearning (adobe.com) https://elearning.adobe.com/2020/05/what-is-instructional-design/#:~:text=3%5D,ensure%20the%20quality%20of%20instruction.

Miner, K. R., Childers, W. K., Alperin, M., Cioffi, J., & Hunt, N. (2005). The mach model: From competencies to instruction and performance of the public health workforce. *Public Health Reports*, *120*(1 Suppl), 9–15.

Moallem, M. (2001). Applying constructivist and objectivist learning theories in the design of a web-based course: Implications for practice. *Educational Technology and Society*, *4*(3), 113–125.

Morrison, G. R., Ross, S. M. & Kemp, J. E. (2004). *Designing effective instruction* (4th ed.). New York: John Wiley & Sons.

Mustaro, P. N., Silveira, I. F., Omar, N., & Stump, S. M. D. (2007). Structure of Storyboard for Interactive Learning Objects Development, In Koohang, A. & Harman, K. (Eds.), *Learning Objects and Instructional Design* (pp. 253–280), Santa Rosa, California: Informing Science Press.

Reigeluth, C. M. (1983). *Instructional design theories and models: An overview of their current status*. New York: Routledge.

Reiser, R. A., & Dempsey, J. V. (2007). *Trends and issues in instructional design* (2nd ed.). Upper Saddle River, NJ: Pearson Education, Inc.

Royce, W. (1970). Managing the development of large software systems. *Proceedings of the IEEE Wescon*, *26*(August), 1–9.

Seels, B. & Glasgow, Z. (1998). *Making Instructional Design Decision*. The United State of America: Merrill Upper Saddle River, NJ.

Siemens, G. (2002). Instructional design in e-learning. Retrieved January 21, 2013, from http://www.elearnspace.org/Articles/InstructionalDesign.htm.

Smith, P. L., & Ragan, T. J. (1999). *Instructional design* (2nd ed.). Upper Saddle River, NJ: Prentice-Hall.

Smith, P. L., & Ragan, T. J. (2005). *Instructional design* (3rd ed.). Hoboken, NJ: John Wiley & Sons, Inc.

Snelbecker, G. E. (1974). *Learning theory, instructional theory, and psychoeducational design*. McGraw-Hill.

Swain, P. H. (2003). Psychology of learning for instruction, the art of changing the brain: Enriching the practice of teaching by exploring the biology of learning. *Journal of Engineering Education*, *92*(4), 283.

Suggested Readings

Branch, R. M., & Merrill, M. D. (2012). Characteristics of instructional design models. *Trends and Issues in Instructional Design and Technology*, 8–16.

Gredler, M. E. (2001). *Learning and instruction: Theory into practice* (4th ed.). Columbus, OH: Merrill Prentice-Hall.

Gustafson, K. L., & Branch, R. M. (2007). What is instructional design? In R. A. Reiser & J. V. Dempsey (Eds.), *Trends and Issues in instructional design and technology* (2nd ed., pp. 16–25). Upper Saddle River, NJ: Merrill-Prentice Hall.

McNeil, S. Retrieved from http://www.coe.uh.edu/courses/cuin6373/whatisid.html.

Merrill, M. D., Drake, L., Lacy, M. J., & Pratt, J. (1996). Reclaiming instructional design. *Educational Technology*, *36*(5), 5–7.

Miner, K. R., Childers, W. K., Alperin, M., Cioffi, J., & Hunt, N. (2005). The mach model: From competencies to instruction and performance of the public health workforce. *Public Health Reports*, *120*(1 Suppl), 9–15.

Moore, M. (1989). The theory of distance education: Some recent literature. In A. Tight (Ed.), *Integration and independence: Student support in distance education and open learning*. Routledge Pub.

Mustaro, P. N., Silveira, I. F., Omar, N., & Stump, S. M. D. (2007). Structure of Storyboard for Interactive Learning Objects Development, In Koohang, A. & Harman, K. (Eds.), *Learning Objects and Instructional Design* (pp. 253–280), Santa Rosa, California: Informing Science Press.

Power, M. (2008). The emergence of a blended online learning environment. *Merlot Journal of Online Learning and Teaching, 4*(4). Retrieved from http://jolt.merlot.org/vol4no4/power_1208.htm.

PricewaterhouseCoopers. (2010). *Survey of ICTs for education in India and South Asia.* New Delhi, India: PricewaterhouseCoopers.

Reiser, R. A., & Dempsey, J. V. (2007). *Trends and issues in instructional design* (2nd ed.). Upper Saddle River, NJ: Pearson Education, Inc.

Siemens, G. (2002). Instructional design in elearning. Retrieved January 21, 2013, from http://www.elearnspace.org/Articles/InstructionalDesign.htm.

Smith, P. L., & Ragan, T. J. (1999). *Instructional design* (2nd ed.). Upper Saddle River, NJ: Prentice Hall.

Smith, P. L., & Ragan, T. J. (2005). *Instructional design* (3rd ed.). Hoboken, NJ: John Wiley & Sons, Inc.

5
COMMUNICATION AND COMMUNICATION STRATEGIES

> "Communication – the human connection – is the key to personal and career success".
> —*Paul J. Meyer https://thenewsstrike.com/communication-the-human-connection-is-the-key-to-personal-and-career-growth-success-paul-j-meyer/*

Communication is crucial and fundamental to human existence. It is fundamental in the sense that every moment brings in numerous communications that take place with talking, listening, writing, and thinking or by conversation or interaction with one another. However, in a literal sense, communication is a process of transfer of feeling, thought, emotion, idea, information, etc. On the other hand, it is also a continuous process.

Meaning and Definition of Communication

In general terms, communication is an essential aspect and inseparable from everyday life. In day-to-day life, every moment involves sharing thoughts, giving direction to each other, sharing emotion, information, etc. by the sensory channels. If one views communication as a process, it is both an "art" and "science". Communication as art involves psychological aspects such as human nature, stimulus, and response, etc. and as a science it emphasizes tools or technological use of communication.

In various fields, communications are concerned in various ways. In the field of education, it denotes communication between teacher and student, the student with a student, the institution with the government, etc. In addition, from the industrial or business point of view, communication may be between employer and employee, between company owner and worker, etc. In addition, similarly, various communications are involved between doctor and patient, engineer, researcher, in everyday general communication, and many more.

Let us describe the precise meaning of the term "communication". The origin of the word "communication" is derived from two Latin words "*communis*" (noun) and "*communicare*" (verb). However, both words emphasize "*communis*" as "commonality" and "*communicare*" as "to make common". From the etymological perspective, communication refers to "to share" or "to participate" in something. Something means information or knowledge or meaning. Therefore, here communication is the process of sharing information, knowledge, or meaning (Adhikary, 2008, Communication and Media Journalism). Nevertheless, communication is much more. In the following section are some definitions which might shed light on the scope of the word and expression of communication.

Definitions of Communications

Brown (2010)(n.d.): "Communication is the transfer of information from one person to another, whether or not it elicits confidence. But the information transferred must be understandable to the receiver".

Meyer (n.d.): "Communication is the intercourse by words, letters or messages".

Dale (1961): "Communication is defined as the sharing of ideas and feeling in a mood of mutuality".

Tubbs (2000): "Communication has been broadly defined as "the sharing of experience", and to some extent, all living organisms can be said to share the experience. What makes human communication unique is the superior ability to create and to use symbols, for it is this ability that enables humans to share experiences indirectly and vicariously. A symbol can be defined as something used for or regarded as representing something else. For the time being, though, let us say that human communication is the process of creating meaning between two or more people.

Webster's New World Law Dictionary (2010) defines "communication as the exchange, imparting, or transmission of ideas, information, opinions, or thoughts, transmitted electronically or by gestures, speech, or writing".

The American Heritage (2013) defines communication as "The exchange of thoughts, messages, or information, as by speech, signals, writing, or behavior".

Little, P. (1977) says "Communication is the process by which information is transmitted between individuals and/or organizations so that an understanding response results".

Keith Davis (1967 cited in Singla, 2008–9, p.236):
Communication is the transfer of information and understanding from one person to another person. It is a way of reaching others with facts, ideas, thoughts, and values. It is a "bridge" of meaning among people so that they can share what they feel and know. By using this bridge, a person can cross safely the river of misunderstanding that sometimes separates people.

From the above discussions and definitions of communication, the following three essential features are extracted:

Transmission and reception of message: One of the essential features of communication is the transmission and reception of the message. The message may be in both verbal and nonverbal forms. The person uses messages to share his thoughts, feelings, emotions, experiences, information, etc. As an example, if one draws a picture this is the message of thought of the artist, in a similar way a person encodes a message to express themselves.

Sender and receiver: In the communication process, there must be two points—one sender and another receiver. Both the points are essential as the sender encodes the message and the receiver takes the role of the decoder.

Communication is a process: Communication is a process in the sense that it is continuous, dynamic, and reciprocal. Thus, communication processes can be described as sender, receiver, or message as if they are static and discrete.

Objective of Communication

Every day brings numerous opportunities for communicating with others. In this orientation, communication has many objectives and forms. Our general discussion will mainly focus on two major objectives which are the most important in the teaching-learning process as well as for a business organization.

Basic Essential Features of Communication

1. *Information* (education, training, instruction, etc.)
2. *Persuasion* (motivation, suggestion, advice, etc.)

Information

Information is related to our knowledge. The major objective of communication is sharing information. However, the purpose of sharing information varies with the situation and organization, such that information sharing in the business sector is different from the education sector. Although the fundamental process of sharing information is based on how one communicates the information. The following are the various objectives of communication from an information-sharing point of view:

Education or sharing knowledge: By communication, knowledge or education is provided to the receiver to gather new information or for up-to-date existing information about new technology.

Training: Another objective of institutional communication is to provide proper training to the receiver. Training is the essential part of the educational setting for habit formation and mastery of learning objectives. In addition, in business or corporate organizations training is for sharpening the knowledge of employees. However, in both situations, effective communication is taken as an important role.

Provide order or instruction: In education or corporate organizations order- or instruction-based communication is common and it is one of the objectives of communication. In classroom situations through communication the teacher provides proper instruction to the students regarding learning objectives. In addition, the head of the institution provides orders or instructions to their assistant teachers about the curriculum of the instruction, circulations from government, policy, etc. Also, in corporate or business situations various rules, strategies, and plans are provided to the workers from higher authority.

Persuasion

Persuasion is a process to change or influence the behavior and attitude of others. Effective communication is the key element in the persuasion process. From an educational point of view a teacher is always engaged in persuading students, as are researchers and writers through their work. Nevertheless, in a business situation, everyone is busy with how their product is accepted by the buyer and, in all of the mentioned situations, their needs are the persuasive power which comes from effective verbal or written communication. So, persuasion is another essential objective of communication. The persuasion process can be divided up in various ways as follows.

Motivation: Motivation is one of the inner characteristics of a human being that provides reinforcement. However, various factors are directly involved for positive motivation in organizational situations viz., a reward for good, incentive, high marks, appreciation, etc. which act as a stimulator related to better learning or high productivity. An effective communication leads to high motivation, so it is another important objective.

Advice or counseling: To provide advice or counseling is another important objective of communication. In the organizational setting of educational situations, the teacher provides advice to their students for the betterment of results or achievement of learning objectives. In a classroom situation the teacher provides oral face-to-face counseling to difficult or maladjusted learners. In the same way, in a corporate or business organization a higher authority provides advice or counseling to an employee who habitually leaves the office early, takes leave frequently, does not have a healthy productive attitude, etc. However, the entire situation needs an effective communication power/ability.

Suggestion: To provide suggestions is another objective of communications. Suggestions in a productive way provide more strategies to overcome problems or create new effective situations. In an organization or educational setting, by suggestions one could develop various new processes of teaching or develop a new curriculum, etc. In a single sentence, suggestions deal with the improvement in service, speed, and expenses for a better result in an organization or for human beings.

Nature of Communication

With regard to the existence of human beings such as personal existence, family existence, company existence, cultural existence, etc., communication always plays an important role. However, the following are some specific ways of communication.

Communication and human activity are interrelated: In real situations the exchange of ideas, thoughts, feelings, etc. is interrelated with how the activity of humans is involved in the communication process. So, by an effective communication process, one can increase human activity such as person-to-person interaction.

At least two people are involved in the communication process: For effective communication, there must be a minimum of two points such as the face-to-face communication sender (who encodes the message) and the receiver (who decodes message), and in virtual communication, the information of the communicator or the sender and the device (who is provided with information). However, a sender can also send out a message for many receivers.

Communication could be a one-way or maybe a two-way process: The existing design of communication indicates that communication may be one-way or two-way. In a one-way communication process the sender sends a message to the receiver through a channel or medium but the receiver is not able to provide his or her reaction to the sender. In a two-way communication the receiver can send his or her reaction to the sender.

Understanding of people could increase the effectiveness of communication: Effective communication takes place when the receiver can properly decode the message of the sender and provide proper feedback of his or her reaction to the sender. However, without a proper reaction from the receiver, the sender cannot understand the view of the receiver and thus communication would be inadequate. In addition, it is the responsibility of the sender that he or she should properly encode the message so that the receiver can easily understand it.

In communication information flows in a variety of styles: In an effective communication process there must be variety in the flow of communication. Organizations, businesses, and classroom communications follow various styles of communication viz., upward direction, downward direction, horizontal direction, and many others.

Communication flows through channel or medium: In every communication, one of the essential components is medium or channel. However, in classroom situations the media could be written, oral, nonverbal, etc.

Components or Elements of Communication

As we know from the previous discussion communication is a process of transmitting or exchange of verbal and nonverbal information to the receiver. However, this section discusses various components of communication and function. It is important to become familiarized with each component clearly to understand the communication process and model effectively.

Components of Communication

(a) Context
(b) Source/sender
(c) Receiver
(d) Message
(e) Symbol
(f) Channel
(g) Encoding
(h) Decoding
(i) Feedback
(j) Noise

Context

The heart of communication is context. Every message is processed with a context. The sender chooses a specific communication context. Context may be physical (room, outdoor, party, classroom, etc.), social (status relationship among people), psychological (formality, informality, etc.), and chronological (time, date, period, etc.).

Source/Sender

Source or sender is the event or people who generate the verbal or nonverbal cues and convey the message and produce a requisite response.

Receiver

A receiver is a person for whom the message is sent by the sender. The receiver plays a role in interpreting a message.

Message

The message is the key element of one communication process. It is the key idea of the sender. The message may be verbal or nonverbal such as facial expression, written documents, vocal conversation, etc.

Symbol

The symbol is a verbal or nonverbal cue used to encode the message. Words, signs, etc. are represented as symbols in communication.

Channel

Channel is a medium that bridges sender and receiver. It is a means to exchange or transmit the mass to the sender.

Encoding

Encoding is the process of symbolization of a message as a code. In the encoding process, the sender uses various symbols, words, graphs, and pictures understandable by the receiver to achieve his desired response.

Decoding

Decoding is a process of decompression or translation of a message that is easily understood. A message sent by the sender is decoded by the receiver in many ways which means that the receiver extracts the meaning of the message in an understandable manner.

Feedback

Feedback is another major component and helps the sender in analyzing the efficiency of the message. For instance, when a sender sends a message to the receiver, feedback is provided to ensure that the received message is properly interpreted by the receiver or not.

Noise

Noise is a barrier to the message. Message sent from the sender to the receiver can be distorted by noise and may produce misinformation. However, noise is both internal (noise from communication process) and external (from environment).

Communication Cycle and Process of Communication

The previous section introduced various components of communication. As stated, each component functions systematically in any communication process. However, completion of one message flowing from the sender to the receiver with feedback going on through a process of a cycle is also called a cycle of communication. This section is going to explore further the process of communication and its steps.

In the communication process, the message delivered from sender to receiver consists of some interrelated steps called process and is a continuous acyclic process. However, the process of communication starts with the idea, fact, opinion, or any other information which is generated by the sender and sent to the receiver. The following are some definitions of the process of communication:

Kreitner (2009): "Communication process is a chain made up of identifiable links. The chain includes sender, encoding, message, receiver, decoding, and feedback".

Steps Involved in the Communication Process

However, the definition of the communication process indicates that transfer, as well as feedback, is involved in various steps (see Figure 5.1). The communication process mainly starts

Fundamental Concepts and Theories

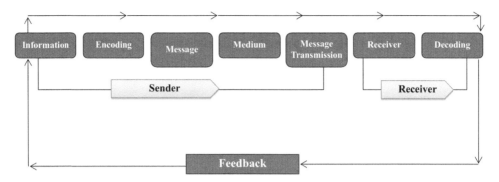

Figure 5.1 Diagrammatic representation of the process or cycle of communication.

with the message of the sender and ends with feedback. The following steps are involved in a communication process:

1) *Information source:* In the first step, the sender generates some idea, thought, information, or any other thing that they wish to convey to the receiver.
2) *Encoding:* After the sender produces an idea or thought it is encoded systematically. Encoding is a process of symbolization or translation of the information in a communicable or logical way. Encoding can take place in various forms viz., oral, written, facial expression, etc.
3) *Development of the message:* After encoding the sender obtains a message that can be delivered to the receiver.
4) *Selection of medium:* The medium or channel is the bridge between sender and receiver. After the development of the message, the sender chooses a proper medium through which the message can be transmitted to the receiver.
5) *Transmission of the message:* In this stage the sender sends a message to the receiver after completion of the medium selection. The role of the sender is to complete one communication cycle.
6) *Receiver:* In this stage the message that is sent by the sender is received by another party called the receiver. The receiver can receive a message in various forms such as hearing, seeing, feeling, etc.
7) *Decoding:* Decoding is the process of message interpretation of the sender. In this stage the receiver tries to understand the message of the sender and analyze it.
8) *Feedback:* Feedback is the final and important stage in communication. After decoding the message from the sender, the receiver provides feedback to ensure that the message is received, understood or not, and the reaction to the message, etc.
9) *Noise:* Noise is a distortion of the message. It is crucial in the sense that the whole process can be a failure by noise. Noise can be internal or external.

Types of Communication

This section will discuss various types of communication used in the classroom and other situations. Before discussing it needs to be remembered that communication is a complex process where people exchange their ideas, thoughts, emotions, feelings, etc. However, now the question arises as to the ways this is done.

Mainly, in a communication process, a sender (encoder) encodes the message and sends it through the media to the receiver (decoder). However, it depends upon the message and its context as to how people communicate with each other. There are several ways which we can divide broadly in two:

1. *Types based on communication channel use*
2. *Types based on the style of communication*

Types Based on Communication Channel Use

In the communication process, it is also important which type of channel is used as it also affects communication. However, based on channel use in communication, it can be divided further in two ways:

i) Verbal communication
ii) Nonverbal communication

Verbal communication

Verbal communication refers to communication through vocal, verbal, or written words, etc. In this mode of communication, the message is transmitted by oral sound or through a piece of writing. In verbal communication, one important acronym is *KISS* (keep it short and simple). Verbal communication is further divided into two types:

A. Oral communication
B. Written communication

ORAL COMMUNICATION

The main attribute of oral communication is spoken words. As per the definition, one can say that oral communication occurs with the help of word of mouth, spoken words, and conversations, and thus any messages or information when shared or exchanged between one another through speech or word of mouth is called oral communication. It also needs to be remembered that oral communication is mainly influenced by face-to-face conversations, speech, telephonic conversations, videos, radio, television, voice-over-Internet, etc.

ADVANTAGES OF ORAL COMMUNICATION

- Through oral communication instant feedback can be sent to the sender from the receiver.
- By face-to-face oral communication, the receiver can read the expression, emotion, and body language of the sender. However, this can help both for effective communication, for example the receiver and sender should trust what's being said or not.
- In oral communication through variations in the tone, pitch, and intensity of voice, the speaker can convey shades of meaning.

DISADVANTAGES OF ORAL COMMUNICATION

- In the oral communication process, the sender sends a message to the sender at their own pace. Sometimes it distracts and it is difficult for the receiver to deeply or meaningfully understand the message.

- In oral communication, without any gadgets or devices, messages are difficult to record. So it is impossible to preserve the message for the future.
- In oral communication, important and secret information may be disclosed (see Figure 5.2).

Written Communication

Written communication refers to communication through any written word or often written signs or symbols. However, in a single sentence, one can use languages in any medium called written communication. The message of written communication may be printed or handwritten, and it can be transmitted through e-mail, letter, report, memo, etc.

Example: For internal written communication memos, reports, bulletins, job descriptions, employee manuals, e-mail, etc. are used. In addition, for external written communication e-mail, websites, letters, proposals, telegrams, faxes, postcards, contracts, advertisements, brochures, and news releases are used.

ADVANTAGES OF WRITTEN COMMUNICATION

- By written communication messages can be recorded permanently. Thus, it is useful where record maintenance is required.
- Written communication is more precise and explicit. In addition, complex subject matter can be presented easily and attractively.
- Written communication can be used as a future reference, and validation and legality of written communication are much higher than oral communication.

DISADVANTAGES OF WRITTEN COMMUNICATION

- Written communication is more expensive compared to oral. In this communication paper, pen, ink, typewriter, and computer are needed. Also, there is a need for some type of expertise and writing ability to execute messages in written form.
- Another, major disadvantage of written communication is the lack of flexibility as written documents cannot be changed easily.
- In written communication, it is impossible to provide instant feedback, it lacks instant misunderstanding and correction, lacks personal intimacy, etc.

Nonverbal Communication

Nonverbal communication is a wordless communication process. In a single sentence, one can say that communication other than oral and written communication is called nonverbal

Figure 5.2 Oral communication process.

communication. Nonverbal communication is all about the body language of the sender and receiver.

Example: Eye contact signs, symbols, colors, gestures, body language, posture, tone of voice, or facial expressions, etc.

Elements of nonverbal communication can be categorized into the following three categories:

Appearance: It is a major part of nonverbal communication, such as clothing, hairstyle, neatness, etc. However, environmental factors viz, room size, lighting, decorations, furnishings, etc. work as an element of nonverbal communication.

Body language: Another essential element of nonverbal communication is body language such as facial expressions, gestures, or posture.

Sound: Volume of communicator, pitch, tone, voice modulation, etc.

ADVANTAGES OF NONVERBAL COMMUNICATION

Meharabian and Wiener (1967) suggested that only 7% of a message is sent through words, with the remaining 93% sent through nonverbal expressions. The following are the advantages of nonverbal communication:

- In this communication, the sender or communicator emphasizes facial expression, voice, appearance, etc. without a spoken or written word so it is helpful for illiterate people.
- Special children, mainly children with hearing impairments, can exchange messages through hands, figures, eye movements, etc.
- Nonverbal communication is mainly expressed through pictures, graphs, signs, etc. that can be seen and can be very attractive.

DISADVANTAGES OF NONVERBAL COMMUNICATION

- In nonverbal communication, long conversations and necessary explanations are not possible.
- It is difficult to understand and requires a lot of repetition (see Figure 5.3).

Figure 5.3 Nonverbal communication process.

Types Based on the Style of Communication

We categorized the communication process based on style and purposes as follows:

i) Formal communication
ii) Informal communication

Formal Communication

By formal communication one can officially interchange information. Officially in the sense that certain rules, conventions, and specific principles are followed while communicating with a message. One of the main attributes of formal communication is that it is controlled in nature and is handled cautiously by authority and organizations. However, due to this and without any interruption the message reaches the desired place at a low cost and in a proper way. Sometimes formal communication is also called "through proper channels communication".

Example: Used usually in professional settings, corporate meetings, and conferences that undergo informal patterns.

CHARACTERISTICS OF FORMAL COMMUNICATION

There are some specific characteristics of formal communication such as:

- *Written and oral:* One of the major attributes of formal communication is it can be delivered through oral and written form. Mainly, our everyday work takes place through oral communication and administrative or official work is handled through written communication.
- *Formal relations:* Formal communication is mainly used when the communicator is formal, such as where communication relations are established by the organization.
- *Prescribed path:* The formal communication message has to be flown through the proper channel. For example, to apply to any organization for a job or fellowship one has to provide an official application form to the higher authority.
- *Organizational message:* Informal communication authorized organizational messages are only taken into consideration, otherwise personal messages are out of its jurisdiction.

ADVANTAGES OF FORMAL COMMUNICATION

Maintenance by higher authority: One of the major advantages of formal communication is it bridges the relationship between higher authority and subordinates. Nonetheless, by this systematic way of communication the higher authority can control the subordinate, which is needed for effective and successful control of communication.

Clear and effective communication: In formal communication, such as educational institutional communication, there is a two-way contact between the higher authority and the teacher. In this way, communication flow is timely and information is concise as well as providing clear and effective interaction.

The systematic flow of information: In the formal communication process information flows systematically from one person to another. Hence, it is more effective compared to unorganized communication.

LIMITATIONS OF FORMAL COMMUNICATION

Overload of messages: Formal communication in the classroom or other organizations generates more information, more messages, and also needs to be provided through a proper channel. Hence, it consumes more time and produces more overload of information.

Distortion of information: As formal communication information flows systematically, it creates a huge distance between sender and receiver. Also, formal communication messages are passed from the sender to receiver in many ways; therefore, they could be distorted when they reach the receiver.

TYPES OF FORMAL COMMUNICATION

I. Vertical communication
II. Downward communication
III. Upward communication

i) *Vertical communication:* Vertical communication refers to communication that takes place among people of different positions and stages (flows the information up and down). It is a kind of internal communication. Ricky and Griffin (2000) defined, "Vertical communication is a communication that flows both up and down the organization, along formal reporting lines".

Vertical communication is further divided into two types:

a) *Downward Communication:* Downward refers to communication from the top hierarchy of the authority to their subordinates. For example, in the school environment communication from the head of the institution to the lower division employee. In downward communication, information includes various rules of the institution, orders, instructions, information, policies, etc. In this communication subordinates or lower members of the organization can get timely information timely.

b) *Upward communication:* Upward communication is the reverse process of downward communication. In this communication information flows from the bottom or subordinates to the higher authority. However, mainly suggestions, reactions, feedback, complaints, and reports are provided to the superior and this type of communication helps in the decision-making process of the institutions.

ii) *Horizontal Communication:* Horizontal communication refers to the communication among people at the same level (position, rank, or status). Horizontal communication helps coordinate information and cooperate and collaborate same and similar ranking people in the organization. However, the benefit of this communication depends on the experience of other people. In horizontal communication, there are various information flows such as mutual problems, suggestions, requests, discussion, etc. (see Table 5.1).

Table 5.1 Difference between vertical and horizontal communication

Basis of Differentiations	Horizontal Communication	Vertical Communication
Purpose of communication	Horizontal communication coordinates various departments and organizations	The main purpose of vertical communication is to provide order, instruction, advice, etc.
Flow of information	In this communication, information flows among the same level and status of people	In this communication, information flows both ways; up and downward
Use of media	Oral communication is mainly used for this communication	Written communication is mainly used for this communication
Relationship	Mainly informal relationship	Mainly formal relationship
Distortion	Free from distortion of the message	There is some possibility of distortion of the message

Informal Communication

Informal communication is also called grapevine communication because there is no absolute channel of communication. In this communication process information is mainly interchanged unofficially. This is informal in the sense that the relation of communication organizational formality is free such as communication among the same club members, friends, those with the same place of birth, and many more. However, such communication is mainly based on comments, suggestions, care, emotional exchanges, etc. For example, two friends are talking about a blood donation camp and its implementation strategies.

CHARACTERISTICS OF INFORMAL COMMUNICATION

Beyond the restriction of the organization: Informal communication is based on social relations and is free from the organization's official rules and regulations. No higher authority and domination are there.

Grapevine-type of communication: As previously mentioned informal communication is free from organizational restrictions and therefore there is no definite channel and it can move in a zigzag way.

Possibility of rumor and distortion: As informal communication has no official rules and regulations, it is not always absolutely true or false and in this communication process there is a higher risk of rumors floating.

ADVANTAGES OF INFORMAL COMMUNICATION

Fast and effective communication: In informal communication the message can flow very fast and effectively, such as we can get news of an accident very fast in an informal way compared to in formal communication.

Creates friendly environment: Informal communication mainly encourages creating a friendly environment as there is no pressure to maintain officially or organizationally. As a result, the flow of communication and reaction of sender and receiver can easily be observed.

Better human relations: Informal communication encourages free speech such that everyone can share their opinion freely with the audience. This helps the establishment of better relations.

Easy solution to difficult problems: In an organizational setting there are many problems and situations which cannot be solved by formal communication because of less freedom. In the informal communication process lower employees/subordinates can provide their opinion to the higher authority which may help to solve difficult problems.

LIMITATIONS OF INFORMAL COMMUNICATION

Unofficial communication: One of the major limitations of informal communication is the unsystematic and unofficial communication process, therefore in many situations it cannot be used or does not have legal validation.

Unreliable information: In informal communication, flow of information is undependable and it means that no one is particularly responsible for information and thus with informal communication no important decisions can be taken.

Principles of Achieving Effective Classroom Communication

In the previous section, we discussed various barriers of communication encountered in classroom situations, which come from various sources. However, effective classroom communication is the key to the success of any teaching-learning situation. It is not only in classroom situations that quick and effective communication can increase productivity, efficiency, and can eliminate redundancies. For example, whether teaching in the classroom, learning from an institution, preparing for a job, etc. one should have strong communication skills for better success. Moreover, revolutions in the computer-based environment encourage more onlinelearning environments. Therefore, this section has been based on various research-based principles for achieving effective classroom communication, many of which are applicable for online communication including distance mode of communication. We can divide effective strategies of classroom communication into two types:

- Principles based on skills and attributes of the teacher and student
- Principles based on classroom-based activity

Seven Cs of Effective Classroom Communication (Based on Teacher and Student Skills and Attributes)

a. *Completeness:* The first and foremost important principle of communication is completeness. Completeness refers to delivering all essential facts to the audience or receiver. In a lecture-based classroom situation the teacher (sender) should take into consideration that the instructional material or learning module should be presented in a complete form that can be conveyed to students' or the receivers' mindset accordingly. Complete classroom communication should improve the following in classroom situations:
    - Complete communication of the teacher in classroom situations enhances desire and fulfills the knowledge of the student on the subject matter.
    - Complete communication in classroom situations provides more and more additional information, for example it answers almost all questions appearing in the mind of a student.
    - Moreover, completeness in classroom communication encourages the provision of all crucial information that the student needs.
    - Complete communication in the classroom helps the teacher with better decision-making through the messages or feedback of the students as to whether they have received all desired and crucial information.
b. *Conciseness:* Classroom communication must emphasize brevity or conciseness. The lyrical prose of the teacher makes the classroom boring and lose focus. So, the teacher should focus on the consciousness of the message or learning material rather than the length of content. Teachers should avoid jargon words and deliver a message which is short and concise.
    - Conciseness focuses on the exact meaning of the message without jargon or needless words.
    - It provides a short and essential message.
    - It is more appealing and acceptable to the audience.
c. *Consideration:* Consideration implies "empathy". For effective communication, empathy is another crucial element. Consideration always encourages giving the receiver first place. In a classroom situation, the teacher should give priority to the viewpoint of the student, their background and level of understanding as per his or her point of view. It is one type of "stepping into the shoes of others". Teachers, as a sender of a message, should be conscious regarding the use of words that may harm the emotions of the receiver. The following are some of the features of consideration:

- Care must be taken about the use of a word such as thanks, sorry, warm, help, etc.
- The empathetic approach increases positive stimulation to the receiver.
- Teachers should flow a positive approach to the whole classroom and emphasize more on "possibility" rather than "impossible".

d. *Clarity:* Clarity implies that the message must flow to the receiver or reader's mind in a specific manner. However, in a classroom situation clarity comes from various aspects such as knowledge or subject matter of the message (what the teacher wants to say), the methods (how he or she wants to say it), the medium (what format he or she wants to use. Lack of insight into clarity may affect effective communication in a classroom situation.
   - By clarity, a message will be easily understandable.
   - Clarity enhances the meaning of the message and also understandability flows to the receiver.
   - Clear messages always encourage the specification of subject matter.

e. *Concreteness:* Another important art in classroom communication is concreteness. Concreteness means the message should be to the point and clear in nature rather than fuzzy, vague, and full of academic loquaciousness. In a classroom situation the teacher should take into consideration that the presented message should be clear and understandable to the student. A teacher should use various components to make his message or learning material clear and concise such as with the use of examples, graphs, images, etc.
   - Concreteness is reinforced with specific facts and figures.
   - It helps to make the message clear which builds the reputation.
   - Concreteness is always clear so that there is a minimum chance of misinterpreting the message of the sender.

f. *Courtesy:* For an effective classroom, communication courtesy is also a crucial element. Courtesy in the communication process refers to the sender's expression and respect for the receiver. In a classroom situation, teachers and students come from diverse backgrounds and cultures thus teachers, as well as students, should respect each culture. However, the teacher or student as a sender of a message should play an important role in being reflective, enthusiastic, judicious, polite, etc. to maintain effective and continuous communication with each other.
   - Courtesy involves giving priority to the feeling, idea, culture, individual differences, etc. of the receiver.
   - A courteous attribute is always positive in nature and involves the student (receiver) in the teaching and learning process.
   - It increases respect to the student and as a result, the student also gives more respect to the teacher as well as the learning environment.

g. *Correctness:* Correctness is another essential principle in classroom communication. Correctness refers to the fact that in classroom situations teachers and students should communicate without grammatical error and with proper pronunciation. The following are the features of correctness in communication.
   - Correctness represents the use of appropriate and correct language in the message.
   - Correctness in communication enhances the confidence level of the sender.
   - In a classroom situation the correct message has a positive impact on student attention and proper learning.
   - The correctness of the teacher helps to ensure the exactness and accurateness of the contents present in teaching-learning scenarios.

Principle of Effective Classroom Communication
(Based on Classroom Activity)

How can communication in classroom-based activities be improved? This is an essential question and has been discussed in various ways in the education field. Arthur W. Chickering and Zelda F. Gamson in their article "Seven Principles for Good Practice in Undergraduate Education" (1987) explained various principles to overcome barriers and establish effective communication in the classroom. Some of them in the classroom scenario are discussed below:

Encourage Contact between Student and Faculty

The student is the most crucial unit in teaching-learning scenarios. The first step toward achieving effective communication in a classroom or any teaching-learning environment is building a healthy relationship with the student. In many classroom situations, teachers fail to create rapport with the student and the student feels they are a separate unit in the classroom which creates a communication gap between teacher and student. However, to minimize the gap the teacher or school authorities should follow the points as suggested by Chickering and Gamson (1987).

- First and foremost, a teacher should share their personal experience and values to the student.
- Teachers should not bound the student to classroom learning, but encourage them to work outside the classroom as well.
- To create effective communication in the classroom, a teacher should provide individual feedback such as calling students by their names or providing personalized corrections or suggestions on their classroom assignments.
- Besides book-based learning teachers should provide information regarding the practical aspect of each learning unit.
- Teachers should help students in their extracurricular activities as well as participate in student events.
- Students should be encouraged in classroom discussion and respected to present their views.
- Teachers should give a feedback sheet to students at the end of class to know more about the achievement of the learning objective and student views regarding the whole class.

Develop Reciprocity and Cooperation among the Students

Another major part of effective classroom communication is a cooperative environment rather than an isolated environment. Communication research unveiled that a cooperative learning environment improves the social activity, thinking, and understanding of the student. To create a more cooperative communicative environment teachers should:

- Encourage students in more group work such as group-based problem-solving, exam preparation, work on assignments, etc.
- Irrespective of culture, race, and religion students should participate in group-based learning which increases more communication with diverse backgrounds and also students to know each other more.
- Provide presentation-based and group projection-based learning environments as well as peer tutoring.

Encourage Active Learning

For effective communication in a classroom environment the teacher should care about inter-activity with the students and teachers must take into consideration that a student is an active unit in the classroom. Students as passive recipients of communication is wrong. Teachers must encourage the students to talk more about what they learn, their past experiences, what they are not able to understand etc. Teachers should:

- Firstly, in every theoretical discussion provide practical justification and implications from a real-life setting.
- Encourage the student to follow new references, projects, and course-based activities.
- Ask the student to present what they learned today.
- Use various realistic software-based applications by which students can understand more effectively the abstract concepts and can manipulate an object as in a real situation.
- Practice stimulation and grow critical thinking skills.
- Create a problem-based situation in the classroom and give the students the opportunity to solve the problem by group-based activity.

Provide Prompt Feedback

From the previous discussion regarding the communication process, we know that feedback is the essential element for effective communication. However, it is also true in a classroom-based teaching-learning situation. Teaching is not a one-way communication process where the teacher teaches only through his or her knowledge and the student listens passively. For effective communication, the teacher must know what the student can learn and be aware of student feedback regarding the subject matter. Appropriate feedback in classroom communication reflects students' prior knowledge, achievement of learning objectives, lack to achievement, etc. Through this the teacher can follow up with the student and can provide appropriate feedback. The following are strategies the teacher should follow for effective feedback:

- For appropriate feedback, the foremost is question and answer. Teachers should encourage question and answer sessions after the completion of the module to gauge the understanding of the student.
- Teachers can arrange short presentations after the learning unit or ask what they have learned.
- Provide more assessment.
- Provide prompt feedback when a student is not able to answer and also provide information on ways of improvement.

Respect Diverse Talents and Ways of Learning

Individual difference is another essential factor taken into consideration for effective communication in the classroom. Every student comes from a diverse background and their pace of learning is also different. Therefore, for effective communication teachers should nurture various learning styles in the classroom in the following ways:

- Encourage a computer-based learning environment where the student chooses his or her learning module on their own interests as well learning at their own pace.
- Teachers should apply diverse teaching activities and techniques to grow interest through the diverse attributes of the students.

- Encourage students to express their problems.
- Provide extra care to the students who lack previous knowledge and are not able to communicate to the teacher as well as their peer group.
- Encourage students from less-advanced classes to provide their opinion in the classroom.

References

Adhikary, N. M. (2008a). *Communication, media and journalism: An integrated study*. Kathmandu: Prashanti Prakashan.

Brown, G. G. (n.d.). Definition of communication. Retrieved June 3, 2013, from http://communicationtheory.org/definition-0f-communications.

Burton, G., & Dimbleby, R. (2002). *Teaching communication*. London: Routledge.

Chickering, A. W., & Gamson, Z. F. (1987). Seven principles for good practice in undergraduate education. *AAHE Bulletin, 3*, 7.

Dale, E. (1961). *Communication in teaching and learning, In Essentials of educational technology* Mangal, S.K., Springer.

Kreitner, R. (2009). *Management* (11TH 09 - Old Edition), 592 pages, South Western Educational Publishing

Little, P. (1977). *Communication in Business*, 345 pages. 3rd ed., Pitman pub.

Mehrabian, A., & Wiener, M. (1967). Decoding of inconsistent communications. *Journal of Personality and Social Psychology*, 6(1), 109–114. https://doi.org/10.1037/h0024532

Meyer, F. G. (n.d.). https://www.communicationtheory.org/definitions-of-communication/

Moorhead, G., Ricky, W., & Griffin, R. W. (2000). *Organizational Behavior*. Jaico Publishing House

Singla, R.K. (2008). *Business Studies: Class XII*. New Delhi: V.K. (India) Enterprises.

The American Heritage Dictionary of the English Language, (2022). *Fifth Edition copyright by HarperCollins Publishers*. All rights reserved.

Webster's New World Law Dictionary, (2010) by Jonathan Wallace (Author), Susan Ellis Wild.

6
MODELS AND PATTERNS OF COMMUNICATION

Patterns of Communication

As previously discussed, communication is the process of sharing information with others. It has various forms such as intrapersonal, interpersonal, and mass communication. This section will discuss some commonly used patterns that have been used in the conventional group communication process. However, a major emphasis of this entire pattern is to communicate with the "group leader" and "group member". The major difference among the pattern is the degree to which they are centralized or decentralized (Ceravolo et al., 2012). Let us discuss briefly all the group communication patterns.

The five patterns are:

1. Wheel network pattern of communication
2. Chain network pattern of communication
3. Y network pattern of communication
4. Circle network pattern of communication
5. Star or all-channel communication pattern

Wheel Network Pattern of Communication

The wheel pattern of communication is the most structured and centralized compared to other communication patterns. One of the most unique attributes of wheel pattern communication is each member can communicate with only one other person.

Example: Suppose a head of an educational institution and his assistant teacher, instructor, or other personnel in a wheel network. The head teacher is "A" and his assistants "B", "C", "D", "E", "F" respectively. However, the five assistants (B, C, D, E, F) or personnel send information to the head (A) and the head (A) sends back he information to them. Usually, this is used in the decision-making process of an institution (see Figure 6.1).

Chain Network Pattern of Communication

As per the centralization point of view, the chain network pattern of communication is the second-highest pattern of communication. In this pattern mainly two people communicate with each other and they have only one person to communicate with.

Models and Patterns of Communication

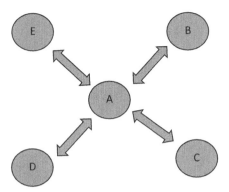

Figure 6.1 Wheel network pattern of communication.

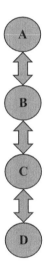

Figure 6.2 Chain network pattern of communication.

Example: Communication in educational institutions is structured like a typical chain. Suppose a higher institutional authority (A) sends a piece of information to the head of the institution (B) who sends the information to the assistant teacher (B), who then reports it to the student (C), and so on. Chain pattern of main communication is used at departments and organizational levels when information is passed throughout the school building to the central level (see Figure 6.2).

Y Network Pattern of Communication

The Y network pattern of communication is similar to the chain network. It differentiates from the chain in the sense that in the Y pattern two members fall outside the chain.

Example: Suppose in an educational institution two assistant teachers (A and B) report to the head I. The head in turn reports to the assistant superintendent (D) who reports to the superintendent (E). One of the important attributes of this pattern of communication is A and B can send the information to C but they cannot receive information from anyone. Similarly, E can receive information from D but cannot send any information (see Figure 6.3).

Fundamental Concepts and Theories

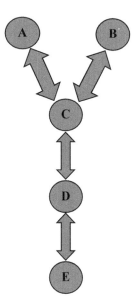

Figure 6.3 Y network pattern of communication.

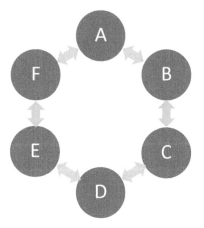

Figure 6.4 Circle network pattern of communication.

Circle Network Pattern of Communication

The foremost attribute of circle pattern communication is three-level hierarchies. However, it is different from wheel, chain, and Y pattern communication in the sense that this communication pattern is symbolic of horizontal and decentralized communication. Besides, these types of communication are democratic. It provides equal opportunity to all the members to communicate with a person from the right and left. Compared to the other three conditions circle pattern is less restricted.

Example: In circle network communication process mainly two-way channels are open for problem-solving and decision-making. Furthermore, in this communication process, every member can take the role of a decision-maker (see Figure 6.4).

Star or All-Channel Communication Pattern

This is an upgraded version or extension of the circle network. Star communication is a feeling process where every member can communicate with each other. It is also a decentralized communication process. Another attribute of the star network is it has no central position, as well as there are no obstacles to communicating with any member.

Example: A committee with no official leadership is a good star network communication (see Figure 6.5).

Forms of Communication

Communication is the mechanism of transferring a message from sender to receiver. However, in the communication process there are various forms or levels of communication which exist such as;

Five major forms of communication:

- Intrapersonal communication
- Dyadic communication
- Small-group communication
- Public communication
- Mass communication

Intrapersonal Communication

Intrapersonal communication refers to communication with one's self. In this communication sender and receiver are the same unit. Thus, the whole communication process and feedback take place without disruption. For instance, thinking, feeling, pain, emotion, etc. are the interpersonal communication process (see Figure 6.6).

Dyadic Communication

The term "dyad" refers to binary or two things related to a similar nature or group. "Dyadic communication" refers to two-person communications or inter-personal relationships between the two. However, this communication process mainly involves dialogue based on face-to-face

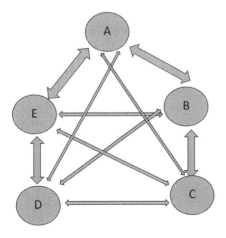

Figure 6.5 Star or all-channel communication pattern.

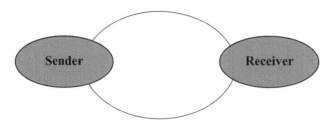

Figure 6.6 Intrapersonal communication process.

Figure 6.7 Dyadic communication process.

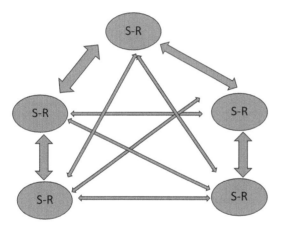

Figure 6.8 Small-group communication process.

verbal communication to share thoughts, mutual ideas, behavior, likes, dislikes, etc. Nevertheless, feedback is shared between the source and the receiver (see Figure 6.7).

Small-Group Communication

Small-group communication refers to the communication between more than two persons to exchange their ideas or thoughts by any medium. Small-group communication is internal communication in nature. However, small-group communication is mainly defined as communication between a minimum of more than two members and a maximum of 12–15 members. Every member plays a role as a sender as well as a receiver. Small-group communication mainly works for making a specific decision, solving a particular problem, submitting a report, policy determination, etc. (see Figure 6.8)

Public Communication

Public communication refers to communication by the sender with a huge number of receivers. In this communication there is no mutual feedback (see Figure 6.9).

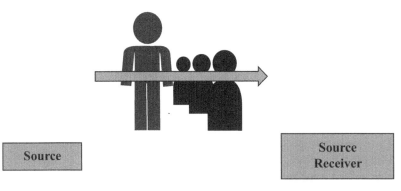

Figure 6.9 Public communication process.

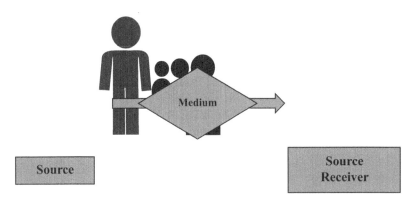

Figure 6.10 Mass communication process.

Mass Communication

Mass communication is also a similar conception of public communication (a large number of audiences) but the difference is in mass communication the receiver or audience is not grouped and needs to use technological tools for communication as a medium. For instance, television, newspaper, radio, etc. are mediums of mass communication. In this communication, feedback is very low (see Figure 6.10).

Models of Communication

This section is going to discuss the various models of communication. However, before discussion one must remember that communication is a complex process. As one knows a model is a replica of a systematic representation of the whole process for understanding how work can be done. In a view of communication, process models show how metaphorically and symbolically communication occurs. By the invention of various communication models researcher and authors convert the process of communication from complex to simple by systematically and orderly organizing its components. From the viewpoint of communication, models not only encourage conventional to stereotypical thinking but also eliminate major obstacles to the human or organizational communication process.

The selection of models of communication is based on the purpose of communication and the types of methods and channels that have been used. However, academics, businesses, and other organizations depend on the proper selection of models to foster their communication. Notwithstanding, communication models also specify how the sender will encode the message and the receiver will decode.

Types of Communication Models

Mainly, communication models are divided into the following categories:

1. Linear models of communication
2. Interactive models of communication
3. Transactional models of communication

Linear Models of Communication

A linear model of communication mainly explains the "one-way communication process" whereby a sender encodes a message and sends it through the medium to the receiver. However, the linear communication model is a simple and straightforward communication model where there is no concept of feedback. The sender, channel or medium, and receiver play a vital role in this communication model. Various business organizations use this model to provide customer support, marketing sales, etc. The fundamental mechanism of linear models of communication is that the "sender" explains his thoughts, feelings, emotions, etc. in a message then the message is transmitted through a "channel". However, here the channel functions as a medium and it helps to change the message into tangible forms such as speech, writing or symbols, or graphics, etc. and then, through the channel, the new form of the message is transferred to the receiver, who acts as a decoder (see Figure 6.11).

However, in a one-way communication processes many things can have an effect, such as choice of channel, disruption by noise (physiological, environmental, etc.). Different researchers and their models following the linear communication models are:

a) Shannon–Weaver model
b) Lasswell's model
c) Aristotle's model
d) Berlo's SMCR model

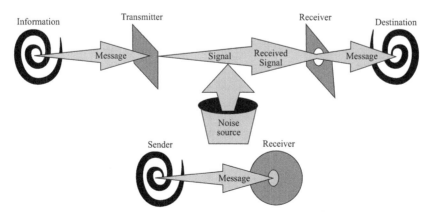

Figure 6.11 A linear model of communication. Source: Wood (2009).

SHANNON–WEAVER MODEL

The Shannon–Weaver model is one of the oldest models in communication and was developed in 1949. It is a linear model of communication and is more technical than other linear models. It was first introduced in "A Mathematical Theory of Communication", an article written by Warren Weaver in the *Bell System Technical Journal*. This model is also known as the "Shannon-Weaver model of communication" and it is the mother of all models.

In the Shannon–Weaver model, major emphasis was given to effective and straight communication between sender and receiver. It also finds that a major factor called "noise" affects the communication process. However, this model mainly aimed to improve technical communication and it is still imperative in various fields of communication (see Table 6.1 and Figure 6.12).

SHANNON–WEAVER MODEL OF COMMUNICATION

In the Shannon–Weaver model, the overall communication process is completed in the following phases.

Table 6.1 Components in the Shannon Weaver communication model

Components	Details
Sender (Source)	The sender is the source of information that creates, chooses, and sends the message to the receiver.
Encoder (transmitter)	The transmitter converts the message into signals. The message of the sender is transformed into binary data for the flow of the message through cable or signal.
Channel	Channel is the bridge or medium used to send a message.
Decoder (receiver)	The decoder may be a machine or receiver functioning to convert the binary data into a message or to translate the message from the signal.
Receiver (destination)	The receiver is the destination of the message providing feedback according to the message.
Noise	Noise is any kind of disturbance such as environmental factors, the physical and psychological condition of the receiver, etc. which hinders the messages while received by the receiver.

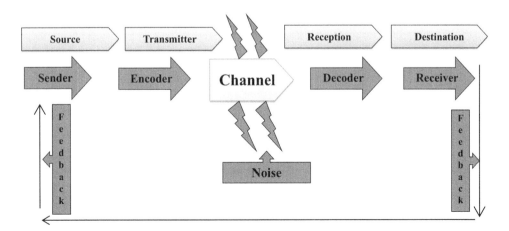

Figure 6.12 Shannon Weaver communication model.

First, a majorly important part of this model is the "sender" whose role is as an "encoder of the message" and sends it to the receiver through a channel. For example, the Shannon–Weaver model is based on a technical model so the major emphasis is on the telephone and telegraph as a channel of communication.

Second, the sender transforms the message into machine language and sends it through the medium.

Third, in this phase the receiver acts as a decoder who decodes, understands, and interprets the message. However, in some cases, the machine receptor takes this responsibility.

Fourth, in this whole process, there is also some probability that the receiver is not able to decode the message which may raise some problems in communication.

For example, in computer-based teaching and learning situations, the teacher or instructional designer is the "sender" and "encoder", the computer is the "channel", and the "receiver" is the student who is also the "decoder". In this whole process, some disturbances create barriers called "noise" (transmission errors, missing text, sound, etc.). Through feedback the student lets the teacher know about errors or incompleteness of the message. However, in the basic Shannon Weaver model, there was no explanation about "noise" and it was added later.

LEVELS OF PROBLEMS IN THE ANALYSIS OF COMMUNICATION

Shannon and Weaver mainly explained three levels of the problem:

1. *Technical problem*: how accurately can the message be transmitted?
2. *Semantic problem*: how precisely is the meaning "conveyed"?
3. *Effectiveness problem*: how effectively does the received message affect behavior?

ADVANTAGES OF THE SHANNON–WEAVER MODEL

- Simplicity
- General validity
- Quantifiability
- Encourages human communication
- Adding the concept of "noise" makes the model more effective as it can help to focus on the problem of noise and the ways to remove it
- The model encourages a two-way process and it is applicable in our daily-life communication as well as in communication theories

CRITICISMS OF THE SHANNON–WEAVER MODEL

The Shannon–Weaver model is criticized on the following grounds:

- The model is not very effective in mass or group communication as it mainly helps in interpersonal communication.
- In this model, the sender is a more important factor compared to the receiver.
- In this model "feedback" is given less importance as it only functions for clarification of noise.

a) **Lasswell's Communication Model**

In 1948, Harold D. Lasswell developed a communication model known as the "action model", "linear model", or "one-way model of communication", which is one of the most influential models of communication.

Components of Lasswell's Communication Model

In Lasswell's model of communication, Harold majorly emphasized five components for analysis and evaluation of the overall communication process. However, these five components are based on a question to be asked and communication will focus on getting answers to all the questions (see Table 6.2 and Figure 6.13).

Table 6.2 Components of Lasswell's model of communication

Components	Meaning	Analysis	Explanation
Who (sender)	In this model who represents the source of the message	Control analysis	Helps the sender to have all the power.
Say what	It represents the subject matter or content of the message	Content analysis	Accompanies categorizing and representation of different groups or media. It helps to unveil the ulterior intentions of the message.
In which channel	Channel represents the media or medium by which message flows	Media analysis	It mentions or indicates which media is more effective.
To whom	The receiver of the message or an audience	Audience analysis	By this, one can find the target population who is to be manipulated or brainwashed.
With what effect	The feedback of the receiver to the sender	Effect analysis	By effect analysis it predicts the effect of the message over the target population to be exploited.

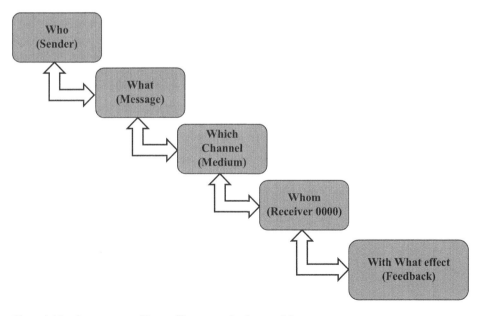

Figure 6.13 Components of Lasswell's communication model.

DISCUSSION ON LASSWELL'S COMMUNICATION MODEL

It is imperative to say that the major focus of Lasswell's model of communication is to analyze mass communication or interpersonal communication or group communication. The flow of the model was developed mainly to analyze mass media as well as business at that time. The main aim of the model was to show media culture such as the presentation of events or facts and their different effects.

However, Lasswell also emphasized the concept of the "effective communication process". This model of communication is used in different media and fields especially for mass communication. This model to some extent is like the Shannon Weaver model. Additionally, this model also generates a similar conception of the "cultivation theory" proposed by George Gerbner, except for the conception of the reaction of the receiver.

DISADVANTAGES AND CRITICISMS OF LASSWELL'S MODEL

Lasswell's model was criticized on the following grounds:

- In this model there is no provision to include "feedback". It has been shown in previous research that without feedback it is hard to complete an effective communication process.
- One important disadvantage was ignorance about "noise". Additionally, the model was too linear and did not consider barriers.
- In this model, Lasswell has used a very traditional concept.
- The model is too simple.
- This model mainly focused on media communication or group communication.

ARISTOTLE'S COMMUNICATION MODEL

The first communication model was developed before 300 BC and was developed by Aristotle a Greek philosopher and writer. Aristotle's model of communication is also a linear communication model. This is one of the earlier communication models (see Figure 6.14).

Aristotle's communication model is based on five elements—speaker, speech, occasion, audience, and effect—and mainly emphasized speaker and speech. In this model speaker plays an important role and it is more active compared to other elements in communication. Speaker sends a message to the audience and the audience takes it passively and influences it by speech. Based on this attribute, the communication process works more as one way and is based on the speaker to the receiver.

EXPLANATION OF ARISTOTLE'S COMMUNICATION MODEL

Aristotle in his communication process indicated that speaker is an organization mechanism of speech. By speaker, the message is sent to the target audience and situation (occasion). In this model, it was also emphasized that preparation of message or speech must be influential and may vary from audience to audience and situation to situation. This model is mainly used in

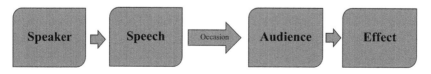

Figure 6.14 Aristotle's communication model.

public communication and group communication. Although this model is based on "speaker" it also emphasizes audience interaction. There is no feedback in Aristotle's communication model.

ELEMENTS OF ARISTOTLE'S COMMUNICATION MODEL

Aristotle emphasized three elements which are most essential for an effective communication process:

- *Ethos*:
  Ethos is one of the essential elements mentioned in Aristotle's communication model. It is related to the credible attribute of the speaker in front of an audience. The belief of the audience is based on the credibility of the audience.
- *Pathos*:
  Pathos emphasized an emotional bonding of the speaker with the audience which increases credibility, as well the audience feeling the speaker as a family member.
- *Logos*:
  Logos is logic. Logic is the most essential part of any communication. Every person finds logic behind any communication. Therefore, besides credibility and emotional bonding, there is a need for strong logic. For example, in a presentation the speaker or presenter uses charts, graphs, statistics, etc. to provide support of his presentation content.

CRITICISMS OF ARISTOTLE'S COMMUNICATION MODEL

The following are criticisms of Aristotle model:

- No feedback, only emphasis on the speaker to audience
- No concept of noise and barriers
- Only based on public speaking or group or mass communication

BERLO'S SMCR COMMUNICATION MODEL

David Berlo is the originator of Berlo's SMCR communication model. SMCR refers to "sender-message-receiver-channel-receiver". It is similar to Shannon 'Weaver's communication model of. This communication model mainly emphasized individual components for more effective communication. In this communication, the process of "encoding" takes place before sending the message from sender to receiver (see Figure 6.15).

COMPONENTS OF BERLO'S COMMUNICATION MODEL

As previously discussed, Berlo's model described four components, viz. sender, message, channel, and receiver, and many factors affecting each component.

SENDER (REPRESENTED AS "S")

As similar to other models, in Berlo's model "sender" is represented as a source of a message. The following attributes of the sender may affect effective communication.

- *Communication skills*: Good communication skills of sender such as modulation of speech, effective presentation of content or message, good reading, writing, and listening skills, etc. affect the communication process.

Fundamental Concepts and Theories

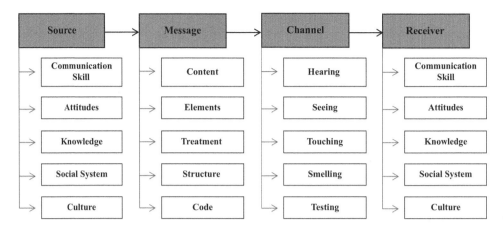

Figure 6.15 Berlo's SMCR communication model. Source: Cited by Stead (1972).

- *Attitude*: Attitude is the most crucial element of the "sender" which includes his/her attitude as well as an attitude toward the receiver affecting communication.
- *Knowledge*: Knowledge of the sender also influences the communication process. A decent knowledge of the topic or subject matter of communication creates an effective communication environment.
- *Social systems*: Social systems refers to beliefs, morality, humanity, values, laws, place, situation, etc. A good sender should maintain the social system effectively.
- *Culture*: The sender should be aware of cultural differences and should respect other cultures.

MESSAGE (REPRESENTED BY "M")

The message is the subject matter sent to the receiver. The message is in various forms such as sound, voice, text, visual, etc. The following are the components of the message:

- *Content or subject matter*: Subject matter or content is the body and heart of the message.
- *Elements*: Elements are the nonverbal components such as facial expression, eye movement, gesture, etc.
- *Treatment*: Treatment is the process by which a message reaches the receiver.
- *Structure*: Structure represents the organization of the message. It also affects effective communication.
- *Code*: Code represents the language or form of message.

CHANNEL (REPRESENTED BY "C")

Channel is the medium of the message. In any communication, there is a need for a channel to communicate with the sender to the receiver and vice versa. However, the channel is in many forms, such as in a physical communication process "air" is the channel and in a technical communication process the telephone, Internet, etc. is the channel of communication. The following may affect effective channels of communication:

- *Hearing*: Receive the message through hearing.
- *Seeing*: Perceive through seeing.

- *Touching*: Mainly the nonverbal message is perceived through touching.
- *Smelling*: Collect information from smelling.
- *Tasting*: Taste also provides information to be sent as a message.

RECEIVER (REPRESENTED BY "R")

The receiver is the destination of the message. In this model it is described that for effective communication all elements must be synchronized properly. As well as good listening skills, the following skills are also important:

- Communication skills
- Attitudes
- Knowledge
- Social systems
- Culture

CRITICISMS OF BERLO'S SMCR COMMUNICATION MODEL

- One-way communication
- No feedback
- No further description about noise

Some factors affecting Transactional model of communication

SOME KEY POINTS OF LINEAR MODELS OF COMMUNICATION

Key features:

- Linear communication is one-way in nature.
- Linear communication is mainly used in mass communication.
- It is straight line in nature, such as the sender sends a message and the receiver receives.
- No feedback and no noise.

Pros of linear communication:

- Linear communication engages audience more effectively.
- This suits one-way processes such as print and broadcast advertising.

Cons of linear communication:

- Linear communication is continuous. It has no feedback.
- No noise conception.

Advantages of a Linear Model

- A linear model of communication is generally effective for marketing communication. As it is generally a direct communication between sender and receiver, it is therefore very easy to analyze the encoding process and it may influence or alter the overall aspect in comparatively easy ways.
- This type of communication is generally very effective for print and broadcast advertising as it is a transactional or circular model of communication.

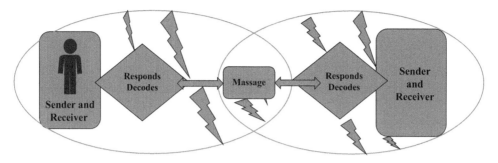

Figure 6.16 Transactional model of communication.

Characteristics of the Transactional Model of Communication

- The transactional model is fluid/simultaneous and each component exchanges their role and people, environment; medium can act in any way they want.
- The transactional model incorporates "environment" such as physical location, personal experience, and cultural background.
- In the transactional model, each "communicator" overlaps with each other.
- Channel plays a vital role in the transactional model.
- This model is more efficient for communication in the same environment.

Factors affecting transactional message

The transactional message pattern of communication depends on various factors such as physical, psychological, social, emotional, etc. In this section, we discussed three major elements of the transactional model such as cultural context, social context, and relational context. However, physical and psychological factors also affect the transactional model of communication.

Social Context

The social context in the transactional message refers to the maintenance of social law and value. It includes various rules that bind people to a specific limit. Societal rules control the communication of a person. For instance, social manners such as thanking, greeting, apologizing, etc. are the social context in the transactional model of communication.

Cultural Context

In the transactional model, cultural contexts refer to the identity of a person such as race, ethnicity, gender, cast, etc. This model explains that better communication takes place when the communicator belongs to the same culture.

Relational Context

Relational context refers to the relationship between communicators. People communicate differently with a friend and a guest. Differences in manners take an important role in communication with the difference in the situation. In the transactional model, the entire context is taken into consideration for effective communication.

Noise in the transactional model of communication

The linear model is straight communication between sender and receiver. Henceforth, noise is solely external such as loud music, environment, etc. but in the transactional model of communication there exists the following two types of noise:

Physiological noise: Biological factors of the communicator (i.e., illness, fatigue, etc.). *Psychological noise*: Mental state of the communicator (i.e., an unwillingness to listen).

Various Transactional Models of Communication

Various models have been developed based on transactional points of view such as:

- Barnlund's transactional model of communication
- Becker's mosaic model of communication

Barnlund's Transactional Model of Communication

Dean Barnlund is the father of the transactional model of communication (2017). In our everyday communication in which sending and receiving messages is going on simultaneously between two people named "communicators" is called Barlund's transactional model of communication.

However, Barlund's transactional model of communication is based on a multilayer feedback system. The foremost attribute of this model is that there is no fixed sender and receiver in communication. Both sender and receiver interchange their role and both are equally important. Based on the message, continuous feedback has been provided by the "communicator". One feedback is a message for another party.

Becker's Mosaic Model of Communication

Sam Becker proposed another transactional model of communication in 1968 known as Becker's Mosaic Model of Communication. The original name was "The Prospect of Rhetoric". He believed that human behavior is complex that is why he proposed a complexity of the human communication process. This model also emphasized the dynamic side of communication and the meaning of the message. Nevertheless, this model mainly adopted the view of Marshall McLuhan's television light and dark spot conception. Mainly, three components are described in this model such as:

Empty cells: Empty cells represent the cell without a message or source.
Vertical layers: Vertical layers represent cells with similar messages or sources.
Cells: Cells represent messages or sources. Receivers go cell to cell in loops every time.

Advantages of the Transactional Model of Communication

- In transactional messages, both sender and receiver are interdependent on each other.
- In this communication model, "communication" is based on background, prior experiences, attitudes, cultural beliefs and self-esteem, etc.

Fundamental Concepts and Theories

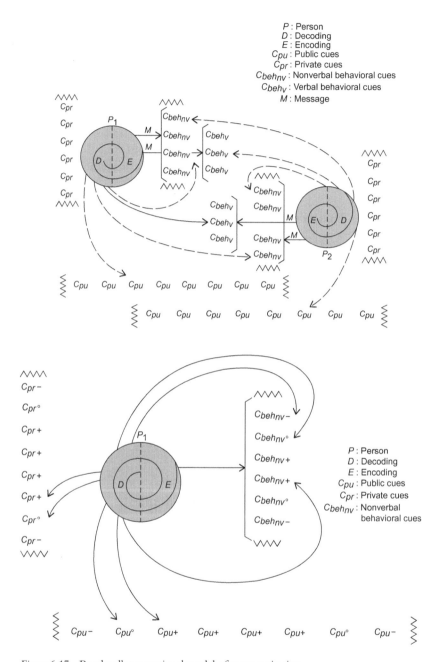

Figure 6.17 Barnlund's transactional model of communication.

Criticisms of the Transactional Model

- This model mainly encourages nonverbal communication and without a verbal response, the sender may not be sure whether the receiver got the message correctly or not.
- Noise is one of the largest disadvantages in the transactional model of communication because communication is simultaneous.

Interactive Model Communication

Schramm (1954) and Wood (2011) majorly focused on the interactive model and explained that in communication is an interactive process where the receiver provides feedback to the sender and the sender listens to the feedback sent by the receiver. In this model of communication, the role is played as a speaker and receiver both, and feedback is provided both ways verbally or nonverbally. Additionally, this model also emphasizes that effective communication takes place when the field of experience (culture, social, behavior, etc.) is common or overlaps. This model is also known as the convergence model. However, various models fall into an interactive model of communication such as:

- Schramm's Model
- Helical Model
- Westley and MacLeans Model

Interactive Model of Communication

Advantages of an interactive model of communication

- Feedback is provided even in mass communication.
- Can provide a new communication channel.
- This model introduces with "field of experience".
- This model is designed for Internet-based online communication.

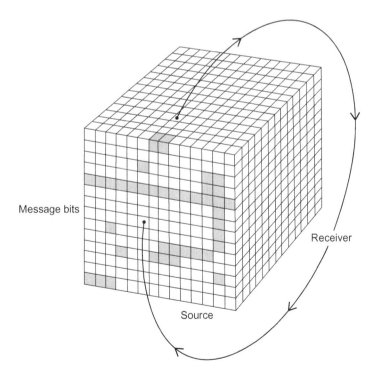

Figure 6.18 Becker's mosaic model of communication.

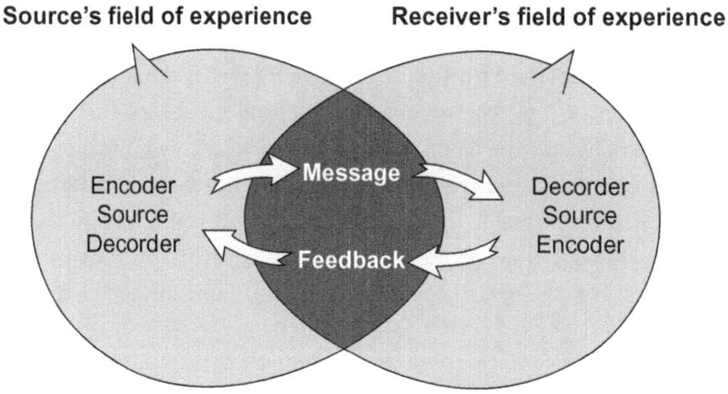

Figure 6.19 An interactive model of communication. Source: Wood (2009).

The disadvantage of the interactive model of communication

- In this model of communication, providing feedback takes more time.
- The sender and receiver are unknown to other people.
- Without the response of the receiver, communication becomes linear.
- No more engagement with the sender and receiver.

Fishbone Diagram or Cause and Effect Diagram

The Fishbone diagram is a cause analysis tool. It helps to identify various causes for a specific problem. Besides, it's also helpful for sorting various ideas into various useful categories.

Use of Fishbone Diagram

A Fishbone diagram is generally used when it is required to identify a list of possible causes for a specific problem.

Procedure to Develop a Fishbone Diagram

Step 1: Find out a specific problem and write it at the center-right of a page with a box around it.
Step 2: Need to list out most of the possible causes for a specific situation and need to categorize them.
Step 3: Needs to write down categories of possible causes on both sides of the main arrow.
Step 4: Brainstorm all the causes with some of the specific questions such as – "why does this happen?"
Step 5: By funneling down each cause, it needs to find out a deeper level of cases responsible for a specific problem and focus attention on the specific points.

Barriers to Effective Classroom Communication

In the previous section, we discussed the nature, components, and models of communication, etc. However, in this section, we are going to discuss barriers to communication with a major focus on barriers to classroom communication. Day-to-day teaching becomes a difficult job and engaging students in the teaching–learning process is also a challenging task. Communication barriers in the classroom create a difficult learning environment as a result where students lose their attention and interest in the learning task. It is also common in a classroom situation that the teacher fails to produce appealing lessons and struggles to engage the student on a one-to-one basis. However, in the opposite situation the attitude of a student, language difficulty, speech difficulty, cultural and personality differences, peer pressure, etc. also may create difficulties in the environment and produce barriers while communicating with their teachers as well as a classmate. The following are some crucial and common barriers in the classroom environment.

Listening Barriers

As we all know listening is an essential factor, not only in the teaching-learning process but also in everyday situations. In classroom situations, teachers must take time to listen to their students to better understand their views and needs. The listening gap in the classroom has been produced as a barrier to bridge between teacher and students. However, to overcome this barrier in classroom situations teachers and students must take care of what the other is saying. Besides, the noise inside and outside classrooms, such as peer talking, loud sounds, phones ringing, etc. creates noise in the environment and makes it difficult to listen in the classroom. For effective classroom communication, noise should be minimized.

Perception Barriers

Differences in perception between teacher and student may create barriers to effective communication. Different people think differently and interpret differently. In a classroom situation, one message or description provided by the teacher may be heard by the whole class simultaneously but will be interpreted differently. However, if teachers do not pay much attention to this it is imperative to take both positive and negative viewpoints of the student to encourage more conversation and engagement in communication in the classroom.

Oral Barriers

In a classroom situation, an essential element of communication is oral communication. Most barriers come from inappropriate oral communication. Effective communication takes place

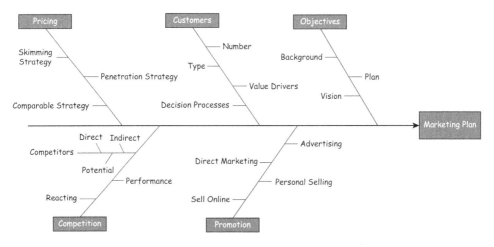

Figure 6.20 Fishbone diagram or cause and effect diagram.

in the classroom or teaching–learning process when a student can listen to his or her teacher properly and vice versa. Sometimes inappropriate communication occurs by using unfamiliar words or words with ambiguous meanings. To overcome barriers to clear oral communication teachers and students should take care to use words with an understandable meaning. In oral communication situations using generalizations and stereotypes are also common barriers. Teachers should maintain specific topics without bias and take caution about drawing premature conclusions. Finally, to overcome the barrier of oral communication teachers need more self-confidence and should deliver the message loudly, meaningfully, and in an understandable manner.

Cultural Barriers

"Culture is the pattern of taken-for-granted assumptions about how a given collection of people should think, act, and feel as they go about their daily affairs" (Joynt & Warner, 1997). Another barrier in classroom communication is cultural differences. In the classroom situation there mainly exists a heterogeneous group of the population, that is, students belonging to various cultures. Henceforth, teacher and student behavior will be different based on their culture. A message will be misinterpreted if delivered without an understanding of the student's culture. So, teachers and students must take care of cultural differences in the classroom to overcome communication barriers.

Bibliography

Barnlund, D. C. (1962). Toward a meaning-centered philosophy of Communication1. *Shared Experiences in Human Communication, 26.*

Barnlund, D. C. (2017). A transactional model of communication. In *Communication theory* (pp. 47–57). Routledge.

Brown, G. G. (n.d.). Definition of communication. Retrieved June 3, 2013, from http://communicationtheory.org/definition-0f-communications.

Burton, G., & Dimbleby, R. (2002). *Teaching communication.* London: Routledge.

Ceravolo, D. J., Schwartz, D. G., Foltz-Ramos, K. M., & Castner, J. (2012). Strengthening communication to overcome lateral violence. *Journal of Nursing Management, 20*(5), 599–606.

Chickering, A. W., & Gamson, Z. F. (1987). Seven principles for good practice in undergraduate education. *AAHE Bulletin, 3,* 7.

Christ, W. (1994). *Assessing communication education* (1st ed.). Hillsdale, NJ: L. Erlbaum Associates.

Daly, J., Friedrich, G., & Vangelisti, A. (1990). *Teaching communication* (1st ed.). Hillsdale, NJ: L. Erlbaum Associates.

Griffin, R. (2000). *Fundamentals of management* (1st ed.). Boston, MA: Houghton Mifflin.

Joynt, P., & Warner, M. (1996). *Managing across cultures.* London: Thomson Business Press.

Joynt, P., & Warner, M. (1997). *Managing across cultures* (1st ed.). London: International Thomson Business Press.

Kumar, K. (2000). *Mass communication in India* (1st ed.). Mumbai: Jaico Pub. House.

Lasswell, H. D. (1948). The structure and function of communication in society. *Communication of Ideas, 37*(1), 136–139.

Little, P. (1977). *Communication in business* (1st ed.). London: Longman.

Mehrabian, A., & Wiener, M. (1967). Decoding of inconsistent communications. *Journal of Personality and Social Psychology, 6*(1), 109–114.

Meyer, F. G. (n.d.). Communication theory. Retrieved June 6, 2012, from http://communicationtheory.org/definition-of communication.

Powell, R., & Powell, D. (2004). *Classroom communication and diversity* (1st ed.). Mahwah, NJ: L. Erlbaum Associates.

Robert, K. (2009). *Principles of management* (11th ed.). Arizona State University.

Schram, W. E. (1954). *The process and effects of mass communication.*

Shannon, C. E., & Weaver, W. (1949). The mathematical theory of communication–University of Illinois Press. *Urbana, 117.*

Stead, B. A. (1972). 'Berlo's communication process model as applied to the behavioral theories of Maslow, Herzberg, and McGregor. *Academy of Management Journal, 15*(3), 389–394.

Tubbs, S. I. (2000). *Human communication.* Singapore: McGraw-Hill International Editions.

Wood, J. T. (2009). Julia Wood's Transactional Model. https://ebrary.net/71373/education/julia_wood_s_transactional_model

Wood, J. T. (2011). *Communication in our lives.* Cengage Learning.

PART II

Design, Evaluation, and Implementations

7
SYSTEM ANALYSIS OR SYSTEM APPROACH IN EDUCATION

We are all living in a world where everything is adhering to a systematic process. It can be assumed that many of us have some basic knowledge about "systems". The system is a combination of the whole, which means various parts of a system work together to carry out a specific task. Just think about the motorcycle; we can start it and accelerate and go from one place to another. But in this whole process, various parts of the motorcycle such as the engine, chain, various small pistons, etc. work together to allow a motorbike to function effectively and accurately. Similarly, the whole education process is a system. The present chapter will discuss system and the system approach and its application in education.

System: An Overview

The system approach is a very common concept that is introduced in the field of education comparatively late. This chapter will discuss the system approach and its functions in the sphere of education. Before doing so the reader must understand what is meant by a system. The following are some definitions of a system given by various eminent scholars from the multidisciplinary field.

Meaning of a System

As discussed in the previous section, a system is a combination of various parts and a pattern of interrelation and interdependence of various elements. Therefore, a system is a unified process where various parts or groups of parts interact with each other to achieve a specific function or objective. The following are some definitions of the system:

- **Webster's dictionary defined (cited by Guralnik, 1972)** a system as an interaction between the various independent, as well as interdependent groups, to form a unified whole.
- **Bertalanffy (1985)** simply defined a system as a holistic approach of a combination of various parts of a whole.
- **Ackoff (1971)** gives a simple definition of a system and says that generally, a system denotes a combination of various elements which are interrelated and independent.

From the above definitions, one gets a view that the system is a dynamic concept that is complex because various interrelated and independent elements work together to achieve predetermined specific objectives. Based on the analysis of the above definitions, it appears that a system means any entity which consists of interrelated, interacting, or interdependent parts. Generally, a system is an organized procedure where the interrelation of various parts works as an orderly whole.

It is also notable that each system consists of a super system and consists of a subsystem. Thus, the notion of a system applies to a cell, a human being, a society, as well as to an atom, a planet, or a galaxy.

Characteristics of System

The following are the characteristics of a system:

1. Unlike other fields, the system approach is also applicable to teaching and instruction.
2. Generally, the system is a dynamic concept. It is not just a combinational aspect of various parts or elements.
3. A system is a complex concept. It consists of various interrelated and independent elements that are systematically organized or designed to achieve specific tasks.
4. Though in a system, all the elements work independently but they have the representative role of specific functions which are interrelated as a whole.
5. Another essential characteristic of a system is it is a goal-oriented approach. Sometimes the goal of the system is stated very clearly and sometimes not.
6. The dynamism of every system depends on the transformation of input to output, the overall process, the functions of an element, etc.
7. Every system has a super system and a subsystem. Therefore, a system is absolutely a relative concept.
8. Every system consists of various elements of the configuration of the component to process desired and systematic outcomes.
9. A system can be open or closed and feedback is one of the essential characteristics of a system.

System Approach Concept

The earliest concept of the "system approach" took place during the time of World War II, when society was going forward toward industrialization, man-machine mechanisms, and management. Generally, in the literature on "systems" various terminologies such as system approach, system engineering, and system analysis are used to provide the knowledge of sophistication of an overall system. The term "system approach" is generally used in education as an approach to managing, strategic orientation, control, and enhancing the overall process and outcome of education as well as the environment. Various researchers and educationists provide different definitions of a systems approach such as the following:

Bertalanfly (1968) mentions that "systems approach involves a consideration of alternative solutions and choosing those promising optimizations at maximum efficiency and minimal cost in a complex network of interactions".

Dearden (1972) mentions that "systems approach is nothing more or less than what a competent, smart, adequate business executive adopts in the ordinary conduct of his business".

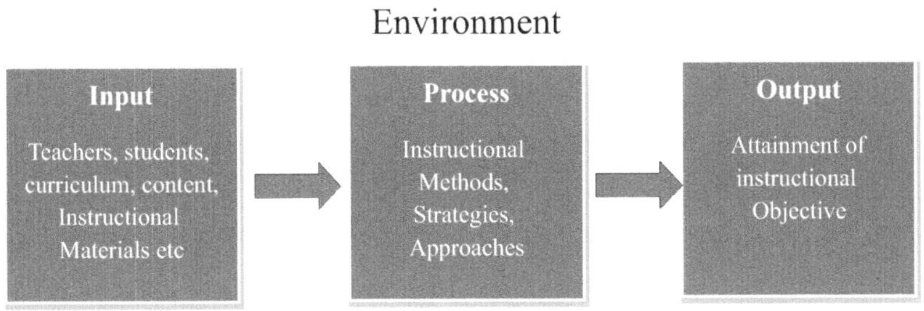

Environment

Input	Process	Output
Teachers, students, curriculum, content, Instructional Materials etc	Instructional Methods, Strategies, Approaches	Attainment of instructional Objective

Figure 7.1 Parameters for instructional system. Source: Adapted from Smith (1966).

Churchman (1985) mentions that "a procedure for characterizing the nature of a system, so that decision making might be made logically and coherently, and the performance of the system might be described".

From the above definition, it can be seen that all defined system approaches are defined in the context of monitoring the progress of systems. Generally, the systems approach is the analysis process of an overall system with feedback and evaluation. This process generally includes the evaluation of the quality and the strength of the contribution of various independent elements of a system as a whole in the context of the achievement and improvement of a system. Therefore, a systems approach is a scientific and rationalized thinking process of functional aspects of any system to enhance the outcome of the system analysis of the whole system step-by-step sequentially.

Stages in the Systems Approach

The systems approach is generally a strategic process of planning, decision-making, and problem-solving in the context of optimizing the functional aspect of a system. Hence, the overall system approach can be divided into the following stages:

- System Analysis
- System Design and Development
- System Operation and Evaluation

I. System Analysis

When a system encounters specific problems, the very first stage of problem-solving strategies starts with "system analysis". System analysis generally tries to find out questions related to the "what" and "how". In this primary stage of identification, system specialists mainly focus on an examination of the structure and function of elements and environment which is involved in a specific system. Moreover, it tries to find various absolute and relative constraints. The most important aspect of this stage is to find "what is required in the context of the system and environment". Following are some set of questions for effective system analysis (Sharma, 1985):

- What is the overall list of elements associated with a system?
- What is the interrelation between each element of a system (in the context of interdependent and independent)?
- What kind of resources are available and what are the specific constraints faced?
- What are the inputs and outputs of the system?

- What is the status of interaction between the system and its environment?
- How does the overall process work?

II. Systems Design and Development

This stage is intended for the design and development of a system. This stage is very important because based on the system analysis, the system developer develops the new system. In this stage task systemization is a major concern. In the stage of design and development of the system the following matters are taken into consideration:

- After the analysis of the overall system, the system developer further specifies the environment and problems.
- After that developer makes explicit statements of objectives.
- At the next stage system developer sets appropriate required strategies, techniques, methods, etc.
- After the completion of the following step, the developer tries out a specific design and evaluates the overall system in the context of functions.

III. System Operation and Evaluation

This is the final and most vital stage of the system approach. In this stage developed or revised system designs are evaluated very carefully to find out any kind of discrepancy in the context of

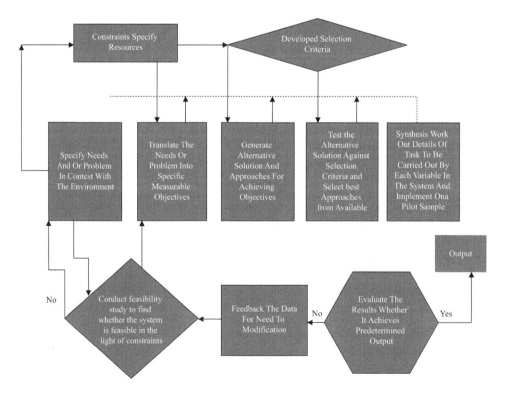

Figure 7.2 Schematic flow chart of the system approach. Source: Adapted from Sharma (1985).

a desirable outcome and system outcome. If any error is still found further modification is taken into consideration and this loop will go on until the system provides a desirable outcome. After the required inspection and modification of elements of the overall system, a final large-scale tryout is considered for summative evaluation.

System Approach to Instruction

Throughout the discussion in this chapter one understands that every aspect of the world is sustained because of the systematic equilibrium of every part of a system. While this chapter mainly focuses on education and the educational system, simultaneously one must know instruction as well.

Instruction is a very crucial aspect of any educational system. Instruction is based on humans or computers and requires a specific and systematic procedure to successfully achieve any instructional objective. In this context, knowledge of the system approach is very crucial to rationalize any instruction systematically through the understanding of the overall process, control, systematic analysis of structure, and function of any instruction, etc. The overall process includes a systematic understanding of every single element, aspect, and problem of any instructional process including finding an effective pathway for a solution that can increase the success of any instruction.

Instructional System

As mentioned instruction is a process of the operation of various interactive and interrelated elements to meet a pre-defined objective of any instructional process, it is generally the broadest term in the context of education. For instance, in designing or developing a curriculum and in the classroom, the meaning of instruction is not an approach of an "instructional system". As per Smith's (1966) definition, "an instructional system is defined as an integrated set of methods, media, equipment, and personnel performing efficiently, the functions required to accomplish one or more teaching objective". From this definition, one can critically understand that Smith has emphasized various elements of instruction such as methods, media, equipment, etc. and their integration. One knows that an instructional process involves various methods such as discussion, lecture, and personalized collaboration; various media such as audio-visual and picture-based; and various equipment such as a blackboard, computer, mobile, etc. In this context, an instructional system provides a systematic pathway for the integration of various elements to achieve any instructional objective effectively.

The term "development" may be used metaphysically in a positive as well as in a negative connotation. However, generally, development is a continuous process that includes planning, designing, application, evaluation, etc. Therefore, in this context, an instructional development system refers to the incorporation or integration of knowledge of the system in the context of the development of any instructional process. The process of instructional development is generally a collaborative approach between the instructor, administrator, curriculum specialist, etc. However, an instructional development system can also be applied by an individual teacher with his or her expert-level knowledge and skill.

Stages and Steps of Systematic Instructional Development

Generally, researchers discuss various systematic steps in the context of instructional development (Sharma, 1985). The systematic steps are the following.

Defining Objective

This is one of the crucial stages for systematic instructional development. This is crucial because in this step the objective of the overall instructional process has been demonstrated based on the defined objective.

Prior Assessment or Pre-assessment of a Learner

Another essential stage, after the establishment of an instructional objective, is the assessment of the learner's prior knowledge and skill. This stage identifies or defines the entry-level knowledge and skill of the learner which he/she is already equipped with.

Conceptualize and Design an Appropriate Approach and Method of Instruction

The next step, after the prior assessment of the skill and knowledge of the learner, is the development or conceptualization of the appropriate method of instruction. An instructor needs to select the appropriate method based on the nature of the content and the student's traits. Specification of the method will optimize the overall instructional process and help to achieve instructional goals effectively.

Specification of Appropriate Material and Media

Based on the instructional objective of the instructional system, the instructional designer requires to specify appropriate material to meet the selected learning experience of a learner. In a classroom, a situation instructor can use various materials or media like a chart, projector for audio-visual material, whiteboard for interactive media, etc. Besides, this instructor needs to ensure an adequate learning environment for the instructional system.

Define and Design the Role of an Instructor

In this step, the instructional professionals or designers will assign the various role of teacher, administrator, para-professional, etc. so that they can perform a specific instructional system effectively to achieve a specific predetermined instructional goal.

Implementation of the Instructional System

This stage is the application stage. After the assignment of all the previous stages successfully it is now time to integrate all the strategies, such as media, and methods into a specific model, and try out a pilot application in a small group to understand how the system works.

Evaluation of Outcome

The evaluation stage of the instructional system is another important stage where students' knowledge and competencies are measured based on their performance against the predetermined objective.

Analysis and Modification of a System

Further modifications or development are being made based on the result of performance in the context of the achievement of students. This process is complex, as it requires an extensive amount of feedback from the learner and expert-level knowledge and rationalization of the designer or instructor to modify the existing instructional system to instructional objectives more effectively.

From the previous discussion of stages of an instructional development system, it is clear that from the planning to execution of any instructional material is required a very systematic understanding. Therefore, the instructional designer must take care of the stage carefully to achieve any instructional objective effectively.

Model of Instructional Development

The system approach is a dynamic process. As discussed by Razik (1985), the following are six-steps of instructional development:

Goal determination: First and foremost, the approach for instructional development is the determination of goals. Following is the flowchart for goal determination:

Task Analysis: As per the model of an instructional development system, the goal of the instructional objective should be divided into general objectives. The general objective consisted of Terminal Performance Objectives (TPOs) and Enabling Objectives (EOs). TPOs refer to the desired behavioral outcome of the learner and EOs are the immediate behavioral outcome. The combinational aspect of TPOs and EOs are generally presented in a logical sequence.

Task Prescription: After the task analysis, another essential stage is task prescription. In this stage, the instructional developer generally sequences the behaviors of a learner and emphasizes established TPOs and EOs to achieve learning objectives successfully. For successful design, the instructional designer must have a good account of knowledge regarding human psychology and knowledge of educational technology.

Implementation: Next stage after the finalization of strategies for the learner is the implementation of software or hardware devices required to implement the task prescription stage.

Evaluation: Based on task analysis, the evaluation will be done by the instructional developer. Summative and formative evaluations will be conducted to find out the overall performance of learners based on a specific instructional development system model.

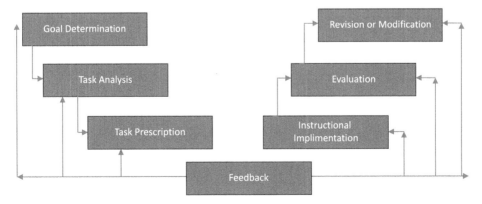

Figure 7.3 Stages of the instructional development system. Source: Adapted from Razik, Taher, and Lester (1985).

Design, Evaluation, and Implementations

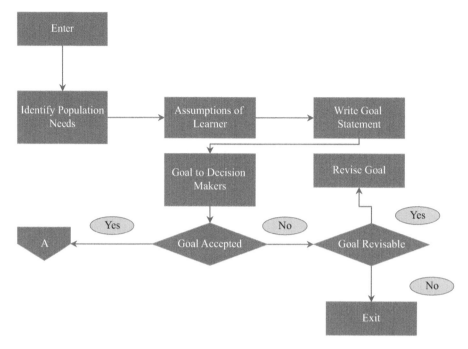

Figure 7.4 Goal determination. Source: Adapted from Razik and Lester (1985).

Revision and Modification: This is the final stage of any instructional development system model. In this stage, an instructional developer makes revisions or modifications of any existing developed model based on learner performance and the context of meeting the learning objective. This stage is very important in the context of the ultimate success of the instructional design model.

Advantages of the System Approach

The following are some advantages of the system approach:

- The system approach generally provides a holistic view of any system and its functionality. It provides some sustainable guidelines of adaptability in the context of any changes in the part or elements of the system or environment.
- The system approach focuses on individual goals as well as the broadest aspect of social goals in a system and synthesized overall aspects in the context of the global economy.
- The functional aspect of any system generally depends on the systematic and conceptual framework. In this context, the system approach provides an overall systematic plan and design to increase the functionality of any system.
- Resource management of a system is crucial for the sustainability of any system. Thus, a system approach generally focuses on the identification and management of resources for the progress of any system.
- The system approach synthesizes interaction between the internal and external environment and increases the performance of a system.
- The system approach provides a guideline for orderly presentation and management of instructional material to enhance the experience of teaching and learning environment.

- The system approach developer sequentially analyzes every system and tries to organize the overall context through various scientific orientations.
- The system approach synthesizes various theories from different fields and design frameworks related to administration, managerial, environmental, etc.

Use of System Approach in Education

Generally, the overall process of education is a systematic endeavor. It consists of various subsystems such as teaching-learning, management, administration, evaluation, etc. The combinational function of each element of the educational system is to fulfill the specific desire of individuals as well as society. Thus, education is a complex system and the system approach is a very beneficial approach for the educational system. Following are some of the aspects where the system approach can be applied:

- **Planning of various programs**: This is very common that for providing and expanding the opportunity, the educational organization has to take various programs. Designing an effective program requires systematic and strategic knowledge that effectively aligns with the broadest educational goal. In this context, the knowledge of the system approach can provide a step-by-step systematic guideline for assigning short-term objectives to achieve a long-term goal.
- **To accelerate systematic control and coordination**: Coordination between administration, management, teaching, and student personnel is a prerequisite for the success of the education system. Besides, control of various elements is also essential for the instructional process. The system approach in education provides a sound systematic strategical overview to increase the coordination between various elements of the education system to achieve specific objectives effectively.
- **Maximize utilization of resources**: Resource management is a very crucial aspect to achieve the success of any system. In the context of education, various resources are involved in the overall process such as teacher, student, educational curriculum, instructional material, etc. Thus, the system approach scientifically utilizes resources to achieve the desired goal.
- **Management of quality of education**: Quality of education is another very essential factor in education. The management of quality involves various interrelated and independent factors. In this aspect, the system approach provides a systematic pathway toward the strategies of control over the quality of education to achieve the educational goal effectively.

Problems of System Approach in Education

Though the system approach is very effective in the context of education, there remain challenges concerning its conceptualization and applicability. These are the following:

- Sometimes, the developer of the system approach is not able to define the exact relationship between the internal and external environment of an organization.
- Designing a framework for an effective system approach in the context of education requires expert-level knowledge, which is very hard to get or avail of in small educational organizations.
- There is a limitation to find the exact nature of various parts and their interdependence for the organization of the system approach.

- Generally, the system approach provides a uniform design. However, in the context of management, the strategies of any organization are variable. For example, managerial strategies need to be changed concerning the environmental aspect. Therefore, it is very hard to maintain a standard set of principles of system approach in the context of a specific design.
- Design and implementation of a system approach require a large amount of time which is very hard to extract by school teachers and administration.
- In the context of the system approach, there is a panacea or a myth that by applying the system approach technique one can change all the aspects of educational problems but that might not be always true.

References

Ackoff, R. L. (1971). "Towards a Systems Concept" *Management Science*, quoted in "System: A Conceptual Framework" by Motilal Sharma, ibid., 5.

Churchman, C. W. (1985). "*The Systems Approach*, "New York, Dell Publishing, 1968, quoted in" Systems Approach: A Conceptual Analysis" by T. A. Ryan. In M. Sharma (Ed.), *Systems approach: Its Application in education* (p. 17). Bombay: Himalaya Publishing House.

Dearden, J. (1972). "Mis is a mirage" in *Harvard Business Review*, quoted in "Systems Approach: an Interdisciplinary Effort", by Motilal Sharma, ibid., p. 36.

Razik, T. A. (1985). Systems Approach to Teacher Training and Curriculum Development: The Case of Developing Countries, UNESCO: International Institute for Educational Planning.

Sharma, M. (1985). System approach: An inter-disciplinary effort. In M. Sharma (Ed.), *System approach: Its application in education* (p. 44). Bombay: Himalaya Publishing House.

Smith, R.G. (1966). *The Design of Instructional Systems*. USA: George Washington University, Human Resources Research Office pub.

Uuralnik, D. B. (1972). *Websters new world dictionary* (p. 760). New Delhi: Oxford and IBH Publishing Company.

Von Bertalanffy, L. (1968). *General systems theory* (pp. 18–19). New York: Gorge Braziller, quoted ibid.

Von Bertalanffy, L. (1985). General system theory: A new approach to unity of science. *Human Biology*, Dec. 1952, 303–361, quoted in "System: A Conceptual Framework", by Motilal Sharma. In M. Sharma (Ed.), *Systems approach: Its application in education* (p. 5). Bombay: Himalaya Publishing House.

Suggested Readings

Kidd, T. (2008). *Handbook of research on instructional systems and technology* (Vol. 2). H. Song (Ed.). USA: Information Science Reference.

Kulkarni, S. S. (1986). *Introduction to educational technology: A system approach to micro level education*. New Delhi: Oxford & IBH.

Miller, D. R. (1970). *A system approach to planned change in education*. Washington, DC: Operation PEP, Bureau of Elementary and Secondary Education (DHEW/OE).

Mitroff, I., Hill, L., & Alpaslan, C. (2013). *Rethinking the education mess: A systems approach to education reform*. Berlin: Springer.

Willems, J. C., & Polderman, J. W. (2013). *Introduction to mathematical systems theory: A behavioral approach* (Vol. 26). New York, USA: Springer Science & Business Media.

Yee, A. H. (1973). *Perspectives on management systems approaches in education: A symposium* (Vol. 44). Chicago, USA.

Ziskovsky, B., & Ziskovsky, J. (2019). *Optimizing student learning: A lean systems approach to improving K-12 education*. Boca Raton, FL: CRC Press.

8
MICRO-TEACHING

What Is Microteaching?

Microteaching is an innovative teacher-training approach. All we know is that there is a strong relationship between the development of a nation and the proper utilization of human resources. In the field of education, the quality of next-generation learning depends on the quality of teacher and their skills. So, it is imperative to provide strategic training to shape the competence of teachers rather than just providing a certificate course or diploma. The present chapter introduces an innovative teacher training technique named "microteaching", a scaled-down teaching approach.

Microteaching Concept, Definition, and Meaning

The term "microteaching" consists of two separate words "micro" and "teaching". The former word "micro" is used to describe the scale of a thing, such as "*small*", and when it is combined with the term "*teaching*" it represents a specific form of teaching which occurs on a "small scale" in all aspects. Therefore, microteaching is a technique that helps trainee teachers to master their teaching skills. The microteaching technique teaches a single concept of content and specified teaching skills in a short amount of time with a small number of trainee teachers. Though it is a widely used technique in the field of teacher training, there is no universal or acceptable definition of microteaching. Various definitions by researchers are a reflection of their context. Following are some commonly used definitions of microteaching:

D. W. Alien (1966), defined microteaching as a "scaled-down teaching encounter with respect to class size and class time".

Cooper and Stroud (1966) defined microteaching as "a scaled-down encounter in which the intern teaches for a short period, to a group of four students on some topic on teaching subjects".

Allen and Eve (1968) defined microteaching as "a system of controlled practice that makes it possible to concentrate on specific teaching behavior and to practice teaching under controlled conditions".

McKnight (1971) explained that "microteaching is a scaled-down but a realistic classroom context which offers a helpful setting for a teacher (experienced or inexperienced) to acquire new teaching skill aid to refine old ones. It does so by reducing the complexity and scope of such classroom components, the number of pupils, and length of the lesson, by providing trainees with information about their performance immediately after completion of their lesson".

Clift et al. (1976) defined microteaching as "a teacher training procedure which reduces the teaching situation to simpler and more controlled encounter achieved by limiting the practice teaching to a specific skill and reducing teaching and class size".

Passi (1976) defined microteaching as "a training technique which requires student teacher to teach a single concept using specified teaching skill to a small number of pupils in short duration of time. The most important point in microteaching is that teaching is practiced in terms of definable, observable, measurable and controllable teaching skill".

It is a scaled-down teaching encounter in terms of task, class size, and time.

Status of Teacher Training Program before Microteaching

Before the introduction of microteaching, traditional teacher education programs mainly emphasized theoretical courses and practice teaching. The theoretical course of teacher education mainly covers philosophy, history, psychology, and sociology of teaching methodology which develops book knowledge and cognitive developmental aspects of teachers rather than behavioral change or practical knowledge. Traditionally, teaching practice also lacked timely feedback and motivational and directional behavioral modification. In India and abroad various researchers compared the improvement of teacher training before and after the introduction of microteaching and envisioned the following status of the teacher training program before the introduction of microteaching:

- Lack of specific training objectives which emphasized teaching rather than doing.
- Lack of needs-based and ability-based training rather is based on rigid curriculum.
- Mostly focused on subjective feedback concerning teacher-training performance.
- No research-based analysis of training effectiveness.
- Unscientific method of supervision and poor connection between theoretical teaching and practical-skill development.
- Lack of uniform program and clear vision for the teacher educator regarding training objectives and evaluation procedures.

What Are the Characteristics of Microteaching?

In light of the above points on traditional teacher-training programs, microteaching is an innovative new approach to teacher education. In the present situation, it is a ubiquitous and essential teacher-training approach all over the world.

Characteristics of Microteaching

It can be seen that each definition carries some common attributes of microteaching. Major characteristics of microteaching based on the definition by R.N. Sharma (2003) and J.C. Aggarwal (1995) are as follows:

- **The new approach**: Microteaching is a comparative innovation in the field of teacher education.
- **Scaled-down teaching**: Compared to other teaching techniques microteaching is a unique approach based on scaled-down characteristics, it reduces the class size (5–10 pupils), the duration of periods (5-10 minutes), the size of the topic to be covered, and teaching skill.
- **Training technique rather than teaching technique**: Microteaching technique is designed to provide training to the teacher regarding effective teaching skills. This is not a method of classroom instruction.
- **Individualized approach**: Microteaching mostly encourages individual training rather than group training.
- **Devices for preparing teachers**: Microteaching techniques mainly work as a device to prepare pre-service or in-service teachers for their future careers.
- **One skill at a time**: Compared to other approaches microteaching is designed to master one specific skill at a time rather than multiple skills.
- **The adequate opportunity for practice**: Microteaching is designed to provide a high degree of opportunity for practice and for controlling one particular skill.
- **Adequate immediate feedback**: Immediate feedback is another unique characteristic of microteaching. Unlike other advanced teaching-learning approaches microteaching is designed to provide immediate feedback to the trainee teacher in terms of their peer-group feedback, tape recorder, and CCTV regarding their present performance and further strategies.

Analytical training approach: Microteaching is an analytical approach to teaching because the teacher can analyze their skills at each stage of the procedure.

History and Development of Microteaching

Origin of Microteaching

In 1963 during the Secondary Teacher Education Program in summer, Dwight Allen and Robert Bush coined the term microteaching at Stanford University. As an early-stage researcher at Stanford University, Acheson started an investigation into teacher training programs by using a portable videotape recorder funded by the Ford Foundation. Later this area majorly concentrated on the design of teaching lessons and the construction of instruments for objective measurement. Research and development in the field of microteaching grew gradually and it accelerated from 1967 onward. In 1969, a survey of microteaching in secondary education reported that 141 out of 442 institutions adopted the microteaching approach as a part of their training and learning and from these only 50 courses for in-service training. Though most of the early research in the field of microteaching was conducted in the United States, in later stages, various countries throughout the world focused their research on microteaching as a teaching approach.

What Is the Origin of Microteaching in India?

Microteaching in India

Early reference to microteaching was documented by Shah G.B in 1970 in his work "Microteaching – without television". An experimental study conducted by Chudasama in 1971 in his M.Ed dissertation found that microteaching is more effective compared to traditional teaching.

Table 8.1 Comparison between microteaching and traditional teaching

Subject	Microteaching	Traditional teaching
Specification of objective	In microteaching, learning objectives are specified in behavioral terms.	Objectives are in general terms.
Nature of teaching	Microteaching is a relatively simple approach.	Teaching as experienced by the teacher is complicated.
Techniques of teaching	This is a scaled-down teaching approach, the number of students in a class is less (5–10 students), the duration is comparatively less, and the sessions are smaller.	Classroom is overcrowded with 60–90 students in a class and the duration of the class is longer (35–45 minutes).
Situation of teaching	Teaching-learning situation is fully controlled by proper supervision which determines the improvement of teaching.	There is a lack of supervision and no control over teaching.
Feedback	One of the unique features is immediate feedback which helps to improve immediate problems and errors of trainee teachers.	No immediate feedback is available.
Practice of skill	Here teachers can practice one skill at a time and can continue to practice one skill until mastery.	Here teacher practices multiple teaching skills at a time.
Studying classroom pattern	Classroom interaction can be studied objectively at each step.	The pattern of classroom interaction cannot be studied objectively.
Teaching environment	This is not authoritative, with no big threat or fear to the teacher.	This is authoritative and poses threat and challenge to the teacher.
Encouragement	This approach encourages trainee teachers to better job performance in future.	Huge pressure may lead to the failure of archive-specific learning objectives that may cause frustration among the pre-service or in-service teachers.

After these two early approaches, various researchers started working in the field of microteaching from various perspectives. For instance, in 1972 Maker compared microteaching and conventional teaching, in the same year, Sing compared microteaching with interaction analysis. In 1974, Passi and Shah started some advanced-level studies and found that microteaching helped to increase questioning skills, reinforcement silence, and nonverbal cues. Furthermore, Passi and other researchers developed various useful teaching skills which were documented in a book named *Becoming Better Teacher: Microteaching Approach*, developed at the Centre of Advanced Study in Education, the M.S. University of Baroda, Baroda by B. K. Passi, Maharaja Sayajirao University of Baroda (Sahitya Mudranalaya, Ahmedabad, pub. (Passi, 1976)) which is the first comprehensive book on microteaching in India.

In the early developmental stage, a large-scale research study was conducted by the National Council of Teacher Education (NCTE) in collaboration with the Center for Advanced Study in Education (CASE). They focused on finding the effectiveness of microteaching as well as variations of microteaching components to find out the relative effectiveness. They found that microteaching and its modified approach helped to acquire higher-teaching competence among the student teachers compared to traditional teacher training techniques.

Comparison between Microteaching and Traditional Teaching
Microteaching Cycle

Generally, six steps are needed to be achieved to complete a cycle of microteaching which can be varied as per the requirement of the objective:

a. Plan
b. Teach
c. Feedback
d. Re-plan
e. Re-teach
f. Re-feedback

What Is the Microteaching Cycle?

Plan: In the planning stage, student teachers plan a topic to teach with the help of their teacher educator or supervisor.

Teach: In this stage, the teacher trainee teaches the planned lesson to a small group of people (5–10 pupils) in a small amount of time (5 minutes) with a supervisor (1 or 2). Here student teacher applies various preplanned components of skills and based on the situation they can modify their behavior. For observation of teaching, if possible, videotape and CCTV could be used.

Feedback: This is one of the crucial aspects of the microteaching cycle. Feedback refers to giving information about performance. Based on the performance of trainee teachers' various information is given on their strengths and weakness. This information helps to improve the further performance of the trainee teacher. Various feedbacks are used in the microteaching process such as supervisor feedback, peer feedback, student feedback, audiofeedback, audio plus supervisor feedback, video feedback and video plus supervisor feedback, etc.

Re-plan: Based on the feedback given by the supervisor or peers, in this stage teacher trainee re-plans their lesson. They incorporate suggested points of strengths and eliminate or rectify the weaknesses which were not skillfully handled during the teaching.

Re-teach: In this stage trainee teacher re-teaches the topic to practice the same skill with a different group of people or the same group of people if the topic is different, to overcome the boredom or monotony of the pupil. In this stage teaching of the trainee teacher is also observed by a supervisor, videotape, or CCTV.

Re-feedback: Feedback is again provided to the trainees for discussion, to make suggestions, and to encourage teacher performance as well as to review strengths and weaknesses.

Through this discussion, major aspects of the microteaching cycle are explained, viz, recording or observing, reviewing skills, responding or feedback on performance, refining, and re-doing. It is also notable that the cycle of microteaching continues until the teacher trainee achieves the desired level of skill. *Figure 8.1* represents the diagrammatical representation of the microteaching cycle.

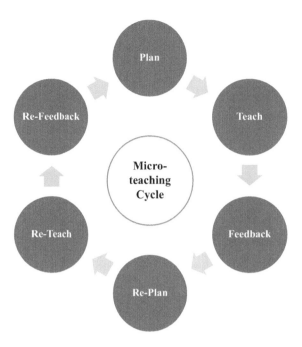

Figure 8.1 The microteaching cycle.

Phases of Microteaching

Clift and other researchers have classified three phases of microteaching, they are the following:

1. Knowledge acquisition phase (pre-active phase)
2. Skill acquisition phase (inter-active phase)
3. Transfer acquisition phase (post-active phase)

1. **Knowledge acquisition phase (pre-active phase)**: Knowledge acquisition mainly encourages the learning aspect of teacher trainees. For instance, in this phase, they gather knowledge about various teaching-learning skills and its component from the expert or supervisor through discussion, illustration, and demonstration. Besides, the teacher trainee also learns how to, and under which conditions, they can apply a specific skill and how they handle it.
2. **Skill acquisition phase (inter-active phase)**: This is a more active phase in the microteaching process. Based on knowledge acquisition about various skills from the expert, in this stage, the teacher trainee plans a lesson to practice the acquired skills. The acquired skills are continued for practice through the microteaching cycle (as discussed in the previous section) until the attainment of mastery-level skills acquisition. In this stage, feedback plays an important role to modify or shape the learned skill.
3. **Transfer acquisition phase (post-active phase)**: In this stage teacher trainee mainly emphasizes the integration process. For instance, after acquiring a mastery level of knowledge or expertise over each of the skills, in this phase, they integrate all skills and transfer them to actual classroom teaching.

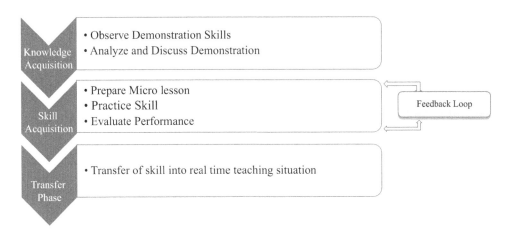

Figure 8.2 The phases of microteaching.

Table 8.2 Phases of microteaching with specific activities and components

Phases	Activities	Components
Knowledge acquisition	Reading Listening Observing Analyzing	Modeling
Skills acquisition	Planning Observing Analyzing Re-planning Re-teaching Re-observing Re-analyzing	Setting Feedback
Skill transfer	Planning Teaching Link Analyzing Teaching Feedback	Integration

What Are the Phases of Microteaching?

In the microteaching procedure, we follow this phase sequentially with specific activities and components. Table 8.2 presents the phases of microteaching with specific activities and components.

Teaching Skills for Microteaching

Teaching is one of the most complex tasks in the whole teaching and learning scenario. From the previous section, we know that microteaching is a unique approach that reduces the complexity of teaching and helps to acquire each teaching skill at a mastery level.

Table 8.3 Presents various teaching skills explained by Allen and Ryan (1969)

Skills	Brief discussion
Stimulus variation	This skill refers to the use of various stimuli to attract the attention of the student. Teacher trainees need to acquire various body movements, gestures, effective eye contact, vocal modulation, interactional style, etc.
Set induction	Set induction skill refers to creating a relationship with students and lessons to induce them to maximum level.
Closure	It refers to the skill of connecting the existing knowledge of the student to the new knowledge.
Silence and nonverbal cues	This skill refers to providing a cue to the student to encourage them effectively.
Reinforcement or student participation	Student participation is a major aim of every teaching-learning approach. Reinforcement or student participation skill refers to the utilization of positive reinforcement and how to avoid or balance negative reinforcement.
Fluency in making question	This skill refers to the fluency of putting a question in the classroom to get a possible answer.
Probing questions	This is one of the important skills that refers to effectively or strategically putting the question to the students to dig out some unique view from the students or lead students to respond correctly.
Higher-order questioning	It is also a questioning strategy. In this skill, the trainee teacher learns how to put a question to the student to enable the student to answer in a generalized way.
Divergent questions	This questioning strategy skill enables the student to think and answer logically and creatively.
Recognizing attending behavior	This refers to the skill of using visual cues to judge how far students are feeling interested and concentrating on their lesson.
Illustration and use of example	It refers to the skill of illustration and giving an example of the trainee teacher to capture attention and attain the desired goal.
Lecturing	Lecturing is the skill of using the right technique and the right way for the presentation of material in the classroom environment.
Planned repetition	It refers to the repetition of any topic or term in a planned way to focus attention on some important point.
Completeness	Completeness refers to an effective two-way communication process to disseminate knowledge and develop the attitude and interest of the student.

The question arises, what is the teaching skill? How many skills are involved? What are the components of those skills? And how effectively can one evaluate the skill acquisition of teacher trainees based on their performance?

What Are the Various Microteaching Skills?

Generally, teaching skills are a set of teaching behaviors of a teacher to change a student's behavior. Gage (1968) defines teaching skills as "specific instructional activities and procedures that a teacher may use in the classroom". These are related to various stages of teaching or through a continuous flow of teacher performance.

Micro-teaching

Various researchers in their way tried to identify the required skills for microteaching. As Allen and Ryan (1969) listed 14 skills which increased to 18 skills based on the work of Borg and his associates. In the Indian scenario, Passi (1976), based on the work of CASE, included 21 skills. However, no lists are universal or exhaustive. A list of skills could be changed, added to, or subtracted from based on situation, fund, and time. Here, some of the important skills could be applied majorly in teaching-learning scenarios. Before the detailed discussion of skills let us see a comprehensive list of skills discussed by the various researchers in their work. Those are the following:

A list of teaching skills is provided by Allen and Ryan (1969) (in Figure 8.3).

Additionally, B.K Passi (1976) in his book *Becoming Better Teacher: Microteaching Approach* describes the following 13 skills:

1. Writing instructional objective
2. Introducing a lesson
3. Fluency in questioning
4. Probing questions
5. Explaining
6. Illustration with example
7. Stimulus variation
8. Silence and nonverbal cues
9. Reinforcement
10. Increasing pupil participation
11. Using blackboard

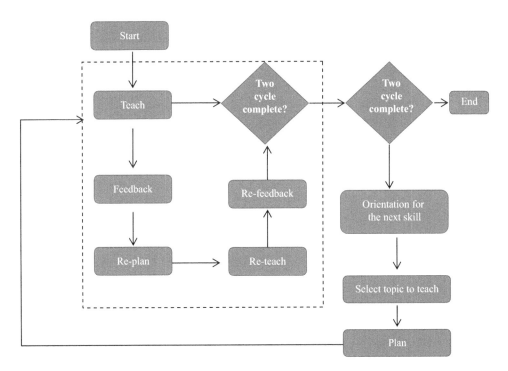

Figure 8.3 The standard microteaching model.

12. Achieving closure
13. Recognizing attending behavior

From the above skills, different skills can be categorized as shown (see Figure 8.4):

As discussed previously it is hard to use all the mentioned skills because of constraints of funds, resources, and time. Thus, various teacher training institutions take into consideration some set of skills as per their available funds, resources, and requirements. However, it is also notable that the rationale for the use of any skill must be clear. This section is going to discuss some of the commonly accepted sets of microteaching skills in terms of concept, components, micro-lesson plans, evaluation, and schedule which is useful for every teacher. Those are as follows:

1. Skill of introducing a lesson
2. Skill of using probing questions
3. Skill of explaining
4. Skill of illustrating with examples
5. Skill of reinforcement
6. Skill of stimulus variation
7. Skill of classroom management
8. Skill of using a blackboard

Skill of Explaining

Situation: In classroom settings, it generally happens that the teacher teaches one concept or topic but the learned topic doesn't make any sense to the student. In this situation, a teacher needs to provide a proper explanation to make the concept explicit.

The skill of explanation is one of the teaching arts that enables the teacher to provide a more supportive and interrelated statement to the student to achieve the desired learning goal.

Components of the skill: To achieve effective explanation one trainee teacher must take into consideration various components that are related to these skills. The component of explanation consists of two types, desirable behavior and undesirable behavior. *Table 8.4* presents components of explaining skills for microteaching.

Observation Schedule for the Skill of Explanation

THE SKILL OF ILLUSTRATING WITH AN EXAMPLE

Situation: In classroom settings, quite often teachers encounter some situations when they are unable to convey the actual meaning of any concept. This mainly happens when the learning concept is abstract. To overcome this problem, teachers need to properly adapt the skill of illustration.

What Is the Skill of Illustrating?

What is the skill of illustration: The skill of illustration refers to a formulation of various exampling strategies to convey the true sense and meaning of the learning concept.

Components of illustration skill: The components of the skill of illustrations are as follows:
- Formulation of simple examples
- Formulation of relevant examples

Table 8.4 Present list of different stages of the lesson and the components of teaching skills

Stage of lesson	Components of teaching skills
Planning stage	Writing instructional objective
	Selection of content
	Organizing content
	Selection of audiovisual aids
Introductory stage	Creating set induction
	Introducing the lesson
Presentation stage	Structuring classroom questions.
Four sub-stages fall into this category	Fluency in asking a question
	Question delivery and distribution
Questioning skills	Higher-order questions
	Divergent questions.
	Responses management
Presentation skills	Pacing of lesson
	Lecturing
	Explaining discussion
	Illustration with examples
	Discussing
	Demonstrating
Add using skills	Using teaching aids
	Using blackboard
	Stimulus variation
	Silence and nonverbal cues
	Reinforcement managerial skills
Managerial skills	Promoting pupil participation
	Recognizing attending behavior
	Management of the class
	Closing stage
	1. Achieving closure
	2. Planned repetition
	3. Giving assignments.
	4. Evaluating the pupils' progress
	5. Diagnosing pupil learning difficulties and remedial measures

- Using appropriate media for examples
- Using examples by the inducto-deductive approach

Formulation of simple examples: In the basic stage of illustration the teacher formulates basic examples of teaching concepts. Formulation of a basic example mainly relates to existing or prior knowledge of the learner. By the formulation of simple examples teachers just try to connect the new knowledge with existing knowledge.

Formulation of relevant examples: For effective illustrations, the teacher must provide an example that is relevant to the learning content. For instance, to teach the shape of our earth, the teacher can use the example of the shape of an orange as a relevant example.

Formulating an interesting example: An example can only be interesting when it arouses curiosity and interest among the learner. To effectively illustrate the content being taught, it is imperative to formulate interesting examples. Interest can be judged by the behavior of the student.

Table 8.5 Present components of explaining skills for microteaching

Component	Explanation
Desirable behaviors: Desirable behavior refers to that behavior that is needed to take into consideration.	
Beginning statement	This is an introductory component to start the explanation. The beginning statement helps to create an environment where students can give attention to the beginning point of the topic.
Explaining links	This component is a list of conjunction, compliment, or contrast word that helps to link one concept to another. Generally, used terms are; but, the purpose of, therefore, so that, to, as a result, thus, such that, the consequence of, hence, because, etc.
Concluding statement	This is the final remarks or statement after the completion of the explanation. This is the summary of all explanations or discussions.
Question to test understanding	The questioning component is used to ensure whether the desired goal of explanation is achieved or not. It involves putting questions related to explaining the topic to test the understanding of students regarding learned concepts or principles. Moreover, with the help of the questioning component teacher trainee can rectify the confusion in the mind of the student.
Undesirable behavior	
Undesirable behavior refers to that behavior that is needed to be ignored for the skill of explanation.	
Irrelevant statement	An irrelevant statement refers to those explanations which do not contribute to any interrelated link with the teaching concept. Besides, irrelevant statements can create confusion in understanding the subject matter.
Lacking in continuity	The flow of explanation must be complete and comprehensive. Lack of continuity refers to incomplete, jargon, or illogical statement, which creates confusion. Various causes of lacking continuity are: • Illogical or unrelated statements in respect of the previous statement. • Without showing any interrelation with the existing concept of the student. • Presentation of concept without sequence. • Unnecessary use of technical terms and inappropriate vocabulary.
Vague words and Phases	Appropriate choice of words and phrases is the most crucial aspect of explanation. Teacher trainees should avoid the use of vague words or phrases to achieve effective expiations of subject matter. For instance, something, somewhat, seems, many, much, probable, actually, etc.

Table 8.6 Format sample

Name of pupil-teacher:	Date:
Name of supervisor:	Class:
Subject:	Time:
Topic:	Teach/Re-teach

Using appropriate media for examples: Appropriate media for example refers to the selection of an example based on the age level, maturity, and culture of the student. When a teacher illustrates something, he or she must take into consideration the nature of media such as verbal or nonverbal based on the nature of the content.

Using examples by the inducto-deductive approach: This is a reverse approach. The teacher gives the example related to the subject matter and based on the example students

Table 8.7 Gradation index

Gradation index
"A" means 95–100% correct use of the component.
"B" means 85–94% correct use of the components.
"C" means 75–84% correct use of the component.
"D" means 65–74% correct use of the component.
"F" means below 65% correct use of the component.

Table 8.8 Component-wise grading

Sl. No	Components	Grading	Remarks
1	Beginning statement	A, B, C, D, E	
2	Explaining links	A, B, C, D, E	
3	Concluding statement	A, B, C, D, E	
4	Questions to test understanding	A, B, C, D, E	
5	Questions followed by correct responses	A, B, C, D, E	
6	No irrelevant statement	A, B, C, D, E	
7	No lacking of continuity	A, B, C, D, E	
8	No inappropriate vocabulary	A, B, C, D, E	
9	No lacking of fluency	A, B, C, D, E	
10	No vague words or phrases	A, B, C, D, E	

formulate the rules. After completion of this process, the teacher tests students by asking for parallel examples of the learned concept. Through this, the teacher gets knowledge about the understanding of students regarding the learned concept.

Observation Schedule for the Skill of Illustration

SKILL OF REINFORCEMENT

Situation: Reinforcement is one of the major aspects of any effective teaching-learning process. Every student in the classroom is eager to get positive reinforcement from the teacher for his activity such as answering questions, having creative discussions, attempting to answer any question, etc. Teachers can reinforce students in various ways such as using verbal statements such as "very good", "good attempt", and "that's right"; or other nonverbal expressions such as smiling, nodding your head, paying attention to the student, etc., by which student participation in the classroom is maximized.

What is the skill of reinforcement? The skill of reinforcement refers to the response of the teacher regarding the activity of the student in the classroom. Reinforcement in the classroom may be positive or negative. Both reinforcements directly affect student participation in the learning process. Inappropriate use of reinforcement may hamper the learning process.

Components of reinforcement skills: The following are the components of the reinforcement skills in the teaching-learning process:
- Positive verbal reinforcement
- Positive nonverbal reinforcement

- Negative verbal reinforcement
- Negative nonverbal reinforcement
- Wrong use of reinforcement
- Inappropriate use of reinforcement

What Is the Skill of Reinforcement?

Positive verbal reinforcement: Positive verbal responses refer to the statements or comments given by the teacher on the correct response of the student. These are the following:
- An example of positive verbal reinforcement is the use of a word such as "good", "fine", "nice", "keep it up", "all right", excellent", "carry on", "think again" and also using some extra verbal cues such as "um", "aha", etc.
- Another situation of positive reinforcement is when the teacher accepts the answer of the student and asks to repeat it once more for the whole classroom by using a statement such as "Please … Repeat it".
- Also, when the teacher loudly repeats the correct answer given by the student either the same way or with a little bit of modification for the whole classroom.

Positive nonverbal reinforcement: Another major component is positive nonverbal reinforcement. It refers to the response of the teacher to the student without using any words. This can be done by "clapping", "smiling", "nodding your head", "patting", "looking attentively", or "writing an answer on the blackboard", etc.

Negative verbal reinforcement: Negative verbal reinforcement refers to a statement given to the student in response to their incorrect answer. Various negative verbal reinforcement with using of words such as "idiot", "stupid", "no", "wrong", "incorrect", "I don't think so", or "I don't like your answer", etc. These words may discourage students' participation.

Negative nonverbal reinforcement: It refers to the use of negative gestures or signs in response to the answer or activity of the student such as "frowning", "moving a hand to show 'no' 'no'", "staring", or "looking angrily", etc. This reinforcement as a result decreases students' participation and generates fear in a classroom environment.

Table 8.9 Sample format skill of illustration

Name of pupil-teacher:	Date:
Name of supervisor:	Class:
Subject:	Time:
Topic:	Teach/Re-teach:

Table 8.10 Gradation Index

Gradation index

"A" means 95 to 100% correct use of components.
"B" means 85 to 94% correct use of components.
"C" means 75 to 84% correct use of components.
"D" means 65 to 74% correct use of components.
"F" means below 65% correct use of components.

Table 8.11 Component-wise grading

S.No.	Components	Grading	Remarks
1	Simple examples	A,B,C,D,F	
2	Relevant examples	A,B,C,D,F	
3	Interesting examples	A,B,C,D,F	
4	Media for appropriate examples	A,B,C,D,F	
5	Pupils give examples to show understanding	A,B,C,D,F	
6	Inducto-deductive approach	A,B,C,D,F	
7	The number of examples before the formulation rule was adequate	A,B,C,D,F	
8	Examples to test whether pupils' understanding was adequate	A,B,C,D,F	
9	Pupils have clearly understood the concept	A,B,C,D,F	

Wrong use of reinforcement: In the classroom situation sometimes teachers are unable to reinforce at a specific time or when the situation is demanding encouragement.

Inappropriate use of reinforcement: This is a situation when teachers lack the appropriate knowledge about how to use reinforcement. Which reinforcements are to be used in a specific situation? For this scarcity of knowledge, teachers use the same types of reinforcement in every situation.

The Skill of Probing Question

Situation: It is sometimes an identical situation in every classroom, that arises when the teacher asks any question to the students and they are given mixed responses. For instance, some students give an incorrect answer, some are partially correct, some correct, and some have no response.

What Is the Skill of Probing Questions?

To probe means to dig out. "*Skill of probing questioning is the art of response management. It comprises a set of techniques used for going deep into pupil's responses to have the desired responses*". This skill is also called the skill of response management.

Components of the skill:
- Prompting technique
- Seeking further information technique
- Redirection technique
- Refocusing technique
- Increasing critical awareness technique

Prompting technique: Prompting is a technique that activates students' response when it is incorrect or a no response. This technique helps to go deep into the mind of the student. To achieve the desired correct answer from the student, the teacher provides a set of prompts following a step-by-step questing order.

Table 8.12 Sample format for the skill of reinforcement

Name of pupil-teacher:	Date:
Name of supervisor:	Class:
Subject:	Time:
Topic:	Teach/Re-teach

Table 8.13 Grading index

Gradation index

"A" means 95 to 100 % correct use of the component.
"B" means 85 to 94 % correct use of the component.
"C" means 75 to 84 % correct use of the component.
"D" means 65 to 74 % correct use of the component.
"F" means below 65 % correct use of the component.

Example:

Teacher: What are the characteristics of the Sun?
Mihika: No response.
Teacher: From where do we get light in the morning?
Mihika: Sun.

Seeking further information: This technique is used when the teacher desires to dig out more explicit or complete answers from the student. In this technique, the teacher provides more related questions to get details about an understanding of the student or facilitate the student to think more.

Example:

Teacher: What are the characteristics of the Sun?
Mihika: Sun gives us light.
Teacher: Well done … What are the other characteristics of the sun?

Redirection: In this technique, the same question is asked to the other students in the classroom by the teacher. This technique mainly helps to increase more active participation when there is a situation of no response, limited response, or incorrect responses in the classroom.

Example:

Teacher: What are the characteristics of the Sun?
Mihika: Sun gives us light and heat.
Abir: No response
Alokesh: It helps trees/ plants in photosynthesis. (Redirection).

Refocusing: This is a comparison technique. In this technique, the teacher compares the phenomenon with another possible phenomenon to provide knowledge between two situations. This technique is used when a student gives the correct response. The refocusing technique helps students to point out comparisons, relations, and similarities in respect of a given question and answer.

Increasing critical awareness: Like refocusing, this technique is also used when a response of the students is correct. In this technique, the teacher further simulates students by providing higher-order questioning.

Example:
1. Why is sunlight important for photosynthesis?
2. What happens if sunlight does not come to the earth?

Observation Schedule for the Skill of Reinforcement

What Is the Indian Model of Microteaching?

The Indian Model of Microteaching (IMM)

A major initiative of the microteaching approach in India was taken by educational organizations such as CASE, Baroda, the Department of Teacher Education, NCERT Delhi, etc. The early stages of research mainly focused on the development of basic apparatus of teaching material for training the teacher educators (Passi, 1976, Passi & Lalitha, 1976). Salient features of the Indian model of microteaching are as follows:

Low-cost devices for skill presentation: Notably, the presentation of skills of trainee teachers is a complex approach. Therefore, various developed countries such as the USA, the UK, and Australia used various technological devices such as films, video, CCTV, tape recorders, etc. However, as per the Indian model, it was simplified, and major emphasis was laid on the written material, lectures, demonstration, and discussion for the presentation of skills. Without using high-cost devices, the effectiveness of the Indian model of microteaching remained the same and did not differ significantly except in verbal skill (where a marginally significant difference was observed) (Das et al., 1976, 1980).

Observation schedules are used for recording and providing feedback: The Indian model of microteaching mainly focuses on low-cost devices and observation schedules are used to record the teaching performance as well as to provide feedback to trainee teachers. Research conducted by Das et al. (1976) found no significant difference in using low-cost devices compared to high-cost devices.

Peer role-play as a student: The Indian model of microteaching is more flexible compared to other microteaching models in the sense that here trainee teacher can use his/her peers to role-play as a student where participation of the real student is not available without losing the effectiveness of microteaching.

Table 8.14 Component-wise grading

S.No.	Components	Grading	Remarks
1	Prompting	A, B, C, D, F	
2	Seeking further information	A, B, C, D, F	
3	Refocusing	A, B, C, D, F	
4	Redirection	A, B, C, D, F	
5	Increasing critical awareness	A, B, C, D, F	

Designed based on minimum facilities or equipment: One of the major characteristics of the Indian model of microteaching is that it can be provided to those classrooms where minimum facilities are not available. For instance, feedback sessions can be organized in open spaces where adequate classrooms are not available without hampering their effectiveness.

Timing of microteaching phases is simplified: In the Indian model of microteaching the various phases of the cycle are as shown in Table 8.15.

The Indian model of microteaching has been successfully implemented in various universities and teacher training colleges throughout India. *Figure 8.3* presents the standard Indian model of microteaching phases.

Advantage of Microteaching

Microteaching is one of the most popular and effective innovations in the field of education. The following are some of the specific advantages of microteaching:

- Microteaching helps to increase the teaching efficiency of pre-service as well as in-service teachers through educational programs.
- Microteaching is helpful for scientific teaching practices.
- It works as an effective feedback device which in turn is effective for modification of a teacher's behavior.
- Microteaching always encourages highly individualized training.
- To achieve desired learning goal in the classroom one of the basic elements is organized and scientific teaching skills. The microteaching innovative approach helps teachers to acquire various scientific skills for their future teaching.
- It provides a specific observation schedule which is helpful for systematic, objective, as well as scientific observation in the classroom.
- It divides the whole classroom situation into small segments by reducing class time and size. Therefore, it helps diminish the complexity of a typical/conventional classroom.
- By using various scientific approaches, microteaching helps to increase the confidence of teacher trainees.
- By using various technological devices such as CCTV, tape recorders, films, etc., teacher trainees can analyze their performances in teaching.
- Microteaching is more flexible and can be used in a real classroom or simulated conditions.

Table 8.15 Phases and timing for microteaching

Phases	Timing
Teach	6 minutes
Feedback	6 minutes
Re-plan	12 minutes
Re-teach	6 minutes
Re-feedback	6 minutes
Total	**36 minutes**

What Are the Disadvantages and Advantages of Microteaching?

Disadvantage of Microteaching

The following are the disadvantages or drawbacks of microteaching:

- Microteaching is time-consuming as it takes 35 minutes to provide mastery-level skills to only one teacher.
- One of the features of microteaching is that immediate feedback may not be feasible in all conditions.
- Due to a shortage of time, many situations or providing all the skills may be hard to grasp effectively.
- It ignores the creativity of the teacher by providing a structural environment.
- It presents a fragmented view of teaching.
- In the Indian scenario, it is hard to fit microteaching in every classroom situation due to an overwhelming number of students with a high teacher and student ratio.
- Only using microteaching may not be enough for adequate training. It is needed to be embedded with other supplemented teaching techniques.
- The list of skills is not exhaustive. A few of the microteaching skills don't apply to all subjects.

Bibliography

Aggarwal, J. C. (1995). *Essentials of educational technology*. New Delhi, India: Vikas Publishing House.
Allen, D. W. (1967). *Micro-teaching, a description*, CA, USA: Stanford Univ.
Allen, D. W., & Eve, A. W. (1968). Microteaching. *Theory into Practice*, 7(5), 181–185.
Allen, D. W., & Ryan, K. (1969). *Microteaching*. Reading, MA: Addison-Wesley.
Clift, J. C., Batten, H., Burke, G., & Malley, J. (1976). Structure of the skill acquisition phase of a microteaching program. *British Journal of Educational Psychology*, 46(2), 190–197.
Cooper, J. M., & Stroud, T. (1966). *The Stanford summer micro-teaching clinic, 1966*. CA, USA: Stanford University, School of Education.
Das, R. C., Passi, B. K., & Singh, K. C. (1976). A study of the effectiveness of micro-teaching in the training of teachers. In M. B. Buch (Ed.), *Second survey of research in education* (pp. 428–429). Baroda: Centre for Advanced Studies in Education.
Das, R. C., Passi, B. K., & Singh, L. C. (1980). *Differential effectiveness of microteaching components*. New Delhi: NCERT.
Gage, N. L. (1968). An analytical approach to research instructional methods. *Journal of Experimental Education*, 37(1), 119–125.
McKnight, P. C. (1971). Microteaching in teacher training. *Research in Education*, 6(1), 24–38.
Passi, B. K. (1976). *Becoming better teacher: Microteaching approach, developed at the centre of advanced study in education, the MS University of Baroda, Baroda*. Ahamadabad, India: Sahitya Mudranalaya
Passi, B.K. & Lalita, M S (1976). Micro-Teaching Skill Based Approach. in B. K. Passi (ed) *Becoming Better Teacher Micro Teaching approach*. Ahmedabad: Sahitya Mudranalya.
Shah, G. (1970). Micro-teaching–without television. *Nutan Shikshan*.
Sharma, R. N., & Chandra, S. S. (2003). *Advanced educational technology* (Vol. 2). New Delhi: Atlantic Publishers & Dist.

Suggested Readings

Lakshmi, M. J. (2009). *Microteaching and prospective teachers*. New Delhi: Discovery Publishing House
Mangal, S. K., & Mangal, U. (2009). *Essentials of educational technology*. India: PHI learning Pvt
Passi, B. K., & Shah, M. M. (1974). *Microteaching in teacher education* (Vol. 3). Baroda: Centre of Advanced Study in Education, MS University of Baroda.

Pathak, R. P. (2012). *Educational technology*. Pearson Education India.
Singh, Y. K. (2007). *Teaching practice: Lesson planning*. New Delhi: APH Publishing.

9
PROGRAMMED INSTRUCTION

In the past, several revolutionary researchers supported the idea that education should be individualized in nature. Jack R. Faymier in his book, *The Nature of Educational Method* (C.E. Merrill Books, 1965) explained that the whole environment of the educational system should be democratic. A democratic environment in education encourages a student to be more creative and energetic, be more engaging, and participate in multidisciplinary ways in learning activities. In contrast, an authoritative learning environment increases shyness, anxiety, and a withdrawn nature. Therefore, researchers feel that there is a need for a unique method of teaching that can flourish the hidden creative ability of students and which is only possible through the active participation of the student in the teaching-learning process rather than being the mere passive recipient of information. Researchers have shown learners become more involved in a learning process when they perceive that they can apply or transfer whatever knowledge they get from the teacher in the classroom. Therefore, just a discussion-based teaching approach is not enough to discover the inner spark of the student. The present chapter discusses "Programmed Instruction" or "Programmed Learning", which is a unique approach toward the encouragement of individualized learning.

Meaning and Definitions of Programmed Instruction

From the 1950s onward, researchers in the field of education perceived that each learner has his/her own rate or pace and capability in the processing of information as well as intellectual ability. Therefore, there was a huge demand for individualized learning approaches or self-learning approaches. Consequently, a voluminous amount of research evolved out of the unique learning method namely "Programmed Learning".

Programmed learning is an instructional approach and is also commonly known as programmed instruction. It is mainly a student-centric learning approach, where students are allowed to progress at their own pace. Furthermore, researchers have defined programmed learning from various perspectives some of which are as follows:

Smith (1962): "Programmed instruction is the process of arranging the material to be learned into a series of sequential steps, usually it moves the student from a familiar background into a complex and new set of concepts, principles, and understanding".

- **Leith (1966)**: "A program is a sequence of small steps of institutional material (called frames), most of which requires a response to be made by completing a blank space in a sentence. To ensure that required responses are given, a system of cueing is applied, and each response is verified by the provision of immediate knowledge of results. Such a sequence is intended to be worked at the learners' own pace as individualized self-instruction".
- **Espich and Williams (1967)**: "Programmed instruction is a planned sequence of instruction, leading to proficiency in terms of the stimulus-response relationship that has proven to be effective".
- **Markle, S. (1976)**: "It is a method of designing a reproducible sequence of instructional events to produce a measurable and consistent effect on the behavior of every acceptable student".
- **Skinner (1954)**: "Programmed learning is the first application of laboratory technique utilized in the study of the learning process to the practical problems of education".
- **Gulati and Gulati (1976)**: "Programmed learning as popularly understood is a method of giving individualized instruction, in which the student is active and proceeds at his own pace and is provided with immediate knowledge of results. The teacher is not physically present".
- **The Columbia, Encyclopedia, Sixth Edition (2001–05)**: "Programmed Instruction is a method of presenting new subject matters to students in a graded sequence of controlled steps. Students work through the programmed material by themselves at their speed and after each step tests their comprehension by answering an examination question or filling in a diagram. They are then immediately shown the correct answer or given additional information. Computers and other types of teaching machines are often used to present the material, although books may also be used".
- **Stephen M. Corey (1969)**: "Programmed instruction refers to a well-disciplined and experimental approach to the development of instances of systems of instruction".
- **Lysaught and Williams (1962)** stated that "programming is a process of arranging materials to be learned in a series of small steps designed to lead a learner through self-instruction from what he knows to the unknown and toward new and more complex knowledge and principles".

Historical Background of Programmed Instruction

Program instruction is not a new concept. The origin of program instruction can be found in the work of the great philosopher Socrates, who first time developed a program in geometry which was documented by his student Plato (Suppes, 1968). After that, the second phase of the revolution took place when British universities adopted the tutorial system. The uniqueness of the tutorial system was a small segment of knowledge was exchanged throughout the learning scenarios and learners can ask their questions and can get feedback immediately. In a general view, the theory of the "Law of Effect", proposed by Thorndike has a direct relation to program instruction. In this theory, he stated that learning will last long when satisfying the situation of the learner which otherwise becomes weak. Besides, it also stated that learners repeat those activities which are pleasurable and successful compared to displeasure.

Another historical initiative in the context of program instruction can be found when Pressy (1927) developed a teaching machine at Ohio State University, where students were provided a set of questions and each consisted of four alternative options or choices. In this teaching machine, students can only go to the next item when he or she chooses the correct alternative. When a student provides the wrong answer immediate feedback is provided. This process goes on until the student responds with the correct alternative. There was a huge impact of using this type of learning machine to achieve learning outcomes in less time (Dececco, 1968).

A huge revolution has taken place in the mid-90s. Lots of learning theories have been developed in that period. One of them was "Operant Conditioning" proposed by Skinner (1954). Based on his conditioning theory he proposed a new kind of teaching-learning technique namely "Programmed Instruction". After coining the term program instruction which is based on Skinner's operant conditioning, this theory and methods have been applied in the development of various self-instructional books and teaching the machine. One can find a constructive view of program instruction in a paper namely "Science of learning and Art of Teaching" published (Feldman & McPhee, 2007). Based on his research and theory Skinner claimed that providing continuous feedback or reinforcement for desirable responses can bring desirable behavioral change in humans. Here Skinner has applied his conditioning theory in the context of a teaching machine. Furthermore, Pressy emphasized assignments and questioning to evaluate student performance. He designed a teaching machine specifically for testing purposes. The approach of Skinner and Pressy was solely based on "Linear Programming". Crowder, a psychologist in the USA proposed a new strategic design of programming called "Branching Programming" or "Intrinsic Programming", "where he was given the major focus on task analysis rather than conditioning and he developed a device namely "Automatic Tutoring". Mager, in 1964 developed a technique namely "Learner-Controlled Instruction" and Gilbert, in 1962 developed a programming style called "Mathetics". After that, in 1965, Stolurow developed a modern program of instructional method namely "Computer-Assisted Instruction".

Program Instruction in India

The concept of program instruction penetrated India in the early-60s when the National Council of Teacher Education (NCTE), started doing research in the area of program instruction. They spread information about the effectiveness of program instruction in various educational institutes. An enormous amount of research work was started related to program instruction in the field of "Educational Technology". The first course of program-based teaching-learning started in 1966 at the University of Baroda. The name of the program was "Educational Technology and Programmed Learning" initiated for M.Ed level teaching. In 1967 the "Indian Association of Programmed Learning" was formed, to promote research in the field of Educational Technology and Programmed Instruction. During this time NCERT and other various organizations conducted various research and found out that program instruction is an effective approach compared to traditional lecture-based teaching.

Characteristics of Programmed Instruction

1. The program should have planned criteria for entering behavior and terminal behavior.
2. Each content of the learning materials is divided into a small segment of knowledge called "Frames".
3. Frames are arranged sequentially from simple to complex.
4. Each frame requires a response from the learner.
5. Immediate feedback is another essential characteristic of Program Instruction. The immediate response confirms the learner's response in the context of right or wrong. A right response obtains confirmation and an incorrect receives correction.
6. In program instruction, each learning unit is arranged systematically to enhance the behavior of the learner.

7. Program learning encourages active participation and interaction between learners and learning material.
8. Another essential characteristic of program instruction is the self-pacing or individualistic learning approach. In a program instruction learning scenario, anyone can learn at his/her own pace depending on learning style, speed, nature, etc.
9. In program instruction, any activity of learning can be observed, measured, and controlled by the teacher.
10. Continuous evaluation is another essential characteristic of program instruction. Based on this characteristic, teachers can evaluate the quality of the learning material as well as the performance of the learner.
11. The stability or success of program learning solely depends on the designer and learner, if the designer or learner makes a mistake the whole program learning structure would be rejected.

What Are the Principles of Programmed Instruction?

Fundamental Principles of Programmed Instruction

This section is going to discuss various principles or assumptions connected to program learning or automatic-learning machines for use in educational purposes. Various scientific, as well as experimental, theories are involved to develop the concept of programmed learning. For instance, Thorndike emphasized three basic laws for effective learning those are the law of readiness, the law of exercise, and the law of effect. Pavlov emphasized laws of conditioning or stimulate learning, Tolman explained cues in sign learning, Hull enforced reinforcement in response learning, Skinner in his theory of operant behavior, and Gestalt's school of psychology emphasized on insightful cognitive approach. If we try to explore all the mentioned theories, we will find that they all are focused on learning by doing, trial and error, and learning by discovery approaches which strengthens the bond between Stimulus-Response (S-R) in a learning process. The following are some of the major assumptions or principles related to programmed learning:

The principle of small steps: This is a very essential step. In this first stage the teacher or instructional designer needs to divide the whole content of learning materials into a small segment of knowledge. This is important because research shows that learning is very much motivating, attractive, and engaging when teaching-learning material is provided in small segments. After the breakdown of the whole learning material, a teacher can provide each segment one after another. Each segment or piece of information is called a "Frame" or "Didule".

Principle of immediate confirmation of feedback: This is the second important step to consider when designing the program instruction. In program instruction when a student responds or answers any specific question, he/she needs "knowledge of the result" immediately. Research shows that, if a student gets the result of his activity immediately, he can perform better compared to a delayed result. When the response of a student is correct then he/she gets confirmation.

The principle of active responding: This principle is mainly based on the assumption that students will learn better if he/she actively engages with learning materials. Properly designed program instruction aims to provide scopes of active participation and induce sustained activeness in the learner.

Self-Pacing: As discussed previously, programmed learning always encourages a personalized or individualized learning environment. Based on various research it is found that learning can take place better when learners get an opportunity to perform at his/her own pace. As each individual is different in many ways, some are very rapid learners while some may be slow compared to others. So, in the context of designing program instruction one needs to follow this principle so that no one is left behind in a specific learning environment. This principle encourages individual differences in the teaching and learning process.

The principle of student testing: The fifth very important principle in program instruction is student testing. Student testing means the teacher can assess the progress of the student immediately. This principle is mainly based on the assumption that continuous evaluation can maximize motivation or engagement in the teaching-learning process. In this principle, the teacher or instructional designer, as well as the student, gets the benefit. For instance, a teacher or instructional designer can evaluate the weak or defective part of the developed program and can modify it as per requirement. Besides, a student can get a continuous evaluation of his/her performance which keeps them engaged with learning materials.

Type or Paradigm of Programmed Instruction

Since the early stage of the development of program instruction, various types of programmed instruction have been developed in the context of the versatility of theoretical assumption. Voluminous research has been conducted in the field of programmed instruction:

- Linear or Extrinsic Programming
- Branching Programming/Branching Sequences
- Rule/Egrule System of Programming
- Mathetics
- Computer-Assisted Instruction (CAI)
- Learner-Controlled Instruction (LCI)

Linear or Extrinsic Programming

B. F Skinner was the proponent of the extrinsic program. This is based on B. F. Skinner's "Operant Conditioning" theory. Skinner proposed linear programming on the assumption that human behavior can be conditioned or shaped by providing suitable and step-by-step reinforcement for each desired response. This style of programming is also called the Skinnerian style of programming. It was proposed by Skinner that a "certain direction can be given to human behavior". In this approach, instructions are provided by breaking down the content material into several steps, called a frame. A linear program is also called a straight-line program, because, hereby the design has some protocol that the learner has to start with his initial behavior and end with terminal behaviors following a straight-line sequence. But the student had the liberty to work with the program at his/her own pace. Furthermore, in a linear programmed approach learners can receive knowledge of the result (right or wrong) immediately after the response. Here one crucial aspect that needs to be taken into consideration for designing a linear program is that arrangement of frames should be systematic and linear. The linear program is also called an extrinsic program because it can be extrinsically controlled by the programmer itself.

The basic formula of Liner programming is: **S, -^ R, ^ KR, ^ S, ^ R, -> KR**
Where: S – Stimulus, R – Response, and KR –Knowledge of Result

Characteristics of a Linear or Extrinsic Programming

A small amount of information: One of the basic characteristics of linear programming is that it is exposed to a small amount of information at a time. The whole learning process goes from one frame to the next in a systematic way.

Immediate knowledge of response: In linear programming, the result of the response is given to the learner immediately.

Self-paced: Linear program is solely based on its own pace or self-paced approach, where the learner can learn based on his/her level of capability or pace.

Features of a Linear or Extrinsic Programming

Straight-line approach: In linear programming, a learner needs to go forward from one frame to another in a straight line. Generally, in linear programming, the whole information of learning content is broken into small segments called frames. A frame can consist of 45–50 words in length. A learner needs to go forward from one frame to another in a straight-line manner to achieve the learning objective.

Controlled responses: In linear programming, the program designer pre-sets the response and its order. A learner has no freedom to answer in his way. Besides, in a linear program response of the learner is very crucial because to achieve the learning objective learner needs to answer each frame in order.

Immediate feedback: In a linear program a learner, after responding to one frame, can immediately compare his/her answer to the correct response of the program. Therefore, a learner can get immediate knowledge of the result regarding the correctness of the given responses.

Prompt: Another important feature of a linear program is the applicability of prompts. If required, in the beginning, a prompt or cue can be provided to facilitate the learning process.

Fundamental principles of a linear or extrinsic programming

Logical order: In the linear programming style each frame is designed or presented in logical order so the learner can go forward systematically without missing any frame or without mistakes.

Limitations of a Linear or extrinsic Programming

Lack of freedom of choice: In a linear program, programs are controlled, so, the choice of a learner is limited in nature. Therefore, the creativity of learners is not flourished in this process.

Guessing: In this style of programming another limitation is learners can guess some of the answers by using cues or prompts. This is one of the limitations of a fair evaluation to measure the achievement of learning objectives.

Limited student and teacher contract: Since linear programming is a personalized learning process, therefore, students' and teachers' communication or relationship are limited.

Lack of convergent thinking: In linear programmed-based learning, there is limited scope for the performance of students concerning differentiation among the answers; therefore, in this learning process this can act as a hindrance in the convergent thinking process of a learner.

The limited scope of applicability: Linear programs cannot be effectively applied in all areas of subject matter. It can only be an effective approach where the behavior is measurable as well as observable. For instance, science or math subjects commonly have more scope for practical observation.

Time-consuming: The subject matter is in small steps therefore, it takes a lot of time to complete one subject matter.

Branching Programming/Branching Sequences

Branching programming or branching sequences are based on the configuration theory of learning. This is a unique style of programming, proposed by Norman A Crowder; therefore, it is also called the Crowderian model of programming. This is based on a stimulus-centric and problem-solving approach in a learning process. The term "Branching" denotes a subdivision of stem or trunk. Simply, branching programming processes the whole subject matter sequence into small frames followed by multiple-choice questions, and by providing the right answer the student can get reinforcement or rewards in response to a correct response and goes to the next frame otherwise the learner goes through a remedial frame where a learner can know the right answer with additional explanation and after that can go back to the mainframe.

This is a concept similar to the trunk of a tree. Here the overall content of a subject matter is subdivided into a smaller concept like a stem of a tree. It is also called the "intrinsic" style of programming because the learner can decide according to his/her background of the subject. Cowder has defined a branching program as "a program which adapts to the needs of the student without the medium of an extrinsic device such as a computer". this programming is based on assumption that the needs of the student are different so the instructional material should be different so that the learner student can learn from his/her error. Branching program is different from linear programming in many ways one of the major differences is students can follow uniformly the same sequence of frames irrespective of their background of the subject. Generally, a branching program consists of two types of frames, such as a content frame and a remedial frame. The content frame includes repeating student responses, positive confirmation, new information, questions, etc. Besides, a remedial frame includes repeating the response of students, alert regarding negative confirmation, explanations regarding wrong, further explanation of correct response, direction regarding going to the required frame, etc.

Limitation of Branching Program

Guessing: In a branching program, one of the major limitations is learners can guess the possible answer without having proper knowledge of the subject matter.

Confusion: Since in a branching program infinite branch can be created, learners can be confused or face difficulty understanding the total number of branches.

Costly: Compared to a linear program, the preparation of a branching program is costly.

Rule/Egrule System of Programming

This style of programming mainly is based on a deductive and inductive approach to teaching. Here some specific examples or rules are being used as a stimulus in respect of imperfect rules. Homme and Glaser are the first proponents of the "rule" system of programming.

Mathetics

The term "mathetics" originated from the Greek word "mathein" which means to "learn". This is based on two distinct types of programming processes one is based on subject material and another is the programming of behavior. Mathetics is based on the realization of objectives through performance. Dr. F. Gilbert first developed the mathetics type of programming. He defined it as "mathetics is the systematic application of reinforcement theory for analysis and reconstruction of those complex behavior usually known as subject matter mastery, knowledge, and skills". Mathetics, if applied diligently, produces teaching material that exceeds the efficiency of lessons produced by any known method.

Computer-Assisted Instruction (CAI)

Computer-assisted instruction is a newly introduced program learning style. As program learning is personalized instruction so there is a need for a device where a massive amount of information or learning materials can be stored and retrieved flexibly. Since the revolution of the personal computer, it has been used for learning purposes in many ways, one of which is program instruction. In this style of program instruction, a computer is used to present the learning materials and instruction to the learner. Here the computer is used as a tutorial machine to present the instructional material and monitor learning.

Learner-Controlled Instruction (LCI)

Learner-controlled instruction or LCI was propagated and proposed by Mager (1962). The fundamental aspect of LCI is that the whole teaching-learning is controlled by the learner itself. In conventional teaching, a teacher is one of the major aspects who control the entire teaching-learning environment. In linear programming, it is the designer, developer, or teacher who prefixes the path of learning. However, LCI is a breakthrough in this rigid teacher-based learning path. In this learning process, the learner has the freedom to choose his learning pathway and use his/her learning resources as well as learning sequences to create a comfortable learning environment.

Development of Program Material

In the previous section, attempts were made to acquire a brief knowledge of programmed learning and its function. Now this section is going to discuss how a teacher or instructor can develop an effective programmed learning material (PLM). The following phases are used to develop an effective PLM.

Phase One: Preparation Phase

The first stage is the preparation stage. This is an initial but important stage in the context of writing a program instruction. The vital aspects that need to be defined or organized in this stage to develop effective programmed instructions are as follows:

1. Analysis of the course content
2. Behavior specification
    - Terminal behavior

- Entering behaviors and target population
- Criterion test
3. Task analysis
4. Programming style, presentation format, response mode

1. **Analysis of the course content**

    In the initial stage of preparation of programmed instruction, the designer or developer needs to consider in-depth analysis of course content. Suppose one wishes to prepare course content on the "solar system" for a 10th-grade geography class and the learning objective is to develop theoretical and conceptual knowledge about the solar system in the context of day-to-day knowledge, then the developer needs to arrange the course unit in some required sequential order. The arrangement of the unit sequence will be based on the learning objective. Furthermore, a flow chart needs to be developed based on the presentation of content. The following are the six conceptual aspects of sequencing for any content material:

    - The concept and theory of evaluation
    - Taxonomy of educational objective
    - Technique of evaluation
    - Types of questions
    - Acquaintance with tools of evaluation
    - Unit test

2. **Behavior specification**

    In the preparation stage, another vital aspect is the specifications of behavior. That can be conducted through the following three steps:

    - **Terminal behavior**: This is the initial step of behavior specifications. In this stage, the major aim is to specify the purpose and objectives of learning that needs to be achieved in a specific learning context. Generally, in a learning environment the "end product" is the behavior of the student. Glaser and Resnick (1972) defined "terminal behavior" as "a specific performance that a student should display at the end of specific instructional situations". Terminal behavior is a kind of roadmap of learning objectives that a student needs to acquire in a process of specific learning scenarios. The effective design of programmed instruction depends on the skillful description of terminal behavior and how students should acquire this behavior.
    - **Entering behavior and target population**: Entering behavior refers to the assumption regarding certain behavior of the learner before providing the learning material. Besides, the target population is a specific learner community for whom the course material is to be developed. Decacco (1970) explained that "entering behavior is the present status of the student's knowledge and skill about a future status the teacher wants him to take". The developer needs to be careful about effectively formulating entering behavior which can help in the feasibility and accuracy of the terminal behavior. In programmed learning the major objective of learning is to move the student forward from entering behavior to terminal behavior.
    - **Criterion test**: Pipe (1965) says a criterion test "helps to sharpen the objectives and the pre-requisite skill does a great deal in showing how to approach the subject-matter when programming starts". The major aim of the criterion test is to find out the achievement of the pre-specified terminal behavior of the learner. One of the basic advantages of this test is to get feedback regarding the pros and cons of the present program for further development.

3. **Task analysis**

   Task analysis is another important stage coming after the criterion test. Task analysis focuses on a methodological aspect, such as how a specific material is developed. In the previous discussion, one can understand that terminal behavior can be broken down into specific tasks. Task analysis refers to an in-depth analysis of students' behavior and activities during the time of the overall instructional process. It is also notable that task analysis is mainly based on terminal behavior formulated for the student.

Programming style, presentation format, and response mode

The next step after the task analysis is the specification of style, presentation format, and mode of response. That means in this stage the program designer will be primarily focused on the design of a specific style of programming, such as linear, branching, etc. Besides this, they will also focus on frame size, type of questions, selection of appropriate diagrams, tables, illustrations, etc.

Phase Two: Writing the Program

After the preparation of the overall basic outline of the design of the program, the next stage is writing it. The following steps are followed to write a program:

1. Writing frame
2. Prompts
3. The first draft of the program

Phase Three: Writing Frames

After following all the previous stages such as a specification of behavior, analysis of the task, and presentation format, it is time to write the program frames. Before writing a program, the frame designer should consider the following matters:

- Program writers should care about the use of wording. Ambiguous or complex words that are difficult to understand should be avoided.
- Program writers should be focused on the responses of the learner.
- The programmed frames should be challenging and stimulating in nature.
- Each frame needs to be structurally crafted so that it can increase the probability of success of the program.

Types of Programmed Frame

In the context of developing program instructions, another essential aspect is the development of programmed frames properly. Because the program frame is a pathway through which a learner can proceed from entering behaviors to terminal behavior. Margulies (1964) defined this as a "Frame presents a small unit of information, requires active responses and may be arranged to give immediate reinforcement". The following are some types of frames in programmed instruction:

1. Introductory frame
2. Teaching frame

3. Practice frame
4. Review frame
5. Criterion frame

Introductory frame: An introductory frame is generally, designed to provide information to learners regarding the overall introductory aspects of programmed instruction.

Teaching Frame: The teaching frame is generally used to provide new information or teaching material to the learner for a specific purpose. To develop an effective teaching frame, it is imperative to provide adequate prompts in a specific frame.

Practice frame: After learning new information, the practice frame repeatedly provides the same information to the learner to strengthen the taught material. In this frame, a student can make an unprompted response.

Review frame: Review frame is another essential aspect. The design of the review frame is focused on two contexts; one is for reviewing the learned concept and the second is for making interconnections between various concepts.

Criterion frame: The criterion frame is basically for the evaluation of a student's acquired knowledge. The criterion frame does make a judgment of how effective content has been learned by the student. Generally, the criterion frame is provided without prompts.

Design of Frame

In the context of designing a frame in programmed instruction, the designer must consider the following three components:

Stimulus: The designer must be focused on the availability of adequate stimulus in every frame to motivate learners effectively.

Response: Another essential component is the opportunity for the response of the learner.

Reinforcement: Reinforcement is another vital component that helps the responses of the learner as a programmer designed it. Therefore, the learner gets stimulated within specific aspects of learning.

Prompts in Programmed Instruction

Prompts are additional information for getting the required correct answers/responses from the student. For example, in a question of "what is the name of your country?" if the student is unable to give the right answer, the teacher can provide the first two letters of the answer as a formal prompt such as "IN" (if the student is from India). It is also noted that prompts can be provided in many ways.

In programmed learning, prompts play a very important role. Using prompts in a program-based teaching and learning process may reduce the error rate. Strategically, the use of prompts can increase the correct responses. Generally, prompts are the mechanism of improving stimulus control.

Classification of Prompts

As discussed earlier, prompts can be classified in various ways. Many researchers of programmed learning classify prompts in various ways. Some of the prompts are:

Formal prompts:

The formal prompt is very commonly used in the programmed learning process. In a formal prompt, a general indication is provided to get correct responses. The following is an example of a formal prompt:
"S—is the biggest star on the earth"

Response: SUN

Thematic prompt:

Thematic prompts are also called hints. It mainly provides general properties of prompting rather than an exact form. A thematic prompt is generally an indirect form of prompt. The following is an example of a thematic prompt:
"The sun gives us heat and _____"

Response: LIGHT

First Draft of a Program

After the analysis of the overall aspect of programmed learning, such as the specification of behavior and analysis of content based on program learning theories, the next step is the preparation of the first draft of the written program. In the first draft of a program, a designer needs to consider the development of appropriate frames, prompts, etc.

It is also notable that, after the development of the first draft of programmed learning needs to be evaluated in the context of its effectiveness and applicability. To evaluate any programmed learning generally two strategies are used for the evaluation of learning material. The first is developmental testing and the second is field testing.

In the developmental testing, the program material is drafted. After the development of the first draft of the program material, the next stage is field testing. Field testing is a more formal way to evaluate teaching and learning material. Through field testing of any program material, it is generally ensured whether the specifically developed learning material is appropriate to achieve the stated learning objectives.

Generally, the basic procedure of field testing is the application of written programmed material on students and analysis of students' responses through the proper scientific and statistical procedure.

Revision of the Final Draft

Based on the data obtained from the field testing, the designer or developer revises or restructures the student and finalizes the validation and application of programmed material.

Bibliography

DeCecco, J. P. (1968). *The psychology of language, thought, and instruction: Educational psychology*. Prentice-Hall.
Espich, J. E., & Williams, B. (1967). Developing programmed instructional materials, a handbook for program writers. ERIC Number: ED018142.
Feldman, J. & McPhee, D. (2007). *The Science of Learning and the Art of Teaching*, Delmar Cengage Learning; 1st edition
Gilbert, T. F. (1962). Mathetics: The technology of education. *Journal of Mathetics, 1*(1), 7–74.
Glaser, R., & Resnick, L. B. (1972). Instructional psychology. *Annual Review of Psychology, 23*(1), 207–276.

Leith, G. O. M., Curr, W., & Peel, E. A. (1966). *A handbook of programmed learning*. Birmingham: University of Birmingham.

Mager, R. F. (1962). Preparing instructional objectives. ERIC Number: ED018143.

Mager, R. F. (1964). Learner-controlled instruction-1958-1964. *Programmed Instruction, 4*(2), 1.

Markle, S. M. (1976). Evaluating instructional programs: How much is enough? *NSPI Journal, 15*(2), 1–5.

Pressey, S. L. (1927). A machine for automatic teaching of drill material. *School and Society, 25*, 549–552.

Skinner, B. F. (1954). *The science of learning and the art of teaching*. Harvard Educational Review (Harvard Education Publishing Group), 24, 86–97.

Smith, N. H. (1962). The teaching of elementary statistics by the conventional classroom method versus the method of programmed instruction. *Journal of Educational Research, 55*(9), 417–420.

Stolurow, L. M. (1965). *Computer-based instruction* (No. Tr-9). Illinois Univ Urbana Training Research Lab.

Suppes, P. (1968). Can There Be a Normative Philosophy of Education?, in G. L. Newsome Jr. (Ed.), *Philosophy of Education 1968, Studies in Philosophy and Education*. Southern Illinois University, Edwardsville, Ill., pp. 1–12

10
MODELS OF TEACHING

Teaching is a complex task. In the past, various researchers and educationists have developed various theories to enhance the teaching and learning process. Based on these theories, various teaching strategies have been developed. Generally, the strategies which were developed to achieve a specific instructional goal and enhance teaching and learning processes are called "models of teaching". The term "model" is used to mean the prototype of a specific real situation. This section is going to discuss "models of teaching", which is the current development of the teaching and learning process. This chapter is very important for the teachers, as well as a student. The knowledge of the teaching model, can help the educator to have applied extensive methodology for making a legitimate intelligent condition for learning. Various educationists and instructional designers have proposed various models of teaching strategies to deal with the barriers and obstacles in teaching.

Meaning and Definitions of Models of Teaching

- **Allen and Ryan (1969)** give the definition: "Modeling is an individual demonstrating particular pattern with the trainee through imitation".
- **B. K. Passi, L. C. Singh, and D. N. Sansanwal (1991)** define it as "A model of teaching consists of guidelines for designing educational activities and environments. Model of teaching is a plan that can also be utilized to shape courses of studies, to design instructional material and to guide instruction".
- According to **Joyce and Weil (1972)**, "Teaching of the model is a pattern or plan, which can be a curriculum or course to select instructional materials and to guide a teacher's actions".
- **Joyce and Weil (1972)** define models of teaching as "Teaching model as just instructional design. They describe the process of specifying and producing particular environmental situations which cause the student to interact in such a way that specific change occurs in his behavior".
- **Weil and Joyce (1978)** define teaching models as "A model of teaching consists of guideline for designing educational activities and environment. It specifies ways of teaching and learning that are intended to achieve certain kind of goals".

Paul D. et al. (1979) propose that "Models are prescriptive teaching strategies designed to accomplish particular instructional goals".

According to N. K. Jangira and A. Singh (1983), "A model of teaching is a set of interrelated components arranged in a sequence which provides guidelines to realize a specific goal. It helps in designing instructional activities and environmental facilities, carrying out of these activities and realization of the stipulated objectives".

Characteristics of Models of Teaching (MOT)

Encourages the teaching and learning process: We all know that teaching is a complex task and it involves various strategies and methods to successfully achieve the teaching-learning goal. In this context, the teaching model provides a design of a scientific learning environment to encourage an effective teaching-learning process.

Increases teaching competencies: Another essential characteristic of the model of teaching is the development of teachers' social competencies and style of instruction through various scientific guidelines. It also brings qualitative development of the teaching environment and the personal development of the teacher.

Considers individual differences: Every individual is unique. It is a very challenging task to maintain every individual in a specific teaching-learning scenario. Teaching design is based on the interests and abilities of students and emphasizes individual differences in the learning environment.

Designed to achieve a specific learning goal: Unlike various general teaching techniques, models of teaching are different in the context of the design and application of the scientific method to achieve specific learning objectives or goals.

Based on a specific philosophy of education: Every teaching strategy is based on various philosophical aspects of teaching. Hence, a model of teaching is also influenced by various philosophies and beliefs of teachers in the context of the teaching-learning process.

Systematic procedure: A model of teaching is a systematic procedure for providing instruction and organized design to the learner with an effort to modify students' behavior in a specific learning environment.

Step-by-step teaching-learning approach: In a model of teaching the whole learning design outcomes are based on behavior terms and then take a step-by-step approach to achieve learning objectives through a scientific design model.

Maximization of teaching: The model of teaching is a scientific procedure for providing instruction. Therefore, it increases the maximization of teaching by investing limited energy, time, and effort.

Specifications of Models of Teaching

Specification of learning outcome: As discussed previously models of teaching are a scientific approach to the teaching-learning process. Therefore, in the context of a specific design specification, a model of teaching provides an explicit outline or specification that a student should learn or perform after the completion of a specific instructional sequence.

Specification of teaching-learning environment: The model of teaching generally specifies an ideal condition of teaching where student response should be observed.

Specification of a criterion of performance: The model of teaching specifies the criteria of teacher performance and the method of instructional design in terms of acceptance of students.

Specification of operation: The model of teaching generally specifies a mechanism of operation that can increase the reaction of students as well as interaction with the environment.

Specification of a scientific procedure: The model of teaching is a systematic and scientific procedure to modify the behavior of the learner. This is an organized approach rather than a haphazard combination of facts.

Assumptions of a Model of Teaching

The existing literature exposes the following assumptions of the teaching model:

- The first and foremost assumption is mainly based on a basic aspect of learning, which is the creation of an environment. It believes that a specific and effective teaching-learning environment can only bring a desirable change in student behavior.
- Another major assumption in the context of a teaching model is that effective teaching-learning involves a lot of individual factors. Therefore, creating an effective learning environment requires a specific teaching model that nurtures as well as controls every single aspect to make teaching-learning effective.
- It also believes that the effective design of instruction and the competency of the teacher can increase the interaction between students and teachers.
- It also assumes that a specific design or model of teaching can increase the physical and social efficiency of a teacher as well as a student.
- Another basic assumption in the context of a teaching model is that effective utilization of teaching elements can bring desirable changes in student behavior.
- It is also assumed that the teaching model can make the teaching experience more effective, engaging, and motivational.

Effects of a Model of Teaching

The previous discussion gives some basic knowledge that teaching by modeling helps students achieve their desired goal of implementing various scientific strategies in the teaching-learning process. Through a model of teaching, students can get a positive impact on how they process information, their way of thinking, their acquisitions of skills, etc. In a general view, it can be said that modeling increases the capability of the learner by providing necessary knowledge and skills through a mastery-learning process. This section intends to provide a basic overview of the effects of modeling on teaching as discussed by various eminent researchers based on their research work. These are the following:

Views of Joyce and Weil

Joyce and Weil in their research work discussed two types of effects of teaching by modeling, which are as follows:

- **Instructional effect**: This is mainly focused on the activities of learning. As per the view of Joyce and Weil, an instructional effect is a more direct effect on a specific teaching model which is mostly based on the development of content and skill of a student.
- **Nurturant effect**: This is mostly an indirect effect of a teaching model as per the explanation given by Joyce and Weil. This is indirect in the sense that this effect is mostly based on the development of a learning environment.

Views of Bandura and Walters

Other eminent researchers, Bandura and Walters, discussed three types of effects in the context of teaching modeling, which are as follows:

- **Modeling effect**: The modeling effect mainly focuses on the acquiring of new kinds of response patterns in students. For instance, when a teacher demonstrates to the student how to read a passage effectively, through this learning process the student acquires a new pattern of behavior of reading a passage or rhymes.
- **Inhibitory and disinhibitory effect**: Here learners increase or decrease the frequency of their responses compared to the entry-level behavior.
- **Eliciting effect**: Learners receive various cues for realizing a response.

Families of Models of Teaching

As discussed earlier, every teaching model has its own style and structure to attain a specific learning objective. That is a teacher or administrator, who needs to find out the specific objective of any specific teaching-learning scenario and needs to choose an appropriate type of model for the benefit of students. Through a comprehensive review of all the teaching models, eminent researchers Joyce and Weil (1980) have identified 23 teaching models. These 23 models are divided into four basic and distinct categories of families based on their nature, structure, and process. The following are the four families of models of teaching:

- Information Processing Model
- Personal Model
- Social Interaction Model
- Behavior Modification Model

Information Processing Model

The information processing model mostly focuses on the intellectual capacity and skill of the learner. This model mostly focuses on the mastery of information, organization of information, the building of information, test hypotheses, etc. The following are some of the primary purposes of the information processing model:

- Mastery over the acquisition of information.
- Mastery over academic concepts and facts.
- Development of intellectual skills of the learners to increase the ability to think more logically.
- Information processing models mostly focus on inductive thinking, concept attainment, advance organizer, etc.

The following is a list of the information processing family:

- Concept Attainment Model
- Inductive Thinking Model
- Inquiry Training Model
- Advance Organizer Model

- Memory Model
- Cognitive Development Model
- Biological Science Inquiry Model

Personal Models

This family mostly focuses on the personal development of the student. The personal model is all about the focus on the personalization of the teaching and learning process where the major objective of any teaching-learning process is the development of confidence, competence, and self-realization (educating themselves on their own). A personal model of teaching is effective to develop the creativity and self-expression of learners. The following are some of the basic goals of this model of teaching:

- Increase the self-expression and self-worth of a learner.
- Increase the ability of self-understanding of students.
- Increase the emotional aspect of a learner in the context of their behavior and way of learning.
- Help to increase the competence of the student based on their developed plan.
- Increase the creativity and openness of learners.

The following is a list of personal models:

- Non-Directive Teaching Model
- Synthetics Model
- Awareness Training Model
- Classroom Meeting Model

Social Interaction Model

The social interaction model of teaching emphasizes the development of the interpersonal relationship capability of the learners. The primary goal of this model is to develop appropriate social skills for the learner to successfully survive in society. This model of teaching mainly focuses on collaboration, cooperation, and problem-solving skill based on the social aspect. The following are some of the primary objectives of the social interaction model:

- Increase the skill of collaboration and cooperation of the learner.
- To develop the value of social relationships and personal relationships.
- Increase personal and social values.

The following are some of the social interaction models:

- Group Investigation model
- Role-Playing Model
- Jurisprudential Inquiry Model
- Laboratory Training Model
- Social Simulation Model
- Social Inquiry Model

Behavior Modification Model

One of the major goals of the behavioral modification model is to manipulate the stimulus and reinforcement to shape the behavior of a learner. Generally, the behavior modification model emphasizes changing learner behavior. The following are some of the basic models belonging to the family of behavior modification:

- Contingency Management Model
- Self-Control Model
- Training Model
- Stress Reduction Model
- Desensitization Model
- Assertiveness Training Models

Fundamental Elements of a Teaching Model

After the previous discussion, one gets a view that every model of teaching has its definite structure. Joyce, Will, and Calhoun in their book *Model of Teaching* (Pearson 2014, 9th edition) discuss six essential and common elements in the context of the teaching model. They are the following:

- Focus
- Syntax
- Principles of Reaction
- The Social System
- Support System
- Application and Effects

Focus

Focus is the pivotal aspect of any teaching model. It mainly constitutes the objective of teaching and the environment of teaching. As shown, every teaching-learning process takes one specific objective or multiple objectives into consideration as its focal point. For example, a master teaching model developed by Madeline Hunter focuses on presenting the learning material with strict control and in a repetitive manner so that a learner can get an opportunity to optimize knowledge of the content and learn the concept most effectively. In a cooperative learning model, a major focus is on social interaction, peer communication, and a collaborative learning approach to learning new things. It is very important to know that every teaching model is different from the other models based on its learning objectives, therefore the focus is on any teaching model which deals with the objective of any process.

Syntax

Syntax is an active part of any teaching model. It involves the sequential steps or organization of any teaching-learning scenario scientifically. Each model has a distinct syntax through which the overall teaching activities and interaction between student and teacher can be determined. Therefore, it can be said that syntax is a design part of any teaching model which defines patterns of specific teaching strategies, the interaction between student and teacher, specific teaching activities, etc., to achieve the objective of any teaching-learning process defined as a focal part in a teaching model. Unlike the focal element of a teaching model, syntax is also different from the teaching model as it permits functions.

Principle of Reaction

A principle of reaction mainly describes the reaction and response of the teacher to the learner in a specific learning scenario. This is a guideline or rule of thumb for the teacher regarding responding to the student appropriately.

The Social System

This is mainly focused on the interpersonal relationship between student and teacher. The social system as an element of any teaching model mainly focuses on the interaction between student and teacher as well as their mutual relationship. The social system provides the norm to the teacher in the context of observing student behavior in specific activities of the student. The social system, distinct from one model to another is based on their learning objectives. For example, in some models teachers have to play a dominant role or use autocratic behavior during a teaching process, on the other hand, some models are more flexible and student-centric, and the whole activity is equally distributed to every student differently. In any teaching model the so-called "social system" is based on the assumption that every classroom is a miniature of society. In a teaching model, the social system also discusses the motivational strategy for the student.

Support System

Generally, the term "support" refers to additional requirements except for human capacity and technical facilities. A teaching model's support system includes special skills and knowledge of the teacher or other special equipment or technological devices to enhance the learning process which could be audiovisual devices, computers, various teaching aids, projectors, films, laboratory kits, etc.

Application and Effect

This is another crucial element in a teaching model. It mainly focuses on the application of any change in behavior of the student in another situation. For example, in any teaching-learning process, students learn how to interact with other peers, how to emotionally respond in a specific situation, how to socially interact with the teacher, various physical movements, etc. The application and effect element of any teaching model is designed in a way so that a student can transfer or apply learned changes to other situations and experiences.

Concept Attainment Model of Teaching (CAM)

The CAM is one of the most popular and commonly used models of teaching. The main points of the model are indicated in Table 10.1

Advantages of Models of Teaching

Development of social as well as individual abilities: The teaching model is intended to increase the efficiency of the teaching approach in order to achieve the desired change in

Table 10.1 Concept Attainment Model of Teaching

Family	Information Processing Model
Major Theorist	Jerome Bruner
Major objective	In a general way, the concept attainment model aims to enhance the thinking skill of a learner. This model is not intended to form a new concept for the learner but rather encourages the learners to analyze positive and negative examples of any concept which is already formed by someone.
What is the concept?	The concept is a mental representation of some objects or experiences. The followings are some of the definitions of the concept: **According to Bruner**, "a concept is mental imagery of a category of objects, which share common characteristics which distinguish these objects from other objects". **According to Archer (1969)**, "a concept is simply the label of a set of things that have something in common. A concept is different from a fact, a principle and generalization".

Various elements of a concept	As per the Concept Attainment Model, each concept consisted of a set of elements and a learner needs to identify and learn each element separately to create a mental representation of a concept. The following are the set of elements:
	• **Name**: Name is a term or level given to a particular category of objects. For instance, tiger, lion, and elephant are a separate set of labels for specific animals.
	• **Attribution**: Attribution is a characteristic of a particular concept. Attribution is two types:
	  1. *Essential attributes*: are common features or characteristics of a concept.
	  2. *Non-essential attributes*: refers to a slight difference among examples of a category.
	• **Attribution value**: This means a degree of attribution for a specific example.
	• **Example**: Example is a very essential element in the context of the CAM model. Bruner has discussed two types of exemplars:
	  1. *Positive exemplars*: are a set of examples that contain all the essential attributes of any concept.
	  2. *Negative exemplars*: when in a specific concept one or more essential attributes are absent.
	• **Rule/Definition**: Rule or definition is the last essential element of concepts. The definition is a statement specifying the concept. It helps to summarize the finding of the search for attributes.

Types of concepts	Bruner has described three types of concepts: • **Conjunctive concept**: Joint presence of several attributes. • **Disjunctive concept**: Presence of some attributes and absence of others. • **Relational concept**: Relational concepts have several attributes but these bear some kind of relationship toone another (Weil & Joyce, 1978).
Variations in CAM model	Bruner and his colleagues discussed three types of CAM models those are the following: • **Reception-oriented CAM**: The major aspect of the reception-oriented CAM is the function of student work as the reception of information rather than playing an active role in an overall teaching-learning process. On the other hand, the teacher plays a more active and dominant role in the context of the overall teaching and learning process. • **Selection-oriented CAM**: The major assumption of selection-oriented CAM is an example that cannot be labeled without question asking whether it is a "Yes" or "No". In this context, students control the sequence of the examples. This model is more flexible in the sense that, here the responsibility of concept attainment and attribute tracking is in the hands of the student and students control the sequence of the example.

(Continued)

Table 10.1 Continued

	• **Unorganized material model**: Unorganized material model mostly focuses on group activities. In this context, the role of a teacher is to encourage and facilitate group discussion and group activities to develop a concept in a material.
Syntax of CAM	Generally, the syntax of the reception model of CAM can be divided into three distinct phases. These are the following: 1. **Phase 1: Presentation of data and identification of a concept** In the first phase, a teacher presents various data to the student for the identification of a concept through examples and non-examples: • The teacher presents labeled examples. • The student compares attributes of positive and negative examples. • The student generates and tests the hypothesis. • Students state a definition according to the essential attributes. 2. **Phase 2: Testing attainment of the concept** In this stage, the teacher is intended to test or evaluate how much a student has attained a concept. The following are some of the strategies: • Students identify additional unlabeled examples as yes or no. • Teachers confirm hypotheses, names concept, and restate definitions according to essential attributes. • Students generate examples. 3. **Phase 3: Analysis of thinking strategies** • Here students describe their thoughts. • The student discusses the role of hypothesis and attributes. • The student discusses the type and number of hypotheses.
Social system	As per the social system, the context CAM model is moderately or highly structured. Initially, the teacher plays a more active role in the selection of concepts, organizing and sequencing data, sequences of examples, etc. On the other hand, student interaction is also encouraged.
Principles of reaction	Generally, in the CAM model a teacher functions in three major aspects; record, prompt and present additional data. • At the initial stage, the teacher supports the hypothesis formulated by students. • In the context of testing hypotheses, the teacher plays a vital role to help students testify their formulated hypotheses. • The thinking strategies of students are discussed and evaluated with the assistance of a teacher.
Support system	• Creative and innovative environment for attaining concepts. • Flashcards, blackboard, and other required material. • Selection, observation, and formulation of hypothesis.
Instructional and nurturant effect	**Instructional effect** • To find out and understand the characteristics of a specific concept • Improved concept through building strategies • Inductive reasoning **Nurturant effect** • Logical reasoning in communication • Tolerance of ambiguity • Awareness of alternative perspectives

the behavior of students or learners. To do so the teaching model utilizes social efficiency, personal ability, cognitive ability, and behavioral aspect of students by applying a scientific design.
- **Establishment of teaching and learning relationship**: The teaching model emphasizes the building of an adequate relationship between teaching and learning empirically, which in turn helps to create a teaching-learning environment more effectively as well as efficiently for the teacher.
- **Desirable change in student behavior**: The model of teaching mainly focuses on the design aspect of teaching-learning scenarios by using various scientific technology. Therefore, it helps in bringing about a desirable change in the behavior of the learner.
- **A new model of innovation**: In every situation, the teaching model encourages the development of innovative teaching strategies, methods, processes, tactics, etc., which helps to create a teaching environment more motivating and attractive to the student.
- **Help to the formation of theories**: The teaching model encourages establishing various theoretical foundations of teaching and learning to increase the efficiency of the teaching-learning environment.
- **Encourages creating effective teaching-learning material**: As the teaching model always focuses on the development of various innovative approaches in a teaching-learning process, it creates effective teaching-learning material to utilize the educational scenario for the benefit of the student.
- **Curriculum planning and development of learning material**: The model of teaching provides a scientific guideline to develop a specific course of study and based on the curriculum it also helps to design scientific learning materials to achieve a desired change in students' behavior.
- **Helps to create an effective teaching-learning environment**: In a specific teaching-learning scenario one of the most important aspects is the creation of an effective learning environment for the student. A teaching model is a unique approach that provides a specific guideline for developing a teaching environment that is most beneficial for the student.

Bibliography

Eggen, P. D., Kauchak, D. P., & Harder, R. J. (1979). *Strategies for teachers: Information processing models in the classroom*. Englewood Cliffs, NJ: Prentice-Hall.

Hyman, R. T. (1970). *Ways of teaching*. New York: J.B. Lippincott Company.

Joyce, B., & Weil, M. (1972). *Models of teaching model*. Boston, MA: A Liyn dan Bacon.

Joyce, B., Weil, M., & Calhoun, E. (2008). *Models of teaching* (8th ed.). Englewood Cliffs, NJ: Prentice-Hall. (there is now a 9th, 2014 edition).

Joyce, B.R. & Marsha Weil, M. (1980). *Models of teaching, Prentice-Hall, 1980 - Educational innovations*

Kauchak, D. P., & Eggen, P. D. (1998). *Learning and teaching: Research-based methods*. Needham Heights, MA: Allyn and Bacon.

Miller, J. P. (1988). *The holistic curriculum*. Toronto, ON: The Ontario Institute for Studies in Education (OISE Press).

Miller, J. P., Cassie, B. J. R., & Drake, S. M. (1990). *Holistic learning: A teacher's guide to integrated studies*. Toronto, ON: The Ontario Institute for Studies in Education (OISE Press).

Passi, B. K., Singh, L. C., & Sansanwal, D. N. (1991). Models of teaching: Report of the three-phased study of CAM and ITM. *Independent Study. National Council of Educational Research and Training*, New Delhi.

Weil, M., & Joyce, B. R. (1978). *Information processing models of teaching*. Englewood Cliffs, NJ: Prentice-Hall.

11
COOPERATIVE LEARNING

Introduction

Cooperation is one of the oldest survival strategies since time immemorial. From the stone age to the present information age, the history of human progress is the history of cooperativeness between humans. In the stone age, humans were helpless when encountering predatory animals, they used cooperation as a survival strategy. In the present information age and the scientific revolution, the need for cooperation and interaction to confront future challenges for progress has also become imperative.

However, the present education system is neglecting interaction or cooperation between students. Instead, it is encouraging individualism, competitiveness, and an authoritative knowledge flow from teacher to student. In the education sector, more and more training is provided to the teacher on how to increase interactions between student and content and teacher and student, but the importance of student-to-student interaction is ignored. Consequentially, the present education system majorly focuses on the comparativeness of students to achieve the highest grades, credentials, and appreciation compared to other students, but "cooperative learning" is another educational approach aimed to encourage students more in group-based learning rather than individual learning. The next section will discuss in more detail cooperative learning and its features.

Meaning and Definitions of Cooperative Learning

Did you ever participate in school programs or festivals where you had to take responsibility or work with a team member to successfully achieve the goal? If so, then it would not be very wrong if it is said that you just have to share some knowledge or gather some knowledge from your team member or groups. In the teaching-learning environment, it is called "cooperative learning".

Cooperative learning is an adjective term used to describe working or acting together to achieve a common goal. Cooperative learning is a unique teaching strategy where each student is interdependent with others and works with a team or group to achieve some learning objective. However, in this learning environment, each member of the group is not only responsible for their learning but also for their teammates to create and achieve a cooperative relationship between each group as well as members.

Various researchers define cooperative learning differently. The following are some definitions:

Siegel (2005): "Cooperative learning is an educational situation where learning occurs while two or more students are working together to complete a common task".

Jacobs, Power, and Loh (2002): Cooperative learning is "principles and techniques for helping students work together more effectively".

Johnson and Johnson (1999): Cooperative learning is "[T]he instructional use of small group so that student work together to maximize their own and each other's learning".

Milis (1996): Cooperative learning is a "generic term used to describe a situation where students work together in small groups to help themselves and others to learn".

Slavin (1994): Cooperative learning is an "instructional program in which students work in small groups to help one another master academic content".

From the above definitions, we can see that cooperative learning involves learning strategies used to work together. In cooperative learning, a student is given a task or assignment and encouraged to achieve the task by working with a team. However, each member of a team is responsible for success and achievement. Therefore, the whole learning environment perpetuates friendliness rather than competition. Mainly, in this learning environment students also learn how to take responsibility for their own-self as well as team members and how to work as a part of a team. Figure 11.1 presents a graphical representation of a cooperative learning environment.

Historical Overview of Cooperative Learning

Cooperative learning is not a new concept. Various social theorists such as Alport, Watson, and Shaw have initiated a movement toward cooperativeness in the teaching-learning environment. However, they believed that group work is more effective and productive compared to individual work. Besides, May and Doob (1937) from their research found that cooperation has helped to achieve the desired goal and more successfully attained the outcome compared to the individualistic approach. They further explained that the individualistic approach more implicates competitive behavior.

Early philosophers and psychologists such as John Dewey and Kurt Lewin in the period 1930–1940 also realized the potentiality of cooperative learning in a way that it could enhance the competence and knowledge of the student to effectively encounter the environment or society outside the classroom. They also believed that a cooperative learning environment would be an effective approach to achieving democratization in education.

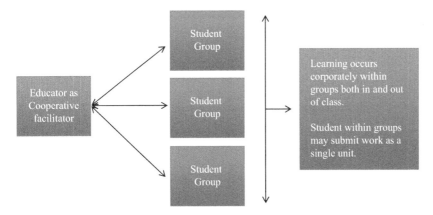

Figure 11.1 Co-operative learning environment. Source: Adapted from Roberts (2004).

However, the strategic movement of the cooperative learning approach took place as a protest against the competitive approach in American schools by James Coleman. In his book, *The Adolescent Society: The Social Life of the Teenager and its Impact on Education* (Coleman, 1961), Coleman envisioned competition as a negative approach to education. Coleman was involved in various empirical scientific studies on cooperative learning. One of the studies was conducted in the school of the Midwest, a two-year study at high schools where Coleman develops two unique conceptions called "climate of value" and "adolescent society". Coleman in his research findings shows that a competitive environment in an academic setting hinders the natural process of learning. He suggested that the school environment should maintain a cooperative approach to teaching-learning.

From the 1970s onward, the field of cooperative learning was enriched by David and Roger Johnson. In 1975 they established the fact that cooperative learning enhances mutual linking, a way of communication, a thinking process, high acceptance, and support among individuals in the group (Johnson and Johnson, 1975). However, he also showed that a more competitive environment caused a lack of interaction and trust with other students in the classroom.

Apart from that, Daniel Holt, Barbara Chips, and Diane Wallace (1991) found in their research that the cooperative learning environment indeed benefited enriching learning linguistically in culturally diverse backgrounds.

Another researcher Robert Slavin (1994) conducted a series of research studies based on cooperative learning. Slavin, in his research, realized the potential of cooperative learning. He also was optimistic toward cooperative learning for "the developmental characteristics of adolescents to harness their peer orientation, enthusiasm, activity, and craving for independence within the same structure". However, Slavin also suggested the following three fundamental features of the cooperative learning environment:

- In the cooperative learning environment, the reward has to be provided to the entire team but needs to be graded individually.
- Team success must be based on the performance of all students not the individual performance of one student. All team members must be involved in helping each other to achieve the learning objective. Success needs to be defined as a combinational effort of all team members.
- Students are expected to improve based on their previous performance to ensure that all students are challenged to do their best (Slavin, 1994).

At the same time as Slavin's research, Johnson and Johnson (1994) published a framework of five elements which are the most important in groups based on a cooperative teaching and learning environment. The details of these elements are discussed in the following section.

Elements of Cooperative Learning

This section will discuss some elements of a cooperative learning environment. However, Kotsopoulos (2010) posits that the implementation of cooperative learning strategies may vary, but some basic elements need to be constant such as social accountability, positive interdependence, and individual, as well as group, accountability, etc. (Kotsopoulos, 2010; Leikin and Zaslavsky, 1999; Walmsley and Muniz, 2003). Johnson, Johnson, and Smith's (1991) book "Active Learning: Cooperation in the College Classroom" outlined some of the elements of cooperative learning. They are as follows:

Table 11.1 Timeline on the history of cooperative learning

Period	Pioneers and their work in the field of Cooperative learning
Before World War II	
1990	John Dewey, Kurt Lewin, Jean Piaget, Lev Vygotsky
The 1960s onward	
The 1960s	Stuart Cook: Research on Cooperation
	Madsen (Kagan): Research on Cooperation and Competition in Children
	Bruner, Suchman: Inquiry (Discovery) Learning Movement:
	B. F. Skinner: Programmed Learning, Behavior Modification
1962s	Morton Deutsch (Nebraska Symposium): Cooperation and Trust, Conflict
	Robert Blake & Jane Mouton: Research on Intergroup Competition
1966–1969	David Johnson, U of MN: Begins training teachers in Cooperative Learning, Roger Johnson: Joins David at University of Minneapolis, Minnesota
The 1970s onward	
1970	David Johnson: Social Psychology of Education
1973	David DeVries and Keith Edwards: Combined Instructional Games Approach with Intergroup Competition, Teams-Games-Tournament
1974–1975	David and Roger Johnson: Research Review on Cooperation/Competition
	David and Roger Johnson: Learning Together and Alone
Mid-1970s	Annual Symposium at APA (David DeVries and Keith Edwards, David & Roger Johnson, Stuart Cook, Elliot Aronson, Elizabeth Cohen, others)
	Robert Slavin: Began Development of Cooperative Curricula
	Spencer Kagan: Continued Research on Cooperation Among Children
1976	Shlomo and Yael Sharan: Small Group Teaching (Group Investigation)
1978	Elliot Aronson: Jigsaw Classroom (Journal of Research & Development in Education, Cooperation Issue) Jeanne Gibbs: Tribes
The 1980s onward	
1981, 1983	David and Roger Johnson: Meta-Analyses of Research on Cooperation
1985	Elizabeth Cohen: Designing Group-work, Spencer Kagan: Developed Structures Approach to Cooperative Learning, AERA, and ASCD Special Interest Groups Founded
1989	David and Roger Johnson: Cooperation and Competition – Theory & Research
The 1990s onward	
Early 1990s	Cooperative Learning Gains Popularity among Educators
1996	First Annual Cooperative Learning Leadership Conference, Minneapolis

Social accountability: One of the prime elements of cooperative learning is social accountability. Social accountability refers to the concern about other group members, in respect of learning (Kotsopoulos, 2010). Maintaining social accountability needs a scope of an equal opportunity to communicate each member with others (Leikin and Zaslavsky, 1999). Therefore, the major concern should be interpersonal communication, trust, and conflict resolution (Walmsley and Muniz, 2003). For example, in classroom settings students are needed to collaborate with other members to make a specific contribution and to achieve learning objectives (Jansen, 2012).

Positive interdependence: In a basic conception positive interdependence refers to trust or reliance on other members of the group (Walmsley and Muniz, 2003). Positive interdependence is another important characteristic of cooperative learning that "one student's success helps another to be successful" (Slavin, 1980, p. 316).

Individual accountability: Individual accountability refers to each member of the group being personally responsible for doing their share of the work (Kotsopoulos, 2010), which is another characteristic of cooperative learning. To engage in individual accountability, each student of the group must be aware of the fact that "what they are learning will be needed or assessed in the future" (Slavin, 1980). However, Slavin (1980) refers to a high level of individual accountability as "individual quantifiable" and a low level of individual accountability as "substitutability". Slavin (1980) to explicit the importance of individual accountability said that group goals can be achieved without individual accountability but all the members of the group may not be able to participate.

Group rewards or accountability: Group rewards work as positive reinforcement in the cooperative learning environment. Group reward means the students' reason to work together (Kotsopoulos, 2010). In teaching-learning when a group reward is taken into consideration rather than an individual reward, students are more likely to care or be responsible for each other's success in the group (Walmsley and Muniz, 2003).

Face-to-face promotive interaction: Promotive interaction is an essential element of cooperative learning. The assigned task is needed to be given in a way that must encourage group interaction rather than individual interaction.

Collaborative skill: Collaborative skill needs an increase in student trust-building, leadership, decision-making, communication, and conflict management.

Heterogeneous Groups: Cooperative learning environments would be more effective in heterogeneous group settings.

To implement a cooperative learning environment in the teaching-learning scenarios these mentioned characteristics need to be taken into consideration. However, from all this, individual accountability and group accountability are the most crucial aspect.

Difference between Traditional and Cooperative Learning

In the previous section, we discussed cooperative learning and its characteristics and features. To gather more distinct knowledge on cooperative learning, we need to know the difference between cooperative learning and traditional learning concerning the characteristics, features, and application of both strategies.

Before discussing the distinction between two types of learning strategies, it is imperative to briefly discuss what exactly is traditional learning. Traditional learning can be characterized in various ways and it is varied in form; therefore, it is hard to provide one universal definition of traditional learning. However, one of the commonly used forms of traditional learning is one-way communication in the teaching-learning process such as a teacher or instructor providing the information to the student, and the student functioning as a passive receptor. Additionally, learning materials are provided in printed form. Therefore, communication in the traditional learning environment is limited to teacher-to-student and student-to-content material. Furthermore, there is no academic communication between students in a formal learning process. Figure 11.2 presents some graphical representations of a traditional learning environment.

Characteristics of Cooperative Learning

As discussed in the previous section the definition of cooperative learning varies and as noted there are some common features that differentiate the cooperative learning method from others. However, this section will discuss some common characteristics of cooperative learning. Though

Cooperative Learning

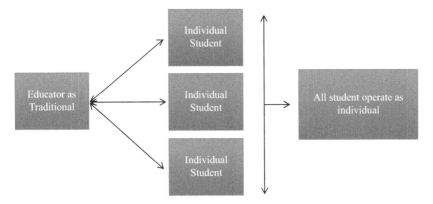

Figure 11.2 Traditional learning environments. Source: Adapted from Roberts (2004).

characteristics may vary with the various educational setting, the following basic characteristics will be shown for an effective cooperative learning environment:

Interdependence: One of the basic characteristics of a cooperative learning environment is "interdependency" such that all students feel like one unit in a group setting. There must be positive feelings and interaction among all the group members to produce or achieve some common goal. Mainly, a cooperative learning environment stimulates the student to work as a team and success together.

Accountability: Accountability is another major characteristic of cooperative learning. A cooperative learning environment provides a structure for social accountability, individual accountability, and group accountability through rubrics, teacher observation, peer evaluation, etc.

Shared leadership: Leadership in a cooperative learning environment is shared in nature. In the shared leadership role, students feel that they all are leaders and owners of the project.

Social and group work skill development: A cooperative learning environment is all about teamwork. Therefore, a major focus must be on the enhancement of student social and group work skills.

Direct involvement of teacher: A cooperative learning environment is all about group dynamics. Therefore, assessing students' work needs more direct teacher involvement, observation, and necessary intervention to ensure effective teamwork within each group.

Group evaluation: In a cooperative learning environment, it is imperative to evaluate how a group works together. A teacher will hand out an evaluation of students' performance after the completion of their assignment.

Types of Cooperative Learning

The cooperative learning environment is the most commonly used teaching strategy in a lab-based learning environment. The modern cooperative learning environment has three types as proposed by Johnson and Johnson, 1994. The three main types of cooperative learning environment as proposed by Johnson and Johnson (1994) are:

- Formal Cooperative Learning Environment
- Informal Cooperative Learning Environment
- The Cooperative Base Group

Table 11.2 Comparison between traditional learning and cooperative learning

Context of Comparison	Traditional Learning	Cooperative Learning
Aim of learning	Content-based knowledge acquisition.	Knowledge acquisition as well as learning the social skill, norms, and strategies of teamwork with fun.
Performance	Major focus is on individual performance.	Always encourages group performance.
Achievement or success	Students believe in self-success. Therefore, each group member competes with each other.	Student believes that they cannot achieve the desired goal unless other members of the group help or are involved.
Accomplishment	Rewards or positive reinforcement are given only for individual accomplishment.	Accomplishments are given based on group achievement as well as individual achievement.
Assignments	Learning material (better to say assignments), are needed to be solved only by commitment with participant self-activity.	Assignments are solved by a group activity, which assists, encourages, and supports other members.
Accountability	Mainly focuses on individual accountability.	Focus on accountability of both individuals as well as the group.
Leadership	One appointed leader.	Shared leadership.
Responsibility	One person takes all the responsibility and does all the work.	Distributed responsibility, teamwork skills, and leadership skills are major premises in the cooperative learning environment.
Interdependence	No interdependence.	Positive interdependence.
Evaluation of work	In a traditional learning environment, no assessments are given on each stage of individual work or for improving their work.	In cooperative learning environment students are given some time to analyze their work and for further strategies.
Group assignment	Student often chooses their group.	Teachers assign groups, based on heterogeneous principles.
Group members and observation	Rarely, groups are assigned that are large (8–10 members) and there is a lack of teacher observation and control.	Typically, small group (3-5 members). Teacher is observed and interaction is timely.

Formal Cooperative Learning Environment

The most widely used cooperative learning method is formal cooperative learning. Structurally, in a formal cooperative learning environment students work for one class period over several weeks to achieve the learning objective. In this environment, a student takes care in regards to sharing learning goals and jointly working to complete given assignments as well as decision-making, problem-solving, etc. (Johnson, Johnson, and Holubec, 1992, 1993). This is more structured in the sense that it maintains pre-instructional learning designs, setting of a task, group monitoring while working, specific evaluation, as well as intervention. Some of the specific procedures needed to be maintained for an effective formal cooperative learning environment are the specification of learning objectives, pre-instructional decisions, explicit explanation of the task, monitoring student learning, evaluation of students' learning, etc.

Informal Cooperative Learning Environment

In an informal cooperative learning environment, students are working together temporarily. Like a formal cooperative learning environment, here also there is a joint learning goal but it is temporary, the ad-hoc group lasts only from a few minutes to one class period (Johnson, Johnson, and Holubec, 1992). However, informal groups are useful to break lectures into small segments and executed through group activity. Besides, it is encouraging to engage students to focus on 3–5 minutes discussions and after that 2–3 minutes of turn-to-your-partner discussion. Though it is a small amount of time, "it will increase the amount of material retained by students as well as their comfort working with each other" (Johnson et al., 2006).

Cooperative base group

Basically, this third type of cooperative learning group is different compared to the other two in the sense that, cooperative base groups work for long-term such as a minimum of one semester up to several years with a stable membership (Johnson, Johnson, and Holubec, 1992). Because base group members have worked together for a long-term commitment, this group involves various complex works rather than just academic problem-solving. A cooperative base group member is attached to encourage and assist academic progress and helps to develop cognitively as well as socially in a healthy way. Cooperative base groups are long-term, heterogeneous cooperative learning groups with stable membership in which students provide support, encouragement, and assistance to each other to make academic progress by attending class, completing assignments, and learning assigned material. These tend to improve attendance, personalize the work required and the school experience, and improve the quality and quantity of learning (Johnson DW, Johnson RT, & Holubec EJ., 2013, 2018)

In this section, we have introduced various types of cooperative learning groups and their attributes. However, it is also imperative to know that, in one learning session teachers can use more than one type of approach. For instance, a teacher can use formal learning groups to project assignments and the same time informal learning groups during teaching time.

Purpose of Cooperative Learning

This section will elaborate on some specific purposes of the use of cooperative learning. Based on research in this field one can extract four pivotal purposes behind the use of cooperative learning in a scientific way such as:

To encourage more active learning: As one finds in the lecture-oriented learning strategies, students are mainly treated as passive recipients of the information. Therefore, the major purpose of a cooperative learning approach is to engage students more actively in the teaching-learning process. However, the cooperative learning environment is based on group learning strategies, it increases the group responsibility of individual learners, and students are actively engaged in learning a task. Previous research also found that students more actively participate in the teaching-learning process by getting actively involved in the teaching-learning, rather than just as a passive recipient of knowledge, as well as only observing or through the note-taking process.

To encourage more cooperation or a helping one another approach: Another more important purpose of cooperative learning is to teach students "how to help others" in the whole learning process. Cooperative learning is based on a "group achievement" approach rather than just "individual achievement". Therefore, the whole group is responsible for the achievement of others to fulfill the learning objective. It increases the "we" feeling of the learner rather than the "I".

To encourage student-to-student learning support: As previously discussed cooperative learning is a unique approach that encourages higher achiever learners to help the lower achiever. However, by this approach higher achiever students are more likely to reach out to other group members and communicate easily with other students than a teacher. With the help of this approach, the connection between student-to-student can be increased further, effectively increasing the overall teaching-learning process.

To encourage learners through group achievement: Cooperative learning encourages the "joy of group success". With this approach, many students can get motivated at a time. In the traditional learning environment where only high achiever gets the chance to enjoy the success of achievement. Eventually, through cooperative learning, the joy of achievement is distributed among high and low achievers.

Advantages of Cooperative Learning

The effectiveness of a cooperative learning environment has been documented in various research studies. Panitz (1996) has provided an outline and listed over 50 benefits of cooperative learning and categorized them into the following major dimensions:

- Academic benefits
- Social benefits
- Psychological benefits

Academic Benefits

In the academic scenario cooperative learning promotes the following benefits:

- **Promotes critical thinking skills**: Cooperative learning helps to develop higher-level thinking and stimulates critical thinking through discussion and debates. It also develops the oral communication and meta-cognition skills of the student.
- **Actively involves the student in the learning process**: Cooperative learning is actively involved in exploratory learning, which increases the responsibility of the student toward learning. It provides training to the next generation of teachers. Furthermore, it encourages the achievement of learning goals rather than performance goals.
- **Classroom results are improved**: A cooperative learning environment helps to obtain higher achievement and class attendance, positive attitude toward the subject matters, increases student retention, increases self-management skills, innovation in teaching and classroom techniques, etc.
- **Large lectures can be personalized**: Cooperative learning can be used to personalize large lecture classes and helps to make large classes more interactive through critical thinking activities during class.
- **To motivate students in a specific curriculum**: This learning technique is mainly helpful in language learning classes where interaction is an important aspect. Besides, it is also helpful for laboratory and design projects.

Social Benefits

In a social setting, cooperative learning techniques are helpful in the following way:

- **Develops social support system for students**: A cooperative learning environment increases interaction between students and faculty that helps to develop social skills as well. Moreover, it develops a stronger social support system and interpersonal relationships and develops responsibility for each other.
- **Helps to build diversity and understanding among student and staff**: In the classroom environment students comes from diverse background. To work with this diverse group student increases positive heterogeneous relationship; understanding of diversity, forester empathetic emotion, and learn how to work with each other, etc.
- **Positive atmosphere for modeling and practice**: Cooperative learning helps to teach constructivist criticisms of the ideas rather than the individualistic.
- **Development learning community**: Cooperative learning helps to create a community-based learning environment. Beyond classroom activity, it promotes social and academic relationships within the classroom, from which the classroom shifts from a teacher-centered to a student-centered learning environment.

Psychological Benefits

The following are the psychological benefits of a cooperative learning environment:

- **Increases self-esteem of the student**: Self-esteem is one of the crucial elements for a satisfactory learning environment. Applying cooperative techniques in the classroom helps to increase students' mastery attribution pattern rather than helpless attribution pattern. This technique encourages creating assistive mentalities in the classroom where students take help from their peers and also help other peers if needed.
- **Reduce anxiety**: It has been found that cooperative learning significantly reduces classroom anxiety that comes from teachers' authoritative behavior including reducing the pressure to gather knowledge without activity. It is also notable that in a conventional classroom where student evaluation is only based on tests that this increases the anxiety of the student.
- **Development of a positive attitude toward the teacher**: Cooperative learning is not a teacher-dominated approach. Therefore, in this learning environment, the teacher plays the role of a helping hand to the student. This creates a more positive attitude among students toward their teacher and vice versa.

Drawbacks of Cooperative Learning

It is clear from the previous section that a cooperative learning environment has lots of benefits in the teaching-learning context; however, without proper knowledge of implementation teachers or instructors can lose control of their classroom. This section discusses some of the disadvantages of a cooperative learning environment. They are as follows:

- Without the proper knowledge, there can be huge chances of irrelevant discussion, chaos, and student involvement outside of the academic content.
- Previous studies showed that in mixed-group learning environments high achievement students are more active compared to low achievers who become passive and lose focus on their task (Slavin, 1987).

- High stakes and praise may increase the chances of conflict among the student.
- Cooperative learning ignores the individual pace of learning; some students are too fast to understand some content matters and some need more time to absorb the full information. In a group learning environment, it is hard to maintain the induvial pace of learning.
- Without proper implementation, a group may become more authoritative, for example, some may take over the group and dictate what everyone does.
- The students who are more introverted or quiet may feel uncomfortable expressing their views and ideas with the group.
- In a cooperative learning environment, the grading process is difficult. Without proper grading discrimination in a group may occur. Some students may work hard in a group but some students who do nothing can also get equal marks or marks quite similar to those who work hard. This scenario may create frustration among the student if not implemented appropriately.

Bibliography and Suggested Readings

Angelo, T. A., & Cross, K. P. (1993). Categorizing grid. In *Classroom assessment techniques* (2nd ed., pp. 160–163). San Francisco, CA: Jossey-Bass Pub.

Aronson, E. (2000). *The Jigsaw classroom.* Retrieved from http://www.jigsaw.org/.

Bean, J. C. (1996). *Engaging ideas: A professor's guide to integrating writing, critical thinking, and active learning in the classroom* (pp. 6–7, 176–177). San Francisco, CA: Jossey-Bass.

Coleman, J. (1961). In his book *The Adolescent Society: The Social Life of the Teenager and its Impact on Education*, Free Press of Glencoe

Cranton, P. (1998). *No one way: Teaching and learning in higher education* (pp. 147–151). Toronto, ON: Wall & Emerson.

Habeshaw, S., Habeshaw, T., & Gibbs, G. (1984). *53 interesting things to do in your seminars and tutorials.* Bristol: Technical & Educational Studies.

Hillebrand, R. P. (1994). Control and cohesion: Collaborative learning and writing. *English Journal, 83*(1), 71–74.

Holt, D., Chips, B., & Wallace, D. (1991). Cooperative learning in the secondary school: Maximizing language acquisition, academic achievement, and social development. *National Clearinghouse for Bilingual Education Program Information Guide Series, 12*(Summer).

Jacobs, G. M., Power, M. A., & Loh, W. I. (2002). *The teacher's sourcebook for cooperative learning: Practical techniques, basic principles, and frequently asked questions.* Thousand Oaks, CA: Corwin Press. Retrieved from http://www.corwinpress.com/index1.asp?id=detail.asp?id=27713.

Jansen, A. (2012). Developing productive dispositions during small-group work in two sixth-grade mathematics classrooms. *Middle Grades Research Journal, 7*(1), 37–56.

Johnson, D. et al. (2006). *Active learning: Cooperation in the college classroom.* Edina, MN: Interaction Book Company.

Johnson, D. W., Johnson, R. T., & Holubec, E. J. (2013). *Cooperation in the Classroom.* 9th ed. Edina, MN: Interaction Book Company

Johnson, D., & Johnson, R. (1975). *Learning together and alone* (1st ed.). Englewood Cliffs, NJ: Prentice-Hall.

Johnson, D., & Johnson, R. (1994). *Learning together and alone* (1st ed.). Boston, MA: Allyn and Bacon.

Johnson, D. W., Johnson, R., & Smith, K. (1991). *Active learning: Cooperation in the college classroom.* Edina, MN: Interaction Bock Company.

Johnson, D. W., Johnson, R., & Smith, K. (1998). *Active learning: Cooperation in the college classroom.* Edina, MN: Interaction Book Company.

Johnson, D. W., & Johnson, R. T. (1999). *Learning together and alone* (5th ed.). Boston, MA: Allyn& Bacon.

Johnson, D. W. & Johnson, R. T. (2018). *Cooperative Learning: The Foundation for Active Learning.* In the edited book, Active Learning Edited by Sílvio Manuel Brito. https://10.5772/intechopen.81086

Johnson, D. W., Johnson, R. T., & Holubec, E. J. (1986). *Circles of learning: Cooperation in the classroom.* Edina, MN: Interaction Book Company.

Johnson, D. W., & Johnson, R. (1992). Positive interdependence: Key to effective cooperation. In R. Hertz-Lazarowitz & N. Miller (Eds.), *Interaction in cooperative groups: The theoretical anatomy of group learning* (pp. 174–199). New York, NY: Cambridge University Press.

Kagan, S. (1992). *Cooperative learning* (2nd ed.). San Juan Capistrano, CA: Resources for Teachers.
Kagan, S. (1994). *Kagan cooperative learning* (2nd ed.). San Clemente, CA: Kagan Publishing.
Kagan, S. (1996). *Cooperative learning*. San Clemente, CA: Kagan Cooperative Learning.
King, R. (1989). *Hoshin planning: The developmental approach*. Methuen, MA: Goal/QPC.
Kotsopoulos, D. (2010). When collaborative learning is not collaborative: Supporting student learning through self-surveillance. *International Journal of Educational Research*, 49(4–5), 129–140.
Leikin, R., & Zaslavsky, O. (1999). Cooperative learning in mathematics. *Mathematics Teacher*, 92(3), 240.
Lochhead, J., & Whimbey, A. (1987). Teaching analytical reasoning through thinking-aloud pair problem solving. In J. E. Stice (Ed.), *Developing critical thinking and problem-solving abilities* (pp. 72–93). New Directions for Teaching and Learning, No. 30. San Francisco, CA: Jossey-Bass.
May, M., & Doob, L. (1937). *Cooperation and Competition*. New York: Social Sciences Research Council.
McKeachie, W. J. (2002). *McKeachie's teaching tips: Strategies, research, and theory for college and university teachers* (pp. 190–191). Boston, MA: Houghton Mifflin.
Millis, B. J., & Cottell, P. G. (1998a). *Cooperative learning for higher education faculty* (pp. 134–138). American Council on Education. Phoenix, AZ: Oryx Press.
Millis, B. J., & Cottell, P. G. (1998b). *Cooperative learning for higher education faculty* (pp. 113–114). American Council on Education, Series on Higher Education. Phoenix, AZ: Oryx Press.
Millis, B. J., & Cottell, P. G. (1998c). *Cooperative learning for higher education faculty* (pp. 95, 101–103). American Council on Education, Series on Higher Education. Phoenix, AZ: Oryx Press.
Panitz, T. (1996). Collaborative versus cooperative learning: A comparison of the two concepts which will help us understand the underlying nature of interactive learning. URL (last checked 16 December 2012). http://home.capecod.net/~tpanitz/tedsarticles/coopdefinition.htm
Plous, S. (2000). Responding to overt displays of prejudice: A role-playing exercise. *Teaching of Psychology*, 27(3), 198–200.
Roberts, T. (2004). *Online collaborative learning* (1st ed.). Hershey PA: Information Science Pub.
Sharan, Y., & Sharan, S. (1994). Group investigation in the cooperative classroom. In S. Sharan (Ed.), *Handbook of cooperative learning* (pp. 97–114). Westport, CT: Greenwood Press.
Siegel, C. (2005). Implementing a research-based model of cooperative learning. *Journal of Educational Research*, 98(6), 1–15.
Slavin, R. (1996). Research on cooperative learning and achievement: What we know, what we need to know. *Contemporary Educational Psychology*, 21(1), 43–69. http://doi.org/10.1006/ceps.1996.0004
Slavin, R. E. (1980). Cooperative learning. *Review of Educational Research*, 50(2), 315–342.
Slavin, R. E. (1987). Cooperative learning and cooperative school. *Educational Leadership*, 45, 7–13.
Slavin, R. E. (1995). *Cooperative learning: Theory, research, and practice*. Boston: Allyn & Bacon.
Swortzel, K. (1997). The effects of cooperative learning methods on achievement, retention, and attitudes of home economics students in north carolina. *Journal of Vocational and Technical Education*, 13(2). Retrieved September 2, 2003, from: http://scholar.lib.vt.edu/ejournals/JVTE/v13n2/Abu.html.
Walmsley, A. L., & Muniz, J. (2003). Cooperative learning and its effects in a high school geometry classroom. *Mathematics Teacher*, 96(2), 112–116.

12
THEORIES AND TECHNIQUES OF COOPERATIVE LEARNING

Theoretical Foundation of Cooperative Learning

The theoretical overview of cooperative learning is mainly based on three perspectives:

- Cognitive Development
- Behavioral Interdependence
- Social Interdependence

Cognitive Development

Two of the early proponents of cognitive development theory are Piaget and Vygotsky. The major assumption of cognitive development theory is the cooperation of individual with the environment that encourages conflicts, creates disequilibrium, and stimulates cognitive development. However, Vygotsky and other related researchers claim that knowledge in society is created by cooperation. A positive attitude toward a cooperative effort to learn, understand, and solve a problem helps to acquire knowledge effectively.

Behavioral Interdependence

Behavioral theories also focus on cooperation, for instance, Skinner explored the effectiveness of group reinforcement and rewards in learning. However, he also explained, "group contingencies" and their effect on learning. Bandura (1977) emphasized "imitation" strategy and Thibaut and Kelley (1959) emphasized the "balance of rewards" and "cost in social exchange" among interdependent individuals.

Besides these two theoretical foundations, "cognitive development" and "behavioral interdependence", which have considered cooperation or group power as a major learning premise, another important theory dealing with cooperation is "social interdependence theory".

Social Interdependence

A major claim of social interdependence is that learning achievements or success are dependent on the action of others. Effective social interdependence takes place when an individual shares common goals (Deutsch, 1949; Johnson and Johnson, 1989). The historical root of social interdependence can be found in the early 1900s with the studies of Kurt Koffka, a Gestalt psychologist who claims groups as a dynamic whole in which interdependence among members could vary (Johnson and Johnson, 1994). In the 1920s and 1930s, Kurt Lewin explained the interdependence of groups as a "dynamic whole" and the accomplishment of the desire for common goals. However, there is a difference between "social interdependence" and "social dependence". Social dependence posits the "outcomes of one person are affected by other people, not vice versa" and social interdependence postulates that "individual outcomes are unaffected by each other's action". As the view of Deutsch (1962) explained that social independence and interdependence are both crucial in the sense that, without these two approaches all efforts will mean individualistic effort. He also stated that social interdependence is fundamental and ubiquitous in all aspects of one's life.

Swortzel (1997) perceived two major aspects associated with successful cooperative learning; the motivational aspect and the cognitive aspect. It was also elaborated that while the cooperative learning approach is based on group success or failure, therefore all member of the group motivate themselves to encourage each other or explores whatever strategies are needed for the success of the group (Johnson and Holubec, 1986). Besides, as per the cognitive approach, it was also explained that cooperative learning helps to train and facilitate our critical thinking and problem-solving approach. Johnson and Holubec (1986) stated that cooperative learning is a unique approach that encourages "elaborative thinking" because to solve one problem or to achieve group success students need more and more discussion with their group peers regarding various probable strategies.

Techniques of Cooperative Learning

The previous section discussed the characteristics, theories, and features of cooperative learning. This section introduces some interesting techniques for cooperative learning. Plenty of research has been conducted in the field of cooperative learning and hundreds of effective cooperative learning techniques have evolved (Kagan, 1994). However, some important techniques are discussed here. Techniques of cooperative learning can be categorized in multiple ways, such as discussion, reciprocal teaching, graphic organizers, writing, and problem-solving (Barkley, Cross, and Major, 2005). It is also notable that any one technique can be used in multiple categories. The following are the more common cooperative learning techniques:

1. **Discussion (i.e., exchanging information, ideas, and opinions)**: It refers to the interaction of students and the exchange of their ideas primarily through spoken word. McKeachie (2002) explained "discussion" as the "prototypic" method that encourages active learning. It also stated that discussion is one of the most valuable tools in the teacher's repertoire. Think-pair-share, round robin, buzz group, talking chips, three-step interviews, and critical debates are the major "discussion" methods of the cooperative learning technique. The following are brief discussions on each technique:
   - **Think-pair-share**
     This technique was originally developed by Frank T. Lyman (1981). In this technique, the instructor poses a question, and students will be given a few minutes to think about a possible response. When prompted, the student shares the generated idea with their partner.
     - **Characteristic**
       This technique needs "pairs", with 5 minutes on task, and single session group durations.

- **Effectiveness**

  This technique encourages more active and effective participation in a whole-class discussion.
- **Round robin**

  It is mainly a brainstorming technique. Here the teacher will pose a question that will have many possible answers. Students have to think of a possible answer at a given specific time. After the "think time", students have to provide their response in another round table style context. This process will go on until all students get their opportunity to answer.
  - **Characteristic**

    This technique needs group sizes of 4–6, with 5–15 minutes on task, and single session group durations.
  - **Effectiveness**

    This technique not only encourages generating more ideas but also ensures equal participation among group members.
- **Buzz group**:

  A buzz group is a quickly formed group approach to respond to course-related questions. Here discussion will be informal and each group can respond to one or more questions.
  - **Characteristic**

    This technique needs group sizes of 4–6, with 10–15 minutes on task, and single session group durations.
  - **Effectiveness**

    To warm up whole-class discussion and the opportunity to involve more students by dividing the whole class into small groups.
- **Talking chips**

  Talking chips are also a group discussion technique. Students are provided a token each time they speak. This technique is used to ensure participation from each group member as well as encourage shy students to speak out.
  - **Characteristics**

    This technique needs group sizes of 4–6, with 10–20 minutes on task, and single session group durations.
  - **Effectiveness**

    It is effective to discuss controversial issues. Moreover, it is helpful to solve communication problems and encourages more participation in the classroom.
- **Three-step interview**

  Three-step interviews are generally a unique and interesting approach. Here each student plays a role as an interviewer, takes turns interviewing their peer, and reports what they learn from another peer group. For instance, in the first step *student A* will be interviewed by *student B*. In the second step, student B will be interviewed by student A. A parallel process will be there for *student C* and *student D*. In the third and final stage students A and B summarize the response of their partner for students C and D, and vice versa (Bean, 1996).
  - **Characteristics**

    This technique first needs group sizes of 2 and then 4, with 15–30 minutes on task, and single session group durations.
  - **Effectiveness**

    This technique mainly helps to increase the communication and network skills of the student.

2. **Reciprocal teaching**

   Generally, reciprocal teaching refers to "students teaching other students". In this approach, students serve both the role of a teacher as well a student. The major assumption in this teaching is a mutual exchange of ideas through dual student roles (McKeachie, Pintrich, Lin, and Smith, 1986). Note-taking pairs, learning cells, fishbowl, roleplay, jigsaw, and test-taking teams are the most discussed reciprocal-teaching methods in the field of cooperative as well as collaborative learning. The following are brief discussions of each technique:

   - **Note-taking pairs**: In the "note-taking pair" technique, students help each other to improve their notes. Through this approach, students can help each other to find out collected missing information and correct this to improve the accuracy of individual notes (Millis & Cottell, 1998).
     - **Characteristics**
       This technique needs pair groups, with 5–15 minutes on task, and single or multiple session group durations.
     - **Effectiveness**
       This technique is effective to increase structural activity to pool information, fill the gap of information, check and correct the mistake, etc. Mainly it encourages collaborative efforts for superior note-taking.
   - **Learning cells**: The learning cell is a reciprocal pair questioning approach. In this technique, one student will generate some questions based on their learned topic or reading assignment and then work with partners to answer the question and vice versa.
     - **Characteristics**
       This is a pair-group technique, with 15–30 minutes on task, and single, multiple, or all-term session group durations.
     - **Effectiveness**
       This approach helps generate thought-provoking questions and encourages students to check their understanding (McKeachie, 2002).
   - **Fishbowl**: In the fishbowl technique (or inside-outside circles), students will be distributed into two groups, the outer circle, and the inner circle (Barkley, Cross, and Major, 2005). The outer circle of the student will sit around the inner circle of the student. The function of inner groups will be to be engaged in deep discussion and the outer circle function will be to listen to the discussion, critique content, and logical group interaction.
     - **Characteristics**
       In this technique 3–5 members will be in the inside group, around which will remain the outside circle members, the time on task will be 15–20 minutes of discussion and 10–15 minutes for debriefing, and single session group durations.
     - **Effectiveness**
       This technique is effective to encourage in-depth discussion and provide the opportunity to model group processing in a discussion setting (Barkley, Cross, and Major, 2005).
   - **Roleplay**: Roleplay is based on the learning-by-doing approach. In this approach, some assumed characters are acted; role and play. "Role" indicates an actionable approach to knowledge, skill, and understanding. "Play" indicates the use of imagination with fun.
     - **Characteristics**
       In this technique, group sizes will be 2–5 members, with time on task at 15–45 minutes, and single session group durations.

- **Effectiveness**

  Roleplaying engages the student in a creative and participatory manner (Plous, 2000).
- **Jigsaw**: Jigsaw is a unique approach to flow knowledge from one group to another. For instance, in the first stage, one group will develop knowledge about a given topic, and after that this "expert" group of students move to the new "jigsaw" group. Each "jigsaw" group will consist of expert students in various subtopics.
  - **Characteristics**

    In this technique, the group size will consist of 4–6 members. Time on task varies based on the situation and with single or multiple session group durations.
  - **Effectiveness**

    The jigsaw technique helps to increase student motivation to learn from their group members (Aronson, 2000).
- **Test-taking teams**: This is another unique approach that involves three steps; (i) student group study for the exam together, (ii) individuals take the exam, and (iii) groups take the exam.
  - **Characteristics**

    In this technique, the group size consists of 4–6 members. Time on the task will be proportional to the exam and the duration of the group will also be proportional to the exam.
  - **Effectiveness**

    This technique helps to increase and deepen the understanding of content. Furthermore, the student can take advantage of the collective knowledge of the group.

3. **Problem-solving**: Problem-solving refers to the growing interest and ability of the student to solve a problem. Generally, a problem can be described as a "puzzle" that encourages exercising the mind. McKeachie (2002) defined it as "problem-based education is based on assumptions that human beings were evolved as individuals who are motivated to solve problems, and that problem solver will seek and learn whatever knowledge is needed for successful problem solving". Think-aloud-pair problem solving (TAPPS), send-a-problem, case study, structured problem solving, analytic teams, and group investigation are all majorly used problem-solving cooperative learning approaches. The following is a brief discussion of the mentioned techniques:
   - **Think-aloud-pair problem solving (TAPPS)**: This is a pair-group approach. In this, technique-specific problems will be given to the pair of a student with the specification of their role such as one student will be a "problem solver" and another student will be a "listener" (the student's role will shift from problem to problem). The problem solver "thinks aloud" and discusses the steps of solving the problem and the "listener" tries to follow the steps, understands the steps, and also suggests correction if needed.
     - **Characteristics**

       In this technique, the group size will be paired. The time on the task will be 30–45 minutes and the duration of the group will also be a single session or multiple.
     - **Effectiveness**

       This process helps to emphasize problem-solving and also helps students to identify logic or process errors (Lochhead and Whimbey, 1987).
   - **Send-a-problem:** In send-a-problem techniques, a problem will be given to each group and they try to solve it. After getting the tentative output of the solution, they will pass the problem and solution to the other group and without looking at the

solution of the previous group they try to solve it in their way. This passing or sending process will continue until they receive a useful solution. Furthermore, each group will be involved in the analysis, synthesis, and evaluation process, and will report the best solution to the class.
- **Characteristics**

  In this technique, the group size will consist of 2–4 members. The time on the task will be 30–45 minutes and the duration of the group will also be a single session.
- **Effectiveness**

  This process helps the student to practice together with one specific problem. Besides, this process will increase the analytical power of a student to find out the best solution by comparing and discriminating among multiple solutions (18Kagan, 1992).
- **Case study**: In this technique, the students' group will be provided "cases" (viz. field-related problematic situation), a brief history of how the specific situation occurred, and the present dilemma of the specific situation. The group members need to apply various concepts they learned and try to find out an alternative approach to solve the problem.
  - **Characteristics**

    In this technique, the group size will consist of 3–6 members. The time on task will be varied based on the situation and the duration of the group will also be a single session.
  - **Effectiveness**

    This process helps the student to increase critical reflection and develops analysis, synthesis, and decision-making skills (McKeache, 2002).
- **Structured problem-solving**: In this technique, the students will be given specific strategies and processes to solve a complex and content-based problem within a specific time limit.
  - **Characteristics**

    In this technique, the group size will consist of 4–6 members. The time on task will be 1–2 hours and the duration of the group will be multiple sessions.
  - **Effectiveness**
  - This process helps to identify, analyze, and solve problems in an organized manner (Millis & Cottell, 1998).
- **Analytic teams**: In this technique, group members "assume roles and specific tasks to perform when critically reading an assignment, listening to a lecture, or watching the video" (Barkley, Patricia, and Claire, 2005).
  - **Characteristics**

    In this technique, the group size will consist of 4–5 members. The time on the task will be 15–45 minutes and the duration of the group will be a single session.
  - **Effectiveness**
  - This technique is specifically helpful to increase the competence of students' critical analysis, including complex problem-solving skills (Johnson, Johnson, and Smith, 1998).
- **Group investigation**: Group investigation is another unique cooperative learning approach, where the students' group has to plan, create, conduct, and report an in-depth research project. In this approach, each student of the group will choose a subject topic based on interest and significance and carry out their research.

- **Characteristics**

  In this technique, the group size will consist of 2–5 members. Time on task can be several hours and the duration of a group will be multiple across terms.
- **Effectiveness**

  Using this technique, the student will understand the importance of invention. Besides, when their project will be reviewed by teachers and peers, they will gain practical experience by giving and receiving various constructive criticisms (Sharan and Sharan, 1994).

4. **Graphics information organizer**: Graphics information organizer refers to converting complex information into meaningful displays. The major assumption in this premise is that the graphic organizer can help students to discover the pattern of relationship among ideas which is impossible in text alone. Affinity grouping, group grid, team matrix, sequence chains, and word webs are majorly used graphic information organization methods in cooperative learning strategy. The following is a brief discussion of each technique:

   - **Affinity grouping**: In this approach students individually will generate various ideas on a given topic and write them down on a specific slip or piece of paper. After completion of idea generation, the whole group will work together on categorization and find out common themes of a given specific topic.
     - **Characteristics**

       In this technique, the group size will consist of 3–5 members. Time on task can be 30–45 minutes and the duration of a group will be a single session.
     - **Effectiveness**

       Using this technique, a student will unveil complicated issues and can increase competence by grouping ideas from separate pieces (King, 1989).
   - **Group grid**: In the group grid approach, students have to sort the provided information such as terminology, names, equation, image, etc. by placing them or sorting them out in the given blank cell.
     - **Characteristics**

       In this technique, the group size will consist of 2–4 members. Time on task can be 15–45 minutes and the duration of the group will be a single session.
     - **Effectiveness**

       This technique is helpful to build a basic schema, learn and remember a large number of newly introduced terms, and learn categorization and classification of information (Angelo & Cross, 1993).
   - **Team matrix**: In the team matrix technique-specific criteria are given to the student and they are asked to differentiate various concepts and determine missing concepts in the given information.
     - **Characteristics**

       In this technique, the group will be in pairs. The time on the task will be 10–20 minutes and the duration of groups will be a single session.
     - **Effectiveness**

       This technique is helpful to increase the ability to recognize and for the distinction of uncommon attributes (Angelo and Cross, 1993).
   - **Sequence chains**: In this approach, students have to create a visual map of logic within a series. After that, applying the knowledge and using reasoning ability students will arrange these points in an orderly and coherent progression (Barkley, Patricia, and Claire, 2005).

- **Characteristics**

  In this technique, the group size will consist of 2–3 members. Time on task can be 15–45 minutes and the duration of the group will be a single session.
- **Effectiveness**

  This technique is helpful to develop logical and sequential thinking (Kagan, 1996).
- **Word webs**: In this technique, a central question, word, or phrase will be used and students need to identify, relate, and organize the relationship in a graphic by drawing lines or arrows to show the connection between each idea.
  - **Characteristics**

    In this technique, the group size will consist of 2–4 members. Time on task can be 30–45 minutes and the duration of the group will be a single session.
  - **Effectiveness**

    This technique is really helpful to relate new ideas to existing knowledge, increase the ability to associate various parts of concept and relate to the central idea, and meaningful organization of facts and principles.

5. **Focusing on writing**: Writing is a means of learning. Generally, writing encourages critical thinking by summarizing, integrating, and synthesizing various elements into a coherent whole. Dialogue journal, round table, dyadic essays, peer editing, collaborative writing, team anthologies, and paper seminar are all techniques used in cooperative learning scenarios.
   - **Dialogue journal**: This is a group pair approach, where each individual keeps note of reading assignments and lecture tasks in their specific journal. After taking notes they exchange their journal with each other and read the reports, comments, and questions for the entry of the journal content.
     - **Characteristics**

       In this technique, the group size will be paired. Time on task can vary based on the situation and the duration of the group can be single or multiple sessions.
     - **Effectiveness**

       This technique is helpful to exchange ideas, correct missing notes, and increase skills for taking notes and recording thoughts (Cranton, 1998).
   - **Round table**: This is a similar technique as discussed previously in "*round robin*". "*Round table*" is a written version of round robin. This technique "takes turns for responding to a prompt by writing one or two words, phrases, or sentences before passing the paper along to others who do the same" (Barkley, Patricia, and Claire, 2005).
     - **Characteristics**

       In this technique, the group size will consist of 3–4 members. Time on task will be 10–20 minutes and the duration of the group will be a single class.
     - **Effectiveness**

       This technique will help student focus their attention, give students time to respond to their answers, and also provide a cumulative record. Moreover, this technique ensures equal participation among group members (Sharan, 1994).
   - **Dyadic essays**: This technique is mainly based on paired group interaction. Each member of the group is to be engaged in writing essay questions and model answers to a given reading assignment or presentation. In the next class or period, the students will share or exchange and compare the response to each other.
     - **Characteristics**

       This technique is mainly based on pair interaction. Time on task is 30–45 minutes and the duration of the group will be single or multiple sessions.

- **Effectiveness**

  This technique facilitates increased competency in identifying learning activities and formulation of answering questions. Furthermore, it is helpful for the student to rehearse how to respond to essay questions and answers (Millis and Cottell, 1998).

- **Peer editing**: This technique is also a critical review process of other peers. In this technique, one member of the peers will review or critically analyze the research paper, essay, report, argument, or writing assignment of the other members and also need to provide editorial feedback regarding each other's writing.
  - **Characteristics**

    This technique is mainly based on pair interactions. Time on task is 2 hours and the duration of the group will be multiple sessions.
  - **Effectiveness**

    This technique helps to increase critical evaluation skills and improves the constructive criticism skills of the student (Millis and Cottell, 1998).

- **Collaborative writing**: Collaborative writing an effective approach in the teaching-learning process. In this technique, 2 or 3 students together will start drafting, organizing ideas, and mind mapping of writing, and thereby will produce a complete writing assignment.
  - **Characteristics**

    This technique is mainly based on 2–3 students' interactions. Time will be several hours and the duration of the group will be multiple sessions.
  - **Effectiveness**

    This technique helps to perform writing more effectively (Millis and Cottell, 1998). Additionally, this technique gains a more professional attitude toward future collaborative participation (Hillebrand, 1994).

- **Team anthologies**: This is mainly organizational techniques of learning approach. In this technique groups of students will do various activities with given course material such as compiling, annotating, preparing print, etc.
  - **Characteristics**

    In this technique, the group size varies session-wise such as it starts with 4 members, and finally ending with 4 members. Time extends for several hours and the duration of the group will be multiple sessions.
  - **Effectiveness**

    This technique is mainly helpful to increase the organization, investigate, and review the competence of the student. Students gain research report writing experience before writing a formal research paper (Millis, 1994).

- **Paper seminar**: This technique mainly emphasizes presentation techniques. Students will make a formal presentation to their peers. Form the group members 2–3 members act as judges or evaluators and all students of the group will critically interact on the presented paper (Habeshaw, Habeshaw, and Gibbs, 1984).
  - **Characteristics**

    In this technique, the group size will be 4–6 members. Time on task varies based on content and situation, and the duration of the group will be multiple sessions.
  - **Effectiveness**

    This technique increases the attention of the student and skills by providing feedback (Millis, 1994).

In present teaching-learning scenarios, a challenging task is to effectively engage the student with the learning environment. The effectiveness mentioned above of various cooperative learning techniques have been empirically proven by various researchers. Before using various techniques, it is imperative to know how to implement or create the environment to apply this technique. The next section answers this question and the entire section will provide a brief outline of the implementation of the cooperative learning approach in a classroom situation.

Implementation of Cooperative Learning

The previous section provided a brief outline of the various techniques which can be used to achieve an effective cooperative learning environment. As one can find that each technique consisted of several characteristics based on their time on task, group size, duration of the group, etc. Whatever techniques and settings are to be used, the most important part is proper design and implementation. Therefore, the biggest challenge to implementing or introducing cooperative learning is proper planning and creating a positive classroom environment. This section will discuss some of the most important issues, which are needed to be taken into consideration before the implementation of cooperative learning (Johnson, Johnson, and Smith, 1991). The entire planning or designing of a cooperative learning environment can be divided into three different stages:

(i) pre-implementation,
(ii) implementation, and
(iii) post-Implementation.

Pre-implementation

After deciding to use cooperative learning the teacher or mentor must ensure the following stages before implementation of various techniques of cooperative learning. According to Johnson, Johnson, and Smith (1991), these are the following:

Specification of instructional objectives: At the outset, the instructor must explain to the student the uses, benefits, results, and effectiveness of cooperative learning. An instructor can give this instruction verbally or by use of printed handouts.
Determination of group size and assigning students to the group: As one knows from the previous section that group size depends on which techniques one is going to use. Groups can be heterogeneous or homogeneous. The instructor must assign the group carefully before the implementation of any groups.
Arrangement of the classroom: The classroom setting must be a crucial part of the implementation of any cooperative learning techniques. The classroom environment needs adequate interaction, moving space, and face-to-face communication space for group work.
Planning of instructional material: Before implementation, the instructor needs to ensure that the instructional material or method that the instructor is going to use must encourage equal contribution space for each member of the group.
Assign group roles and tasks: It is still controversial whether the instructor imposes a group role or not. But the instructor may assist the student to choose their role in a specific group and task.

- **Explaining criteria for success:** The instructor should explain to the student how their skill, group work, and assistance of other members will be evaluated and specific criteria for success.
- **Structure positive independence and accountability:** It is an important role of the instructor to ensure positive independence and accountability. For instance, group tasks should be assigned in a way that encourages equal participation and contribution of each participant.
- **Specify desired behaviors:** Before implementation, the instructor needs to specify specific desired behavior such as the instructor can take mini-classes to learn about how to respect and praise the other group members as well as how to make shared decisions making.

Implementation

Now it's time to start. In the implementation stage instructor must ensure the following role of students:

- Working together
- Listening to one another
- Questioning one another
- Keeping records of their work and progress
- Producing the assessment task (product)
- Assuming personal responsibility

Besides the student's role Johnson, Johnson, and Smith (1991) established various role of instructor that needs to be maintained to acquire an effective cooperative learning environment.

- **Supervision:** The implementation stage should be supervised throughout the groups and by each group member.
- **Intervention:** In the supervision stage if one notices any group conflict or off-task behavior instructor should intervene.
- **Assistance:** If needed instructor should assist the group regarding any additional information or help.
- **Praise:** The instructor should praise the group if they complement the assignment correctly or successfully.

Post-implementation

Johnson, Johnson, and Smith (1991) gave three guidelines for the instructor after students complete the whole procedure and complete or submit the task. The following are the three guidelines:

- **Provide closure through summarization:** In this stage, the instructor should summarize the important point of the unit or lesson.
- **Evaluate student learning:** The instructor should use a rubric (which was created in the implementation stage) to give a grade to group work as well as individual work.
- **Reflect on what happened:** One of the important tasks is a reflection on each event. For instance, the instructor should track or record what worked and why it worked at each stage of the journey.

From pre-implementation to post-implementation, cooperative learning strategies are a long strategical process. An instructor must care about each stage such as feedback on students regarding their problems, enjoyment, and association with other students, and also important is to provide feedback to the student about their work skills and assignment. This is a brief outline that can be used or followed by the teacher or instructor in the classroom environment to successfully achieve the learning goal.

Bibliography and Suggested Readings

Angelo, T. A., & Cross, K. P. (1993). Categorizing grid. In *Classroom assessment techniques* (2nd ed., pp. 160–163). San Francisco, CA: Jossey-Bass.

Aronson, E. (2000). *The Jigsaw classroom*. Retrieved from http://www.jigsaw.org/.

Bandura, A. (1977). *Social Learning Theory*. New York: General Learning Press.

Barbara, J., Millis, B. J. (1994). Conducting Cooperative Cases. *To improve the Academy*, 13(1), 309–328. https://doi.org/10.1002/j.2334-4822.1994.tb00274.x

Barkley, C., Barkley, E. F., Cross, K. P., & Major, C. H. (2005). *Collaborative learning techniques: A handbook for college faculty*. San Francisco, CA: Jossey Bass.

Bean, J. C. (1996). *Engaging ideas: A professor's guide to integrating writing, critical thinking, and active learning in the classroom* (pp. 6–7, 176–177). San Francisco, CA: Jossey-Bass.

Coleman, J. (1961). *The adolescent society* (1st ed.). New York: Free Press of Glencoe.

Cranton, P. (1998). *No one way: Teaching and learning in higher education* (pp. 147–151). Toronto, ON: Wall & Emerson.

Deutsch, M. (1962). Cooperation and trust: Some theoretical notes. In M. R. Jones (Ed.), *Nebraska symposium on motivation* (pp. 275–319). Lincoln, NE: University of Nebraska Press.

Deutsch, M. (1949). A theory of cooperation and competition. *Human Relations*, 2, 129–152.

Habeshaw, S., Habeshaw, T., & Gibbs, G. (1984). *53 interesting things to do in your seminars and tutorials*. Bristol: Technical & Educational Studies.

Hillebrand, R. P. (1994). Control and cohesion: Collaborative learning and writing. *English Journal*, 83(1), 71–74.

Holt, D., Chips, B., & Wallace, D. (1991). Cooperative learning in the secondary school: Maximizing language acquisition, academic achievement, and social development. *National Clearinghouse for Bilingual Education Program Information Guide Series*, 12(Summer).

Jacobs, G. M., Power, M. A., & Loh, W. I. (2002). *The teacher's sourcebook for cooperative learning: Practical techniques, basic principles, and frequently asked questions*. Thousand Oaks, CA: Corwin Press. Retrieved from http://www.corwinpress.com/index1.asp?id=detail.asp?id=27713.

Jansen, A. (2012). Developing productive dispositions during small-group work in two sixth-grade mathematics classrooms. *Middle Grades Research Journal*, 7(1), 37–56.

Johnson, D. et al. (2006). *Active learning: Cooperation in the college classroom*. Edina, MN: Interaction Book Company.

Johnson, D., & Johnson, R. (1975). *Learning together and alone* (1st ed.). Englewood Cliffs, NJ: Prentice-Hall.

Johnson, D. W., & Johnson, R. (1989). *Cooperation and competition: Theory and research*. Edina, MN: Interaction.

Johnson, D., & Johnson, R. (1994). *Learning together and alone* (1st ed.). Boston, MA: Allyn and Bacon.

Johnson, D. W., Johnson, R., & Smith, K. (1991). *Active learning: Cooperation in the college classroom*. Edina, MN: Interaction Bock Company.

Johnson, D. W., Johnson, R., & Smith, K. (1998). *Active learning: Cooperation in the college classroom*. Edina, MN: Interaction Book Company.

Johnson, D. W., & Johnson, R. T. (1999). *Learning together and alone* (5th ed.). Boston, MA: Allyn& Bacon.

Johnson, D. W., Johnson, R. T., & Holubec, E. J. (1986). *Circles of learning: Cooperation in the classroom*. Edina, MN: Interaction Book Company.

Kagan, S. (1992). *Cooperative learning* (2nd ed.). San Juan Capistrano, CA: Resources for Teachers.

Kagan, S. (1994). *Kagan cooperative learning* (2nd ed.). San Clemente, CA: Kagan Publishing.

Kagan, S. (1996). *Cooperative learning*. San Clemente, CA: Kagan Cooperative Learning.

King, R. (1989). *Hoshin planning: The developmental approach*. Methuen, MA: Goal/QPC.

Kotsopoulos, D. (2010). When collaborative learning is not collaborative: Supporting student learning through self-surveillance. *International Journal of Educational Research*, 49(4–5), 129–140.

Leikin, R., & Zaslavsky, O. (1999). Cooperative learning in mathematics. *Mathematics Teacher, 92*(3), 240.

Lochhead, J., & Whimbey, A. (1987). Teaching analytical reasoning through thinking-aloud pair problem solving. In J. E. Stice (Ed.), *Developing critical thinking and problem solving abilities* (pp. 72–93). New Directions for Teaching and Learning, No. 30. San Francisco, CA: Jossey-Bass.

Lyman, F. (1981). The Responsive Classroom Discussion. In A. S. Anderson (Ed.), *Mainstreaming Digest* (pp. 109–113). College Park, MD: University of Maryland College of Education.

McKeachie, W. J. (2002). *McKeachie's teaching tips: Strategies, research, and theory for college and university teachers* (pp. 190–191). Boston, MA: Houghton Mifflin.

Millis, B. J., & Cottell, P. G. (1998a). *Cooperative learning for higher education faculty* (pp. 134–138). American Council on Education. Phoenix, AZ: Oryx Press.

Millis, B. J., & Cottell, P. G. (1998b). *Cooperative learning for higher education faculty* (pp. 113–114). American Council on Education, Series on Higher Education. Phoenix, AZ: Oryx Press.

Millis, B. J., & Cottell, P. G. (1998c). *Cooperative learning for higher education faculty* (pp. 95, 101–103). American Council on Education, Series on Higher Education. Phoenix, AZ: Oryx Press.

Millis, B. J., & Cottell, P. G. (1998). *Cooperative Learning for Higher Education Faculty*. Phoenix, AZ: Oryx Press.

Plous, S. (2000). Responding to overt displays of prejudice: A role-playing exercise. *Teaching of Psychology, 27*(3), 198–200.

Sharan, Y., & Sharan, S. (1994). Group investigation in the cooperative classroom. In S. Sharan (Ed.), *Handbook of cooperative learning* (pp. 97–114). Westport, CT: Greenwood Press.

Siegel, C. (2005). Implementing a research based model of cooperative learning. *Journal of Educational Research, 98*(6), 1–15.

Slavin, R. (1996). Research on cooperative learning and achievement: What we know, what we need to know. *Contemporary Educational Psychology, 21*(1), 43–69. http://doi.org/10.1006/ceps.1996.0004

Slavin, R. E. (1980). Cooperative learning. *Review of Educational Research, 50*(2), 315–342.

Swortzel, K. (1997). The effects of cooperative learning methods on achievement, retention, and attitudes of home economics students in North Carolina. *Journal of Vocational and Technical Education, 13*(2).

Thibaut, J. W. & Kelley, H. H. (1959). *The social psychology of groups*. NY: John Wiley & Sons.

Walmsley, A. L., & Muniz, J. (2003). Cooperative learning and its effects in a high school geometry classroom. *Mathematics Teacher, 96*(2), 112–116.

13
CO-TEACHING APPROACH IN EDUCATION

The present chapter is going to discuss a unique method of teaching namely co-teaching. We all know that teaching is a creative process. Teaching is surely complex. Many times we think that those who have huge subject/content knowledge may become good teachers. However, this statement may be just partially true. As teaching is not just an interaction between teacher and student, it is much more than that. Therefore, a researcher is always concerned with the method of teaching, and experimentally they try to develop various teaching methods which can accelerate the teaching and learning process more effectively. This chapter will discuss co-teaching or collaborative teaching and team teaching.

Overview and Definition of Co-Teaching

Co-teaching denotes collaborative teaching. In the co-teaching approach, two or more educators teach a collaboratively heterogeneous group of students in a specific classroom. Co-teaching is like a synchronized team-based swimming process where team-mates coordinate each member to win the swim and save from drowning.

In co-teaching two or more teachers can teach together to achieve a specific learning objective. Many specific fields such as special education, literacy specialist, technology specialist, social workers, and speech therapists use the co-teaching method as their teaching approach. Moreover, co-teaching differs from collaborative consultation. In collaborative consultation, both educators only discuss specific problems related to instruction, but in the co-teaching approach, both teachers involve and engage in the instructional process.

Co-teaching is defined in different ways in the context of country and culture, some definitions are as follows:

Bacharach, Heck, and Dank (2004) define "co-teaching as where two teachers are working together with groups of students; sharing the planning, organization, delivery, and assessment of instruction as well as the physical space".

Muller, Friend, and Chamberlain (2009) say "Co-teaching is a specific form of collaboration, a special education service that may be delivered to students with disabilities. It has shown promise for blending professional expertise to better serve students with disabilities within general education classrooms".

Murawski (2012) has described co-teaching as "substantively different" from a solo-taught class with isolated services.

Cook and Friend (2017) defined it as "two or more professionals delivering substantive instruction to a diverse or blended group of students in a single physical space".

After analyzing the above and various other definitions, the following points may be extracted:

- Co-teaching includes the strategies to provide instruction simultaneously to a heterogeneous group of students.
- Co-teaching is a process of providing instruction by two or more teachers to achieve a specific learning objective.
- Co-teaching is an instructional process where the whole instruction is provided in the same physical space.
- Co-teaching is a scientific process of instruction that involves the specific design of scientific pre-planning, collaboration, and active participation of students and teachers respectively.
- Co-teaching is a scientific design of instruction where a teacher can communicate with every student individually as well as effectively.
- Co-teaching is a process where the diverse needs of students can learn in the physical space of a classroom.
- Co-teaching is a model based on the philosophy of inclusion.
- Co-teaching increases participation and collaborative practice among the teacher and students.

Characteristics of Co-Teaching

After analyzing the above definitions one can say that co-teaching is a collaborative teaching-learning approach where a heterogeneous group of pupils can learn at the same time and in the same physical space. Since co-teaching is a scientific teaching approach it has some unique characteristics, unlike other instructional approaches. This section is intended to provide some of the important and basic characteristics of co-teaching so that one can differentiate between what is co-teaching and what is not co-teaching. The following are the important characteristics of co-teaching:

Co-teaching involves two or more professionals as teachers: One of the essential characteristics of co-teaching is that it involves two or more experts or professionals to provide the instructional material as well as observation of the whole classroom situation. This teaching-learning approach has the flexibility to modify the whole instructional material as per the requirement of students (Fennick, 2001).

Joint delivery of instruction: Another essential characteristic of co-teaching is an opportunity to provide instruction jointly to achieve specific learning objectives. That means two or more professionals can actively coordinate with each other in a teaching-learning process and have some common goal for attaining mastery of a student in specific learning content. In a co-teaching process, two or more teachers should have a common belief that they are jointly working to achieve a specific instructional goal which is not possible by only one teacher (Austin, 2001).

A diverse group of students learns in the same physical space: In a conventional teaching-learning approach it is challenging to communicate with the diverse needs of students and to create an environment where a student can be evaluated individually. The co-teaching approach is a unique teaching and learning scenario where two or more teachers can teach students from diverse populations. This approach helps to expand the expertise of teachers that can be applied to student needs (Hourcade and Bauwens, 2001).

Shared Classroom Space: As discussed in the previous section that co-teaching is a teaching-learning approach where a diverse population of students can be taught in the same physical space. As we can generally see that in a conventional teaching-learning approach a teacher is not able to communicate with a special or backward student; therefore, this approach needs to take a separate location to achieve a specific learning goal for a special or backward student. In this context, it is a unique teaching-learning approach where any type of student can be taught in a single physical space (Friend and Cook, 2007).

Models of Co-Teaching

From the above discussion, a general view can be agreed, that co-teaching is a special teaching-learning approach where a general education teacher and a special education teacher both teach together to achieve a specific learning goal. Through a co-teaching approach, diverse groups of pupils can be taught in a single physical space. This section is intended to provide a brief overview of the various models of co-teaching and their application in the teaching-learning scenario. Following are some of the basic models of co-teaching:

1. **Parallel Teaching**
2. **Station Teaching**
3. **Teaming**
4. **Alternative Teaching**
5. **One Teaches and One Observes**
6. **One Teaches and One Assists**

Parallel teaching

One of the general aspects of parallel teaching is that the whole classroom is divided into equal groups. Two teachers teach simultaneously the same learning material or information. Parallel teaching is one of the popular co-teaching approaches. This approach is mainly intended to provide effective teaching-learning in heterogeneous groups. It is notable that, in the parallel teaching-learning approach, coordination and timing is the most vital method to provide instruction.

Characteristics

- In the parallel teaching-learning approach, all the students in the classroom are divided into two equal groups.
- In this approach, both teachers teach a specific learning material or the same content in the same amount of time.
- Both teachers can apply a different method of instruction following the parallel teaching-learning model.

Advantages

- In a parallel teaching approach, the teacher is more flexible to provide the instruction in their way or have the liberty to apply their teaching strategies which can enhance the entire teaching-learning process.
- Furthermore, in this model of co-teaching approach, there are more chances for student participation, which can increase the motivation, responses, and engagement of students.

Design, Evaluation, and Implementations

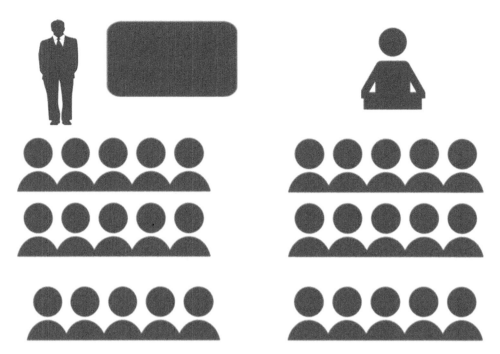

Figure 13.1 The parallel model of co-teaching.

- One of the direct benefits of this teaching-learning approach is that here teacher can play an active role rather than just being a passive lecturer.
- This model is very effective for a heterogeneous group of students.

Challenges

Besides the huge advantage of co-teaching there are also some obstacles or challenges which are listed below:

- The first and foremost challenge is to find out an appropriate physical space. In the context of developing countries where most of the classrooms do not have enough available physical space to divide the classroom into two different groups and also do not have enough space for providing teaching learning material to two different teachers simultaneously.
- Another challenge is a lack of adequate knowledge of the teacher. In the parallel teaching-learning model, there is a huge need for content and pedagogy knowledge to provide equally effective instruction.
- In the parallel model noise level and destruction is comparatively very high. Therefore, both teachers need to be careful about the management of noise levels that come from the student side and the mismanagement that comes from the instruction at the same time by the two teachers.

Station Teaching

Another essential teaching model is station teaching. In a station teaching model, there would be a teacher similar to the parallel teaching model but here the content material would be divided into two segments and presented in the different locations of the classroom. Two teachers teach each segment alternatively through two sessions. However, the 3rd or 4th station can be established depending on the classroom situation. In the 3rd and 4th stations, students can work independently with their peers and learning materials which is called the independent station.

Characteristics

- In the station teaching model, all the students are divided into two equal groups.
- The content in the station teaching model is divided into two segments.
- In the station teaching model, the group rotates from one station to another station.
- The station teaching model is appropriate and effective when the student and teacher ratio is low.

Opportunities

- Through the station teaching model, a teacher can get an opportunity to take care of every student in their classroom equally.
- In the station teaching model, the engagement of students is high due to continuous interactions and participation of the teacher with the student.
- In the station, the teaching model teacher can closely monitor the learning behavior and participation of a student in a specific classroom situation.
- This model is much more appropriate when the content material is complex and not in a hierarchical manner.

Challenges

- One of the biggest challenges in the station teaching model is to get a specific or appropriate physical space to apply station teaching effectively.

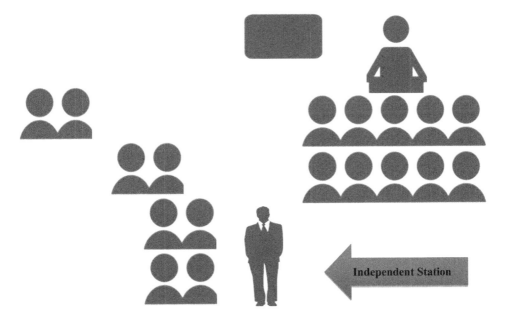

Figure 13.2 The station model of co-teaching.

- Another challenge is to align two types of teaching methods in a specific classroom situation.
- In a station teaching model, teachers need adequate knowledge of the content as well as the method of instruction. In the context of a developing country, there is a lack of trained and expert teachers who can handle a station teaching model most appropriately in their classroom.
- It is a very challenging task to create or design a learning station that can function independently.
- Management of time and management of noise or destruction is a very challenging task in the context of the station teaching model.

Teaming

Teaming is another unique co-teaching approach. In the team teaching-learning approach, both teachers provide their material or instruction at the same time. Sometimes this approach of teaching is also called "one brain in two bodies" or "tag-team teaching". This model of teaching is complex but a more satisfying approach.

Characteristics

- In this model of co-teaching both teachers provides the same teaching-learning material simultaneously.
- In this model, both teachers are responsible for the classroom management, teaching-learning process, and engagement of the student.

Advantages

- This model helps to motivate the student effectively.
- Various instructional strategies can be applied in the specific model of teaching.
- In this model of teaching, the teachers can work collaboratively and cooperatively which can bring about huge engagement from students and increase the opportunity for participation.
- Through this model of teaching, a teacher can introduce various new concepts/topics and methods of instruction in a specific teaching-learning scenario.

Challenges

- The first and foremost challenging task is content knowledge. In the teaming model of co-teaching, both teachers need an accountable expectation in teaching content, otherwise, this model can create disturbance in the teaching-learning environment.
- Teachers need to be significantly planning their classroom management and the strategies of instruction otherwise this model can create huge noise in the classroom.
- Teachers need to know effective collaborative strategies otherwise it can increase ego in both teachers.
- Another challenging task in this model of co-teaching is the maintenance of individual needs in a specific teaching-learning situation and the maintenance of the trust and commitment of both teachers.

Alternative Teaching

In the alternative method of co-teaching, one teacher is responsible to provide instruction to a heterogeneous group of students or a large group of students, and another teacher is responsible to provide instruction to small groups. This model is specifically designed to provide remedies to

Figure 13.3 The teaming model of co-teaching.

the student but it is equally appropriate to engage students in their teaching-learning materials. In an alternative teaching-learning model co-teaching, a small group is not permanent rather it is responsible for various pre-teaching activities such as the enrichment of students, application of special activities, or alternative methods or strategies, etc.

Characteristics

- In this model of teaching one teacher is responsible to provide instruction to a large group of students and the other teacher provides instruction to small groups of students.
- This model is very much effective for remedial class teaching.

Advantages

- This model of co-teaching can increase the content knowledge of the student in a versatile way.
- This approach can scientifically manage student behavior scientifically.
- This approach is very effective to provide immediate feedback, positive reinforcement to the student, and facilitating appropriate behavior among students.

Challenges

- Students may be disappointed by participating in a small group.
- Another challenging task is time management and group collaboration.
- One teacher can dominate the other teacher in the context of content delivery and teaching style.

One Teaches and One Observes

In this model of co-teaching one teacher teaches the whole class and the other teacher works as an observer, who is responsible for systematically gathering data on students' activities. This model is specifically designed to get a review or feedback from the student to know more about the mastery of the concepts.

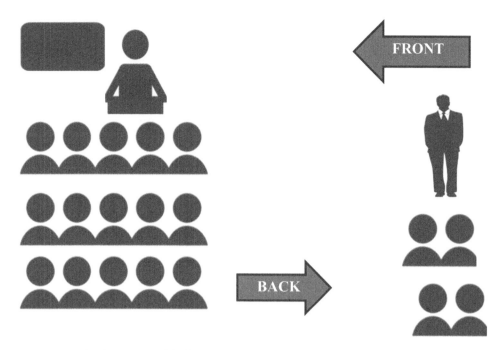

Figure 13.4 The alternative model of co-teaching.

Characteristics

- This model of co-teaching is specifically designed for the evaluation of students' performance.
- In this model, one teacher teaches the whole classroom and another teacher observes the student activities.

Advantages

- Teachers can focus on students more accurately and explicitly.
- Teachers can evaluate their instructional process or method of instruction experimentally.
- Another advantage is an increase in student motivation through instant feedback.
- Teachers can collect data from the students for their future improvement and individualized educational program planning.

Challenges

- One of the greatest challenges is the handling of student data for expert solutions.
- Another challenge is managing student data when the appropriate physical space is not available.
- The maintenance of teacher trust is also a big challenge in this model.

One Teaches and One Assists

One teaches and one assist is another essential teaching model where one teacher takes primary responsibility to provide the learning content or lessons in a classroom, and the other teacher assist the students as required.

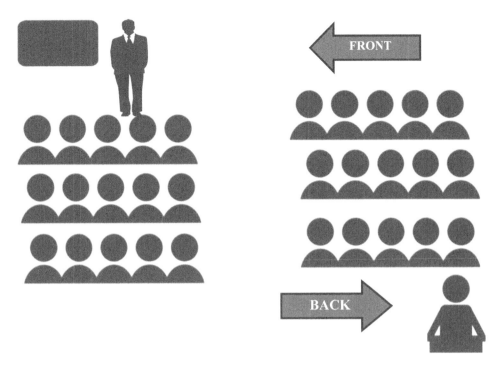

Figure 13.5 The one teaches one observes model of co-teaching.

Characteristics

- In this approach, one teacher takes responsibility to provide learning content material and the other teacher observes all of the student activity and collects data to ensure the understanding or mastery of the learning material.
- An assistant teacher always takes care of struggling students to assist in understanding.
- An assistant teacher takes the role of a monitor of student behavior.
- Instructing teacher is responsible for providing learning content material in an effective manner

Advantages

- In this approach, a teacher can closely monitor students' academic and social behavior.
- Students can get individualized support from the teacher promptly.
- A new teacher can take responsibility for teaching as an assistant teacher in a one teach one assist approach.

Challenges

- One of the greatest challenges of the "one teaches one assists approach" is the authority or ownership of a teacher. In this model of co-teaching one student can perceive the authority or ownership of one specific teacher who is instructing them more than the other teacher who is assisting.
- In this model of co-teaching one teacher can mostly focus on student behavior rather than their learning process.

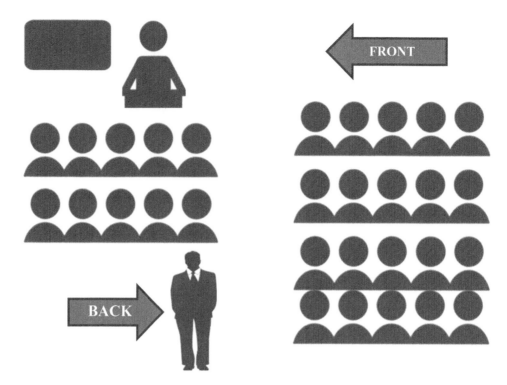

Figure 13.6 The one teaches one assists model of co-teaching.

- In this approach, students may think that the instructing teacher is a "real teacher" and the other is just an assistant.
- Students may distract from their learning when other teachers walk around for supervision.
- This model of co-teaching requires an expert-level teacher to implement this in a classroom situation which is mostly not available in a developing country scenario.
- This model requires a balanced alternative between the role of both teachers which is more challenging.

Applicability of Co-Teaching and Level of Planning

Stages of the Co-Teaching Process

As we all know that co-teaching is a developmental process. Like other methods of instruction co-teaching also has some specific processes and stages. Gately (2001) through extensive research in the field of co-teaching has identified three developmental stages in the co-teaching process. Those are the following:

1. **Beginning Stage**
2. **Compromising Stage**
3. **Collaborating Stage**

Beginning Stage

This stage is a basic level or introductory level communication between two teachers. In this stage, teachers develop their interpersonal relationships as well as professional relationships with

Table 13.1 Present applicability of co-teaching and level of planning

Co-teaching Method	Description of Co-teaching	Applicability	Levels of Planning and Time
Parallel teaching	Two teachers present their instructional material simultaneously by dividing the whole class into two equal groups.	• The student–teacher ratio is low and the teacher likes to provide effective instructional material. • To increase student participation in the classroom. • This model of teaching is more applicable for re-teaching, test review, drill, and practice.	Medium 30%–40% of the time
Station teaching	The classroom and content material is divided into two equal groups. Two teachers teach one group first and after the second group alternatively.	• The content is more complicated and not in a hierarchical manner. • A specific instructional material is comprised of several topics.	Medium 30% of the time
Teaming	Both teachers provide their instructional material at the same time.	• This model is applicable when in a specific lesson instructional conversation is appropriate. • When teachers have considerable experience and knowledge and a high sense of cooperation.	High (as required)
Alternative teaching	One teacher instructs a large student and another teacher works with a small group to provide specialized attention.	• A teacher likes to provide a mastery of content to the student. • Enrichment of students is more important. • Students are working with a parallel curriculum.	High 20%–30% of the time
One teaches one observes	One teacher teaches the whole class and the other teacher work as a supervisor of the whole teaching-learning scenario. After the completion of the overall activity, both teachers sit together to analyze the gathered information from the student.	• This model of teaching is applicable when both teachers are new in a co-teaching situation. • Lots of questions arise from the students. • To in-depth monitor the student activity. • To compare target students with their other classroom peers.	Low <10% of the time
One teaches, one assist	One teacher provides the whole instructional material and another teacher functions as an assistant to monitor the entire activity of the classroom.	• One teacher has knowledge of the subject matter and another teacher has more observation power. • This approach mostly is applicable when the co-teaching scenario is comparatively new. • When a teacher needs to closely monitor the whole classroom situation and analyze it for further improvement.	Low

Design, Evaluation, and Implementations

their co-teacher or colleagues. This stage is crucial, but also hard because in that stage both teachers (e.g., general education teacher and special education teacher) need to create an intimate relationship that will be more professional rather than personal. At the beginning stage, a special education teacher will be more uncomfortable compared to a general education teacher. In that stage, the special education teacher feels detached or excluded from the whole teaching-learning scenario. Therefore at the beginning stage, both teachers need to work very slowly and strategically, so that they can distribute or specify their roles in a classroom situation. Without strategic collaboration and mutual understanding, both teachers can get "stuck" at this level. Therefore at the beginning stage, both teachers need to spend as much time as possible to achieve a concrete interpersonal relationship.

Compromising Stage

This is a second-level communication after the beginning stage. In this stage, both teachers develop an adequate relationship with each other as needed. This stage is comparatively more professional and interactive. In the compromising stage, special education teacher seems more comfortable and play an active role in the whole teaching-learning process. The major focus in this stage is to achieve a mutually accepted educational goal effectively. In that stage, through compromise, both teachers build a level of trust, collaboration, cooperation, etc., and this process moves them from the compromising stage to the collaborative stage.

Collaboration Stage

This is the third and most important level in the co-teaching process. In this stage, both teachers communicate more professionally and openly. This stage is more professional because both teachers mostly focus on successfully achieving an educational goal rather than the role they are playing in a classroom. A high level of communication can be perceived on the stage by a teacher, student, and other visitors. At this stage, both share their work and complement each other. Because of a high level of comfort in communication in the collaborative stage, sometimes it is very hard to differentiate who is a special education teacher and who is a general educator.

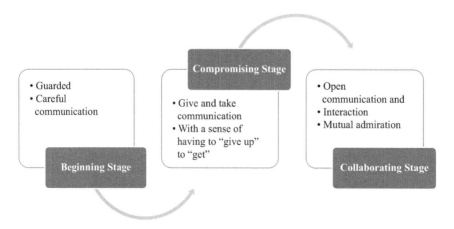

Figure 13.7 Present stages of the co-teaching process.

Components of Co-Teaching

In a co-teaching approach, various components are interrelated between the success and failure of a co-teaching process. Eminent researcher Gately (2001) discussed eight important components which need to be effectively utilized to achieve a specific co-teaching goal; those are as follows:

- Interpersonal communication
- Physical arrangement
- Familiarity with curriculum
- Curriculum goals and modifications
- Instructional planning
- Instructional presentation
- Classroom management
- Assessment

Interpersonal Communication

Interpersonal communication is one of the most essential components of co-teaching. From a basic point of view, interpersonal communication builds up an essential relationship between a teacher with students, or a teacher with another teacher, or students with other students. Interpersonal communication may be a verbal or non-verbal approach. In the initial stage of co-teaching, interpersonal communication may be comprised by a lack of openness, a lack of verbal style, and a level of dissatisfaction. After some time teacher will be familiar with interpersonal communication in an effective manner. In the second stage of interpersonal communication, a teacher will be more open and able to interact with the student more fluently. This stage is very important for relationship-building with the students and co-teachers. After successfully achieving this stage teachers can share their ideas, a broad spectrum of specific educational goals, and strategies to achieve a goal with the students. At the second stage of interpersonal communication, a teacher can successfully increase their use of appreciation for humans in a specific classroom situation. Successful application of humor in a classroom situation is a mark to move from the beginning stage to the compromising stage. In the compromising stage or the collaborative stage, co-teachers begin to create a model for effective communication. The creation of a communication model is very important for people with disabilities as they become role models for effective communication with the students. In that stage students observe the model of communication of the teacher and further apply it in solving problem, future communication, negotiating with other pairs, etc. In the context of effective interpersonal communication in the co-teaching approach if the partner is male and female both together then the student can get an opportunity to learn the communication between both sexes.

Physical Arrangement

In a co-teaching approach, another essential component is an appropriate physical arrangement in the classroom. Appropriate arrangement of teaching-learning material, the seating arrangement of a student, and the arrangement of required devices can increase the opportunity for success in a specific co-teaching model. In the beginning stage, it is hard to arrange the seating arrangement for the entire classroom in a correct manner. It can also show that at the beginning stage there appears to be an invisible wall between the two teachers. At the beginning stage, it can also be felt by the students and teachers that they are seated in two separate classrooms under a single roof. However, after the careful handling of the physical arrangement, teachers can level up to the compromising stage where they feel mutual understanding between two teachers in respect of sharing a physical space. In a compromising state, a teacher will start sharing their space and material without any pre-discussion. It is also noticed by the researcher that in the compromising state special education teacher move more freely in the whole classroom compared to the beginning stage.

Familiarity with Curriculum

After becoming comfortable with the physical arrangement another essential component of a co-teaching approach is being competent and confident in the educational curriculum. This is very important to take into consideration that special education teachers should not take the role of a general education teacher, and vice versa, in the context of the delivery of teaching material. In the context of familiarity or comfort with the curriculum, both teachers need to work with a solid understanding of the content of a curriculum. At the beginning stage, both teachers may not be familiar with the content or methodology used by each other. This kind of lack of understanding may create a challenging situation. However, after leveling up from the beginning stage to the collaborative stage the confidence of both teachers grows in the context of the curriculum. In this stage, competence, as well as confidence, will increase and both teachers will be willing to modify the curriculum and share their plan to increase the effectiveness of a specific teaching-learning scenario.

Curriculum Goals and Modifications

The development of an effective curriculum is the central stage of an effective teaching-learning process. It involves huge planning to align the curriculum with a broader educational goals. In the context of curriculum design and development, both teachers need to be involved to design a curriculum that can meet a border spectrum of education goals. They also need to design a curriculum that can explicitly specify the educational objective. To achieve a successful curriculum design an extensive amount of planning and modification is needed before the start of a school year. However, at the beginning stage, both teachers can complain about "limited planning time" or even "no planning time". Therefore a strong relationship and cooperation are needed to successfully design curriculum goals or to modify an existing curriculum. Without concrete guidelines about curriculum goals, some teachers can move very slowly in relationship building. It is also noted that planning time is very important in co-teaching because without specific planning time co-teachers will not be able to discuss future strategies or modifications to achieve a specific learning objective.

Instructional Planning

We all know that instructional planning is a very important component in any educational scenario. Instructional planning is a very complex job that requires a lot of planning to design effective instructional strategies. Therefore, in a co-teaching approach where two or more teachers are involved in a teaching-learning process, a huge amount of collaboration and cooperation is needed to plan an effective instructional strategy. At the beginning stage of co-teaching, students can experience two types of teaching from two separate teachers. Without proper design of instructional planning, students may feel that one teacher is the prime teacher and another teacher is just an assistant in the classroom. In the compromising stage, both teachers will be more flexible with sharing their plans with each other. This mutual understanding of sharing will help to reach both teachers at a collaborative level. At a collaborative level, both teachers will discuss instructional planning inside as well as outside the classroom environment, or during the continuation of the instructional lesson. Mutual sharing and planning are essential norms in a collaborative stage of instructional planning.

Instructional Presentation

An instructional presentation is another essential component of the co-teaching classroom. Research shows that at the beginning stage of co-teaching teachers are mostly intended to provide a separate instructional presentation in a classroom. In the beginning stage, it seems that one teacher who uses the chalkboard is the main teacher and the other teacher seems to be working as a helper. However, after overcoming the beginning stage, at the compromise stage teachers understand the power of sharing the presentation with their co-teacher. In that stage, both teachers will learn how to make collaborative activities in a specific classroom in the context of instructional presentation. At the collaborative level, both teachers can also learn how to present instructional material, how to provide instruction effectively, and how to structure learning activities inside the classroom.

Classroom Management

Classroom management is another essential component in a co-teaching approach. Effective classroom management requires community building and relationship building with the student and teacher. Structure and relationships are very crucial elements for effective classroom management. A good classroom manager can effectively utilize these two elements. In the core teaching scenario, where the teacher works in a single classroom, they must understand their role and responsibility as a basic requirement of effective classroom management. At the basic stage of classroom management, it seems that the special education teacher plays the role of a "behavior manager" and the general teacher plays a lead role in the classroom as "chief behavior manager". When the teachers move from the beginning stage to the compromising stage, this will generate a mutual understanding in the context of rules and the role of both teachers in the classroom. At this stage, they will discuss the behavior plan and revise it by discussing it with the peer teacher. After achieving the collaborative stage both teachers will be involved in developing a classroom management system through a mutual discussion with co-teachers. This process helps to develop community-building and relationship-building to enhance the management of the classroom effectively.

Assessment

In a classroom situation, the development of an evaluation system for the individual student standard, the expectation, and the performance of a student. A norm is created that students need to achieve. At the beginning stage of assessment in a co-teaching scenario, both teachers will stumble with two separate grading systems. Sometimes a general education teacher authoritatively maintains one grading system which they have developed. In this state, the student evaluation process mostly is objective and mainly focuses on an evaluation of the content knowledge of a student. At the compromising stage, both teachers will discuss a common or alternate assessment idea to improve the assessment process. In this stage, both teachers will also discuss the variously applicable methodology or strategies to capture the student's progress. At the collaborative stage, teachers will understand the effectiveness of various assessment processes to monitor the student's progress in both a subjective and objective manner.

Design, Evaluation, and Implementations

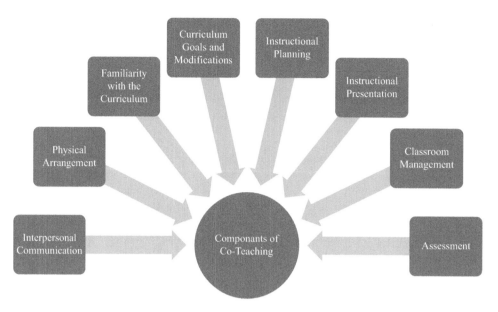

Figure 13.8 Components of the co-teaching approach.

Advantages of a Co-Teaching Approach

From the overall discussion of previous sections, one gets a view that co-teaching is an innovative approach. The effectiveness of co-teaching is not bound to the student or teacher, it is also helpful for the school administration. The following are some of the benefits of co-teaching when constructed carefully:

Benefits for Student

Students can get the following benefit from the well-constructed co-teaching environment:

- Children with special needs and diverse needs can have access to the general education curriculum and general classroom space.
- The co-teaching model can increase the self-esteem of the student which can create a positive environment in the teaching-learning process.
- Co-teaching helps to create a strong relationship between student-to-student, teacher-to-teacher, and teacher-to-student effectively which can bring more motivation and engagement in a teaching-learning process.
- Co-teaching especially promotes an individualized learning environment; therefore, it helps to create a teaching-learning environment that is much more active and fun.
- Co-teaching can enhance academic performance in an effective manner.
- Co-teaching provides opportunity and access to a variety of instructional strategies through two or more highly qualified experts which helps the student in academic achievement.
- Co-teaching works as a support system for educators to address students' needs.
- The ability to access the general education teacher and special education teacher in the teaching model helps to reduce the stigma for the student with a disability.
- Co-teaching helps the student to expose a positive academic and social model.

Benefits for Teachers

A well-constructed co-teaching approach can give the following benefit to the teacher:

- The first and foremost important aspect for a teacher is his or her professional growth. Co-teaching is a well-designed model which can effectively promote professional growth for the teacher.
- A co-teaching platform helps the teacher to share their knowledge, skills, and resources with co-teachers, which helps to develop their interpersonal communication skills.
- A teacher can increase their competence through the utilization of resources and effective communication in the classroom besides they can also increase their understanding in the context of the general education curriculum and classroom expectations.
- The co-teaching model can help the teacher to build strategies for how to adapt or modify a curriculum to meet the need of a student.
- Co-teaching helps to promote collaborative practice between two or more teachers in classroom situations.
- It helps to increase the communication between the classroom teacher and student to effectively achieve a mutually accepted educational goal.
- The co-teaching model provides an opportunity to share the responsibility of one teacher with another, which can lighten the workload of the teacher in a specific teaching-learning scenario compared to the conventional teaching-learning model.
- Co-teaching helps the teacher to increase their expertise in the context of collections and analysis of student performance on a much deeper level for strategy-making and the improvement of a classroom environment.
- Co-teaching helps the teacher in increasing their practice to set a mutual goal of educational objectives.
- In a co-teaching approach, a teacher can feel less isolated compared to the conventional teaching model.

Benefits for Schools

Schools can get the following benefits from the co-teaching model:

- Co-teaching can help to establish a school-based culture of collaboration that will be helpful for a school environment.
- Co-teaching will help to establish a system for all educators in a school environment.
- Co-teaching helps to decrease the student-teacher ratio in a classroom environment.

Disadvantages of a Co-Teaching Approach

There has been a lot of benefits and significant outcome of the co-teaching approach. But still, some situations may not work very well in a co-teaching approach and these are the following:

- **Personality conflict**: Every teacher has his/her own teaching style and personality. In this context people with contradicting personalities are not able to adjust in a co-teaching situation because of a dominating intensity. In that scenario, the overall classroom cannot get benefit from the co-teaching approach.
- **Lack of team management**: For effective co-teaching, there is a huge need for effective management of the team to get good outcomes or results. However, in a realistic situation,

it shows that both teachers may suffer internal conflict and ego problems that may result in a complete failure of the co-teaching approach.
- **The problem of coordination**: As per teaching strategies some teachers prefer to work with hands-on experience and some teachers are more reliable with text-based teaching-learning. Many times it shows that it may be a source of conflict between both teachers to effectively coordinate with each other in the context of teaching strategies.
- **Lack of strategy-making time**: To develop effective coordination and design effective co-teaching it needs a lot of time to design and plan an effective strategy. However, teachers are busy with their classes and have very limited time to study the underlying theme and that may be one of the reasons for the failure of the co-teaching approach.
- **Lack of acceptance of change**: Teachers are very familiar with the conventional approach to teaching and learning; therefore, they fear changing their teaching pattern and often are rigid about their teaching style.
- **Lack of administrative support**: In developing countries such as India there is a lack of administrative support to implement a proper co-teaching approach.

Bibliography and Suggested Readings

Austin, V. L. (2001). Teachers' beliefs about co-teaching. *Remedial and Special Education, 22*(4), 245–255. https://doi.org/10.1177/074193250102200408.

Bacharach, N., Heck, T., & Dank, M. (February, 2004). *Co-teaching in student teaching: A case study.* Paper presented at the annual meeting of the Association of Teacher Educators, Dallas, Texas.

Beninghof, A. M. (2012). *Co-teaching that works: Structures and strategies for maximizing student learning.* Crosspoint Boulevard, Indianapolis, IN: Wiley pub.

Burke, J. (2010). *Effective factors of co-teaching as perceived by general and special education teacher.*

Chisholm, M. A. (n.d.). *Co-teaching: Regular education/special education; and, Co-teaching reference guide.* U.S. Dept. of Education, Office of Educational Research and Improvement.

Conderman, G., Val Bresnahan, E. D. S. E. T., & Pedersen, T. (2008). Purposeful co-teaching: Real cases and effective strategies. *Focus on Exceptional Children, 28*(3). https://10.17161/fec.v28i3.6852

Cook, L., & Friend, M. (2017). Co-teaching: Guidelines for creating effective practices. *Focus on Exceptional Children, 28*(3). https://doi.org/10.17161/fec.v28i3.6852.

Co-teaching regular education/special education co-teaching reference guide. (1991). Distributed by ERIC clearinghouse.

Fattig, M. L., & Taylor, M. T. (2008). *Co-teaching in the differentiated classroom: Successful collaboration, lesson design, and classroom management, grades 5–12.*

Fennick, E. (2001). Coteaching an inclusive curriculum for transition. *Teaching Exceptional Children, 33*(6), 60–66. https://doi.org/10.1177/004005990103300608.

Friend, M. (2014). *Co-teaching: Strategies to improve student outcomes.* Pro-Ed.

Friend, M., & Cook, L. (2003). *Interactions: Collaboration Skills for School Professionals* (4th ed.). Boston, MA: Allyn and Bacon

Gately, S. E., & Gately, F. J. (2001). Understanding coteaching components. *Teaching Exceptional Children, 33*(4), 40–47. https://doi.org/10.1177/004005990103300406.

Hill, J. (2015). *Co-teaching: A difference study in student discipline and attendance in co-taught, regular, and pullout special education.* Weber State University.

Honigsfeld, A., & Dove, M. G. (2010). *Collaboration and co-teaching: Strategies for English learners.* Crowin Press .https://dx.doi.org/10.4135/9781452219516

Hourcade, J., & Bauwens, J. (2001). Cooperative teaching: The renewal of teachers. *Clearing House, 74*(5), 242–247. Retrieved from http://www.jstor.org/stable/30189673.

Jackson, P. D. (2006). *Co-teaching: Bringing specially designed instruction into the general education classroom.*

Muller, E., Hurley-Chamberlain, D., & Friend, M. (n.d.). State-level approaches to co-teaching. *Inforum.* Project Forum at NASDSE. http://www.projectforum.com

Murawski, W. W. (2012). 10 tips for using co-planning time more efficiently. *Teaching Exceptional Children, 44*(4), 8–15. https://doi.org/10.1177/004005991204400401.

Perez, K. D., & Wong, H. K. (2012). *The co-teaching book of lists.*

Potts, E. A., & Howard, L. A. (2011). *How to co-teach: A guide for general and special educators.* Baltimore, MD: Brookes Publishing Company.

Stein, E. (2017). *Two teachers in the room: Strategies for co-teaching success*, (1st edition). Routledge.

Villa, R. A., Thousand, J. S., & Nevin, A. I. (2013). *A guide to co-teaching: New lessons and strategies to facilitate student learning.* San Diego, CA: Ravillabayridge

Wilson, G. L. (2016). *Co-planning for co-teaching: Time-saving routines that work in inclusive classrooms (ASCD arias).* Alexandria, VA: North Beauregard Street.

Wilson, G. L., & Blednick, J. (2011). *Teaching in tandem: Effective co-teaching in the inclusive classroom.* Alexandria, VA: North Beauregard Street.

14
BLENDED LEARNING IN EDUCATION

Introduction

The entire educational system is going through a revolutionary phase. Now, the process of education is more dynamic compared to the previous century. To ensure quality education for all is not only a fundamental aim but also a major challenge in any education system.

Since, the very past educationist and researchers felt that the traditional lecture-based teaching method is limited in its scope to achieve the challenges of teaching-learning. In this context, the blended learning method is an innovative approach in the context of the 21st-century education system. The major focus of the present chapter is to provide expanded knowledge of blended learning in the context of the present education system.

Meaning and Definitions of Blended Learning

In general view, blended learning is a method of instruction that combines both face-to-face teaching and teaching through the use of Information Communication Technology (ICT) It's a combinational process of direct, indirect, collaborative, and computer-based instructional approaches. The following are some of the definitions of blended learning:

Partridge, Ponting, and McCay (2011) explained that blended learning is a balance between face-to-face elements and online activity that varies depending on the purpose and outcomes to be achieved, and is guided by pedagogical design principles.

Krause (2007) defined blended learning as the general integration of various modes of delivery in the context of teaching and style of learning. It is also a systematic approach that can combine the best features of technology and face-to-face interaction in the teaching and learning process.

Dziuban, Hartman, and Moskal (2004) defined blended learning as a model which generally combines the effectiveness of the instructional process and increases the opportunity for socialization in the context of instruction.

Osguthorpe and Graham (2003) defined blended learning as a combinational process of face-to-face and distance-learning environments. Furthermore, they discussed that blended learning can increase the opportunity for the utilization of the benefits of face-to-face and online methods of instruction. From the above definition, it can be said that blended learning is a unique learning approach where multiple methods are combined to achieve a learning objective. In the 21st century, some familiar terms such as "hybrid learning", "mixed learning", and "multiple methods of learning" all denote the integration that blends e-learning equipment and technique with the conventional method of teaching.

However, it is also imperative to say that blended learning is not only the combination of electronic media or online-based teaching approach to the traditional methods of teaching rather it is a broader concept where blended learning is combined following the various level of learning:

- **Theoretical level**: Blended learning combines various theories of instruction such as cognitivism, behaviorism, cognitivism, constructivism, etc.
- **Methodical level**: In the methodological aspects of teaching, blended learning combines an individual learning approach with a collaborative learning approach, a self-directed learning approach with instructor-led instruction, and a receptive learning approach with explorative learning, etc.
- **The medium of instruction level:** In the context of the use of various mediums in teaching-learning; blended learning combines a face-to-face teaching approach with online learning, paper, and pencil-based learning approach with computer-based teaching, etc.

History of Blended Learning

First Attempt (1999–2002)

The history of blended learning is not very old. In the year 2000, Cooney et al. (2000) first coined the term "blended learning" and designed a new learning approach in kindergarten school by combining play and work to achieve learning objectives. However, Cooney's concept of blended learning is not the same as the modern blended learning concept but it is still an important concept to promote instruction in the blended method.

In the context of the modern blended learning approach, Voci and Young (2001) were the first proponents who integrated the e-learning approach into instructor-led programs. The major aim of this experiment was to find out the effectiveness of instructor-led programs and e-learning in a combined way. However, the result revealed that the process increased the sense of teamwork and group learning among the learner (Voci & Young, 2001).

In another revolutionary work conducted by Bonk et al. (2002) the major aim of the study was to find out the effectiveness of the blended learning approach in the context of professional development. They applied the strategies of the blended learning approach for training the military through a high-stake course. They mainly used synchronously internet-based learning in their first phase of research and synchronous learning, virtual collaborative chat, and face-to-face residential learning in the third phase and found out that the blended way of learning is more effective compared to the only internet-led learning process (Bonk et al., 2002).

Besides, they also conducted a focused group interview with the students, instructors, and education advisors, and took a view about this new combined or blended system of learning. The result indicated that internet-based online learning seems interesting among the student but maximum learning participation was found in face-to-face sessions at different times.

Moreover, Bonk's research was not fully designed for blended learning rather it supported "online learning" courses through face-to-face sessions. Therefore, it can be said that the first fully blended learning model approach was proposed by Stewart (2002). He mixed self-paced asynchronous learning with synchronous face-to-face instructor-led learning for intellectual training.

Definition Period of Blended Learning (2003–2005)

After various research conducted by eminent researchers globally, the year 2003–2005 is termed as the defining period of blended learning because a majority of researchers in this period mainly focused on defining blended learning. In this period one of the most cited and acceptable definition were provided by Osguthorpe and Graham (2003). They defined blended learning as it "combines face-to-face with distance delivery systems …, but it's more than showing a page from a website on the classroom screen … those who use blended learning environments are trying to maximize the benefits of both face-to-face and online methods". Osguthorpe and Graham (2003) also discussed three types of blended learning models. First, **a blend of learning activities**, where a student can benefit from both online as well as face-to-face classrooms, Second, **a blend of students**, where the student in the face-to-face classroom can be blended with a different student in online learning activities. Third, **a blend of instructors**, where a student in the face-to-face classroom can benefit from the other instructor through the online learning environment. Moreover, various researchers like Singh (2002), Garrison and Kanuka (2004) enriched the field of blended learning in many ways.

Popularity Period of Blended Learning (2007–2009)

In the years 2007–2009, the blended learning approach gathered more popularity. During this stipulated period, throughout the world, many developed and developing countries adopted the blended learning approach. At the peak of the popularity period researchers pointed out two major concerns in the context of blended learning one is the perception of the participant and another is the effectiveness of blended learning.

Characteristics of Blended Learning

A Combination of Online and Offline Learning

In the previous section, it is explicitly described that blended learning is a combinational process of online and offline learning. In this learning process, students can learn through ICT-based learning environments, where some teachers can also be involved to assist the learner. In some of the blended learning contexts, the responsible teacher teaches one learning module through a face-to-face learning method in the classroom and the rest part of the specific module can be provided as a homework task for the learner.

Involvement of Instructor

In the online learning process, one of the major concerns of the parents is whether their child can fully participate in an online learning process or not. In this context, blended learning is a teacher-dependent online learning environment, where one teacher physically assists the students in the classroom and virtually assists the students when a student learns from home through the online learning process.

Independent Learning

Another important characteristic of blended learning is that it is much an independent learning process compared to conventional learning aspects. This process of learning always encourages self-learning. In a learning process, it shows that some students are faced with difficulty because they are slow-paced learners relative to other peers. In this context, the blended learning process always promotes interaction in the learning process rather than just sitting and listening to the dialogue from the teacher.

Dynamics and Diverse Role of Teachers

Though the blended learning process promotes both online and offline learning processes, this type of learning process encourages the teacher to play a more active, dynamic, and diverse role in the learning process. In this process of learning, teachers need to play a diverse role in a specific learning environment. For instance, they need to be more tech-savvy in the online learning process and more interactive in the conventional learning format.

Increase the Online Experience of the Student

A plethora of changes have taken place after the inclusion of computers. Now it is important for the learner to learn about ICT and 21st-century skills to sustain in present society. In the context of the definition of "literacy", those who do not know modern technology can also be called illiterate. Therefore, one of the essential characteristics of blended learning is it helps to develop the understanding of students regarding modern technology-based learning approaches such as online learning, virtual world, ICT, etc.

Promote 21st-Century Competence to the Learner

Another essential characteristic of blended learning is that it helps to promote various timely competencies of the learner. The current time is the digital era. It is not enough for a learner to just gather book knowledge and learn by rote memory, rather to progress in this present social context learner needs to adopt various learning skills such as effective communication, empathy, self-management, critical thinking, sharing knowledge throughout the world, etc. Blended learning helps to promote all these through the online and offline learning process.

Physical Development of the Learner in the Online Learning Space

In the earlier phases of online learning, many critics blamed online learning, saying it creates a hindrance to the space of physical development of the student. However, the blended learning process helps to overcome this limitation by blending both aspects (online and offline). Therefore, it also encourages various physical activities on the school campus as well as online activities for learning purposes.

From the above discussion, one can learn about some of the specific characteristics of blended learning. It is also imperative to say that in developing countries such as India, the use of blended learning is limited, but increasing very fast. Maybe in the future, blended learning will be treated as a common learning approach.

Types of Blended Learning

As discussed in the earlier section, in a general overview blended learning is not a new concept. In educational scenarios from the past, various methods of the instructional process have been used to develop the competency of the learner as well as to achieve the learning objective. In this point of view, nearly 100 types of blended learning have been developed. However, this section discusses 12 of the most popular and useful types of blended learning models and their outcomes. So that, the reader can understand and identify the best possible method applicable to the educational settings. They are as follows:

1. **Section rotation blended learning**: Section rotation blended learning is a unique blended learning approach commonly used in the "elementary school" settings. In this blended learning approach students are allowed to rotate around a specific station in a fixed schedule. Of the many stations, one station must be an online station.
2. **Lab rotation blended learning**: This is a similar aspect to the station rotation model. Here the student is allowed to rotate through a station on a fixed schedule. Here students are also allowed to communicate with a teacher in the computer lab, which increases the use of a computer lab in school.
3. **Remote blended learning or enriched virtual**: Remote blended learning model is another unique approach in the context of strategies and methods used for instruction. Here the major focus of the student always is on the completion of existing online coursework with the help of the teacher intermittently or as per need. This learning method is different as compared to the flipped classroom because "instructional time" is the context of balance between online and face-to-face communication. Besides, in the remote blended learning model students are allowed to meet with the teacher occasionally rather than on a daily basis such as in the flipped classroom.
4. **Flex blended learning**: In the flex blended learning model "online learning" is the main aspect of learning. Here student learning goes like a fluid or flexible schedule and students learn mainly on the "brick and mortar" campus, except for homework assignments. In this approach the role of the teacher is optional and the teacher will provide face-to-face support only based on the requirements of the students through using various methods such as small group interaction, group projection, individual tutoring, etc.
5. **Flipped classroom blended learning**: This is the most commonly used blended learning model. One of the major characteristics of this type of blended learning is homework provided to the learner to learn any new content or learning module. However, the practice of the newly learned content takes place in a school environment where the teacher physically helps the learner drill and practice the prior learning modules.
6. **Individual rotation blended learning**: This is also like a station learning model where a learner needs to rotate through a specific station but the unique characteristic of individual station learning is that here the teacher or a specific software algorithm specifies the individual learning schedule. Besides, unlike other rotational models, an individual rotational model has very limited opportunity to rotate in any station. A student is only allowed to rotate in a specific pre-mentioned schedule set by the teacher or software algorithms on their playlist.
7. **Project-based blended learning**: The project-based blended learning model promotes both online and face-to-face collaboration in the context of creating project designs, iterations, project-based learning assignments, or artifacts.
8. **Self-directed blended learning:** The self-directed blended learning model is a personalized learning model where a learner sets a role of formal learning on their own. Furthermore, to achieve the prior set learning objective, a student can take help or use it online, face-to-face, or both. In a self-directed blended learning process, the role of online learning and physical communication with the teacher is very flexible.
9. **Inside-out blended learning**: One of the effective examples of the inside-out blended learning model is the "project-based learning approach". One of the essential characteristics of project-based is that the main emphasis is on the "finish or end up" phase of any

learning objective which must be outside the classroom. It may still be required to use the physical and online space both together.

10. **Outside-in blended learning**: In the outside-in blended learning approach learners start any learning module in a non-academic physical space or daily use online or digital space but must "end up or finish" inside the classroom. There is a need for face-to-face guidance and support from the teacher in the outside-in blended learning approach.
11. **Supplemental blended learning**: In this learning approach the major concern is "supplementing the critical learning objective". In this learning approach, either learner completes all the learning module in the "online" space and supplements it with face-to-face learning scenarios or vice versa. Here one space of learning achieves the "critical learning" objective and the opposite space provides a specific supplementing experience that others did not provide.
12. **Mastery-based blended learning:** In this learning space, the student is free to rotate between online and face-to-the face learning process in the context of the activity, assessment, and project to achieve the mastery-based learning objective.

The Process of Blended Learning

From the previous section of this chapter, one can understand that blended learning is a newly introduced unique teaching and learning approach. This is generally a combination of online and offline teaching and learning together. Research shows that the participation of learners is a very crucial aspect of any effective teaching and learning process (Wild, 2007). Therefore, to increase participation in the blended learning a structural process of designing is required so that cognition and collaboration can be increased to enhance the blended approach of the teaching and learning process. As Allen and Seaman (2010) discussed that "thinking and working together creates learning", for a quality learning experience it is required to systematically process and design a learning environment that can help to utilize the resources, time, and money. The following are some of the essential steps needed to be followed to create an effective blended learning environment.

- Planning
- Designing
- Implementing
- Reviewing
- Improving

Planning: In the context of designing any teaching and learning material, one of the essential aspects is planning. As blended learning is a unique teaching and learning environment, it requires an extensive amount of planning before designing a blended learning component. The planning of a blended learning environment can be designed by answering some structured questions related to functions, roles, and application of components of blended learning, in specific course content, resources, activities, and assessment. These four elements are crucial in the context of maintaining the quality of learning courseware. However, before designing blended learning material instructional designers should consider the following:

- The first and foremost aspect to consider is whether the instructional designer wants to develop new courses, likes to work with existing courses, or rather redesign specific courses which are already been used.
- Second, the designer needs to contextualize the scope of the courses. For instance, whether a designer likes to fulfill the specific needs of a particular student or group.
- The third aspect focuses on learning objectives, such as what will be the ultimate goal a student will have achieved after the completion of a specific course.

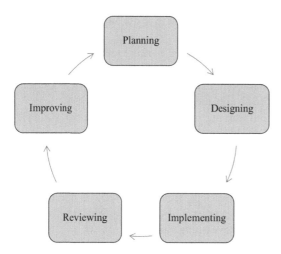

Figure 14.1 Process of blended learning.

- Selection of effective teaching and learning activities in the context of achieving such a specific goal.
- Another essential consideration is the level of course. This includes the teaching and learning environment, the team of teaching personnel, the major contribution of course development and application, a commitment of time, technical skill and knowledge, etc.
- Furthermore, the question related to learning outcomes also needs to be considered, such as whether the use of technology or a blended learning approach is essential to achieve the learning objective. If so, whether the elements of blended learning are capable of scaling its platform as per requirement. Whether designed blended learning technology is sustainable. What is the future of designing blended learning (short-term, mid-term, or long-term).
- In the planning stage, the researcher needs to consider culture and infrastructure as essential considerations. Such as what is the culture of a specific organization. Whether blended learning is applicable in this specific culture. Whether adequate infrastructure or resources are available.
- In the context of student demography, a planner of blended learning should focus on whether or not students have prior experience with blended learning. The level of skill of students using the technology. Whether the number of students is large or small? What is the socioeconomic background of the students. What is the age, language, and location of a student, etc.
- Another important aspect that needs to be considered at this stage of planning is accessibility. It is imperative to get an understanding that the learning environment should meet the needs of a student with disabilities and that the learning environment should be compatible with the diverse nature of learners irrespective of their devices, the speed of the internet, etc.

Design and Development

After planning another essential aspect is designing a blended learning environment. The aspect of design can be divided into two ways one is based on the general design principle and the second is based on special design elements or some of the aspects that can be integrated into a blended learning scenario.

General Design Principles

One of the essential general design principles is the achievement of learning objectives effectively. Therefore, a designer should align teaching and learning activities effectively so that they can directly affect the teaching and learning process.

- Another aspect of the general design principle is constructive alignment, that means allowing a student to participate in or demonstrate the learning objectives (Biggs, 1999).
- The design and development stage needs to be focused on purposeful activities. Besides, the overall activities of learning should be linked with time and content.
- The workload is another essential aspect. In the context of designing blended learning, an instructional designer should maintain a workload that never exceeds the workload in comparison to the traditional model.
- A designer needs to align time, resources, and effort in the context of designing blended learning courseware.

Implementing

After the designing of blended learning courses, another critical aspect is proper implementation in a real educational setting. The following are some of the subject matters that need to be taken into consideration:

- Whether the design of blended learning course material properly trailed.
- Whether students are properly skilled to use various blended learning tools and able to fully participate in specific blended learning scenarios.
- Whether a designer properly analyzed the common problem or difficulties related to using blended learning courseware.
- How much technical supports are available to the student. Whether the designer thinks it is adequate for students.

Reviewing (Evaluating)

After the planning, design, and implementation of teaching and learning course material in a blended learning environment, another essential aspect is evaluation. This is a crucial aspect of the design of any blended learning environment. Throughout the process of evaluation, a developer or instructional designer should maintain the following.

Evaluation in the Context of Feedback

- After the implementation of any course, an instructor needs to wait until the end and collect feedback very carefully by maintaining various appropriate strategies.
- The collection of feedback should be continuous.

Figure 14.2 The constructive alignment model of curriculum design.

- Feedback should be collected strategically and should be taken from various strata of courses, such as after the start of the course, middle of the course, and end of the course.
- The instructor should encourage any critical feedback that comes from the student.

Evaluation in the Context of Course Materials

Like the other teaching and learning scenarios, the process of evaluation in the context of course material is complex. While a blended learning environment involves technical devices, some additional aspects in the context of evaluation need to be taken into consideration.

Herringto et al. (2001) proposed the basic model of an evaluation process that includes three common areas that are pedagogies, resources, and delivery strategies. The instructor needs to be focused on these three aspects to evaluate the blended learning environment very effectively.

It is also notable that Bath and Smith (2004) provide the four "quadrants" or 4Q model of evaluation. In the 4Q model, the four essential aspects are:

- Self-evaluation
- Student learning
- Student experience
- Peer review

Improving

After the completion of the four previous stages and collecting feedback on overall student data, in this stage, an instructional designer needs to include all the required aspects to improve the overall course material. This is the final stage of any blended learning environment.

Advantages and Disadvantages of Blended Learning

From the above discussion, a basic understanding can be sort regarding blended learning and its various model. This section discusses various potential advantages and disadvantages of blended learning.

Advantages of Blended Learning

- **Flexibility**: One of the most crucial advantages of blended learning is flexibility. It provides flexibility in the presentation of learning materials, the methods of learning, and the sched-

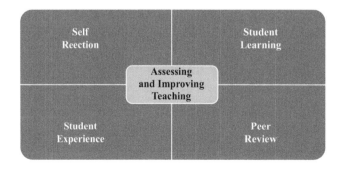

Figure 14.3 The 4Q model of evaluation. Source: Bath and Smith (2004).

ule. Various complex topics can be presented in the classroom and practice can be done online. In this learning approach, the learner is flexible about assigning their role over how and when he or she will participate.

- **Effectiveness**: As discussed previously that various researchers like Garrison Kanuka (2004), Driscoll (2002), Okaz (2015) have found blended learning to be more effective than a purely face-to-face learning approach. Furthermore, it can also impact the level of student achievement, learning motivation, and meaningful learning experiences.
- **Efficiency**: In a well-designed blended learning approach a teacher can provide efficient and quick learning to a broad spectrum of students. In the context of the efficiency of blended learning, the use of digital media such as videos, images, eBooks, and recordings has a huge impact on learning and there is potential to reuse the learning material.
- **Cost-effectiveness**: One of the major challenges in the present education system is that it maintains the cost and saves money for sustainability. Blended learning is a uniquely designed instructional innovation where both online and offline learning can save more time and money in any educational organization. Learning through online modes can save time and money.
- **Personalization**: Every student is unique, therefore without considering this aspect the learning design can result in the isolation of students and an impersonal learning experience. However, a well-crafted blended learning process can overcome this challenge by providing a combinational seamless transition from a computer to the classroom and vice versa. A teacher can design personalized content based on the interest, motivation, and specific job of a learner.
- **Instant diagnosis and student feedback**: Blended learning can provide the ability for the teacher to rapidly analyze, review, and give feedback on the work of the student. Besides, it also provides an opportunity to design learning methods and feedback for each student individually.

Disadvantages of Blended Learning

Like many advantages of blended learning over the instructional process, there are also various disadvantages of blended learning, they are the following:

- Without a proper design, the blended learning process could impact over high dependency of a learner on online and technical resources.
- The group learning aspect could be difficult because of the lack of management of online resources.
- Digital resources available in an online platform are not reliable to use. Therefore, there is a high risk of misleading digital resources.
- As the proper design of blended learning is a complex concept, therefore, it is a great deal of additional workload for the teacher, and all the teachers may not be willing to do so.
- As a great range of possibilities provided by blended learning, it may cause a cognitive overload in the students.

References

Allen, I., & Seaman, J. (2010). *Class Differences: Online Education in the United States, 2010.* Needham, MA: The Sloan Consortium, 1–26. http://sloanconsortium.org/publications/survey/class_differences

Bath, D., & Calvin Smith, C. (2004) *, Sarah Stein & Richard Swann (2004) Beyond mapping and embedding graduate attributes: bringing together quality assurance and action learning to create a validated and living curriculum. *Higher Education Research & Development, 23*(3), 313–328. https://10.1080/0729436042000235427

Biggs, J. (1999) What the student does: teaching for enhanced learning. *Higher Education Research & Development, 18*(1), 57–75. https://10.1080/0729436990180105

Bonk, C. J., Olson, T. M., Wisher, R. A., & Orvis, K. L. (2002). Learning from focus groups: An examination of blended learning. *Journal of Distance Education, 17*(3), 97–118.

Cooney, M. H., Gupton, P., & O'Laughlin, M. (2000). Blurring the lines of play and work to create blended classroom learning experiences. *Early Childhood Education Journal, 27*(3), 165–171. https://doi.org/10.1007/bf02694230.

Driscoll, M. (2002). Blended learning: Let's get beyond the hype. *E-Learning, 1*(4), 1–4.

Dziuban, C., Hartman, J., & Moskal, P. D. (2004, March 30). Blended learning. *ECAR Research Bulletin, 7*. Retrieved from http://educause.edu/ecar/

Garrison, D., & Kanuka, H. (2004). Blended learning: Uncovering its transformative potential in higher education. *Internet and Higher Education, 7*(2), 95–105. https://doi.org/10.1016/j.iheduc.2004.02.001.

Krause, K. (2007). Griffith university blended learning strategy, document number 2008/0016252.

Okaz, A. A. (2015). Integrating blended learning in higher education. *Procedia-Social and Behavioral Sciences, 186*, 600–603.

Oliver, R., & Herrington, J. (2001). *Teaching and learning online: a beginner's guide to e-learning and e-teaching in higher education*. Mount Lawley, Australia: Centre for Research in Information Technology and Communications, Edith Cowan University.

Osguthorpe, R., & Graham, C. (2003). Blended learning environments: Definitions and directions. *Quarterly Review of Distance Education, 4*, 227–233.

Partridge, H., Ponting, D., & McCay, M. (2011, January 1). *Good practice report: Blended learning.*

Singh, H. (2002). Building effective blended learning programs. *Educational Technology, 43*(6), 51–54.

Stewart, J. M. (2002). A blended e-learning approach to intercultural training. *Industrial and Commercial Training, 34*(7), 269–271. https://doi.org/10.1108/00197850210447264.

Voci, E., & Young, K. (2001). Blended learning working in a leadership development program. *Industrial and Commercial Training, 33*(5), 157–161. https://doi.org/10.1108/00197850110398927.

Wild, M. (2007). White Paper: Blending Learning – what's in the mix? *Nine Lanterns.* www.ninelanterns.com.au/iles/9L/pdf/Blended-Learning.pdf (accessed 20 February 2015).

15
ASSISTIVE TECHNOLOGY AND AUGMENTATIVE AND ALTERNATIVE COMMUNICATION

In 2018 the World Health Organization reported that 1 billion people (15% of the overall population of the world) experience some form of disability (WHO, 2018). And another bitter truth is that people with disabilities are the most stigmatized and excluded population in the world. In their overall life span, a person with a disability deals with extreme inequality compared with their non-disabled peers or community. Moreover, the barriers for people with disabilities limit their participation in daily life, family, community, and society. These barriers create an isolative environment around their lives and affect their civic life. To combat these challenges, technology plays a vital role for people with disabilities which helps to improve the functioning of their civic life and increase their opportunity to participate in society. The present chapter is intended to introduce the reader to some new buzz terms such as "assistive technology" and "Augmented Alternative Communication (AAC), that are revolutionary technological innovations to assist a person with a disability.

What Is Assistive Technology

The term "assistive technology" was coined by John Williams decades before the Americans with Disabilities Act (ADA) was passed into law. The legal definition of assistive technology comes from the "Technology-Related Assistance for Individuals With Disabilities Act of 1988" which is also known as the "Tech Act". In 1998 this act was named the "Assistive Technology Act of 1998" (US, 1998).

International Organization for Standardization (ISO) (2016) defines "assistive products more broadly as any product, especially produced or generally available, that is used by or for persons with disability: for participation; to protect, support, train, measure or substitute for body functions/structures and activities; or to prevent impairments, activity limitations or participation restrictions. This includes devices, equipment, instruments, and software".

The International Classification of Functioning, Disability, and Health (ICF) (2013) defines "assistive products and technology as any product, instrument, equipment or technology adapted or specially designed for improving the functioning of a person with a disability" (Draft Version).

The Canadian Association of Occupational Therapy (2012) explains that "AT is any device or product that is useful for a person's enhanced functioning and participation".

Peterson, D. B., Peterson, D. B., and Murray, G. C. (2006) explained that "assistive technology is a systematic application of technologies, engineering methodologies, and scientific principles to meet the needs of, and address the barriers confronted by individuals with handicaps in areas which include education, rehabilitation, employment, transportation, independent living, and recreation".

The World Health Organization (2004) explained that "AT is an umbrella term for any device or system that allows individuals to perform tasks they would otherwise be unable to do or increases the ease and safety with which tasks can be performed".

Individuals with disabilities Education Act (IDEA) (2004) as per services "Assistive Technology means any service that directly assists a child with a disability in the selection, acquisition, or use of an assistive technology device" (From Mittler, J. 2007).

Stead (2002) explained that "Assistive technology (AT) is a service or product that enables independence".

Kraskowsky and Finlayson (2001) defined "Any object or tool that maximizes a person's independence in activities of daily living".

Assistive Technology Act (1998) explained that "Assistive technology is any item, piece of equipment, or product system, whether acquired commercially or off the shelf, modified or customized, that is used to increase, maintain, or improve the functional capabilities of a person with a disability".

In a general aspect, the **Ohio AT Network Assistive Technology Resource Manual (2008)** explained that any *technology-based adaptive device* or service that helps to increase the participation and independence of *people with disability* may be called assistive technology.

If we try to understand the above definition, we can find three major terms that are "people with a disability", "technology" and "adaptation". The following are some brief definitions:

People with a disability: It refers to "any physical or mental impairment that substantially limits a major life activity. Disabilities include but are not limited to, learning disabilities, blindness or low vision, hearing loss, speech impairments, and mobility impairments" (Robitaille, 2010).

Technology: Technology refers to "the science or study of the practical or industrial arts" (Webster, 1984).

Adaption: Here adaption is to "provide enhancements or different ways of interacting with the technology. Adaptations may be as simple as a pencil grip or as complex as an adapted computer system" (Ohio AT Network Assistive Technology Resource Manual, 2008).

It is also notable that, assistive technology by definition includes not only hardware devices but also it includes necessary "services" to increase the participation of people with a disability. The following are definitions of assistive technology based on services.

Augmentative and Alternative Communication (AAC)

As we discussed, assistive technology in the broadest term can be applied to a wide range of individuals with a disability. In this context, assistive technology can be divided into eight categories (Blackhurst & Lahm, 2008). These are the following:

- Augmented Alternative Communication (AAC)
- Adapted computer access
- Device to assist in listening and seeing

Assistive Technology and Alternative Communication

- Environmental control
- Adapted play and recreation
- Seating and positioning
- Mobility and powered mobility
- Prosthetics

In this section, we will discuss Augmented Alternative Communications (AAC). Generally, AAC refers to a specific area of communication disability. Throughout the world, many individuals experience speech or language disorders, and they are unable to communicate with their peers effectively. For instance, an individual with a motor speech disorder is unable to use oral speech effectively. In this context, AAC is a combination of applying various strategies, techniques, symbols, and aids to increase the ability of communication for people with communication disabilities. Beukelman and Mirenda (2005) discussed that AAC is "a system with four primary components; symbols, aids, strategies, and techniques." Johnston (2003) explains that the AAC device can help to compensate for difficulties in expressive and receptive communication. Lloyd et al. (1997) defined AAC as "the supplementation or replacement of natural speech and/or writing".

It is also important to know that, overall AAC systems can be categorized into two categories 1) unaided or no technology and 2) aided or with technology. Unaided or no technology does not require any extra pieces of equipment. It includes manual signs, fingerspelling, body language, gestures, facial expressions, etc. Aided communication requires, as a low-tech aid, external devices, such as objects, pictures, drawings, an alphabet communication board, etc.; and, as a high-tech aid, voice input systems and portable speech-generating devices, etc.

AAC is generally used for two specific purposes, 1) to augment the communication of an individual with dysfluent or unintelligible speech and 2) To provide alternative communication for an individual with a lack of speech or that lack sufficient or effective communication. A variety of conditions can affect an individual with little or no function. Generally, three basic conditions are discussed by Tonsing, Alant, and Lloyd (2005) they are 1) congenital, 2) acquired, and 3) progressive or temporary. From these three conditions, a congenital condition associated with complex communication needs includes disabilities such as a) autism, b) cerebral palsy, c) intellectual disability, and d) developmental apraxia.

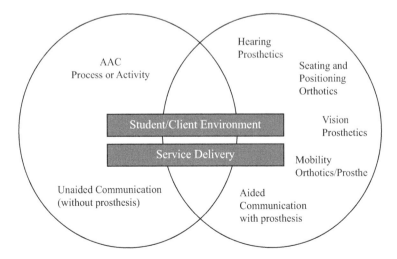

Figure 15.1 Categories of assistive technology by Blackhurst and Lahm, 2008.

Historical Overview of Assistive Technology

The overall historical journey of assistive technology can be divided into three different chronological sections:

The Foundation Period (Before 1900)
The Establishment Period (1900–1972)
The Empowerment Period (1973 to Present)

The Foundation Period (Before 1900)

In the context of the foundation period of assistive technology, we can say that during the Stone Age cavemen used sticks or other natural items for their daily activity when they had an acute injury or other physical disability. From this historical viewpoint, one can see that the first spinal surgery was performed around 600 AD. In those periods assistive technology was not like the present scenario, the major design of assistive technology was mainly focused on providing assistance to injured persons to carry out their daily life activities. As per the historical context, it can be shown that the first autopsies were conducted during the 1600s–1700s, to identify the cause of physical and mental disabilities. From 1817 onwards, Thomas Hopkins first established a school for students with hearing impairment. The name of the school was the "American Asylum for the Education of the Deaf and Dumb"; later the school's name was changed to "American School for the Deaf" (Bryant and Bryant, 2003). Early innovation of assistive technology was developed around 1834 when Louis Braille developed a reading method for people with visual impairment to support their reading. However, the design was mainly developed for French soldiers to increase their ability to read at night. At the same time, Dr. J. G. Blomer developed an institute for individuals with a physical disability and also developed an experimental workroom to make artificial limbs, bandages, and other various assistive technology devices. The name of the institution was the "American printing house for the blind". The first publication for individuals with a disability was published in 1860, named "The Gallaudet Guide, and Deaf Mutes Companion". The foundation period also developed the wheelchair and prosthetic devices around 1869, but that was mainly designed for border soldiers with extreme leg injuries to move from one place to another. However, a major revolution in the field of assistive technology took place in 1876 with the development of the Bell amplifier devices for deaf people (King, 1999). Another significant innovation in the context of assistive technology was the invention of the phonograph in 1877 by Thomas Edison which was very helpful for recording and listening to material, another innovation took place in 1892 when Frank Hall developed the first Braille typewriter for blind people. Therefore, it can be noted that at the foundation period assistive technology took a further important step toward modern innovation of assistive technology.

The Establishment Period (1900–1972)

As discussed by Quist and Lloyd (1997), from 1900 to 1972 is the establishment period of assistive technology. During that period various scientific revolutions took place in the area of people with disabilities. At the early stage of the establishment period of assistive technology the major focus was to serve soldiers whose injuries resulted in various disabilities such as cognitive, language, sensory, physical, etc. However, the major significant footstep in the established period was taken by Barr, Stroud, and Fournier d'Albe in 1920 who developed a reading machine for blind people (Freiberger, 1971). We can say that early innovation of electrical and electronic development in the context of AT took place during the 1920s and 1940s. In that period, lots of innovative technology related to speech synthesis, construction of transistors, etc., were developed. This period is also defined as an incubation period of the development of Augmented Alternative Communication (AAC). Another important innovation is Nemeth Braille Code and computerized braille, which was developed in the 1950s. Besides all such innovations, in the establishment period, lots of organizations related to disability have been growing, for instance, American Association on Mental Retardation, American Speech-Language-Hearing Association, Council for Exceptional Children, United Cerebral Palsy, etc. These were all momentum revolutions in the context of the present development of assistive technology.

The Empowerment Period (1973 to Present)

Quist and Lloyd (1997) in their book, discussed that 1973 is a significant year in the context of the empowerment period for the development of assistive technology. Because in this year Section 504 was added to "The Rehabilitation Act". In that period, plenty of significant legislation was added as a disability right in the context of their education, employability, housing, including other various empowerment aspects. Another significant contribution after 1974 was the invention of the evolutionary closed-circuit television magnifiers that provide low vision aid for a full range of visual needs, specializing in assisting individuals and the development of the first compact braille electronic calculator. From 1970 onward, lots of significant innovations enriched the field of AT market. In that period, the first Braille embosser connected to the microcomputer, which in turn increased the usability of Braille for children and adults. In contemporary times IBM launched a research unit for individuals with disabilities. Furthermore, the most drastic revolutions in the field of assistive technology accelerated during the period of microprocessor innovation. The invention of the microprocessor helped in the development of more complex designs, to reduce the size of devices, lower the cost of devices, and increase the functionality of devices. Another great innovation which helped the field of assistive technology is the innovation of the internet. Through access to the internet, a huge amount of AT devices and resources are immediately available at any time and any place. In the present situation, plenty of assistive technology devices are available in the market for people with hearing impairment, visual impairment, mental retardation, developmental disability, etc. and will be discussed in the next section.

Classifications of Assistive Technology

From the above discussion, one gets the idea that assistive technology is any device or product that is useful for a person's enhanced functioning and participation. Based on the effectiveness and usability of assistive technology worldwide, an increasing number of products related to assistive technology have been developed by various agencies (government as well as private), researchers, and other stakeholders. However, in a general view, the overall innovation of assistive technology can be categorized from various viewpoints. This section will discuss the category of assistive technology based on its level and its comprehensive. They are as follows:

According to the level of assistive technology, it can be classified into two categories:

- Low technology
- High technology

Low technology: Low technology refers to an easy-to-use approach that does not require direct electric power. Glennen and DeCoste (1997) described low technology as a technological approach that requires simple equipment. Cook and Polgar (2008) describe low technology systems as "inexpensive, simple to make and easy to obtain". It is notable that low technology can be electronic or non-electronic. Low technology electronic systems are generally battery-operated with single or multiple switches. Non-electronic low technology is mainly paper-based or physical gesture-based approaches, which can be homemade or can be purchased commercially.

High technology: High technology is more "sophisticated, programmable, types of equipment" (Glennen and DeCoste, 1997). Quest, and Lloyd (1997) described "high-technology" as any device which uses an integrated circuit (IC) such as smaller computer chips, wireless technology, etc.

Furthermore, from the comprehensive definition of Gitlin (as cited by Fuhrer et al., 2003), the following are some forms of categories of assistive technology:

- **Structural alterations**: Changes the original physical structure of the environment, such as widening doors at home.
- **Special equipment**: Connections between attachments to the original structure of the physical environment is established. For example, handrails, stair glides, etc.
- **Assistive devices:** Where physical devices apply to or are directly manipulated by a person such as wheelchairs, voice-output communication aids, or hearing or visual aids.
- **Material adjustment**: Alteration to non-permanent features of the physical environment, for instance, adjusting the light at home, clearing pathways, etc.
- **Environmentally**: Based on behavior modification of personal interaction with the physical environment.

Throughout the different stages of innovation of assistive technology, a lot of assistive technology devices have been developed by the researcher and the designer. We can classify the overall innovation of assistive technology in the following 12 categories (adapted from Ohio AT Network Assistive Technology Resource Manual February, 2008).

1. **Seating and positioning**
   These types of assistive technology devices for the individual with a disability in the context of their sitting and positioning in a particular environment are mentioned below:
   a. Non-slip surface on a chair
   b. Blocks for feet
   c. Bolster or rolled towel for positioning
   d. Adapted alternate chair
   e. Side-lying frames
   f. Standing frames
   g. Floor sitter
   h. Wheelchairs
   i. Custom fitted wheelchair
   j. Straps
   k. Head supports
   l. Trays
   m. Adapted desk/table
   n. Bean bag chairs

2. **Activities of daily living (ADLs)**
   These kinds of assistive technology help the individual with a disability to live independently in the context of their daily life and are as mentioned below:
   a. Adapted eating utensils
   b. Adapted drinking devices
   c. Adaptive dressing devices
   d. Specially designed toilet seat
   e. Restroom modification
   f. Aids for grooming
   g. Robotic and electronic feeders
   h. Adapted cooking tools
   i. Universal cuffs to hold the item
3. **Environmental control**
   This kind of assistive technology device helps individual with a disability perform independently by using various equipment to control their environment. Those are the following:
   a. Switch interfaces for appliances (such as VCR tape recorders).
   b. Adaptable on/off switches
   c. Remote control switch access
   d. Switch latch timers
   e. Switch interface for battery
   f. Operated devices
4. **Mobility**
   This kind of assistive technology helps the person with a disability in getting around in their environment. They are as follows:
   a. Walkers
   b. Grab rails
   c. Manual or powered wheelchairs
   d. Powered recreational vehicles
   e. Building modifications and
   f. Adaptations
   g. White canes
   h. Electronic image sensors
   i. Telescopic aids
5. **Assistive listening**
   This kind of assistive technology helps the individual with hearing-impairment gain their auditory capabilities. These are as follows:
   a. Hearing aids
   b. Classroom amplification
   c. Personal FM system
   d. Captioning
   e. Signaling device
   f. TDD/TTY
   g. Screen flash on the computer
   h. Phone amplification
6. **Visual aids**
   This kind of assistive technology helps individuals with a disability to gain sight in the context of effective communication. They are as follows:

a. Increased contrast
   b. Enlarged images
   c. Use of tactile and auditory materials
   d. Books on tape
   e. Eyeglasses
   f. Magnifier
   g. Large print books
   h. Low vision aids
   i. Screen magnifier
   j. Screen magnification software
   k. Closed circuit TV (CCTV)
   l. Screen reader
   m. Braille keyboard or note taker
   n. Braille translator software
   o. Braille printer/embosser
   p. Brailled materials
   q. Scanners
   r. Optical character readers
   s. Reading machine
7. **Augmentative communication**
   This kind of assistive technology helps an individual with a communication disability to communicate effectively. They are as follows:
   a. Communication boards and wallets with pictures, words, or letters
   b. Eye gaze board
   c. Simple voice output device
   d. Electronic communication devices
   e. Speech synthesizers for typing
   f. Communication enhancement software
   g. Computer-based communication systems
8. **Physical education, leisure, and play**
   These kinds of assistive technology help the individual with a disability's social interactions and participation. They are as follows:
   a. Adapted toys and games
   b. Adapted puzzles
   c. Switch activations with a battery interrupter
   d. Adapted sporting equipment
   e. Universal cuffs to hold crayons, markers, etc.
   f. Modified stampers and scissors
   g. Beeping balls
   h. Arm support for drawing
   i. Graphic design software (e.g., Kid Pix)
   j. Adaptive computer games
9. **Reading**
   This kind of assistive technology helps individuals with a disability to gain reading accessibility. They are as follows:
   a. Change in text size, spacing, color, or background-color
   b. Use of pictures with text
   c. Adapted page turning

d. Bookstands
   e. Talking electronic dictionary
   f. Scanner with talking word processor
   g. Electronic textbooks
   h. Highlighted text
   i. Recorded material
   j. Multimedia presentation formats
   k. Books on tape, CD, or MP3
   l. Optical character reader
   m. Braille books
   n. Screen reader/text reader
10. **Writing**
    This kind of assistive technology helps individuals with a disability to increase their writing efficiency. They are as follows:
    a. Pencil with adaptive grip
    b. Adapted paper (e.g., raised lines, highlighting)
    c. Slant board
    d. Typewriter
    e. Portable word processor
    f. Talk-to-text word processing
    g. Computer with word processing
    h. Word processing with spell/grammar checking
    i. Text prediction
    j. Electronic dictionary/thesaurus/spell checker
    k. Word cards/word book/word wall
    l. Voice recognition software
    m. Braille keyboard or notetaker
    n. Braille printer
11. **Learning/studying**
    This kind of assistive technology assists a student with a disability to organize or complete educational tasks. They are as follows:
    a. Picture/print schedules
    b. Low-tech aids (e.g., page tabs, color coding)
    c. Highlighted text
    d. Voice output reminder
    e. Electronic organizer
    f. Low- or mid-tech timer
    g. Software for organizing ideas
    h. Software for concept development
12. **Computer access**
    This kind of assistive technology assists a student with a disability to access a computer (including input and output).
    a. Keyboard with built-in accessibility options on a standard computer
    b. Keyguard
    c. Arm support
    d. Trackball/trackpad
    e. Joystick with an onscreen keyboard
    f. Alternate keyboard (e.g., IntelliKeys)

g. Mouth stick/head pointer
h. Head mouse/headmaster, tracker
i. Touch screen
j. Voice recognition software
k. Switch with Morse code
l. Switch with scanning
m. Screen reader
n. Word prediction/abbreviated expansion

It is also notable that the above list of classifications is not inclusive of all assistive technologies; rather it is an overview of some assistive technology options that are available.

Application of Assistive Technology for a Person with a Disability

UN convention has recognized "Artificial Intelligence as one of the powerful algorithms or tools to increase participation and independence for person with a disability" (UNCRPD, 2006). Globally, various tech giants are working to develop various AI-based applications to enhance accessibility for children with disabilities. Here is a list of some of the technologies:

AI-Based Visual Aids

Microsoft has developed a revolutionary AI-based application for people who are visually impaired named "SEEING AI". This application is very powerful because this application can describe the look, hair color, age, and emotion of a person standing in front of a visually impaired person. Moreover, a visually impaired person can point this application, through a smartphone to any product to get further details about it.

Smarter Glasses

A team of neuroscientists and computer scientists at the University of Oxford innovates "smarter glasses". Through these glasses, the content and features of an image can be increased. Google has already invested US$658,000 in this project.

Cognitive Hearing Aids

Columbia University's School of Engineering has developed cognitive hearing aids that can track brainwaves and brain activity to find out what the person wants to hear.

Sign-to-Text

Sign-to-text is a powerful tool that can help to transform sign language into text or audio. It is equipped with a 3D camera that can recognize and track the movements of the signer with a claim of 98% accuracy.

Advantages and Disadvantages of Assistive Technology for People with Disability

As discussed earlier, assistive technology helps to enhance the daily lives and participation of people with disabilities. It helps people with disabilities to perform tasks to the same level as people without disabilities. The following are some of the advantages of assistive technology:

- **Increased inclusiveness**: One of the major advantages of using assistive technologies is that it increases the participation of people with disabilities.
- **Increase equality of participation**: Every individual has the right to equal opportunities. However, people with a disability face a lot of obstacles in the context of daily living and participation with peers. Through using assistive technology, the scope for people with disabilities to participate in the world equally is increased.
- **Scope to work at their own pace**: Every individual is unique in this world; therefore, every individual has a different pace for learning and working. As per the classroom teaching-learning scenario, students with a disability's ability to learn content at their own pace by using assistive technology is increased. No one feels like they are being rushed.
- **Increase the academic standard**: Assistive technology helps to increase the academic standard of a student with disabilities through using various technological assistance.
- **Increase socialization**: People with disabilities experience isolation from mainstream society and technology helps to increase their participation in a social context as a result of increasing their socialization and interactions in any context.
- **Increases organizational skills and social competencies**: With the help of assistive technology, a person with a disability can perform at a much higher level of performance/achievement, which in turn can increase their organizational skills and social competencies.
- **It helps to build bridges:** Assistive technology increases the scope to create a bridge between people with a disability and people without a disability. It also increases the social communication between these two communities.

Disadvantages of Assistive Technology

- **Costly**: Though assistive technology is a very effective approach for people with disabilities, many of these are extremely costly. Therefore, it is difficult to avail assistive technologies individually as well as in classroom situations due to the unavailability of sufficient funds.
- **Time-consuming**: Another disadvantage of using assistive technology is that sometimes it takes a lot of time to get expert-level knowledge or it requires an extensive amount of training for the student as well as a teacher to use this technology.
- **Technology can never be fully relied on**: Though technology is very helpful for daily living as well as our social participation, one cannot fully depend on technology solely as it may break down at the time when it is most required.
- **Privacy**: Sometimes there is a concern about the privacy of student data in the context of using assistive technology in a classroom situation.

Bibliography

Aarts, E. (2006). *True visions: The emergence of ambient intelligence* (p. 37). Berlin: Springer.
Ahmed, T., Hoyle, R., Shaffer, P., Connelly, K., Crandall, D., & Kapadia, A. (2017). Understanding physical safety, security, and privacy concerns of people with visual impairments. *IEEE Internet Computing*.
Assistive technology act of 1998. *Pub. L.*, 105–394.
Beukelman, D. R., & Mirenda, P. (2005). *Augmentative and alternative communication: Supporting children and adults with complex communication needs* (3rd ed.). Baltimore, MD.
Blackhurst, A. E., & Lahm, E. A. (2008). Technology and exceptionality foundations. In J. D. Lindsey (Ed.), *Technology and exceptional individuals* (4th ed., pp. 65–126). Austin, TX: Pro-Ed.
Bloom, L. (1970). *Language development: Form and function in emerging grammars*. Cambridge, MA: MIT Press.
Bryant, D. P., & Bryant, B. R. (2011). *Assistive technology for people with disabilities*. Pearson Higher Ed.
Bryant, D. P. & Bryant, B. R. (2003). *Assistive Technology for People with Disabilities*. Upper Saddle River, NJ: Pearson Education, Inc.

Cook, A., & Polgar, J. M. (2008). *Assistive technologies: Principles and practice.* St Louis, MI: Mosby.
Cook, A. M., & Hussey, S. M. (2002). *Assistive technologies.* St. Louis, MI: Mosby.
Freiberger, H. (1971). Deployment of reading machines for the blind. *Bulletin of prosthetics research —Spring, 10*(15), 144-156.
Fuhrer, M. J., Jutai, J. W., Scherer, M. J., & DeRuyter, F. (2003). A framework for the conceptual modeling of assistive technology device outcomes. *Disability and Rehabilitation, 25*(22), 1243–1251.
Glennen, S. L., & DeCoste, D. C. (1997). Augmentative and alternative communication systems. In *The handbook of augmentative and alternative communication.*
Hayhoe, S. (2014). *The need for inclusive accessible technologies for students with disabilities and learning difficulties.*
International Organization for Standardization (ISO). (2016). *Assistive product for person with disability-classification and terminology* (6th ed.). Retrieved from https://www.sis.se/api/document/preview/920988/.
Johnston, S. S. (2003). Assistive technology. In J. J. McDonnell, M. L. Hardman, & A. P. McDonnell (Eds.).
Jones, M. L. (2002). Human factors and environmental access. In D. A. Olson & F. DeRuyter (Eds.), *Clinician's guide to assistive technology* (pp. 41–53). St. Louis, MO: Mosby.
King, T. W. (1999). *Assistive technology: Essential human factors.* Needham Heights, MA: Allyn & Bacon.
Kraskowsky, L. H., & Finlayson, M. (2001). Factors affecting older adults' use of adaptive equipment: A review of the literature. *American Journal of Occupational Therapy, 55*(3), 303–310.
Krug. (2006). *Don't make me think.* Pearson India.
Krüger, S. & Berberian, A.P. (2015). Augmentative and Alternative Communication System (AAC) for social inclusion of people with complex communication needs in the industry. *Assistive technology: the official journal of RESNA, 27*(2), 101–111. https://10.1080/10400435.2014.984261
Lee, H., & Johnson, C. (2017). Perspectives of teachers on the use of assistive technology with students with disabilities. *Journal of Special Education & Rehabilitation Science, 56*(4), 357–377. http://doi.org/10.23944/jsers.2017.12.56.4.16.
Lloyd, L., Fuller, D. R., & Arvidson, H. H. (1997). *Augmentative and alternative communication: A handbook of principles and practices.* Allyn and Bacon.
Logemann, J. A. (2000). What is evidence-based practice and why should we care. *ASHA Leader, 5*(5), 3.
Malcolm, M., & Roll, M. (2016). The impact of assistive technology services in post-secondary education for students with disabilities: Intervention outcomes, use-profiles, and user-experiences. *Assistive Technology, 29*(2), 91–98. http://doi.org/10.1080/10400435.2016.1214932.
Malcolm, M., & Roll, M. (2017). Self-reported assistive technology outcomes and personal characteristics in college students with less-apparent disabilities. *Assistive Technology,* 1–11. http://doi.org/10.1080/10400435.2017.1406414.
McDonnell, J. J., Hardman, M. L., & McDonnell, A. P. (2003). *An introduction to persons with moderate and severe disabilities: Emotional and social issues* (2nd ed.). Boston, MA: Pearson Education.
Merriam-Webster. (1984). *Webster's New Reference Library, An Encyclopedia of Dictionaries.* Canby, Oregon, United States: Merriam-Webster, Inc.
Mittler, J. (2007). Assistive technology and IDEA. In C. Warger (Ed.), *Technology integration: Providing access to the curriculum for students with disabilities.* Arlington, VA: Technology and Media Division (TAM).
Ohio AT Network Assistive Technology Resource. (2008). *Assistive technology resource guide.* Retrieve from https://assistedtechnology.weebly.com/uploads/3/4/1/9/3419723/at_guide.pdf.
Peterson, D. B., Peterson, D. B., & Murray, G. C. (2006). Ethics and assistive technology service provision. *Disability and Rehabilitation: Assistive Technology, 1*(1–2), 59–67.
Quist, R., & Lloyd, L. (1997). Principles and uses of technology. In *Augmentative and alternative communication.* Boston, MA: Allyn & Bacon.
Robitaille, S. (2010). *The illustrated guide to assistive technology and devices: Tools and gadgets for living independently: Easyread super large 18pt edition.* ReadHowYouWant.com.
Schlosser, R. W. (2003). Evidence-based practice: Frequently asked questions, myths, and resources. *Perspectives on Augmentative and Alternative Communication, 12*(4), 4–7.
Schlosser, R. W., & Raghavendra, P. (2004). Evidence-based practice in augmentative and alternative communication. *Augmentative and Alternative Communication, 20*(1), 1–21.
Schlosser, R. W., & Sigafoos, J. (2009). Navigating evidence-based information sources in augmentative and alternative communication. *Augmentative and Alternative Communication, 25*(4), 225–235.
Stead, A. (2002). The future of assistive technology services in the United Kingdom. *Technology and Disability, 14*(4), 149–156.
The Canadian Association of Occupational Therapy. (2003). *CAOT position statement assistive technology and occupational therapy (2012).* https://caot.in1touch.org/document/3655/assistivetechnology.pdf.

The World Health Organization. (2004). *The world health report 2004 - Changing history*. Retrieved from https://www.who.int/whr/2004/en/.

Thistle, J. J., & Wilkinson, K. M. (2015). Building evidence-based practice in AAC display design for young children: Current practices and future directions. *Augmentative and Alternative Communication*, 31(2), 124–136.

Tonsing, K. M., Alant, E., & Lloyd, L. L. (2005). Augmentative and alternative communication. *Augmentative and Alternative Communication and Severe Disabilities: Beyond Poverty*, 30–67.

The International Classification of Functioning, Disability, and Health (ICF). (2013). World Health Organization. How to use the ICF: A practical manual for using the international classification of functioning, disability, and health (ICF). Exposure draft for comment. October 2013. Geneva: WHO.

United States. (2012). *Assistive Technology Act of 1998*. Bethesda, MD: ProQuest.

UNCRPD. (2006). United Nations Convention on the Rights of Persons with Disabilities. Available from: https://www.un.org/development/desa/disabilities/convention-on-the-rights-of-persons-with-disabilities. Last accessed on Dec 28, 2018.

WHO (2018). *Disability and Development Report, Realizing the Sustainable Development Goals by, for and with persons with disabilities*. NY, USA: Department of Economic and Social Welfare, United Nations Pub.

16
MODELS AND UNIVERSAL DESIGN PRINCIPLES OF ASSISTIVE TECHNOLOGY

Models of Assistive Technology

Various models have been developed for innovations in both Assistive Technology (AT) and Augmented Alternative Communication (AAC). We all know that a model is an organized prototype of any real-world context. Researchers in the field of AT and AAC provide plenty of models; however, still no single model is universally accepted. Every model is unique in its own context. Table 16.1 presents some of the AT-specific models and their features.

As discussed earlier, several AT devices have been developed for individuals with various disabilities. The next section provides an overview of some of the common and effective assistive devices for an individual with a disability.

Universal Design Principle of Assistive Technology and AAC

This section focuses on the designing principle provided by Quist and Lloyd (1997). Quist and Lloyd (1997) portrayed six standards of AT that need to be considered when designing any assistive devices. The six standards are as follows:

- Principle of Parsimony,
- Principle of Minimal Effort,
- Principle of Minimal Energy,
- Principle of Minimal Interference,
- Principle of Best Fit,
- Principle of Practicality and Use, and
- Principle of Evidence-Based Practice.

Principle of Parsimony

"Everything should be made as simple as possible, but not simpler"
—*Albert Einstein (*Reader's Digest, *July 1977)*

The "Principle of parsimony" refers to a design of AT that should be at its simplest, to increase effectiveness and efficiency (Quist & Lloyd, 1997). A complex design can be a very effec-

Table 16.1 Present various models of assistive technology

Name of the Model	Author(s)	Year	Description of the Model	Components and Levels
Parallel Interventions Model	Angelo, J., and Smith, R. O.	1989	• This model mainly focused on the dynamics of matching technology. • Emphasized "adaptation" and "training". • Explained that AT cannot be implemented without a parallel training track. • Furthermore, training has an impact on the type of technology required.	Ten
Human Activity Assistive Technology (HAAT) Model	Cook, A. Cook, M. and Hussey, S. M.	2002	• This model discussed four major elements of AT systems such as "*activity*", "*context*", "*human*", and "*assistive technology*". • ***Activities*** have three basic performance areas; the activity of daily living, work and productive activity, and play and leisure. • Context includes four categories; the setting, social context, cultural context, and physical context. • In this model, a person with a disability is considered an operator. • In the HAAT model the general ability of an individual to perform a specific task is called "intrinsic enabler". That includes- sensory input, central processing, and effectors (motor). • The unique part of this model is that here assistive technology is considered an "extrinsic enabler" because its only function is to improve the performance of an individual with a disability. • This model also explained that assistive technology consisted of four interacting components; the human/technology interface, the processor, the environmental interface, and the activity output.	Four components and four subcomponents
Matching Person and Technology (MPT) Model	Scherer, M.J.	1992	• MPT is mainly a person-centered model. • This model mainly focused on three basic aspects, they are person, milieu, and technology to determine the best devices for an individual. • From these three aspects, people are divided into consumers and providers, a milieu is physical/architectural and attitudinal/cultural, and technology is service and product.	Three
Framework for conceptual modeling of AT device outcomes	Fuhrer, M.J., Jutai, J.W. Scherer, M.J., and De Ruyter, F.	2003	• This model has taken three basic aspects into consideration they are the need for devices, the type of devices, and the services involved. • This model shows that outcome is a result of interaction among characteristics of interventions, reception of intervention, and environment.	Nine components with 18 subcomponents
The AT CoPlanner Model	Haines, L., and Sanche, B.		• This model focused on four stages for facilitating AT-based communication, they are orientation, assessment and planning, evaluation, and reporting. • In the orientation stage, it is required to identify AT services and development of AT team. • The assessment and planning stage mainly focuses on gathering information and learning context. • The implementation and evaluation stage, "translate the assessment information into action to determine the effectiveness of instruction".	Four components and four subcomponents

tive solution, but can also create barriers for users, especially those who have struggled with various physical and mental challenges. Therefore, when designing or selecting any technological devices the designer and end-user should be concerned with unnecessary complexity and implement easy-to-understand approaches (Jones, 2002). Generally, in daily activities, people use various complex solutions which can easily be substituted for simple solutions (viz. inexpensive, reliable, and easy to transport) (Lee and Johnson, 2017). For example, for those who have "Tourette's syndrome" or difficulty in a motor pattern for learning, one of the major struggles is "writing". Therefore, he or she can easily buy "voice recognition software" for writing or can use low technology such as "pencil grips". But if both these technologies help in writing then choosing a simple one that is expensive, easy to transport, and less time-consuming is best (Quist & Lloyd, 1997). By reducing complexity, active participation may be enhanced and hence inclusion can be improved.

Principle of Minimal Effort

"Don't Make Me Think"

—*Steve Krug (Krug, 2006)*

Another hindrance to active participation or "inclusion" for people with disabilities is the use of a poor design while developing AT devices that require additional thinking or mental effort to use or understand their function (Malcolm and Roll, 2016). The principle of minimal learning refers to less cognitive load aspects when using devices. For example, in 9th grade, the teacher gifted a new design pen to all the students in the class. There were various instructions given by the pen company regarding how to open the pen and write. However, after some time the classroom was getting too noisy, and lots of queries were directed at the teacher, lots of broken pens due to inappropriate opening, and lots of frustrated faces. So, why does such a situation happen? The answer is as the designer of the pen company did not maintain the principle of minimal learning. Therefore, to use or understand the function of the pen, the users required more mental effort which increased the cognitive load and decreased the motivation to use it (Malcolm and Roll, 2017).

Therefore, in the context of designing AT devices designers should be concerned about less instruction on how to use them. King (1999) pointed out it as "operational knowledge", knowledge regarding "how to use" or "operate" any devices. Quist and Lloyd (1997) noted that if any device required more "operational knowledge", it likely reduces the use of the device over time by the user.

Principle of Minimal Energy

"Minimum effort means maximum comfort"

—*Cited by Aarts (2006)*

Minimal energy refers to the least necessary mental and physical effort for any task to be performed. Research has shown that for tasks that required huge energy for task performance there will be less motivation for specific task completion (McDonnell et al., 2003). This can be worse for people with disabilities. Quist and Lloyd (1997) found that AT users are most likely to avoid any task performance if there is a need for too much energy. Therefore, the designer of AT must take into consideration this principle to increase performance for a long period. From the designing perspective, the Center for Universal Design at North Carolina State University

(1997) provides some guidelines to minimize effort in task performance. For instance, the natural body position of the user should be maintained in any design. The rest are as follow:

- Reasonable operating forces should be executed.
- Repetitive action should be minimized.
- Sustained physical effort should be minimized.

In the context of AT devices, this principle can be utilized for motivation or to execute a behavior. Any user can be withdrawn from any task-related cognitive load or mental effort and physical effort that is more than the motivation of the user.

Principle of Minimal Interference

"Stop bothering me!"

—Cited by Quist and Lloyd (1997)

This principle emphasizes that any design of AT should create a distraction-free environment. This principle is important to consider because if any AT design has complex or multiple features then the attention of the user will be engaged in operating the device rather than the task performance (Ahmed et al., 2017). In such a situation extrinsic cognitive load will be increased, therefore the user may experience less motivation for the required task such as learning activities or communication.

Principle of Best Fit

"Is it me?"

—Cited by Quist and Lloyd (1997)

This principle emphasizes the individualized design of any AT. A designer should be aware of the target group or individual to design a "best fit" device based on the personality or need of the individual or community to the maximum extent possible. Quist and Lloyd (1997) stated that a design that is compatible with user needs and the personality of a user becomes more effective for people with disabilities. Ergonomic or understanding of the human factor is a major study area in the field of any technological design. King (1999) claimed that 75% of the success of any AT device is related to the human factor.

Principle of Practicality and Use

"Never forget why you started"

—Cited by Quist and Lloyd (1997)

This principle supports the feasibility and practicality of any AT device. The design of any device needs to be consistent with the availability of resources. Therefore, this principle emphasizes applying all the principles from a practical viewpoint. For instance, mental effort, cognitive aspect, and physical or environmental aspects need to be considered based on the availability of resources. Simply put, this principle encourages the development of a solution that can be used in the real world. Therefore, the designer should keep in mind economic, social, mobility, psychological aspects, etc. while designing devices (Hayhoe, 2014).

Table 16.2 Assistive technology for people with visually impaired

Type of Devices	Name of the Assistive Devices	Description
Non-optical low-vision devices	Acetate or color filters	This is a very simple but effective technology that enhances the contrast or darkness of an ant through a printing page. This color filter needs to be placed over any printing page to enhance the depth of any printing.
	Bold line paper	Bold line paper helps the dark line of paper. It helps to write the script online and create a graph with increased contrast.
	Book stands and slant boards	This is another mechanism for enlarging text through automatic magnification.
	Felt tip pens	This is a specially designed pen for people with VI to make a darker line and to increase the contrast.
	Graphite pencils	This pencil is designed to draw a bold line.
	Large print keyboards	This is a specially designed keyboard for people with VI. This keyboard has a large number and alphabets.
	Low vision watches	This specially designed watch helps to show the clock efficiently.
	Reading guides with highlighters	The reading guide is a highlighter mechanism as a reading guide for people with VI.
	Task lighting	Task lighting is supplementing adequate lighting for people with VI to increase contrast, distance, and size.
	Typoscopes	This is specially designed for VI learners to increase focus. It blackouts other text in a specific passage and mostly highlights the required one.
Low/medium-technology devices	Braille compass	Braille compasses help to find North, South, East, and West independently for people with blindness.
	Braille labelers	Braille labelers help to create levels for people who are new or not familiar with braille.
	Braille watches	Braille watches are embedded with braille in the watch to identify the time very efficiently.
	Bump dots	This is ideal for a person with blindness and low vision to easily identify various items.
	Cranmer abacus	This is specially designed for a person who is blind to learn basic mathematics operations.
	Script letter board	It provides the student with VI an opportunity to explore upper- and lower-case cursive letters.
	Full-page writing guide	This is a full-page writing guide that helps the visually impaired student to stay within writing space.
	Perkins braille writer	This is a six-key machines braille writer used to produce braille.

	Signature guide	Signature guides help people with VI simply cut out various shapes. It has a flexible rubber cord that is used to create shapes.
	Slate and stylus	This is a portable mechanism to produce braille.
	Work play trays	This tray help person with VI to keep an object from rolling out.
Optical devices for near viewing	**Type of lenses** • Convex lens • Bi-aspheric lens • Single aspheric lens • Flat field magnifiers	These types of lenses help the person with VI spot any small objects such as labels, tags, writing, image, etc.
	Type of Magnifiers • Handheld magnifiers • Stan-mounted and dome magnifiers • Illuminated magnifiers • Globe, dome, and bar magnifiers • Bar magnifier • Magnifiers on adjustable arms • Pocket magnifiers • Spectacle-mounted magnifiers for near viewing	Magnifiers help to increase the size of objects and increase visual functioning.
Optical devices for distance viewing	• Handheld monocular • Binoculars • Spectacle-mounted telescopes • BiOptic telescopes	These devices help the student with low vision access information from a certain distance.
Video magnifiers	• Stand video magnifiers • X-y tables • Video magnifiers with distance capabilities • Portable video magnifiers • Optical character recognition	These devices help to access print and other information as near.
Screen enlargement and readers	• CDs • JAWS® • NVDA (free) • Serotek	These devices are a mechanism of screen magnification built into the computer.

(Continued)

Table 16.2 (Continued)

Type of Devices	Name of the Assistive Devices	Description
	• TalkButton • Thunder • Virtual magnifying glass (Free) • WebAnywhere (free) • Window-eyes (free) • Word talk (Free)	
Braille technology	• Braille printer/embosser • Braille translation software (Duxbury, MegaDots, and Braille, 2000) • Electronic Braille Note Takers	These devices help to access and produce braille.
Tactile graphics technology	• Brailleable labels and sheets • Feel'n peel sheets: Carousel of textures • Graphic art tape • Textured paper • Crafty Graphics II Kit • Swail dot inverter • DRAFTSMAN tactile drawing board • Crafty graphics, stencil embossing kit • inTACT eraser • Thermoform machine • Swell-form graphics II machine	These devices help to read tactual graphics and charts.
Auditory access devices	• Auditory books • Electronic dictionary w/ speech • Audible gym equipment • Screen reading software • Speech recognition software • Talking or large print calculators • Talking watches	These devices help to access any written documents in auditory format.

Table 16.3 Assistive Technology for Hearing Impaired

Type of Devices	Name of the Assistive Devices
Technologies for non-aid users	• Loud telephones • Amplified handsets • Headphones and headsets • Personal listeners
Technologies for aided users	• Cochlear implants (CI) • In-the-ear (ITE) • Behind-the-ear (BTE) • Telecoil (t-coil)
Telephone accessories	• Ear hooks and neckloops • Bluetooth
Music and other audio accessories	• NoiZfree's • iNoiZ-Music • Sensorcom's MusicLink • Geemarc's iLOOP
Assistive listening systems	• FM systems • Sound field systems • Loop systems • Infrared systems • Communications gateway devices
Alerting devices	• Doorbell signalers • Smoke and carbon monoxide detectors • Baby monitors • Telephone signalers • Multiuse alerting systems • Travel
Non-audio technologies for aided users	• iCommunicator • Closed-captioning • Computer-assisted note-taking • Communication access real-time translation • TypeWell and C-print • Voice writing • Text telephones • TTY relay service • Videophones • Video relay services • Video remote interpreting • Captioned telephones • E-mail and visual voicemail

Principle of Evidence-Based Practice

"Stand on the shoulders of giants"

—*Isaac Newton in a Letter to Robert Hooke (1676)*

Another important principle for designing an AT device is evidence-based practice (EBP) (Thistle and Wilkinson, 2015). Schlosser (2003a) stated three aspects of EBP, (a) the use of best and most current research as a reference for design, (b) the focus on multidisciplinary teams or expert approach, and (c) the need to consider all stakeholders' perspectives for best services. EBP

Table 16.4 Assistive Technology for People with Physical Disabilities

Type of Devices	Name of the Assistive Devices
Alternative input devices	• Trackballs • Joysticks • Switches • Eye gaze systems • Head tracking systems • Foot control systems • Mouth control systems • Pen tablets • Touch screens • TouchPads • MouseKeys
Alternative keyboards	• Expanded keyboards • Miniature keyboards • Ergonomic keyboards • One-handed keyboards • Onscreen keyboards • StickyKeys
Software	• Word prediction • Speech recognition software
Technologies for daily living	• Manual wheelchairs • Scooters • Powered wheelchairs • Specialized wheelchairs • Prosthetics • Environmental control units (ECUs)

Table 16.5 Assistive Technology for People with a Communication Disability

Type of Devices	Name of the Assistive Devices
Assistive technologies for developmental disabilities	• Scan/read programs • Text-to-speech software • Dictation software • Web and e-mail • Electronic helpers • Books and audiobooks • Writing and spelling • Math and numbers • Personal digital assistant
Assistive technologies for intellectual disabilities	• Personal digital assistants • Keyboards • Communications boards

Table 16.6 Assistive Technology for People with Cognitive Disability and Learning Disorder

Type of Devices	Name of the Assistive Devices
Assistive technology for reading	<ul><li>Enlarged text</li><li>Handheld magnifiers</li><li>Video magnifier</li><li>Braille</li><li>Braille labeler</li><li>Audio books</li><li>Digital text</li></ul>
Assistive technology for writing	<ul><li>Writing tools</li><li>Adaptive paper</li><li>Slate and stylus</li><li>Handheld digital recorder</li><li>Video magnification/CCTV</li><li>Word processor</li><li>Word processor with specialized software</li><li>Word processor with a refreshable braille display</li><li>Manual and electric braille writer</li><li>Braille notetaker</li><li>Braille embosser</li></ul>
Assistive technology for math	<ul><li>Abacus</li><li>Tactile, braille. and visually enhanced manipulative</li><li>Low-tech refreshable braille cubes</li><li>Manual and electronic braille writers</li><li>Adaptive calculators</li><li>Adaptive measurement tools</li><li>Adaptive timepieces</li><li>Talking money identifier</li><li>Adaptive paper and tactile graphics</li><li>Specialized math software</li></ul>
Assistive technology to support Social studies and science	<ul><li>Magnification</li><li>Visually enhanced or tactile graphics</li><li>Models and 3D objects</li><li>Large print, tactile, or braille measuring tools</li><li>Specialized software</li><li>Handheld Computing Device</li></ul>
Assistive technology for computer access	<ul><li>Adaptive hardware</li><li>Operating system accessibility</li><li>Specialized accessibility software</li><li>Refreshable braille display</li></ul>
Assistive technology to support orientation and mobility	<ul><li>Low-tech adaptations in environment</li><li>Cane</li><li>Enlarged, braille, or talking compass</li><li>Electronic travel aids</li><li>GPS devices</li></ul>
Assistive technology for art, music, and physical education	<ul><li>Textures and materials</li><li>Specialized materials</li><li>Low-tech adaptations for music</li><li>Mid- to high-tech support for music</li><li>Adaptive tools for physical education</li></ul>

Table 16.7 Agencies and organizations for assistive technology

Name of the Organization	Website
American Association of Blind Teachers	http://www.blindteachers.net/
American Foundation for the Blind	http://www.afb.org
AppleVis	http://www.applevis.com/
Paths to Literacy	http://www.pathstoliteracy.org/
Perkins School for the Blind	http://www.perkins.org/
Special Education Technology British Columbia	http://www.setbc.org/lcindexer/default.aspx
Texas School for the Blind and Visually Impaired	http://www.tsbvi.edu/
United States Association of Blind Athletes	http://www.usaba.org/

Table 16.8 Some vendors for assistive technology resources

Some of the Vendors	Website Address
Ai Squared	http://www.aisquared.com/
American Printing House for the Blind	http://www.aph.org/
C-Tech Low Vision Products	http://www.lowvisionproducts.com
Dancing Dots	http://www.dancingdots.com
Enablemart	http://www.enablemart.com
Freedom Scientific	http://www.freedomscientific.com/
Humanware	http://www.humanware.com
Independent Living Aids	http://www.independentliving.com
Independent Science	http://www.independencescience.com
Maxi Aids	http://www.maxiaids.com
National Foundation for the Blind	http://nfb.org

is the most critical aspect of AT development for any technological design for the following ground:

- Research-based pieces of evidence can help educators or designers toward effective implementation of AT for assessment and intervention (Schlosser and Raghavendra, 2004).
- EBP increases accountability through a literature survey and helps to find out effective strategies and interventions for the present and future design of AT (Logemann, 2000).
- EBP helps to provide insight regarding the equal weight to the unique client (Schlosser and Sigafoos, 2009) (Tables 16.2–16.8).

Bibliography

Aarts, E. (2006). *True visions: The emergence of ambient intelligence* (p. 37). Berlin: Springer.
Ahmed, T., Hoyle, R., Shaffer, P., Connelly, K., Crandall, D., & Kapadia, A. (2017). Understanding physical safety, security, and privacy concerns of people with visual impairments. *IEEE Internet Computing*. 3523–3532.
Assistive technology act of 1998. *Pub. L.*, 105–394.
Beukelman, D. R., & Mirenda, P. (2005). *Augmentative and alternative communication: Supporting children and adults with complex communication needs* (3rd ed.). Baltimore, MD.
Blackhurst, A. E., & Lahm, E. A. (2008). Technology and exceptionality foundations. In J. D. Lindsey (Ed.), *Technology and exceptional individuals* (4th ed., pp. 65–126). Austin, TX: Pro-Ed.

Bloom, L. (1970). *Language development: Form and function in emerging grammars.* Cambridge, MA: MIT Press.
Bryant, D. P., & Bryant, B. R. (2011). *Assistive technology for people with disabilities.* Pearson Higher Ed. 2nd Ed
Cook, A., & Polgar, J. M. (2008). *Assistive technologies: Principles and practice.* St Louis, MI: Mosby.
Cook, A. M., & Hussey, S. M. (2002). *Assistive technologies.* St. Louis, MI: Mosby.
Fuhrer, M. J., Jutai, J. W., Scherer, M. J., & DeRuyter, F. (2003). A framework for the conceptual modeling of assistive technology device outcomes. *Disability and Rehabilitation, 25*(22), 1243–1251.
Glennen, S. L., & DeCoste, D. C. (1997). Augmentative and alternative communication systems. In S. L. Glennen, & D. C. DeCoste (Eds.), *The handbook of augmentative and alternative communication,* (pp. 547–597). Sandiego
Hayhoe, S. (2014). The need for inclusive accessible technologies for students with disabilities and learning difficulties. In: Burke, L., (ed.) *Learning in a Digitalized Age: Plugged in, Turned on, Totally Engaged?,* (pp. 257–274). Melton, UK: John Catt Educational Publishing. ISBN 9781909717084
International Organization for Standardization (ISO). (2016). *Assistive product for person with disability-classification and terminology* (6th ed.). Retrieved from https://www.sis.se/api/document/preview/920988/.
Johnston, S. S. (2003). Assistive technology. In J. J. McDonnell, M. L. Hardman, & A. P. McDonnell (Eds.) *An introduction to persons with moderate and severe disabilities: Educational and social issues.* Boston: Allyn & Bacon
Jones, M. L. (2002). Human factors and environmental access. In D. A. Olson & F. DeRuyter (Eds.), *Clinician's guide to assistive technology* (pp. 41–53). St. Louis, MO: Mosby.
King, T. W. (1999). *Assistive technology: Essential human factors.* Needham Heights, MA: Allyn & Bacon.
Kraskowsky, L. H., & Finlayson, M. (2001). Factors affecting older adults' use of adaptive equipment: A review of the literature. *American Journal of Occupational Therapy, 55*(3), 303–310.
Krug. (2006). *Don't make me think.* Berkeley California: New Riders Publisher.
Lee, H., & Johnson, C. (2017). Perspectives of teachers on the use of assistive technology with students with disabilities. *Journal of Special Education & Rehabilitation Science, 56*(4), 357–377. http://doi.org/10.23944/jsers.2017.12.56.4.16.
Logemann, J. A. (2000). What is evidence-based practice and why should we care. *ASHA Leader, 5*(5), 3.
Malcolm, M., & Roll, M. (2016). The impact of assistive technology services in post-secondary education for students with disabilities: Intervention outcomes, use-profiles, and user-experiences. *Assistive Technology, 29*(2), 91–98. http://doi.org/10.1080/10400435.2016.1214932.
Malcolm, M., & Roll, M. (2017). Self-reported assistive technology outcomes and personal characteristics in college students with less-apparent disabilities. *Assistive Technology,* 1–11. http://doi.org/10.1080/10400435.2017.1406414.
McDonnell, J. J., Hardman, M. L., & McDonnell, A. P. (2003). *An introduction to persons with moderate and severe disabilities: Emotional and social issues* (2nd ed.). Boston, MA: Pearson Education.
Mittler, J. (2007). Assistive technology and IDEA. In C. Warger (Ed.), *Technology integration: Providing access to the curriculum for students with disabilities.* Arlington, VA: Technology and Media Division (TAM).
Ohio AT Network Assistive Technology Resource. (2008). *Assistive technology resource guide.* Retrieve from https://assistedtechnology.weebly.com/uploads/3/4/1/9/3419723/at_guide.pdf.
Peterson, D. B., Peterson, D. B., & Murray, G. C. (2006). Ethics and assistive technology service provision. *Disability and Rehabilitation: Assistive Technology, 1*(1–2), 59–67.
Quist, R., & Lloyd, L. (1997). Principles and uses of technology. In *Augmentative and alternative communication.* Boston, MA: Allyn & Bacon. Vol4, https://doi.org/10.1163/9781780522951_001
Robitaille, S. (2010). *The illustrated guide to assistive technology and devices: Tools and gadgets for living independently: Easy read super large 18pt edition.* ReadHowYouWant.com.
Schlosser, R. W. (2003). Evidence-based practice: Frequently asked questions, myths, and resources. *Perspectives on Augmentative and Alternative Communication, 12*(4), 4–7.
Schlosser, R. W., & Raghavendra, P. (2004). Evidence-based practice in augmentative and alternative communication. *Augmentative and Alternative Communication, 20*(1), 1–21.
Schlosser, R. W., & Sigafoos, J. (2009). Navigating evidence-based information sources in augmentative and alternative communication. *Augmentative and Alternative Communication, 25*(4), 225–235.
Stead, A. (2002). The future of assistive technology services in the United Kingdom. *Technology and Disability, 14*(4), 149–156.
The Canadian Association of Occupational Therapy. (2003). *CAOT position statement assistive technology and occupational therapy (2012).* https://caot.in1touch.org/document/3655/assistivetechnology.pdf.
The World Health Organization. (2004). *The world health report 2004 - Changing history.* Retrieved from https://www.who.int/whr/2004/en/.

Thistle, J. J., & Wilkinson, K. M. (2015). Building evidence-based practice in AAC display design for young children: Current practices and future directions. *Augmentative and Alternative Communication, 31*(2), 124–136.

Tonsing, K. M., Alant, E., & Lloyd, L. L. (2005). Augmentative and alternative communication. *Augmentative and Alternative Communication and Severe Disabilities: Beyond Poverty*, 30–67. Wilurr Publisher, 186

The International Classification of Functioning, Disability, and Health (ICF). (2013). World Health Organization. How to use the ICF: A practical manual for using the international classification of functioning, disability, and health (ICF). Exposure draft for comment. October 2013. Geneva: WHO.

17
INTELLIGENT TUTORING SYSTEM (ITS) IN EDUCATION

Introduction

Some researchers explained that application of various modern technological innovations appropriately in the field of education can be beneficial for the learning process. Technology has been changing the whole pattern of present lifestyle as is evident in the sphere of education through the application of various technologies. Now education is no longer limited to just the listening aspect of a boring lecture by a teacher or instructor passively; rather it is more active and engaging due to the use of various technology-based devices and scientific instructional processes. The present chapter discusses another important innovation of the education system, namely the "Intelligent Tutoring system" (ITS). For some readers, it may be a first-time encounter with the word. In this context, it needs to be known that ITS is a highly sophisticated and complex learning software that is based on modern Artificial Intelligence (AI) to facilitate instruction. The present chapter aims to provide a broader spectrum of knowledge regarding the ITS and its functions in education.

Meaning and Definitions of Intelligent Tutoring System

As discussed previously, the computer is now a fundamental aspect that plays a vital role in the present education system. The revolutionary inclusion of computers and information and communication technology has entered present-day life including education allowing more independence with respect to time and place. Moreover, various software technologies make education opportunities open for all through the automated education process. However, out of the list of various categories of software technology, one essential software is the Intelligent Tutoring System (ITS). ITS is a complex teaching and learning design approach which integrates various software systems and principle methods of AI. It is a unique design of the teaching and learning approach enabling knowledge seeking of the student, problem-solving skills, and correction of student knowledge through various instant feedback strategies that use artificial intelligence. Besides, an ITS promotes the mastery level of learning and individuality of the learner. The following are definitions of an ITS:

VanLehn (2011), defined ITS as a kind of machine that functions in multiple ways in the context of instruction. For instance, it can function as a subject expert, diagnostic mechanisms, teacher expert, etc.

Hafner (2004) has defined ITS broadly. They explained that ITS is a kind of educational software that is intended to provide instruction by using the components of AI. The mechanism of ITS can maintain or track student performance and provide hints of feedback to the learner effectively and immediately. ITS also has some advanced-level features that can collect student data and can generate a report of the strength and weaknesses of learners and suggest additional remedies.

Murray (1997) defined ITS as generally computer-oriented tutoring or instructional system. It consisted of a systematic database or knowledge base which helps to specify what to teach and also specifies strategies about how to teach.

Woolf and Murray (1993) defined ITS in the context of its elements. They also discussed that there are three basic elements as a mechanism that models the thinking pattern of an expert teacher, student, and tutor. The creation of an environment that can produce a world-class laboratory for the learner so that they can build their reality and ITS supports the diverse complex discovery of learners through a computer partner which helps the recognized intention of students and provides advice accordingly.

Tobias (1993) defines the term as generally referring to a systematic presentation of instructional material to the student. Besides, ITS can provide personalized instructional parameters to the learner by collecting student data prior to the instruction or at the time of instruction. Moreover, it can provide feedback or opinion to the student regarding their status of performance as well as required remedies.

Psotka and Mutter (1988) defined ITS in a very simplistic way. They explained ITS as a computer program that can execute immediate feedback and customized and personalized instruction without the help of human interaction.

Hartley and Sleeman (1973) provided the early approach of ITS and notified that a complete ITS must have three common elements they are (a) knowledge of the domain (expert model), (b) knowledge of the learner (student model), and (c) knowledge of teaching strategies (tutor). This is still prevaling.

Historical Perspective of Intelligent Tutoring System (ITS)

It was a revolutionary time when the world introduced the computer. However, that was not as similar to the current version of what we call a computer. If one digs deeply into the historical scenario one can see that the modern computer is a dream of Charles Babbage from the early 1900s. He was the first person who thought about a multi-purpose machine that can be used in every aspect of human life which he named the "analytic engine". However, that dream of an analytic engine forced him to build an automatic machine for calculating logarithm tables which is, in fact, an actual form of a modern computer. After the computer revolution, ITS has been using intelligence in many ways. In the context of the instructional process the name "intelligent machine" was first used by Pressy in 1926. He built an instructional machine to provide multiple-choice questions to the learner and provided immediate feedback to each learner.

While it was absolutely an intelligent process or innovation for teaching and learning it was; however, based on a mechanical set with only pre-specified questions and answers which did not incorporate contemporary learning theories and pedagogical strategies.

In the mid-1900s, when the digital computer was introduced, it paved the way for what can truly be called "intelligent (artificial) machine". This machine was based on a numerical processor and an electronic and binary system. It was designed to make a logical decision or manipulation of data and the ability to store and access data for future.

In this period Alan Turing, a British mathematician and logician, developed the "Turing test" based on machine intelligence. He believed not only in "number crunching" but also in "symbolic manipulation". The "Turing test" was based on a mechanism of what is called the modern "Intelligent Tutoring System" with the features of an individual asking questions in real-time. The major question behind the "Turing test" was to distinguish the difference between a person and the respective responses of the computer whatever question or statements the integrator renders. This question of inquiring helps the future researcher toward the development of what is called ITS (Merrill et al., 1992).

From 1950 onward, various researchers like Allen Newell, Clifford Show, Herb Simon, etc. realized that "Turing's work and program are capable of creating logical proofs and theorems and by using the symbolic manipulation process they developed information to process without direct human control which is the early innovation of artificial intelligence. However, the name "Artificial Intelligence" was first coined by John Mccarthy in 1956 at the Dartmouth conference.

The next part of the computer-based instructional process mainly focused on the newly introduced Computer Assisted Instruction (CAI) process. In that period, various program languages such as ALGOL in 1958, LOGO in 1967, etc. were developed by various eminent researchers such as Wally Feuzzeig, Cynthia Solomon, and Seymour Papert. After that phase of development, Jaime Carbonell shared his view that the computer could act as a teacher rather than just a tool. During that time many researchers used computer intelligently that was called "Intelligent Computer Assisted Instruction" or "Intelligent Tutoring System".

Besides, the above-mentioned design of the intelligent tutoring system, there are also various advanced methods of ITS such as; Method Man by Crampe, Intelligent Labeling Explorer (ILEX) by Cox et al, Instruction in Scientific Inquiry Skill (ISIS) by Meyer, PACT by Aleven, etc.

Architectures of Intelligent Tutoring System (ITS)

The earlier discussion provides a general view of ITS and its development in the context of a historical overview. This section is going to discuss a vital aspect that is the architecture of ITS and its model. To get a concrete view of ITS, one needs to understand three categories of architecture:

- Three models of ITS
- Four models of the ITS
- New generation architecture model

Three Models of ITS

Three models of architecture are the basic design aspect. It comprises three major components:

- System domain expertise
- Student knowledge and skill
- Tutoring expertise

The following are the two very common architectures of ITS:

Derry, Hawkes, and Ziegler (1988) Architecture

In 1988, educational researchers namely Derry, Howkes, and Ziegler proposed a model or architecture of ITS that includes, Tutoring Model, Expert Domain Model, and a Student Knowledge Model.

Table 17.1 Historical chronology of intelligent tutoring system

Proponent and Year	Name of ITS	Functions
Carbonell, Collins, et al. (1969)	SCHOLAR	It is the earliest form of ITS, designed to teach South African Geography. It was based on Socratic dialog in tutoring.
Collins and Stevens (1977)	WHY	It was an extension of the SCHOLAR design. Here both tutorial dialog and Socratic dialog were used to provide the learner's ability to generalize and experience.
Suppes (1981)	Buggy	This was designed to identify misconceptions about learners' math problems. Here a teacher provides examples of an incorrect math problem (buggy solutions). Now the intelligent system helped the instructor to generate his own system to solve incorrect responses. This is designed to understand the nature of specific misconceptions made by the student.
Burton and Brown (1982)	SOPHisticated Instructional Environment (SOPHIE)	SOPHIE is based on an electronic circuit debugging tutor that aims to provide expert problem-solving strategies to the student.
Sleeman and Brown (1982)	WEST	This is for a basic mathematics solution. WEST is a game-based pedagogical approach. It helps to critique student decisions and provide guidelines or comments for improving student performance.
Clancey (1983)	GUIDON	This instructional program was mainly inspired by the medical diagnostic program MYCIN. This is a dialog strategy method to diagnose disease.
John R. Anderson, et al. (1984)	LISP	This method of design is based on a learning theory called ACT. It helps to identify procedural and declarative knowledge as a part of the problem-solving model.
Tennyson and Park (1987)	MAIS	This model is based on a system approach to instructional design. MAIS stands for Minnesota Adaptive Instructional System. It helps to provide a prediction level of student achievement based on analyzing the history of student performances.

Tutoring Model

The tutoring model of ITS provides a guideline to perform three levels of instructional activity namely; planning an individual route through the curriculum (the agenda), planning lessons (using action schemata), and online tutorial intervention. Student performance data of each level can be compiled and available to other levels. In this model, three sub-components are used for three active levels of instructional activities such as curriculum planner, lesson planner, and intervening monitor.

Expert Domain Model

This model particularly provides a guide in the tutoring model by using the expert domain model. An expert can make a comparison of the learner's solution to problems using their expert knowledge.

Student Knowledge Model

The model of Darry et al. (1988) in the context of an ITS is a combinational process of planning and opportunity by using a global model of domain knowledge. The major advantage of this model is it provides explicit tutoring. This model is particularly important for the problem-solving aspect of learning.

Siemer and Angelides (1998) Architecture

This model was proposed by Siemer and Angelides in 1998. This model is also based on domain expertise, student knowledge, and skill and tutoring expertise. However, the difference between Derry's model and Siemer and Angelides' model is the process of manipulation of three knowledge bases. Overall system control of Siemer and Angelides model are as follows:

The Domain Model

The domain model of this specific model denotes the knowledge related to the subject matter. Here the ITS will work to utilize the domain knowledge in the context of problem-solving and answering the question posed by a student.

The Tutoring Model

The tutoring model is the didactic aspect that helps in determining appropriate teaching strategies for learning based on the student model, learner needs, learning experience, etc. The tutoring system takes control over the selection of presented subject material, response mechanism, etc.

The Student Model

This is a representation of emerging knowledge of learner skills. The student model will record the learner's error or misconceptions. In general terms, it is a diagnostic and analysis process of a student's behavior.

This model requires an overall system of control mechanisms to coordinate the previously mentioned three models. However, this model explicitly described the knowledge and functional requirement of various components related to this model.

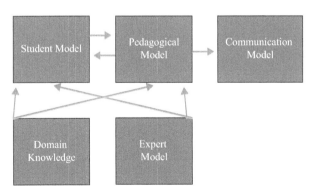

Figure 17.1 Interaction in components in an intelligent tutoring system. Source: Adapted from Beck, Stern, and Haugsjaa (1996).

The three models of architecture are a conventional model of ITS which is mainly based on the domain model, student model, and tutoring model. The next section will discuss the four-model architecture of ITS which is based on the "three models of architecture".

Four Models of Architecture of ITS

This is identical to the three models of architecture the only added components are for the fourth model architecture called "user interface". This is the classical architecture model of ITS (Dede, 1986). Dede's model has the following components:

Dede's Architecture of ITS

Dede in his four models of architecture discussed four components namely knowledge base, student model, pedagogical module, and user interface.

Knowledge Base

Knowledge base components are similar to the concept of domain knowledge in the three-model architecture of ITS. Here, the instructor or tutor incorporates various knowledge such as declarative knowledge, procedural knowledge, and metacognitive knowledge.

Student Model

This is also a similar conception of the student model in the three-model architecture of ITS. This model represents the cognitive processes, metacognitive strategies, and psychological attributes of each learner.

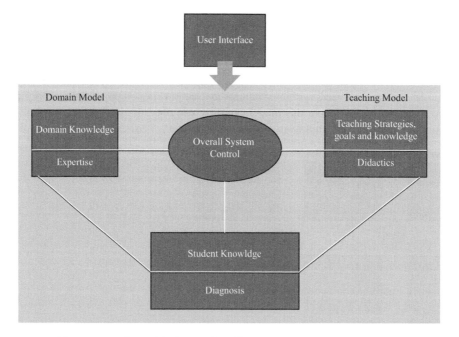

Figure 17.2 Siemer and Angelides's general intelligent tutoring system architecture. Source: Siemer and Angelides (1998:87).

Pedagogical Module

A pedagogical module is a similar conception of the tutoring model of the previous architecture of ITS. The major aim of this aspect is to generate expert behavior by the learner. This model is based on various teaching strategies and instructional theories to find out effective pedagogical aspects. Here a recommendation is made in the context of integration and coordination of the other components.

User Interface

The user interface is an added feature in the four-model architecture of ITS. A user interface is communicating components of ITS that interact between students and the system. It translates the system language into language the student can understand. It includes the pattern of interpretation (i.e., to understand a speaker), action within dialogues, domain knowledge to communicate with content, and knowledge for communicating intent.

The four-model architecture of ITS incorporates a separate user interface which is very essential in the context of learning. Besides, it also takes into consideration various psychological aspects such as cognitive strategies, learning style, etc. This model is a classic model of ITS because it provides an industry standard for ITS construction.

New Generation Architecture for ITSs

This is an upgraded model compared to the traditional three models and the classical four models. This is more advanced because of the integration of various complex software programming and the implementation of various learning theories. One of the models, namely multi-agent architecture, is discussed below.

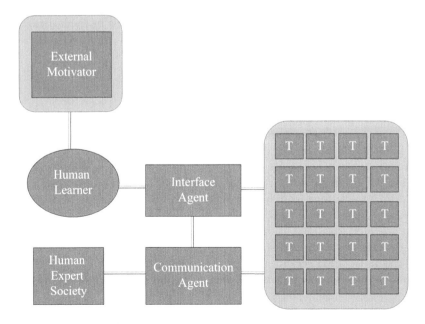

Figure 17.3 Costa and Perskuchisk's Architecture of MATHEMA for IT learning environment. Source: Costa and Perkusich (1996:170).

Multi-Agent Architecture

A multi-agent architecture was proposed by Costa and Perkusich in 1996, which they called MATHEMA. This is a computer-based intelligent learning environment that is comprised of six components:

1. **External motivator**: It is a basic element of an external motivator (human) that works in MATHEMA. For instance, the teacher can be a direct external motivator.
2. **A human learner**: It is the students who are going to learn through MATHEMA.
3. **Micro-society of artificial tutoring agents (MARTA)**: This design unit cooperates with the other two elements to achieve problem-solving.
4. **Human experts society (HES)**: This is a source of knowledge house or MARTA.
5. **Interface Agent:** This is a bridge between human learners and MARTA, responsible for communication and selection of tutor agents.
6. **Communication agent**: This is responsible for making the interaction between MARTA, HES and its communication process.

The major aspect of this multi-agent architecture is the integration of human learners into a micro-society to promote learning. This model can be used in a formal and well-structured knowledge domain, for instance, the classical logic domain.

Design and Development of ITS

The previous sections briefly discussed the architecture of the intelligent tutoring system from various theoretical points of view. This section provides another essential aspect namely the design and development of ITS. This is most important because without proper knowledge of design a whole intelligent system may fail to achieve a required learning objective. The design aspect as proposed by Corbett et al. in 1997 is given below. They discussed four essential stages of the development process namely, need assessment, cognitive task analysis, initial tutor implementation, and evaluation. A detailed discussion of these four stages is below:

Needs Assessment

This is the first and most common stage required for development of instructional design. This stage mainly focuses on learner analysis with the basis of common discussion with an expert or instructor based on the development of knowledge in the context of the student domain. The major objective of this stage is to specify the learning objective and development or design of the curriculum. It is not mandatory to computerize the whole concept rather the need is to develop a new curriculum structure based on learning objective. In this context, the designer needs to consider three essential dimensions:

1. The problem-solving probability of students.
2. The time it takes to reach this performance level.
3. Probability analysis of how many students will actively use the gathered knowledge in the future.

Besides such analysis, there is also a need for a cost-effective analysis and prior knowledge analysis of the learner.

Cognitive Task Analysis

This is the second stage in the context of ITS development. This stage is more complex as the designer needs to make an expert system program in the context of valid problem-solving knowledge. To design an effective domain model, the designer needs to interview a domain expert, needs to apply a "think-aloud" for the domain expert, needs to conduct a think-aloud study with a novice, and observe teaching and learning behavior.

Many times, it shows that experts do not know about reporting cognitive components. In this context by applying the "think aloud" method, a designer needs to ask the expert what he/s is thinking while solving a problem. Sometimes a designer needs to track the interaction between teacher and student in an online learning environment to get a more detailed view of the problem-solving method used by students and teachers in a specific situation. This record of information is very essential for building dialog or interactivity into a tutoring system.

Initial tutor implementation

This is the third stage of the design and development of ITS. This stage initiates setting up a problem-solving environment to promote an authentic learning process. Like any software development project, this stage also needs to take various evaluation activities to ensure effectiveness.

Evaluation

This is the final stage of design and development. In this stage, a designer needs to ensure the following:

- Basic usability and educational impact of design.
- Formative evaluation of each part system.
- Final summative evaluation of the whole system.

Anderson et al. in 1987 provided a simple guideline for designing and developing an intelligent tutoring system. He proposed eight essential principles that are required for designing an effective ITS. They are the following:

- Need to designate student competence as a production set.
- Need to communicate with goal structure to underlie the problem-solving.
- Provide instruction in a problem-solving context.
- Need to promote an understanding of problem-solving knowledge.
- Minimize cognitive and work memory load.
- Need to provide immediate feedback for error responses.
- Facilitate successive approximation to the target skill.

Practical Application of Intelligent Tutoring System

Automated Debugger in Learning System (ADIL): This is a software-based application intended to provide automated debugging-based knowledge to the learner. This program was developed by Syed Abdullah Mohd Zin, Ahmad Aljuinid Zarina Shukur, et al. (2000) at the University of Teknologi Mara (UiTM). This software is mostly applicable to computer-programming students for mastering basic debugging skills for program languages like C++, Python, etc. It displays specified syntax errors and locates programming errors with proper explanations.

Animated Data Structure Intelligent Tutoring System (ADIS): In 1997 Kai Warendorf and Colin Tan developed the application Intelligent System Laboratory (ISL). This is a Java-based application that aims to provide a comprehensive understanding of various data structures to students for lists, stacks, queues, trees, graphs, etc. This application can also provide graphical manipulation of a created data structure. This application also facilitates tutorial opportunities for students on the incorporation of data, learning basic algorithms (insertion and deletion), etc.

Bayesian Intelligent Tutoring System (BITS): This is also an ITS-based platform for computer application programming. This application was developed by C.J Butz, S. Hua, and R.B Maguire (2004) at the Department of Computer Science, at the University of Regina, Canada. BITS was mostly designed to provide the opportunity for a student to navigate through online generated materials suitable for learning sequences.

Dynamic Courseware Generation (DSG): This application is based on ITS-shell architecture. DCG was developed by Julia Vassileva and Ralph Deters in 1992 at Bundeswehr University Munich, Germany. This application is mainly based on AI-planning techniques to determine the content of instruction.

Decision-Making Tutor (DM-Tutor): This is a constraint-based ITS embedded with Management Information System (MIS) and its application is generally designed for oil palm plantation management. The major function of DM-Tutor is that it provides real-time experiences to the learner for plantation analysis and decision-making. This application was developed by Sagaya Amalathas and Antonija Mitrovic in 2009 at the University of Canterbury, New Zealand.

Episodic Learner Model-ART (ELM-ART): This is a Web-Based Intelligent Tutoring System (WITS) that aims to provide knowledge of the List Processing (LISP) programming language. It is specially designed based on a combinational aspect of an intelligent education system and electronic textbook by the application of which students can broaden and deepen their prior knowledge.

Java Intelligent Tutoring System (JITS): This is a unique Java-based programming tutor that aims to provide a design-based guideline to students in their first programming course in Java. It was developed by Edward R. Sykes at the School of Computing and Information Management and Franya Franek at the Department of Computing and Software, McMaster University, Canada in 2003.

Knowledge-Based Entity Relationship Modeling Intelligent Tutoring (KERMIT): This intelligent tutoring was mainly developed to provide knowledge about entity relationship (ER) modeling. It was mainly designed to teach a database language (SQL-Tutor) and punctuation and capitalization rules (CAPIT). It was developed by Pramuditha Suraweera and Antonija Mitrovic at the University of Canterbury, New Zealand.

Multicriteria Bayesian Intelligent Tutoring System (MBITS): It is designed to assist the student to increase understanding of any course content by using a multicriteria approach. It was developed by EttarresYamna and Khaled Melluli at Laboratoire de Recherche Opérationnelle, de Décision et de Contrôle de Processus (LARODEC).

Machine Learning Tutor (ML-Tutor): It was developed by A. Serengul Smith-Atakan, at Middlesex University, School of Computing Science. The major aim of this ITS is to combine internet technology with educational hypertext.

Normalization Intelligent Tutor (NORMIT): It helps to teach database normalization to university students. It was developed by Antonija Mitrović, at the Department of Computer Science, University of Canterbury, New Zealand.

ChatBots in Education

In the era of modern technological innovation "Intelligent Tutoring Systems" are one of the powerful personalized learning environments for teaching and learning scenarios. "Chatbots" are based on AI algorithms used to communicate with students in a more natural conversation style. It can be used to access student performance and understanding levels repeatedly as required to achieve the learning goal. ChatBots can help the teaching-learning process in the following ways:

1. It can enhance the student's engagement effectively.
2. It can provide more natural, smart, and secure feedback to the student.
3. It can work as a teaching assistant process.
4. Can provide instant feedback based on student performance.
5. It can be used as a tool for student support.
6. Can provide up-to-date information to the student as required.

Some educational ChatBots are Botsify, CouseQ, etc.

Advantages and Limitations of Intelligent Tutoring System

Tutoring advantage: In the context of teaching and learning it is very effective to provide a teacher or instructor for each student respectively in a specific subject area. But in the real context, it is very hard to meet such aspects due to physical and financial constraints. It is a special design aspect of the teaching and learning process that encourages personalization of learning by providing different required treatments to the learner on a single basis at a low cost.

The versatility of uses: ITS is a unique learning approach that promotes versatility in the learning process. For instance, a navy officer can use it for tactical training, a doctor can use it for the simulation of a medical operation, and a pilot can use it to simulate a flight. Furthermore, ITS can also be used in soft skill training like selling, negotiating, working collaboratively, etc.

Cost-effectiveness: Another greatest advantage of ITS is cost-effectiveness compared to the conventional tutoring approach. The only costs to set up ITS are the hardware and software which is comparatively low in the context of classroom setup and teacher wages.

Increase Motivation of learner: Davidovic, Warren, and Trichina (2003) in their research found that by using an ITS-based learning system, students were comparatively more motivated to complete the assignments and experienced greater satisfaction and motivation in participation in a learning process.

Academic achievement: Ong and Ramachandran (2000) in their research showed that students scored 43% higher in the final exam of computer programming when they participated in learning through ITS compared to traditional learning.

An increased speed of learning: Recent research shows that an ITS-based learning environment helps to increase the cognition process of a learner and move through assignments faster compared to a face-to-face learning environment.

Limitation of ITS

Lack of subject-based design: Notably, the model of ITS is the best fit for mathematics, science, and technology where problem-solving is more objective in nature but ITS may lack in design when it comes to various social science-based subjects like geography, literature, history, etc. which are more subjective and also due to the way it is taught. However, the future development of ITS has a more sophisticated design aspect to encounter these challenges.

Bibliography

Anderson, J. R., Boyle, C. F., & Reiser, B. J. (1985). Intelligent tutoring systems. *Science, 228*(4698), 456–462.

Beck, J., Stern, M., & Haugsjaa, E. (1996). Applications of AI in education. *Crossroads, 3*(1), 11–15.

Burton, R. B., & Brown, J. S. (1982). An investigation of computer coaching for informal learning activities. *Intelligent Tutoring Systems*. Information Analysis Reports

Butz, C.J., Hua, S., and Maguire, R.B., (2004). A Web-based Intelligent Tutoring System for Computer Programming, in: Preceedings of the IEEE/WIC/ACM Conference on Web Intelligence, Beijing, China, 159–165.

Clancey, W. J. (1983). Guidon. *Journal of Computer-Based Instruction, 10*(1-2), 8–15.

Corbett, A. T., Koedinger, K. R., & Anderson, J. R. (1997). Intelligent tutoring systems (Chapter 37). In M. G. Helander, T. K. Landauer, & P. Prabhu, (Eds.) *Handbook of Human-Computer Interaction*, 2nd edition, pp. 849–874. Amsterdam, The Netherlands: Elsevier Science

Davidovic, A., Warren, J., & Trichina, E. (2003). Learning benefits of structural example-based adaptive tutoring systems. *IEEE Transactions on Education, 46*(2), 241–251.

de Barros Costa, E., & Perkusich, A. (1996, June). Modeling the cooperative interactions in a teaching/learning situation. In Frasson, C., Gauthier, G., Lesgold, A. (Eds.) *International Conference on Intelligent Tutoring Systems* (pp. 168–176). Berlin, Heidelberg: Springer.

Dede, C. (1986). A review and synthesis of recent research in Intelligent computer-assisted instruction. *Int. J. Man Machine Studies*, 24, 329–353. Academic Press Inc. (London) Limited, 19

Derry, S. J., Hawkes, L. W., & Ziegler, U. (1988). A plan-based opportunistic architecture for intelligent tutoring. In *Proceedings of the intelligent tutoring systems (ITS-88)* (pp. 116–123). Springer.

Hafner, K. A. T. I. E. (2004). Software tutors offer help and customized hints. *The New York Times*.

Hartley, J. R., & Sleeman, D. H. (1973). Towards more intelligent teaching systems. *International Journal of Man-Machine Studies*.

Jim, O., & Ramachandran, S. (2000). Intelligent tutoring systems: The what and the how. *Learning Circuits*. Retrieved March 8, 2002, from http://www.learningcircuits.org/feb2000/ong.html.

Merrill, D. C., Reiser, B. J., Ranney, M., & Trafton, J. G. (1992). Effective tutoring techniques: A comparison of human tutors and intelligent tutoring systems. *Journal of the Learning Sciences, 2*(3), 277–305.

Murray, T. (1997). Expanding the knowledge acquisition bottleneck for intelligent tutoring systems. *International Journal of Artificial Intelligence in Education, 8*(3–4), 222–232.

Murray, T., & Woolf, B. (1993). Design and implementation of an intelligent multimedia tutor. *AAAI'93 tutorials*.

Psotka, J., Massey, L. D., & Mutter, S. A. (Eds.). (1988). *Intelligent tutoring systems: Lessons learned*, (pp. 1–14). Hillsdale, NJ: Lawrence Erlbaum.

Siemer, J., & Angelides, M.C. (1998). Towards an Intelligent Tutoring System Architecture that Supports Remedial Tutoring. *Artificial Intelligence Review, 12*, 469–511 (1998). https://doi.org/10.1023/A:1006588626632

Siemer, J., & Angelides, M. C. (1998). Towards an intelligent tutoring system architecture that supports remedial tutoring. *Artificial Intelligence Review, 12*(6), 469–511.

Sleeman, D., & Brown, J. S. (1982). *Intelligent tutoring systems*. New York, USA: Academic Press

Suppes, P. (1981). *University-level computer-assisted instruction at Stanford: 1968–1980*. Stanford, CA: Institute for Mathematical Studies in Social Science, Stanford University

Tennyson, R. D., & Park, O. C. (1987). Artificial intelligence and computer-based learning. In R. M. Gagné (Ed.), *Instructional technology: Foundations*, (pp. 319–342). Lawrence Erlbaum Associates, Inc.

Van Lehn, K. (2011). The relative effectiveness of human tutoring, intelligent tutoring systems, and other tutoring systems. *Educational Psychologist, 46*(4), 197–221.

Zin, A.M., Aljunid, S.A., Shukur, Z., & Nordin, M.J. (2000). A Knowledge-based Automated Debugger in Learning System. *arXiv: Software Engineering*

PART III

Large-Scale Instructional/Administration Tools, Techniques, and Initiatives

18
DISTANCE EDUCATION

Introduction

Education is the basic requirement of any civilized society. Therefore, learning opportunities need to be more open, and should not be bound by the formal education institution. However, there are number of formal educational institutions failing to achieve "education for all". Additionally, the formal education system has not been able to cope with the challenges of an increasing number of students, the demand for upgraded knowledge for employment, the continuation of learning of dropout students, part-time learning of in-service employers, etc. However, there was the greatest demand for an alternative learning approach where learning opportunities could be open for all with no binding as per time, age, gender, demographic background, subject of study, etc. Non-formal education is an alternative learning approach compared with formal institutional learning and distance education and Open education are examples of non-formal education. This chapter focuses on the "distance education" learning approach.

Meaning and Definition of Distance Education

As discussed in the introductory part of this chapter there is greater demand for a non-formal educational approach along with a formal education system to cope with various social, demographical, personal, and organizational problems of the formal educational process. Coombs (1977) defines non-formal education as an organized teaching-learning activity outside the formal education system which would be able to meet specific needs of learning.

Distance education is one of the non-formal educational processes that can be defined as an educational process imparted from a distance. However, from time to time definition of distance education has changed. The following are some of the definitions provided by various researcher:

United States Distance Learning Association (1998) defined it as "the acquisition of knowledge and skill through mediated information and instruction, encompassing all technologies and other forms of learning at a distance" (p. 192).

These definitions majorly focused on the organizational structure of distance learning and do not clearly distinguish the types of learning (viz. formal and informal) as well as the types of distance (viz. temporal and physical). However, in the next definition Newby, Stepich, Lehman, and Russell tried to define distance education more concisely.

Newby, Stepich, Lehman, and Russell (2000) described distance education "as an organizational instructional program in which teacher and learner are physically separated" (p. 210). However, this definition is also contradicted on the ground that it ignored any interaction effect of teacher and learner.

Peters (1985) described distance education as a method of indirect instruction implying a geographical and emotional separation of teacher and taught whereas in mainstream education the relationship between a teacher and student is in the classroom, based upon technological rules.

Moore (1990), the editor of the *American Journal of Distance Education*, defines distance education as arrangements for providing instruction through print or electronic communications media to persons engaged in planned learning in a place or time different from that of the instructor or instructions.

Portway and Lane (1994) in the book, *Guide to Teleconferencing and Distance Learning* (Applied Business, 1994) defined distance education as a teaching and learning process where instructor and learners are geographically separated that's why the learning materials are provided through print or electronic devices for instructional delivery.

Picciano (2002) describes that distance education uses three current and popular forms of media: (a) broadcast, (b) two-way video conferencing, and (c) asynchronous learning networks (multi-modal, wave-based delivery of instruction that can be reviewed by the students at any time).

History of Distance Education

The concept of distance education is quite old mainly introduced in the late 1800s. The University of Chicago, IL was established through a correspondence program where the teacher and students were in different locations and the teaching-learning process occurred without face-to-face connection between teachers and students. However, prior to that, one of the best ways of learning was to gather all the students in one place at a specific time and be taught by one teacher. Education was dominated in those times by males and the opportunity for education was mostly amidst the higher level of society. The earlier efforts to break the traditional way of learning were made by William Rainey Harper who designed an alternative way and tried to spread educational opportunities irrespective of all students. In the early phase, critics were seen as correspondence to shape education for business orientation.

However, the greatest demand for distance education as a new medium for delivering instruction was during the period of WWI through the invention of the radio and thereafter television in 1950. The early attempt was taken by establishing the Wisconsin School of the Air in 1920 where the major aim was that schools must not be restricted by walls rather the entire state would represent the school boundary.

Historical View of Distance Education in Various Countries

Germany: In 1856 Charles Toussaint established postal service language teaching. Although, academic distance education in Germany started in 1960. In 1966 educational radio broadcast was initiated by Hessian Broadcasting Corporation and the University of Frankfurt, Frankfurt.

USA: Sir Issac Pitman, in 1840, invented an idea to deliver instruction to a limitless audience based on a correspondence course through the mail. Thereafter, the International Correspondence School (ICS) started in the USA.

Australia: The Australia University of Queensland, Brisbane initiated the Department of External Studies in 1911. However, before that Grundy, a health inspector used the correspondence instruction method to train the rural health inspectors.

United Kingdom: The Open University idea grew in 1963 by Harold Wilson, an opposition leader, and in 1977, the first open university was established in the UK.

India: In 1962, the University of Delhi, New Delhi, was established as the directorate of correspondence. Thereafter, 31 universities adopted this scheme by 1985 such as the University of Punjab, Lahore, which started correspondence education in 1967. Following these two universities, Delhi and Punjab, and other universities followed suit such as Mysore University, Mysore, (1969) and Himachal Pradesh University, Shimlas, (1971) also established their correspondence course. However, overall, 40,000 students were enrolled in correspondence education at various levels. At the primary level correspondence education was mainly media-based; however, a great demand in different universities was found in various stages. As a result, Indira Gandhi National Open University (IGNOU), New Delhi, was established in 1985 with various courses of study.

Characteristics of Distance Education

The previous discussion provides some knowledge about distance education and a historical overview of distance education. However, this present section is going to explore the characteristics of distance education based on various definitions and synthesis of Valentine (2002) and Encyclopedia Britannica (2012) the following characteristics of distance education are highlighted:

1. **Spatial and temporal separation**: One of the major characteristics of distance education is distance or separation between teacher and learner through space (geographical) and time.
2. **Self-learning methods**: Distance education mainly encourage self-learning methods.
3. **Self-motivation:** Due to the separation between teacher and learner success of distance education primarily depends on the self-motivation of the student.
4. **Instructional material mixed in nature**: In a distance learning environment, teaching-learning material provides various mediums such as printed material, radio, television, video/audio recording, computer-based, and most recently Internet-based online mediums.
5. **Democratic**: Through distance education, a large number of students gets the opportunity to fulfill their academic aspiration without institutional boundaries. Mainly this view embellishes distance education as a democratic learning environment.
6. **Self-paced learning environment**: In a distance learning environment learners can learn at their own pace and achieve the learning objective in their own way. In this learning environment, teaching-learning material does not impose from outside therefore, it maintains learning methods based on psychological principles.
7. **Equality of educational opportunity**: Distance education has opened the door for education for all. It provides learning opportunities irrespective of all and increases participation in education scenarios and equality of educational opportunity.
8. **Competency-based knowledge**: Distance education merely encourages the skill, competence, and productivity of learners rather than just earning a university degree.
9. **Promote aesthetic culture and intellectual knowledge**: In a distance learning environment, learners mainly focus on learning. Many of the learners try to enrich various

subjective knowledge, cultural knowledge, literature of various regions, etc. In a distance learning environment, learners can learn any topic without the boundary of age, or demographic background, etc.
10. **Innovative as well as less expensive**: Compared to traditional organizational-based learning environments distance education is innovative, flexible, and less expensive.

Purposes of Distance Education

As previously discussed, distance education was in great demand in society from various levels. Various institutions have taken initiatives to spread distance learning environments. However, the purpose and rationale vary in many ways. The fundamental purpose of distance education can be categorized in four broad ways:

1. **To expand educational opportunity and access**: Distance education expands the potentialities to promote the educational opportunity to a new audience, those who are not able to learn in formal organization because of various barriers.
2. **Alleviating capacity constraints**: The population increasing each day and the demand for educational institutions has been increasing in the same proportion. Therefore, to accommodate, facilitate, or include more people in the educational scenarios, there must be some alternative approach, and distance education has been shouldering this responsibility over decades. Besides, future research on distance education mainly focuses on the scalability of distance education to avoid the pressure of overwhelming student inclusion in education.
3. **Promote opportunities for the fulfillment of lifelong learning**: Apart from academic degree-based education, various learners are intended to enrich themselves with additional knowledge better to say education for its own sake. They view education as a hobby or source of personal development. From this point of view distance education opens the opportunity to fulfill the demand for education.
4. **To promote education to the employer for their professional enhancement**: Another purpose of distance education is that various people who are the employer and seek to learn more or want to upgrade their knowledge and skill for their professional enrichment, distance education opens the door to get educated at their own time and space.
5. **To deliver education to remote areas**: One of the major purposes of distance education is to provide education to the remote areas where formal education is a dream due to lack of infrastructure such as hill areas, desert areas, etc. However, enabling technology such as radio, television, and correspondence, etc. as a medium of distance education helps to include more people in education in remote areas.
6. **To encourage the democratizing of education**: A distance learning environment encourages democratizing higher education by opening the scope to a huge number of populations including disadvantaged groups such as working people, women, people in remote areas, etc.
7. **To promote flexible learning**: Flexibility is also an important purpose of distance education. Distance education is more open in terms of place of learning, methods of learning, a combination of courses, enrolment eligibility, examination, implementation of courses, etc.

Distance Education in India

India has the second-highest distance education system in the world after China. Presently, India offers six types of distance education institutions.

Structure of Distance Education in India

1. National Open University
2. State Open University
3. Distance Education Institutions (DEIs) at:
   - Institutions of National Importance
   - Central Universities
   - State Universities
   - Deemed Universities
   - State Private Universities
4. DEIs at Stand-Alone Institutions
   - Professional Associations
   - Government Institutions
   - Private Institutions

Facts and Overview of DE in India

- After independence, there was a great need to include the majority of people in education. Therefore, to expand higher education, the government of India realized that distance education (DE) is an important and alternative approach. In this regard, the University Grant Commission (UGC) 1956–60 recommended evening college and correspondence courses. Besides this, the focus was also given to external degree courses and accreditation.
- Major preliminary initiatives in regard to DE have been recommended in the third five-year plan (1961-66) where expert committees raised their voice about correspondence education in India. Based on this observation of the planning commission the Central Advisory Board on Education (CABE) recommended Dr. Kothari and the chairman of UGC to look into the matter of correspondence courses in India.
- The expert committee approved the recommendation suggested by CABE and suggested that only universities should administer the correspondence courses in the first instance. Following this, the first initiatives were undertaken by the University of Delhi, New Delhi, as a pilot project in 1962 by setting up a school based on correspondence courses and continuing education.
- From 1970 onward it was perceived that the growth and spread of correspondence education grew and it was also noted that more universities started correspondence course institutions that were named Directorates of Distance Education or Centers of Distance Education.
- DE was more effective in respect of access and flexibility; however; it had limited access to the disadvantaged learner. Therefore, there was the greatest demand to open educational opportunities by breaking the structural barrier of the conventional education system and the inclusion of communication technology.
- Based on this societal demand, from 1980 onward government of India introduced Open Universities (OU) with the broadest objective such as the democratization of higher education to a large number of populations, reaching education to remote and rural areas, the inclusion of working people, woman, and other disadvantaged/ marginalized group of people to acquire and upgrade their knowledge and skill.
- The Ministry of Human Resource Development (MHRD) stated a clear vision that OU would be different from conventional education. In the National Policy on Education

(1986), MHRD explicitly documented the OU system as a means to "augment opportunity for higher education as an instrument of democratizing education".
- Therefore, a major initiative has been taken by the establishment of Dr. BR Ambedkar Open University in Hyderabad in 1982. After that 1985 Indira Gandhi National Open University (IGNOU) was established. Moreover, various OU such as Nalanda Open University (NOU) Patna, Bihar; Vardhman Mahaveer Open University (VMOU), Kota, Rajasthan; and Yashwantrao Chavan Maharashtra Open University (YCMOU) Nashik, Maharashtra, were established from 1989 onward.
- After the establishment of IGNOU, it was getting more responsible regarding the promotion and coordination of OU and DE instead of UGC. To fulfill this responsibility the Distance Education Council (DEC) was set up by IGNOU in 1991 which became optional in February 1992.
- DEC was responsible for various initiatives such as promotions, coordination, and maintenance of standards of the open and distance education system in India.
- In August 2010 MHRD constituted a committee under the chairmanship of Prof. Madhava Menon, and based on the committee report MHRD recommended a new regulatory body for the Open Distance Learning (ODL) system namely the Distance Education Council of India (DECI) and decided to shift the DEC of IGNOU to UGC.
- On 29 December 2012 MHRD transferred distance education from IGNOU to UGC.

Theories of Distance Education

To enrich the development of any field, theories are imperative that directly affect the practice of any area of research. In the context of distance education; however, various indigenous definitions and systematic theories have emerged over time from various leading scholars in this area. Holmberg (1986) stated that systematic theoretical explanations regarding distance education provide an insightful view to the distance educator to take decisions confidently.

As discussed in the previous section the advantage of distance education was documented by various earlier pioneers such as William Rainey Harper, Willam H. Lightly, Hermod, etc. in their research. A systematic theoretical view of distance education was postulated in 1970. In 1972 Moore raised his voice regarding various hindrances which slowed the progress of distance education, one of them was a "lack of attention" Moore named it a "micro factor". Moore also felt a serious need for explicitly defining, describing, discriminating various components, and identifying critical elements of various forms of distance education.

This section explicitly discusses various theories underpinning the influence of the field of distance education.

Types of Distance Education Theories

One of the landmark works in the field of distance education is namely "The foundations of distance education" by Keegan (1986) which categorized distance education into three broad categories:

1. Theories of Autonomy and Independence
2. Theories of Industrialization of Teaching
3. Theories of Interaction and Communication

Table 18.1 Details of the name of the theory and contributors with year

Name of the Theory	Contributors	Year
Independence and autonomy	Major proponents are Rudolf Manfred Delling (Germany), Charles A. Wedemeyer (USA), and Michael G. Moore (USA)	late 1960 and early 1970
Industrialization of teaching	Otto Peters (Germany)	The early 1970s
Theories of interaction and communication	Borje Holmberg (Sweden), John A Bååth (Sweden), Devid Sewart (UK), Kelvin C. Smith (Australia) John S. Daniel (Canada/UK)	

1. **Theories of Autonomy and Independence**

Systematic theorization of distance education has been developed in various ways. Although, there are no omnipresent theories in this field, each theory provides various insightful orientations in a spectrum of distance education. In the autonomy and distance education theories the learner is one of the centers and distinguishing features (Saba, 2003, 2007). Therefore, it encourages the student role and the teacher role. Various researchers have worked in this specific domain such as Rudolf Delling, Charles Wedemeyer, Michael G. Moore, etc. The following are brief discussions of these theories.

Theory of A Helping Organization: Rudolf Delling

A helping organization view of distance education was provided by Rudolf Delling, University of Tübingen, Tübingen. Delling was a historian and bibliographer and took the distance educational process from a multidimensional point of view. From 1968–78 many of his writing reflected the dimension of distance education (Keegan, 1986, 2013). He listed eight dimensions as central to his view; they are:

1. A learner or student
2. Society (including legislation, administration, family, etc.)
3. A helping organization
4. A learning objective
5. The content to be learned
6. The result of learning
7. Distance
8. A single carrier

Rudolf Delling did think that if distance education is cognizant as a teaching process, then it could disrupt the whole aim of distance education. Perhaps, in his above-mentioned eight dimensions, he intentionally omitted the "teacher" conception. The rationale behind ignoring "teaching" and "teacher" as a characteristic of distance education was that he thought that learning encompasses helping an organization that is to be performed by machines, people, and material. Mainly he emphasized "autonomy and independence of the learner". He believed that in the distance education model adults are the most targeted population and the adult group generally do not accept the relationship of educator-student. However, apart from this, he was given the major emphasis on "helping organization", functionally it would maintain the facility of the learner as per their needs and provide the information, documentation, library facilities, etc.

However, Delling conceptualized distance education as an "artificial signal carrier" process where he described the course content of distance education as an artificial distance between learners and helping the organization to bridge the artificial signal carrier. Additionally, two-way communication and feedback were some of the central quests in his theory. Besides, the whole learning opportunity was divided into two different segments; they are:

(b) **Monologues**: It includes books, newspapers, journals, documentary films, lectures without discussion, broadcasts, self-learning material, etc. However, monologues are considered one-way communication.
(c) **Dialogic**: As per the dialogic method, it includes normal classroom or school teaching, conversation, distance education course, etc. Dialogic is considered two-way communication.

In brief conclusion, it seems that Delling has taken distance education as a communication process rather than an educational process. It is characterized by industrial mechanisms and took distance education as an "artificial signal carrier" and eliminated the function of "teacher" in the ground that students should learn independently and autonomously.

(b) Theory of Independent Study: Charles A. Wedemeyer

Another ground-breaking theory in this area is the "theory of independent study" proposed by Charles A. Wedemeyer, a professor at the University of Wisconsin, WI. The central idea of his theoretical reflection was the independence of students and he used the term "independent study" that reflected the freedom of students in the learning process.

Wedemeyer defined "independent study" as a learning process which changes the behavior of students, an activity-based learning process, the environment of the learner differs from the school, the teacher may be there but the student does not depend upon them, and the learner accepts the degree of freedom and responsibility that lead to learning (Keegan, 1986).

Wedemeyer was ardently influenced by the philosophy of Carl Rogers. Therefore, the basis of this theory stands on two major views such as democratic and liberal orientation in educational scenarios. He believes that education should not be a barrier owing to poor, geographical isolation, social disadvantage, health condition, organizational base, etc. He believed that to eliminate the mentioned barrier it is imperative that the design of education should be individualized and self-paced, and freedom should be the goal.

Wedemeyer also provides the conception of "independent learner" or "proto" learner "whose success in learning enable him/her to survive". Conversely, he also provided the conception of "dependent learner" this group of learners mainly depends on the teacher, policy, and practice for the goal of learning, activity, rewards as well as punishment.

He discussed six successive stages to eliminate the barrier regarding space and time. Those are the following (Wedemeyer, 1973):

1. Invention of writing
2. Invention of printing
3. The invention of correspondence education
4. Development of democratic and egalitarian philosophy
5. Application of telecommunication media in teaching
6. Development of programmed learning theory

Wedemeyer emphasized the above-mentioned factors as the development of all these factors enables the opportunity for the student to take part in education to a large extent. From 1960 onward he felt the importance of the re-emergence of the independent learner and programs in those areas where formal education is less enabling to success. Indeed, he was a critic of the contemporary structure of teaching and learning in the higher education scenario that he felt is outdated and impedes the utilization of modern technology.

In this context, Wedemeyer (1968) set a fourth systematic view of distance education with ten characteristics of the proposed system to maintain the balance of student autonomy and technological adaptation and implementation. The following are the ten characteristics:

1. **Operation from any place**: The system should be capable of operating the learning process at any place where there are students, even only one student. However, it may not be a problem if there are no teachers at the same place and at the same time.
2. **Greater responsibility**: The system should place greater responsibility for the learning of the student.
3. **Custodial-type duties:** Free faculty members form custodial-type duties, so more time can be given to truly educational tasks.
4. **Wider choice opportunity**: The system should offer students and adults more opportunities (wider choice) in course format and methodology.
5. **Use of effective media and method**: Use of teaching media and method which is proven to be effective.
6. **The appropriate combination of media and method**: The system needs to appropriately combine effective technology, media, and method to facilitate the best way of learning within the subject area and topic.
7. **Redesign the course:** The system needs to redesign the course program and appropriate development, of course, to fit into an "articulated media program".
8. **Individual difference**: The system should enhance the opportunity for adaptation to individual differences.
9. **Simple evaluation process**: The evaluation process should be simple not by barriers concerned with the place, rate, method, or sequence.
10. **Own Pace of learning**: The system should give freedom to a student so that they could stop, start, and learn the course material at their own pace.

However, in this discussion, it is notable that Wedemeyer ardently anticipate the term "teaching-learning" rather he proposed to separate teaching from learning to diminish the "space and time" barrier. He suggested six characteristics to maintain an "independent study" system; they are:

1. **Separation**: In the scenario of "independent study" separation of teacher and student is one of the important characteristics as per the proposed theory of Wedemeyer.
2. **Normalization**: Teaching and learning should be carried out in a normalized way through writing or some other medium.
3. **Individualization**: Emphasized individual learning as a key characteristic. Every student is different from the others. Therefore, in the "independent study environment" this factor should be taken care of.
4. **Student activity**: Learning takes place through student activity.
5. **Student's environment**: Learning is made convenient for the student in his environment.
6. **Responsibility of learner**: In the "independent learning" scenario the learner takes responsibility for his progress and the freedom to start and stop at any time or pace.

Wedemeyer's Proposed Teaching-Learning Situation

Illustrating teaching and learning scenarios Wedemeyer said that a traditional classroom is comprised of four elements and he discussed his thought through the diagram. *Figure 18.1* presents a diagram of the classroom as a teaching-learning situation:

1. A teacher
2. A learner or learners
3. A communication system or mode
4. Something to be taught/learned

The whole structure is discussed in this diagram and Wedemeyer named it the "classroom box". In this scenario, communication must be face-to-face, eyeball-to-eyeball, earpan-to-earpan speech. Besides, he also said that if one wants to achieve teaching-learning which can fit any place, any time, with one or many learners, then it is imperative to reconstruct or structure the diagram of "classroom box" as discussed in Figure 18.1. However, Wedemeyer did not change any of the four elements of the "classroom box" diagram, and just accommodated the physical space to enable the teaching-learning process any time, any place and as per single and multiple learner requirements. Table 18.2 presents teaching-learning situations to accommodate physical distance.

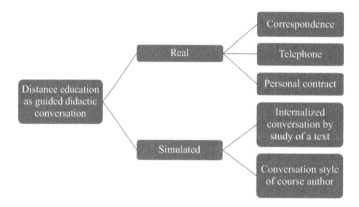

Figure 18.1 Guided didactic conversation: BorjeHolmburg (1995).

Table 18.2 Distance teaching program based on dialog and structure

Distance	Type	Program Type	Example
Most distance	(–D) (–S)	Programs with no dialog no structure	Independent reading, "self-directed" etc.
	(–D) (+S)	Programs with no dialog but with structure	When the communication method is television or radio
	(+D) (+S)	Programs with dialog and structure	Correspondence method
Least distance	(+D) (–S)	Programs with dialog and no structure	A Rogerian type of tutorial program

Source: Adapted from Moore (1977).

Based, on this Wedemeyer conceptualized three views for independent distance programs:

- Encouragement of a self-paced based learning environment, and learning should take place based on the circumstances of the learner and their needs
- Encouragement of an individualized learning environment
- Freedom to set the learning goal, activity, and content

At the end of the Wedemeyer "independent study" theory, one can say that this theory was a blueprint to transcend all barriers regarding the liberal vision of distance education. His theory overwhelmingly influenced various policymakers, writers, and educational activists to further contribute to this field.

Theory of Autonomy and Distance: Michael G. Moore

In 1970, Michael G. Moore, a professor at Pennsylvania State University, PA, formulated the theory of distance education based on two variables viz. "autonomy" and "distance". However, from 1973 onward, Moore realized some complications in the distance education environment "micro factors" such as:

- Description
- Definition
- Discrimination
- Identification
- Build a theoretical framework

Moore deliberately focused Moore focused on two types of learning environments; they are:

- **School environment**: The classroom, lecture, or seminar, the setting in which the event of teaching is contemporaneous and co-terminus with the event of learning.
- **Distance education**: It refers to an autonomous learning environment where the learner is separated from the teacher by time and space so that communication is by a non-human medium.

Moore systematically divided distance education into three separate sub-systems, viz. a learner, a teacher, and a method of communication and distinguishing them from learning, teaching, and communication as another form of education.

However, Moore in the early development stage of his theories tried to explicitly use the term "distance education" and he deliberately studied various previous conceptions regarding distance he found terms listed in educational provisions related to distance teaching such as open university, university without a wall, on-campus university study program, external degree program, teach yourself books, etc. Moore realized that all are wider classifications in the distance education scenario. In this orientation, Moore considered distance education as two-way, face-to-face or contiguous and "distance teaching". However, based on this view Moore found two essential components for independent study one falls under *distance teaching* and the other falls under *learner autonomy*, and in both, the component learner is the most crucial element. The two elements are:

- **Distance teaching**: In this component programs are designed for the learner in an environment apart from the instructor.
- **Learner autonomy**: In this component programs are designed for the encouragement of independent/self-directed learning.

Concept of "Distance" and "Autonomy" and Classification of "Program" in Moore's Theory

Concept of Distance

First, in the conception of the term "distance", Moore identifies the origin by the separation of learner and teacher in an educational environment. Therefore, Moore found the two elements in distance education, which can be measured. First, in the provision of two-way communication (dialog), Moore gave the example that some medium has the capacity of two-way communication such as a telephone network which is two-way communication that denotes (+D) and some do not such as radio broadcast, denotes (–D). Therefore (–D) would not be counted as distance education as per the definition of Moore (Moore, 1994). It is notable that Moore mainly focused on the use of media rather than communication media. Besides, the second element is the extent to which a program is responsive to the need of individual learners (structure). However, in some program structures, no variation is possible that denotes (+S) and some are more responsive to the need and goals of individual student denotes (–S). Therefore, Moore understood to measure 'dialog' and 'structure' separately. He presents a table to understand both concepts. Table 18.2 present the details of the distance teaching program based on dialog and structure, adapted from Moore (1977).

Concept of Autonomy

In the second part of Moore's theory, he addressed the concept of learner "autonomy". He started his thought with some general operation, he found that learners are very much dependent on teachers for guidance, explanation, questions, and simulation in conventional and distance programs. Moore, shows in these scenarios teachers are more active and students are passive. Moore felt a gap between teacher and student, he suggested that students should take responsibility to conduct the learning program. He seeks learner autonomy in:

- The setting of objectives
- Methods of study
- Evaluation

However, Moore also stated that autonomous learner proceeds without any need for a teacher or may only need a little direction. Although, for highly autonomous learners the teacher functions as a respondent rather than a director, and the institution becomes a helping organization. Moore has set forth some characteristic components which are important for any teaching-learning process (Moore, 1977b).

- **Establishment of preparatory activity**: Problems are identified, goals are set, and strategies are planned.
- **Executive activity**: Information and ideas are patterned and experiments and tests take place for an institutional solution.
- **Evaluatory activity**: Judgment about appropriateness, ideas for solving the problem, and meeting the goal.

Classification of Programs

As discussed previously, Moore classifies distance education programs in two ways one is "autonomy" (learner-determined) and "non-autonomy" (teacher-determined). Therefore, Moore set three questions that can help the student to exercise autonomy in learning:

- **Autonomy in the setting of objectives**: Is the section of the learning objective in the program the responsibility of the learner or the teacher?
- **Autonomy in the method of study**: Is the selection of various resources, media, and content based on learner decisions or teacher decisions?
- **Autonomy in evaluation**: Are the use of the method of evaluation or criteria decided by the learner or teacher?

However, based on the questions asked by the student, Moore classified the whole situation as shown in Table 18.3.

In this regard, one can say that Moore has classified the whole procedure of educational programs based on two variables "distance" and "autonomy". Based on these two variables and classification, Moore has also categorized the "most independent" and "less independent" educational environment in the teaching and learning process. *Figure 18.3* represents the tropology of educational programs (Moore, 1977a).

As a description of tropology, Moore stated that *AAA–D–S* is the most independent form of education, which is characterized as a totally private study without two-way communication. It is also unstructured and the learner is autonomous based on the setting of goal, method of learning, and also evaluation.

Besides, *NNN+D–S* represents less independence, autonomy and distance are very low and most importantly learner is fully controlled by the teacher.

As discussed, Moore believes in the separation of "learning program" and "teaching program" by "time" and "space". Moore stated that this separation is important because, the learner and teacher can equally influence the whole teaching-learning process such as setting learning goals, resource utilization, methods of learning, decision-making, the process of evaluation, etc.

Moore also stated that it is important and challenging to match the program in a way that learners can exercise maximum autonomy and growth. Because, the high autonomy-based program could damage the learning environment and learner compared to low autonomy (Moore, 1993).

Theory of Industrialization of Teaching

An extensive amount of research on distance education was accomplished in the early 1960s. Otto Peters was one of the eminent scholars in the field of distance education, who worked at the German Institute of Distance education (DIFF). However, in his early career, Peters published a comparative survey of distance education and authoritative analytical discourse of distance education in higher education.

Table 18.3 Types of independent study programs by learner autonomy

Example	Objective Setting	Implementation	Evaluation
Private study	A	A	A
University of London external degree	A	A	N
Learning sports skill	A	N	–
Learning car driving	A	N	N
Learner control course and evaluation	N	A	N
Learner control evaluation	N	N	A
Many independent course study	N	A	N
Independent study for credit	N	N	N

After a comparative analysis of the distance teaching system, Peter realized that in the conventional model of teaching where the method of teaching mostly is based on oral lecture, group education is a mainly pre-industrial form of education. Therefore, Peter mostly focused on the industrial production process and teaching-learning. To support his argument, Peters stated that distance education is a comparatively new form of learning, better to say post-industrial innovation, began as early as, 130 years ago, (Peters, 1980). The industrial revolution increased the possibility of various ways of communication and the pace of society. Distance education was not possible without fast and regular postal service and fast railway service which was established in the period of the industrial era.

Peters Didactical Analysis of Distance Education

Peters theory of distance education was based on a didactic analysis. His didactic structure of distance education (1979) was closely similar to the model proposed by two German theorists, Heiman and Wolfgang Schultz, their model also refers to as the Hamburg model (Heidt, 1978; Holmberg, 1982). However, the major assumption of the Hamburg model was based on six intrinsic elements which are aim, content, methods, choice of medium, human prerequisites, and socio-cultural prerequisites. Peters also analyzed distance education based on the Hamburg model as follows:

- **Aim**: Peters realized that structural consideration is the major aim in the distance education program. In the distance education process, the structural difference is in the domains of cognitive, emotional, and practical.
- **Content**: The content of distance education is considered as teaching of knowledge, skills, practical "hands-on" learning, etc.
- **Methods**: Reduction of interpersonal communication and use of written information carriers and motivation use as a substitute for interpersonal communication.
- **Choice of medium**: Communication suffers or loses from human speech to the written word. Therefore, the possible role of other media is considered.
- **Human prerequisites**: Employment condition, age, and entry-level counseling are juxtaposed with the condition of conventional students.
- **Socio-cultural prerequisites**: Considered various ideological, political, academic statuses of a different culture.

However, based on these six components, Peters has proposed two types of teaching; direct and indirect. Peters has claimed that in the educational scenarios researcher and theorist have emphasized more on direct teaching such as the form of conventional, oral, and group-based. However, he stated that distance education is one of the indirect modes of teaching.

Later, based on economic and industrial theories Peters made a distinct comparison between distance education and industrial production of the good. Peters proposed the following new terminologies to understand or analyze distance education:

- **Rationalization**: Peters emphasized methodical measurement and its rational application which helps to achieve desired outputs by providing lower input of power, money, and time.
- **Division of labor**: Labor must be divided or distributed within the subject matter expert; educationist and experienced practitioner to develop required course material for the development of the distance education program.

- **Mechanization**: Communication is one of the crucial elements in the teaching-learning process. Therefore, the distance learning situation needs to use modern or updated means of communication medium and electrical data processing.
- **Assembly line**: In the development of distance education material such as a manuscript is passed from one area to another and specific changes are made at each stage.
- **Mass production**: Peters envisioned that the traditional method of learning mostly mechanizes to teach a small group of learners and can only be applied to the masses artificially by using a loudspeaker in a long lecture hall. But in distance education situations instructional material is mass-produced and delivered to the learner with the help of modern innovation.
- **Preparatory work**: Preparation was also a more important part of the distance education program regarding production situations such as division of labor, economy, quality, speed, etc.
- **Planning**: Planning on the other hand is the primary requirement of effective preparation. Planning needs to be more comprehensive and detailed. Also, required coordination of various interacting factor.
- **Organization**: Immediate connection between effective teaching methods and rational organization is crucial in a distance learning environment. Organizations maintain an essential role for a student to accommodate a predetermined instructional unit at appointment time.
- **Scientific control method**: Scientific control means the efforts to measure the success of teaching method by which systematic analysis or can measure time study by following result extracted from measurement and empirical data.
- **Formalization**: In distance education, various phase needs to be predetermined formally rather manually by the division of labor and manufacturing.
- **Standardization**: Standardization means, a limitation or norm to restrict the number of production or type of one product to make it more purposeful, cheaper, and flexible.
- **Change of function**: In the industrial form of education functional change of workers is the most important aspect concerning the production process. In distance education situations, the functional role of the teacher is distributed in three-way such as (a) knowledge provider (author), (b) evaluator of knowledge and progress (marker or tutor), and (c) counselor (subject program advisor).
- **Objectification**: Organization principles and machine is responsible for more production process, the loss in the production process, its subjective element which is used to determine the craftsman's work to a considerable degree.
- **Concentration and centralization**: In the industrial process capital is the most fundamental element. For mass production, division of labor, there has been a movement toward concentration of capital, centralized administration, and monopolized market.

From the above-mentioned factors, he realized that division of labor is most crucial and mechanization and automation help to restructure the teaching process. However, as per concern about teaching and learning, Peter stated that the industrial structure of the distance education model should be taken into consideration.

Educational Technology and Peters View

Before his industrial model, Peters extensively analyzed a plethora of information regarding distance mode of teaching in the focal point of modern technology potentiality in the educational scenarios. As per theoretical orientation, he mainly followed five groups of models of learning, which are:

- Simulation model
- Planning model
- Material development strategies
- System approach
- Curriculum development model

Peter was an optimist about technological potentiality and believed that effective planning and proper utilization of technological advantage will help to accelerate the teaching-learning environment as well as educational achievement.

Criticism and Conclusion

The theoretical view of Peter has been criticized by various educationists in various ways. Such as, Christ of Ehmann, Kari-Heinz Rebel, Manfred Hamann who are the leading critics of the Peters model. They criticized Peter in terms of faith in the value of planning and technological progress in education (Ehmann, 1981). Besides this, Rebel (1983) criticized Peter on his assumption of six interdependence elements (as previously discussed, Berlin Didactic School). Rebel reflected those six interdependence elements could never be expressed in such a way as Peters explained.

Although Peter's theories were criticized in many ways, he found milestones to enquire the industrialization education and it is still considered as a unique contribution in the field of distance education.

Theories of Interaction and Communication

The field of distance education has been enriched by many conceptual discussions and theories. If we summarize the previous discussion, notably, Moore, Wedemeyer, and Delling in their theories emphasized the conception of "*Autonomy and Independence*" and Peter's focus on the "development of learning material". This section introduces another central conception of distance education theories called "theories of interaction and communication".

Five researchers namely Bååth, Holmberg, Daniel, Stewart, and Smith emphasized interaction and communication as central aspects in the field of distance education. The first two of the following theories are discussed:

- Two-way communication: John A. Bååth
- Guided didactic conversation: Borje Holmberg
- Interaction and independence: John Daniel
- Continuity of concern: David Sewart
- An integrated mode: K. C. Smith

Two-Way Communication: John A. Bååth

John A. Bååth, a Swedish philosopher, created the concept of "two-way communication" as a mode of distance learning from 1970 onward. He was mostly influenced by the existence of the teaching model of Skinner, Rothkopf, Ausubel, Eagan, Gagne, and the applicability of this model in distance education. Based on various existing teaching models, Bååth developed his two-way communication model in the field of distance education. In 1980 Bååth provided some theoretical and conceptual outlines of "two-way communication" which applied in the scenarios of Swedish distance education (Bååth, 1982). Those are the following:

> **Ensure two-way communication:** Bååth elaborated that before writing any course material of distance education one needs to ensure that is it possible to have some kind of two-way communication within the material, for example, means of exercise, question, or self-check test with specimen answer.

Guided Didactic Conversation: Borje Holmburg (1995)

Another significant theoretical contribution falls under the interaction communication theories of distance education that is called "guided didactic conversation" by Borjeholmburg.

Borje Holmberg stated that "*My theory of distance education as a method of guided didactic conversation implies that the character of good distance education resembles that of a guided conversation aiming at learning and that presence of the typical traits of such conversation facilitates learning*".

Seven assumptions based on Holmberg's guided didactic conversation are as follows:

1. Personal relation between teaching and learning can foster or promote pleasure and motivation.
2. A personal relationship can be increased by self-instructional material and two-way communication.
3. Proper study processes and methods increase intellectual pleasure and motivation which in turn helps to attain learning goals.
4. Learning atmosphere, language, the conversation can be in favor of feeling of personal relationship.
5. The communicative message must be easily understandable and remembered.
6. Conversation concepts can be translated or used by the media available through distance education.
7. That planning and guiding the work, whether provided by the teaching organization or the student, are necessary for organized study, which is characterized by explicit or implicit goal concepts. (Holmberg, 1978: 20, repeated 1983: 115–116).

Major characteristics of learning material were developed based on Holmberg's theory of guided didactic conversation they are as follows:

1. Easily accessible study material in respect of language as well as readable and moderate density of information
2. Explicate advice to the student regarding what to do, how to do it, what to avoid etc.
3. Exchange view about what to be accepted and what to be rejected
4. Increased emotional attachment of student by which they can take part in subject and its problem
5. Use of personal and possessive pronoun

Bibliography

Bååth, J. A. (1982). Distance students' learning—Empirical findings and theoretical deliberations. *Distance Education, 3*(1), 6–27.

Coombs, P. H. (1977). *A Fresh Look at the World Educational Crisis in Commonwealth Secretariat. Report of the Seventh Commonwealth Conference.* London: The Commonwealth Secretariat.

Dictionary, M.W. (2012). Encyclopedia britannica. In *Encyclopedia britannica ultimate reference suite.* Chicago, IL: Encyclopedia Britannica.

Ehmann, C. (1981). Fernstudium/fernunterricht. Reflection on Otto Peters' research. *Distance Education, 2*(2), 228–233.

Heidt, E. U. (1978). *Instructional media and the individual learner: A classification and systems appraisal.* London: Kogan Page.

Holmberg, B. (1981). *Status and trends of distance education.* London: Kogan Page.

Holmberg, B. (1983). Guided didactic conversation in distance education. In D. Sewart, D. Keegan, and B. Holmberg (Eds.), *Distance education: International perspectives* (pp. 114–122). London: Croom Helm.

Holmberg, B. (1985). The feasibility of a theory of teaching for distance education and a proposed theory. ZIFFPapiere 60. ERIC, ED 290013.

Holmberg, B. (1986). *Growth and structure of distance education.* London: Croom Helm.

Holmberg, B. (1988). Guided didactic conversations in distance education. In D. Sewart, D. Keegan, & B. Holmberg (Eds.), *Distance education: International perspectives* (pp. 114–122). New York: Routledge.

Holmberg, B. (1989). *Theory and practice of distance education.* London: Routledge.

Holmberg, B. (1991). Open and Distance Learning in Continuing Education. *IFLA Journal, 17*(3), 274–282. https://doi.org/10.1177/034003529101700314

Holmberg, B. (1995). The evolution of the character and practice of distance education. *Openlearning 10*(2), 47–53.

Keegan, D. (1986). *The foundations of distance education.* London: Croom Helm.

Keegan, D. (Ed.). (1993) *Theoretical principles of distance education.* London: Routledge.

Keegan, D. (1994). Autonomy and interdependence. *American Journal of Distance Education, 8*(2), 15.

Keegan, D. (1995). Distance education technology for the new millennium: Compressed video teaching. ZIFFPapiere IO 1. ERIC, ED 3 89–93 1.

Keegan, D. (2013). *Foundations of distance education,* (3rd ed.). London: Routledge.https://doi.org/10.4324/9781315004822

Levy, M., Stewart, D. E. & Kent, C. H. W. (2020, October 20). Encyclopædia Britannica. Encyclopedia Britannica. https://www.britannica.com/topic/Encyclopaedia-Britannica-English-language-reference-work

Moore, M. (1990). Recent contributions to the theory of distance education. *Open Learning, 5*(3), 10–15.

Moore, M. G. (1972). Learner autonomy: The second dimension of independent learning. *Convergence, 5*(Fall), 76–88.

Moore, M. G. (1994). Autonomy and interdependence. *The American Journal of Distance Education, 8*(2), 15.

Moore, M. G. (1993). Theory of Transactional Distance. In D. Keegan (Ed.), *Theoretical principles of distance education* (pp. 22–29). New York: Routledge.

Moore, M. (1977). On a theory of independent study. In *ZIFFPapiere, No. 16,* W. Germany: Fernuniversitat.

Moore, M.G. (1977a). A model of independent study. *Epistolodidaktika, 1*(6) 40.

Moore, M.G. (1977b). *On a theory of independentstudy (ZIFF PAPIERE 16).* Hagen: FernUniversitat.

Newby, T. J., Stepich, D. A., Lehman, J. D., & Russell, J. D. (2000). *Educational technology for teaching and learning.* New Jersey: Prentice Hall.

Newby, T. J., Stepich, D. A., Russell, J. D., & Lehman, J. D. (2006). *Educational technology for teaching and learning.* Englewood Cliffs, NJ: Prentice Hall.

Perraton, H. (1988). A theory for distance education. In D. Sewart, D. Keegan, & B. Holmberg (Eds.), *Distance education: International perspectives* (pp. 34–45). New York: Routledge.

Peters, O. (1988). Distance teaching and industrial production: A comparative interpretation in outline. In D. Sewart, D. Keegan, & B. Holmberg (Eds.) *Distance education: International perspectives,* (pp. 95–113). New York: Routledge.

Peters, O. (1989). The iceberg has not melted: Further reflections on the concept of industrialization and distance teaching. *Open Learning: The Journal of Open, Distance and E-Learning, 4*(3), 3–8.

Peters, O. (1994a). Distance education and industrial production: A comparative interpretation in outline (1973). In D. Keegan (Ed.), *Otto Peters on distance education: The industrialization of teaching and learning* (pp. 107–127). London: Routledge.

Picciano, A. G. (2002). Beyond student perceptions: Issues of interaction, presence, and performance in online course. *Journal of Asynchronous Learning Networks, 6*(1). Retrieved from http://www.aln.org/alnweb/journal/jaln-vol6issue1.htm

Portway, P. S., & Lane, C. (1994). History of telecourses. In *Guide to Teleconferencing and Distance Learning* (3rd ed.). Retrieved from http://www.tecweb.org/eddevel/telecon/de92.html

Saba, F. (2003). Distance education theory, methodology, and epistemology: A pragmatic paradigm. In M. G. Moore & W. G. Anderson (Eds.), *Handbook of distance education* (pp. 3–21). Mahwah, NJ: Lawrence Erlbaum.

Saba, F. (2007). A systems approach in theory building. In M. G. Moore (Ed.), *Handbook of distance education* (pp. 43–57). Mahwah, NJ: Lawrence Erlbaum.

Shale, D. (1988). Toward a reconceptualization of distance education. *American Journal of Distance Education, 2*(3), 25–35.

Simonson, M. (1995). Does anyone really want to learn at a distance? *Tech. Trends, 40*(5), 12.

Simonson, M., & Schlosser, C. (1995). More than fiber: Distance education in Iowa. *Tech. Trends, 40*(3), 13–15.

United States Distance Learning Association. (1998). Distance learning definition (online). Retrieved from http:/www.usdla.org/pages/define.htm.

Valentine, D. (2002). Distance learning: Promises, problems, and possibilities. *Online Journal of Distance Learning Administration, 5*(3), 1–11.

Wedemeyer, C. A. (1973). Characteristics of Open Learning Systems. Report of NAEB Advisory Committee on Open Learning Systems to NAEB Conference, New Orleans, Louisiana, USA

Wedemeyer, C. (Ed.). (1963). *The Brandenburg memorial essays on correspondence instruction I.* Madison, WI: University of Wisconsin, University Extension.

19
E-LEARNING IN EDUCATION

Introduction

Time is changing so fast, every single analog device is going digital, becoming smaller, and more user-friendly. If one thinks about the early stage, computer devices were very big and the use of a computer was considered a privilege, but now it is a necessity. Currently, we are living in a world where many classrooms are equipped with electronic devices such as computers, projectors, various electronic learning gadgets, etc. Electronic is denoted by "e" and when one uses any electronic device for learning it is called "e-learning". Information and communication technology expands that scope, now everyone can learn through electronics from anywhere and at any time. So, it is very important to know about e-learning in detail. The present chapter intends to explore a comprehensive discussion about e-learning as a mode of teaching and learning.

Meaning and Definitions of E-Learning

To know what "e-learning" is let us simplify the term "e" and "learning" separately. The word "e" stands for "electronic". Therefore, e-learning is a process of education through any kind of electronic device. Therefore, e-learning refers to electronically and technologically supported learning and teaching (Luskin, 2010). The term "e-learning" was first introduced in 1999 in a CBT seminar in Los Angeles and meant "web-enabled material deployed using net". E-learning comprises a teaching-learning process that is not directly through a book or a face-to-face lecture by a teacher rather learning is through the intentional use of network information and communication technology (Naidu, 2006). Therefore, e-learning comprises various related terms such as online learning, networked learning, web-based learning or instruction, distributed learning environment, etc. Plenty of research has been conducted in the field of e-learning and various researchers define e-learning in many aspects. These are as follows:

Urdan and Weggen (2004) explained e-learning as a process of providing instruction through electronic media which includes television, radio, tape recorder, CD-ROM, etc.

Oblinger and Hawkins (2005) provided a narrow definition of e-learning and explained e-learning areas solely based on an online learning approach that includes various course management systems.

Organisation for Economic Development and Co-operation (OECD, 2005) elucidated that e-learning is generally referred to as the applicability of Information and Communication Technology (ICT) to promote learning in tertiary education. This organization also explained that in the context of education e-learning acts both in campus-based and also the distance education context.

European Commission (2001) explained that e-learning is the use of various new electronic and multimedia technologies as well as an internet-based online medium to promote effective learning through service, exchange, and collaboration facilities. (Arkorful and Abaidoo, 2014).

Joint Information Systems Committee (JISC, 2003) defined e-learning from a different point of view, this committee explained e-learning as a mechanism of facilitating and supporting of teaching and learning process by using the method of ICT.

Abbad and Juan (2009) defined e-learning as any learning scenario that is electronically enabled.

Downey, Wentling, Wentling, and Wadsworth (2005) noted that e-learning refers to the acquisition and distribution of knowledge through electronic means.

Welsh et al. (2003) mainly focused on hard technology such as computer networks and the internet in the context of providing information and instruction to the masses or individuals.

Tao et al. (2006) described that e-learning is a new learning environment that is enabled on electronic networks for learning, allowing the learner to receive individual support and a learning schedule from one learner to another.

Stockley (2005) defines e-learning as the medium of providing instruction or educational programs through various electronic mediums such as TV, mobile, computer, etc.

Suzan Kwegyir (2008) defined e-learning as a unique approach to teaching and learning which may comprise various electronic instructional mediums such as TV, audio/videotapes, the internet, computers, etc. E-learning facilitates access to relevant knowledge from anywhere at any time.

From the above definitions, it can be concluded that e-learning can be defined in many ways based on its application and orientation. One can extract some basic points from the above definitions regarding e-learning such as the following:

- E-learning includes numerous types of electronic media such as TV, CD-ROM, DVD, mobile phone, computer, audio devices, satellite, etc.
- It facilitates providing knowledge that is relevant or useful.
- E-learning encourages education from anywhere at any time.
- E-learning can occur through face-to-face and distance modes of the learning environment.
- E-learning can be asynchronous, instructor-led, synchronous, self-paced, etc.
- E-learning uses various media elements such as words, pictures, animation or video, etc.

Characteristics of E-Learning

Technology enhances learning: E-learning is based on Technology Enhanced Learning (TEL) where learning only takes place through the use of various electronic mediums such as TV, radio, computers, etc.

More than online learning: E-learning is the broader concept in the context of online learning as online learning only refers to the internet or network-based learning through any electronic medium.

Lifelong learning approach: E-learning increases access to learning with various knowledge-based resources, therefore, it encourages lifelong learning among various stakeholders.

The social aspect of learning: The e-learning mode of learning provides the opportunity for the learner to learn collaboratively through peer interaction. This mode of learning fosters the social attribute of the learner.

Personalization: Another important characteristic of e-learning is its personalization nature. For instance, the learner can learn at his/her own pace and choice based on his/her learning style, career goal, personal preference, job requirements, etc.

Multiple ways of communication: E-learning expands the opportunity for multi-level communication in the teaching-learning process rather than one-way communication such as lecture-based teaching-learning. Modern e-learning provides various stand-alone tools with Learning Management Systems (LMS) that can increase collaboration and engagement in learning.

Flexible: E-learning is flexible. There is no necessity to learn in a specific place and at a specific time and learners can learn at his/her convenience.

Learner-centric approach: E-learning is a teaching and learning revolution toward a learner-centric approach to teaching. It enables the liberty of the learner regarding their love of learning. Such as they can choose their learning content, place, and method of learning.

Historical Perspective of E-Learning

Unlike the definition of e-learning, there is no specific point or universal acceptable time frame for the evolution of e-learning. As the term e-learning consisted of electronic devices for learning from time to time various devices were being developed. Therefore, the concept of e-learning evolved in many ways based on aspects, components, delivery methods, etc. Some of the basic parallel conception related to e-learning is multimedia learning, technology-enhanced learning (TEL), virtual education, online learning, mobile learning, computer-mediated communication, etc. Each term advocates based on some basic distinction. Henceforth, discussing the historical orientation of e-learning will mostly initially emphasize the origin of a specific term or concept related to e-learning. The following are the historical journeys of e-learning as explained by Roberta Gogos (2016) in his scientific work.

Beginning from the core aspect it is imperative to focus on the early invention of e-learning that is "The Testing Machine" developed by Sidney Pressey in early 1920. The major educational aspect of the testing machine was to provide drills and practice to the student in a systematic way.

After that, another revolution in the context of e-learning is the "Teaching Machine" invented by Skinner in 1954. The major focuses of the teaching machine were to provide information in small amounts and systematic ways. That is also called programmed instruction.

However, a huge revolution in the field of e-learning took place after the revolutionary introduction of the computer in the field of learning and teaching. At the early stage of the invention of the computer, the first-time use of a computer-based program for teaching and learning was the Programmed Logic for Automated Teaching Operations (PLATO) that was also the first Computer-Based Training (CBT) program used for drills and practice through the computer.

In 1966, two professors at Stanford University, California, Patrick Suppes and Richard Atkinson, used Computer Assisted Instruction (CAI) for teaching and learning. At this time the first computer was installed in community colleges for instructional work.

In 1969, The Advanced Research Projects Agency Network (ARPANET) was introduced to create the internet by the US Department of defense. Only one year later computer-based training began at the New Jersey Institute of Technology and at this specific time, computer mice and Graphical User Interface (GUI) were also being invented.

In the early 1980s, the personal computer was used for teaching-learning purposes. From this time onward online communities started sharing information and gradually enriching the field of e-learning.

In the 1990s, the field of e-learning took different shapes. That is a time of digital natives and started a new era of learning. During that time the term e-learning started being popular and widely recognized. The virtual learning environment and Learning Management Systems (LMS) started emerging by the end of this century.

In the first decades of the 2000s, e-learning started to be used, not only in the academic sector but also in the field of business training. At this time, plenty of online learning materials were being developed by experts from all over the world. Various authoring tools were created and learning material became more accessible than ever.

At present, (2010–2018) e-learning is developing as an important learning approach for the scope of various unique innovations, one of them being Massive Open Online Courses (MOOC). Throughout the globe, various government and private organizations developed an open-learning platform based on e-learning. Besides, various social media-based platforms such as YouTube, Twitter, Facebook, etc., promote e-learning by providing an opportunity to connect, share, and learn from anywhere at any time.

Components of E-Learning

In the previous section, one may get a brief conception of e-learning and its characteristics. Also, it is understood that e-learning is a process of learning through an electronic medium. To understand the concept of e-learning one needs to know its various essential components related to e-learning. Here one presents some of the crucial components of e-learning proposed by Andrew (2001). These are the following:

1. Audience
2. Course structure
3. Page design
4. Content engagement
5. Usability

Expectation

Expectation means a specific learning goal of a specific learning community in the context of participation in a specific e-learning course. The following context is needed to be analyzed carefully before the development of an e-learning course:

Who will be the course audience or for whom will the courseware be developed?
Where will the outcome of this course be used by the participant or audience?
Which kind of existing skills are required for a specific e-learning course?

After a nuanced analysis of these specific requirements of the audience, the concept can grow further regarding the structure, format, and specific design of content.

Learning abilities

This is also a quintessential aspect that is needed to be taken into consideration. Generally, every learner has individual differences in the context of his/her learning abilities. Therefore, the designer of the e-learning course needs to consider this matter for the development of effective e-learning material.

Availability of resources

This is another prerequisite aspect for the development of e-learning material. To develop an e-learning courseware various resources of software, hardware, and content material needs to be chosen very carefully so that learners can access or take benefit of learning material effectively.

Learning environment

The learning environment is one of the very crucial aspects of any teaching and learning process. In the context of e-learning, the developer or designer should clarify the following:

- In which environment the learner is going to complete this course?
- Whether the learning environment will be a classroom, workstation, or virtual?
- Whether learning will be face-to-face, blended, or fully self-paced?

Job responsibilities

Besides all these aspects a developer or instructional designer should be clear about the job responsibility of learners or audiences such as current skills and required skills.

Diverse need of preference

It is a known fact that a learner has diverse needs of preferences with respect to learning. In the context of e-learning, the developer should take care of these attributes of the learner by providing various customized learning aspects. For instance, some learners prefer to learn through audio or video, some by simulation, some by fully hands-on experiences, etc.

Ethics in E-Learning

One of the greatest issues which needs to be focused on, with the unprecedented growing market of online or e-learning scenarios is an ethical consideration. After the innovation of the effectiveness of e-learning in the context of teaching and instruction, the government started developing multiple online learning platforms many of which are with ethical parameters. Now the question is what kind of ethical aspect mostly affects the e-learning platform? The answer to this question is not a single or simple one. For example, recently an e-mail was received by someone from a world-renowned e-learning provider where it was written "You may already have a degree and not know it" with an eye-catching and colorful banner. This is a representative answer to such related moral issues and ethical aspects in the context of online learning. Another, scary piece of information in the context of e-learning was a survey conducted by NSSE in 2007 that out of the 59% of US student who uses e-learning programs, 27% "very often" and 32% "often" make some sort of a fault. The present section intends to provide knowledge on the ethical aspect of e-learning in the context of the e-learner and e-teacher.

Ethical Issues in the Context of E-Learning

Academic fraud is not a new concept. This kind of fraud occurs from the student side either face-to-face or in an online learning environment. However, what is new in the context of the ICT-based e-learning environment is "psychological distance" which is a new phenomenon in the present online-based teaching and learning situation (Savin, 1992). Another distinguishing factor in the context of ethical violation or academic fraud compared to face-to-face learning approaches and e-learning-based teaching and learning scenarios is monitoring. In the context of a face-to-face learning scenario, the teacher or instructor may be able to monitor the behavior of students instantly. However, it is hard to monitor student activities specifically subtle insults, mockery, or unusual body language in an effective way. Besides, in the online learning environment, the learner or e-learner cannot regret his/her behavior because they are unable to see or hear other people physically.

R. A. Fass discussed academic fraud in the context of "psychological distance" in a study for the American Council on Education. The following are some of the lists of the pattern of academic fraud in the e-learning environment discussed by R. A. Fass (Cited by Brown, 2008, in "Ethics in eLearning").

- Inappropriate assistance in examinations
- Misuse of sources on papers and projects
- Writing assistance and other inappropriate tutoring
- Misrepresentation in the collection and reporting of data
- Improper use of academic resources
- Disrespecting the work of others
- Lack of protection for human subjects in research
- Breaches of computer ethics
- Lack of adherence to copyright and copy-protection
- Providing inappropriate assistance to others
- Lack of adherence to academic regulation

This list of academic fraud in the e-learning aspect is similar to the academic fraud in traditional face-to-face teaching and learning environment. Furthermore, there is a list of causes for this kind of academic fraud in the context of student on-campus settings. They are:

- Pressure for grades
- Anxiety in the testing environment
- Lack of knowledge related to academic regulation
- Personality characteristics and lack of development of moral reasoning

From the above list, some of the factors are also applicable in the context of the e-learning environment of "psychological distance" conditions.

Ethical Issues for the E-Teacher

Before discussing the ethical consideration for the "e-teacher", it is necessary to understand what is meant by "e-teacher". In this discussion, "e-teacher" denotes an "e-learning instructor or provider". Ethical considerations with respect to teaching and learning are not a new phenomenon for the teacher in actual face-to-face learning scenarios. But the teacher or institution that provides an e-learning environment and a face-to-face environment faces far more and unique academic ethical violations. One of the greatest challenges faced by the e-teacher (those who have additional virtual teacher-learner connections) is the quality assurance or maintenance of the quality of the educational process (Brown, 2008). The determinism of educational values and morality is the primary aim of education. Besides, it is also true that accreditation does not always ensure the quality of education; however; still, accreditation is a very essential identity toward the achievement of learning objectives. However, throughout the world, various organizations and e-learning service providers are providing e-teachers accreditation for specific courses without evaluation of student learning achievement.

Moreover, throughout the world, various organization are providing learning material to make a profit; therefore, they always try to develop learning material based on market demand. To do so, sometimes they overlook the learning objective to follow the market demand. In this context, the ethical aspect or challenge of the e-teacher is to ensure the quality of learning context material that must be addressed or fulfill a specific learning objective effectively.

Besides, another essential challenge is to maintain copyright issues and acknowledgment. There is a plethora of information available after the revolution of information and communication technology. Therefore, curating various content materials from multiple sources is very easy now. This situation increases the probability of ethical violations in academia. E-teachers sometimes do not properly acknowledge the original creator and sometimes plagiarize original content material without taking prior consent from the original author or publisher and use it to develop e-learning material.

Ethical Issue in the Context of Research

Another malpractice in the context of academic ethics comes from the various researchers, teachers, and organizations who are working with human subjects and/or internet-based research. Sometimes this type of fraud comes in the form of undocumented or poor documentation of online resources or survey resources. In this aspect, Frankel and Siang (1999) have discussed, two basic protocols for researchers or educators who work in the field of human subject internet-based research. They are the following:

- **Autonomy**: All subjects are to be treated with respect as autonomous agents.
- **Beneficence**: Researchers are obligated to maximize the benefits of the research and minimize the harms and risks to the subjects, including taking informed consent and the protection of privacy and confidentiality (cited by Brown, 2008).

We all know that e-learning or an online-based learning platform is a sharp, innovative, and essential weapon for making the whole teaching-learning more accessible. Therefore, it is our responsibility to create an effective learning environment for the utmost utilization of this greatest innovation in the view of moral goods.

Quality of E-Learning Measuring System (D&M IS Model)

The earlier section elucidates the historical overview of e-learning and shows how in the early 1960s television was used as an e-learning tool. From then until now the field of e-learning has shifted in many ways. Presently throughout the world, a plethora of e-learning tools are developed by various organizations (government as well as private). Though this is a good sign in the context of accessibility and usability of educational material, there is concern regarding the quality and subjective aspects of e-learning.

This section discusses an interesting and important model of e-learning that is the success model developed by DeLone and McLean. This model is designed to provide a blueprint for the success of information systems in the context of eLearning (DeLone and McLean, 1992). The model of information success (IS) of D&M consists of two distinct versions. The early version of the D&M model proposed in 1992 has six different aspects such as "system quality", "information quality", "use", "user satisfaction", "individual impact", and "organizational impact".

An updated version of DeLone and McLean's information success model has been published in 2003. The major change between the model of 1992 and the model of 2003 was the inclusion of two dimensions namely "quality" and "service quality". As per quality DeLone and McLean (2003) discussed three major dimensions such as "information quality", "system quality", and "service quality". Besides, in the updated model DeLone and McLean added a dimension called "intention to use" and replaced two separate dimensions called "individual impact" and "organizational impact" with a dimension namely "net benefits". Moreover, DeLone and McLean added a feedback loop between "intention to use" and "user satisfaction". The following is a brief discussion of each dimension of the DeLone and McLean IS model (Petter, DeLone, and McLean, 2008):

- **System quality**: The dimension of system quality is an indication of a desirable characteristic of an information system. Some of the characteristics are ease of use, flexibility, response time, sophistication, system reliability, etc.
- **Information quality**: Information quality is the desirable characteristic of system output that is a management report and web page. For example, relevance, understandability, accuracy, conciseness, completeness, etc.
- **Service quality**: Service quality is to some extent the technical part of the system users will receive from the IS department or IT support personnel. For instance, SERVQUAL, responsiveness, accuracy, reliability, etc. (Pitt et al., 1995).

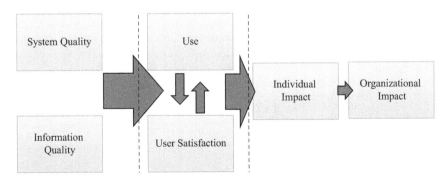

Figure 19.1 Information systems success model. Source: DeLone and McLean (1992).

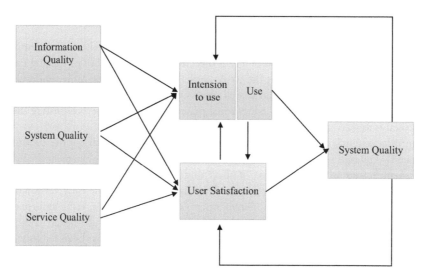

Figure 19.2 Updated information systems success model. Source: DeLone and McLean (2002, 2003).

- **System use**: "The degree and manner in which staff and customers utilize the capability of an information system" (Petter, DeLone, and McLean, 2008). For instance, amount of use, frequency of use, nature of use, appropriateness of use, etc.
- **User satisfaction**: This is an indication of the user's level of satisfaction with reports, websites, and support services.
- **Net benefits**: Net benefits denote the overall success in the context of individuals, groups, organizations, industries, and nations. For example, improved productivity, sales, cost reduction, market efficiency, etc.

It is notable that the application of the IS model of D&M depends upon the context of any organization. To successfully apply this model one must have a sound understanding of the information system (Petter, DeLone, and McLean, 2008). Generally, the D&M model of IS can be applied in various contexts such as education, e-commerce, the IT industry, etc.

Synchronous and Asynchronous E-Learning

In a general aspect, synchronous e-learning denotes an online learning environment where the learner can interact with content materials, teachers, as well as peers, and engage in real-time interaction such as through video conferencing, instant chat, etc. In synchronous learning scenarios, students can engage with learning material every time and can directly interact with the course material, lecture, or classes in real time. The following are some of the characteristics of synchronous e-learning:

Characteristics of Synchronous E-Learning

- This is an online learning activity where some of the learning activities are similar to a traditional classroom setting in the context of real-time communication between student and instructor.
- The synchronous online learning environment encourages meaningful interaction between student and teacher also refers to as synchronous learning activities (Simonson et al., 2011).

- In an asynchronous learning environment, overall teaching and learning activities occur at a specific time and point; therefore, a student needs to participate in a specific teaching and learning scenario in that specific period.
- The synchronous learning environment encourages multiple ways of interacting with students and instructors. Sharing content materials increases collaboration, real-time questions and answers, as well as feedback, etc.
- Videoconferencing, webcasts, interactive learning models, instant messaging, teleconferences, etc. are some examples of synchronous learning.

Advantages of Synchronous E-Learning

- One of the major advantages of synchronous e-learning is real-time interaction that may increase student attention and engagement in a specific learning environment.
- As an asynchronous learning environment has a similar essence to a traditional learning environment, therefore, students may not feel isolated from a specific learning environment.
- Synchronous e-learning is very unique in the sense that it provides an opportunity for the learners and instructor to work collaboratively and participate in a specific discussion actively and in real time.
- Synchronous e-learning always encourages meaningful learning because every time the students learn about a specific topic they can discuss it with the teacher and other peers instantly that in turn increases the motivation of the learner creating a more meaningful teaching and learning environment.
- The role of a teacher or learning professional is more active in the synchronous e-learning environment. They can also actively participate in a specific learning environment by providing guidance and assistance, and facilitating the progress of their learner.
- Synchronous e-learning can create an advanced learning environment by providing instant information to the learner without time delay.

Disadvantages of Synchronous E-Learning

- Synchronous e-learning is fully technology-based. Therefore, sometimes it is very hard to maintain a learning environment where a sufficiently skilled trainer is not available.
- Synchronous e-learning is real-time instant video, audio, or text-based communication which requires a high bandwidth internet connection which is sometimes not available in various developing countries. Therefore, a student from these countries or with a low bandwidth internet connection may not fully participate in a synchronous e-learning environment.
- Though synchronous e-learning eliminates the barriers of distance, there is still some problem with the synchronization of time. This is a challenging task to align different time zone throughout the globe. As a result, all the students are not able to participate due to time barriers.
- Designing an effective synchronous learning environment is a very challenging task and requires very concrete planning. Sometimes it is very hard to find a skillful instructor who can handle the overall teaching-learning environment very effectively.

Asynchronous E-Learning

Most simply it can be said that asynchronous e-learning is a kind of e-learning environment where the learner is not required to be online at a specific point in time. The following are some of the characteristics of asynchronous e-learning.

Characteristics of Asynchronous E-Learning

- Generally, asynchronous e-learning is delivered via a web-based learning environment.
- In an asynchronous e-learning environment, the learner has the liberty to participate in the specific learning program at his or her own choice, pace, and time. Sometimes asynchronous e-learning has no deadline to start or complete.
- In the asynchronous e-learning environment, teaching and learning and dissemination of course material may be completed "off-line".

Advantages of Asynchronous E-Learning

- One of the greatest advantages of an asynchronous e-learning environment is learning can take place without any rigidity of schedule.
- A student may follow the curriculum at their own pace.
- In an asynchronous e-learning environment, the student can get much time for reflection on his or her teaching and learning environment as well as the material, which in turn increases the understanding of the material very explicitly without any time pressure.
- In asynchronous e-learning, students can get more control over learning which means a student can decide when, how, what, and where he or she will learn. There are no time barriers, therefore, a learner can personalize their schedule of learning.
- Online communication and participation increase interactivity; however, some learners feel shy or uncomfortable in the context of participation in a specific learning environment that requires social interaction or participation in a discussion. Thus, the asynchronous learning environment is more convenient where a student has control over participation in discussion.

Disadvantages of the Asynchronous E-Learning Environment

- In the asynchronous learning environment, there is very limited scope for instant feedback.
- In an asynchronous learning environment, there is no scope for live participation in a specific learning environment, therefore, no scope for personal interaction with the instructor or other peers.
- In the asynchronous learning environment, there is no scope for collaboration and real-time participation.
- In this learning environment, the student may not be motivated due to a lack of interaction.
- Another challenging aspect of asynchronous teaching and learning environment is "self-discipline". In this teaching-learning scenario, the student needs to maintain their time, goal, and be motivated on their own, that sometimes is a very challenging task for the learner.

E-Learning in India: A Contextual Overview

India has a very rich history in the context of education which is going through various changes and reformation continuously. In the early stages, Indian education was mainly based on the "*Gurukul*" system which was teacher-centric and imparted by the "guru". In the "gurukul" system student mainly learned about various skills of living or lifelong learning. However, during the British period, the overall aim of education was to create white-collar professions and clerks and to spread religious narratives. The demand for the reformation of the education system was felt after 300 years when India got independence from British rule on 15 August 1947. Later after this period, the demand for education increased and schools and universities were insufficient to meet the educational needs of a huge number of students. In this context, the distance model of education or open-education system was introduced to increase the opportunity for those students who were not able to access the formal education system due to various social, economic, and cultural constraints. After the revolution of information and technology, this open-learning model expanded the scope of learning more widely and globally.

Compared with other developed or developing countries, the revolution of information and communication technology took place later in India. However, recently, the growth of the information and communication sector is very high. In the context of education, one of the essential aims of education is to provide education for all and increase access to educational opportunities and diminish the inequality gap. To achieve this goal one of the essential and effective weapons is the utilization of technological innovations. Based on the demand for the proper use of technology in education, the government, as well as a private organization, have been taking various significant initiatives such as the following:

- From 2006 onwards, Indira Gandhi National Open University (IGNOU) established an e-learning repository namely "eGyanKosh" which was operated by an open-source software, namely Dspace. The major aim was to store and use eLearning course material appropriately.
- Another great initiative taken by IGNOU was National Open and Distance Learners Library and Information Network (NODLINET). The major part of this network was to collect and publish various e-learning materials throughout the world to use for formal as well as non-formal education.
- In February 2009, the National Mission of Education developed which mostly emphasized information and communication technology. One of the vital aims of this commission was to provide a high-speed internet connection to 2,000 or more schools, colleges, and universities.
- United Nations Educational Scientific and Cultural Organization (UNESCO) has taken initiatives to spread and distribute e-learning material throughout the world created by three Indian Institutes of Technology (IITs).
- From 2004 onwards, one board was set up with financial support by UGC namely UGC-INFONET. The major responsibility of this board was to connect various universities in India and research organizations through an internet-based platform as well as increase access to educational materials utmost to everyone.
- In the context of e-learning, another significant footstep is the Memorandum of Understanding (MOU) between India and the United States to develop an e-learning satellite network where six American universities participated and on the Indian side the Indian Space Research Organization (ISRO), the Department of Science and Technology (DST), and Amrita University participated in this project.
- Other initiatives were taken by the Government of India, Ministry of Human Resource Development (MHRD) in 2006 with the "National Programme on Technology Enhanced Learning". This was a web-based training platform that aims to enhance knowledge about science and engineering by using multimedia and other advanced technology. Another significant aspect of this program was to develop 110 new and 10 existing courses into e-learning formats such as multimedia and visual-based. Various organizations like seven IITs, IISC, and various other organizations helped in this project.

- The National Council of Educational Research and Training (NCERT) has taken the initiative to digitize school textbooks by using various media such as images, graphics, video, etc. The major aim of this project was to increase access to school textbooks and other educational materials. All books are in Hindi and English languages.
- Another e-learning portal was developed jointly by UNESCO and the Indian Society for Advancement of Library and Information Science. The major aim of this portal was to increase the knowledge regarding "information literacy" and "assessment". This portal was a self-learning portal.
- Most recently the Chairman of Microsoft (a software company) Bill Gates visited India with a branch of amendment in the context of the digital divide, a bridge between those who have access to digital platforms and those who have done. In this context, Microsoft has taken initiatives to provide training to the teachers and students in the next 3 to 5 years. The entire initiative was taken jointly by Microsoft and the Department of Information Technology.
- Besides, the above initiatives another most recent initiative taken is the development of MOOC-based learning platforms namely Study Webs of Active Learning for Young Aspiring Minds (SWAYAM). The major aim of this platform was to create an open-learning platform for all.

The above discussion depicts the various initiatives taken by India to accelerate education by using e-learning. The next section will discuss the market and structure of e-learning in India.

Market and Structure of E-Learning in India

From the above discussion, it is clear that the context of e-learning in India is very significant. Besides, in the context of India, the market for e-learning has been exponentially growing. The present section intends to provide some knowledge about the present market of e-learning in India and the structure of the e-learning scenario in India.

Before getting some knowledge about what is the present market of e-learning in India, it is imperative to know what is the overall market of the Indian Education System. The present market of the Indian education system is US$100 billion (IBEF, 2007). In the context of the advancement of e-learning, the market of e-learning has increased by 31% between 2011–2016 (Google Report, 2017). It is also predicted by various market researcher that by 2021 the number of internet users in India will increase from 409 million to 735 million (Google Report, 2017). Not only the internet but also the number of users of the smartphone will increase, which was 290 million in 2016.

It is also notable that presently the overall online market in India is US$247 million, of which 1.57 million students are paid customers. To understand or get a more explicit view of the e-learning market in India, one needs to understand the present structure of e-learning in India. The next section discusses the present structure of e-learning in India.

Structure of E-Learning in India

Categorizing the overall e-learning structure in India, one can get a view of five different structures of e-learning provided in India, which are as follows:

- Complimentary supplementary courses for primary and secondary students.
- Higher education courses.

- Test preparation courses.
- Reskill and certificate courses.
- Language and general education courses.
- **Complimentary supplement courses for primary and secondary students**: This is complimentary learning material or additional learning material in the context of the primary and secondary level textbook. The present e-learning market size in India reached US$ 5.6 Billion in 2021 of which 1.57 million are paying customers. Between 2019 and 2020 the number of internet users in India increased by 128 million
- **Higher education**: Higher education is one of the biggest markets in the context of the online learning market in India. The online education market in India was worth $247 million USD in 2016 and is expected to reach approximately $1.96 billion USD by 2021. Concurrently, it is estimated that the number of paid online education users was as high as 9.5 million in 2021 (https://assets.kpmg/content/dam/kpmg/in/pdf/2017/05/Online-Education-in-India-2021.pdf).
- **Test preparation courses**: This kind of online education market mainly provides learning material for the competitive exams of students. The present market for test preparation for the supplement courses is worth US$30 million and 146,000 are paying customers.
- **Reskill and certificate courses**: The primary aim of this kind of course is to increase the skill of learners and to provide certificates after the successful completion of specific courses. The paid market for this kind of course is worth US$93 million.
- **Language and general education**: This kind of course is mainly intended for language learning. The trend in English language learning is very high. Besides, various non-formal and informal learning such as guitar playing, handcrafts, and photography are also very famous in the context of online learning. The present market for this kind of learning is worth US$5 billion and paying customers are 355,000.

Barriers to E-Learning in the Context of India

This section very briefly, points out the various obstacles or hindrances in the context of eLearning in India which are as follows:

- One of the major challenges is the inadequate structure, supply, and support of hardware and software material for e-learning and online learning which in turn affects acceptance of e-learning by a teacher in the classroom situation.
- Lack of knowledge of the teacher, school administrator, and parents regarding the effectiveness and elements of e-learning in the context of effective teaching and learning.
- Lack of cooperation and supervision and huge cultural diversity.
- Lack of skilled and knowledgeable experts who can provide proper training and support to learning in the classroom.
- Lack of encouragement in the context of community-based participation to the student and teacher.
- Lack of knowledge regarding the development of various teaching and learning materials as per the requirement of e-learning or online learning.
- Lack of internet speed and lack of infrastructural scarcity on the rural side of India.
- The majority of online learning materials are in the English language. Therefore, students face various problems working with an online platform. There are very limited numbers of e-learning materials developed based on the local language.
- Teachers and parents have a fear to accept new technology for teaching and learning.

Bibliography

Abbas, A.R., Juan, L. (2009). Supporting E-Learning System with Modified Bayesian Rough Set Model. In: W. Yu, H. He, N. Zhang (eds) *Advances in Neural Networks*Berlin, Heidelberg: Lecture Notes in Computer Science, Springer, vol 5552. https://doi.org/10.1007/978-3-642-01510-6_22, – ISNN 2009. ISNN 2009

Arkorful, V. & Abaidoo, N. (2014) The Role of e-Learning, the Advantages and Disadvantages of Its Adoption in Higher Education. *International Journal of Education and Research, 2*, 397–410.

Brown, T. (2008). Ethics in e-learning. *Revista de EDUCAÇÃO do Cogeime, 17*(32/33), 211–216.

DeLone, W. H., & McLean, E. R. (1992). Information systems success: The quest for the dependent variable. *Information Systems Research, 3*(1), 60–95.

DeLone, W. H., & McLean, E. R. (2002, January). Information systems success revisited. In *Proceedings of the 35th annual Hawaii international conference on system sciences* (pp. 2966–2976). IEEE.

DeLone, W. H., & McLean, E. R. (2003). The DeLone and McLean model of information systems success: A ten-year update. *Journal of Management Information Systems, 19*(4), 9–30.

Downey, S., Wentling, R. M., Wentling, T., & Wadsworth, A. (2005). The relationship between national culture and the usability of an e-learning system. *Human Resource Development International, 8*(1), 47–64.

Frankel, M. S., & Siang, S. (1999). *Ethical and legal aspects of human subject research on the internet.* Published by AAAS online.

Gogos, R. (2016). A brief history of elearning (infographic). Retrieved from https://www.efrontlearning.com/blog/2013/08/abrief-history-of-elearning-infographic.html.

IBEF. (2007). *Education sector in India.* India Brand Equity Foundation. Retrieved from https://www.ibef.org/download/education-report-291012.pdf.

Joint Information Systems Committee (JISC). (2003). *E-learning: Identifying how e-learning benefits students, practitioners and institutions and advising on its implementation.* Retrieved from https://www.jisc.ac.uk/rd/projects/e-learning.

Kwegyir, S. (2008). *Development of e-learning content and delivery for self-learning environment.* Karlskrona, Sweden.

Luskin, B. (2010). Think "exciting": E-learning and the big "E". *Educause Review Online, 33*(1).

Naidu, S. (2006). *E-learning: A guidebook of principles, procedures and practices.* Commonwealth Educational Media Centre for Asia (CEMCA). http://hdl.handle.net/11599/53 https://doi.org/10.56059/11599/53

OECD. (2005). *E-learning in tertiary education [online].* Retrieved September 23, 2018, from http://www.cumex.org.

Oblinger, D. G., & Hawkins, B. L. (2005). The myth about e-learning. *Educause Review, 40*(4), 14–15.

Petter, S., DeLone, W., & McLean, E. (2008). Measuring information systems success: Models, dimensions, measures, and interrelationships. *European Journal of Information Systems, 17*(3), 236–263.

Pitt, L. F., Watson, R. T., & Kavan, C. B. (1995). Service Quality: A measure of information systems effectiveness. *MIS Quarterly, 19*(2), 173–187.

Simonson, M., Schlosser, C., & Orellana, A. (2011). Distance education research: A review of the literature. *Journal of Computing in Higher Education, 23*(2–3), 124.

Sivin, J. P., & Bialo, E. R. (1992). *The ethical use of information technology in education.* Rockville, MD: National Institute of Justice.

Stockley, D. (2005). *Definition of e-learning.* Retrieved July. http://www.derekstockley.com.au/elearning-definition.html

Urdan, T., & Weggen, C. (2004). *Corporate e-learning: Exploring a new frontier, 2000* (pp. 1–95). WR Hambrecht & Co.

Welsh, E. T., Wanberg, C. R., Brown, K. G., & Simmering, M. J. (2003). E-learning: Emerging uses, empirical results and future directions. *International Journal of Training and Development, 7*(4), 245–258.

Suggested Readings

Bates, A. T. (2005). *Technology, e-learning and distance education.* London: Routledge. https://doi.org/10.4324/9780203463772.

Buzzetto-More, N. A. (Ed.). (2007). *Advanced principles of effective e-learning.* USA: California Informing Science.

Campbell, K. (2004). *E-ffective writing for e-learning environments*. Canada: IGI Global. https://10.4018/978-1-59140-124-7

Clark, R. C., & Mayer, R. E. (2016). *E-learning and the science of instruction: Proven guidelines for consumers and designers of multimedia learning*. Chichester: John Wiley & Sons.

Ehlers, U. D., & Pawlowski, J. M. (Eds.). (2006). *Handbook on quality and standardisation in e-learning*. Springer Science & Business Media. https://10.1007/3-540-32788-6

Garrison, D. R. (2011). *E-learning in the 21st century: A framework for research and practice*. New York: Routledge. https://doi.org/10.4324/9780203838761

Holmes, B., & Gardner, J. (2006). *E-learning: Concepts and practice*. Sage. https://dx.doi.org/10.4135/9781446212585

Horton, W. (2001). *Evaluating e-learning*. American Society for Training and Development. *Book Library*. 189. https://digitalcommons.georgiasouthern.edu/ct2-library/189

Horton, W. (2011). *E-learning by design*. Chichester: John Wiley & Sons.

Khan, B. H. (2005a). *E-learning quick checklist*. IGI Global.

Khan, B. H. (Ed.). (2005b). *Managing e-learning: Design, delivery, implementation, and evaluation*. IGI Global.

Phillips, R., McNaught, C., & Kennedy, G. (2012). *Evaluating e-learning: Guiding research and practice*. New York: Routledge. URL https://assets.kpmg/content/dam/kpmg/in/pdf/2017/05/Online-Education-in-India-2021.pdf

20
MASSIVE OPEN ONLINE COURSE (MOOC)

Introduction

Web 2.0 technologies have changed the form of learning. It provides the opportunity and scope of education in a more "open" and "massive" way. The present chapter introduces a revolutionary 21st-century learning approach called MOOC (Massive Open Online Course). It is revolutionary in the sense that it is based on a "connectivist" learning approach that aims to include more participation, is open access, and is a free-of-cost learning platform in the field of higher education (HE).

Meaning and Definition of MOOCs

Massive Open Online Courses (MOOCs) is a relatively new open online learning platform. From 2008 onwards Dave Cormier, Stephen Downes, and George Siemens coined the term MOOC as a learning approach based on the "connectivist" distributed peer learning model. However, MOOCs could be defined by their name "massive", "open", "online", and "course". "Massive" refers to the prudential scale of MOOCs such as a large number of participants no matter where they belong can participate in this course. It is "open" in the sense that anyone from anywhere can openly access, regardless of learner background, prior experience, and current context, as well as at no cost, and "online" in the sense that it is mainly based on "Internet" access. "Course" refers to being united by common themes. However, as it is a new concept therefore there is no universal definition of MOOC. Hence, here we are providing the following dictionary-based definition of MOOC:

Grajek, Bischel, and Dahlstrom (2013) explain MOOC as a model for delivering learning content online to any person who wants to take a course, with no limit on attendance. MOOC incorporates both traditional and modern course materials for learning such as videos, readings, projects, assignments, and many more.

Cormier and Siemens (2010) define MOOC as an online course with the option of free and open registration, a publicly shared curriculum, and open-ended outcomes. MOOCs integrate social networking, resources that are accessible online, and are facilitated by leading practitioners in the field of study. Most significantly, MOOCs are built on the engagement of learners who self-organize their participation according to learning goals, prior knowledge and skills, and common interests.

Characteristics of MOOCs

As discussed in the previous section, "MOOC" is an acronym for "Massive Open Online Course" which aims to provide active learning and a community-based learning environment by incorporating thousands of diverse learners into education. The following are the fundamental characteristics of a MOOC:

Participatory in nature: One of the most important characteristics of a MOOC is that it is mainly based on participation features. A MOOC's learning environment encourages the participant to create, interact, and share content material with others as well as provide an opportunity to gather expert knowledge from various fields. Consequently, all participation is voluntary.

Open learning environment: "Openness" is the core characteristic of a MOOC-based learning environment. We can define the term "open" in two ways; first, it is open to anyone who could access the internet regardless of caste, creed, gender, demographic background, etc. Second, it is "open" in the sense that content material which is generated through both participant and facilitator is shareable and publicly published. Also, it is open because there is no entry-level requirement for prior knowledge of the course content.

MOOC is massive: As potential scales of MOOC, it is massive. Massive in the sense a large number of participants can learn at a time. The design of the MOOC platform is the fundamental attribute that could provide large scaling amidst the learning environment (Downes, 2013).

Online learning environment: MOOC is mainly a web-based learning environment where each course material is provided through the internet.

Connectivist learning approach: MOOC is based on newly introduced "connectivist" learning theories. In this theory, the major focus of learning is network creation. Besides, it seems in this theory that knowledge should be created and distributed across the network.

Interactive learning orientation: The MOOC platform is interactive where the participant can interact with the instructor, with peer participants, with course material, and with content. However, MOOC-based learning interaction encourages building a community of learning.

Blended course material: As per course material design MOOC is blended in nature. To develop learning material both traditional and modern approach is taken into consideration such as video, collaboration, reading, games, assignment, etc.

University level course: A MOOC is an international level learning approach because various elite universities such as Harvard, Yale, Stanford, IIT Bombay, and other various universities provide learning platforms globally.

Free of cost: The MOOC-based learning platform is free of cost, and participants are not required to pay a single penny to learn. However, some university charges money for accreditation.

Fun learning environment: MOOC is a video and picture-based learning approach. However, presently many learning modules also provide game-based learning facilities. Therefore, a combination of various visual and interactive-based learning initiatives makes the MOOC platform more fun and engaging.

Types of MOOC

MOOC was developed because from the connectivist learning approach. However, after a certain period, MOOC was divided into two types based on their theoretical view. The following are the two types of MOOCs:

1. cMOOC (based on connectivism approach)
2. xMOOC (based on instructionism approach)
    - **cMOOC (connectivist MOOC)**: As discussed MOOC was developed from a view of connectivist learning approach. However, here "c" refers to "connectivism". As described by George Siemens (2012) cMOOC is mainly social network learning where the major focus is on knowledge creation based on communication between peer-to-peer and building a learning network. The ultimate aim of the cMOOC is that knowledge is open and learners can play the role of a content creator as well as a learner. A cMOOC-based learning approach encourages gathering knowledge through peer-to-peer, peer-expert, and peer-to-content communication. Consequently, in this learning approach knowledge develops via blogs, instant messengers, images, videos, etc. like a distributed learning mechanism.
    - **xMOOC (instructivist MOOC)**: xMOOC on the other hand has taken an opposite view of cMOOC. Here the learning environment is authoritative in the sense that it is mainly a teacher-based traditional learning approach. In the xMOOC learning approach, the major focus is on content delivery, assign reading, video lectures, quizzes, feedback, etc. However, the utmost functional difference between cMOOC and xMOOC is that cMOOC is driven by learner-generated content but xMOOC comprises expert-generated content. Besides, the major aim of xMOOC is to help the learner achieve mastery level of the content.

However, besides these two types of MOOC learning environment, there are various other MOOC-based learning platforms that have been developed based on scale and structural differences. A taxonomy of MOOC as provided by Pilli and Admiraal (2016) is discussed here. However, Pilli and Admiraal categorized MOOC into four major parts based on their massiveness and openness as follows:

1. Small Scale Less Open
2. Small Scale More Open
3. Large Scale Open
4. Large Scale More Open

Types of Learners in MOOCs

In a teaching-learning environment, every student participates with some intention such as acquiring knowledge, earning a credential, etc. When students are not able to achieve, they either lack his/her interest or escape from the system. We all know that the MOOC learning environment is an online learning platform where a diverse learner gets enrolled to complete his/her learning interest. In this learning platform, every student is enrolled with some interest. For example, some students are enrolled to see what the course is about, some students only try to find out whether the particular learning material is worthwhile to pursue, etc.

Based on the learning interest and learning style various researchers have categorized types of learners that tend to stay engaged throughout the classes. The following are some of the categories of learners that various researchers explain based on student engagement and disengagement:

Kizilcec et al. (2013) in their research categorized four types of learners based on their engaging behavior as follows:

- **On track**: Those students who complete their assignments on time.
- **Behind**: This type of student always delays submitting their assignment.
- **Auditing**: This type of learner does not complete the assignment but tends to show the video lecture and takes some interest.
- **Out**: They do not participate in a course at all.

Koller et al. (2013) have categorized the MOOC learner into two major categories: one is "browser" and the other is "committed learner".

- **Browser**: Browser is this kind of learner who sometimes signs up for the class with overwhelming interest but after some time they lack interest in completing the task.
- **Committed learner**: Committed learners always tends to stay engaged in a specific course for a certain period. The committed learner can be divided into three separate categories:
- Passive participants
- Active participants
- Community contributor

1. **Passive participant**: This kind of participant participates in a learning environment only through watching lecture videos and some basic assignments. They generally participate limitedly such as attending some of the video questions and a few quiz assignments.
2. **Active participant**: These participants always show interest in learning course content and they always tend to complete their assignments, quizzes, exams, and peer-graded assessments. They are generally labeled as "course completers" who complete all the necessary work related to a specific course and earn a statement of accomplishment.
3. **Community contributor**: This kind of participant also actively participates in a specific course but their major aim is to generate new content and participate in a forum discussion.

Anderson et al. (2014) have defined five patterns of the learner in a learning environment based on their pattern of engagement: the viewers, solvers, all-rounders, collectors, and bystanders.

Difference between Online Learning and MOOC

In the field of online learning, there has been a huge debate on MOOC-based learning and online learning. However, as per definition and characteristic, the following differentiation may be identified: (see table 20.1)

Components of MOOC

In a MOOC-based learning environment, various components are used to increase learner engagement (Grainger, 2013). The following are some of the components:

Table 20.1 Difference between online learning and MOOC

Subject	Online Learning	MOOC
Cost	To make an online learning course the learner needs to provide fees to the organizer.	MOOC-based learning is free but some providers demand an accreditation fee.
Joining the course	There is a fixed date and time to join the course. The learner is unable to join in the middle of the course.	As per MOOC, there is no set time to register and start the course. Anyone can join even in the middle of the course.
Pre-requisites knowledge	Here participant needs some prerequisite knowledge to join one particular course.	In MOOC-based learning, any learner can participate one course without any demand for prior knowledge.
Scale	The scale of online learning is limited such as in an online learning platform, only a limited number of participants can take advantage.	The scale of MOOC-based learning platforms is massive. Thousands of participants can join this learning environment.
Copyright	The majority of online learning course material is copy-protected or proprietary.	There is copyright content material in MOOC-based learning platform; some are proprietary and some are open. Content is generated by a participant in cMOOC-based learning and the platform is open.
Provider	Distance education provider.	Various universities with private companies.
Learning analytics	Learning analytics Might not be there.	Various MOOC providers use learning analytics to track the student.
Accreditation	Conventional.	Non-conventional.
Quality	Formal in nature.	Non-formal in nature.

Table 20.2 Categorization of MOOC-based on their massiveness and openness

Types	Descriptions	Example
Small scale less open	It is typically similar to a traditional online course. The major characteristic is that it has a small number of participants and less open content.	SPOC (Small Private Online Courses), group MOOC and task-based MOOCs.
Small scale more open	It is highly open but based on learning networks and social media tools. The major attribute is network-based learning that is based on the connectivist approach.	MOOC taxonomy, cMOOCs, BOOCs (Big Open Online Course), COOCs (Community Open Online Courses), DOCCs, POOCs, LOOCs, gMOOCs, pMOOCs, adaptive MOOCs, and network-based MOOCs can be listed.
Large scale less open	It provides the learning opportunity to a large number of participants with limited open content as per registration fee, course duration, course design, etc.	VOOC (Vocational Open Online Courses), SMOC (Synchronous Massive Online Course), HOOC (Hybrid Open Online Course), miniMOOC and POOC (Personalized Open Online Course).
Large scale more open	Large scale more open provide a centralized platform with no binding such as there is no starting and ending, and anyone can participate at any time. Also, no need for any prerequisite knowledge.	xMOOC, transfer MOOC, made MOOC, a synch MOOC, SPOC (Self-Paced Online Course), Content-based MOOC, FlexMOOC, iMOOC (Learner-centeredness), MOOC-Eds, and MOOR. (Massive Open Online Research).

1. **Video lecture**: We all are more familiar with pre-recorded video-based lectures on the YouTube learning platform. However, similar to that various MOOC providers have been using video lectures with various presentation styles such as talking head, lecture instruction, live broadcasts, video with various regional subtitles, etc. Usually, the majority of videos are 5–10 minutes long and some of them are embedded with an interactive quiz.
2. **Syllabus**: MOOC-based learning platform courses are structured with the pre-defined specific learning objective, scope, topic, accompanied reading, discussion, assignments, quizzes, tests, etc., which may be termed as the syllabus of the course. However, the syllabus also includes weekly schedules and assignment submissions.
3. **Learning material**: Another essential component of MOOC-based learning platforms is that learning material in each of the supportive learning resources is provided by the provider. Learners do not need to buy the book and all reading material is available online from the course instructor. However, various providers make money in affiliation various online retailers (Rivard, 2013).
4. **Assessment**: Like a traditional learning environment various MOOCs also have built-in components with student evaluation and grade assessment. However, to do so instructors use auto-graded multiple-choice questions or programming-based interactive assessments, peer review assessments, etc. So, the student can be a part of the assessment. etc.
5. **Forums**: One of the unique features of the MOOC-based learning environment is the opportunity for forum-based communication. A forum is a platform provided by various service providers to post a question, share an idea, peer communication, student and teacher interaction, etc. However, it mainly consists of a general discussion, idea sharing, questioning, technical feedback, and subject-specific discussions.
6. **Face-to-face live video-based communication**: Live video-based communication is another component in MOOC-based learning environment. The live video session is provided frequently by the instructor as a weekly lecture.
7. **Activity**: Various range of activities are provided by the instructor to enrich engagement such as games, questionings, etc.
8. **Social media**: Social media–based linking is one of the unique features of MOOCs. In this learning platform students are encouraged to share their learning experience and various learning discussion on social media such as Facebook, Google+, ResearchGate, etc.

History of MOOC

This section will provide a glimpse of enlightenment regarding the historical journey of MOOC through a distance education lens. About 150 years ago in Great Britain correspondence course was designed to promote various training and skills to the people who were unable to attend any formal educational institution due to financial or geographical obstacles. However, based on the technological revolution the form of distance education has changed over time and various technologies such as radio, television, etc. were used to broadcast the course. Consequently, the innovation of computers dramatically changed the way of education, as a result, a new educational approach was introduced, such as e-learning innovation. However, besides this online presence, online learning opportunities and MOOC innovation took place giving a completely new dimension.

The development of Online Educational Resource (OER) and the open education movement changed the form of learning innovation resulting in MOOC innovation. However, in a practical way, Siemens and Downes were the first to develop MOOC-based learning on the topic of "connectivism and connective knowledge". Initially, the primary design of the first

MOOC was focused on including students worldwide through free registration. Now, this initiative was historic in the sense that an overwhelming participation of over 2,300 students were registered in this course without paying a single penny. Next, a major initiative of MOOC was taken by Sebastian Thrun and his colleagues with the course "Introduction to artificial intelligence" at Stanford University. It also had a huge response with 160,000 learners attached all around the world, participants from 190 countries were registered in this course. Perhaps, MOOC has taken the serious attention of academics as well as researchers. As a result, various initiatives have been taken by commercial organizations, individuals, and institutions to further develop MOOC-based learning platforms in various ways.

As we discussed in the previous section MOOC was rooted and differentiated from the other traditional online course by "openness" and "massiveness". However, from the beginning, MOOC was operationalized in various ways by MOOC providers. Therefore, we can find taxonomical architectures of MOOCs such as some MOOCs are massive but not more open, some are more open but less massive.

MOOC has been theoretically justified by the presently developed "connectivism" theory. The major view in this theory is that sharing knowledge and creating a network of learning facilitates the learning process more. Henceforth, learning content should be free and the scale of learning area should be spread worldwide irrespective of demographics, culture, or economic boundaries.

The concept of open education was mainly initiated in the early 20th century as the Massachusetts Institute of Technology (MIT) established open courseware in 2002 and Open Learn in 2006 (Peters, 2008). However, the early steps of MOOC and its huge response were encouraged or influenced by various major elite universities to develop their own MOOC platform such as MIT designed edX and Open University (OU) designed Future Learn. However, in the present situation, various MOOC providers and universities are working in this area to provide education worldwide.

MOOC as a Medium of Learning

As we know MOOCs have opened a revolutionary potential way of learning. However, it can be used not only as a web-based self-learning medium rather it can also be used in traditional classroom settings or institutions. This section will discuss the various potential uses of MOOCs in the higher education teaching-learning scenarios.

- **To create universal learning content and environment**: To provide the same course, the same assignment, and the same online learning environment teachers can use MOOC as a learning medium. In the classroom learning environment, MOOCs can be used as additional learning support additional to traditional classroom learning. However, not only that but students who are not able to get attached to universities can benefit from MOOC-based self-pacing learning anywhere and anytime.
- **To assign students to the different online courses**: In MOOC-based learning platforms, teachers can encourage the student to assign various online courses and complete those by involving them together.
- **To share knowledge**: Knowledge sharing is the major objective of the MOOC-based learning medium. Students can share their knowledge through social media platforms and can gain knowledge from each other.
- **To enhance creative and critical thinking**: MOOCs as a medium of learning can provide an opportunity not only to hear the knowledge of students but also to share their practical

projects to create a discussion-based learning environment. Through this discussion, students can gain creative and critical thinking skills.

List of MOOC-Based Learning Platforms

As we discussed various universities and commercial organizations provide MOOC-based learning platforms for learning purposes. However, they have created MOOCs based on various taxonomy. This section is going to discuss some of the MOOC providers that have been launched to provide learning opportunities, resources, and course material in various subjects.

Coursera: It is one of the majorly used MOOC-based learning platforms. It is a commercially profitable organization with a US$22 million total investment. However, Coursera widely collaborates with four elite universities such as Stanford, Michigan, Pennsylvania, and Princeton. It provides many courses in 18 subjects. Coursera also provides certificates to collaborate with universities but students have to pay money for that.

Features of Coursera

- It provides the opportunity for a free learning environment.
- Coursera offers a large number of courses, presently there are 197 courses in 18 subject areas such as computer science, electronics, public health, etc.
- There are various opportunities to keep track of student progress such as various quizzes, assignments, etc.

edX: The edX learning platform is developed by two elite universities; the Massachusetts Institute of Technology (MIT) and Harvard University. The edX is a non-profit learning platform and currently provides eight courses. As the edX learning platform is absolutely free and anyone can benefit from any part of the world. However, if anyone wants to get a certificate for their mastery of learning then have to provide a modest or minimum fee.

Features of edX

- Students can join edX all around the world and it is absolutely free.
- Teachers, as well as the professor, can join in edX platform both together to carry out learning.

Udacity: Another MOOC-based learning platform is Udacity. It is also a for profit organization. The founder of this learning platform is Sebastian Thrun, Devid Stavens, and Mike Sokolsky. However, like Coursera, Udacity also provides 18 online courses on various subjects. It is also notable that Udacity provides a certificate for each course at no cost. Certificates are provided based on the level of performance of participants.

Features of Udacity

- Udacity is a large-scale MOOC therefore a massive number of participants can participate in this learning platform.
- Udacity provides learning material free of cost and also provides a certificate depending on the level of performance.

Alison: Alison is also a well-known MOOC-based learning platform. It provides 600 courses on various subject areas such as digital literacy and IT skills, diploma courses, financial literacy, etc. Alison also maintains standard-based learning modules and certified courses.

Features of Alison

- Participants can learn at their own pace.
- Certification is provided upon completion of the course.
- Alison also provides the opportunity for online classes.
- Alison's courses are absolutely free.

Canvas network: The Canvas network is the simplest form of MOOC-based online learning platform. Canvas network can connect millions of learners and provide opportunities for discussion and knowledge sharing among users. Like other mentioned MOOC-based platforms, the Canvas network is also absolutely free of cost. However, it is organized and comprehensive in the sense that it includes course objectives, syllables, quizzes, study plans, etc.

Features of Canvas network

- It is a discussion-based and forum-based learning environment.
- It is free and registration is open.
- It provides an opportunity for the student to learn at their own needs and pace.

OpenLearning: OpenLearning is also a MOOC-based learning environment. It is designed by Adam Brimo, Richard Buckland, and David Collien. OpenLearning does not provide assessment and completion certificates. The major aim is to provide knowledge, not a certificate or grade. Here learners also learn at their own pace.

Features of OpenLearning

- User-friendly design.
- Courses are free.
- No assessment, only grades or certificates are given.
- Users can participate from all around the world.

Academic Earth: Academic Earth is another MOOC-based platform. However, users do not need any registration at all. What is only needed is to choose their required course and work with all assignments and projects as listed. It is also self-learning in nature.

Features of Academic Earth

- Absolutely free.
- No registration is needed.
- Self-paced.
- Provide information about scholarships and fellowships all around the world.

Udemy: Udemy, founded in 2010, is a majorly used MOOC-based learning environment. It offers over 5,000 courses. However, it is a profitable organization, therefore 1,500 courses are payment-based with an average price between US$20 and US$200 (1,400 INR to 14,000 INR).

Peer-to-Peer University (P2Pu): P2Pu is another MOOC-based learning platform. It was founded in 2009 by the Howlett and Shuttleworth Foundation. It has been providing nearly 50 courses and is free. However, it is an integrated gamification of the learning process.

Khan Academy: Another well-known online learning platform is Khan Academy. It provides learning free of cost. It is a non-profit organization started by Salman Khan. It provides video lectures based on various assessments and exercises.

Future Learn: It is also an online learning platform. It provides a free wide range of online learning courses. The unique part of the Future Learn platform is that it can be accessed through mobile, tablets, as well as computers.

Saylor: Saylor is an online-based learning platform created by professional educators. The best part of this learning platform is that student can share their education and learn at their own pace. It is also based on discussion forums and the learner can participate in debates and can communicate peer to peer.

Advantages and Disadvantages of MOOC

In the overall discussion, it is understood that a MOOC-based learning platform is a boon for higher-education learning. However, besides its huge potential, certain challenges need to be taken into consideration while pursuing MOOC-based learning courses. The following are the advantages and disadvantages of MOOC-based courses:

Advantages of MOOC

- **Potentiality of sharing ideas and knowledge**: MOOC-based learning platform offers a learning environment based on the "sharing knowledge" principle which helps to improve the skills of the learner and improves the opportunity to assess global learning resources.
- **Enhance active learning**: MOOC-based learning platform provides their learning material in a way to enhance the engagement of the learner. For instance, instructors use small videos with various problem-based activities, assignments, quizzes, forum-based discussions, and peer-to-peer communication which enhances more active learning.
- **Cross-cultural relationship**: In MOOC-based learning platforms worldwide various participants are involved in the learning process that belongs to various cultures. Therefore, it helps to collaborate with cross-cultural educators and peers all around the world.
- **Encourages to learn anytime anywhere**: MOOC is an online learning environment that mostly encourages learning from all around the world beyond time and place.
- **Encourages peer evaluation**: MOOC is based on a connectivist approach, the theoretical view of this approach is that knowledge is gained by sharing. Therefore, most MOOC platforms provide an opportunity for grading via other peers.
- **Provides an opportunity to connect with worldclass universities and instructors**: MOOC opens the door to participate and interact worldwide with various elite universities. The best part is it is absolutely free and one can learn while sitting in any corner of the world.
- **Worldclass accomplishment and certification**: MOOC provides the opportunity to earn verified certificates of their level of achievement at a minimum cost. However, participants can use this certificate for job applications. Although, some universities allow fulfilling the credit requirement from MOOCs. For instance, recently UGC India (Credit Framework for Online Learning Course through SWAYAM), Regulation 2016 has been finalized, and as per the regulation, online courses are made on the SWAYAM platform.

Table 20.3 MOOC-based learning platforms and their web addresses

MOOC provider	Website
Coursera	https://www.coursera.org/
edX	https://www.edx.org/
Udacity	https://www.udacity.com/
Alison	http://alison.com/
Canvas Network	http://www.instructure.com/
Open Learning	https://www.openlearning.com/
Academic Earth	http://academicearth.org/
Udemy	https://www.udemy.com/
P2Pu (Peer-to-Peer University)	https://p2pu.org/en/
Khan Academy	https://www.khanacademy.org/
Future Learn	https://www.futurelearn.com/
Saylor	http://www.saylor.org/

Disadvantages of MOOC-Based Learning Platform

- **Lack of real-time interaction**: Real-time face-to-face interaction is not possible in MOOC-based learning platforms.
- **Lack of physical hand on practice**: Various technical courses needs to be explored through hands-on experiences which is not possible in MOOC-based learning.
- **No proper evaluation**: In MOOC-based learning environment all the evaluation process is based on a computer-generated automated process. Besides, participants are not very interested in the peer evaluation process which may lead to discouragement among participants.
- **Lack of empathy and respect**: MOOC-based education involves computers and participants so in this learning environment there is a possibility and scope for a lack of empathy. It only encourages the growth of a virtual community of participants.

Reference

Anderson, A., Huttenlocher, D., Kleinberg, J., Leskovec, J. (2014). Engaging with Massive Online Courses. WWW '14: Proceedings of the 23rd international conference on World wide web. 687–698. https://doi.org/10.1145/2566486.256804210.1145/2566486.2568042

Cormier, D., & Siemens, G. (2010). Through the open door: Open courses as research, learning, and engagement. *Educause, 45*(4), 30–39. Retrieved October 20, 2010, from http://www.educause.edu/EDUCAUSE+Review/EDUCAUSEReviewMagazineVolume45/ThroughtheOpenDoorOpenCoursesa/209320.

Downes, S. (2013). The semantic condition: Connectivism and open learning. Keynote presentation delivered to Instituto Iberoamericano de TIC y Educación – IBERTIC, July 11. Retrieved from http://www.downes.ca/presentation/323.

Grainger, B. (2013). Massive open online course (MOOC) report. Retrieved from http://www.londoninternational.ac.uk/sites/default/files/documents/mooc_report-2013.pdf.

Grajek, S., Bischel, J., & Dahlstrom, E. (2013). What MOOC means to today's students and instructions. Retrieved June 2016, from https://library.educause.edu/~/media/files/library/2013/10/erb1309-pdf.pdf.

KIzilcec, R. F. (2013). In Proceedings of the 1st Workshop on Massive Open Online Courses at the 16th Annual Conference on Artificial Intelligence in Education (2013). Memphis, TN. http://www.moocshop.org

Koller, D., Ng, A., Do, C., & Chen, Z. (2013). Retention and Intention in Massive Open Online Courses. *Educause Review Review, 48*(3) (May/June 2013)

Peters, M. (2008). Paper presented at economic and social research council (ERSC, UK) seminar series on 'educationand the knowledge economy', University of Bath.

Pilli, O., & Admiraal, W. (2016). A taxonomy for massive open online courses. *Contemporary Educational Technology*, 7, 223–240.

Rivard, R. (2013, April 8). Free to profit. Inside Higher Ed. Retrieved from http://www.insidehighered.com/news/2013/04/08/coursera-beginsmake-money.

Shirky, C. (2012). Napster, Udacity, and the academy. http://www.shirky.com/weblog/2012/11/napster-udacity-and-the-academy/.

Siemens, G. (2012, July 25). MOOCs are really a platform. Elearnspace. Retrieved from http://www.elearnspace.org/blog/2012/07/25/moocs-are-really-a-platform/

Suggested readings

Bonk, C. J., Lee, M. M., Reeves, T. C., & Reynolds, T. H. (Eds.). (2015). *MOOCs and open education around the world*. New York: Routledge.

Haber, J. (2014). *MOOCs*. Cambridge, MA: MIT Press.

Hollands, F. M., & Tirthali, D. (2015). *MOOCs in higher education: Institutional goals and paths forward*. New York: Palgrave Macmillan.

Rhoads, R. A. (2015). *MOOCs, high technology, and higher learning*. Baltimore, MD: JHU Press.

Sharma, Y. P. (2015). Massive open online courses (MOOCs) for school education in India: Advantages, challenges and suggestions for implementation. *Microcosmos International Journal of Research*. 1(2), 1–5

21
LEARNING MANAGEMENT SYSTEM (LMS) AND LEARNING CONTENT MANAGEMENT SYSTEM (LCMS) IN EDUCATION

Introduction

We are living in an unprecedented information era. The deluge of technological advancement keeps changing every aspect of our life. Therefore, In the field of education, a revolution is being witnessed from the classical classroom to a smart and virtual classroom. This chapter will discuss the Learning Management System (LMS) and Learning Content Management System (LCMS). Both concepts are newly introduced in the field of education to provide administration, tracking, reporting, and delivery of educational courses and training programs through software and its applications. Before the introduction of the learning management system in the conventional classroom, it is seen that the whole administration process, student assessment, feedback on student performance, etc, is provided manually, which was more time-consuming and required lots of human resources. Conversely, LMS provides more sophisticated teaching-learning and administrative environment through the application of technological advancement. In the present scenario, LMS is ubiquitous, with billions of dollars in the market throughout the world in the field of education. The present chapter provides an overview and detailed discussion of the LMS and LCMS so that a reader can gain a rich knowledge of modern and sophisticated technologies.

Definitions of Learning Management Systems (LMSs)

In a single sentence, it can be said that a learning management system is a process of administering education and training.

About E-learning (2016) discussed that LMS is generally, a software approach designed to plan, implement, and promote or access the learning process. It includes various features like interactive communication, discussion forums, instant messaging, video conferencing, etc.

Shawar et al. (2010) explained that LMS is a software-oriented platform designed to create, manage, and distribute instructional material for various courses.

Ellis (2009) defined LMS as a software-based application intended to administer various tasks related to instruction such as tracking and management of various online events, training content, etc.

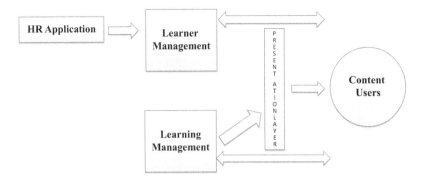

Figure 21.1 Components of Learning Management System (LMS).

Klonoski (2008) described that "LMSs is a process of student integration, learning objective repositories, branding, content sharing, and an improved user interface".

Szabo and Flesher (2002) described LMS as a framework that can enable the management of all aspects of the learning process. For instance, it can manage and deliver various instructional materials appropriately and effectively, can access or track various learning goals, can generate automated progress reports based on learner performance, can collect learner data for the supervised learning process, etc.

Recesso (2001) explained LMS as a software mechanism that can facilitate and handle effectively the various administrative task as well as the participation of the student in the context of e-learning scenarios.

Hall (2003) defined LMS as a software approach that can manage and administer learning or training. It includes various effective functions related to instruction such as user registration, a record of student data, a report to management, etc.

Commonwealth of learning (2003) (as cited by Naidu, 2006) "Learning Management System typically contains features for administration, assessment, course management, possibly content management, and authoring".

Learning Content Management System (LCMS)

The major aspect of the LMS is the administration of learning-related activities. In contrast to an LMS, a major aspect of the Learning Content Management System is "content management or authoring". The term LCMS has been defined in many ways such as to organize and facilitate collaborative content creation or management of website content (Renaux et al., 2005). Following are some of the definitions of LCMS given by various researchers:

Leiserson (2003) defined LCMS as a design approach that can function both as administrative as well as content management. LCMS is generally specially designed so that it can handle the course management capacity of a learning management system.

Jones (2001) explained that LCMS is a complex designed software approach that can organize and distribute learning objects to a mass audience.

Hall (2001) gave a very simplistic definition of LCMS. It has been discussed that a learning content management system is a designed learning environment through which an instructor can develop, store, manage, and distribute learning content from a specially designed central database.

Donello (2002) proposed the core components of an LCMS and reflects that it is a kind of tool that is basically for non-programmers and its interface is generally designed for administration such as recording student enrollment, delivering content, tracking the progress of learners, a repository for learning objects, control of the overall instructional process through a central database, etc.

Flate Paulsen Morten (2003) explained that a learning content management system is a type of environment where an instructor can generally create, reuse, and distribute content to an individual as well as a mass learner. This is based on a model of the learning object.

From the above definitions, one can see that LCMS is a complex software program that enables the storage, management, and reusability of online content through database functionality. In the LCMS system, multiple collaborators can work together or participate in the content creation process.

Historical Overview of Learning Management System

Though the learning management system is a comparatively new concept in the field of education it has a long history. The early invention of the learning management system can be noted in 1924 when the first teaching machine was introduced by Sydney Pressey. The teaching machine could administer and evaluate multiple-choice questions automatically. Another significant innovation after the teaching machine was a "problem cylinder" invented by M. E. Lazerte in 1929. A significant innovation in 1956 was an adaptive system that can arrange or adjust questions for the learner as per their performance level. However, the modern LMS system was introduced after the innovation of the personal computer in 1970 by HP. After the innovation of the internet, the first LMS was introduced by SoftArc in 1990. The modern learning management system is mostly cloud-based and more sophisticated compared to early innovations.

Features of Learning Management System

Management of courses, instructor, and learner: One of the major features of a learning management system is the management of the entire teaching-learning scenarios. It includes generating reports, uploading courses, recommendations for courses, roles assignment, etc.

Establishment of course calendar: This is one of the essential features of LMS, which enables the learner to know about available and upcoming training programs so that they can register or request for the specific training program.

Message and notification: Another great feature is a notification or message to the registered learner about new courses, deadlines of assignments, and upcoming events so that they can be more aware or involved in their learning.

Handle given assignment or test: By these features, LMS can follow up by giving an assignment to the learner. Besides, it can also diagnose pre-test and post-test assessments to assess the level of knowledge.

Performance measurement and certification: LMS can track learner performance and display a score of learners. It can also record, transcript, and maintain the performance of the learner. From the LMS teachers can auto-generate or manually generate certificates of performance of the learner.

Table 21.1 Historical overview of Learning Management System

Year	Significant Innovations	Initiated By/In
The 1950s innovations		
1874	First institutional-sponsored distance education began in the United States.	Illinois Wesleyan University.
1892	First introduced the term 'Distance Education' in the catalog.	Wisconsin Madison catalog.
1906–1907	The first distance education institution was introduced.	Namely, The University of Wisconsin-Extension.
1909	An audiovisual communication network was used to provide Australian music.	A story by E. M. Forster (The machine stops).
1920	The first teaching machine was introduced.	Sidney Pressey.
1929	Various instructional devices were developed to minimize the effort of instruction.	M. E. Lazerte.
1953	First television college.	University of Hudson.
1956	The first adjective teaching system namely SAKI was developed.	Gordon Park & Robin McKinnon-wood.
1957	First attempt to understand the human memory and cognition process.	Frank Rosenblatt.
The 1960s innovations		
1960	First Programmed Logic for Automated Teaching Operations PLATO was developed.	University of Illinois.
1963	First computer instruction was introduced.	Orange coast college, California.
1964	Introduced first authoring tools for the development of computer courses.	—
1965	Introduced COURSEWRITER for interactive computer systems.	IBM and its subsidiary Science Research Associations.
1968	First installed computer base online courses at the University of Alberta to provide training in cardiology for the university medical school.	IBM.
1969	Introduced first associate committee for Instructional Technology.	In the National Research Council of Canada.
1970s Innovations		
1970	The Havering Computer-Managed Learning System.	London.
1972	Develop a Computer-Based Course in logic and set a theory.	Patrick Suppes, Professor at Stanford University.
1974	Invented Computerized conferencing and communication center.	Murray Turoff, New Jersey Institute of Technology (NJIT).
1976	CICERO project was initiated at Open University, UK.	—
1979	Invented Unix Path structure A storage of information in the file system tree.	The Athabasca University.
1980s Innovations		
1980	TLM was invented, intended to access remotely student by using a terminal emulator.	
1981	• Started online program School of Management and strategic studies.	• Western Behavioral Science Institute.
	• Introduced the first commercial interactive video disc.	• Allen communication.

(Continued)

Table 21.1 Continued

Year	Significant Innovations	Initiated By/In
1985	The decision was taken to found ASCILITE.	Australian Society of Computer in Learning.
1986	Installed the first CSILE.	An elementary school in Toronto, Canada.
1990s Innovations		
1991	Introduced smartboard system, touch screen intelligence whiteboard.	
1995	Introduced Microsoft Online Institute (MOLI) for the future of technology-based learning.	Neville Gordon-Carroll and Vaughn Taylor.
1997	Introduced "Internet active learning network".	CourseInfo LLC.
2000s Innovations		
2000	Introduced the first online LMS, ePath learning to manage, create, and maintain online learning and training.	
2001	Introduced a full-featured course management system namely Coursework version 1.	Stanford University academic computing.
2002	Version 1.0 of Moodle was released.	
2004	Open-source collaboration and learning environment.	Sakai Project.
2005	'E-xcellence' project was introduced to support a learning program and maintain the standard and quality of e-learning.	The European Association of Distance Teaching University.
2007	Introduced SharePoint learning kit and SCORM to provide LMS functionality.	Microsoft Corporation.
2013	Introduced first Moodle LMS, SugarCube LMS.	
2013–2018	Developed various advanced levels of learning management systems.	

Automated task: Automated task is the most interesting feature of LMS that enables the administrator to automatically use grouping, enrollment of group, new user alert, or deactivation of the existing account.

Social learning: A useful feature of the learning management system is social learning. Social learning refers to a process of learning where the learner can learn in collaborative ways. Most LMS encourage learner peer mentorship, knowledge curation, collaborative learning, etc.

Mobility: Learning must be flexible and learning content should be open that can be accessed anytime and anywhere. The software of LMS can enable the learner to learn from a desktop as well as a mobile device.

Integration: LMS allows integration with other third-party features such as CRM, video conferencing tools, etc.

Gamification: Through LMS one can use gamification-based learning content that can encourage learner engagement by allowing them with more active participation and achievement of point badges, awards, etc.

Interoperability: LMS supports learning content in an interoperable manner such as SCORM, AICC, xAPI, etc.

Functional Aspects of LMS

Management of skills and competency: Every organization or higher education institution has its own pre-set goals to achieve. In this context, LMS can track, manage, monitor, and analyse the performance skills of learners or employees, analysis of knowledge gaps, recommendations for correction of the gap, etc. This kind of complex scientific analysis and management can increase the chance to achieve the goal in time and is also cost-effective.

Development of course timing and calendar: This is another great feature of LMS, that it can generate and manage a specific date for a course and can provide information about the availability of a trainer or instructor in a specific course. With these features, learners or employees can easily choose and access a specific course as per their requirements.

Instructor-led course management: Another great feature of the LMS system is instructor-led course management which is very time-saving and an efficient centralized tracking system of course material.

Tracking and reporting: Learning management system functions to track and report a wide range of standard and custom detailed reports of students so that a learner can view and access the average test score, final test score, single-user report, report of the company or institutional login, a summary of overall test, etc.

Administration: Another essential function of a learning management system is that it helps to facilitate the means of administration of the teaching-learning process through enrollment of students, registration of students, and verifying the prerequisite of students.

Table 21.2 Comparison of LMS and LCMS

Subject of Comparison	Learning Management System (LMS)	Learning Content Management System (LCMS)
Purpose of use	To manage, track or maintain the whole course	To develop and assemble course material.
Level of content management	Only curriculum and course level	Whole lesson includes pages, media, etc.
Level of tracking	In LMS learners can be tracked by their needs, preference, and abilities. Besides, also with course start, completion, and test management	In LCMS learners can track based on course, lesson, and a specific page.
generating report	LMS can generate learner performance reports in respect of curricula, courses, and grade	LCMS can generate learner reports based on activities, tests, courses, and lesson.
Authoring	Authoring tools are not built-in	Authoring tools are built-in or can access through add-on.
Test and practice activities	LMS has built-in facilities for test creation and administration	LCMS can track tests at the whole page, lesson, and course level.

** Many advanced-level LMS product or LCMS product includes all the features of LMS and LCMS together.

Table 21.3 Learning management platform commercial and open-source

Commercial	Open-Source
ANGEL Learning	A Tutor Bazaar
	Mitechsoft
SAP Enterprise Learning	Bodington
Blackboard Inc.	Docebo LMS
Apex Learning	Dokeos e-Learning XHTML Editor
Desire2Learn	Fle3
eCollege	GaneshaLMS
Learn.com	Moodle
Meridian KSI	ILIAS
Saba Software	interact
	KEWL.Nextgen
	OLAT
	LRN

Overview of LMS

It is previously discussed that a learning management system is a web-based software application that can help to develop learning material and track, evaluate, and predict student performance. It consists of various unique features such as student registration adding course material, enrollment of the learner into a course, grading, etc. The actual features of a learning management system depend upon the requirement of the product and its performance. Worldwide, government and private organizations innovate various features in the LMS as per student or as per employee requirements. However, some common elements can be seen in the inner structure of a learning management system as a database, course, curriculum, web interface, etc.

Therefore, it is noted that the learning management system work as a central repository to serve various educational needs. In this context, the functional aspect of a learning management system can be divided into four independent but interrelated aspects. They are as follows:

- Curriculum planning
- Content management
- Learner engagement
- Instant evaluation

Curriculum planning: We all know that curriculum is an overview of the overall course of study in the context of what to teach and how to teach (time frame). Prior to starting any course, generally, in an organization, different authorities or teacher councils take responsibility to develop a specific course of study, a specific schedule of completion, etc. In a curriculum planning framework, the total number of lecturers is also specified, the number of classes, the amount of code coverage, any advanced-level learning management system software equipped with a design, a specific curriculum planning in a specific or general way, etc.

Content management: In teaching and learning scenarios one of the essential aspects is the management of content material. A common problem in a content management scenario in a specific classroom situation is a repetition of designing the same content material for a course of study by a different teacher. To encounter these challenges there is a need to

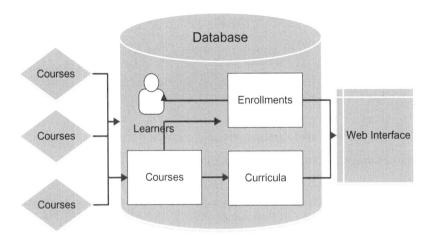

Figure 21.2 Overview of the functional aspect of Learning Management System.

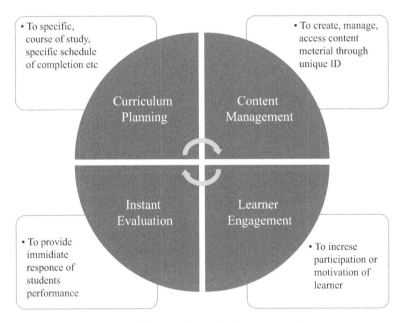

Figure 21.3 Overview and features of Learning Management System.

develop a specific content management platform where each teacher can access the overall content in central repositories (if required). The LMS is a unique platform where every teacher can access, create, manage, and store learning content material through a unique login ID. Furthermore, LMS can also provide the opportunity to store previous note files in the mode of Private Files.

Learner engagement: Learner engagement in the teaching-learning process denotes increasing the motivation and participation of the learner. From the various research, it is proved that participation of students increases by getting the opportunity to perform in specific learning groups and interaction with a student from a different cultural background. An LMS provides various social and collaborative learning tools such as chat, forum, group

messaging, gamification, etc. through which a learner can easily learn a difficult concept at their own pace.
- **Instant evaluation**: Another important element in an LMS is tools for instant evaluation. Instant evaluation denotes, the immediate result of a student's performance in the context of asking questions. Besides, LMS can also track overall student performance and prediction for the future performance of the student.

Advantages of Learning Management System

Efficient Management of the Overall Teaching-Learning Scenario

The teaching and learning process is a complex task. It requires effective control over administration, development of curriculum, effective communication, management of content materials, training of teachers for trainers, etc. It is also imperative to say that in a teaching-learning process or any training situation teachers, students and administrators have different roles to manage effective communication. In this context, an LMS is a very powerful tool that allows the creation, management, and monitoring of the overall teaching-learning scenario in an automated manner through using various software algorithms. Therefore, it helps to create an environment that is more effective, efficient, and organized.

Cost-Effective and Time-Saving

Another very notable advantage of an LMS is its cost-effectiveness and time-saving features. Effective LMS provides an automated and online communication process in the context of education and training programs. Therefore, it reduces the involvement of human resources in the context of management, so more human resources can be allocated to other important aspects. LMS-based learning platforms can simultaneously train a mass audience from different geographical locations and community-based learners which helps to save money and time compared to the traditional teaching and training approach.

Easy Accessibility of Resources

LMS structures and organizes all the pieces of information in the same place, therefore, it is very helpful to access any required resources anytime from any place. Besides, students and teachers can access the calendar, multimedia material, archives, and evaluation results anytime where internet access is available and they can get information about any change in the calendar or update resources as per requirement.

Personalization

LMS-based learning platform provides a complete overview as never before. An institution or organization can access, report, evaluate, analyze, and predict every student separately in just one click. Besides students can learn at their own pace and choice.

Easy Content Addition or Update

Through LMS administrators and teachers can update any content or add material and resources for students anytime for immediate access and the unique part is students can get a notification about the update or addition of teaching material in real time.

Advanced Reporting and Instant Evaluation

LMS allows the ability to provide instant feedback about student performance and generate or create personalized detail reports of the progress of students regarding their group activity, performance in specific content, completion of work, activity during learning situations, etc., which helps in instant evaluation of student either in a group or individually.

Multimedia-Based Learning Situation

LMS provides an opportunity to create a teaching-learning material more sophisticated by using various video images, audio, and text to increase the motivation of the student. Furthermore, various barriers to multimedia-based tools are available in LMS that can increase engagement and participation of the learner in a specific teaching-learning scenario.

Improve the Accessibility of Communication

Most of the learning management systems are equipped with an online forum, instant messenger, access to social media, etc. that can facilitate the creation of more collaborative and interactive teaching-learning sessions for the student as well as the teacher.

Disadvantages of LMS

Not Applicable to Every Teaching-Learning or Training Scenario

A learning management system is a very efficient and effective approach to teaching-learning and training. Still, in various training scenarios, specifically for performance that is more important than the theoretical aspect, the learning management system fails to report skill of performance effectively. Besides some jobs require physical skill and practice such as medical operation, skill, and training for facial and body language expressions for the salesman, etc. that cannot be trained or evaluated through online-based teaching and learning scenarios or LMS.

Expensive for the Initial Setup

Though a learning management system is a very expensive approach compared to the traditional way of teaching, the initial setup of the installation, management, and maintenance of a learning management system is very expensive due to the use of complex software and hardware application.

Needs an Expert Administrator

To effectively maintain a learning management system requires an expert administrator who can manage the overall courses, database, software, and hardware and knows where to access it in the context of developing countries.

Bibliography

Donello, J. (2002). *Theory & practice: Learning content management systems.* Retrieved February 17, 2018, from http://www.elearningmag.com.

Ellis, R. K. (2009). Field guide to learning management system. Retrieved April 6, 2018, from http://www.astd.org/NR/rdonlyres/12ECDB99-3B91-403E-9B157E597444645D/23395/LMS_fieldguide_20091.pdf.

Flate Paulsen, M. (2003). Experiences with learning management systems in 113 European institutions. *Educational Technology and Society*, *6*(4), 134–148.

Hall, B. (2001). *Learning management and knowledge management. Is the holy grail of integration close at hand?* Retrieved April 1, 2018, from http://www.brandonhall.com.

Hall, B. (2003). *Learning management systems and learning content management systems demystified*. Retrieved April, 2018, from http://www.brandonhall.com.

Jones, C. (2001, June). Rules of the game. *Online Learning Magazine*, *5*(6).

Kaplan-Leiserson, E. (2000). E-learning glossary. Retrieved April, 2018, from http://www.learningcircuits.org/glossary.html.

Klonoski, E. (2008). *Cost-saving collaboration: Purchasing and deploying a statewide learning management system, 2008*. Retrieved April, 2018, from http://www.innovateonline.info/index.php?view=article&id=69.

Leiserson, K. (2003). E-learning glossary. Retrieved June 12, 2018, from www.learningcircuits.org/glossary.html.

Naidu, S. (2006, January 1). *E-learning: A guidebook of principles, procedures and practices*. Commonwealth Education Media Center for Asia. https://doi.org/10.56059/11599/53

Paulsen, M. F. (2003). Experiences with learning management systems in 113 European institutions. *Journal of Educational Technology and Society*, *6*(4), 134–148.

Recesso, A. (2001). Prospect of a technology-based learner interface for schools. *Educational Technology and Society*, *4*(1),1436–4522

Renaux,E., Caron, P. A., & Le Pallec, X. (2005). *Learning management system component based design: A model driven approach, NOCE Team*, Trigone Laboratory, University of Lille 1, FRANCE, MCETECH', Conference submission paper n 26.

Shawar, B. A., & Al-Sadi, J. A. (2010). Learning management systems: Are they knowledge management tools? *International Journal of Emerging Technologies in Learning (iJET)*, *5*(1), 4–10. https://doi.org/10.3991/ijet.v5i1.887.

Szabo, M., & Flesher, K. (2002). CMI theory and practice: Historical roots of learning managment systems. Paper presented at the E-Learn 2002 World Conference on E-Learning in Corporate, Government, Healthcare, & Higher Education, Montreal, Canada.

Suggested Readings

Baker, K. M. (2018). Lms success: A step-by-step guide to learning management system administration, 52(2)

Burke, J. J., & Tumbleson, B. E. (2016). *Learning management systems*. American Library Association.

Clossen, A. (2018). Integrating the library in the learning management system, *54*(5), 7.

Dias, S. B., Diniz, J. A., & Hadjileontiadis, L. J. (2013). *Towards an intelligent learning management system under blended learning: Trends, profiles and modeling perspectives*, Springer.

Foreman, S. (2017). *The LMS guidebook: Learning management systems demystified*. Association for Talent Development, ATD Press.

Fyffe, D. N. (2015). *Learning management system efficiency vs. staff proficiency*, (1st ed). Jamaica Pen Publishers.

Kats, Y. (2010). Learning management system technologies and software solutions for online teaching: Tools and applications, https:// 10.4018/978-1-61520-853-1

Kats, Y. (2013). *Learning management systems and instructional design: Best practices in online education*. https://10.4018/978-1-4666-3930-0

Momani, A. M. (n.d.). *Easy way to evaluate learning management systems*, USA: Scholar's Press.

Tinschert, S. (2007). *Implementation of a learning management system for a small American company*.

22
SOCIAL MEDIA APPLICATIONS IN EDUCATION

The advancement of technology allows us to digitally connect in a meaningful way. Yes, it is meaningful because in the present situation communication is more than just only "Hi" or "Hello". The abundance of technology helps to shift our communication from "face-to-face" to a "digital one", and it creates an interactive communicative environment for everyday update, feedback, as well conversations with others. However, it is social media which allows people to exchange their ideas, interest, pictures/video, and many other things with others through virtual community networks.

Meaning and Definition of Social Media

The term social media generally refers to a virtual technological platform that people use to communicate and socialize with each other online. However, presently the term "social media" has become a buzzword. Today social media technology has taken an essential part of our life to share thoughts, visuals, information, and communication with others. Nevertheless, varied definitions have been provided by researchers for academic use. Following are some of the comprehensive definitions given by researchers:

Buettner (2016) defines social media as computer-mediated tools that allow people or companies to create, share, or exchange information, career interests, ideas, and pictures/videos in virtual communities and networks.

Howard and Parks (2012) provide a more complex definition of social media with three parts: (a) the information infrastructure and tools used to produce and distribute content; (b) the content that takes the digital form of personal messages, news, ideas, and cultural products; and (c) the people, organizations, and industries that produce and consume digital content (p. 362).

Russo, Watkins, Kelly, and Chan (2008) defined social media as "those that facilitate online communication, networking, and/or collaboration".

Boyd and Ellison (2007) defined social network sites (SNSs) as web-based services that allow individuals to (i) construct a public or semi-public profile within a bounded system, (ii) articulate a list of other users with whom they share a connection, and (iii) view and traverse their list of connections and those made by others within the system (p. 211).

From the above definitions, it can be said that social media are internet-based web 2.0 technology that provides the opportunity for users to interact with one another in real-time or asynchronously, with various audiences in the world.

Characteristics of Social Media

From the above discussion regarding social media, it can be summarized that social media is the collection of online communication channels dedicated to community-based input, interaction, content-sharing, and collaboration. Now some characteristics of social media are discussed.

Two-Way Interactive Communicative Processes

First and foremost a characteristic of modern social media is that it is *interactive* and not a one-way medium. Compared with past "broadcast" media where the content was transmitted or distributed to an audience in a one-way process, social media serves two-way communication and blurs the line between media and audience. Posting any content on social media has the potential to start a conversation between authors and content writers with the reader via chatroom or many other alternative ways, thereby shaping the conversation. Besides, people can share information or make contact with multiple people at the same time.

User-Generated Content

Another important characteristic of social media is amidst the area of social networking all are participants, authors, and content creators. It is built and directed through user-generated content and without user content, social media would be an empty area stuffed with empty boards, applications, and chat rooms. Users generate various content for the social community with conversations and content material. The direction of that content material is dependent upon anyone who takes part in the dialogue. That is why social networks are enjoyable and dynamic for internet users.

Community Driven

Social network or media is mainly based on the community conception. So, similar to the real-life community or social groups around the world, social media takes a similar responsibility in a virtual environment. It is a known fact that community or social groups hold common beliefs, hobbies, as well as other common attributes. However, social media is based on the same principle and it is notable that in modern-day online social media one can find a sub-community of people who share a commonality such as a love of photography, a political issue, or a favorite TV show, school management system, social welfare attribute, etc. Social media also helps to connect with new friends as well as find some old friends. Besides, most social media is product or company-focused, social media is about building community, and functions as such. The members (both consumer and company/organization) are participants in the community. It is the community that dictates the shape and scope of the content.

Information Sharing

Social media encourages information sharing. Interesting articles or discussions in the newspaper or online sources can be shared with multiple people at a time. In the conventional method, there was a need for photocopying or hand distributing. Now, with just one click one can share information globally with multiple people.

Openness

Most social media services are open to suggestions and active participation. They motivate vote casting, feedback, and the sharing of knowledge.

Active Global Relationship

Social networks thrive on the attributes of active relationships. The active relationships within the network will establish one toward the center of that network. It is a similar conception of a pyramid scheme. Relation or communication in social media is not bound to only one single country rather it also helps to encourage or establish a global relationship.

Emotional Expression

A different targeted characteristic of social media is the emotional component. Social media provides users with emotional satisfaction and a way that it doesn't matter what happens, their buddies are within effortless attainment. Whether or not struggling through a divorce, breakup, or any different household crisis, men and women are discovering that the ability to leap online and communicate directly with a circle of neighbors provides the best deal of support for an unmanageable problem.

Classifications of Social Media

Social Networks Site

A social networking site supplies an established platform for constructing social communication or social relations among various people globally. This type of social media site is mainly based on communication of shared interests or hobbies. This networking site furnishes an approach to engage over the internet, email, and now even present situations through cell phones/ mobiles. The most standard used social network sites are MySpace that started in 2003, LinkedIn started in 2003, Facebook in 2004, and Twitter in 2006. However, presently there are many social networking site users for various purposes. A social networking site would enable a consumer or user to create profiles or personal pages with password protection and create a virtual communicative environment. The profile as a consequence is created for an understanding of the user's demography, and personal and professional information such as gender, religion, orientation, interests, place of origin, present location, marital status, books appreciated, etc. The page can be customized as the person desires and incorporate video clips, song documents, or images on their page. Additionally, integrated into the profile is a list of friends with community attributes. In most cases, these friends are actual pals, acquaintances, and even strangers, who may have dispatched a friend request and the person has included them in his/her record. These sites permit persons to build private group pages or open group pages and then join with neighbors or another common interested person to share content material and verbal exchange.

Blogs

Blogs are probably the most known forms of social media, online journals, with entries showing the latest/recent first. The word blog (derived from the word web-blog) is an online journal, the place of an individual, group, or manufacturer that offers a record of hobbies, ideas, or beliefs. Blogs are like an open diary concept that enables the writer to explore their thinking or ideas on his or her webpage. Many websites enable customers to create blogs without paying any fees like wordpress.com, blogspot.com, or blogger.com, etc. Anyone can create a web publication on these websites and these blogs can be accessed by anyone typing the web page or URL (uniform resource locator).

Content Material and Sharing Communities

Communities that organize and share specific sorts of content material. This type of user-generated content community site is also known as crowdsourcing. These sites function as a source of unconventional knowledge for various issues. Presently websites are taking these initiatives for photos such as flicker.com, picasa web, google.com and video sharing sites such as youtube.com, slide sharing websites such as slideshare.com, document sharing websites such as docstoc.com, and many others all fall beneath this category. The content of these sites is free for all customers. Users can search for content material, download, and use the content material available on these websites at any rate. The content can be generated via the users or any organization. From an educational point of view, these sites are an important advantage to those people who are unable to get entry to educational resources.

User Appraisal Sites

User appraisal sites function as a platform for value determinations of more than a few merchandise and offerings. Although it is viable for customers to precise their view in any of the media, person appraisal sites commonly deal with such stories. Websites such as mouthshut.com and pagalguy.com are common examples of such websites. These internet sites serve as an establishing factor of customers' choice-making model for gathering information about products or services they are contemplating for shopping. As such these sites serve as fundamental word of mouth for consumers and a supply of expressions put up by suggestions.

Wikis

These internet sites allow persons to add content to or edit the information on them, performing as a communal document or database. Wikipedia, the online encyclopedia which has over 2 million English language articles.

Podcasts

Audio and video records which might be at hand by using subscriptions, through offerings like Apple iTunes.

Boards

Boards are areas for online dialogue usually around specified issues and interests. Boards came about before the time period when social media was strong and well-known element of online communities.

Micro-Blogging

Social networking is combined with bite-sized blogging, where small amounts of content updates are distributed online through the mobile phone network. Twitter can be treated a leader in this field.

Evolution or History of Social Media

In the present situation when thinking of social media the first instance that comes to our mind is the name Facebook, Twitter, etc. However, in reality, it is more than that. The following are the historical evolutionary phase of social media.

Social Media before 1900

The earliest approaches to speaking throughout exceptional distances used written correspondence delivered by hand from one person to another with letters. The earliest type of postal carrier dates back to 550 BC and this primitive supply process would turn out to be well-known and streamlined in future centuries.

In 1792, the telegraph was invented allowing messages to be delivered over an extended distance more rapidly than a horse and rider could. Although telegraph messages were brief, they were an innovative strategy to carry news and know-how.

Even though no longer general outside of pressure-by means of banking, the pneumatic publish, developed in 1865, created another means for letters to be delivered swiftly between recipients. A pneumatic publish utilizes underground pressurized air tubes to hold pills from one discipline to an additional one.

The telephone was developed in 1890 and the radio (viz., Italian inventor Guglielmo Marconi first developed the idea of a radio, or wireless telegraph) in 1891 (https://theradius.eu/the-effect-of-social-media-on-society/). Telephone lines and radio signals were two of the most important inventions that enabled people to communicate across great distances, something that mankind had never experienced before. Each technology is nonetheless in use these days, even though the latest models are much extra refined than their predecessors. Phone strains and radio indicators enabled persons to keep in touch across exceptional distances immediately, something that mankind had in no way experienced before.

Social Media in the 20th Century

Technological know-how started to alter very swiftly in the 20th Century. After the first computers were created in the 1940s, scientists and engineers started to advance methods to create networks between those computers, and this later resulted in the beginning of the internet.

The earliest forms of the internet, equivalent to CompuServe, have been developed in the 1960s. Primitive types of email were additionally developed for the period of this time. By the 1970s, networking technology had improved, and 1979s UseNet allowed users to be in contact by way of a virtual e-newsletter. By the 1980s, home computers were becoming extra common, and social media was becoming more refined. Web relay chats, or IRCs, have been first used in 1988 and persisted to be trendy in the 1990s.

The primary recognizable social media site, six levels, was created in 1997. It enabled users to upload a profile and make friends with different customers. In 1999, the first blogging sites became trendy, making a social media sensation that is nonetheless fashionable these days.

Social Media in the 21st Century

After the invention of blogging, social media started to grow in repute. Websites such as MySpace and LinkedIn gained prominence in the early 2000s, and sites like Photobucket and Flickr facilitated online photo sharing. YouTube launched in 2005, developing an utterly new approach for people to communicate and share with each other across vast distances. By 2006, Facebook and Twitter both grew to be available to users globally. These sites projected some of the most trendy social networks on the internet. Different websites such as Tumblr, Spotify, Foursquare, and Pinterest commenced popping up to fill special social networking niches.

Soon social media became a conference of the web panorama. Predominant social networks and social media websites make changes and enhancements on a particularly normal basis, so it is sure to keep evolving in the coming years.

Comparison of Social Media with Conventional Media

Social media is an innovative proposition that gained its position and popularity in our existence as a recent result of web 2.0 technology. It refers to places with extremely accessible and sharable content. It has become more standardized through social interaction by making use of the internet and web-based technologies. In other words, the suggestion of social media refers to platforms equivalent to social networks, blogs, micro-blogs, and forums where the self-generated content of users is shared with the aid of a person like a publisher. Social media are specified from conventional or usual media comparable to newspapers, TV, and film as they are comparatively low cost and available. They enable any person (even private members) to post or access knowledge. Some of the attributes that make differences between social and industrial media are given in Table 22.1.

Table 22.1 Differences between social and industrial media

Causes of Differentiations	Social Media	Conventional Media
Accessibility	Production for conventional media is generally possessed by private companies and governments.	Social media tools can be in general, used by everybody at a low cost or no cost.
Availability	Production of conventional media usually requires specialized skills and training.	This is not valid for most productions of social media or in some cases, skills are completely different and everybody may complete production.
Immediacy	The time difference in conventional media communications (days, weeks, and even months) can be longer.	Social media enables instant effect and reaction. The time difference of reaction is decided by participants.
Permanence	Conventional media once created, cannot be altered (once a magazine article is printed and distributed, changes cannot be made to the same article).	Social media can be immediately changed via comments and repurposing.
Access	Access to conventional media doesn't need an internet connection.	To access social media internet connections are mandatory.
Usability	Conventional media production typically requires specialized skills and training.	Social media production requires only a modest reinterpretation of existing skills.
Reach	Conventional media typically use a centralized framework for organization, production, and dissemination.	Social media are by their very nature more decentralized, less hierarchical, and distinguished by multiple points of production and utility.

Advantages and Disadvantages of Social Media

The previous discussion regarding social media in education elicits an overview of the structural and functional aspects of social media in educational scenarios. Albeit, the use of social media in education has been criticized on various grounds and argued by various researchers that it is a serious risk to use social media in classrooms or teaching-learning settings. Various potential advantages and disadvantages of social media in education will be discussed.

Advantages of Social Media in Education

Student collaboration: social media provides an open platform for the entire student community to connect for their project assignments, group assignments, homework task, and many more opportunities.

Accessibility: social media-based learning platform is a revolutionary invention to connect each unit of the world without any demographic barrier. The student can access their learning environment from any corner of the globe.

Encourage more participation: Many students in the classroom situation are not able to express their thoughts. Through social media, many students can express their thought through instant chat or text messages. Not only that but also many students are not able to access their school regularly. Hence, through social media, they can connect with their class from home and increase participation.

Helpful for homework tasks: Earlier, students were not able to communicate with their peers or teachers if clarification or questions needed to be asked for help from home. Through social media now students can chat or ask any questions to teachers or peers for feedback at any time or place.

Share learning resources and events: Through social media, the teacher is now directly able to provide learning resources in specific schools or organization pages through Facebook or Twitter, for example, for student access.

Connect teachers, students, and parents all together: Social media provides an opportunity to connect teachers, students, and parents in one specific community. For instance, in one school community page on Facebook everyone such as teachers, parents, and students could communicate altogether.

Increase social interaction: Social media encourages students and provides opportunities and various discussions through the chat room and discussion forum. It provides the opportunity for knowledge sharing with the whole world.

The Disadvantage of Social Media in Education

Distraction in class: One of the major criticisms of using social media in education is it distracts the attention of the student from the classroom. Various features such as unessential graphics, newsfeed messages, etc., could affect student attention.

Discourage face-to-face communication: Another disadvantage of social media-based teaching-learning is the lack of face-to-face communication. Students are missing social learning, social skills, face-to-face communication with instructors, etc.

Privacy concern: Critics raise their voices regarding privacy concerns of the social media-based learning environment. They argue that social media-based environments have a high chance of privacy violation. Teachers and employees are now accessing the profile of the student and making judgments by their community-based activity which has a negative consequence for student learning and job.

Posting inappropriate content: In a social media-based learning environment, it is hard to monitor students and their activities. A student may post irrelevant content or may conduct inappropriate activity which could negatively impact the teaching and learning process.

Social Media: Dos or Don'ts

Abundance and rapid technological revolution raise questions on how one can use digital social communication safely. Here some guidelines are provided by the various researcher for teachers and students to be taken into consideration while using social media:

Dos for Teachers and Students

- Teachers should maintain the confidentiality of students regarding their exam questions, grades, and personal information from the other "social page or network" except "school page".
- Social media-based communication needs more encouragement from the student. Hence, the teacher should use more interactive media, graphics, video sharing, etc. to encourage more student participation.
- Needs to separate private or personal chat with students.
- Teachers and students should maintain personal and professional accounts separately.
- Teachers should have rich knowledge about the privacy maintenance of social media.

Don'ts for Teachers and Student

- Teachers or students need to be careful about the use of their language in a digital social media environment because it can affect the learning activity of others.
- An instant chatting feature is the most powerful feature in social media but it needs to be maintained properly. Such as, too many chats with peers and students with teachers may affect the interpersonal relationship between students and teachers.
- Besides, students and teachers should be more careful about posting their images on Facebook profiles.
- Bullying is a serious problem in social media-based learning platforms. The inappropriate use of the word could hurt others and students often leading to suicide, depression, and discrimination.
- Students shouldn't post inappropriate content which could lead to distraction from teaching and learning scenarios.

Bibliography

Badeeb, H. (2021). The Effect of social media on Society, Rise, Realise, Redefine. https://theradius.eu/the-effect-of-social-media-on-society/

Boyd, D. M., & Ellison, N. B. (2007). Social network sites: Definition, history, and scholarship. *Journal of Computer-Mediated Communication, 13*, 210–230. https://doi.org/10.1111/j.1083-6101.2007.00393.x.

Brown, E., Krústeva, A., & Ranieri, M. (2016). *E-learning & social media* (1st ed.). Information Age Publishing.

Buettner, R. (2016). *Getting a job via career-oriented social networking sites: The weakness of ties.* Kauai, HI: Hawaii International Conference on System Sciences (HICSS-49).

Cheal, C., Moore, S., & Coughlin, J. (2012). *Transformation in teaching* (1st ed.). Santa Rosa, CA: Informing Science Press.

Howard, P., & Parks, M. (2012). Social media and political change: Capacity, constraint, and consequence. *Journal of Communication, 62*(2), 359–362. http://doi.org/10.1111/j.1460-2466.2012.01626.x.

Issa, T., Isaias, P., & Kommers, P. (2015). *Social networking and education* (1st ed.). Berlin: Springer.

Mallia, G. (2013). *The social classroom* (1st ed.). IGI Global.

Noor Al-Deen, H., & Hendricks, J. (2011). *Social media* (1st ed.). Blue Ridge Summit, PA: Lexington Books.

Petrakou, A. (2010). Interacting through avatars: Virtual worlds as a context for online education. *Computers and Education, 54*(4), 1020–1027.

Poore, M. (2013). *Using social media in the classroom* (1st ed.). Los Angeles, CA: Sage.

Russo, A., Watkins, J., Kelly, L., & Chan, S. (2008). Participatory communication with social media. *Curator: the Museum Journal, 51*(1), 21–31. https://doi.org/10.1111/j.2151-6952.2008.tb00292.x.

Wankel, C. (2011). Copyright page, C. Wankel (Ed.) *Educating Educators with Social Media (Cutting-Edge Technologies in Higher Education, Vol. 1)*, (p. iv). Bingley: Emerald Group Publishing Limited. https://doi.org/10.1108/S2044-9968(2011)0000001027

White, B., King, I., & Tsang, P. (2011). *Social media tools and platforms in learning environments* (1st ed.). Heidelberg, Germany: Springer.

Suggested Readings

Balkin, J., Warschauer, M., Bélair-Gagnon, V., Dede, C., Palfrey, J., Lu, Y. J., ... Mai, M. (2016). *Education and social media: Toward a digital future*. Cambridge, MA: MIT Press.

Buckingham, D. (2007). *Youth, identity, and digital media* (p. 216). Cambridge, MA: The MIT Press.

Cheal, C. (Ed.). (2012). *Transformation in teaching: Social media strategies in higher education*. Informing Science.

Flew, T. (2007). *New media: An introduction*. Oxford: Oxford University Press.

Harasim, L. M. (Ed.). (1993). *Global networks: Computers and international communication*. Cambridge, MA: MIT press.

Information Resources Management Association. (2018). *Social media in education: Breakthroughs in Research and practice*. IGI Global.

Lievrouw, L. A., & Livingstone, S. (Eds.). (2002). *Handbook of new media: Social shaping and consequences of ICTs*. London: Sage.

Mallia, G. (Ed.). (2013). *The social classroom: Integrating social network use in education: Integrating social network use in education*. IGI Global.

Patrut, M., & Patrut, B. (Eds.). (2013). *Social media in higher education: Teaching in web 2.0*. IGI Global.

Poore, M. (2015). *Using social media in the classroom: A best practice guide*, (1st Ed).. Sage.

Wankel, C. (Ed.). (2011). *Teaching arts and science with the new social media*. Bingley: Emerald Group Publishing Limited., p. i. https://doi.org/10.1108/S2044-9968(2011)0000003024

Westwood, J. (Ed.). (2014). *Social media in social work education*. Critical Publishing.

23
VARIOUS SOCIAL MEDIA PLATFORMS AND APPLICATIONS IN EDUCATION

Types of Social Media Used in Education

Education is no longer a passive communication process. The various abundant phases of social media have already been discussed. However, to date, numerous types of social media have been developed and each play various effective roles in teaching and learning scenarios. The following are the majorly used social media outlets in the sphere of education:

1. **eNewsletters**

An eNewsletter is an innovative way to keep in touch with community members. It provides a platform for the customization of message content, incorporation of various social media and pictures in messages, etc. However, it is valuable in the sense that it saves time and cost compared to the conventional way of communication. Besides, there are a lot of features such as constant contact, a contact management panel, user tracking, etc. for collecting emails and communicating effectively and systematically.

Function of eNewsletters

All must be familiar with email but compared to traditional email, an eNewsletter is different in many ways. The following are the functions of an eNewsletter:

- The first and foremost important function is an eNewsletter user not only saves or retrieves the email address of the sender but also can provide more information about the recipient. Additionally, users can customize his/her message.
- As eNewsletters are digital, henceforth, writing and drafting messages is more flexible.
- Not only the write up is as per the sending process of the message, but it is also more functionally advanced such as the user could schedule his message on a specific time and date, features categorization such as one message can be sent automatically to multiple people, by the recipient etc.
- Another innovative feature of eNewsletters is the "message tracker", for instance, users can track the delivery report of the message, view details of who clicked and opened the message, the sender whom to forward, etc. With these features, users can not only track the

recipient but can also follow up such as resending the message, providing a reminder to open the message, etc.

Advantages of eNewsletter

Customizable: eNewsletters are more customizable, for example, users can change a template that is inherent in professional design. Besides, it is more flexible to change the orientation, incorporation of picture and front, categorization of contact (parents, school organization, faculty, etc.), the option to include video, etc. We cannot work with this kind of flexibility in a traditional newsletter.

Automation as well as time and cost-saving: As previously discussed an eNewsletter is digital, therefore, one can set a schedule for message sending, there is no need for paper, stamps, and copies, the message tracks automatically, and you can follow-up, etc., thus it helps to save time and money, and helps organize the communication process.

Educational Implication of eNewsletter

The previous discussion specified the various features and effectiveness of an eNewsletter in a general way. However, in educational scenarios an eNewsletter provides the following opportunities:

Awareness Program

An eNewsletter is a platform for digital communication. Therefore, teachers or school organizations can frequently communicate with the student, as well as peer instructors, and can send information regarding various awareness programs, the schedule of the school play, various cultural programs announcements, etc., with minimum cost and effort.

Provide Feedback

In the eNewsletter platform, there is scope for various opportunities to provide feedback from the audience. Suppose, in a classroom or school-based situation head of the institution need to

Table 23.1 Comparison between traditional newsletter and eNewsletter

Subject of Comparison	Traditional Newsletter	eNewsletter
Process of sending the newsletter	Needs more physical involvement as well as paper, envelopes, photo-copy of the message, etc.	It has a lot of features such as schedule management, feedback automatically, and a delivery report analyzer to organize the whole process.
Message received by the receiver	Needs to communicate individually to get confirmation about message reception, and their feedback.	Message sender can track the status of delivery, views, clicks, read notifications, etc. and the receiver can send instant feedback.
Categorization of the communication group	Needs to find out the list of specific community members for communication of specific community.	This is customizable and can be categorized based on a specific community.

take an opinion regarding the improvement of teaching-learning strategies and he or she creates one opinion poll. In these scenarios, peer staff or specific groups could provide feedback and it can be tracked with just one click, by comment box, online survey, etc., and can take important decisions based on the opinion of peers or parents.

Collaboration

In educational scenarios, an eNewsletter helps to create a collaborative environment with various groups. For instance, the head of the institution or other higher authority could collaborate with other members of their community for feedback and can provide a voting poll for decision-making.

2. **Facebook**

Facebook is one of the most popular social networking sites. It was officially launched on 4th February 2004. The primary aim of Facebook was to provide information and create an educational community for Harvard University students. However, after that, it expanded worldwide and now it has 1.65 billion monthly active users as of April 2016. In the present scenario, Facebook has become an essential communication tool not only for social communication but also for academic communication such as classroom event organization, news of exam schedules, and active communication from teacher to student, student to student, and teacher to teacher.

Functions of Facebook

Facebook functions as a communication process on a virtual platform. However, for discussion, we functionally divide Facebook users into two categories:

i) Individual user
ii) Organization- or community-based user

i) **Individual user**
Individual user refers to the personal account of a Facebook user. To join as a new individual user on Facebook one has to follow the following steps:
User registration
To newly join on Facebook the first step is registration. By registration, Facebook grants an active member status. For registration, the user needs to go to the website facebook.com, click the "sign up" button, and provide the personal details of a registered phone or email address, name, etc. After fulfillment of these steps, one can go to the next steps.
Create profile
After completion of registration, the second step is to create a user profile with proper details of the individual. In this stage, users have to provide their details such as name, date of birth, address, school name year, college name, year of enrollment, etc. Besides this, the user also may provide a profile picture for picture identification as a user.
Add friends
The third step is to search for and add friends. In this step, users have to add their friends by searching or by default suggestions from Facebook based on the details of the user. However, the user has to ensure that one knows the people personally. After the confirma-

tion of a friend, one can see the newsfeed of a friend, can personally chat with a friend, and can post his or her information.

ii) **Organization or community-based user**

For an organization or community-based communication such as a school or organization one needs to create a "page" instead of a personal account. On a Facebook page, there are a variety of extra features to effectively communicate with community members. First and foremost, the step is registration with Facebook. One member of the school authority has to register his or her school with proper details of the school such as a picture of the school, school name, address, contact information, etc., to create a "page of the school". After the development of the "page" admins can control and give priority to the group member about the update on school events, exam schedules, cultural events, etc. Through the school community page, faculty and student can engage with every update of the school.

The Implication of Facebook on Educational Scenarios

In the 21st century, Facebook as a social media provides lots of opportunities in education and teaching-learning situations. Facebook as a social media not only provides status updates, photo posts, and an add comments mechanism, but also provides direct learning through communication. The following are some of the basic implications of Facebook in Education:

Ask for opinions: Instead of a Google search or search through Wikipedia, one can get information by asking his or her peers for comments including many expert opinions that can be taken from the information collected or decision-making.

Mass education: Through various educational community pages on Facebook one can learn from remote areas, thus there are no demographic bindings for Facebook-based education.

Development of century skill: With Facebook as an educational tool teachers could engage the student in various skills such as collaborative learning, news, community-based learning, networking, etc.

Brainstorming: Students can be encouraged more on collaborative attributes and brainstorming on Facebook-based learning situations.

Exam practice: On the Facebook page students and teachers could generate subject-based question-and-answer sessions for online practice.

Writing workshop: The collaborative nature of Facebook helps the student to participate in various writing workshops with peer review.

Table 23.2 Comparison between traditional classroom communication and Facebook-based classroom communication

Subject of Comparison	Traditional Classroom	Facebook-Based Classroom
Promoting various announcements	To promote or announce various program schedules, wall posters, vocal announcements, etc.	Students can communicate with the official Facebook page of the school to know updated announcements regarding the school program.
Teacher-student communication	Student and teacher communication is mainly based on the classroom situation.	Students can communicate with a teacher anytime and anywhere without any demographical boundaries.

3. **Twitter**

In July 2006 Jack Dorsey, Evan Williams, Biz Stone, and Noah Glass launched Twitter, and presently there are 332 million (January 2016) active users on Twitter. As previously discussed, Twitter is a microblogging site that enables one to communicate with the entire world in 280 characters. Messages on Twitter are known as "tweets".

The Function of Twitter

Twitter is one type of instant messaging service for mass communication. However, in the 21st century, it is an essential tool for mass communication. Twitter is also essential for teaching-learning scenarios. Before describing Twitter as an educational tool, one should know more about how Twitter works. The following are the various procedures for the use of Twitter:

Registration and Making a Profile

Like Facebook, Twitter also needs a registered account to communicate or tweet. However, without a Twitter account, one can read the tweets of others. To register on Twitter, the user needs to fill up a form regarding personal and demographic details and that helps to create one's profile with a secure username and password. After, registration a user can modify their profile with an appropriate user name denoted with an "@" sign such as @Example.

Posting a Tweet

To post a tweet just simply type on the status box as it appears on the upper side of the Twitter page which indicated by the sample text "What's happening". The user has to remember that a Twitter post is bound to only 280 characters currently in 2017 including punctuation. However, users can also post website links or the address of their blog site for more information regarding their tweets. Once tweeted it spreads to the whole world.

Reading Tweets

Reading tweets is a simple procedure. Users can read any tweet without any binding. Twitter is also an essential tool for reading. Users can search and read specific topics from the search bar.

However, the following are some specific "terms" and "symbols" Twitter users must be familiar with:

@Username: In Twitter, the name before the "@" sign indicates a particular user account or user name. For instance, one can find this book author on Twitter with usernames @anita_Ed_Tech and @Angik_Ed_Teach.

#Tag: As a Twitter user one can encounter the sign "#" also called 'hashtag' which indicates a keyword, topic, or content on Twitter. For instance, "#Educational technology" indicates a topic regarding educational technology.

Following and Followers: On Twitter, through the "following" feature users can follow various experts, colleague, peers, etc., to know more about their activity and for linkup and personal communication. Besides this, "followers" are those who follow the user. One can update his or her message for their followers.

Educational Implication of Twitter

Twitter in the field of the education industry has had an abundant impact. Twitter is ubiquitous social networking. However, Twitter in teaching-learning has the following impact:

a) **Tweet about the assignment**: In classroom scenarios, Twitter could play a role as an announcement process of assignment. The teacher can create a schedule of the school's program, tests, quizzes, etc.
b) **Coordinates assignment**: With the help of Twitter students can communicate with peers, collaborate on various projects, etc.
c) **Track Hashtag**: With the help of the Twitter hashtag features students can find out the recent trend and also can track the content features in educational settings.
d) **Connect with the community**: Twitter is a community-based social platform. School organizations can create pages and students can communicate with the page for further information and community-based communication.
e) **Chat with teacher or experts**: Through Twitter, students can effectively communicate with teachers to solve various problems, including communication with a field expert for more advanced discussion.
f) **Engaging parents**: Twitter not only encourages teacher and student communication but also encourages the communication of parents with the school community. However, parents can be updated about school events and can communicate with school faculty.

4. **YouTube**

YouTube is a video-sharing platform. This site allows users to upload videos, view videos, comment, like, share with social media, etc. YouTube was developed by Steve Chen, Chad Hurley, and Jawed Karim in February 2005, later it was bought by Google in November 2006 for US$1.65 billion. At present YouTube is a powerful tool for gathering and sharing information worldwide. However, YouTube as an educational tool plays a major role in the 21st-century teaching and learning process.

Function of YouTube

YouTube as a social media involves various steps from the creation of videos to publishing a video on the website. We can divide the functional side of YouTube into two ways such as a developer or creator and a viewer or user. The subsequent section briefly discusses some of them.

Procedure for a Developer or Creator

- **Creation or collection of videos**: To communicate with or work with YouTube users need to create a video by using various video recording devices such as a webcam, high-definition video cameras, etc. After that, the video could be directly uploaded or it can be made with various editing such as title, sound, voice-over, the addition of graphics, etc., to make the video presentable.
- **Upload and publishing of video**: The second step after the creation of the video is to upload the created video to YouTube. To upload the video, the user needs to register on YouTube. It has two options; sign in and sign up. For a new user, one needs to click on sign

up and needs to provide the required details. Additionally, for existing users, one needs to log in with their existing username and password. However, after the mentioned procedure user can upload their video by clicking the "upload" button which appears in the right upper corner. After, completion of the upload procedure a user can publish their video by clicking the publish button.

- **Sharing or posting a video on various other websites**: In this stage, a user can share their created video on various other sites for publicity purposes. To do so, the developer or creator needs to click on the sharing button present on Facebook, Twitter, LinkedIn, etc.
- **Further analysis**: The creator can analyze their posts by addressing the viewer count, like count, comments, subscriptions, etc. to further improve the video.

Procedure for Viewer

As a viewer, YouTube has various features to express viewer response regarding the specific video such as:

- **Rating video**: Viewers can rate the video by clicking the like and dislike button. It is helpful for the creator to judge their video, as well as more "like" rated video comes in front during search result of YouTube thereby accelerating the promotion of the created video.
- **Comments**: The viewer can provide comments such as suggestions, opinions, reports, etc., regarding the video for future evaluation.
- **Share in social media**: The viewer is also able to share the video on various social media platforms.
- **Subscription in channel**: The viewer can subscribe to one particular channel for future access to a particular specific video.

Table 23.3 Some other social media platforms for education

Name of the Website	Basic Function of Educational Practice	Official Website
EdConnectr	Used to share learning material, curriculum, and model, rate and track vendors for better results, collaborative environment through virtual dialog, etc.	http://edconnector.org
Edmodo	Edmodo can connect teachers, students, and parents, together at a time. Edmodo teachers can create a blended learning classroom, join global learning communities, etc.	https://www.edmodo.com
TedEd	It offers various teaching-learning materials, a short talk, an animated learning clip, subject-based teaching material and also learning collaboration.	http://ed.ted.com
Google+	Besides social picture and video sharing Google+ also provides community-based learning platforms.	https://plus.google.com
Instagram	On the Instagram, platform teachers can create picture-based assignments and students can learn by taking photo uploads and by captions.	https://www.instagram.com
Vimeo	Vimeo is a video-based online platform. Through video sharing and video, creation the teacher can teach the student or provide various learning materials.	https://vimeo.com

Table 23.4 Name of the websites, their functions, and official website link

Name of the Website	Basic Function and Educational Practice	Official Website
WordPress	WordPress becomes a popular way for teachers to create learning material and encourage students to write their blogs.	https://wordpress.com
Skype	Skype is a face-to-face video calling platform. In teaching-learning, Skype provides an opportunity to connect the teacher with the student through face-to-face calls for teaching or discussions.	https://web.skype.com
Pinterest	Pinterest provides online teaching to connect a student with various infographic learning materials. Also, the teacher can create community-based learning on Pinterest.	https://in.pinterest.com
TeacherTube	TeacherTube provides a platform for all sorts of education, from the basics to more complicated work.	https://www.teachertube.com
Academia.edu	Academia is mainly a research-based learning platform that connects millions of academicians and researchers to promote and discuss their work.	https://www.academia.edu
Research Gate	Bringing researchers, academics, and students together for collaboration.	https://www.researchgate.net
LinkedIn	LinkedIn provides a platform to connect employers to employees. For educational scenarios, the student can post their resume to attach to a job or educational institution.	https://in.linkedin.com

Educational Implication of YouTube

YouTube is a worldwide video-hosting site that has an enormous educational impact. It provides an educational platform for learning, sharing, and creating a collaborative learning environment over a global educational network. The following are the basic educational impacts of YouTube for teaching-learning scenarios.

(a) **Learning content and pedagogic uses**: For educational purposes, YouTube is an important tool that provides an opportunity to create an audio-visual-based learning environment. Various private and government organizations, teachers, and educational activists upload various learning modules on YouTube for student learning all free of cost.
(b) **Feedback**: YouTube provides an interactive platform, based on the learning material students can provide their feedback by comments and also ask questions regarding content and the teacher could provide their comments or responses.
(c) **Collaboration**: YouTube also provides a collaborative learning environment. For instance, the content creator of the teacher could communicate with global viewers and can follow their comments for future purposes. However, based on one video one user collaborates with other viewers by comments and re-comments and continuing the conversation.

Some Other Social Media Platforms for Education

In the previous section, we discussed the majorly used social media platforms for educational purposes. However, social media has the power to connect with a worldwide educational network such as one teacher could teach one student 2,000 miles away. This section is going to introduce concisely most of the common social networking web-based platforms which are used for various educational purposes.

Social Media in Educational Practice

Web-based technological revolution expands the scope of education beyond demographic boundaries. As discussed in the previous section the ubiquitous nature of the technology-based revolution can change the form of teaching-learning. Now, education is not situated in a specific place and time but any time anywhere with the help of the internet. However, social media or networking is not only an effective tool for teaching-learning but also essential for the functional maintenance of school organizations such as event organization, job announcement and recruitment of faculty, relief and searching for funds, arranging a conference, publishing studies, etc. This section discusses briefly some major educational practices of social media.

Social Media in the Teaching-Learning Process

The entire discussion above depicts that social media–based websites provide a platform for students and teachers globally to connect using teaching and learning. Day to day, each website improves and incorporates various features such as Learning Management System (LMS) and Virtual Learning Environment (VLE) to accelerate communication. Hence, there are various features for the teacher to create learning modules, post assignments, analyze students responses or answers to questions, provide features, communicate live with the student, etc., as well as this, there are various advanced features for a student such as communicating with learning module, discussion with a peer group, collaborative learning environment, etc. However, in the present situation, some of the larger users of social media are Moodle, EdX, Blackboard, etc., and it has been commonly used by the University of Illinois, Urbana-Champaign, Illinois, etc. It has been found by various researchers that a major challenge in the online learning environment is lack of "face-to-face communication" and "interaction" between students (Petrakou, 2010). Nevertheless, with this problem in mind social media-based sites have updated their features with live video communication and live chat to eliminate various obstacles and accelerate the teaching-learning process. Various research has shown that social media increase the possibility to gain more social attributes, the ability to communicate worldwide, enrichment by sharing content, enrichment of knowledge, etc. (Petrakou, 2010). Henceforth, a revolutionary step has been taken by various universities to properly use social media in teaching-learning scenarios.

Social Media for Institutional-Based Management

Not only for the teaching and learning process but also social media–based communication is an important tool for the school management process. The subsequent section discusses the potential use of social media:

- *First*, through community-based social media schools or other institutional authorities could communicate with other faculty, student, staff, etc.
- *Second*, each organization has various activities or events to arrange or maintain the whole event systematically such as sending invitations, contacts, phone calls, and schedule announcements, and for more human involvement social media has the advantage over the

others. Now, teachers are more flexible to communicate with the student to announce and change the class schedule.
- *Third*, With the help of social media, broadcasting school events to the whole world is just a matter of clicking a button.

Job Announcement and Recruitment of Faculty

The social media revolution provides various innovative opportunities for faculty recruitment, job announcement, etc. such as:

- The school could announce any job openings and the job specification with the help of social media.
- An application portal could be made on the school website for applicants.
- Not only that, for hiring teachers, there are various features in social media such as LinkedIn, YouTube, Craigslist, and multi-posting services to screen and recruit hire potential applicants.
- With the help of social media, school organizations can know more about the interests, activities, and attitudes of applicants if needed through the help of Facebook, Twitter, and other social activity.

Grant Funding and Solicitation for Donation

With the help of social media, an educational organization could find, apply, and track grants or funding. The following are some specific implications of social media for the grant funding process:

- The educational organization could search on Google for the specific term "grant funding organization for schools" to find out and list the funding organization.
- Also, they could follow the Twitter page to know more about the new grant announcement as well as communicate and discuss with the members of the grant funding organization.
- Tracking the grant application process is also more important. Traditionally, one needs to send a follow-up letter to the organization to know the status of the application process. But now it has become easy with the help of the website of the grant funding organization for tracking portal or by email.
- Not only for funding but social media also provides a great platform for solicitation of donations on various social media or educational communities.

Academic News, Conferences, and Publishing Studies

Another vital use of social media in educational scenarios is conference arrangement and the publishing of research work or another update in the website to spread information worldwide. Now, one can follow the information of any ongoing and upcoming conference details on the confarencealert.com website. Nevertheless, there are various websites that mainly provide various academic news and conference details. The school community could arrange a conference and provide a detailed announcement on the website and also on Facebook and Twitter, etc. Additionally, various academic and research-based activities could be published on the school website as well as research-based social networking sites such as academia, ResearchGate, etc.

Bibliography

Boyd, D. M., & Ellison, N. B. (2007). Social network sites: Definition, history, and scholarship. *Journal of Computer-Mediated Communication, 13*, 210–230.

Brown, E., Krŭsteva, A., & Ranieri, M. (2016). *E-learning & social media* (1st ed.). Information Age Publishing.

Buettner, R. (2016). *Getting a job via career-oriented social networking sites: The weakness of ties.* Kauai, HI: Hawaii International Conference on System Sciences (HICSS-49).

Cheal, C., Moore, S., & Coughlin, J. (2012). *Transformation in teaching* (1st ed.). Santa Rosa, CA: Informing Science Press.

Howard, P., & Parks, M. (2012). Social media and political change: Capacity, constraint, and consequence. *Journal of Communication, 62*(2), 359–362. http://doi.org/10.1111/j.1460-2466.2012.01626.x.

Issa, T., Isaias, P., & Kommers, P. (2015). *Social networking and education* (1st ed.). Berlin: Springer.

Mallia, G. (2013). *The social classroom* (1st ed.). IGI Global.

Noor Al-Deen, H., & Hendricks, J. (2011). *Social media* (1st ed.). Blue Ridge Summit, PA: Lexington Books.

Petrakou, A. (2010). Interacting through avatars: Virtual worlds as a context for online education. *Computers and Education, 54*(4), 1020–1027.

Poore, M. (2013). *Using social media in the classroom* (1st ed.). Los Angeles, CA: Sage. https://doi.org/10.1111/j.1083-6101.2007.00393.x.

Russo, A., Watkins, J., Kelly, L., & Chan, S. (2008). Participatory communication with social media. *Curator: The Museum Journal, 51*(1), 21–31. https://doi.org/10.1111/j.2151-6952.2008.tb00292.x.

Wankel, C. (2011). *Educating educators with social media* (1st ed.). Emerald Group Publishing.

White, B., King, I., & Tsang, P. (2011). *Social media tools and platforms in learning environments* (1st ed.). Heidelberg, Germany: Springer.

Suggested Reading

Balkin, J., Warschauer, M., Bélair-Gagnon, V., Dede, C., Palfrey, J., Lu, Y. J., … Mai, M. (2016). *Education and social media: Toward a digital future.* Cambridge, MA: MIT Press.

Buckingham, D. (2007). *Youth, identity, and digital media* (p. 216). Cambridge, MA: MIT Press.

Cheal, C. (Ed.). (2012). *Transformation in teaching: Social media strategies in higher education.* Santa Rosa, California: Informing Science.

Flew, T. (2007). *New media: An introduction.* Oxford: Oxford University Press.

Harasim, L. M. (Ed.). (1993). *Global networks: Computers and international communication.* Cambridge, MA: MIT Press.

Information Resources Management Association. (2018). *Social media in education: Breakthroughs in Research and practice.* IGI Global.

Lievrouw, L. A., & Livingstone, S. (Eds.). (2002). *Handbook of new media: Social shaping and consequences of ICTs.* London: Sage.

Mallia, G. (Ed.). (2013). *The social classroom: Integrating social network use in education: Integrating social network use in education.* IGI Global.

Patrut, M., & Patrut, B. (Eds.). (2013). *Social media in higher education: Teaching in web 2.0.* Portland, OR: IGI Global.

Poore, M. (2015). *Using social media in the classroom: A best practice guide*, (2nd Ed). Sage.

Wankel, C. (Ed.). (2011). *Teaching arts and science with the new social media.* Emerald Group Publishing Limited.

Westwood, J. (Ed.). (2014). *Social media in social work education.* Critical Publishing.

24
OPEN EDUCATIONAL RESOURCES (OER)

Introduction

Worldwide, every country is trying to enhance its educational framework as it gives back in the form of financial, social, and natural advancement of any country. The major aim of the 21st-century educational system is not only to produce bookish or educated individuals but rather to enhance the quality of education and enhance the skills and competence of learners to encounter the future challenges of our society. If the aim of education is the all-round development of learners then every student must be equipped with creative energy, innovativeness, and other various 21st-century skills. However, the traditional education system is not enough to learn such skills, therefore, there is a need for some alternative approaches to acquiring knowledge from different sources. The present chapter aims to provide explicit knowledge about different educational resources that are not structured as authoritative sources of knowledge but rather alternative educational resources that are more open and authorizing in nature, that foster free reuse and free repurposing by others for educational purposes namely "Open Education Resources (OER)".

Conceptualization and Definitions of Open Educational Resources

The **Berlin Declaration** on Open Access to Knowledge in the Sciences and Humanities characterizes Open Access "as an exhaustive wellspring of human learning and social legacy that has been affirmed by established researchers" and invigorates the signatory organizations "to advance the Internet as a utilitarian instrument for a worldwide logical learning base and human reflection".

The **Budapest Open Access Initiative (BOAI, 2002)** characterizes OA as the "free accessibility on the general population web, allowing any clients to use, download, duplicate, circulate, print, inquire, or connect to the full writings of these articles, slither them for ordering, pass them as information to programming, or utilize them for any other legitimate reason, without monetary, lawful, or specialized obstructions other than those indivisible from accessing the web itself. The main requirement on multiplication and circulation, and the role for copyright in this area, ought to give creators authority over the trustworthiness of their work and the privileged to be legitimately recognized and referred to".

UNESCO (October 23, 2018) referred to OER as diverse instructional or research materials that are primarily free of cost and residing in the public domain or as an open licensing paradigm with limited restriction or no restriction of access and distribution. In addition, open licensing is based on intellectual property rights which are surrounded by international conventions to acknowledge the authorship of work properly.

Commonwealth of Learning (July 20, 2017) defines OER as a free and open substance that is generally acclimated to an instructional process, research, and development.

Wikieducator OER Handbook (n.d.) specified OER as a combination of varied educational resources such as simulation, teaching-learning materials, modules for learning, quizzes, etc. that are generally based on the doctrine of cost-free access, adaption, sharing, and reproduction with no restriction or limited restriction.

Historical Background of OER

From the previous section, one can get an understanding that OER is a revolutionary movement toward free and open access worldwide. But this revolution did not happen overnight. It has a rich long history in the context of its revolution. The present section is intended to provide contextualization of the historical journey of open educational resources by highlighting some milestone years of innovation and activities.

Characteristics of OER

From the above discussion and definition, the following characteristics can be extracted:

- **Open access**: One of the notable characteristics of OER is the open accessibility of educational resources with free and limited restrictions. The open accessibility characteristics of OER expand the scope of mass use of any resources without or with limited monetary or legal bindings.
- **Open sources**: OER is a community-based content development approach therefore, it is open source. Anyone from any part of the world can contribute to learning without any bindings.
- **Openness in uses**: Irrespective of caste, creed, gender, religion, etc., one can use open content. For example, OER can be used for people with disabilities and it is usable for teaching and studying. In a general sense, there is no participation limit in the context of using OER.
- **Reusability**: Another essential characteristic of OER is the reusability of material. That means any material of OER can be republished, allowing for modification, and commercially used by maintaining a limited aspect. This characteristic of OER increases the sustainability of OER-based resources.
- **Flexible in nature**: Compared to other educational materials OER is a very flexible learning content that can be upgraded very easily and in a flexible manner.

Various Types of OER Websites

In the context of OER, there is a multitude of resources available throughout the world. Various government and private organizations have taken initiatives to open content material and make it free and accessible for all. This intends to discuss some of the open educational resources, in the context of global scenarios. Table 24.2 presents some well-known OER-based learning materials available online.

Table 24.1 Present historical overview of open educational resources

Year	Who/Which Organization Has Taken an Initiative	What Is the Significance
1994	Wayne Hodgins	Introduced the term "learning objects". The role of learning objects in the context of OER is an idea that digital material can be designed in a way that can be reused in a variety of pedagogical situations.
1998	David Wiley	First coined the term "open content". The concept of open content extended the idea that unlike the open-source "software movement", a revolution can be in the context of free/open educational resources.
1999 (January)	University of Tubingen (Germany)	Public video series lecture online. This was considered the first OER.
2003 (November)	China Open Resources for Education (CORE)	Aims to provide MIT OpenCourseWare at the University of China.
2005 (January)	OECD's Centre for Educational Research and Innovation	Undertook a 20-month study on the scale and scope of open educational resources.
2006 (September)	Khan Academy	K–12 learning material is basically on a subject basis available for free throughout the world.
2007 (September)	University of Michigan Medical school	Developed describes publishing all pre-clinical curricula material for free.
2008 (January)	The Open Society Institute and the Shuttleworth Foundation	A report namely the Open Education Declaration was released. This report argued with the world government and was published to make all education free over the internet.
2009 (February)	Hewlett	Hewlett provided a grant to the University of Michigan, OER Africa, and four African universities to further develop and support OER in the context of health education.
2009 (March)	YouTube	YouTube EDU is launched by Google to provide a free channel for organized premium educational material from various colleges and universities.
2009 (August)	Governor Arnold Schwarzenegger	Supports free digital initiatives namely "California's Free Digital Textbook" to provide free access to digital textbooks at the high school level.
2010 September	Stanford University	Offered free online courses where more than 350,000 students were enrolled throughout the world.
2011 (April)	Bangladesh digitized a complete set of textbook material for grades 1–12.	Bangladesh private and government organization.
2011 (August)	Codeacademy	Launched the first open educational resources for computer programming, funded by Y-Combinator.
2012 (March)	TED-Ed	Provide a platform for a top-quality educational speech from various communities.

Copyright and Open Licensing in the Context of Education

The present section discusses "copyright" and "open licensing" in the context of online and offline resources. So, what is meant by copyright? Some comprehensive definitions are as follows:

Wikipedia (2019) defines copyright as usually intellectual property in the context of creative work. This is primarily a guideline for legal rights of reproduction, reuse, distribution, and public performance. It also focuses on "moral rights", such as attribution.

Neil. (2015) (commonwealth of learning) defines copyright as generally a safeguard of intellectual property by law to the author/creator within a specific period in the context of copy, reuse, print, derivation, etc.

From the above definitions, one can say that "copyright" is:

- A legal right in the context of the use and distribution of any original work.
- Copyright law is created by different countries as per their laws.
- Copyright is usually for a limited time.

Throughout the world, copyright law is different per different jurisdictions. However; there is a common attribution of any copyright law that is termed "fair use" or "fair dealing" (COL, 2015; https://en.wikipedia.org/wiki/Copyright). Generally, "fair use" denotes permission to use any copyrighted material with some basic precaution. For instance, a written work in the context of "fair use" means permission for use of this specific material for private study, research, book review, reporting, and other non-commercial uses. It is also notable that "fair use" does not permit the reproduction of any material in the full form of any documents.

The traditional approach to copyright context is very restrictive. Therefore, in the context of teaching and learning, a teacher, as well as a student, is very much bound to use copyrighted material freely and effectively. In this concept, the concept of OER has emerged and encouraged the creation of an alternative and flexible copyright strategy called an "open licensing system". The following are some brief discussions about various copyright strategies such as all rights reserved, public domain, open licensing system, etc.

- **All rights reserved**: This is very restrictive; all rights reserved copyright means the copyright holder restricted its material by copyright laws. Generally, if content material is bound with all rights reserved copyright agreement, then any user is not allowed to republish the content material without prior permission of the copyright holder.
- **Public domain**: Public domain content is purely open and free content material. There is no control over the distribution of public domain material. Generally, public domain content is produced by the government of any country or organization of a country that is supported by the public fund.
- **Open licensing system**: An open licensing system is a mechanism of balance between traditional "all rights reserved" copyright and "public domain" copyright. Therefore, an open licensing system is open and free like the public domain, there is also clear and specific ownership of intellectual property like all rights reserved copyright. Besides, there is an explicit guideline to attribute the work to the original author when using openly licensed materials.

Table 24.2 Present repository-based OER platform

Name of the Resources	Detail Context	Website
SOL*R	SOL*R is a repository service of online open educational resources. This service is provided by BCampus. It allows access to the license of post-secondary material in the context of sharing, discovery, and reuse of a plethora of educational content.	https://solr.bccampus.ca/wp/about-bccampus-shareable-online-learning-resources/
Creative Commons Search	This is also an online repository of educational context that provides access to educators and students to various types of media such as images, music, videos, etc.	https://search.creativecommons.org/
OER Commons	This online repository is specifically for accessing various types of textbooks, courses, and ancillary materials. OER was commonly launched by ISKME in 2007.	https://www.oercommons.org/about
MERLOT	MERLOT is an online repository where millions of educational content are curated and accessed for free and open teaching. It is led by the international community of educators, learners, and researchers.	https://www.merlot.org/merlot/index.htm
OER Handbook for educators	This platform is designed for novice educators who just started the creation of open educational resources.	http://wikieducator.org/OER_Handbook
Mason OER Metafinder	This is a real-time federated search engine for OER content.	https://oer.deepwebaccess.com/oer/desktop/en/search.html
Connexions	This is a large repository for individual teacher.	https://cnx.org/
Orange Grove	This is Florida's collection of open-text resources. The overall search engine is categorized as Open collection, higher education resources, K–12 resources, and institutional collection.	https://www.floridashines.org/orange-grove
Quantitative Undergraduate Biology Education and Synthesis (QUBES)	QUBES is a specific repository for online resources intended to provide learning material, software, data, and model for teaching quantitative skills in graduate biological courses.	https://qubeshub.org/resources
Curriki	Curriki is a platform to create, share and explore educational resources of the K–12 context.	https://www.curriki.org/
Open Scout	This is a database for business skill development-based teaching resources.	http://learn.openscout.net/
AMSER	This online open resource repository is based on applied math and science education. This is basically for the high school and community college levels.	
Excitement!	This is mainly based on learning objects and lessons from National Endowment for humanity.	https://edsitement.neh.gov/
Community of Online Research Assignments	This is open resources for research assignment of faculty and librarians.	https://www.projectcora.org/
OpenCulture	This is blog based online repository intended to provide free resources on culture and education.	http://www.openculture.com/

Table 24.3 OER for complete courses

Name	Details	Website
Academic Earth	Academic Earth was created around 2009 and intended to provide free online college courses from the world's top universities.	https://academicearth.org/
Coursera	MOOC-based online learning platform intended to provide free online education from top universities and educational institutions.	https://www.coursera.org/
EdX	EdX Founded by Harvard University and MIT, it aims to provide high-quality educational courses from the world's top universities.	ttps://www.edx.org/
LearningSpace from the open university	Open University gives the platform to access an article and video games created by various experts throughout the world. A learner can explore various new topics and can join in debates besides learning.	https://www.open.edu/openlearn/
Open Course Library (OCL)	This is also a free-to-use high-quality open learning platform. The uniqueness of OCL is all the learning material is available in Google docs for easy access and download.	http://opencourselibrary.org/
Saylor Academy	Saylor Academy offers a learning platform to build new skills among learners.	https://www.saylor.org/
Online Learning Intuitive (OLI)	OLI provides online courses for traditional and independent students.	http://oli.cmu.edu/
NOBA	NOBA is an open-learning platform in the field of psychology. It has a complete list of course material from introductory to advanced topics.	https://nobaproject.com/

Before getting an overall understanding of "open licensing" as a whole it will be helpful to know about the terms separately related to open licensing that is "open" and "licensing". The term "open" denotes free to use or access for all. Besides that, the term, "licensing" denotes a set of documents that are legal rules that specify the boundary regarding what can and cannot be done in the context of original work. As per the definition given in opendefinition.org:

"An open license grants permission to access, reuse and distribute work with few or no restriction".

Besides, another term is very famous in the context of open licensing that is "copyleft". The term "copyleft" is used to encourage openness in the licensing system. It symbolizes mirror C or ☺.

The "open licensing" system is a revolutionary movement that has developed and evolved over the past two decades. The following are some of the open licensing systems available in the present scenario:

- GNU General Public License (for software)
- GNU Free Documentation License (for manuals)
- Open Publication License (content)
- Open Game License (computer games)
- Free Art License (art, image, graphics)
- Creative Commons Licences (content)

From the above list, as per educational content "Creative Commons License" is an extremely used and common open license approach.

Creative Commons Licensing

As discussed previously, creative commons is a famous licensing system in the context of educational content. If one looks back to the early stage of the open licensing movement, one can find that in 1983 the free software movement occurred that opened the door to use/modify/share the source code of software with limited restriction or non-restriction. After this the open licensing movement has been influenced by the other sector of open licensing such as database licenses and open game licenses.

But the open licensing in the context of non-computer-related programs had been introduced from 2001 onwards. Throughout the world, various people from various communities such as educationists, legal scholars, technologists, investors, and philanthropists came forward with the work for the development of copyright licenses so that everyone can share material such as blog posts, slides, photos, written content, films, books, etc. in an effective way. With initiatives, they developed a non-profit organization called "creative commons" in 2002.

Types of Creative Common Licensing

The following are six types of creative commons licensing adopted from the creative commons website (https://creativecommons.org/licenses/).

Some OER Movements in India

India stepped forward toward an open educational movement in 2007. Currently, various government and private organizations are working together to increase the scope and access to open resources. The following are some of the significant steps toward OER in India:

Digital library of India: This is a collaborative project. In this project, 21 institutions in India are working together to provide open access to non-copyrighted books from various libraries. Presently this project is handled by the Indian Institute of Science (IISc), Bangalore. This project was started in 2000, the primary aim of this project was to increase the opportunity to access non-copyrighted literacy, artistic, and scientific books free for everyone. This project also partnered with the "million book project" led by Carnegie Mellon University.

Shodhganga: The term "Shodh" denotes "Sanskrit" and "Ganga", which stands for the largest and longest river of the Indian subcontinent. In a Holistic view "Shodhganga" is a reservoir of Indian intellectual output. Overall the Shodhganga project is maintained by the Information and Library Network (INFLIBNET). The shodhganga@INFLIBNET uses open-source software called DSpace and was developed by the Massachusetts Institute of Technology (MIT) with a partner organization Hewlett-Packard (HP). The Shodhganga repository, export the opportunity to open access thesis and dissertation of doctoral and other research work produced in Indian University.

National Digital Library of India (NDL India): Ministry of Human Resources Development (MHRD) of India under its National Mission on Education through Information and Communication Technology (NMEICT) has initiated the development of an actual repository of a learning resource with a single-window search facility called National Digital Library of India (NDL India). The major name of this project is to provide support to formal as well as non-formal aspects of education. NDL India is designed and developed by the Indian Institute of Technology (IIT) Kharagpur.

National Knowledge Network (NKN): The major aim of the National Knowledge Network (NKN) is to establish and create a strong Indian network that will be capable of producing secure and reliable connectivity. NKN was established in 2010 recommended by National Knowledge Commission (NKC). This is a step toward the creation of a knowledge society.

Vidyanidhi: This is a comparatively new open-access institutional repository set up in 2013. The major aim of "vidyanidhi" is to provide free access to scholarly publications, journals, articles, books, book reviews, presentations, etc.

Shodhgangotri: Shodhgangotri is another free-access digital repository that aims to provide and submit an electronic version of the approved synopsis of research registered for the PhD program. This is an initiative of the Information and Library Network (INFLIBNET) center started in 2011.

Advantages and Disadvantages of OER

OER has increased learning opportunities as it is more open and accessible to the learner. Unlike other educational resources, OER has also the following advantages and disadvantages.

Advantages of OER

- **Increase the scope of access**: OER is globally accessible learning material. A learner can access educational material anytime from anywhere repeatedly.
- **Enhance the quality of education**: As there is a huge scope in the context of OER to develop by various experts in a specific field it can therefore increase the quality of educational resources as well as increase the quality of education.
- **Personalization**: OER-based learning material encourages a learner-centered, self-directed, informal learning approach.

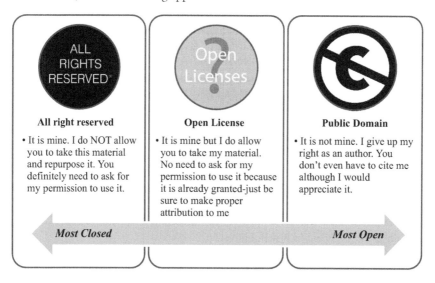

Figure 24.1 Difference between all right reserved, open license, and public domain.

Table 24.4 Six types of Creative Commons licensing

Name	Details	Symbol
Attribution CC BY	This license lets others distribute, remix, tweak, and build upon one's work, even commercially, as long as they credit one for the original creation. These are the most accommodating licenses offered. Recommended for maximum dissemination and use of licensed materials.	
Attribution-ShareAlike CC BY-SA	This license lets others remix, tweak, and build upon one's work even for commercial purposes, as long as they credit you and license their new creations under identical terms. This license is often compared to "copyleft", free, and open-source software licenses. All new works based on yours will carry the same license, so any derivatives will also allow commercial use. This is the license used by Wikipedia and is recommended for materials that would benefit from incorporating content from Wikipedia and similarly licensed projects.	
Attribution-NoDerivs CC BY-ND	This license lets others reuse the work for any purpose, including commercially; however, it cannot be shared with others in adapted form, and credit must be provided to you.	
Attribution-Non-Commercial CC BY-NC	This license lets others remix, tweak, and build upon your work non-commercially, and although their new works must also acknowledge you and in non-commercial, they don't have to license their derivative works on the same terms.	
Attribution-Non-commercial-ShareAlike CC BY-NC-SA	This license lets others remix, tweak, and build upon one work non-commercially, as long as they credit and license their new creations under identical terms.	
Attribution-NonCommercial-NoDerivs CC BY-NC-ND	This license is the most restrictive of the six main licenses, only allowing others to download one's works and share them with others as long as they credit you, but they can't change them in any way or use them commercially.	

Table 24.5 Present various institutional repositories in India

Name	Host Institution	URL	No. of Items	Types of Documents	Software Used
Librarian's Digital Library (LDL)	Documentation Research & Training Centre (DRTC)	https://drtc.isibang.ac.in/	236	Research Papers, Articles, Reports, etc.	DSpace
DSpace at GBPUAT University	G.B. Pant University of Agriculture & Technology	http://202.141.116.205/dspace/	82	Research Papers, Articles, Reports, Thesis, etc.	DSpace
IIA Repository	Indian Institute of Astrophysics	http://prints.iiap.res.in/	725	Research Papers, Articles, Reports, Thesis, etc.	DSpace
EPrints@IIITA	Indian Institute of Information Technology, Allahabad	http://eprints.iiita.ac.in/	22	Research Papers, Articles, Reports, etc.	EPrints
DSpace@IIMK	Indian Institute of Management, Kozhikode (IIMK)	http://dspace.iimk.ac.in/	133	Research Papers, Articles, Reports, etc.	DSpace
EPrints@IIMK	Kozhikode (IIMK) Indian Institute of Management,	http://eprints.iimk.ac.in/	25	Research Papers, Articles, Reports, etc.	EPrints
EPrints@IISc	Indian Institute of Science (IISC)	http://eprints.iisc.ernet.in/	3645	Research Papers, Articles, Reports, etc.	EPrints
ETD@IISc	Indian Institute of Science (IISC)	http://etd.ncsi.iisc.cern.et.in/	153	Theses & Dissertations	DSpace
EPrints@IITD	Institute of Technology, Delhi (IITD)	http://eprint.iitd.ac.in/dspace/	1296	Indian Research Papers, Articles, Reports, etc.	DSpace
DSpace at INSA	Indian National Science Academy (INSA)	http://61.16.154.195/dspace/	818	Conference Papers, Articles, Reports, etc.	DSpace
ISI Library, Bangalore	Indian Statistical Institute, Bangalore	http://library.isibang.ac.in:8080/dspace/	10	Research Papers, Articles, Reports, etc.	DSpace
DSpace at INFLIBNET	INFLIBNET	http://dspace.inflibnet.ac.in	428	Research Papers, Articles, Reports, etc.	DSpace
NAL Institutional Repository	National Aerospace Laboratories (NAL)	http://nal-ir.nal.res.in/	418	Research Papers, Articles, Reports, etc.	EPrints
DSpace at NCRA	National Centre for Radio Astrophysics	http://ncralib.ncra.tifr.res.in/dspace/	22	Research Papers, Articles, Reports, Thesis, etc.	DSpace
EPrints at NCL	National Chemical Laboratory (NCL)	http://dspace.ncl.res.in/	290	Theses, Research Papers, Articles, Reports, etc.	DSpace
OpenMED@NIC	National Informatics Centre (NIC)	http://openmed.nic.in/	1035	Research Papers, Articles, Reports,	EPrints
Digital Repository Service of NIO	National Institute of Oceanography	http://drs.nio.org/drs/	55	Journal articles, conference proceeding articles, Technical reports, thesis, dissertations, etc.	DSpace
DSpace@NITR	National Institute of Technology, Rourkela	http://dspace.nitrkl.ac.in/dspace/	223	Theses, Research Papers, Articles, Reports, etc.	DSpace
Digital Repository of RRI Research	Raman Research Institute	http://dspace.rri.res.in/	1064	Papers, Articles, Reports, Thesis, etc.	DSpace
Vidyanidhi DSpace	University of Mysore	http://www.vidyanidhi.org.in/	1835	Theses & Dissertations	DSpace

Source: Adapted from Chakraborty and Ghosh (2011).

- **Collection of indigenous information**: OER expands the scope of collection and archive of information coming from various communities.
- **Scalability**: The distribution of OER material can be expanded anytime with little or no cost.
- **Fast distribution**: OER material can be distributed very fast compared to the publishing of a book or journal or any other learning material.
- **Low cost**: OER is comparatively very low cost compared to traditional books or educational material packages.
- **The flexibility of change or modification**: Unlike textbooks or other static educational material OER is very flexible in the context of change or modification of content material.
- **Translate learning material**: In the context of OER, resources can be translated into any language in a very flexible manner.
- **Ensure learning as a public property**: By OER, it can be ensured that publicly funded resources are available to the public.

Disadvantages of OER

- **Quality control**: As OER is an open repository to provide learning material, therefore, it opens the scope to create an account and post-learning material by anyone in the world. As a result, some material may not be relevant or accurate so it can increase the quality issues in the context of OER.
- **Technological issues**: The majority of open educational resources are based on internet access. However, in the context of a developing country, there is a scarcity of sufficient internet or a lack of high-speed internet. Besides, some of the resources may require some additional software that students do not have or are not able to afford.
- **Copyright concern**: Another biggest issue in the context of OER is its "fair use". As open educational resources are open-sharing approaches of any educational material, therefore, it can increase the concern about intellectual property or copyright issues.
- **Sustainability and upgradation issues**: Since those who are creating open educational resources do not get any monetary support for their development, therefore, it may be the initiative of a developer to update their learning material as a future initiative.
- **Language and cultural barriers**: As per open educational resources there is a huge concern about the language and cultural barriers in the context of available learning material. However, a lot of initiative is being taken currently to encounter these issues by developing learning material in multiple languages that are culture-free.
- **Lack of human interaction between teacher and student**: OER material is designed to access outside the classroom environment. As a result, it can decrease the interaction between a teacher and a student and a student may find it hard to find out how to solve a specific problem related to the learning material if required.

Bibliography

BOAI. (2002). Budapest open access initiative. Retrieved April 18, 2018, from http://www.soros.org/openaccess/read.shtml.

Chakraborty, S., & Ghosh, S. B. (2011). Open resources for higher education: The Indian scenario. *Proceedings of the IATUL Conferences*, Paper 32. http://docs.lib.purdue.edu/iatul/2011/papers/32.

Commonwealth of Learning. (2017, July 20). *Open educational resources (OER)*. Retrieved from https://www.thecommonwealth-educationhub.net/oer/.

DeBarger, A., & Redstone Strategy Group. (2016, August 3). Education, education, & education. *Open educational resources*. Retrieved from https://hewlett.org/strategy/open-educational-resources/.

Neil, B. (1970, January 1). A basic guide to open educational resources (OER). Retrieved from http://oasis.col.org/handle/11599/36.

Neil, B. (2015). A basic guide to open educational resources (OER). Retrieved from http://www.unesco.org/new/en/communication-and-information/resources/publications-and-communication-materials/publications/full-list/a-basic-guide-to-open-educational-resources-oer/.

Open Educational Resources (OER). (2018, October 23). Retrieved from https://en.unesco.org/themes/building-knowledge-societies/oer.

Wikieducator OER Handbook. (n.d.). Retrieved from http://wikieducator.org/OER_Handbook.

Wikipedia. (2019). Retrieved from https://en.wikipedia.org/wiki/Copyright.

Suggested Readings

Bonk, C. J., Lee, M. M., Reeves, T. C., & Reynolds, T. H. (2015). *MOOCs and open education around the world*. New York: Routledge

D'Antoni, S., Savage, C., & UNESCO. (2009). *Open educational resources: Conversations in cyberspace*. Paris: UNESCO.

Dominic, O., Michele, R., & Dirk, D. (2015). *Educational research and innovation open educational resources a catalyst for innovation: A catalyst for innovation*.

Green, T. D., & Brown, A. H. (2017). *The educator's guide to producing new media and open educational resources*. Routledge

Miao, F., Mishra, S., & McGreal, R. (2016). *Open educational resources: Policy, costs, transformation*. Paris: UNESCO, Commonwealth of Learning.

Okada, A. (2012). *Collaborative learning 2.0: Open educational resources: Open educational resources*. IGI Pub

PART IV
Emerging Trends

25
COMPUTER IN EDUCATION AND ITS APPLICATION

Introduction

Metaphorically one can say that "we are living in the future" because the innovations that were hard to imagine some decades ago are now our reality and we are living with it. The computer is the kind of innovation that changed our lifestyle, culture, socio-economic background, etc. The computer is one of the greatest innovations of this era. The computer brings various changes in our education system and its impact on methods of teaching and learning as well as educational management and administration. The present chapter discusses computers and their functions and application in education.

Meaning and Definitions of Computer

In a simplistic way, it can be said that a computer is an electronic device intended to work with information. The term "computer" is derived from the Latin term "comutare" which means calculate or programmable machine. From this term, one can say that a computer can only function in the context of some pre-defined programming. The following are some of the definitions of a computer:

Vermaat (2013): "A computer is an electronic device, operating under the control of instructions stored in its memory that can accept data (input), process the data according to specified rules, produce information (output), and store the information for future use".
Microsoft® Encarta® (2009): "Computer, a machine that performs tasks, such as calculations or electronic communication, under the control of a set of instructions is called a program".
Oxford University Press (2000): "An electronic machine that can store, organize and find information, do calculations and control other machines".
Merriam-Webster dictionary: "A programmable usually electronic device that can store, retrieve, and process data".

Characteristics of a Computer

From the above definition, one can see that a computer is a powerful tool that can complete various tasks accurately and consistently and can store and retrieve a large amount of data instantaneously. This section discusses various characteristics of computers that make this device so unique and powerful, they are the following:

Accuracy

One of the greatest characteristics of a computer is accuracy. That means a computer can produce information and work accurately over time if there is no human error in the context of developed programming.

Consistent in Nature

Another essential characteristic of a computer is consistency. That means a computer can work repeatedly and consistently without human limitations such as boredom and tiredness.

High Speed

This is a significant characteristic of a computer that can produce information very fast, for example, a powerful computer can calculate with 3–4 million simple pieces of information at a time.

Multiple Functions

Besides speed, computers can perform various works at a time, for example, they can work as a learning device, and parallelly one can watch movies, news, and listen to the radio in the device at the same time.

Storage Device

Another essential characteristic of a computer is its large volume of storage capability. A powerful computer can store an abundance of information that can be retrieved instantly.

Computer-Assisted Instruction (CAI)

The term CAI denotes "Computer-Assisted Instruction". Computer-assisted instruction means the use of computer devices to carry out an instruction which is sometimes also called computer-aided instruction. Simply, one can say that CAI is a specific type of instruction that makes use of computers in education. Throughout the historical overview of instruction in education, it seems that the method of instruction has evolved over time. Sometimes instruction is lecture-oriented, sometimes project-based, and sometimes individualistic as well as computer-assisted. In that sense, CAI is an instructional process through which purposeful instruction happens between the learner and the computer to achieve the desired instructional objectives.

Definitions of CAI

Bhatt and Sharma (1992): "CAI is an interaction between a student, a computer-controlled display and a response entry device to achieve the educational outcomes".
Hilgard and Bower (1977): "Computer-assisted instruction has now taken so many dimensions that it can no longer be considered as a simple derivative of the teaching machine or the kind of programmed learning that Skinner introduced".

Cotton (2001): Explained that "CAI is a narrower term and most often refers to drill and practice, tutorial, or simulation activities offered either by themselves or as a supplement to traditional, teacher-directed instruction".

Characteristics of Computer-Assisted Instruction

A computer is a powerful tool and when it is used for educational purposes it can change the way of instruction and the learning process. The following are some of the characteristics of computer-assisted instruction.

Interactivity

One of the essential characteristics of computer-assisted instruction is interactivity. Interactive means students can interact with a computer in various aspects. For instance, they can work with a computer, get instant feedback from the computer, and instantly evaluate their performance through the computer. It is a systematic process and interaction between computer devices, teaching material, and learners. It can automatically produce instant feedback to the learner with some encouraging words like "ok", "very good", "you did it correctly", or "excellent" etc. That can produce reinforcement to the learner in the context of their performance.

Individuality

Another unique characteristic of computer-assisted instruction is it encourages the individual aspect of the learner. Individual aspect means a learner can perform based on their own pace and own learning style. Through computer-assisted instruction, it is possible to produce individual instructional material for the learner as per their own needs and capability.

Multimedia-Based

Computer-assisted instruction is mainly multimedia-based. Multimedia includes graphics, sound, animation, motion, film, clips, and various other features. All of these features of media help to make computer-assisted instruction more sophisticated and interesting in the context of teaching-learning.

Small Chunk Content

The content material involved in computer-assisted instructions is mainly based on the principle of small steps. That means the overall content material is broken into small chunks, sections, subsections, units, etc. By these characteristics of CAI, a learner can perform very effectively through a step-by-step learning approach.

Use of Narrator

Computer-assisted instruction can be equipped with a guideline narrator which can help the learner by narrating the topic of content or it can direct the learner on how to use the specific learning package.

Basic Assumptions of CAI

Computer-assisted instruction is based on the following assumptions of learning:

- **Instruction to a mass number of learners at a time through an individualized learning approach**: It is scientifically proven that a learner can perform better when they perform individually at their own pace. In this context, computer-assisted instruction helps to produce a learning environment that encourages the individualistic approach to learning and at the same time can provide education to thousands of learners at a time. Through computer-assisted instruction, learners can choose their learning material based on their ability and interest in a particular subject or topic. Besides computers can help to provide instructional material in an individualized way. Therefore, it can be said that computer-assisted instruction can provide quality instruction to a large number of people by considering individual differentiation.
- **Instant feedback and automatic recording of learner performance**: Another assumption is that learners can perform better when they can get a response immediately. Besides this, another assumption is that by tracking the learner performance an instructor can get desired knowledge and make a prediction about student learning for the future. Computer-assisted instruction can produce instant feedback to the learner regarding their performance and can record it for evaluation. That is helpful for further planning instructions for the learner for more effective instruction.
- **Use of multiple media can help enhance performance and engagement in learning**: Computer-assisted instruction is based on an assumption that learners can perform better when they use multiple components of media in their learning process rather than just using a single component of media. The learning material which is based on computer-assisted instruction is consistent with multiple types of media like graphics, sound, text, vector graphics, video clips, etc. Besides this, computer-assisted instruction can produce various strategies and methods of learning at a time such as program learning, drills, practice, etc.

Types or Modes of Computer-Assisted Instruction

Computer-assisted instruction can be divided into the following types based on their functions.

Information on Instruction

This type of CAI provides the learner with the desired information effectively. In this context, the computer functions as an information office that is responsible to retrieve the pre-stored information to the learner based on their input. This type of computer-assisted instruction provides very limited opportunities for interaction between students and computer programming. The major purpose of this type of instructional process is to provide essential knowledge and skills to the learner through self-learning instruction.

Drill and Practice

Computer-assisted instruction can provide a learning environment where students can drill and practice their lessons effectively. These features of computer-assisted instruction can help the learner practice the instructional material which they have already learned. For example, a student can practice various math problems over time with instant feedback. Drill and practice are a continuous process in a computer-assisted instruction system until the student achieves mastery.

Discovery Method

This type of computer-assisted instruction mainly focuses on the problem-solving aspect of student learning. In this mode of instruction, a problem is presented before the student and they are asked to discover the solution through the trial-and-error method. In this, the computer works as a support instrument to find the best possible solution. This is based on the inductive method of teaching principle.

Tutorial Method

This is another mode of the computer-assisted instruction process. In this mode computer functions and engages in actual teaching. In this method, the computer maintains interaction and dialogue with an individual student. Here, the computer provides an environment for the learner where they can learn at their own pace, ability, and requirement. Only if the student is mastering specific content, the computer provides the next step of instruction otherwise it provides remedial instruction.

Game-Based and Simulation

This type of computer-assisted instruction is mainly based on the principle of gamification or game-based learning. In this mode of instruction, students are provided with a well-designed learning platform which is developed by considering various principles of the game. The major aim of this kind of instruction is to provide an intellectual challenge, stimulation of curiosity, and urge to achieve various levels of learning through self-motivation. Various rewards, badges, and accomplishments are provided as reinforcement for such kind of computer-assisted learning.

Simulation-Based

Simulation provides a teaching-learning environment that is near to a real-life scenario. It provides a representation of real-life situations, phenomena, and processes in a learning environment. This kind of computer-assisted instruction provides an opportunity for the learner to perform in a realistic environment without time, expenses, and the risk associated with a real situation. In a simplistic view, one can say that simulation provides a safe learning environment where a student can feel free to perform.

Theoretical Foundation of Computer-Assisted Instruction

The application of any strategies or technological devices should have a strong base of theoretical justification of existing knowledge postulated by various researchers. As learning is a complex phenomenon it is, therefore, required to get an understanding of how the application of devices works in the context of modification of the behavior of a learner. Figure 25.1 presents the process of computer-assisted instruction (CAI). Computer-assisted instructional process is based on various theoretical foundations such as behaviorist, cognitivist, constructivist, and their interrelation or connections. The subsequent section will discuss briefly each of the theories and their application in CAI.

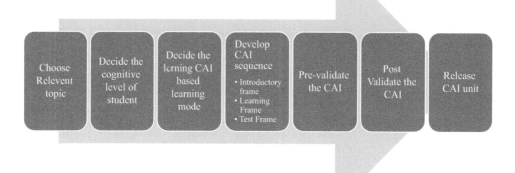

Figure 25.1 Process of computer-assisted instruction.

As a student of education, one is well aware that the majority of educationists and researchers, tried to answer some of the basic philosophical questions related to learning such as what is meant by learning? How does learning takes place? What elements or factors affect the process of learning? How it can be made more effective, etc. In the past, all such questions related to learning have been attempted to answer through the focal point of the "objectivist theoretical approach" and "connectivist" theoretical approach.

These two theoretical aspects describe the questions related to learning from their philosophical focal point and there is a certain degree of differentiation between these two approaches (Roblyer and Edward, 2000). From the computer-assisted instructional point of view, both approaches support and discuss how computer-assisted instruction is an effective platform to promote teaching and learning effectively.

The objective point of view, which emphasized mainly direct instruction, as well as systematic and structured instruction, focused on two learning theories namely:

1. Behavioral Theories
2. Cognitivist Theories

Behavioral Theories

Behavioral theorists believe that learning is a mechanism of interaction between stimulus and response. They also believe that learning is a process of behavioral change of the learner which is measurable. Behaviorists also believed that the mind is a reservoir of information and the idea and structure of the real world, in general, is an independent understanding of a learner.

In the context of the ideological aspect, the behavioral theorist can be divided into the following two categories:

1. Contiguity Theorist
2. Reinforcement Theorist

Contiguity Theorist

Contiguity theorists generally believe that the combination of stimuli affects the process of responding to the learner. Contiguity theories did not give major emphasis on positive or negative reinforcement such as rewards or punishment to make an association between stimulus and response. Edwin Gutherie was the chief proponent of the contiguity theory.

Reinforcement Theorist

Reinforcement theorists emphasized the aspect of reinforcement to strengthen the connections between stimulus and response. As per the reinforcement theorist, reinforcement can be provided positively as well as negatively. A stimulus occurring through positive reinforcement is called "conditioned positive reinforcement" and in the same way if the stimulus occurred through negative reinforcement it is called "conditioned negative reinforcement".

Application of Behaviorism in the Context of CAI

One of the greatest applications of behaviorist theories in CAI is the specification and predetermination of the learning goal. As per behaviorism if a learner can understand what exactly they are going to learn and how it will meet their expectation, the learner automatically responds toward a predetermined goal. Besides, behaviorists emphasized that behavioral change is measurable, therefore, by applying the principle of behavior the outcome based on CAI is also measurable. By following the principle of behaviorism, the subject matter of CAI is also presented in small steps and each step consisting of questions and responses can be reinforced through the positive and negative aspects of reinforcement.

Cognitive Theories

The CAI environment is mostly influenced by cognitive theories. Cognitive theories mostly dealt with the processing of information and functions of the mind, memory, etc. The principle concern of cognitive theorists is how humans process information from external stimuli, how short- and long-term memory store information, how the encoding and decoding process of information occurs, how the retrieval of information happens in the brain, how virtual and audio information process differently, how cognitive load affect the brain, etc.

Application of Cognitive Theories in CAI

Generally, the theoretical knowledge of cognition is applied in the development and design of CAI-based learning modules. Various scientific factors are taken into consideration to develop instructional material such as:

- How a specific learning objective can be defined (Gagne, R.M., 1984).
- How to design a learning material so that it processes quickly and interacts with long-term memory.
- How an instructional designer can design a specific learning material so that, it can help to decode the learner very effectively?

- In which medium (audio, video, interactive) a learning material can be developed to process easily and effectively?
- How a learning material or computer-based software can be developed so that it can reduce the cognitive load of learners?

Generally, cognitive theories provide a pathway to develop effective CAI. Teachers or instructional designers can follow cognitive theories for the development and presentation of learning materials. Cognitive theories deal with the attention of learners' metacognition, elaboration, coding and decoding abilities, etc.

Constructivism

Another great theory that influences the field of CAI is constructivism. Generally, great educationists such as Max Wertheimer, Jean Piaget, Jerome Brunner, Albert Bandura are some of the major theorists of constructivism. Constructivism gives major emphasis on the active construction of knowledge by a learner in the context of their realization of the world. Constructivist believes that learners can create their mental model based on the experience they have gained, prior knowledge, beliefs, etc. Learning occurs through the creation of a mental model. Constructivism generally believes in the following:

- The learner creates his or her mental schema or representations.
- Any aspect of the construction of knowledge is made based on the experience of the learner.
- Learning is actively searching for meaning.

Application of the Constructivist Approach to CAI

Based on the constructivist approach, the application of computers as a technology in the context of education is mainly as follows:

- From the cognitivist point of view, a computer is taken as a cognitive tool to enhance the teaching and learning process.
- The role of a computer will be an enhancement mechanism to accelerate the learning process.

As a cognitive tool computers will enhance the cognitive power of learners in the context of their thinking, problem-solving, etc. Therefore, in this orientation computers will promote productivity in the learning process through the features of the network, research, problem-solving, etc.

From the cognitivist point of view, Duffy and Cunningham (1996) explained that "culture creates tools, but tools change the culture". In this context, the computer can function as a tool as well as a sign that can participate to create a culture of the overall learning process and can also change the overall existing culture of learning as per requirement.

Connectivism

Connectivism is a recent learning theory introduced in 2004 by Gorge Siemens and Stephens Downes. This theory is developed based on technological development and learning network.

Connectivism theory accumulated various ideas from "chaos theory", "self-organization", "network", etc. George Siemens (2005) discussed that "connectivism theories do not address learning that occurs outside people (learning that is stored and manipulated by technology). They also fail to describe how learning happens within an organization. One can no longer personally experience and acquire learning that one needs to act. One derives our competence from forming connections".

According to Siemens (2005), the elements of network learning are:

- Content (data or information).
- Interaction (forming tentative connections).
- Dynamic nodes (continuously changing based on new data, since knowledge does change over time).
- Self-updating nodes (nodes tightly linked to the original information source).
- Emotive element (emotions that influence the prospect of connection).

Generally, knowledge is formed when the connections between nodes and the network of nodes are established.

Application of Connectivism in CAI

As we see the theory of connectivism provides a new insightful orientation regarding the facilitation of learning in the digital age. They focused on learning through networking. The following are some of the applicability of CAI in the context of connectivism:

- Connectivism believes in the generation of knowledge through diverse options. Computer-based instruction also helps to promote learning in a diverse community.
- In connectivism Siemens emphasized the connection of nodes or information sources to promote the effective learning process. Taking this aspect into consideration, in a classroom situation through CAI a teacher can connect learners from various demography and community in a single computer-based learning platform.
- Another focal point in the connectivism aspect is the learner's ability to connect ideas, concepts, and skills. In that way, CAI can connect the diverse idea of the learner through a collaborative learning approach.

Various Concepts Related to the Computer in Education

Computer-Assisted/Aided Instruction (CAI) or Computer-Assisted Learning (CAL): "Computer-assisted instruction (CAI) also called computer-aided instruction (CAI) is a narrower meaning and most often refers to drill and practice, tutorial, or simulation activities offered either by themselves or as supplements to traditional, teacher-directed instruction" (cited by Cotton, 2008).

Computer-Based Education (CBE) and Computer-Based Instruction (CBI): "CBE and CBI broadly refer to virtually any kind of computer use in educational settings, including drill and practice, tutorials, simulations, instructional management, supplementary exercises, programming, database development, writing using word processors, and other applications. These terms may refer either to stand-alone computer learning activities or to computer activities which reinforce material introduced and taught by teachers" (quoted Cotton, 2008).

Computer Enriched Instruction (CEI): "is defined as learning activities in which computers (1) generate data at the students' request to illustrate relationships in models of social or physical reality, (2) execute programs developed by the students, or (3) provide general enrichment in relatively unstructured exercises designed to stimulate and motivate students" (quoted in the paper by Cotton, 2008).

Computer-Managed Instruction (CMI): This is the administrative part of an instructional process through the computer. In this context, a computer is used by organizational staff or instructors to evaluate through test student performance, provide instruction for required appropriate instructional material, track student progress and keep a record of student performance (discussed by Cotton, 2008).

Computer-Based Training (CBT): CBT is generally a computer-based training approach where one of the essential instruments is a computer through which specific training is provided to the learner. This is a software-based approach and the CBT-based learning material called courseware. (Defined by Cotton, 2008)

Computer-Managed Learning (CML): CML is a learning platform where a computer system managed and administer a teaching and learning framework where a learner performs or interact with an overall process such as enrolment, selection of learning module, study material, etc., as per the guideline provided by a pre-defined computer program. Here computer manages the assessment and feedback of learner responses simultaneously (discussed in Cotton, 2008).

New Terminology

Web-Based Training (WBT): Web-based training is another innovative approach in teaching and learning. This is generally effective for the distance mode of teaching and learning scenarios. This is a similar conception to computer-based training the only difference is that WBT is an online platform where instructional material is provided through hypermedia.

Web-Based Learning (WBL): Web-based learning or WBL is also called online learning. This is generally a web-based instructional approach through various online-based techniques such as forums, instant messaging, live video conferencing, etc. Furthermore, in WBL educational resources can be provided through web pages in printable format or online access mode.

Web-Based Instruction (WBI): "Web-based instruction (WBI) is a hypermedia-based instructional program which utilizes the attributes and resources of the World Wide Web to create a meaningful learning environment where learning is fostered and supported" (Khan, 1997).

Instructor-Led Training (ILT): Instructor-led training or ILT is generally an instructional approach where the training of any instructional courses happens through the real-time interaction between instructor and learner. This kind of training can be provided to the individual or group.

Web-Based Training (WBT): Web-based training is different from ILT. WBT is generally a self-paced teaching and learning approach. This is a kind of asynchronous learning approach where there are very limited facilities for real-time collaboration.

Table 25.1 Advantages and Disadvantages of Computer-Based Instructional Visualization

Advantages	Disadvantages
Increases interest and motivation.	Less motivated learners can fall behind.
CAI is a compatible learning style.	Without adequate proper training, the student may be confused about course activities and deadlines.
It can provide immediate feedback and reinforcement.	Students may feel isolated from the instructor and other peers.
It can instantly analyze the error of the learner and can provide remedies.	Students may not get help in the context of immediate confusion and required help.
It can provide an opportunity for personalized learning as well as collaborative learning.	A slow internet connection or slow computer may lead to frustration for the learner in accessing course materials.
CAI is an outcome-oriented process.	Managing advanced-level CAI required advanced-level computer skills which are very limited in the context of a developing country.
It can increase the effective communication of learners.	The initial setup of CAI is very costly.
Promote enthusiasm.	Overuse of multimedia-based instruction may lead to distraction from specific learning objectives.

Advantages and Disadvantages of CAI in Education

Table 25.1 shows some of the advantages and disadvantages of computer-based instruction in education:

Bibliography

Bhatt, B. D., & Sharma, S. R. (1992). *Educational technology*. New Delhi: Kanishka Publishing House.

Cotton, K. (2001). *Computer-assisted instruction*. North West Regional Educational Laboratory. Retrieved from http://www.nwrel.org/scpd/sirs/5/cu10.html.

Cotton, K. (2008). Computer-assisted instruction. *Encyclopedia of Special Education*, 514–520. https://doi.org/10.1002/9780470373699.speced0481

Duffy, T. M., & Cunningham, D. J. (1996). Constructivism: Implications for the Design and Delivery of Instruction. In D. H. Jonassen (Ed.), *Handbook of Research for Educational Communications and Technology*. NY: Macmillan Library Reference USA.

Encarta, M. (2009). *Microsoft Encarta premium*. https://www.shouldiremoveit.com/microsoft-encarta-premium-2009-31598-program.aspx

Gagne, R. & Driscoll, M. (1988). *Essentials of Learning for Instruction* (2nd Ed.). Englewood Cliffs, NJ: Prentice-Hall.

Gagne, R., Briggs, L. & Wager, W. (1992). *Principles of Instructional Design (4th Ed.)*. Fort Worth, TX: HBJ College Publishers.

Hilgard, E. R., & Bower, G. H. (1966). *Theories of learning* (3rd ed.). New York: Appleton-Century-Crofts.

Khan, B.H. (1997) Web-Based Instruction: What Is It and Why Is It? In: B.H. Khan, Ed., *Web-Based Instruction, Educational Technology Publications* pp. 5–18. Englewood Cliffs.

Microsoft® Encarta®. (2009). Retrieved from http://microsoftencarta-in english.blogspot.com/2009/01/computer.html.

Roblyer, M. D., & Edwards, J. (2000). *Integrating educational technology into teaching* (2nd Ed.). Upper Saddle River, NJ: Prentice-Hall, Inc

Siemens, G. (2005). Connectivism: A learning theory for the digital age. *International Journal of Instructional Technology & Distance Learning*, 2, 3–10.

Vermaat, M. E. (2013). *Discovering computers & Microsoft Office 2013: A fundamental combined approach* (1st ed). Lydia: Cengage Learning.

Suggested Reading

Banerjee, U. K. (1996). *Computer education in India: Past, present and future.* New Delhi: Concept Publishing Company.

Jain, A. (2005). *Computer in education.* New Delhi: Gyan Publishing House.

Kelsey, S. (Ed.). (2011). *Computer-mediated communication: Issues and approaches in education: Issues and approaches in education.* IGI Global.

Singh, U. K., & Sudarshan, K. N. (1996). *Computer education.* New Delhi: Discovery Publishing.

Watson, P. G. (1972). Using the computer in education: A briefing for school decision-makers. Educational Technology Publications, Inc, 18(4), 47–49.

26
INFORMATION COMMUNICATION TECHNOLOGY (ICT) IN EDUCATION

Introduction

The term ICT is an acronym for "Information Communication Technologies". Information Communication Technology (ICT) together was first introduced in the early 1980s. However, in the late 1990s, major emphasis was given to communication then ICT. ICT also refers to as Information Technology (IT) is limited to only computers or the internet. Australasia uses the term IT&T instead of ICT, and Singapore uses the term Z "Infocomm" for ICT. In some countries, ICT refers to information and content technology. However, here the foremost question is what is ICT? Whether it is possible to integrate ICT into classroom processes? What are the efforts made by the department in this direction? What do various organizations and government policies say about ICT in education? These are some of the important questions one needs to probe into to understand ICT and its effect on our society as well as education. The present chapter aims to answer this question with a detailed discussion.

Meaning and Definitions of ICT

As discussed, Information Communication Technology or ICT is combined with three terms "information", that refers to the knowledge obtained from reading, investigation, study, or research. Besides this there is "communication", that refers to information exchanged between individuals using symbols, signs, or verbal instructions, thus it is the transmission of the message. "Technology" refers to the use of scientific knowledge, experience, and resources to create processes and products that fulfill human needs. In a combined way, one can say ICT is concerned with any storage, retrieval, manipulation, transmission, or receipt of digital data. ICT has been defined in many ways by various organizations and researchers. These are the following:

SER (1997): "ICT is a generic term referring to technologies, that are being used for collecting, storing, editing and passing on information in various forms".
QCA Scheme of Work for ICT (2000): "ICTs are the computing and communication facilities and features that supports teaching, learning and a range of activities in education."
British Computer Society (2008): "ICT as a scientific, technological, and engineering discipline as well as management technologies that help in processing, handling, and dis-

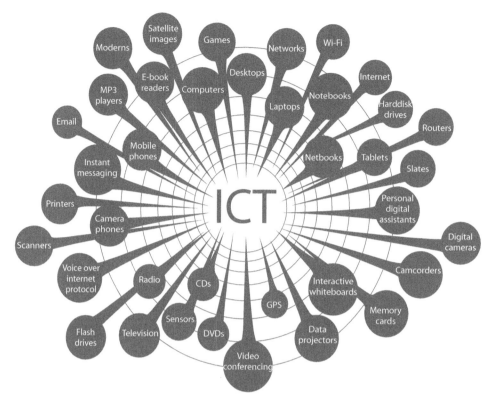

Figure 26.1 Representation of ICT and its various uses. Source: Adapted from UNESCO (2010).

seminating of information along with their applications; computers, networking, and communication. This process integrates men and machines and associated social, economic, and cultural aspects" (Cited by Harris et al., 2008).

Turban et al. (2002) define ICT as "an organization and management process of information resources and their uses. It includes the IT infrastructure and all other information systems in the organization".

From the above definitions, ICT can be defined comprehensively as follows:

ICT is a technology of information processing through electronic computers, communication devices, and application software such as radio, television, cellular phones, computer, and network hardware and software, satellite systems, etc., which helps to convert, store, protect, process, transmit, and retrieve information from anywhere, anytime.

ICT is often used in a particular field or context such as ICT in education, ICT in healthcare, ICT in libraries, etc.

ICT in Education

"*Information communication technology in education is the processing of information and its communication facilities and features that variously support teaching, learning, and range of activities in education*". (https://edufocus.blogspot.com/p/information-technology.html)

Table 26.1 ICT tools in education

Input Source	Output Source	Others
Visualizer/ camera	Projector	Digital camera
Personal computer/tablet	Interactive whiteboard	Switcher
Student response system	Display monitor	Digital recorder
Application software	Television, radio	Other technology

Henceforth, it is necessary to know that "ICT" is "information and communication technology" and "ICT in education" means "teaching, learning, and educational activity through ICT". ICT in education tools can be divided into three categories input source, output source, and other. Table 26.1 presents ICT tools for education. Table 26.1 presents the ICT tools in education.

Characteristics of ICT in Education

Information communication technology is one of the most effective weapons to help to revolutionize the 21st-century education system. Laudon and Laudon (2010) stated that one of the most important drives behind globalization is ICT. They explained the following major characteristics of ICT in education:

1. **Ubiquitous learning**: One of the major characteristics of ICT in the field of education is it helps to provide the opportunity of learning to students globally irrespective of their global boundary that means anyone can learn anytime and anywhere.
2. **Personalized learning**: In teaching-learning scenarios, one of the major challenges is individual differences. The use of ICT is encouraged to personalize learning and tailor the teaching process to address the learning gap, pace of learning, and learning style of learners.
3. **Open educational resource**: ICT in the field of education increases the opportunity to assess open educational resources from any corner of the world. It helps to create network opportunities between teachers and students to identify the learning resources that they find more effective for learning.
4. **Use of modern devices**: ICT increases the opportunity to use a range of digital devices such as computers, laptops, smartphones, etc., which in turn helps in the teaching-learning process.
5. **Interactivity**: Another characteristic of ICT in education is the emphasis on interactivity. In the present situation education is more reciprocal rather than one-way communication. The use of various devices related to information and communication increases the opportunity for interactive communication in the teaching and learning process.
6. **Schooling opportunities for both formal and informal settings**: ICT broadens the thinking process, now students are members of a bigger community or the global school where one can select their learning material, institution, and teacher based on their choice, that means there are no more boundaries of four walls like in a traditional classroom.

Scopes of ICT in Education

Professional development: Professional development is one of the key elements in the teaching-learning process. ICT expands the scope for professional development and also upgrades the teacher and the student with the help of various online training, virtual workshop, the use of modern devices, etc.

Lifelong learning: Education is a continuous and lifelong process. Students must learn throughout their life span, not only for a specific period. Therefore, ICT is a revolutionary approach that expands the scope of learning. Currently, anyone can learn anything at any stage of his or her life.

Universal accessibility and quality of learning: In the teaching-learning scenario one of the major barriers is universal accessibility of education. Because of geographical, economical, or physical hindrances a huge number of students are still out of school and unable to access quality education. ICT expands the scope as now education is open to all without any boundary.

Open educational resource: Open educational resource (OER) is an educational movement of the 21st century. The major aim of this movement is to open universal access to "world-class educational resources to all through ICT". Therefore, the open education resource movement is one of the major scopes of ICT.

Educational management and evaluation: The scope of ICT is also in the educational management and evaluation process. Using various ICT tools in the educational management process helps save time and labor and decreases errors. Besides, the student evaluation process is dramatically changed by the use of modern ICT tools namely "learning analytics" that continuously evaluate students' performance and diagnose the problem of students based on their academic performance through day-to-day activity and thereby suggest possible remedies to the teacher.

Expand educational opportunity: ICT helps to spread education to the masses and expands the educational opportunity. Now even a student from a rural remote village can access education by using ICT tools.

Inclusiveness: Inclusiveness is another major scope of ICT. Now diverse student groups can take part or be included in the same educational process irrespective of disability, economic, demographical barriers/limitations, etc. Figure 26.2 presents the scope of ICT in education.

Figure 26.2 Scope of ICT in education.

Increasing competence and enhancing skill acquisition: In the last 15 decades, the teaching-learning environment has dramatically changed. However, to effectively survive in this field teachers and students need to adopt effective skills and strategies. Various tools of ICT provide scope to the teacher as well as the learner.

Enhance the quality of learning and teaching: ICT increases the scope to use plenty of teacher learning gadgets and instructional strategies such as computers, smartphones, multimedia-based instructions, and game-based learning, which in turn enhances the quality of teaching-learning.

Creativity exploration: Student creativity is a matter of concern in 21st-century learning because of the knowledge economy. Thus, the teacher needs to care about nurturing the creativity of the student. In this viewpoint, ICT provides huge scope to the learner regarding flourishing their creativity and extending it throughout the world.

Maintain community relationship or linkage: Networking and virtual community creation is another crucial scope of ICT. By using this, one can maintain community relationships as well as links to other community members.

Application of ICT in Education

Distance education and open learning: Distance education and open education are some of the innovative approaches in the field of education. It helps to narrow down the gap between geographical and affordability barriers to education access. The use of ICT in the field of distance and open education is revolutionary because it enhances the quality of education as well as makes the learning environment more interactive. Presently massive open online course (MOOC) is the largest online distance and open learning environment which is fully ICT based.

Classroom-based application: The classroom-based teaching-learning applications of ICT dramatically changed it to make it more innovative. For instance, the teacher can now use ICT-based gadgets or devices such as computers, mobile phones, whiteboard technology, etc. to present abstract or difficult content more effectively to the students. It changes classroom communication from one way to more interactive. Besides, the teacher applies ICT to access lesson plans, network with other teachers, pedagogical techniques, and information resources.

Technical and vocal training: ICT in the field of technical and vocational education increases the opportunity to train workers with various modern technology and simultaneous approaches. For instance, by using ICT students can get real-time field-based experience in the classroom environment.

Educational testing and evaluation: The application of ICT in education changes the process of student evaluation and testing. Learning analytics is one of the innovative approaches based on ICT technology that helps to track and diagnose students' activity and performance in more detail and provides possible future predictions and remedies.

Educational administration: ICT also applies in educational management and administration such as student admission and tracking, financial management of the educational organization, data record, distribution and management, library record, placement cell, progress report, etc.

Scientific research and publication: Research and development (R&D) is a major aspect of any organizational development. ICT applies in the field of educational research and publication in various ways such as through the use of the internet, Google, the creation of a virtual research community, collaboration with other researchers and projects, information distribution and publication, etc.

Technological Pedagogical Content Knowledge (TPACK)

The previous discussion on the topic throws light on ICT and some of its applications. The present section is going to provide some knowledge about how one can integrate structural knowledge of ICT in the teaching and learning process. This section will discuss a very famous framework in the context of teaching with technology that is Technological Pedagogical Content Knowledge (TPACK).

One knows that teaching is complex for it requires advanced level skills and knowledge to promote effectively. Furthermore, in a changing scenario where technology is ubiquitous and in an educational scenario lots of different advanced-level teaching learning devices penetrate, a teacher faces various challenges to keep up with the application of modern advanced technological devices in a classroom situation. The use of technology in a classroom apart from the advantages also has side effects. Sometimes it effectively promotes learning and sometimes it can create chaos in a classroom. One of the major notable aspects in both situations is the appropriate application of technology in the teaching and learning context. Teachers very often have adequate knowledge of the integration of technology compared with the application of domain-specific knowledge (Koehler and Mishra, 2009). Therefore, there would be no wonder that the teacher will have a lack of confidence in the context of the application of newly introduced technology in the classroom.

Based on these challenges Matthew Koehler and Punya Mishra described a framework in 2006 and 2008. In this framework, they have focused on the basic three components of a teacher's knowledge such as content, pedagogy, and technology (Koehler and Mishra, 2008).

Components of the TPACK Framework

In the TPACK model, the major focus is on the basic three elements such as content knowledge, pedagogical knowledge, and technological knowledge. Besides, it also discussed interaction constraint with each element. Following are a brief discussion of each element under the TPACK framework.

Content Knowledge

As discussed in the TPACK model, content knowledge is very versatile. For instance, knowledge of Geography and knowledge of History are different. Therefore, one of the essential aspects of the teacher is to be skilled in content knowledge. Content knowledge generally includes ideas, theories, knowledge of evidence, etc. (Shulman, 1986). The content knowledge is varied based on the field of study and it is the responsibility of teachers to be skilled in his or her field of expertise. Various research revealed that limited knowledge of the content of teachers may lead to misconceptions among the learner (Pfundt and Duit, 2000). Henceforth, this aspect has been taken very seriously in the model of TPACK.

Pedagogical Knowledge (PK)

Pedagogical knowledge (PK) mainly deals with the methodological aspect of teaching and learning. This also includes the purpose, values, and aims of education. Pedagogical knowledge includes an understanding of how a student learns, how can one manage a skill in the classroom, assessments of a student, etc. Furthermore, pedagogical knowledge also focuses on the design of instructional strategies as well as evaluating student understanding. If a teacher gains expertise in pedagogical knowledge, then he or she can understand how knowledge can construct, how student acquires their skills, how habits can be developed, etc. Generally, it can be said that pedagogical knowledge demands an adequate level of understanding of cognitive, social, and developmental theories of learning and their application in the classroom (Koehler and Mishra, 2009).

Technological Knowledge (TK)

In the context of technological knowledge in the TPACK framework, Koehler and Mishra (2009) explained that it is very difficult and dangerous to define technological knowledge because the technological knowledge domain is changeable and dynamic therefore, there will be chances definitions become outdated. However, the author of this framework provides a general view of technological knowledge in the TPACK framework that is, "certain ways of thinking about and working with technology can apply to all technology tools and resources" if the given definition is simplified, it can be said that Technological Knowledge (TK) is understanding and knowledge of the use of new technology in the educational context.

Technological Content Knowledge (TCK)

Technological Content Knowledge (TCK) is a general understanding of the interrelation between technology and content. It means TCK dealt with how modern technological innovation is related to various subject areas such as physics, math, chemistry, etc. In the context of the application of TCK in a classroom situation, it is required that a teacher should have adequate knowledge about the subject matter as a well deeper understanding of how technology can be applied to advent the whole aspects of subject knowledge.

Pedagogical Content Knowledge (PCK)

Koehler and Mishra (2009) discussed that Pedagogical Content Knowledge (PCK) is a similar concept as discussed by Shulman (1986). PCK is generally, knowledge of pedagogy which applies to teaching specific content knowledge. The overall procedure of TCK is very systematic as first, teachers select a subject area after that find out various ways of representation then design various strategies, required material, etc. This is generally an aspect that interrelates pedagogical knowledge and content knowledge together.

Technological Pedagogical Knowledge (TPK)

Technological Pedagogical Knowledge (TPK) mainly focuses on how technology impacts specific teaching and learning process. This is a deeper understanding of the "constraints and affordance of technology and disciplinary context within which the functions are needed" (Koehler and Mishra, 2009).

Technology, Pedagogy, and Content Knowledge (TPACK)

Technology, Pedagogy, and Content Knowledge (TPACK) is generally an emergent form of knowledge. This is beyond all three core components such as content, pedagogy, and technology

(Koehler and Mishra, 2009). TPACK is generally the interaction of content, pedagogy, and content knowledge. TPACK is a unique form of knowledge that is equipped with a combination of three elements of knowledge.

Implications of the TPACK Framework

Henceforth, TPACK is a kind of scientific framework that provides a guideline on how a teacher can skillfully integrate content, pedagogical and technological knowledge into a specific teaching and learning scenario. This is a well-known fact that the overall aspect of education emphasizes the process and knowledge as well as teacher action and their fact. TPACK generally extends and integrates three essential elements and their interaction which is essential in the context of considering teaching methods. Furthermore, the TPACK framework assists the teacher to develop a better technique to apply technology related to professional knowledge.

Challenges of Integration of ICT in Education

Many potentialities of ICT as modern technology is already discussed. However; the application of ICT in education has various limitations. This section will focus on some of the limitations or disadvantages of ICT which can be categorized into three -sub-dimensions (a) teacher-related barriers, (b) infrastructure and administration-related, and (c) technological access and adoption-related. Details are as follows:

(a) **Teacher-related barriers**: For successful implementation and application of ICT in classroom settings, many potential limits come from the teacher such as:
- **Teacher's attitude**: The attitude of teachers toward the use of technology plays a vital role in the successful implementation of ICT in education. In contrast, various research reveals that in developing countries, such as India, the majority of teachers lack knowledge regarding the potential or benefits of ICT for the enhancement of teaching-learning. Brosnan (2001) found that attitude, motivation, and computer anxiety are vital factors that affect the enthusiasm of teachers.
- **Inadequate IT skills**: Furthermore, another potential barrier to ICT in education is the lack of IT skills. Many teachers have no or limited IT skills; therefore, they feel uncomfortable using technology as a tool for teaching-learning. To overcome this factor there is a serious need to develop a willingness toward acceptance and adopt some basic technical skills among the teacher community.
- **Lack of teacher motivation regarding the adaption of new technology**: The adoption of new technology by the teacher as well as the student is also a major challenge for the integration of ICT in school education. For a major shift from the traditional learning environment to ICT-based teaching-learning, the majority of teachers and students fear adopting a new ICT-based environment as they feel it is challenging. Therefore, to overcome these challenges there needs to be more pre-implementation motivational training for the teacher and student for increasing their positive attitude toward preparedness and acceptance of new technology.

(b) **Infrastructure and administration-related**: There are various barriers related to infrastructure and administration in the sphere of ICT. Those are mentioned and described as follows:

- **Lack of infrastructure**: One of the major challenges in the integration of ICT in schools is the appropriate availability of infrastructure. In developing countries such as India where most of the schools have no proper internet connection, telephone connection, electric supply, etc., those are the major challenges for launching ICT-based learning platform. Therefore, before implementing any ICT-based program the policymaker, planner, as well as a teacher must need to take into consideration the following components namely appropriate building, electricity, telephone and internet connection, availability of ICT devices, etc.
- **Lack of leadership**: Leadership is a fundamental element to achieve any goal in school education. Lack of leadership skills is also a major challenge to the integration of ICT in school education. Proper leadership is needed to discuss the new technological model, awareness about the concept and future impact of any new project, etc. To overcome this challenge, it is needed to initiate proper leadership and management training before integrating any ICT-based program in the classroom.
- **Lack of time**: A classroom is bound with a limited and fixed amount of time. One teacher teaches more than one subject a day with huge curriculum pressure. Therefore, they get limited time to design, develop, and incorporate ICT-based teaching into the classroom and learning quite often.
- **Lack of equipment**: To integrate ICT into the classroom needs, various supportive resources and equipment such as electricity, proper classroom infrastructure, and hardware and software devices, such as computers, printers, projectors, scanners, etc. can be used. But most rural educational institutions lack the availability of minimum resources to implement ICT.
- **Insufficient funds**: To get the best benefits from ICT, it is imperative to have up-to-date versions of the hardware, software, and resources. In developing countries such as India, most educational organizations are unable to utilize the benefits of ICT due to a lack of sufficient funds.
- **Maintenance**: Every technology-based piece of equipment is upgraded day by day. In the scenario of developing countries, the educational organization faces various challenges to maintain or upgrade ICT devices in the classroom.

(c) **Technological access and adoption-related:** The barriers related to technology and adoption are described as follows:
- **Lack of language**: English has been the dominant language in ICT-based platforms which is a major challenge for those countries where English is a second language. Eighty percent of educational software programs produced in the world market are in English. Therefore, it is a real challenge for countries such as India, Malaysia, and the Philippines, where English is the second language, to effectively adapt to ICT without adequate knowledge of English. To overcome this challenge software or web developer must need to take into consideration of the development of software and web-based educational content in the local language.
- **No or limited electricity**: Electricity is one of the crucial elements for the successful implementation of ICT. Most rural educational organizations don't have electricity or limited availability of electricity.
- **Limited or low internet access**: To create an ICT-based teaching-learning environment, there is a great need for sufficient internet access. However, in the context of various developing countries, especially India, most of the rural schools face the problems of lack of internet connection or slow internet connections.

Advantages of ICT in Education

As pointed out in the previous section ICT has numerous advantages in the field of education. The teaching and learning environment has been dramatically changed when ICT emerged with education. The following are some of the advantages of ICT in education:

- **Enhances motivation**: Over the past one of the major challenges in the field of education is a lack of motivation or engagement. Thus, ICT is one of the innovative approaches where the teacher can use a variety of modes of instructional techniques to increase students' motivation.
- **Globalized educational approach**: With ICT, education is no longer bound to any specific geographical location. ICT makes education more open and massively available. Presently any student can learn anything they want from any corner of the world.
- **Equality and equity**: Since earlier times education was mainly open to some elite classes. Education was too costly; therefore, it was unavailable for all. However, ICT-based education increases the scope of participation of more students irrespective of their demographic background. ICT also increases equity by providing scope for personalized education.
- **Enhances speed of communication**: The present era is the fastest ever. ICT increases the speed of communication. Now the student can collaborate with other students from different districts, states, countries, or continents within a fraction of a second. This unique learning approach is not possible without internet-based communication.
- **Promote independent learning**: ICT-based educational communication increases the scope so that the student is no longer a passive recipient of the educational process. Based on various online learning communication students can independently take part in any educational platform without the physical presence of any teacher or guidance.
- **Encourage the teacher to develop exciting ways or methods of teaching**: Traditional teaching-learning depends on printed learning material with little instructional strategies. With the ICT-based educational approach, teachers can use a variety of exciting instructional materials and teaching methods such as multimedia-based learning, interactive visualization, etc.
- **Immediate feedback and evaluation**: ICT also changes the way student feedback is given. Now students can get instant feedback based on their activity. Researchers found that instant feedback is more effective for student cognition. Not only that student assessment and evaluation process has also changed due to information and communication technology as in the automatic process student can track their performance and activity at any time throughout the learning process.
- **Enhance collaborative and cooperative learning**: Collaboration and cooperation are important 21st-century skills. ICT increases this scope of learning by providing various collaborative communication tools such as GoogleDocs, Endnote, Microsoft-project, etc.
- **Availability of resources**: Before the introduction of ICT, the student had to depend on the library or teacher for any educational resource. It was hard to get resources from a different country. However, this situation no longer exists due to the ICT revolution. Presently, anyone can assess any educational resources throughout the world by simply clicking on a mouse. OER (Open Education Resources) movement is one of the greatest movements for the availability of educational resources for all.
- **Acquiring a variety of skills**: To effectively survive in the 21st century it is imperative to learn various skills such as digital knowledge skills, skills for collaborative work, etc. ICT provides the scope for the student to flourish, grow their skills and effectively adjust to the environment.

- **Cost-effectiveness**: With more availability of resources and an abundance of learning material, the cost of a textbook or other educational material is comparatively low after the introduction of ICT in education. It is also notable that students no longer need any printed books rather they convert to digital means. Besides, tuition fees also decreased due to online-based education. For instance, teachers, as well as students, no longer need to travel to any other place which saves on transportation costs, resulting in reduced cost of education overall.
- **Bridging the cultural gap**: Various states, countries, or continents have their own culture, and education is also designed based on this. ICT increases the scope to link or connect these diverse cultural dots. For instance, through online communication one student from India can share their culture with a student from the United States, which bridges the cultural gap and eventually assimilates one culture with another.

Disadvantages of ICT in Education

Apart from the huge potentiality of ICT, there are some disadvantages these are as follows:

- **Plagiarism**: Plagiarism is one of the unique challenges of ICT-based education. As lots of information is available on the internet, many times students download and copy this information without taking consent or acknowledgment of the author. To prevent these challenges teacher needs to provide various awareness and knowledge about citations, author acknowledgment, etc. to the student. Also, the teacher can take the help of various plagiarism software like iThenticate, plagiarism checker (free), Quetext (free), etc. to detect plagiarism or copy content.
- **Student confusion and access to unnecessary information**: The abundance of availability of information increases the confusion of the student regarding authenticity. Many times, they learn or access the wrong information available on the internet. To encounter these challenges students, have to be conscious about accessing information as well as there is a need to get it verified.
- **Students' privacy**: Students' online activity can be easily hacked by criminals and marketers which is a violation of the privacy of students. Therefore, teachers need to provide adequate knowledge to the student regarding safe online activity.
- **Costly equipment for setting up ICT and digital divides**: Though ICT-based educational resources are low cost the first-time set-up of ICT-based equipment is too costly such as computers, printers, the internet, etc. Many people belonging to low socio-economic class families and rural schools cannot afford this cost which to some extent may create digital divides.
- **Lack of physical interaction with teacher**: As ICT is an independent learning approach it increases the gap between the physical attachment of teacher and student. Students get habituated to virtual communication rather than physical face-to-face communication/interaction.
- **Raise various instructional challenges**: To effectively use an ICT-based educational approach there needs to be some appropriate pre-requisite skills. Without proper competence to handle the ICT-based equipment or instructional material, there may result in an instructional challenge among the students.
- **Need fluent English**: The internet is dominated by the English language. Therefore, to access online platforms for education, students need adequate English knowledge which may be challenging for many of the students belonging to underdeveloped areas.

References

British Computer Society. (2008). *Helping ICT professionals to assess ethical issues in new and emerging technologies*. ©British Computer Society 2008.

Brosnan, T. (2001). Teaching using ICT. University of London: Institute of Education.

Harris, I., Jennings, R., Pullinger, D., Rogerson, S., & Duquenoy, P. (2008). Helping ICT professionals to assess ethical issues in new and emerging technologies. In *MINAmI workshop on ambient intelligence and ethics* (Vol. 15, p. 2008). Mantua, Italy: University of Pavia. http://www.fp6-minami.org/.

Koehler, M.J., & Mishra, P. (2008). Introducing TPCK. AACTE Committee on Innovation and Technology (Ed.), *The handbook of technological pedagogical content knowledge (TPCK) for educators* (pp. 3–29). Mahwah, NJ: Lawrence Erlbaum Associates.

Koehler, M., & Mishra, P. (2009). What Is Technological Pedagogical Content Knowledge (TPACK)? *Contemporary Issues in Technology and Teacher Education, 9*, 60–70.

Laudon, K. C., & Laudon, J. P. (2010). *Management information systems: Managing the digital firm*. Upper Saddle River, NJ: Pearson Education.

Mishra, P., & Koehler, M. J. (2006). Technological Pedagogical Content Knowledge: A Framework for Teacher Knowledge. *Teachers College Record, 108*(6), 1017–1054. https://doi.org/10.1111/j.1467-9620.2006.00684.x

Pfundt, H., & Duit, R. (2000). *Bibliography: student's alternative frameworks and science education* 5th edn. Kiel: University of Kiel.

QCA. (2000). *Information and communication technology: A scheme of work for key stage 3*. London: Qualifications and Curriculum Authority.

SER. (1997). *ICT en arbeid: Advies informatie- en communicatietechnologie en arbeid*. Den Haag: SER Sociaal-Economische Raad.

Shulman, L. S. (1986). Those who understand: Knowledge growth in teaching. *Educational Researcher, 15*(2), 4–14.

Turban, E., King, D., Lee, J., Warkentin, M., & Chung, H. M. (2002). *Electronic Commerce 2002: A managerial perspective*. Englewood Cliffs, NJ: Prentice-Hall.

Suggested Readings

Abbott, C. (2001). *ICT: Changing education*. Psychology Press.

Fallows, S. J., & Bhanot, R. (2005). *Quality issues in ICT-based higher education*. Psychology Press.

Gillespie, H. (2014). *Unlocking learning and teaching with ICT: Identifying and overcoming barriers*. Routledge.

Jimoyiannis, A. (2016). *Research on e-learning and ICT in education*. New York: Springer.

Karagiannidis, C., Politis, P., & Karasavvidis, I. (2014). *Research on e-learning and ICT in education: Technological, pedagogical and instructional perspectives*. Berlin: Springer.

Lawrence, A. T. (2010). *Online courses and ICT in education: Emerging practices and applications: Emerging practices and applications*. IGI Global.

Manichander, T. (n.d.). *ICT in education*. Lulu.com.

Nwokeafor, C. U. (2015). *Information communication technology (ICT) integration to educational curricula: A new direction for Africa*. University Press of America.

Passey, D., & Tatnall, A. (2014). Key competencies in ICT and informatics: Implications and issues for educational professionals and management: IFIP WG 3.4/3.7 international conferences, KCICTP and ITEM 2014, Potsdam, Germany, July 1–4, 2014, revised selected papers. Berlin: Springer.

Pelgrum, W. J., & Law, N. (2003). *ICT in education around the world: Trends, problems and prospects*. Unesco, International Institute for Educational Planning.

Selwood, I. D., Fung, A., & O'Mahoney, C. D. (2012). *Management of education in the information age: The role of ICT*. Berlin: Springer.

Shaikh, I. R. (n.d.). *Introduction to educational technology & ICT*. Tata: McGraw-Hill Education.

Taylor, H., & Hogenbirk, P. (2001). Information and communication technologies in education: The school of the future. In *IFIP TC3/WG3.1 international conference on the bookmark of the school of the future April 9–14, 2000*. Viña del Mar, Chile: Springer Science & Business Media.

Thakur, D. G. (n.d.). *Recent trends in ICT in education*. Lulu.com.

Vrasidas, C., Zembylas, M., & Glass, G. V. (2009). *ICT for education, development, and social justice*. IAP.

27
GAMES, GAMIFICATION, AND SIMULATION IN EDUCATION

Introduction

It can be rightly claimed that we are living in an information age (Bates, 2000; Reigeluth, 1996). The unprecedented rate of progress was a dream for a long time. The technology advancement which is the transmitter and generator of information has been changing very fast and is achieving a increasingly multicultural audience every moment. This deluge of information and technological advancement has impacted the education system in a paradigm shift from the industrial age to the information age. The present model of instruction and method of teaching is getting insufficient day by day. Consequently, in the field of education researchers worldwide are trying to find out a more innovative and sophisticated approach to meet the needs and demands of the present century (Gustafson and Branch, 1997).

One such unique innovative instructional method is "games and simulation". It may be a wrong claim to say that the "games and simulation" approach is an innovation in the field of education because, since childhood, one is involved with various games (Riber, 1996). However, the uniqueness of childhood games and modern games or simulations is a scientific design of a game based on learning objectives. This chapter will discuss simulation and games in teaching-learning.

Meaning and Definitions of Game

It would be hard to find someone who hates to play games. Most of our childhood is spent playing various physical games such as cricket, football, kabaddi, etc. In the past, well-known educational researchers such as John Dewey, Montessori, Froebel, and Pestalozzi identified the power of the physical game in the teaching-learning process. Meanwhile, due to the inclusion of computer and mobile technology in the 21st century, the mode of playing games is being shifted from the physical to the virtual. McGonigal (2012) in his survey explored that, worldwide people spend more than 3 million hours playing various virtual games. Presently people of all ages spend hours and hours playing games such as Candy Crush, Angry Bird, Temple Run, etc. to achieve arbitrary levels, ranks, or positions. Considering this aspect, researchers, especially educational researchers, are researching how to use game components in the teaching-learning process, to increase the active participation of students in their tasks. This is called "gamifica-

Table 27.1 Difference between game, game-based learning, and gamification

Subject of Difference	Game	Game-Based Learning (GBL)	Gamification
Definition	Game includes all other categories except gamification	Game-based learning generally refers to the process and practice of learning through games.	By definition, gamification refers to the application of variable game elements to a non-game context.
Achievement	In a game situation, there must be a winning and losing scenario.	In a game-based learning environment winning or losing situations is not possible because the points used in a game-based learning environment are only for motivational purposes.	Winning or losing is not possible because gamification is intentionally designed to motivate learners in specific learning contexts.
Objective	In a game, there may be some objective or purpose.	Game-based learning in management is not a game that is specially designed for learning purposes.	Sometimes gamification is used to motivate the learner but the major aim of gamification is to make something playful or joyful.
Cost and skills	Games are very expensive and require an extensive amount of knowledge and skill to develop.	Game-based learning is also expensive and hard to develop.	Compared to game and game-based learning, gamification is cheap and easy to develop.
Contents	Game is generally based on stories and scenes.	Game-based learning is based on learning content.	Gamification learning environment based on content with some learning management system.
Business orientation	In a game, the user has to pay for its application.	In game-based learning, environment institutions pay for the overall environment.	As per the gamification context, the producer has to pay for the overall learning environment.
Core aspect	Games are generally used for solely amusement purposes.	Game-based learning environments mainly deal with learning and learning content.	The core aspect of gamification is usually how a thing can be taught and administered rather than learned.

tion". There is a misconception about the three interrelated concepts of game, gamification, and simulation.

Gamification is a newly introduced term or concept in the field of education. Therefore, before opening an in-depth discussion regarding gamification, we first need to know what is a "game"?

Many researchers define the term "game" in various ways. However, a more viable definition of a game is given by Kapp (2012). Kapp defined "Game as a system in which players engage in an abstract challenge, defined by rules, interactivity, and feedback, that results in a quantifiable outcome often eliciting an emotional reaction".

The definition that Kapp provides a broader view of "game" but it fails to provide enlightenment on various types of games that can be used to achieve specific learning objectives. Generally, games can be categorized from different perspectives such as puzzle games, fighting games, collecting/capture, war games, matching games, role-playing games, simulation games, science fiction games, etc. Therefore, one needs to take into consideration many aspects when talking about games, gamification, and simulation. First, content-related games (i.e., Game's audio-visual content or the visual appearances of its characters, etc.), and second, the concept between testing games versus teaching games. Third, and the important aspect is the activities occurring within the game, because based on activity one may differentiate between game, gamification, or simulation. The next section will discuss briefly various types of game activities for a better understanding of game elements that may help the instructional designer to design future games.

Types of Game Activities

As discussed previously, the activity within the game is a crucial aspect to better understand learning games and their design. Each activity leads to a specific type of learning. The following are some of the common activities involved in learning games.

Matching

One of the common activities seen in a game is the matching activity. In this activity, players require similar matching elements within the space of gaming. Matching can be card-based, word-based, or picture-based. For instance, 50 pictures were given to the student with 25 similar pairs. Now, students have to match the 25 pairs from the face-down random-order pictures.

Puzzle Solving

Puzzle solving is a unique genre of game activity. In puzzle solving, students are required to figure something out. This activity can explore the problem-solving skills of learners such as logic, pattern recognition, sequence solving, word completion, etc. Some of the puzzle activities are action puzzles, hidden object puzzles, traditional puzzles, etc.

Role-Playing

Role-playing is another common activity in the game. In this activity, players are required to assume the role of a fictional character and need to play out a specific role either through literal acting or structured character development. One of the most complicated role-playing games is Assassin's Creed III.

Helping

Helping is another great activity in some games. It involves features of helping or assisting other players. Some of the helping activity-based games are Kindness Cook-Off, Trash Competition, Collection Box, etc.

Exploring

Exploring is another special type of game that mainly emphasizes exploring a specific game-based environment and interacting with the variously available element to find valuable items. This type of game encourages learners in strategy making such as what to do next, how to interact, how to progress, and how to achieve the winning stage within the game. Some conventional computer-based exploring games are Myst and Riven.

Building

Building is another type of game activity where learners/players are encouraged to create an object out of a given material. Minecraft and Jenga are types of building game.

Strategizing

Strategizing games emphasize a strategy-making process in the specific game-based situation. In strategizing games one player competes with another to acquire various resources such as land, cultural influence, etc.

Meaning and Definitions of Gamification

The term "gamification" originated from the digital media industry and dates back to 2008. But it was popularized in the second half of 2010 by commercial industries and conference organizations (Deterding, 2011). In the field of educational research or game design research, the term gamification has been heavily contested and until now there is no explicit academic definition of gamification.

However, the following are some of the operational definitions of gamification as proposed by various researchers:

Attali and Arieli (2015) defined gamification as the use of various elements of game design such as points, leaderboards, badges, etc. and are used in a non-game situation to uplift or promote user engagement.

Alliance (2015) explained that gamification is the robust design of the game or program design and behavioral economics for the optimization of behavioral change and outcome.

Kim (2015) defined gamification as a design process that can be used to enhance user participation as well as engagement and instruction.

Buckley and Doyle (2014) defined that gamification applies game dynamics to non-game applications.

Kapp (2012) defined more explicitly that gamification is game-based mechanics, aesthetics, and game-thinking "to engage people, motivate action, promote learning, and solve the problem".

From the above definitions given by various researchers, one can elaborate that gamification is a design process where various elements of the game are used to promote engagement of the user in the non-game context. It is a much higher-order design than only game design because the primary focus of gamification is to make sure that the user is motivated toward task completion.

Very well-crafted explanations regarding "gamification" have been provided by Scot Osterweil, a creative director at Education Arcade at Massachusetts Institute of Technology (MIT). He explained the "Four Freedom of Play", which are the following:

- **Freedom to fail**: One of the essential freedom in the context of gamification is that games allow the learner to make mistakes.
- **Freedom to experiment**: Another freedom is the scope of more and more exploration and discovery of new strategies to encounter a specific challenge.

- **Freedom to assume different identities**: Every problem has various perspectives for solutions. Games encourage the player to find out the utmost effective solutions by analyzing the problems through different modes or points of view.
- **The freedom of effort**: The game gives freedom to the player in the context of effort. For example, the player can pause at any time by his/her choice for relaxation before exploring further strategies.

Characteristics of Gamification

From the above discussion, one can understand that gamification is a process that seeks to enhance the motivation and commitment of the user regarding task completion. Based on the well-grounded definition of gamification given by various researchers, it can be characterized by different aspects. However, to provide more specific characteristics of gamification, a list of characteristics of gamification discussed by Kai Erenli (2013) in his article "The Impact of Gamification: Recommending Education Scenarios" are given below:

- **Use of game elements in non-game context**: One of the major characteristics of gamification is the use of game elements such as badges, points/scoreboards, levels, ranks, etc. in a non-game context.
- **Blend of fun and instruction**: Gamification mainly balances the fun and instruction aspects to facilitate effective learning. In the gamification process, there must be some specific instructional goal that the user or learner achieves in a more fun way.
- **Uncertain**: The outcome of gamification is uncertain by nature. The user is unable to predict what would happen next.
- **Engaging storyline and challenges**: Another major effective characteristic of gamification is the well-crafted storyline and well-presented challenges which are more powerful elements to increase engagement and attention.
- **Separate**: Generally, gamification is limited to a specific time and place.
- **Governed by rules**: The activity of gamification is based on some specific rules that may differ from everyday lifestyle.
- **Fictitious**: Gamification is fictitious which is accompanied by the awareness of a different reality.
- **More interactive**: Unlike other educational learning material gamification creates a more complex and sophisticated interactive learning environment for enhancing the efficiency of the course.
- **Step-by-step progress toward learning goal**: In a gamification-based learning environment the learner encounters some specific problem or challenges and the learner can only archive some specific goals by performing towards the learning goal in the given situation. In this process, the learner gradually achieves the learning objective as a whole (Table 27.1).

Elements for Gamification in Education

The above discussion gives an overview that gamification is the application of various principles and elements of a game into education. Now the question is what are those game elements that are used extensively in an educational or learning context? Some of the essential and extensive uses of game elements are listed below:

Table 27.2 Brief history of gamification trajectory

Year	Innovation
1958	Dr. William Higinbotham an American physicist developed the first graphical display-based game namely "Tennis for Two". This was mainly a simulation-based table tennis game using an oscilloscope.
1970	In the early 1970s Multi-User Dungeon (MUD1) was developed by Roy Trubshow, a UK-based researcher. That was the oldest form of the virtual world. Another innovation in this same age was developed by John Hunter, an elementary school teacher. He designed the "World Peace Game" which was based on a simulation approach using geopolitical fictional aspects.
1980	Revolutionary research work was published by Thomas Malone namely "What makes things fun to learn? Heuristics for designing instructional computer game". Besides this, "British Legends", a textbook-based game was developed using TELNET.
1982	Microsoft, a software company released an early version of flight simulator.
1984	This is the year when the first world-famous game "Tetris" was released, which was developed and designed by Alexey Pajitnov, a Russian computer engineer. 425 million copies were sold out after release.
1989	During this period application of game or computer games in various aspects of life took place.
1993	The first shooter game was released.
1999	The first multiplayer and role-playing MMORPG game was released namely, Everquest.
2002	The term "gamification" was coined by Nick Pelling, a British programmer and entrepreneur.
2005	The first visual programming language was developed namely "Scratch".
2007	The Institute of play was initiated in New York. Besides, a revolutionary book namely "What Video Games have to Teach us about Learning and Literacy" was published by renowned researcher James Paul.
2009	The first gamified course "Quest to Learn (Q2L)" was initiated by the Institute of Play.
2010	The term "gamification" became popular and researchers in the field of education were given the major focus on academic literature related to gamification. Sweden used gamified techniques in traffic laws namely "Speed Camera Lottery".
2011	The first conference on gamification was held in San Francisco, CA. Besides this, the Oxford English Dictionary added the word gamification as the word of the year.
2012	Gamification consultancy was implemented by the Deloitte Leadership Academy. Mozilla Open Badges initiative is launched.
2014	M2 research predicted that the whole market of gamification will be US$2.8 billion by 2016.
2015	Gamified web design Fantasy Geopolitics was developed which mostly encouraged the student to earn more about the world's news.
2016	The first PC-based virtual reality head-mounted was released namely "Oculus Rift".
2018	Gamification became mainstream for both businesses and consumers.

- **Points**: Points are one of the very essential and common elements of a game used in education. Generally, points were used as a measurement score of achievement or success in any gaming process. The point as an element of the game was used in various forms such as rewards, investment for further progression, an indication of one's level, credit in the academic environment, etc. In the context of the education-based game various points are used such as "Experience Points" (XP) (i.e., points earned by completing the task), which is mostly earned after the successful completion of a specific task, and Steam Point, this point is generally used for the role-playing game in education.
- **Level/Stages**: The level or stage is generally an indication of the progression of the learner/player. A well-designed game always follows the easy to complex level of design. The level

is also used as a form of reward in the context of task assignments, measurement of student learning ability, etc.
- **Leaderboard**: A leaderboard is a display of progression in the context of compassion for other learners. A leaderboard is one of the motivational elements in the game design because it creates a competitive learning environment where the learner is always motivated to achieve a higher score to keep him/her at the top of a specific leaderboard.
- **Prizes and rewards**: Another effective game element are prizes and rewards. These are very conventional elements for reinforcement in any learning process. Rewards or prizes provide positive reinforcement to the learner to motivate them in a specific task. Research shows that multiple small rewards are a more effective strategy to keep consistency in a learning process rather than providing big rewards at the end of learning.
- **Progress bars**: The progress bar is an effective element to track or display the overall progression of the learner. This element is effective in a dichotomous way, first, it helps the learner to navigate how close he/she is to achieving their goal and encourages or motivates them to achieve the learning objective faster.
- **Storyline**: A storyline is a narrative or story element of a specific game. Sometimes a storyline helps in the navigation of goals and works as a catalyst for the motivation of a specific game-based learning process.
- **Feedback**: Feedback is another extensively used element in games. Feedback is an indication tool to analyze whether a learner has met a specific goal or expectation or if a learner needs more efforts in a specific learning cycle to achieve the learning goal.
- **Avatars**: Avatars are another frequently used element. They are the representation of one learner to other learners. Avatars vary as per representation such as a 3D avatar, symbolic avatar, picture-based avatar, etc.

Various Concepts Related to Gamification

In the context of the use of games or gaming in education, four interrelated concepts can be found and those are the following (Sandusky, 2015).

1. Gamification
2. Game-based learning
3. Serious games
4. Simulations
    - **Gamification**: In a general view, gamification is the application of a game design element or mechanism into a non-game context. As discussed in the previous section, those elements include levels, badges, leaderboards, rewards, etc.
    - **Game-based learning**: Game-based learning is the actual application of games in the classroom to promote the teaching and learning process more effectively. In this aspect, the entire learning process is converted into a game.
    - **Serious games**: By definition, a serious game is "a game designed for a primary purpose other than pure entertainment". Therefore, from this definition, it is clear that a serious game is designed to achieve a specific purpose rather than just for fun. A serious game looks like a game but it has a specific predetermined objective to achieve.
    - **Simulations**: In a general view simulation is the imitation or operation of a real-world process, system, or mechanism. Simulation is a replica of a realistic situation,

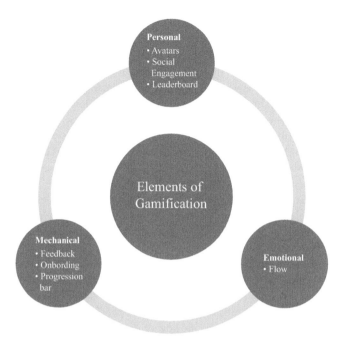

Figure 27.1 Elements of gamification classified by Oxford Analytica in a global analysis report. Source: World Government Summit & Oxford Analytica (2016).

Table 27.3 Present game-design elements and motives

Game Mechanics	Game Dynamics	Motives
Documentation of behavior	Exploration	Intellectual curiosity
Scoring system, badges, trophies	Collection	Achievement
Ranking	Competition	Social recognition
Ranks, levels, reputation point	Acquisitions of status	
Group tasks	Collaboration	Social exchange
Time, pressure, task, quests	Challenge	Cognitive stimulation
Avatars, virtual worlds, virtual trade	Development/organization	Self-determination

Source: (Blohm and Leimeister, 2013.

which acts upon a minimal risk environment where the learner can practice learned behavior repeatedly and experience the impact of learned context. Simulation is a technique for practice and learning that can be applied to many different disciplines and trainees. It is a technique (not a technology) to replace and amplify real experiences with guided ones, often "immersive" in nature, that evoke or replicate substantial aspects of the real world in a fully interactive fashion (Lateef, 2010). In some contexts, simulation is similar to a serious game but it resembles a real context or situation.

Some of the Gamification Tools Used in Education

The field of gamification is enriched in many ways since the earlier days till today and within the space of every aspect of education such as mathematics, language, biology, and geography, more and more gamification has impact over the decades. This section is intended to provide a brief overview of some of the extensively used gamification software and their application. They are as follows:

Code Academy

Code Academy is one of the most used online gamified learning platforms. It was founded in August 2011. This platform provides a rich gamified experience to the learner in the online learning space. Code Academy is mainly designed for web as well as mobile-based teaching and learning platforms with various online tools for students and course curators. It offers free coding classes in 12 different languages that show learners how to develop and code computer programs. It had 25 million users in 2016 (https://www.codecademy.com/).

Mozilla Open Badges or IMS Open Badges

In 2011 Mozilla Foundation funded by MacArthur Foundation developed open technical standards namely "Mozilla Open Badges". The major aim of Open Badges is to create, as well as build, a common system for the collection and display of digital badges on multiple sites. Besides, it is also intended to serve a broad range of digital badges for both academic and non-academic uses. Initially, Open Badges are specified into three types of badges:

- **Assertion**: It contains a single badge for the individual.
- **Badge class**: It contains information on the accomplishment of a specific badge recognizer.
- **Issuer organization**: It contains a collection of information regarding the person and organization which issues a badge.

Website: https://openbadges.org/

Classcraft

Classcraft is an engagement management platform for K–12 educators. Classcraft is intended to provide a classroom that is entirely made of gamified learning experiences. In this learning, the platform learner needs to assume the role of a distinct character and the teacher helps to create a team of students. In this overall teaching and learning situation, a student can earn experience points and upgrade their level which can be further applied to the class privilege.

Website: https://www.classcraft.com/

Quest To Learn

Quest To Learn (Q2L) is another gamified teaching and learning scenario. This learning platform is fully embedded with game-based elements. The significant approach in Q2L is it provides a challenging situation to the learner and the student has to encounter using distinct knowledge, feedback, reflection, etc.

Website: https://www.instituteofplay.org/quest-school

Knowre

Knowre is a math-based gamified teaching and learning platform. This is intended to provide the right content at the right time. The best part of Knowre is it helps to identify the weaknesses of a student by using an adaptive learning platform. It provides step by step guide to the learner through a learning map and distinct game to create a learning environment with more fun in the context of math equations.

Website: http://www.knowre.com/

Apart from the above discussion on the extensive use of gamified learning platforms *Table 27.4.* represent some more gamified learning platforms and their websites.

The Implication of Gamification in Education

The previous section provides a brief knowledge of gamification and the various contexts of the use of game elements in education. This section aims to provide knowledge about what are the implications of gamification in the context of education. From the previous discussion, one understands that one of the major aspects of the use of gamification in the context of education is to engage students more effectively with their learning materials. Through the gamification process, the teacher provides a problem for students to solve which is related to the objective of education that generally increases problem-solving skills and creative thinking. The following are some of the implications of gamification in education:

Increase the motivation and engagement of students: One of the greatest challenges in any educational scenario is to increase student motivation and increase learner engagement. It is also a proven fact that to increase the motivation of a learner, students need to participate actively in a specific learning situation. Talent LMS (2018) provides the following information about the active participation of learners through gamification. For 89% of students who participated in any kind of game-based learning environment gamification increases their motivation and engagement more effectively compared to those who do not use gamification. To add to this, 82% of students mentioned that learning through gamification increased their motivation in the context of problem-solving and active participation.

An increased retention rate of learners: Research conducted by University of Colorado, CO, revealed the fact that by using gamification the retention rate of students increased to a large extent Therefore, one can say that gamification helps students in increasing the processing of information effectively from short-term memory to long time memory.

Increase skill-based knowledge: As said earlier, gamification is a uniquely designed learning platform through which various problems are provided to the learner to increase participation and engagement of learners which in turn increases the efficiency and competence of learners to achieve a specific learning objective. The University of Colorado also explored that the competency of students increased to 11% through using the gamification method.

Worldwide, the majority of educational institutions accepted the gamification method in the teaching and learning process. As a result, students from K–12 to university are all using various game-based software to solve complex mathematical equations and learn languages. The various private organization also are involved in the development of various game-based learning platforms in various subjects such as history, mathematics, geography, literature, etc., which in turn increases the market demand for gamification-based learning platforms. For instance, throughout the world, the market for game-based learning platforms was 150 Cr INR in 2012 September, which was supposed to increase by more than 230 Cr INR in 2017.

Meaning and Definition of Simulation

In the simplest view "simulation is a representation of a real environment". In general, simulation is open-ended involving situations that may emerge with various interrelating variables.

Table 27.4 Some of the various gamification-based learning applications/platforms

Name of the Application	Specification	Website
ClassDojo	This is mainly an interconnection of the learning platform with students, teachers, and parents. This is a web, as well as a mobile-based, platform where the teacher can give instant feedback to the learner on their performance and student can earn points based on positive responses.	https://www.classdojo.com/
Socrative	In present times, Socrative is one of the famous game-based learning platforms. Socrative provides an extensive number of tools for the teacher to use. It provides three different customized modes first, a question-based game mode. Second, "space race", which aims to combine accuracy and speed. Third is "exit ticket", which is intended to take the pulse of the classroom at the end of the whole session.	http://www.socrative.com/
MinecraftEdu	MinecraftEdu is designed for classrooms and educators. MinecraftEdu is a classroom server that connects teachers and students. Over 5,500 teachers in 40+ countries use MinecraftEdu to teach distinct subject areas such as STEM, language, art, etc.	https://education.minecraft.net/
Play Brighter	Play Brighter is a game-like platform that helps a teacher to manage and create their learning environment in their own ways. This platform has an overall game-based environment that encourages and motivate student more effectively.	http://playbrighter.com/
Zondle	This is a free website where various educationalist provides their own created games for the learner. By using this platform one can create a game-based platform by using the Scratch application.	https://www.zondle.com/
Virtonomics	This is mainly a business simulation game. This gamified learning platform mostly is focused on higher education students. This virtual site is populated with 1 million players all over the world. On this platform, players shares their knowledge and experience to grow business strategies. This is a business game for managers, entrepreneurs, and students.	https://virtonomics.com/
Course Hero	Course Hero is mainly developed for high school and higher education. From the 5,000 universities more than 7,000,000 student-uploaded documents. by using this platform. A teacher can teach a massive number of students around the world. Course Hero has also built its game-like courses for the student and allows them to submit a course to any learner from any corner of the world.	https://www.coursehero.com/
Duolingo	Duolingo is a gamified language-learning platform. More than 80 million students around the world use this gamified learning platform. It helps the overall language learning platform that motivates the learner more and is also fun.	https://www.duolingo.com/
VeriShow	VeriShow is a gamified question-based learning platform. On this platform, learners interact with a distinct question through embedded video, images, games, etc., which helps the learner to learn faster and ineffective ways. This is mainly a customer engagement platform.	https://www.verishow.com/

(Continued)

Table 27.4 Continued

Name of the Application	Specification	Website
Maven	Maven is an advanced gamification tool for an educator. It builds with advanced GUI techniques for the LAMS system. It provides educators with a rich visual authoring environment for effective teaching and learning.	http://www.playwarestudios.com/
Class Realm	This is a gamified learning platform where students can earn points, achieve extra book reading, complete a specific test, help other classmates, etc.	http://classrealm.com/
Kahoot!	Kahoot! is a famous game-based teaching and learning platform. In this platform, the teacher can use various fun tools like geographical location, multiplication table, the periodic table, etc. Additionally, Kahoot!'s platform promotes a point system as an element of gamification which makes this learning platform more fun.	https://kahoot.it/

This is similar to a real-world context in which a girl can play the role of her mother by wearing a saree and acting similarly to her mother. Therefore, simulation is an exact imitation of the same context, situation, object, person, etc. The following are some of the definitions of simulation:

Barton (1970): Simulation is an attempt to give the appearance and or to give the effect of something.

Robert Gagne (1977): Defined simulation as a model of reality reflecting some or all of its properties. He also identified some of the critical properties of simulation those are:
- It represents a real situation in which the operation is carried out.
- A certain level of control over a situation or problem.
- Simulation is based on the formula: Simulation = (reality)−(task-irrelevant elements)

Heinich et al. (2002): Simulation is an interactive abstraction or simplification of some real life.

Alessi and Trollip (2001): Simulation is an attempt to imitate a real or imaginary environment or system.

Tessmer, Jonassen, and Caverly (1989): Simulation is a real-life scenario in which the student has to act upon.

Margaret E. Gredler (2004): Simulation is an evolving case study of a particular social or physical reality in which the participants take on bonafide roles with well-defined responsibilities and constraints.

From the above definitions and discussions one can say that:

> Simulation is a replica of a realistic situation, which acts upon a minimal-risk environment where the learner can practice learned behaviors repeatedly and experience the impact of learned context.

If one breaks down the above definition one will get four important terminologies which are important to understand the concept of simulation. They are as follows:

Replica of the realistic situation: As previously discussed, simulation is near about (if not the same) replica of the realistic event, context, object, person, etc.
Minimal risk environment: Compared to a real context, simulation is a minimal risk environment. For instance, it will be very risky to drive a car without the knowledge of driving, compared to using a simulation-based car driving approach.
Practice learned behavior repeatedly: In a simulation, a learner can repeatedly act on what they learned and can apply it to the needful situation.
Experience the impact of learned context: In a simulative environment, a learner can experience near to real context. Therefore, they can judge the impact of specific activity by the contextualization of reality.

Simulation-Based Teaching and Learning

Simulation-based teaching and learning designate the use of simulation techniques in the teaching and learning process. It is mainly based on a socio-drama approach. Simulation in teaching and learning is not a very old concept in the field of education. It can be defined in the following way:

Simulation teaching is a technique of learning and teaching that helps students improve their problem-solving behavior. This is a kind of role-playing in which students or teachers perform a specific role in an artificially created environment.

Characteristics of Simulated Teaching

Children in their childhood have been experiencing or learning from various simulated environments. For instance, those children who imitate the activity of his or her parents, also experience those through simulation of real context. Here are some of the fundamental characteristics of simulated teaching:

Analogous situation: Simulated teaching starts with an analogous situation. It is analogous in the sense that it puts the students in a specific situation that is identified in a real context.
Low-risk learning environment: As previously discussed simulated teaching and learning environment is a safer or low-risk learning environment compared to a real context. Suppose a student wants to learn to swim, so it will be safe to learn hand movement, leg movement, body movement, etc. through a simulation process rather than learn it directly in the swimming pool.
Symbolic feedback: In the simulation-based teaching and learning process another significant characteristic is symbolic feedback. Symbolic feedback refers to what would happen if a student does some wrong/different activities in a specific situation. For instance, a student who learned to swim through simulation can get instant feedback about drowning if he stops the proper hand movement or leg movement, etc.
It is replicable: Besides, the characteristic of low-risk and symbolic consequences of feedback another important characteristic of simulation-based teaching is that the whole scenario of the physical learning climate can be changed if required. For an instance, the whole climate or structure of the swimming pool can be changed wherever required. This replicable attribute of simulated teaching can increase the opportunity for an interactive procedure to achieve the best solution.
Personalization: Simulation-based teaching-learning environments can be personalized in nature. It can be changed based on discipline and conceptual structure. For example, the

environment of simulated learning will be different in the context of education, besides, it will be more mathematical in the context of economics.

Varies in style and complexity: The style and complexity of simulation may be varied based on context and subject matter. Such as paper-pencil-based or physical aspects can be used to teach some simple concepts of social interaction, besides, it may require some different styles of simulation such as a computer-based program to teach some complex concepts such as social administration or legislation in sociology.

Deep learning: Instructional simulation encourages a deep learning process that needs a high capacity for abstract thinking rather than just surface learning. which may demand rote memorization.

Unique circumstance: Various unique learning circumstances can be created through simulation-based teaching and learning by changing the parameter of a specific situation.

Types of Simulated Teaching

In the process of teaching and learning various types of simulation have been invented. Some of them are discussed here. They are as follows:

Branching storyline: This is the most simple and commonly used simulation approach in the teaching and learning process. This is mainly based on discussion. In a branching storyline approach, the teacher or instructor tells a story or presents a situation through text, graphics, video, etc. and tries to create a learning environment where the learner engages himself or herself as an active participant or character of a specific story or context. In this situation, after some time learner encounters a specific point and the simulation goes forward like "branches". In this type of simulation, learners can reply multiple times in different branches by making different decisions.

System dynamics simulation: This is a complex type of simulation process and is used to understand and define complex as well as dynamic scenarios. For example, in a business simulation, there will be thousands of dynamic complex ideas related to revenue generation, market share, costing, product design, stock price, etc. and every time one tries to find some predictive view such as how the entire system will function when a single part of the system changes. That is often called "process simulation".

Equipment or software simulation: This type of simulation is based on computer software. An equipment simulation accurately envisioned a specific learning concept. For instance, one of the most commonly accepted software-based simulations is train simulation or airplane simulator where learners manipulate every part of the train or airplane required to drive or fly it. Equipment- or software-based simulation is also used to teach the use of new software systems. Equipment simulation demands more accuracy in the context of design and function.

Bibliography

Alessi, S. M., & Trollip, S. R. (2001). *Multimedia for learning: Methods and development* (3rd ed., Vol. 214, pp. 254–257). Boston, MA: Allyn & Bacon.

Attali, Y., & Arieli-Attali, M. (2015). Gamification in assessment: Do points affect test performance? *Computers and Education, 83*, 57–63. https://doi.org/10.1016/j.compedu.2014.12.012.

Barton, R. F. (1970). *A primer on simulation and gaming*. Prentice-Hall, Inc.

Bates, T.. (2000). Managing Technological Change: Strategies for College and University Leaders. https://venturebeat.com/business/venturebeats-12-most-popular-stories-from-2013/

Blohm, I., & Leimeister, J. M. (2013). Gamification. *Wirtschaftsinformatik, 55*(4), 275–278.

Buckley, P., & Doyle, E. (2014). Gamication and student motivation. *Interactive Learning Environments*, 1–14. https://10.1080/10494820.2014.964263

Carmichael, S. (2018, December 6). *The best games of 2013 (GamesBeat staff picks)*. Retrieved from https://venturebeat.com/2013/12/31/the-best-games-of-2013/.

Deterding, S. (2011, May). Situated motivational affordances of game elements: A conceptual model. In *Gamification: Using game design elements in non-gaming contexts, a workshop at CHI*.Vancouver, Canada

Employees, Motivation, and Games. (2019, May 22). *The 2018 gamification survey is out!* Retrieved from https://www.talentlms.com/blog/gamification-survey-results/.

Erenli, K. (2013). The Impact of Gamification - Recommending Education Scenarios. *International Journal of Emerging Technologies in Learning (iJET), 8*(S1), pp. 15–21. https://doi.org/10.3991/ijet.v8iS1.2320

Gagne, R. M. (1977). *The conditions of learning* (3rd ed.). New York: Holt, Rine-hart and Winston.

Gee, J. P. (2007). *What Video Games Have to Teach Us About Learning and Literacy* Second Edition. Macmillan Publishers.

Gredler, M. E. (2004). Games and simulations and their relationships to learning. *Handbook of research on educational communications and technology, 2*, 571–581.

Gustafson, K. L., & Branch, R. M. (1997). *Survey of instructional development models.* Information Resources Publications, Syracuse University, 4-194. Center for Science and Technology, Syracuse, NY 13244-4100.

Heinich, R., Molenda, M., Russell, J. D., & Smaldino, S. E. (2002). *Instructional media and technologies for learning.* Upper Saddle River, NJ: Prentice Hall Merrill Education.

Kapp, K. M. (2012). *The gamification of learning and instruction: Case-based methods and strategies for training and education*. New York: Pfieffer: An imprint of John Wiley & Sons.

Kim, B. (2015). *Understanding gamification.* ALA TechSource. Chicago, IL: ALA TechSource.

Lateef, F. (2010). Simulation-based learning: Just like the real thing. *J Emerg Trauma Shock, 3*(4), 348–52. https://10.4103/0974-2700.70743.

McGonigal, J. (2012). *Reality is broken.* London:Vintage.

Reigeluth, C. M. (1996). A new paradigm of ISD? *Educational Technology-Saddle Brook NJ, 36*, 13–20.

Rieber, L. P. (1996). Seriously considering play: Designing interactive learning environments based on blending microworlds, simulations, and games. *Educational Technology Research and Development, 44*, 43–58.

Sandusky, S. (2015). *Gamification in education.* https://repository.arizona.edu/bitstream/handle/10150/556222/GamificationinEducatio n.pdf?sequence=1&isAllowed=y

Tèssmer, M., Jonassen, D., & Caverly, D. C. (1989). *Designing and planning computer assisted instruction: A workbook.* Littleton, CO: Libraries Unlimited.

Thomas, W., Malone, T. W. (1980). *SIGSMALL '80: Proceedings of the 3rd ACM SIGSMALL symposium and the first SIGPC symposium on Small systems*, pp. 162–169. September 1980.

What is Gamification. (n.d.). Retrieved from http://engagementalliance.org/what-is-gamification/.

World Government Summit & Oxford Analytica. (2016). Gamification and the Future of Education. World Government Summit. https://www.worldgovernmentsummit.org/api/publications/document?id=2b0d6ac4-e97c-6578-b2f8-ff0000a7ddb6 [accessed 25 May 2020].

Suggested Readings

Campbell, A. A. (2016). *Gamification in higher education: Not a trivial pursuit Doctoral thesis.* Tallahassee, FL, USA: St. Thomas University Miami Gardens.

Gamification in education: Breakthroughs in research and practice (2018). IGI Global.

Kapp, K. M. (2012). *The gamification of learning and instruction: Game-based methods and strategies for training and education.*

Marczewski, A. (2013). *Gamification: A simple introduction.* Raleigh: Lulu

McMunn-Tetangco, E. (2017). *Gamification: A practical guide for librarians.* Rowman & Littlefield Pub

Niman, N. (2014). *The gamification of higher education: Developing a game-based business strategy in a disrupted marketplace.*NY: Palgrame Mcmillan.

Reiners, T., & Wood, L. C. (2014). *Gamification in education and business.* Switzerland: Springer International Publishing. https://doi.org/10.1007/978-3-319-10208-5

Shea, T. M. (2013). *Gamification: Using gaming technology for achieving goals.* Rosen Pub Group.

Stieglitz, S., Lattemann, C., Robra-Bissantz, S., Zarnekow, R., & Brockmann, T. (2016). *Gamification: Using game elements in serious contexts* (1st ed.). Springer.

Zichermann, G., & Cunningham, C. (2011). *Gamification by design: Implementing game mechanics in web and mobile apps.* CA: O'Reilly Media.

Zichermann, G., & Linder, J. (2013). *The gamification revolution: How leaders leverage game mechanics to crush the competition* (1st ed.). McGraw-Hill Education.

28
MOBILE OR M-LEARNING IN EDUCATION

Introduction

Times are changing so fast; every single analog device is becoming digital, smaller, and more user-friendly with upgraded features to make life more convenient. We have come a long way from the earlier huge computer device to smaller mobile devices. Technology has been changing drastically as per the needs and demands of society and people. The present chapter intends to explore a comprehensive discussion about M-learning as a mode of teaching and learning.

Meaning and Definition of Mobile or M-Learning

Presently the mobile-based teaching-learning approach is one of the unprecedented learning approaches in the context of teaching and instruction. Various researchers throughout the world support utilization of the advantages of technological equipment to accelerate the effectiveness of teaching and learning scenarios. As mobile learning is a more modern learning approach, therefore, there is a huge scarcity of universally agreed definitions of mobile learning or M-learning. Some of the well-known definitions are provided here by various researchers throughout the world.

Quinn (2000) postulates mobile learning is the same as the e-learning process and explained that mobile learning is a kind of e-learning through a mobile computational device, Windows CE machines, and even your digital cell phone.

O'Malley et al, (2003) defined mobile learning as "any sort of learning that happens when the learner is not in a fixed, predetermined location, or learning that happens when the learner takes advantage of the learning opportunities offered by mobile technologies."

Wang (2004) defined mobile learning as a learning approach where a learner can access e-learning content independently within a specific location, and utilization of services is created dynamically including communication with others.

Keegan (2005) explained mobile learning as a learning environment that is designed by wireless technologies.

Barbosa and Geyer (2005) state that mobile learning is a learning approach where the learning environment follows the learner's movement.

Harris (2001) is a mobile computer technology or internet-based learning technology which encourages learning to happen at "any time" and "anywhere".

Inceoglu et al. (2006) defined mobile learning as a candidate system to fill the efficiency of former distance learning systems with mobile technology as well.

From the above definition, it can be broadly defined that "mobile learning is the exploitation of ubiquitous handheld technologies, together with the wireless and mobile phone network, to facilitate, support to enhance and extend the reach of teaching and learning" (Molenet, 2017).

Characteristics of Mobile Learning

From the above definitions, one can get a brief overview of mobile learning or m-learning. However, to understand mobile learning some essential characteristics of mobile learning need to be discussed. The following are some of the basic characteristics of mobile learning:

1. **The mobility of learning in physical space**: One essential characteristic of mobile learning is mobility in the learning process. That means the learner no longer needs to be the static recipient of information rather a learner can be a dynamic unit who can learn anywhere at any time. Such as a traveler can learn and find a travel route map during travel, an interactive learning module can be used by a learner when he or she is on a school bus, etc. This is a combined experience that constitutes dynamism and learning together.

2. **The mobility of technology**: In the past, technological devices that were used to provide instruction were complex and large. However, in the mobile learning process, various portable technology and resources are available which can easily be carried around conveniently. It can be said that one can carry a technology from one place to another.

    Interactivity: Interactivity is one of the essential characteristics of any effective teaching and learning process. In this context, another essential characteristic of mobile learning is that it promotes three kinds of interactivities in any learning and instruction.

    First, it promotes educational cognitive development by enhancing the learning environment. Now a learner can interact with an instructor, course material as well as social communication through virtual platforms anytime which can help a learner to enhance their cognitive environment.

    Second, interactive features in mobile learning are self-directive. In mobile learning, process learners have the liberty to choose his or her learning material, schedule of learning, place of learning, etc. Therefore, the learner is no longer a passive recipient. They can independently interact and create required learning material.

    Third, competency-based interactivity is another unique interactive characteristic of a mobile learning process. For instance, mobile learning provides an opportunity for the learner to use various learning applications that may influence learners to enact such learning material to increase their learning competency such as how text messaging enacts competence for social communication and voice application increases the oral communication process of the learner, etc.

3. **Provides multiple cues**: Mobile learning can provide multiple cues to the learner by providing an opportunity for the learner to access learning material from anywhere and anytime which can help in the comprehension and retention of the learner.

4. **Mobile learning is private**: One of the revolutionary features of mobile learning is that it provides space for the learner to learn privately. Private is not in the context of sharing information with others or rather it is private because only one learner can learn or access a mobile device at a time or the learner can learn independently as per their comfortability.
5. **Mobile learning is collaborative**: Mobile learning always encourages a collaborative learning process. By mobile learning platform, one learner may connect with his or her peers and teacher for a collaborative problem-solving project. In this context, mobile learning works to support communicative devices or connectors that can enhance the collaborative learning process.
6. **Instant information**: Mobile learning provides an opportunity for the learner to access any information or answer any question immediately. Such as a learner needs to know how an airplane flies, in this context, a learner can instantly search for it on the internet or can connect with any teacher or peers to know the answer instantly.
7. **Blended learning process**: One spontaneous characteristic of mobile learning is it encourages a blended learning model. For instance, in a learning scenario, a learner can learn from his school and use a mobile learning platform for homework, projects, etc. In that way, a learner can take advantage of face-to-face learning and mobile learning together.
8. **Mobile learning is collaborative**: Mobile learning always encourages a collaborative learning process. In a mobile learning platform, one learner may connect with his or her peers and teacher for collaborative problem-solving projects. In this context mobile learning work as a communicative support device or connector that can enhance the collaborative learning process.
9. **Combinational learning process**: Mobile learning is a bridge between learners and learning material and a combinational process of electronic learning and mobile learning.

Components Used for Mobile Technology

As discussed earlier mobile learning is a complex but effective learning approach. A mobile device comprises various components to function properly. Some of the essential components used for mobile technology are mentioned below:

Wireless network: Wireless network is communication technology used for global networks of internet and intranet (domestic networks). This is very common in any mobile device. Generally, a wireless network establishes a connection between network nodes. Example of a wireless network is cell phone networks, wireless local area networks (WLANs), wireless sensor networks, satellite communication networks, and terrestrial microwave networks.

Global system for mobile (GSM): This is a second-generation cellular network developed by the European Telecommunications Standards Institute (ETSI). In December 1991, Finland first deployed GSM network services. The frequency range of GSM is 900–1,900 and bandwidth is 9.6–28.8 Kbps.

General packet radio service (GPRS): GPRS is a mobile communication system, which is based on 2G technology. GPRS is "packet-oriented mobile data". The first GPRS system was established by the European Telecommunications Standards Institute (ETSI) which is maintained by the 3rd generation partnership project (3GPP). In a 2G system, GPRS provides a data rate of 56–114 Kbit/sec. Its frequency range is 900–1900 and the bandwidth is 171.2–384 Kbps.

Bluetooth: Bluetooth is a data transfer device used in mobile and laptops for short-range data transfer. It uses a UHF radio wave in the ISM band from 2.4 to 2.485 GHz. It is a personal area network (PAN) initiated in 1989 by Nils Rydbeck, CTO at Ericsson Mobile in Lund, Sweden, and by Johan Ullman.

Infrared (IrDA): Infrared is an external device that is build-in in mobiles, laptops, pocket computers, etc. This is a basic-level data transfer communication system and the rate of transmission is slow and low in the range.

Enhanced data rates for GSM evolution (EDGE): The full form of EDGE is "enhanced data rates for global system for mobile (GSM) evolution". It is a former level of the 3G network. This is a type of GSM network used to increase the data transmission rate. The possible data transfer rate of EDGE is 380 kbps. EDGE can transmit three times more data as compared to GPRS and EDGE works as an add-on to GRPS.

3G and 4G technology: 3G and 4G technology is an abbreviated form of 3rd generation communication and 4th generation service respectively. 3G technology is based on WCDMA, UMTS, and HSDPA standards. Japan was the first country to launch a 3G network in 1998 by NTT DoCoMo, branded as FOMA. In India, 3G technology was introduced quite late, on 11 December 2008, by the government-owned Mahanagar Telephone Nigam Ltd (MTNL) in Delhi and later in Mumbai. The frequency range of the 3G communication process is 1,900–2,000 and the bandwidth is near about 2,000 kbps. In the 3G communication process, voice and numeral data are being transferred. One of the major characteristics of the 3G communication process is navigation.

Besides this, 4G network communication is quite new in the arena of mobile technology. In late 2009, the mobile operator TeliaSonera first introduced the 4G in the city of Stockholm and Oslo. On 10 April 2012, Bharti Airtel launched 4G LTE in Kolkata, the first in India. The connection speed of a 4G network in a mobile phone is 100 Mbps and a wireless network is 1 Gbps. 4G produces high data speed. It balances network service, quality, and safety altogether.

Basic Elements of Mobile Learning

This is a common aspect that, every teaching and learning scenario required various basic sets of elements to promote the overall teaching and learning process. Basic elements of mobile learning is presented in Figure 28.1. These elements vary from one another. For example, some common elements of a classroom situation are teacher, learner, learning environment, content material, etc. Mobile learning also requires the following sets of elements to perform the overall teaching and learning scenario. They are as follows:

- Learner
- Teacher
- Content
- Environment
- Assessment

Learner

This is true that in teaching and learning, a learner is a quintessential or pivotal factor in all the teaching activities. The learner is a central factor because all the other factors, strategies, methods, etc. only focus on the development of the learner. In mobile learning scenarios, every development in the context of a pedagogical approach is built to meet the interest and experience of the learner. In the context of the learner's role in mobile learning, Makoe (2010) explained that the pedagogical approach of mobile learning should always place the student in the center

Emerging Trends

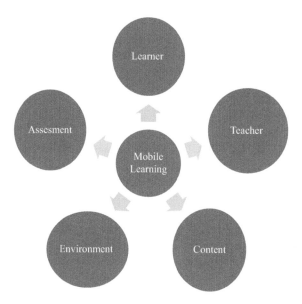

Figure 28.1 Basic elements of mobile learning.

of learning. In mobile learning, the process learner plays an active role in the overall teaching and learning process. The following are some of the roles of the learner as discussed by Ozdamil and Cavus (2011):

- Students should access the information whenever they need it.
- Students should be responsible for their learning.
- Students should have space to learn at their own pace.
- Students should discover and use their learning styles.
- Students should have the capability to create at their own pace.
- Students should increase their skills to adapt to collaborative and culturally diverse teaching and learning situations.
- The last and foremost important aspect is to gain the ability to evaluate own self as well as other peers.

Teacher

Another essential element is the teacher or instructor who is majorly responsible to convey any media or teaching-learning material to the learner in a blended or traditional learning environment. However, the role of a teacher in a mobile learning environment is different in comparison to a traditional learning environment. The role of a teacher is ever-changing. At the time of the television and media revolution, the role of the teacher was mainly to promote domain-based expert-level knowledge to the student. However, throughout the transition of the technological revolution the role of a teacher transit from expert to presenter. Moreover, at the time of the web 2.0 revolution, the availability of information is becoming ubiquitous and is spread all over the globe. Henceforth the role of a teacher is mainly as a moderator or consultant. The teacher's role in present technology era is presented in Figure 28.2. The following are some of the roles of teachers discussed by Ozdamil and Cavus (2011):

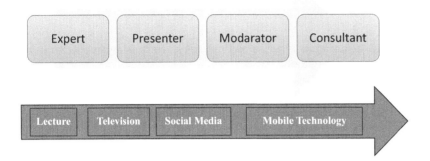

Figure 28.2 Teacher role in the present technology era. Source: Ghaln (2011).

- Teachers should have adequate or qualified knowledge and skill to use various mobile tools and technology.
- Should have sound knowledge about the strength and weaknesses of various methods related to mobile learning.
- Teachers should take the role of facilitator, guide, and advisor.
- Teachers should have high-level self-confidence regarding the application of various courses.
- Teachers should have an open-minded attitude or openness to learn from or with their students.
- Teachers should encourage and motivate a learner to prepare them to face any new challenges and learning scenarios.
- Another role of a teacher is to promote and support an interactive and collaborative learning environment.
- Arrange various activities for the evaluation process.

Content

The selection of content for learning materials is another essential aspect in the context of a mobile learning environment. The following are some of the contexts that need to be taken into consideration before the selection of content material:

- Content of learning material should be selected before prior discussion with a learner, teacher parents, etc.
- Learning content material should be easily accessible and interactive.
- Content material should follow a small amount of content in a single frame so that, a learner can work with it easily.
- Content should be equipped with multiple media such as graphics, video, interactive elements, etc.
- Content should be organized in a manner so that it can grasp the attention of the learner.
- Siragusa et al. (2007) suggested that content should meet the pedagogical needs of a learner.

Environment

The success of any teaching and learning mostly depends on the availability of appropriate teaching and learning environment. Therefore, it is imperative to take special attention in the context of promoting a learning environment. The following are some of the issues that need to be taken into consideration in the context of the teaching and learning environment of mobile learning:

- Students must have opportunities to access all the learning content, assignment, or other relevant learning resources very easily.
- A learning environment should encourage the personalized experience of learning.
- In instructor-led teaching and learning approaches, the instructor should facilitate a learning environment so that learners can enjoy their learning experiences.
- Learning content needs to be designed in a way so that learners can access it anywhere and anytime.
- The environment should encourage a collaborative learning environment.
- The environment should increase communication between student-to-student, student-to-teacher, and student-to-learning content.
- In a learning environment, Wikis, social media, and blogs need to be used to increase social interaction.

Assessment

Assessment is another important component in the context of mobile learning. The following are some essential aspects for the assessment of mobile learning:

- Need to use appropriate LMS to track learner performance in any instructional aspect.
- For effective student assessment, a mobile learning environment should be equipped with a database log, software package, instant messenger, discussion forum, etc.
- There must be an opportunity for assessment of a student by themselves and assessment of others.
- As discussed by Behera (2011), in a mobile learning environment an assessment process should clear all the doubts of learners based on specific courses.
- The design of a mobile learning environment must be capable to access learner performance and can produce immediate feedback.
- It is imperative to provide a good feeling of experience to the learner after a certain assessment.

Challenges of Mobile Learning

As discussed in the previous section, mobile learning is an effective learning approach in the context of learner engagement. However, the implementation of an effective mobile learning environment is very challenging due to the complexity of various related issues such as management, pedagogy, culture, privacy, accessibility, etc. The present section aims to provide a brief overview of challenges related to mobile learning. They are as follows:

Management and institutional challenges: One of the major challenges related to mobile learning is ambiguous policies and pedagogical support in the context of widespread implementation of the mobile learning environment. One of the greatest obstacles is that the mindset of the higher authority of any organization is very rigid and when it comes to the establishment of new technology these challenges become double. To encounter these challenges, change within the institution is needed. Besides this, there is a need to manage the change in the context of processes, activities, components, teachers, decision-makers, content designers, developers, students, etc. The application of M-learning in an educational institution is a major shift, therefore, an organization needs to adopt appropriate change management techniques to cope with the changing situation and accept new technology.

Designing learning materials for mobile devices: Design issues are the greatest challenge in a mobile learning process because a mobile device is equipped with various powerful features such as a camera, voice recording, location, sensor, calculator, media player, etc. Therefore, there is a huge challenge for a designer to effectively utilize various features and to design effective learning material. In the context of the design of mobile-based instructional material, a designer needs to take into consideration three aspects. (a) an instructional design that is related to the educational design of any educational application, (b) interface design which is related to the transparency of the user, and (c) screen design which is related to graphics and visual design.

Technical challenges: This is a pivotal aspect faced by any organization to establish a mobile learning platform. Various technical challenges such as the installation of mobile devices, scarcity of upgraded technology, slow internet connection, low voltage or no electric supply, an absence of technical support, etc. This kind of challenge is very explicit in developing countries compared to developed ones. Besides, other challenging factors directly related to mobile devices are the small screen, the limited capacity of memory, network reliability, limited software application, limited battery, etc.

Privacy and security issues: This leads to varied challenging situations to maintain the privacy and security of student personal data, academic plans, and learning content in mobile learning. Privacy is a fundamental right of any responsible citizen. As mobile learning is an online learning platform; therefore, there is a need to be careful using a secure LMS, data protection algorithm, automatic backup, password protection techniques, etc.

Connectivity of battery life: Battery life of any mobile device is limited to 8–10 hours. Therefore, it affects the continuation of the learning process. To deal with this challenge institutions need to adopt upgraded technology and plan B (or backup) for uninterrupted learning.

Cultural and social challenges: In the context of M-learning, there are basic concerns and challenges related to cultural and social issues. As it is a new learning world and new social communication platform, therefore, students need to learn ethical practice and sensitivity during communication with various cultures. However, without this basic knowledge, a learner can be isolated from a learning platform or may misuse it with bullying, cybercrime, etc.

Various Mobile Learning Software Available in the Market

Throughout the world, plenty of Android and iOS-based mobile applications are available to promote an effective educational process. Some of them are as follows:

Speakabook Reading App

This app is very famous in the market. The major uniqueness of this app is the interactive storytelling mechanism. The database of this platform consisted of 200+ interactive stories for kids. In the cognitive aspect, this app generally increases the motivation of learners and promotes effective habits of reading by providing various eye-catching graphics and interactive features. It can also track the progress of learners and can generate reports for further evaluation of learners. This app is mainly based on the iOS platform. The language is English and it is 73 MB in size.

Noggin

Noggin is a video streaming app for preschool children. This platform is free to use and download. The special aspect of this platform is the availability of various award-winning shows and cartoons such as Backyardigans, Blue's Clues, Yo Gabba Gabba, etc. This app is 70.1 MB in size and available on iOS platform. The language of this application is English.

Chegg

Chegg is a unique mobile learning platform. It provides various educational materials such as textbook solutions, help with homework, etc. The best part of this application is the book rental features. Chegg provides a 2.5 million books database and 24/7 support in the context of homework solutions and subject help. This is a paid app. The monthly rental of this app is US$14.95.

Elevate

Elevate is a brain training app. It is specially designed to improve math skills, rational thinking skills, concentration, etc. for the learner. Elevate is available for Android and iOS-based platforms. Elevate generally consisted of 40+ games that are scientifically designed to improve the memory and cognitive abilities of a learner. It also provides opportunities for the learner to work with daily brain workout activities. Another award-winning feature of the app is that it can track the performance of a learner very accurately and effectively. Furthermore, the learner can earn points and levels based on his or her performance. This app is 1877.3 MB in size on the iOS platform and 46 MB in size on the Android platform.

Udemy Online Courses

Udemy is an online learning platform. This is an open-source learning platform available for web-based as well as mobile-based learning platforms. The Udemy platform is equipped with 42,000+ online courses and has 14 million active users. This platform is available for free with premium courses. Multiple types of learning materials are available such as self-paced, on-demand access, etc.

Peak

Peak is another brain-based training and learning platform. It is based on a neuroscience mechanism. Peak provides various brain-based activities for daily workouts to improve skills of memory. This application consists of 40 fun games that are also designed based on various expert-level neuroscience theories. It can also track and provide details of learner performance. This is paid app with per month charges of US$4.99. This app is available in various languages such as English, French, German, Italian, Chinese, etc.

Learn Language with Rosetta Stone

This is another very effective mobile learning platform for language learning. This app consists of an advanced-level speech recognition mechanism as per the requirement of the learner. This app is available on Android as well as on the iOS platform.

Mathways

Mathway is a math problem-solving platform. This is specially designed to provide instant solutions to various tricky math problems. It can provide solutions to complex Algebra, Pre-algebra, Trigonometry, Chemistry problems, etc. This software is free to download and it is free to get a solution at no charge. The learner can get step-by-step solutions at a meager cost of US$7.99 per month. This software is available in various languages such as Arabic, Portuguese, Russian, English, etc.

Epic!

Epic! is a children's learning platform that consists of 20,000 high-quality books and educational materials for children. Besides this, it also offers various audiobooks and educational videos. This is a paid app costing US$7.99 per month. The subscription of one month is free and supports four profiles. Students get recommendations based on their interests, level of reading, and performance.

ABCmouse.com

This is a mobile-based platform for early learning consisting of 8,500 interactive learning activities. This is a multiple purpose site used for reading, games, puzzle animation, etc. Subscriptions to ABCmouse.com cost US$79.99 per year.

Advantages of Mobile Learning

- **Flexibility in learning**: Mobile learning is a unique learning approach in the context of flexibility in a learning process. In respect of flexibility, mobile learning not only provides an opportunity for the learner to learn from anywhere and at any time but rather it is also flexible to use various modes of learning content such as pictures, videos, interactive learning materials, game-based learning environments, etc.
- **Better completion and higher retention**: Mobile learning platform based on the contextualization of a small unit of learning content, means that any content material present in the mobile learning platform is small in a segment and concise. Therefore, the completion rate of any learning material is high compared to a traditional lecture-based learning environment. Besides, the versatility of the mode of presentation in a mobile learning platform encourages the motivation of a learner and leads to a higher retention rate.
- **Collaborative learning**: In the past, the majority of researchers found that teaching and learning are more effective and fun when a learner can get a chance to learn collaboratively. In this context mobile learning is a more innovative and effective approach to establishing a collaborative learning environment.
- **Higher engagement**: There is a plethora of research in the field of mobile learning that reveals that the engagement of the student in a specific learning content is high when learning materials are presented through a mobile platform. As mobile learning is flexible a learner can access their learning content at any time and track his or her learning progress whenever needed which results in fewer dropouts in an instructional process.
- **Multiple device support**: Another essential advantage of a mobile learning process is it supports learning through multiple devices. It means that a learner can learn his or her learning content material through any device ranging from PCs, laptops, tablets, smartphone, etc.

Instant feedback: Through mobile learning, a learner can track his or her learning performance instantly and a software algorithm program can provide possible remedial feedback to the learner instantly.

Increase the motivation of learners: In a mobile learning process, various addictive learning theories can be applied such as the gamification method. Various scientific methods related to gamification such as learner leaderboards, badges, levels, and virtual social status can increase the learner's motivation as a result learning environment becomes more fun and engaging.

Fit for multiple learning styles: Individual differences are one of the major challenges in any learning environment. Every learner is unique and also has a unique learning style. Mobile learning minimizes these challenges by providing a personalized learning environment.

Disadvantages of Mobile Learning

Cost: One of the major disadvantages of the adaption of mobile technology in the teaching and learning process is that the cost of smartphone-based mobile technology is too high. This is a very common challenge in the context of a developing country. Besides, in the mobile-based teaching-learning process learners need to upgrade their devices occasionally which is also very costly. Furthermore, the data charges for the internet and access to various learning material is also very expensive.

Size of Device: Another basic disadvantage of mobile learning technology it is small in size. This small size of the mobile device is a disadvantage in three core aspects (a) small screen size can result in eye strain in the context of learning over a long-time, (b) in mobile-based learning, only a small amount of information can be provided at a time, and (c) a mobile device is small in size, therefore, it can be lost or stolen very easily.

Battery life: This is a very common disadvantage of mobile learning. Generally, a smartphone can only run 8–10 hours at a time. Therefore, if the battery of any mobile device is run out then it is no longer possible to continue learning unless again charging it. This kind of interruption is very common in a mobile learning process.

Limited capacity of storage: Every mobile device has a limited amount of storage capacity. Therefore, a student is unable to store required documents or learning material if there is no adequate space. Also, there is no universal operation space for mobile learning; therefore, this is very challenging for a designer to design instructional material for everyone on a single platform.

Usability: The design of a mobile is based on calling and texting each other. But the use of any mobile device for learning is very challenging in the context of usability. For instance, if a learner wishes to type very fast, then the style of the keyboard is very small or tricky for some people to operate. Besides this, it is very hard to get access to various features such as printing, drawing, and pointing very efficiently until a learner can use a high-cost mobile phone.

Unexpected distraction: There is also a high chance of distractions for learners due to unnecessary notifications, calls, SMS, etc.

References

Barbosa, D. N. F., & Geyer, C. F. R. (2005). Pervasive personal pedagogical agent: mobile agent shall always be with a learner. Proceedings of the IADIS international conference on mobile learning 2005 (pp. 281–285), Qawra, Malta.

Behara, S.K. (2013). E- and M. learning: A comparative study. International Journal on New Trends in Education and Their Implications, *4*(3).

Harris, P. (2001). Goin' Mobile, Web Site. Retrieved August 20, 2010, from http://www.astd.org/LC/2001/0701_harris.htm.

Inceoglu, M. M., Donmez, O., & Gelibolu, M. F. (2006). *The new face of technology in education: Mobile learning.* IETC 19-21.04.2006 Gazimagusa KKTC

Keegan, D. (2005) The Incorporation of Mobile Learning into Mainstream Education and Training. Proceedings of mLearn2005- 4th World Conference on mLearning, Cape Town, South Africa, 25-28 October 2005. http://www.mlearn.org.za/CD/papers/keegan1.pdf

Makoe, M. (2010). Linking mobile learning to the student-centred approach. Retrieved May 12, 2011, from http://www.checkpointelearning.com/article/8044.html.

MoLeNET. 2014. Molenet. http://www.molenet.org.uk. Accessed 10 May 2014.

O'Malley, C., Vavoula, G., Glew, J. P., Taylor, J., Sharples, M., Lefrere, P., Lonsdale, P., Naismith, L., & Waycott, J. (2005). MOBIlearn. WP 4—Pedagogical Methodologies and Paradigms. Guidelines for Learning/Teaching/Tutoring in a Mobile Environment (82 p). Nottingham: University of Nottingham. https://curve.coventry.ac.uk/open/file/8ff033fc-e97d-4cb8-aed3-29be7915e6b0/1/Review%20of%20e-learning%20theories.pdf

Ozdamli, F., & Cavus, N. (2011). Basic elements and characteristics of mobile learning. *Procedia - Social and Behavioral Sciences, 28*, 937–942

Quinn, C. (2000, Fall). mLearning: mobile, wireless, In-Your-Pocket Learning. *Line Zine*. Retrieved May 11, 2011, from <http://www.linezine.com/2.1/features/Cqmmwiyp.htm>.

Siragusa, L., Dixon, K. & Dixon, R. (2007). Designing quality e-learning environments in higher education. Paper preseted at the Proceedings ascilite, Singapore

Wang, Y. K. (2004, March). Context-awareness and adaptation in mobile learning. In *The 2nd IEEE international workshop on wireless and mobile technologies in education, 2004 proceedings* (pp. 154–158). IEEE. WMTE '04: Proceedings of the 2nd IEEE International Workshop on Wireless and Mobile Technologies in Education (WMTE'04)

Suggested Readings

Ally, M. (Ed.). (2009). *Mobile learning: Transforming the delivery of education and training.* Athabasca University Press.

Ally, M. (2010). *Mobile learning: Transforming the delivery of education and training.* AU Press.

Ally, M., & Tsinakos, A. (2014). *Increasing access through mobile learning.* Commonwealth of Learning (COL); Athabasca University. . https://doi.org/10.56059/11599/558

Berge, Z. L. (2017). *Handbook of mobile learning.* NY: Taylor & Francis.

Guy, R. (Ed.). (2009). *The evolution of mobile teaching and learning.* Informing Science. Santa Rosa, California: Infonning Science Press.

Kukulska-Hulme, A., & Traxler, J. (Eds.). (2005). *Mobile learning: A handbook for educators and trainers.* London, England: Psychology Press.

McQuiggan, S., Kosturko, L., McQuiggan, J., & Sabourin, J. (2015). *Mobile learning: A handbook for developers, educators, and learners.* Chichester: Wiley.

Quinn, C. N. (2011). *The mobile academy: mLearning for higher education.* Chichester: John Wiley & Sons.

29
ARTIFICIAL INTELLIGENCE IN EDUCATION

Introduction

Technological innovation is a dynamic process. All the technological innovations so far discussed in the field of education in previous chapters have highlighted various aspects of current education. The present chapter will discuss another technological innovation that can be considered part of the 21st-century revolution in the sphere of education. By "intelligence" one usually refers to a special characteristic of human beings that helps them to appropriately plan and solve problems. The idea that a machine can also have intelligence would be an abstract idea. Current machine intelligence is a much-discussed topic. Machine intelligence is the artificially created intelligence of a machine that enables the machine to take on human-like problem-solving planning and logical action. Therefore, Artificial Intelligence (AI) is also a demanding area right now with many advantages and benefits.

Significant advancements in computer systems have been acquired over the past few decades. The pioneers of this innovation have always engaged in how computers can be utilized more. Artificial intelligence has become a part of our daily lives currently. Artificial intelligence provides us with a variety of technical facilities that make it easy to gather and analyze large amounts of information and personal data for further application and various purposes. Therefore, it is easy to apply AI to human decision-making and automation of any task. Since artificial intelligence is a state-of-the-art concept, in many cases a huge application-related controversy can be found in various cases. Various eminent scholars have questioned the application of artificial intelligence following appropriate ethical considerations. They have revealed how artificial intelligence could harm humankind and the world in the future. One thing to note in this context is that the use of AI has been presented in some cases as a very challenging such as in the sphere of healthcare, agriculture learning management system in the classroom where the privacy of humans is a serious concern. However, as discussed in the application of artificial intelligence (AI) in the present chapter, it is good to note that teachers and instructional designers need to be aware of the practical and ethical aspects of AI before applying it in a classroom situation.

Definitions of AI in Education

To gain an overall idea of AI it is necessary to form an idea about its definition. The definition of AI has changed over the years in different ways. At the outset, definitions of AI found at different times will be provided.

Mechanical Concept

The definitions we get in the early stages of AI reflected the mechanical concept of AI. Artificial intelligence is described as the key to the science and engineering of making intelligent machines, with John McCarthy coining the term AI. He elucidated what intelligence is in the general sense as a machine.

Definitions of AI

Intelligent Agent

At a later stage when various books or writings on AI were being published, the concept of AI was revealed as a kind of intelligent agent. Given the idea of AI, he said that AI is a type of intelligent agent that analyzes the overall environment of an event or problem and takes appropriate action in terms of analysis which increases the success rate of problem-solving. Wikipedia also uses the concept of AI as an intelligence agency, stating that AI is a mechanical concept where a machine learns through various experiences and performs human intelligence, such as problem-solving and understanding of language.

Non-neutrally Occurring System

Subsequently, we noticed a change in the concept of AI, and with it the definition of AI. At this stage, the artificial intelligence key has been described as a non-neutrally occurring system. During this period, it has been said that AI is the application of knowledge to fulfill a goal. Rich and Knight (2004) said that an artificial system is designed to perform better than humans.

Artificial Intelligence Is a Machine

A closer look at the evolution of the concept of AI reveals that day after day the concept evolved first into a mechanical device, then a system, and later a machine. Defining AI during this time provided researchers to see if AI is a type of machine that can respond in a way that is consistent with human response. In this concept, AI was a machine rich in experience and sharpness that can perform various normal functions.

Artificial Intelligence Is a Simulation Process

The next step is when AI is shown as a simulation process and where it is shown that a machine AI system can mimic human cognitive content and process information.

Classification of Artificial Intelligence

The scope of AI is very wide and it has been influenced by various fields such as mathematics, philosophy, computer science, psychology, and economics. An important point to note here is that the conceptual changes in the various fields mentioned have changed the definition and scope of AI. For example, the concept of intelligence, which has been described as better human thinking in the subject of psychology, has been re-introduced as cognitive computing in the field of AI.

Artificial intelligence can generally be divided into different categories. Taking a closer look at the classifications of AI, one can notice two main classifications, one based on capabilities and the other based on functionality.

Artificial Intelligence Based on Capabilities

Artificial intelligence is generally divided into three categories based on capabilities.

1. Artificial Narrow Intelligence (ANI) or Weak AI/Narrow AI
2. Artificial General Intelligence (AGI)/Strong AI or Deep AI
3. Artificial Superintelligence (ASI)

1. Artificial Narrow Intelligence (ANI) or Weak AI/Narrow AI

Narrow Artificial intelligence refers to the design of AI that is pre-meditated to perform a single task based on a specific goal. Although they may seem extremely intelligent in a general sense, there are some limitations in their functionality. This type of AI performs based on certain parameters. Below some of the characteristics of narrow or weak AI are mentioned:

Characteristics of Narrow AI

1. Narrow AI can generally accomplish in a very short time and is low in capabilities.
2. Narrow AI is limited by a particular field and cannot perform outside its boundaries. This is because this type of AI is designed to be trained for certain tasks and it is also called weak AI. Another point to note is that weak or narrow AI can fail miserably if it exceeds its limits.
3. The Apple series is a perfect example of narrow artificial intelligence because it can perform certain predefined activities.
4. Some more examples of artificial intelligence are chess-playing robots, e-commercial websites, driverless cars, speech recognition software, etc.

Examples of Narrow AI

1. Facial or speech recognition software
2. Email spam filter software
3. Disaster prediction tools and disaster mapping software
4. IBM's Watson

2. Artificial General Intelligence (AGI)/Strong AI or Deep AI

Artificial General Intelligence (AGI) is often referred to as the strongest AI. This kind of AI can think and act like a normal human being. Strong artificial intelligence uses various psychological theories as a framework and applies them to the machine by analyzing a person's needs, emotions, beliefs, and ability to think.

Characteristics of AGI

1. Just as a human being can easily understand intellectual work, so artificial general intelligence performs various tasks in a way that is as efficient and rich as human beings.
2. Strong artificial intelligence systems are designed to enable a machine to easily think like a human.
3. However, no strong AI has yet been developed that can work perfectly as a human. Researchers around the world are now focusing on developing machines with general AI.
4. General artificial intelligence is very limited in nature. Further research work is ongoing and further development of such systems will require a lot of effort and time.

Example of Strong AI

Fujitsu-built K, a supercomputer that is still considered a significant step in the field of strong artificial intelligence. But it took 40 minutes to stimulate neural activity. So, it is notable to say that still it is not known exactly how long it will take humans to build a strong AI platform. However, it can be said that with the advancement of image and facial recognition technology, the capabilities and visual skills of machines can be improved.

3. Artificial Superintelligence (ASI)

Artificial superintelligence still exists at an imaginary level. Researchers believe that artificial superintelligence will bring out the equivalence of human intelligence and behavior. Not only that but it is also thought that artificial superintelligence can in some cases overwhelm human intelligence. Generally, the concept of artificial superintelligence has been explored in various science fiction movies. Where it is seen that robots are using human beings as their slaves beyond humanity. And at the same time, it is seen that artificial superintelligence has developed on its own by gaining knowledge from human emotions and experiences and can increase emotional needs, beliefs, and aspirations to a greater extent.

Characteristics of ASI

1. Some researchers believe that the use of AI will improve, theoretically, the fields of mathematics, science, sports, etc.
2. Describing the potential of future artificial superintelligence, the researchers suggest that this super-mechanism will easily have more memory and analytical ability. As a result, this type of machine will show very good decision-making and problem-solving ability.
3. Researchers looking at the capabilities of artificial superintelligence have found that such superintelligence machines will have very intelligent and self-defense capabilities that can affect our survival and well-being.
4. Artificial superintelligence will have some more features such as the ability to think, reason, solve problem-solving, learn judgment plans, and the ability to communicate by oneself and express in one's language.

Types of Artificial Intelligence Based on Functionalities

In terms of functionality, AI can be divided into four categories:

1. Reactive Machine
2. Limited Memory

3. Theory of Mind
4. Self-Awareness

1. Reactive Machine

A reactive machine is a primitive and fundamental form of AI. This type of machine has no previous memory and cannot use information from the past to accomplish any future work. A perfect example of a reactive machine is IBM's chess program that defeated Garry Kasparov in 1990.

Characteristics of Reactive Machine

1. Reactive machines in general cannot use any previous memory.
2. It is based on information about what is currently happening and controls current activity.
3. Reactive machines usually perform activities in the external world and perceive the world and react.
4. Such machines cannot interact with the world.
5. Reactive machines perform a task based on their predetermined design and cannot work outside of this type of machine design.
6. Such machines only look at the current situation and give the best possible response to that situation.

2. Limited Memory

Limited memory AI-based machine is the second type of AI. This type of machine can store experience and learn from that experience and make decisions. Limited memory machines can use past data but they cannot store it. This type of technology is commonly used in self-driving cars. Self-driving cars, for example, monitor the speed of different vehicles and make decisions accordingly. This whole activity cannot be done all of a sudden but requires the identification and observation of different objects. The information that is collected from long-term monitoring of driver-driven activities is presented as a program in the self-driving car. Such programs include traffic lights, various lane signs, and other important elements. So, when a self-driving car changes the road lane, one car does not collide with another. Mitsubishi Electric is working on such technological development.

Characteristics of Limited Memory AI

1. Limited memory AI's data storage capacity is very short-lived.
2. Building a system with limited memory depends on the representation of certain information and the use of experience.

3. Theory of Mind

Theory of mind is a type of AI that can socialize with human emotions, beliefs, thoughts, expectations, etc. Although this type of machine has many important aspects, it is yet to fully develop such a machine. This type of machine can be called the complete division of what the AI machine has developed and the AI machine that will be created in the future.

General psychology claims humans or other creatures have thoughts and emotions. But the theory of mind believes that a machine could express different emotions and thinking abilities just like humans.

Characteristics of the Theory of Mind AI

1. The theory of mind-based AI technology represents an advanced form of AI that still exists as a concept.
2. Researchers believe that this type of AI will be able to work between people and the environment to absorb their feelings and change their behavior.
3. Researchers believe that machines rich in theories of Mind AI cannot detect human attention.
4. Although the concept of this type of AI has not been widely developed, it is imperative to say that researchers are working tirelessly to bring improvement.

An example of AI in the theory of mind is the Kismet robot, which can easily mimic human feelings and emotions and use them later when performing other specific performances such as interactions with humans. Another great example of the theory of mind AI is the Sophia robot that is created by Hanson Robotics. The Sophia robot can easily make eye contact with humans and identify any human beings through advanced computer algorithms and deep learning technology.

4. Self-Awareness

The concept of self-awareness in AI has not yet been fully realized. The concept of such AI is hypothetical. It is thought that such AI systems would be able to perceive the inner state and emotions of human beings. It is also thought that the machines of this type of AI will be much more intelligent than humans; not only will they be able to understand emotions, but they will also be able to arouse emotions.

Characteristics of Self-Awareness AI

1. Researchers are considering introducing self-awareness in AI machines.
2. Researchers also believe that this type of AI will be able to represent itself on its own.
3. The concept of such AI will be able to easily predict human emotions.
4. It is thought that self-awareness will be an important feature of future AI machines and these machines will be so intelligent that they will have their own sense of self and self-awareness.

Application of AI in Education

Every aspect of our current life is being managed and changed by AI. So, it is not surprising that educational institutions or the current education system will be affected in various ways by AI. The impact of AI is not only affecting certain subjects such as science, technology, engineering, and mathematics but also changing the entire education structure. These advanced technological strategies are playing a special role in helping students to learn and acquire education in the field of vocational education as well as primary to higher education. We know that the biggest challenge in education is to impart education keeping in mind the individual differences of the learners. There is variation in terms of the nature of learning and learning patterns including the pace that differs one learner from another. Over the past few decades, various scientific stories, literary predictions, and filmmakers have predicted the emergence of AI. Although we have not yet been able to move forward with the work of creating high-quality conscious robots seen in movies we have seen the use of many robots in daily life that have brought unprecedented changes in various fields. Although human robots have not yet been widely used in education, it is needless to say that robots with AI have emerged in different ways and in different forms. And using this advanced technology using computer intelligence, students and teachers are able to gain a variety of educational experiences. Here we will look at the application of the use of AI in several fields of education.

Assistance of Teachers and Artificial Intelligence

We know that the role of a teacher in a school environment is not only to impart education but also to evaluate their students and to engage in preparing various lessons. Now the point is that by using AI, both the teacher and the machine can easily share several tasks, such as assigning question papers to students in a school and evaluating them can be done effortlessly using machine algorithms. AI has now reached such a level that it is possible to evaluate a student's handwritten answer sheet.

We have to keep in mind that to apply AI in the field of education, teachers of educational institutions have to be much more active than ever before and increase their ability to accept new things. Using AI can easily spread personalization education and AI can very easily undermine the work of an organization's administration.

Artificial Intelligence Inspires Personalized Learning

Each student learns according to his or her ability. It is at this stage that it becomes impossible for a teacher to teach each student separately in an education system. Artificial intelligence plays an important role in the practical field and the machines are designed in such a way that each student can master the subject matter according to his/her learning ability. It is possible to create customized profiles for each student using advanced AI science algorithms. Each student can adopt the desired learning method according to his or her skills. It is expected that by 2024, 47% of educational equipment used in education will be powered by AI. And it will be possible for each student to tailor the curriculum as per their needs. It is also estimated that the market for AI in the sphere of learning will exceed several billion dollars by 2024. Machine learning is being used to prepare textbooks with hyper-personalization in mind and class card technology is being used to shorten very large chapters. With the use of digital technology, it will be possible to easily prepare paperless education in the field of education where the use of hardcopy textbooks is rarely seen. The use of personal learning and conversation-assisting tutoring machines is enhanced through customized learning materials as well as AI. And they are designed to communicate with students, ask them questions and respond to their questions appropriately. In addition, these machines can provide assignments to students and provide them with the assistance they need in their assignments. This allows a student to participate in learning at their own pace and ability. Artificial intelligence plays a special role in providing trading to students. Providing homework and reading to students in educational institutions is a very tedious task. Assigning an assignment to a student for assessment and assigning their marks based on that assignment is a very important task. In some educational infrastructures, there are fewer teachers than they used to be. In those situations, the use of AI makes it easier for students to complete the assessment process. Although the grading of students through AI is still not equivalent to the provision of human-guided grading; however, nevertheless very easy to evaluate student assignments by applying AI algorithms.

Forming an Education Structure According to the Needs of Students

One thing we have come to realize is that AI will have a profound effect on everything from kindergarten to university education. Currently, some applications using AI such as learning programs, games, software, etc. have received special attention. These systems are designed so that a machine algorithm can easily respond to student needs. How much a student has to read a subject matter? How much the student has mastered and the ability of the student to repeat is being understood through the machine algorithm. This type of custom learning process enables teachers to help a student work together in the classroom. Teachers are embracing the benefits of using AI in educational institutions. Over the next several years, the advancement of AI may reach a point where it is possible to develop and expand various adaptive programs.

Impact of AI on Improving the Academic Environment

Usually when a teacher teaches in the classroom most of the time students have trouble realizing what they don't understand. Many times, the student gets confused about a particular idea. In addition, teachers are often unaware of the difficulty of their lectures and teaching materials. The role of AI in all these cases is unprecedented. Artificial intelligence-enabled machine algorithms specifically in identifying student difficulties and determine how much a student needs to learn. The AI system alerts the teacher and encourages the students to give correct answers in the future in case a student submits a wrong answer in a large online educational institution.

Teaching the Teacher New Things

Using AI, a teacher can come at any time of the day and learn new things for students because AI collects a lot of information and provides it according to the teacher's specific needs. Teachers can easily master the knowledge of different techniques in learning new languages sitting at home. As well as mastering knowledge about various complex programming techniques or content will at just one click.

Bringing the Whole World Together

Since the field of AI is computer-based, it is very easy to connect different educational institutions from all over the world. As well as the role of AI in collaborating with different educational institutions and building a spirit of empathy is notable.

Identify and Address Various Shortcomings in the Field of Education

In the field of education, the assimilation of a student's content depends a lot on the teacher's presentation of the lesson. A teacher can't determine exactly how much content a student in a huge class with numerous students understood from the presentation. The use of AI technology has made this much easier. Using machine algorithms, it is very easy to determine how much content a teacher has mastered in a student's presentation. Also, when a large number of students do homework, it is often not possible for a teacher to test it accurately. With this in mind, AI is currently being designed in such a way that students can easily determine if a wrong assignment is submitted by a student. And with the help of AI machines, the teacher can warn the student in the future so that he does not make mistakes again.

Encouraging Extracurricular Activities

Using the current technology of AI, robots are being created that can easily interact with children, such as hand gestures, mental movements, choreographies, dances, etc. As a result, a lot of enthusiasm is instilled in a student and they can proceed through learning forward by interacting with more and more machines.

Virtual Reality (VR), Augmented Reality (AR), and Mixed Reality (MR)

Technological advancement has allowed us to mimic the real-world context and produce it on-screen through visualization. Sometimes it is very hard to provide training to the learner in a real-world situation because of various reasons related to the context. For example, it is very hard to show the inner human body in a real-world context but it can be visualized through various technological innovations namely virtual reality (VR), augmented reality (AR), and mixed reality (MR). This section discusses each category separately:

- **Virtual reality**: Virtual reality generally refers to a powerful computer simulation that can reproduce any realistic situation to the user. This technological simulation is equipped with various screens, speakers, sensors, headsets, etc. that can help to translate the user's motions into a simulation.
- **Augmented reality**: Augmented reality provides the next-level opportunity for the user to feel any activities and entertainment realistically. Augmented reality also provides the opportunity for the user to feel the physical world through computer-generated visuals and sound. One of the great examples of augmented reality is Google Maps where a user can get a camera view of any real road map.
- **Mixed reality**: Mixed reality is based on the systematic orientation of hybrid reality. One of the interesting things about mixed reality is the synchronization between real and virtual objects in real time. In a mixed reality scenario virtual and real-world work together. One of the great examples of mixed reality is a game namely Pokémon GO where a user can play it in a real situation.

Application of AI in the Indian Education System

Every country has taken important steps to use AI in education and India is not lagging behind. The current market for educational technology in India is estimated to reach US$2 billion by 2021. If we get an idea of the educational technology start-up companies in India today, we will see that there are more than 3,500 educational technology startups, of which about 56 have invested 700 million USD. The use of AI in India has been noticed in various fields ranging from personal education, skills development, to generating employability, etc. In the case of India, every public and private organization has participated in the dissemination and promotion of AI in various ways and they have come up with ideas on how to further apply AI in education effectively and efficiently. And looking at the current trend of AI, it can be seen that the use of ICT technology in government schools and colleges is day by day increasing in India.

Therefore, the interest of various educational technology startups and various foreign companies in creating a market for AI in India has increased tremendously. Companies such as Mindspark and Leverage Edu, and other various public-private schools in India, have focused on creating personal learning software and are motivated to create a platform to further enhance the personalization of education by using various AI-based software and gadget. In India, AI has added a special dimension to education. In some cases, it is noteworthy that various government and non-government organizations like Del, Microsoft, etc. have started working hand-in-hand with the Indian government to think about how to better use AI in education.

Bibliography

Archer, B. (1986). *The three R's in technology in schools* (A. Cross & B. McCormick, Eds.). Milton Keynes: Open University Press.
Gilchrist, R. S. (1951). Are schools meeting the imperative needs of youth? *Bulletin of the National Association of Secondary School Principals*, *35*(180), 82–87.
Knight, G. (1982). *Issues and alternatives in educational philosophy*. Berrien Springs, MI: Andrews University Press.
Mitcham, C. (1994). *Thinking through technology: The path between engineering and philosophy*. Chicago, IL: University of Chicago Press.
Pacey, A. (1984). *The culture of technology*. Cambridge, MA: MIT Press.
Rich, E. & Knight, K. (2004). *Artificial Intelligence* (p.3). Tata McGraw.
Vries, M. J. de (2012). Philosophy of technology. In P. J. Williams (Ed.), *Technology education for teachers* (pp. 15–34). The Netherlands: Sense Publishers

Suggested Readings

Benson, C., & Lunt, J. (Eds.). (2011). *International handbook of primary technology education: Reviewing the past twenty years* (Vol. 7). New York: Springer Science & Business Media.
De Vries, M. J. (2016). *Teaching about technology: An introduction to the philosophy of technology for non-philosophers*. Berlin: Springer.
Erneling, C. E. (2010). *Towards discursive education: Philosophy, technology, and modern education*. Cambridge: Cambridge University Press.
Ihde, D. (2012). *Technics and praxis: A philosophy of technology* (Vol. 24). Springer Science & Business Media.
Scharff, R. C., & Dusek, V. (Eds.). (2013). *Philosophy of technology: The technological condition: An anthology*. Chichester: John Wiley & Sons.

30
COVID-19 PANDEMIC

Educational Strategies and Resources during Crises and Emergencies

"Hard times come again no more" is a line of a very famous song written by Stephen C. Foster (1954), America's pioneer songwriter in 1984 which is still relevant in the present unprecedented pandemic situation. One of the most significant threats to the world today is the COVID-19 pandemic, which has significantly disrupted the overall education system worldwide. Since early 2020 COVID-19 has severely impacted human beings in terms of maintaining social distancing, suspension of regular direct communication and activities, managing physical and psychological vulnerability, etc. COVID-19 is a shockwave that impacted almost every sector of our society from economics to education.

The recent data furnished by UNESCO (2020) reveals that, presently, 1.6 million students were unable to access formal education because of strict lockdowns in most countries. In such conditions, the only option open for continuing education is to shift to online alternative teaching-learning. Taking decisions in such extreme situations is most challenging as most of the institutions were not fully prepared for this shift. Hence, most educational institutions had to formulate their new education plans within a very short period and a comprehensive plan was needed on how to adapt to this new environment. The sudden school closures not only affected the educational institutions but also created an attitude of confrontation between the students, their parents, and teachers. The only thought in everyone's mind was how to continue the teaching and learning process in such a situation. Besides the goal, the educators had a hard time coming up with a creative plan that would allow them to continue their work in the same way as in the school environment.

In terms of Indian education, it is noticed that about 300 million students in India have been affected by the COVID-19 virus. In this context, a glimmer of hope is that 37.6 million children in 16 states in India can continue their education through various educational initiatives. However, the picture is a bit different in many parts of the world for example child labor has increased by 105% due to the impact of the pandemic. A recent survey by "Save the Children" found that 62% of children in households dropped out of education, compared to 67% in rural areas and 55% in urban areas. In addition, what worries us, even more, is the impact of poverty and the fact that families are failing to finance their children due to less or no earnings during the lockdown period.

Thanks to technology in education that created a scope for a flexible environment for all thereby making it possible to deliver education outside the school environment and to the children. The enormous capacity of technological innovation has increased the level of communication between teachers and students. Now a student can access learning materials, video lectures, mobile apps, and software applications anytime and anywhere (Huang et al., 2020; Liang, 2020; Smart Learning Institute, 2020). Various online education mediums have shown the light of hope in this case. Teachers have agreed to continue teaching using various online software such as Zoom, Google Meet, YouTube, WhatsApp, Facebook, etc. in immediate preparation.

Strategies for Teachers in the Time of Pandemic
Prepare and Practice

1. **Ensure digital equity**
   If we are talking of a major problem in online learning, then it must be said that not every student has the proper infrastructure for online learning. From a practical point of view, it is not possible for the government of any country, especially for economically weak countries, to provide every student with a laptop or mobile phone to have access to online education. In such circumstances, the government or the educational institutions should conduct a proper survey to identify all the students who do not yet have a proper device to access or participate in online learning and initiatives should be taken strategically to provide the same at the earliest.

   In addition, various research surveys have shown that some families have only one laptop or mobile phone that is used to work from the home of the working parent. In this case the government, software developers, and teachers, all need to take into serious consideration the fact that the software should be designed in such a way so that it can be used properly on both computer and mobile as per the availability.

   Another problem, especially in economically weaker countries, is that not every teacher has access to high-speed internet services, so the government has to go through a well-planned survey to find out the real situation and provide adequate services.

2. **Practice makes perfect**
   In a country such as India where the online education system is not considered a conventional system, the big problem for many is that teachers or students suddenly find it very difficult to adapt to a new environment because of their fear of new technology, as they do not want to get out of their comfort zone. The most important thing in this situation is to explain to the teachers the benefits of online learning and to teach the students how they can participate in learning in a home environment. We know that more skills can be acquired through practice so teachers need to practice more online learning. Teachers can emulate the following steps in practice:
   a) An important aspect of online teaching is to communicate with the student through audio and visual methods. So, a teacher has to practice extensively to know how to manage audio and visual media appropriately.
   b) The second important thing is to respond to emails or other queries through various modes sent by the students as soon as possible. That's why teachers should be careful about checking emails and other modes every day and respond to students' questions frequently.

3. **Teachers and students should be given clear expectations**
   One of the most important things during this epidemic is to get the school administration teachers, students, and parents to communicate properly. In many cases, the lack of proper

communication causes concern between teachers, students, and their parents. The important thing to do in this case is to prepare a FAQ (Frequently Asked Question) sheet.

In addition to preparing the FAQ, the school needs to see how to reach every stakeholder easily and quickly. Besides this, the school needs to teach a student and a member of his/her family how to log in to a new software application and how to use it properly for learning purposes. Teachers need to be aware of all the nuances of the new software and its application. Teachers must have an idea of how to use this software to take student attendance, how to properly plan the learning, and how to evaluate them properly in an online learning platform.

The school administration needs to develop a step-by-step guideline that will provide accurate information on how students can access online materials. It needs to be kept in mind that this information needs to be presented in various formats such as video, text screenshots, etc. The subsequent section provides various tools that teachers and students can use in online learning.

4. **Planning is the key to success**
We know that proper planning is an important means of dealing with any difficult situation. Since the COVID-19 situation is a new problem for us, it is necessary to plan properly to deal with it and to continue the education process in this difficult situation. As physical interaction between teachers and students was not possible online was the only means of communication and learning. So, if a teacher is preparing an online learning plan, he needs to pay special attention to some crucial aspects of planning a learning design. Suddenly jumping into online teaching-learning without a plan will lead to more failure.

5. **Daily schedule in small segments**
Student onscreen scheduling is an important factor in providing online education. Throughout the lockdown process, it has become mandatory for students to take classes online, while their parents have to work from home. When a teacher prepares a routine for an online class, it is important to keep in mind the schedule and how to design it strategically so that the student and his/her parents can access it with ease and interest. As there is very little space for direct interaction like in the school learning environment, it is very important to make a schedule for students based on their attention.

6. **Preparation of effective learning design**
We know that learning design is an important part of teaching. Therefore, the topic of learning design should be discussed seriously. Since online teaching is a new medium of instruction, the teacher must emphasize several important instructional strategies in the field of online teaching design. These are some of the goal-setting considerations that a teacher may use:
- Shorten the content with a small pause in between each presentation.
- When providing online education, the student should first be clear about the objectives and expectations of his/her learning.
- Various online assessments such as chats, interactive forms, question-and-answer sessions, feedback, etc., should be arranged properly to check the progress of the students.
- In addition, some virtual conferences, video-sharing tutorials, and one-to-one communication with the students need to be designed properly to strengthen the connection between students and teachers.

7. **Learning design should encourage independent learning for student**
As it is not possible to directly substantiate how a student behaves through online education and how much progress is being made in his/her knowledge, special attention needs to be

paid during online education. Besides this, parents have to do their office work from home, so it is not always possible for them to constantly assist the students in teaching-learning. Therefore, learning design should be prepared in such a manner that a student can complete the process and do the evaluation process by themselves.

8. **Sensitivity is a means to success**

    The medium of online education is a new initiative that teacher and student groups were not previously aware of. In such a situation, the teacher needs to extend a helping hand to their fellow teachers and help each other so that every teacher and student can feel comfortable in the digital medium. Moreover, teaching at home can be a new challenge for the teacher, so it is important to keep the following in mind:
    - Take a break in the middle of each presentation.
    - It is important to practice regular exercise.
    - Everyday sleep schedule needs to be made properly.
    - It is important to stay away from various disruptive media if possible.
    - It is important to set daily and weekly goals and prepare routines based on the goals.
    - If a teacher or student is in trouble, the matter should be looked into emphatically.

9. **Proper equipment must be prepared and designed**

    It is important to acquire knowledge of various technical tools for managing online education plans as well as how to apply them properly. Various tools have been developed for online media all over the world but it is up to the planning level to decide what kind of gazette a teacher will use to conduct his/her education. some applications may seem tempting to use but it is important to review how useful such applications are, if at all. We know that many kinds of distractions can occur in the field of online education but to control them, teachers need to be aware of various scientific instructional techniques.

    The following tables subsequently provides a list of open-source software that can be useful for teachers and students to continue education during a pandemic.

Tools to Create Infographics and Charts for Teachers

We all know that charts and infographics are very important elements to illustrate complex concepts in a systematic way. In a classroom situation sometimes, it is very hard to communicate with the student only using verbal or written instructions. Therefore, charts and infographics are powerful tools to help make sense of concepts effectively and efficiently. Tables 30.1 to 30.15 list very useful tools for teachers to make charts and infographics in an easy way to capture the attention of students and covey information uniquely.

Table 30.1 Tools to create infographics and charts for teachers

Name of Tools	Web Address
Am Charts	https://live.amcharts.com/
ChartsBin	http://chartsbin.com/about/apply
Easel.ly	https://www.easel.ly/
Gapminder	https://www.gapminder.org/
Gliffy	https://www.gliffy.com/
Google Chart Tools	https://developers.google.com/chart/
Hohli Charts	http://charts.hohli.com/

Tools to Create Text-to-Speech for Teachers

Text-to-Speech (TTS) is another essential tool for teaching-learning. Generally, in asynchronous online or distance mode teaching and learning where real-time lectures of the teacher are not available, TTS helps to increase the attention of students while reading text material by machine. Besides this, it is also effective for students to focus on comprehension as well as fix errors in their writing (see Tables 30.3).

Table 30.2 Tools to create infographics for teachers

Name of Tools	What It Is	Web Address
infogr.am	Infogr.am is a web-based infographics tool with a variety of powerful features such as interactivity, collaboration, custom tracking links, etc.	https://infogram.com/
Inkscape	Inkscape is a flexible drawing tool and vector graphics editor. Teachers can use this software to create various learning prototypes and graphics designs.	https://inkscape.org/en/
Lucidchart	Lucidchart is free for students and teachers. This intelligent diagramming tool is very helpful for the teacher to create a visual understanding of various information effectively and efficiently.	https://www.lucidchart.com/
Piktochart	Piktochart is a platform to develop visual content effectively. This web-based platform can turn any text or data into a stunning presentation and report very quickly.	https://piktochart.com/
Pixlr	Pixlr is a photo editing tool with powerful AI-based features.	https://pixlr.com/
Stat Planet	StatPlanet is a powerful tool to create rich infographics maps. Features of this software enable teachers and students to explore, analyze, and filter 8,000+ indicators through interactive maps and graphs.	https://www.statsilk.com/maps/statplanet-world-bank-open-data
Tableau Public	Tableau Public is a visual analytics tool to solve various data problems.	https://www.tableau.com/
Venngage	Venngage is another infographic tool that is equipped with various charts and visuals. Users can choose from a rich amount of template designs or can customize designs by changing fonts and colors.	https://venngage.com/
Visual.ly	Visual.ly is an infographics platform that helps to create premium visual content simply and affordably. Teachers can use this platform to develop interesting learning material for students.	https://visual.ly/
Wordle	Wordle is generally used to create "Word Clouds". It is equipped with lots of useful features that help to identify important or frequently used words and highlight them in a systematic manner.	http://www.wordle.net/

Table 30.3 Tools to create text-to-speech for teachers

Name of Tools	Web Address
Announcify	http://www.announcify.com/
Balabolka	http://www.cross-plus-a.com/balabolka.htm
DSpeech	http://dimio.altervista.org/eng/
Free Natural Reader	https://www.naturalreaders.com/
QR voice	http://ww1.qrvoice.net/
text2speech	https://www.text2speech.org/
Voki	http://www.voki.com/
vozMe	https://vozme.com/index.php?lang=en
WordTalk	https://www.wordtalk.org.uk/Home/

Table 30.4 Digital storytelling tools for teachers

Name of Tools	Web Address
Animoto	https://animoto.com/business/education
Cartoonist	https://www.creaza.com/this-is-creaza/Cartoonist
Generator	https://www.acmi.net.au/education/film-it/
MakeBeliefsComix	https://www.makebeliefscomix.com/
Pixton	https://edu.pixton.com/educators/
Smilebox	https://www.smilebox.com/about-us/
Storybird	https://storybird.com/
Puppet Pals	https://apps.apple.com/us/app/puppet-pals-hd/id342076546
ShowMe Interactive Whiteboard	https://apps.apple.com/us/app/showme-interactive-whiteboard/id445066279
Toontastic	https://toontastic.withgoogle.com/

Table 30.5 Podcast tools for teachers

Name of Tools	Web Address
Ardour	http://ardour.org/
HuffDuffer	https://huffduffer.com/
Podbean	https://www.podbean.com/
PodOmatic	https://www.podomatic.com/
SoundCloud	https://soundcloud.com/

Table 30.6 Screen recorder tools for teachers

Name of Tools	Web Address
Free Cam	https://www.freescreenrecording.com/
Free Screen Video Recorder	http://www.dvdvideosoft.com/products/dvd/Free-Screen-Video-Recorder.htm
ShareX	https://getsharex.com/
CamStudio	http://camstudio.org/
Ezvid	https://www.ezvid.com/download
OBS Studio	https://obsproject.com/
iSpring Suite	https://www.ispringsolutions.com/ispring-suite
Camtasia	https://www.techsmith.com/video-editor.html
Filmora Scrn	https://filmora.wondershare.com/screen-recorder/
Movavi Screen Recorder	https://www.movavi.ru/
My Screen Recorder Pro	https://www.deskshare.com/video-screen-capture.aspx
FlashBack	https://www.flashbackrecorder.com/home

Table 30.7 Social bookmarking for teachers

Name of Tools	Web Address
Symbalooedu	https://www.symbalooedu.com/
Pearltrees	https://www.pearltrees.com/
A1-Webmarks	https://a1-webmarks.com/
All my favorites	http://go.surftown.com/
BibSonomy	http://www.bibsonomy.org/
Diigo Education Edition	http://www.diigo.com/teacher_entry/educationupgrades
Edshelf	https://edshelf.com/
Evernote	https://evernote.com/
Givealink	http://cnets.indiana.edu/groups/nan/givealink/
Historious	https://historio.us/
ikeepbookmarks.com	http://ww2.ikeepbookmarks.com/Default.asp
Jog The Web	http://www.jogtheweb.com/
Learn Fizz	https://www.happy.co.uk/
linkaGoGo	http://www.linkagogo.com/
Livebinder	http://www.livebinders.com/
Livebinder	http://www.livebinders.com/
Netvibes	http://www.netvibes.com/en
Pinboard	http://pinboard.in/
Pinterest	https://www.pinterest.com/
Reddit	https://www.reddit.com/
Sharetivity	http://sharetivity.com/
Smub	http://smub.it/
Stumbleupon	https://www.stumbleupon.com/

Table 30.8 Bibliography and citation tools for teachers

Name of Tools	Web Address
CitationGenerator	https://www.citationgenerator.com/
Citation Machine - Free	http://www.citationmachine.net/
Citefast - Free	https://www.citefast.com/
Recipes4Success - Free	http://recipes.tech4learning.com/
Zotero - Free	https://www.zotero.org/
EndNote	http://buy.endnote.com/store/endnote/DisplayHomePage
NoodleTools	https://www.noodletools.com/
RefWorks	https://www.refworks.com/refworks2/default.aspx?r=authentication::init
EasyBib	http://www.easybib.com/
Citelighter	http://www.citelighter.com/
Citation Machine	http://citationmachine.net/index2.php
Bibme	http://www.bibme.org/
RefDot	https://chrome.google.com/webstore/detail/refdot/
Citefast	http://www.citefast.com/
Mendely	http://www.mendeley.com/

Table 30.9 Sticky notes tools for teachers

Name of Tools	Web address
Corkboard	http://www.corkboard.it/
Hott Notes	http://www.hottnotes.com/
Linoit	http://en.linoit.com/
Listings	https://pinup.com/
Notepad2	http://www.flos-freeware.ch/notepad2.html
Padlet	https://padlet.com/
Scrumblr	http://scrumblr.ca/
Simple Sticky Notes	http://www.simplestickynotes.com/
Stickies	http://www.zhornsoftware.co.uk/stickies/
StickyPad	http://www.greeneclipse.com/stickypad.html

Table 30.10 Photo and image editing tools for teachers

Name of Tools	Web Address
Cacoo	https://cacoo.com/
Chart Chooser	http://labs.juiceanalytics.com/chartchooser/index.html
ChartGizmo	http://chartgizmo.com/
ChartTool	https://www.onlinecharttool.com/
CoSketch	http://cosketch.com/
Creately	https://creately.com/
Creative Docs.net	http://www.creativedocs.net/
diagram.ly	https://www.draw.io/
DoppelMe	http://www.doppelme.com/
Flash PAINT	http://www.searchingmagnified.com/?dn=flashpaint.com&pid=7PO217VO5
Flowchart.com	https://flowchart.com/
Gickr.com	http://gickr.com/
Glogster	http://edu.glogster.com/?ref=com
GoAnimate	https://goanimate.com/
Google SketchUp	https://www.sketchup.com/
Inkscape	https://inkscape.org/en/
PhotoPeach	https://photopeach.com/
Pixlr	https://pixlr.com/
Reshade	http://reshade.com/
Rich Chart Live	https://planning-strategy.com/
Roxio PhotoShow	http://www.photoshow.com/home
SUMO Paint	http://www.sumo.fm/
Toondoo	http://www.toondoo.com/
Voki	http://www.voki.com/

Table 30.11 Testing and quizzing tool for teachers

Name of Tools	Web Address
ClassMarker	https://www.classmarker.com/
ClassTools	http://www.classtools.net/
Easy Test Maker	https://www.easytestmaker.com/
Hot Potatoes	http://web.uvic.ca/hrd/hotpot/
ProProfs Quiz SchoolC	https://www.proprofs.com/quiz-school/
Quandary	http://www.halfbakedsoftware.com/quandary.php
Quiz Revolution	http://www.mystudiyo.com/
Yacapaca	https://yacapaca.com/
Jeopardy	https://jeopardylabs.com/
Edgames	http://people.uncw.edu/ertzbergerj/ppt_games.html
QuizSlides	https://quizslides.com/
What2Learn	http://www.what2learn.com/

Table 30.12 Web or video conferencing tools for teachers

Name of Tools	Web Address
AnyMeeting	https://www.anymeeting.com/
BigBlueButton	https://bigbluebutton.org/
Google+ Hangout	https://plus.google.com/browser-not-supported/?ref=/
Meetin.Gs	http://www.meetin.gs/
Mikogo	https://www.mikogo.com/
Sync.in	http://sync.in/
TokBox Video Chat	https://tokbox.com/
Twiddla	https://www.twiddla.com/
Zoho Meeting	https://www.zoho.com/meeting/
Zoom	https://zoom.us/
Google Meet	https://meet.google.com/

Table 30.13 Authoring tools for teachers

Name of Tools	Web Address
Easygenerator	https://www.easygenerator.com/
LCDS	https://www.microsoft.com/en-us/learning/lcds-tool.aspx#tab1
SmartBuilder	http://www.smartbuilder.com/
authorPOINT	http://www.authorgen.com/authorpoint/index.htm
Document Suite 2008	http://www.jetdraft.com/eng/jds/about/
Jackdaw	http://www.openelms.org/page/jackdaw-cloud-authoring-system
LessonWriter	http://www.lessonwriter.com/
MOS Solo	https://www.mindonsite.com/
myUdutu	https://www.udutu.com/
QuickLessons Authoring Tool	http://www.quicklessons.com/
Scratch	https://scratch.mit.edu/

Table 30.14 Video tools for teachers

Name of Tools	Web Address
Ezvid	https://www.ezvid.com/
BlueBerry Flashback Express Recorder	https://www.flashbackrecorder.com/express/download/
CamStudio	http://camstudio.org/
Webineria	http://www.webinaria.com/
Screen-O-Matic	http://www.screencast-o-matic.com/

Table 30.15 PDF tools for teachers

Name of Tools	Web Address
Adobe Reader XI	https://get.adobe.com/reader/
Doro PDF Writer	https://doro-pdf-writer.en.softonic.com/?
BullZip PDF Printer	http://www.bullzip.com/products/pdf/info.php
PDFTK Builder	https://portableapps.com/apps/office/pdftk_builder_portable
PDFill PDF Tool	http://www.pdfill.com/pdf_tools_free.html
PDF Annotator	https://www.pdfannotator.com/en/
Xodo	https://www.xodo.com/
Drawboard	https://www.drawboard.com/
Annotate	https://www.annotate.com/

Digital Storytelling Tools for Teachers

Storytelling has been presented at various times as a special medium of learning. Since ancient times and even now the process of storytelling has been specially recognized in the field of education. In the current era of digital globalization, the style of storytelling has changed. Through various software, a teacher can present educational content through stories. This whole process is called digital storytelling. Digital storytelling completes the process of learning while entertaining the students and the student can happily absorb the whole content of the story. The following are some of the benefits of digital storytelling in education:

- Students can easily assimilate the medium of digital storytelling and remember the content learned for a long time.
- Another special feature of learning through digital storytelling is that in these cases students can increase a stronger sense of hearing and can easily complete the learning process.
- Another special feature of this process is that any curriculum can be easily presented through digital storytelling.
- The digital storytelling process can increase the students' attention effectively.

Podcast Tools for Teachers

We know that different new technologies have affected the education system in different ways. A podcast is one such technology. Teachers and school authorities are focusing more on education through podcasts to make education more dynamic during uncertain times. Through podcasts, a teacher can record audio of his/her educational content, and students can listen to that audio at any time and learn from it. To complete this process the student only needs to subscribe to a podcast. Since online education is an important medium in the current situation, the use of podcasts can make the education system more dynamic. Below are some of the educational benefits of the podcast:

- A special advantage of podcasts is that a student can easily continue his/her learning process 24 hours a day through their usability.
- Another advantage of podcasts is that a student will be able to hear far more than what they see and read.
- It usually takes a long time for a student to read a book and watch a video but in the case of podcasts it becomes much easier and the student's attention span is much improved.

- Another important point is that when a student misses a certain class, he can easily learn using the podcast provided by the teacher.
- In addition, there may be times when a teacher may not be able to take classes for a few weeks, in such circumstances the teacher may record his/her lessons through a podcast for the students.
- It can often be tedious for a student to read a book continuously. In this situation, by using podcasts, a student can easily learn his/her learning content through podcasts.

Screen Recording Tools for Teachers

We all know that screen recording works like video recording, which helps to capture a specific thing from a screen. Through screen recording, a teacher can give instructions to the student and it can capture the mouse movement and help the student to understand the specific features. During the pandemic, many teachers have used screen casting to increase student learning opportunities. To get a more detailed idea of the use of screen casting the example of Khan Academy can be given that provides screen casting with more than 6,000 subjects and more than 10 million students take the opportunity to learn through this unique technique every month. The advantages of screen recording in education are described below:

- Through screen recording, a student gets an audio and visual learning environment that attracts and captures their attention a lot more compared to just reading a book.
- Screen recording gives students the opportunity for self-learning which helps them to automate their learning.
- Through screen recording, a teacher can bring hands-on experience to the student.
- Presenting a subject through screen recording allows the student to learn a lot more than just presenting the text.
- Screen recording plays a special role in improving the student's perception.
- Through screen recording, a teacher can easily share his ideas with the students making the learning environment much easier.

Social Bookmarking for Teachers

Social bookmarking is usually a centralized online service where a user can bookmark their web documents, edit them and share them with other users. Hence social bookmarking is an application service where a teacher can combine different materials found online and edit them and share them with students if necessary. It is a process of saving various web links and it can be added to these saved links in the form of metadata so users can download them for themselves at any time and share them with others.

Social bookmarking is a very important medium for teachers and students as when we search the world for information online, we come across a variety of web links and one wants to keep the important and necessary web links separate. In this context, various social bookmarking applications are especially helpful for the student to save different websites as specific categories and reuse them. Teachers can bookmark various educational materials and share them with student groups and students can effortlessly learn their subject matter from those bookmarks.

Bibliography and Citation Tools for Teachers

Research papers need to be analyzed not only for research work but also to mention the right sources. Enlisting different research papers is an important task. However, it is time-consuming so we need to use the right technology techniques to make it easier. Nowadays with the advancement of technology many applications are assisting researchers to complete their bibliography or citations. The advantages of preparing a bibliography using different applications are described below:

- A bibliography can be presented with just one click using the application.
- The bibliography style can be changed very easily.
- The application has manually edited features.
- Different notes and tags can be added to each bibliography separately.
- Bibliography and citation can be updated automatically.

Sticky Notes Tools for Teachers

The use of sticky notes in education is a creative process. Many teachers use sticky notes when creating their teaching content. Sticky notes not only help the teacher but also help a student to accurately assess what they are learning. Currently, the invention of digital sticky notes can be noticed in various software technologies. We can generally describe the following advantages of sticky notes in education:

- Using digital sticky notes, a student and teacher can easily embellish their learning content with information and use it in the future.
- Students can indicate their subject matter with cards and note papers with sticky notes.
- Sticky notes are an important way to easily identify a topic and find each of the learning items effectively.
- Teachers can teach their students disciplinary action through sticky notes such as green sticky notes for imitation behavior and red sticky notes can be shown as modified behavior for students.

Photo and Image Editing Tools for Teachers

Digital photo editing tools are very important in the online teaching platform through which a teacher can easily make his/her subject matter much more interesting. We know that videos and pictures are especially helpful in attracting students' attention. Using digital photo editing tools, a teacher can easily and effectively prepare his/her educational content. Below we will highlight some of the effective aspects of using digital photo editing tools:

- The use of digital photo editing tools enhances a teacher's ability to prepare educational contacts so that a student can easily master the subject matter.
- Using digital photo editing tools, teachers can get a scope to increase their planning and presentation skills incrementally.
- The use of digital photo editing tools greatly enhances the creativity of the teacher.
- We know that preparing subject matter is an innovative task and the use of digital photo editing software greatly enhances the teacher's ability to innovate.
- Communication with students grows using digital photo-editing tools.

- A teacher can present his/her content in a much more beautiful way and the teacher can bring out new ideas, thoughts, and feelings in the student.
- Digital photo-editing tools are very effective in instilling more simulation in students and designing new ideas.

Testing and Quizzing Tool for Teachers

Test and quiz software plays an important role in e-learning in planning any education process during the pandemic. Such platforms help both students and teachers carry on the learning process to a sufficient extent. The benefits of testing and quizzes on the e-learning platform are discussed below:

- The virtual online test and quiz process saves both time and labor.
- This platform allows a student to take exams automatically and feel comfortable in the exam process.
- Virtual online exams and quizzes give students instant grades and feedback on their answers.
- It is very easy to prepare a set of questions for the exam on this platform and it can be done in a very short time.
- Students can be properly assessed and their performance can be predicted through the use of embedded LMS in testing and quizzing software to evaluate students' performance effectively.
- Using test and quiz software, a student can prepare his/her question paper and arrange the mock test easily.

Web or Video Conferencing Tools for Teachers

The coronavirus outbreak forced all education processes to go online. Web conferencing is an important tool to manage the online learning process where teachers can easily establish a means of communication with students through video conferencing. There are several potential benefits of video conferencing that are explained below:

- The use of video conferencing eliminates the need for teachers to provide their learning materials only by email or in the classroom. If the teacher wishes, he/she can easily provide his/her teaching materials or teaching content to the student through video conferencing.
- Video conferencing is an important way to bring together a group of teachers from different schools in a common virtual platform.
- Another advantage of video conferencing is that it allows recording so that a student can listen and learn from video conferencing at any time and across multiple viewings.
- Video conferencing facilitates communication between teachers and students as well as with the school administration which makes the learning process much easier.
- In case of any problem for the student, the teacher can easily talk directly through video conferencing and the teacher can be aware of the problem and give him/her appropriate assistance.

Authoring Tools for Teachers

One of the most important steps a teacher can take to begin the process of online learning is to use a variety of advanced and popular online tools. As different tools or applications make the learning process much easier and very little time investment is needed to excel in this field of education. In the present section, we will learn about authoring tools. Authoring tools are a type of software application where advanced quality learning materials can be prepared using various multimedia elements such as pictures, videos, etc. This is a lot like expressing a creative idea. A teacher will combine different learning materials through his/her creativity to help make the learning process more streamlined by using various graphics designs or other multimedia objects. Several benefits of authoring tools are described below:

- Using authoring tools allows a teacher to make their learning materials much more personal and student-friendly.
- Using authorings tool makes it possible to prepare suitable learning materials through several groups by dividing different learning materials into different segments.
- In each case, there are various new demands from the student. Using the authoring tool, a teacher can easily adapt to the student's demands and prepare new on-demand learning materials to improve the overall teaching and learning process.

Video Tools for Teachers

We all know that the visual medium is an important mode of communication with multiple advantages. A special advantage of using the video medium is that the student can easily assimilate the subject matter and complete the whole learning process with great enthusiasm and attention. Since it is not possible to have physical contact with the student in the event of a pandemic, video education is being integrated as one of the effective and essential educational tools. Some of the notable advantages of providing education through visuals/videos are:

- Teaching through video makes the subject matter more appealing to the student and the teacher can easily communicate with the student anytime and anywhere.
- Learning through video is much more acceptable to the new generation of students.
- Teaching through visuals increases the enthusiasm of the students and the students are eager to learn new content with new enthusiasm.
- Another special advantage of providing visual-based education is that a lot of information can be presented simultaneously together and students can improve their learning by listening and watching.
- By providing online visual education, any student from all over the world gets the opportunity to learn any subject, and the whole world is transformed into a classroom where teachers from any part of the world can teach students from a particular village.
- Boredom can come to the student in teaching only through lectures but since the visual medium is a combination of text, pictures, sound, and visuals the subject matter of learning is much more interesting to the student.
- A difficult subject can be presented very easily through a visual medium with a lot of benefits for students in terms of the students' understanding of any concept.

PDF Tools Teachers

In the current situation, teachers need to work with different documents and media. As the digital revolution unfolded, some of the pictures changed drastically such as, now the pile of paper covering the desk of teachers has gradually disappeared.

The digital PDF format is one of the most popular formats for the secure and versatile use of any important document. PDF format is also a popular format for making it easy for students to access any educational content. The advantage of the use of PDF format is that it does not cost anything and everyone can use this file very easily. Besides, when a subject matter is presented in other than PDF format some changes are made but there is no change in the formatting of any documents edited in PDF format. Table 30.15 provides some popular PDF editors and their web links for teachers and students.

Conclusion

If we look at the current situation in terms of history, one thing that will be very clear is that it has become mandatory to close educational institutions due to different incidents at different times. Therefore, policymakers and educational leaders need to be better prepared for the near future as we may face a bigger challenge. Lessons learned from the current pandemic situation can help to tackle many similar problems in near future and to better prepare beforehand. It is understood quite well that planning during a global crisis is not an easy task but it is also true that overcoming effectively certain situations may help us to explore and facilitate through our creativity. Although the current pandemic is a nightmare for all, it is significant to say that this pandemic has allowed learning many new and crucial things. Though different educational institutions and groups of teachers have developed their form of education based on their needs, their overall thinking has brought about a radical change in the whole education system.

Bibliography

Archer, B. (1986). *The three R's in technology in schools* (A. Cross & B. McCormick, Eds.). Milton Keynes: Open University Press.

Foster, S. (1954). "Hard Times come again no more:, Firth, Pond & Co., NY, USA. iFoster's Melodies No. 28. https://en.wikipedia.org/wiki/Hard_Times_Come_Again_No_More

Gilchrist, R. S. (1951). Are schools meeting the imperative needs of youth? *Bulletin of the National Association of Secondary School Principals, 35*(180), 82–87.

Huang, C., Wang, Y., Li, X., Ren, L., Zhao, J., Hu, Y., Zhang, L., Fan, G., Xu, J., Gu, X., Cheng, Z., Yu, T., Xia, J., Wei, Y., Wu, W., Xie, X., Yin, W., Li, H., Liu, M., Cao, B. (2020). Clinical features of patients infected with 2019 novel coronavirus in Wuhan, China. *The Lancet, 395,* 497–506. https://doi.org/10.1016/S0140-6736(20)30183-5

Knight, G. (1982). *Issues and alternatives in educational philosophy*. Berrien Springs, MI: Andrews University Press.

Liang, L., Ren, H., Cao, R., Hu, Y., Qin, Z., Li, C., Mei, S. (2020). The Effect of COVID-19 on Youth Mental Health. *Psychiatr Q, 91*(3):841–852. https:// 10.1007/s11126-020-09744-3.

Mitcham, C. (1994). *Thinking through technology: The path between engineering and philosophy*. Chicago, IL: University of Chicago Press.

Pacey, A. (1984). *The culture of technology*. Cambridge, MA: MIT Press.

UNESCO (2020). *Global Education Monitoring Report: Inclusion and Education, All Means*. Paris: UNESCO.

Vries, M. J. de (2012). Philosophy of technology. In P. J. Williams (Ed.), *Technology education for teachers* (pp. 15–34). The Netherland: Sense Publishers URL http://iasle.net/icsle-2020/ http://www.fredsakademiet.dk/abase/sange/Indledning%20til%20fredssange.pdf

Suggested Reading

Benson, C., & Lunt, J. (Eds.). (2011). *International handbook of primary technology education: Reviewing the past twenty years* (Vol. 7). Springer Science & Business Media.

De Vries, M. J. (2016). *Teaching about technology: An introduction to the philosophy of technology for non-philosophers*. Berlin: Springer.
Erneling, C. E. (2010). *Towards discursive education: Philosophy, technology, and modern education*. Cambridge: Cambridge University Press.
Ihde, D. (2012). *Technics and praxis: A philosophy of technology* (Vol. 24). Springer Science & Business Media.
Scharff, R. C., & Dusek, V. (Eds.). (2013). *Philosophy of technology: The technological condition: An anthology*. Chichester: John Wiley & Sons.

INDEX

**Pages in bold reference tables.
**Pages in italics reference figures.

3G technology 381
4G technology 381
16 mm film 25–26

AAC (augmentative and alternative communication) 208–209
abacus 22
ABCD formation 44
ABCmouse.com 387
Academia.edu **321**
Academic Earth 290, **330**
academic fraud 271
academic news, social media 323
accountability, cooperative learning 155–157
achieving effective classroom communication 68–72
action model 82–84
active learning 11, 72
active participants 285
active responding 132
activities of daily living (ADLs), assistive technology 213
activity, Massive Open Online Courses (MOOC) 287
adaptation 208
ADDIE model, instructional design (ID) 37–43
ADIL (Automated Debugger in Learning System) 241–242
ADIS (Animated Data Structure Intelligent Tutoring System) 242
ADLs (activities of daily living), assistive technology 213
Advanced Research Projects Agency Network (ARPANET) 268

advice, communication 59
affective mode of learning 35
affinity grouping 170
age of book and chalkboard 20
agencies for assistive technology **230**
AGI (artificial general intelligence) 392–393
AI *see* artificial intelligence
AI-based visual aids 216
Alison 290
all rights reserved copyright 328
all-channel communication pattern 77
alternative teaching 182–183, **187**
American Asylum for the Education of the Deaf and Dumb 210
American printing house for the blind 210
American School for the Deaf 210
AMSER **329**
analysis phase, ADDIE model of instructional design 38–39
analytic teams, cooperative learning 169
ANI (artificial narrow intelligence) 392
Animated Data Structure Intelligent Tutoring System (ADIS) 242
appearance, nonverbal communication 65
application and effect element of teaching models 148
approaches of educational technology 11–14
AR (augmented reality) 398
ARCS model of motivation (Keller) 50–52
Aristotle's communication model 84–85
ARPANET (Advanced Research Projects Agency Network) 268
artificial general intelligence (AGI) 392–393
artificial intelligence (AI) 29, 235, 390; artificial general intelligence (AGI) 392–393; artificial narrow intelligence (ANI) 392; artificial superintelligence (ASI) 393; classifications of

391–392; definitions 391; in education 395–398; in Indian education system 398–399; Intelligent Tutoring System (ITS) *see* Intelligent Tutoring System (ITS); limited memory 394; reactive machines 394; self-awareness 395; theory of mind 394–395
artificial narrow intelligence (ANI) 392
artificial superintelligence (ASI) 393
assessments: co-teaching 191; Massive Open Online Courses (MOOC) 287; mobile learning (M-learning) 384
assistive listening 213
assistive technology 207–208, 216–217; agencies for **230**; application for a person with disability 216; augmentative and alternative communication (AAC) 208–209; classifications of 211–216; for hearing impaired **227**; history of 210–211; for people with cognitive disability and learning disorder **229**; for people with physical disabilities **228**; principle of best fit 223; principle of evidence-based practice 227, 230; principle of minimal effort 222; principle of minimal energy 222–223; principle of minimal interference 223; principle of parsimony 220–222; principle of practicality and use 223; various models of **221**; vendors for **230**; for visually impaired **224–226**
ASSURE model, instructional design (ID) 43–46
asynchronous e-learning 275–276
AT CoPlanner Model **221**
audience, e-learning 269
augmentative and alternative communication (AAC) 208–209, 211; *see also* universal design principle of assistive technology and AAC
augmentative communication, assistive technology 214
augmented reality (AR) 398
Australia, distance education 249
authoring tools **409**, 413–414
Automated Debugger in Learning System (ADIL) 241–242
automated task, learning management system (LMS) 298
Automatic Tutoring 131
autonomy: concept of 258; and distance theory 257–259, 272
avatars 369

Bååth, John A. 262–263
Barnlund's transactional model of communication 89–90
Bayesian Intelligent Tutoring System (BITS) 242
Becker's mosaic model of communication 89, *91*
behavior modification model, models of teaching (MOT) 147
behavior specification, development of program material 137
behavioral interdependence, cooperative learning 164

behavioral technology 13, 16–17
behavioral theories, computer-assisted instruction (CAI) 344–345
behaviorism, computer-assisted instruction (CAI) 345
beneficence, researchers 272
Berlo's SMCR communication model 85–87
bibliography, tools for creating **407**, 412
BITS (Bayesian Intelligent Tutoring System) 242
blackboard 20
blended learning: advantages of 204–205; characteristics of 198–199; definitions 196–197; disadvantages of 205; history of 197–198; process of 201–204; types of 199–201
blogs 307–308
bluetooth 380–381
boards, social media 308
body language 65
Braille typewriter 210
branching programming/branching sequences 131, 135
branching storyline 376
browsers 285
building games 366
buzz groups 166

CAI (computer-assisted instruction) 28, 136, 268
CAL (computer-assisted learning) 347
calculator 23
CAM (concept attainment model of teaching) **149–150**
Canvas network 290
case studies, cooperative learning 169
categorization of Massive Open Online Courses (MOOC) **286**
Cause and Effect diagram 92
CBE (computer-based education) 347–348
CBI (computer-based instruction) 347–348
CBT (computer-based training) 268, 348
CEI (computer enriched instruction) 348
chain network pattern of communication 74–75
chalkboard 20
channels, communication 61
charts, tools for creating 403
ChatBots 243
Chegg 386
circle network pattern of communication 76
citation tools for teachers **407**, 412
Class Realm **374**
Classcraft 371
ClassDojo **373**
classroom box 256
classroom communication 68–72
classroom management, co-teaching 191
closure **116**
CMI (computer-managed instruction) 348
CML (computer-managed learning) 348

Index

cMOOC (connectivist MOOC) 284
Code Academy 371
cognitive development, cooperative learning 164
cognitive disability, assistive technology **229**
cognitive hearing aids 216
cognitive psychology 33
cognitive task analysis, Intelligent Tutoring System (ITS) 241
cognitive theories 345–347
collaboration stage, co-teaching 188
collaborative skill, cooperative learning 156
collaborative writing 172
committed learners 285
communication: achieving effective classroom communication 68–72; all-channel communication pattern 77; barriers to 92–94; chain network pattern 74–75; circle network pattern 76; components of 60–61; cycle 61; definitions 56–57; dyadic communication 77–78; forms of 77–79; interactive models 91–92; intrapersonal communication 77–78; linear models *see* linear models of communication; mass communication 79; nature of 59–60; objective of 58–59; process 61–62; public communication 78–79; small-group communication 78; star communication pattern 77; transactional models 88–90; types of 62–68; wheel network pattern 74–75; Y network pattern 75–76
communication disabilities, assistive technology **228**
community contributors 285
Community of Online Research Assignments 329
completeness **116**
component-wise grading **121, 123, 125**
compromising stage, co-teaching 188
computer access, assistive technology 215–216
computer age 20
computer enriched instruction (CEI) 348
computer-assisted instruction (CAI) 28, 131, 136, 235, 268, 340, 347–349; assumptions of 342; characteristics of 341; definitions 340–341; process of *344*; theories 343–347; types of 342–343
computer-assisted learning (CAL) 347
computer-based education (CBE) 347
computer-based instruction (CBI) 347–348
computer-based instructional visualization **349**
computer-based training (CBT) 268, 348
computer-managed instruction (CMI) 348
computer-managed learning (CML) 348
computers 339–340
concept attainment model of teaching (CAM) 148–151
concept of education and technology 3–4, 6–9
conferences, social media 323
connectivism, computer-assisted instruction (CAI) 346–347
connectivist MOOC (cMOOC) 284
Connexions Orange Grove **329**
constructive educational technology 12
constructivism, computer-assisted instruction (CAI) 346
content, mobile learning (M-learning) 383
content knowledge, TPACK (Technological Pedagogical Content Knowledge) 356
content management, learning management system (LMS) 300–301
contiguity theorists 345
controlled responses, linear or extrinsic programming 134
conventional media, versus social media 310
cooperation, among students 71
cooperative base group 159
cooperative learning: academic benefits of 160; behavioral interdependence 164; characteristics of 156–157; cognitive development 164; cooperative base group 159; definitions 152–153; discussions 165–166; drawbacks of 161–162; elements of 154–156; formal cooperative learning environment 158; graphics information organizer 170–171; history of 153–**155**; implementing 173–175; informal cooperative learning environment 159; problem-solving 168–170; psychological benefits 161; purpose of 159–160; reciprocal teaching 167–168; social benefits 161; social interdependence 164–165; versus traditional learning 156, **158**; writing 171–172
copyright, open educational resources (OER) 328–331
cost-effectiveness 11
co-teaching: advantages of 192–193; alternative teaching 182–183, **187**; characteristics of 178–179; components of 189–192; definitions 177–178; disadvantages of 193–194; one teaches and one assists 184–**187**; one teaches and one observes 183–184, **187**; parallel teaching 179–180, **187**; present applicability of co-teaching and level of planning **187**; stages of 186–188; station teaching 180–182, **187**; teaming 182, **187**
counseling, communication 59
Course Hero 373
Coursera 289, **330**
COVID-19 pandemic 400–401; strategies for teachers 401–403
creative commons licensing **329**, 331, **333**
criterion test 137
critical awareness, increasing 125
crowdsourcing 308
cultivation theory 84
cultural barriers to communication 94
curriculum 31
curriculum goals, co-teaching 190
curriculum planning, learning management system (LMS) 300

D&M model, measuring e-learning 273–274
Decision-Making Tutor (DM-Tutor) 242
decoding, communication 61
Dede's architecture of Intelligent Tutoring System 238
delivery strategies, instructional design (ID) 34–35
Delling, Rudolf, theory of a helping organization 253–254
Derry, Hawkes, and Ziegler (1988) architecture, Intelligent Tutoring System (ITS) 235–236
design: blended learning 202–203; Intelligent Tutoring System (ITS) 240–241; *see also* universal design principle of assistive technology and AAC
design phase, ADDIE model of instructional design 39–40
development of program material, programmed instruction or learning 136–140
developmental phase, ADDIE model of instructional design 40–41
dialogic 254
dialogue journals 171
Dick and Carey (DC) model, instructional design (ID) 46–48
differentiate analyzer 26
digital library of India 331
digital storytelling tools 410
disabilities: people with a disability 208, 216–217, people with cognitive disability and learning disorders, assistive technology **229**; people with communication disability, assistive technology **228**; people with physical disabilities, assistive technology **228**
discovery method, computer-assisted instruction (CAI) 343
discussion, cooperative learning 165–166
distance, concept of 258
distance education 247–248; characteristics of 249–250; classification of programs 258–259; helping organization theory (Delling) 254–255; history of 248–249; in India 250–252; Information and Communications Technology (ICT) 355; purpose of 250; theories 252–253; theories of autonomy and distance 257–259; theories of interaction and communication 262–263; theory of independent study 254–255; theory of industrialization of teaching 259–262
distance learning 35; *see also* e-learning; mobile learning (M-learning)
distance teaching program, dialog and structure **256**
distortion of information 67
divergent questions **116**
diverse needs of preference, e-learning 270
DM-Tutor (Decision-Making Tutor) 242
domain model, Intelligent Tutoring System (ITS) 237
donations, social media 323
downward communication 67
DSG (Dynamic Courseware Generation) 242
Duolingo **373**
dyadic communication 77–78
dyadic essays 171–172
Dynamic Courseware Generation (DSG) 242

EdConnectr **320**
EDGE (enhanced data rates for GSM evolution) 381
Edmodo **320**
educational film 23–24
educational radio 26
educational technology 261–262; approaches of 11–14; assumptions of 11; characteristics of 9–10; concept of 3–4, 6–9; definition 6–9; overview 14–15; scope of 10–11
Educational Technology I (hardware approach) 11–12
Educational Technology II (software approach) 12–13
Educational Technology III (system approach) 13–14
EdX 289, **330**
effective communication process 84
eGyanKosh 277
e-learning 35; asynchronous e-learning 275–276; characteristics of 267–268; components of 269–270; definitions 266–267; ethics 270–272; history of 268–269; in India 276–279; measuring system 273–274; synchronous e-learning 274–275
Electronic Numerical Integrator and Computer (ENIAC) 26
Elevate 386
eliciting effect, models of teaching (MOT) 145
ELM-ART (Episodic Learner Model-ART) 242
Empowerment Period (1973 to Present), assistive technology 211
Enabling Objectives (EOs) 105
encoding, communication 61
eNewsletters 314–316
enhanced data rates for GSM evolution (EDGE) 381
ENIAC (Electronic Numerical Integrator and Computer) 26
enriched virtual learning 200
entering behavior 137
environmental control, assistive technology 213
environments, mobile learning (M-learning) 383–384; *see also* learning environments
EOs (Enabling Objectives) 105
Epic! 387
Episodic Learner Model-ART (ELM-ART) 242
equipment simulation 376
Establishment Period (1900-1972), assistive technology 210–211
e-teachers, ethics 272
ethics, e-learning 270–272
ethos 85
evaluating: blended learning 203–204; Intelligent Tutoring System (ITS) 241

evaluation: ADDIE model of instructional design 42–43; learning management system (LMS) 302
examples, illustrating with 118–121
Excitement! **329**
expectations, e-learning 269
expert domain model, Intelligent Tutoring System (ITS) 236
explaining, teaching skills 118–121
exploring games 365–366

Facebook 307, 310, 316–317
face-to-face live video-based communication, Massive Open Online Courses (MOOC) 287
face-to-face promotive interaction, cooperative learning 156
familiarity with curriculum, co-teaching 190
FAQ (Frequently Asked Questions) 402
feedback 72; blended learning 205; communication 61; computer-assisted instruction (CAI) 342; eNewsletters 315; evaluating blended learning 203–204; gamification 369; linear or extrinsic programming 134; programmed instruction or learning 132
film 23–24; 16 mm film 25–26
Fishbone diagram 92–93
fishbowl technique 167
five "Ps," ASSURE model 45
flex blended learning 200
flipped classroom blended learning 200
fluency in making question **116**
focus, teaching model 147
formal communication 66–67
formal cooperative learning environment 158
formal prompts 140
forms of educational technology 15–17
FORTRAN (formula translation) 28
forums, Massive Open Online Courses (MOOC) 287
Foundation Period (Before 1900), assistive technology 210
Four models of architecture of Intelligent Tutoring System (ITS) 238–239
frames, programmed frames 138–139
Framework for conceptual modeling of AT device outcomes **221**
fraud, e-learning 271
Frequently Asked Questions (FAQ) 402
Future Learn 291

Gagne's Nine Events of Instruction 48–50
game-based learning **364**, 369; computer-assisted instruction (CAI) 343
game-design elements **370**
games **364**; definitions 363–365; types of 365–366
gamification **364**, 369–370; characteristics of 367; Code Academy 371; definitions 366–367; elements of *370*; history of 367–368; implications in education 372; Open Badges 371
gamification-based learning applications/platforms **373–374**
general packet radio service (GPRS) 380
Germany, distance education 248
GLIDER 27
global system for mobile (GSM) 380
goal determination 105–106
Google+ **320**
GPRS (general packet radio service) 380
grading index **124**
graduation index **121–122**
grant funding, social media 323
graphics information organizer, cooperative learning 170–171
group evaluation, cooperative learning 157
group grids 170
group investigation, cooperative learning 169–170
group rewards, cooperative learning 156
GSM (global system for mobile) 380
guided didactic conversation 263
gurukul system, India 276
Gutenberg printing press 23–24

Hamburg model 260
hardware approach (Educational Technology I) 11–12
hearing impaired, assistive technology **227**
helping games 365
helping organization theory (Delling) 253–254
heterogeneous groups, cooperative learning 156
high technology, assistive technology 212
higher-order questioning **116**
historical development of educational technology 19–20
Holburg, Borje 263
horizontal communication 67
Human Activity Assistive Technology (HAAT) Model **221**

ICs (integrated circuits) 28
ICT (Information and Communications Technology) 28, 351
ID *see* instructional design
IGNOU 277
Illustrating: with an example **116**, 118–121; reinforcement 121–123
ILT (instructor-led training) 348
IMM (Indian Model of Microteaching) 125–127
implementation phase, ADDIE model of instructional design 41–42
implementing: blended learning 203; cooperative learning 173–175
inappropriate use of reinforcement 123
increasing critical awareness 125

Index

independent learning 198–199
independent study programs by learner autonomy **259**
independent study theory 254–255
India: artificial intelligence (AI) 398–399; COVID-19 pandemic 400–401; distance education 249–252; e-learning 276–279; microteaching 111–112; open educational resources (OER) 331–332; programmed instruction or learning 131
Indian Association of Programmed Learning 131
Indian Model of Microteaching (IMM) 125–127
Indian Society for Advancement of Library and Information Science 278
individual accountability, cooperative learning 156
individual quantifiable 156
individual rotation blended learning 200
inducto-deductive approach 120–121
industrialization of teaching theory 259–262
infographics, tools for creating 403
informal communication 68
informal cooperative learning environment 159
information, communication 58
Information Age 20
Information and Communications Technology (ICT) 28; advantages of 360–361; application of 355; challenges of 358–359; characteristics of 353; definitions 351–353; disadvantages of 361; scopes of 353–355
information communication age/computer age 20
information processing model, models of teaching (MOT) 145–146
information sharing 306
information success (IS), D&M model 273–274
infrared (IrDA) 381
inhibitory and disinhibitory effect, models of teaching (MOT) 145
initial tutor implementation, Intelligent Tutoring System (ITS) 241
innovations in education and technology 22–29
inside-out blended learning 200–201
Instagram **320**
institutional repositories in India **334**
institutional-based management, social media 322–323
instruction 31
instructional design (ID): ADDIE model 37–43; ARCS model of motivation (Keller) 50–52; ASSURE model 43–46; AT CoPlanner Model **221**; Becker's mosaic model of communication 89, *91*; behavior modification model, models of teaching (MOT) 147; Berlo's SMCR communication model 85–87; concept attainment model of teaching (CAM) 148–151; of co-teaching 179–186; D&M model 273–274; domain model, Intelligent Tutoring System (ITS) 237; expert domain model, Intelligent Tutoring System (ITS) 236; Hamburg model 260; Indian Model of Microteaching (IMM) 125–127; instructional design models 37; instructional development 105–106; interactive models of communication 91–92; linear models of communication *see* linear models of communication; Parallel Intervention Model **221**; personal models, models of teaching (MOT) 146; teaching model, elements of 147–148; transactional models of communication 88–90; tutoring model, Intelligent Tutoring System (ITS) 236–237
instructional design models 37
instructional effect, models of teaching (MOT) 144
instructional planning, co-teaching 190–191
instructional presentation, co-teaching 191
instructional system, system approach 103
instructional system design (ISD) 33; versus instructional design (ID) **34**
instructional technology 13, 16
instructivist MOOC (xMOOC) 284
instructor-led training (ILT) 348
integrated circuits (ICs) 28
intelligence 390; *see also* artificial intelligence (AI)
intelligent agents, artificial intelligence (AI) 391
intelligent machines 234
Intelligent Tutoring System (ITS): advantages of 243; architectures of 235–240; ChatBots 243; definitions 233–234; design 240–241; disadvantages of 243; history of 234–**236**; new generation architecture 239–240; practical application of 241–242; Technological Pedagogical Content Knowledge (TPACK) 356–358
interaction and communication theories, distance education 262–263
interactive models of communication 91–92
interdependence 157
interpersonal communication 189
intrapersonal communication 77–78
Intrinsic Programming 131
IrDA (infrared) 381
IS (information success), D&M model 273–274
ISD *see* instructional system design
ITS *see* Intelligent Tutoring System

Jacquard loom 23, *25*
Java Intelligent Tutoring System (JITS) 242
jigsaw 168
JITS (Java Intelligent Tutoring System) 242
job announcement and recruitment, social media 323
job responsibilities, e-learning 270

Kahoot! **374**
Keller, John, ARCS model of motivation 50–52
KERMIT (Knowledge-Based Entity Relationship Modeling Intelligent Tutoring) 242
Khan Academy 291
knowledge acquisition phase, microteaching 114

knowledge base, Intelligent Tutoring System (ITS) 238
Knowledge-Based Entity Relationship Modeling Intelligent Tutoring (KERMIT) 242
Knowre 371–372

lab rotation blended learning 200
Lasswell's communication model 82–84
Law of Effect 130
LCI (learner-controlled instruction) 136
LCMS *see* learning content management system
leaderboards, gamification 369
leadership, shared leadership 157
learner engagement, learning management system (LMS) 301
learner-controlled instruction (LCI) 131, 136
learners: committed learners 285; Massive Open Online Courses (MOOC) 284–285; mobile learning (M-learning) 381–382
learning cells 167
learning content management system (LCMS) 295–296; versus learning management system 299–300
learning disorders, assistive technology **229**
learning environments 257; e-learning 270; mobile learning (M-learning) 383–384
learning management system (LMS): advantages of 302–303; definitions 294–295; disadvantages of 303; features of 296–298; history of 296–**298**; versus learning content management system 299–300; overview of 300–302; platforms **300**
learning material, Massive Open Online Courses (MOOC) 287
learning platforms, MOOC-based **292**
LearningSpace **330**
lecturing **116**
Leonardo da Vinci calculator 23
levels/stages, gamification 368–369
limited memory 394
linear models of communication: advantages of 87–88; Aristotle's communication model 84–85; Berlo's SMCR communication model 85–87; Lasswell's communication model 82–84; Shannon-Weaver model 80–82
linear or extrinsic programming 133–135
linguistic learning mode 35
LinkedIn 307, **321**
listening barriers 93
LMS *see* learning management system
logical order, linear or extrinsic programming 134
logos 85
low technology, assistive technology 212

Machine Learning Tutor (ML-Tutor) 242
machine technology 12
Magin Cataoprica 23
management strategies, instructional design (ID) 35

management technology 13
market, e-learning in India 278
Mason OER Metafinder **329**
mass communication 79
mass communication age 20
Massive Open Online Courses (MOOC) 269; Academic Earth 290; advantages of 291; Alison 290; Canvas network 290; categorization of **286**; characteristics of 283; components of 285–287; connectivist MOOC (cMOOC) 284; Coursera 289; definitions 282–283; disadvantages of 292; edX 289; Future Learn 291; history of 287–288; instructivist MOOC (xMOOC) 284; Khan Academy 291; as medium of learning 288–289; versus online learning 285–286; OpenLearning 290; Peer-to-Peer University (P2Pu) 291; Saylor 291; types of learners 284–285; Udacity 289; Udemy 290
mastery-based blended learning 201
matching games 365
Matching Person and Technology (MPT) model **221**
MATHEMA for IT learning environment *239*
mathetics 131, 136
Mathways 387
Maven **374**
MBITS (Multicriteria Bayesian Intelligent Tutoring System) 242
measuring e-learning, DYM model 273–274
MERLOT **329**
messages, communication 60
micro-blogging 308
Microsoft 278
microteaching 109; advantages of 126; characteristics of 110–111; definition 109–110; disadvantages of 127; explaining 118–121; history of 111; illustrating 118–121; in India 111–112; models *117*; phases of 114–115; probing questions 123–125; reinforcement 121–123; skill of illustration 121–123; teaching skills 115–118; versus traditional teaching **112**
microteaching cycle 113–114
MincraftEdu **373**
minicomputers 28–29
mixed reality (MR) 398
M-learning *see* mobile learning (M-learning)
ML-Tutor (Machine Learning sTutor) 242
mobile learning (M-learning): ABCmouse.com 387; advantages of 387–388; challenges of 384–385; characteristics of 379–380; Chegg 386; definitions 378–379; disadvantages of 388; elements of 381–384; Elevate 386; Epic! 387; Mathways 387; Noggin 386; Peak 386; Rosetta Stone 386; Speakabook Reading app 385–387; Udemy 386
mobile technology, components used for 380–381
mobility, assistive technology 213
modeling effect, models of teaching (MOT) 145

models: ADDIE model 37–43; ARCS model of motivation (Keller) 50–52; ASSURE model 43–46; AT CoPlanner Model **221**; Becker's mosaic model of communication 89, *91*; behavior modification model, models of teaching (MOT) 147; Berlo's SMCR communication model 85–87; concept attainment model of teaching (CAM) 148–151; domain model, Intelligent Tutoring System (ITS) 237; expert domain model, Intelligent Tutoring System (ITS) 236; Hamburg model 260; Indian Model of Microteaching (IMM) 125–127; instructional design models 37; interactive models of communication 91–92; of co-teaching 179–186; D&M model 273–274; instructional development 105–106; linear models of communication *see* linear models of communication; Parallel Intervention Model **221**; personal models, models of teaching (MOT) 146; teaching model, elements of 147–148; transactional models of communication 88–90; tutoring model, Intelligent Tutoring System (ITS) 236–237

models of teaching (MOT): advantages of 151; assumptions of 144; behavior modification model 147; characteristics of 143; concept attainment model of teaching (CAM) 148–151; definitions 142–143; effects of 144–145; information processing model 145–146; personal models 146; social interaction model 146; specifications of 143–144; teaching model 147–148

monologues 254

MOOC *see* Massive Open Online Courses

Moore, Michael G., autonomy and distance theory 257–259

MOT *see* models of teaching

motivation 58–59

motivational design 50–52

Mozilla Open Badges 371

MR (mixed reality) 398

multi-agent architecture, Intelligent Tutoring System (ITS) 240

Multicriteria Bayesian Intelligent Tutoring System (MBITS) 242

MySpace 307

Napier's bones 23–24

narrow AI 392

National Council of Educational Research and Training (NCERT) 278

National Digital Library of India (NDL India) 331–332

National Knowledge Network (NKN) 332

National Open and Distance Learners Library and Information Network (NODLINET) 277

NCERT (National Council of Educational Research and Training) 278

needs assessment, Intelligent Tutoring System (ITS) 240

negative nonverbal reinforcement 122

negative verbal reinforcement 122

new generation architecture, Intelligent Tutoring System (ITS) 239–240

Nine Events of Instruction 48–50

NKN (National Knowledge Network) 332

NOBA **330**

NODLINET (National Open and Distance Learners Library and Information Network) 277

Noggin 386

noise, communication 61

nonlinguistic learning mode 35

nonverbal communication 64–65

Normalization Intelligent Tutor (NORMIT) 242

note-taking pairs 167

nurturant effect, models of teaching (MOT) 144

OA (Open Access) 325

observation schedules 126

OCL (Open Course Library) **330**

OER *see* open educational resources

OER Commons 329

OER Handbook for educators **329**

offline learning, blended learning 198–199

OLI (Online Learning Intuitive) **330**

one teaches and one assists 184–**187**

one teaches and one observes 183–184, **187**

one-way model of communication 82–84

Online Educational Resource (OER) 287

online learning: blended learning 198–199; versus Massive Open Online Courses (MOOC) 285–286; *see also* e-learning; mobile learning (M-learning)

Online Learning Intuitive (OLI) **330**

Open Access (OA) 325

Open Badges 371

Open Course Library (OCL) **330**

open education 288

open educational resources (OER): advantages of 332, 335; characteristics of 326; complete courses **330**; copyright and open licensing 328–331; creative commons licensing 331, **333**; definitions 325–326; disadvantages of 335; history of 326–327; in India 331–332; repository-based OER platforms **329**

open licensing, open educational resources (OER) 328–331

Open Scout **329**

Open University **330**

OpenCulture **329**

OpenLearning 290

Operant Conditioning 131, 133

oral barriers 93–94

oral communication 63–64

outside-in blended learning 201

P2Pu (Peer-to-Peer University) 291
paper seminars 172
Parallel Intervention Model **221**
parallel teaching 179–180, **187**
passive participants 285
pathos 85
PCK (pedagogical content knowledge) 357
PDF tools for teachers **410**, 414–415
Peak 386
pedagogical content knowledge (PCK) 357
pedagogical knowledge (PK) 356–357
pedagogical module, Intelligent Tutoring System (ITS) 239
peer editing 172
peer role-play as a student 126
Peer-to-Peer University (P2Pu) 291
people with cognitive disability and learning disorders, assistive technology **229**
people with communication disability, assistive technology **228**
people with a disability 208; assistive technology 216–217
people with physical disabilities, assistive technology **228**
perception barriers 93
personal models, models of teaching (MOT) 146
personalized learning, artificial intelligence (AI) 396
persuasion, communication 58–59
Peters, Otto, distance education 259–262
philosophy of technology education 4–5
phonographs 210
photo and image editing tools **408**, 412–413
physical arrangements, co-teaching 189–190
physical disabilities, assistive technology **228**
physical education, leisure, and play, assistive technology 214
Pinterest **321**
PK (pedagogical knowledge) 356–357
plagiarism 361
planned repetition **116**
planning, blended learning 201–202
PLATO (Programmed Logic for Automatic Teaching Operations) 28, 268
Play Brighter **373**
podcasts 308; tools for creating **405**, 410–411
points, gamification 368
positive interdependence, cooperative learning 155
positive nonverbal reinforcement 122
positive verbal reinforcement 122
principle of active responding 132
principle of best fit 223
principle of evidence-based practice 227, 230
principle of immediate confirmation of feedback 132
principle of minimal effort 222
principle of minimal energy 222–223
principle of minimal interference 223
principle of parsimony 220–222

principle of practicality and use 223
principle of reaction 148
principle of small steps 132
principle of student testing 133
printing press 23–24
privacy 361
prizes, gamification 369
probing questions **116**, 123–125
problem cylinders 296
problem-solving, cooperative learning 168–170
productivity 11
programmed instruction or learning 28, 268; branching programming/branching sequences 135; characteristics of 131–132; computer-assisted instruction (CAI) 136; definitions 129–130; development of program material 136–140; history of 130–131; India 131; learner-controlled instruction (LCI) 136; linear or extrinsic programming 133–135; mathetics 136; principles of 132–133; prompts 139–140; rule/egrule system of programming 135
Programmed Logic for Automatic Teaching Operations (PLATO) 28, 268
progress bars, gamification 369
project-based blended learning 200
prompting technique 123
prompts: linear or extrinsic programming 134; programmed instruction or learning 139–140
"The Prospect of Rhetoric" 89
psychological benefits of cooperative learning 161
psychological distance, academic fraud 271
psychology, cognitive psychology 33
public communication 78–79
public domain 328
publishing studies, social media 323
puzzle solving games 365

quality of e-learning measuring system (D&M success model) 273–274
Quantitative Undergraduate Biology Education and Synthesis (QUBES) **329**
Quest To Learn (Q2L) 371

radio 26
reactive machines 394
reading, assistive technology 214–215
reading machine for blind people 211
receivers, communication 60
reception-oriented CAM **149**
reciprocal teaching 167–168
reciprocity, among students 71
recognizing attending behavior **116**
redirection 124
refocusing 124
reinforcement **116**, 121–123, **124**
reinforcement theorists 345
Relational technology 12

remote blended learning 200
research, ethics 272
Research Gate **321**
respecting diverse talents and ways of learning 72–73
reviewing, blended learning 203
rewards, gamification 369
role-playing 167–168, 365
Rosetta Stone 386
round robin 166
round tables 171
rule/egrule system of programming 135

Saylor 291
Saylor Academy **330**
screen recorder tools **406**, 411
seating and positioning, assistive technology 212
section rotation blended learning 200
seeking further information technique 124
selection-oriented CAM **149**
self-awareness, artificial intelligence (AI) 395
self-directed blended learning 200
self-pacing 133
send-a-problem technique 168–169
sequence chains 170–171
sequencing techniques, instructional design (ID) 34
serious games 369
set induction **116**
seven Cs of effective classroom communication 69–70
Shannon-Weaver model 80–82
shared leadership, cooperative learning 157
Shodhganga 331
Shodhgangotri 332
Siemer and Angelides (1998) architecture, Intelligent Tutoring System (ITS) 237
sign-to-text 216
silence and nonverbal cues **116**
simulated teaching 375–377
simulation 369–370; computer-assisted instruction (CAI) 343; definitions 372, 375
simulation-based teaching and learning 374–375
skill acquisition phase, microteaching 114
skills, teaching skills **116**
Skype 321
slide rule 23, *25*
small-group communication 78
smarter glasses 216
SMCR (sender-message-receiver-channel-receiver) 85
social accountability, cooperative learning 155
social benefits, of cooperative learning 161
social bookmarking **406**, 411
social interaction model, models of teaching (MOT) 146
social interdependence, cooperative learning 164–165

social learning, learning management system (LMS) 298
social media: academic news 323; advantages of 311; characteristics of 306–307; classifications of 307–308; conferences 323; versus conventional media 310; definitions 305–306; disadvantages of 311–312; dos and don'ts 312; eNewsletters 314–316; Facebook 316–317; grant funding 323; history of 309–310; institutional-based management 322–323; job announcement and recruitment 323; Massive Open Online Courses (MOOC) 287; platforms **320**; publishing studies 323; teaching-learning process 322; Twitter 318–319; YouTube 319–320
social networking sites 307
social system, teaching model 148
Socrative **373**
software approach (Educational Technology II) 12–13
software simulation 376
soroban 22
sound, nonverbal communication 65
sources/senders, communication 60
Speakabook Reading app 385–386
Sputnik 1 27
SQL*R **329**
star communication pattern 77
station teaching 180–182, **187**
sticky notes **407**, 412
stimulus variation **116**
Stone Age 19–20
Stonehenge 23
storylines, gamification 369
straight-line approach, linear or extrinsic programming 134
strategizing games 366
strong AI 392–393
structured problem-solving 169
student knowledge model 237
student model, Intelligent Tutoring System (ITS) 237–238
student participation **116**
student testing 133
students' privacy 361
Study Webs of Active Learning for Young Aspiring Minds (SWAYAM) 278
suan pan 22
substitutability 156
success model, measuring e-learning 273–274
suggestion, communication 59
supplemental blended learning 201
support system, teaching model 148
SWAYAM (Study Webs of Active Learning for Young Aspiring Minds) 278
syllabus, Massive Open Online Courses (MOOC) 287
symbols, communication 60

synchronous e-learning 274–275
syntax, teaching model 147–148
system: characteristics of 100; definition 99–100
system approach 99; advantages of 106–107; concept of 100–101; to instruction 103; model of instructional development 105–106; problems in education 107–108; stages of 101–103; use in education 107
system approach (Educational Technology III) 13–14
system dynamics simulation 376
systematic instructional development 103–105

talking chips 166
TAPPS (think-aloud-pair problem solving) 168
task analysis, development of program material 138
task prescription 105
TCK (technological content knowledge) 357
teacher training programs, status before microteaching 110
teachers: COVID-19 pandemic 401–403; mobile learning (M-learning) 382–383; role in blended learning 198–199
TeacherTube **321**
teaching machines 27, 268, 296
teaching model, elements of 147–148
teaching skills **119**; explaining 118–121; illustrating with an example 118–121; for microteaching 115–118; probing questions 123–125; reinforcement 121–123
teaching technology 13, 15–16
teaching-learning process, social media 322
teaching-learning situation 256–257
team anthologies 172
team matrix 170
teaming 182, **187**
teamwork, cooperative learning 157
technological activity 4
technological content knowledge (TCK) 357
technological knowledge (TK) 4, 357
Technological Pedagogical Content Knowledge (TPACK) 356–358
technological pedagogical knowledge (TPK) 357
technology 5–7, 11, 208; development of (1500 BC to AD 2018) 21; in education 15–16; of education 15–16; *see also* assistive technology
TedEd **320**
television 26
terminal behavior 137
Terminal Performance Objectives (TPOs) 105
testing, student testing 133
testing and quizzing tools for teachers **408**, 413
test-taking teams 168
Text-to-Speech (TTS) 404
theories of autonomy and independence 252–253; helping organization 253–254; independent study theory 254–255; theories of autonomy and distance 257–259
theories of interaction and communication 262–263
theory of industrialization of teaching 259–262
theory of mind 394–395
thematic prompts 140
think-aloud-pair-problem solving (TAPPS) 168
think-pair-share 165
Three models of Intelligent Tutoring System (ITS) 235–237
three-step interviews 166
TK (technological knowledge) 4, 357
TPACK (Technological Pedagogical Content Knowledge) 356–358
TPK (technological pedagogical knowledge) 357
TPOs (Terminal Performance Objectives) 105
traditional learning, versus cooperative learning **158**
traditional learning environments *157*
traditional teaching, versus microteaching **112**
transactional models of communication 88–90
transfer acquisition phase, microteaching 114
trial-and-error learning method 4
TTS (Text-to-Speech) 404
turing machine 26
Turing test 235
tutorial method, computer-assisted instruction (CAI) 343
tutoring model, Intelligent Tutoring System (ITS) 236–237
Twitter 307, 310, 318–319
two-way communication: distance education 262–263; social media 306

Udacity 289
Udemy 290, 386
UGC-INFONET 277
United Kingdom, distance education 249
United States, distance education 248
universal design principle of assistive technology and AAC: principle of best fit 223; principle of evidence-based practice 227–228; principle of minimal effort 222; principle of minimal energy 222–223; principle of minimal interference 223; principle of parsimony 220–222; principle of practicality and use 223
upward communication 67
user appraisal sites 308
user interface, Intelligent Tutoring System (ITS) 239
user-generated content, social media 306

vendors for assisted technology **230**
verbal communication 63
VeriShow **373**
vertical communication 67
video lectures, Massive Open Online Courses (MOOC) 287

video tools **409**, 414
Vidyanidhi 332
Vimeo **320**
Virtonomics **373**
virtual reality (VR) 398
visual aids, assistive technology 213–214
visually impaired, assistive technology **224–226**
VR (virtual reality) 398

WBI (web-based instruction) 348
WBL (web-based learning) 348
WBT (web-based training) 348
web or video conferencing tools **409**, 413
web-based instruction (WBI) 348
Web-Based Intelligent Tutoring System (WITS) 242
web-based learning (WBL) 348
web-based training (WBT) 348
Wedemeyer, Charles A.: proposed teaching-learning situation 256–257; theory of independent study 254
wheel network pattern of communication 74–75
wikis 308
wireless networks 380
WITS (Web-Based Intelligent Tutoring System) 242
word webs 171
WordPress **321**
writing: assistive technology 215, 222; cooperative learning 171–172
written communication 64
wrong use of reinforcement 123

xMOOC (instructivist MOOC) 284

Y network pattern of communication 75–76
YouTube 319–320

Zondle **373**